Biofeedback,
Behavior Therapy
and Hypnosis

Biofeedback, Behavior Therapy and Hypnosis:

Potentiating the Verbal Control of Behavior for Clinicians

Introduced and Edited by

Ian Wickramasekera, Ph.D.

Assistant Professor of Psychiatry
Peoria School of Medicine
University of Illinois College of
Medicine and Private Practice
Peoria, Illinois

Nelson-Hall, Chicago

Library of Congress Cataloging in Publication Data
Main entry under title:

Biofeedback behavior therapy and hypnosis.

 Bibliography: p.
 Includes index.
 1. Behavior therapy. 2. Biofeedback training.
3. Hypnotism—Therapeutic use. I. Wickramasekera, Ian.
RC489.B4B5   616.8'914   76-18294
ISBN 0-88229-193-9

To Trooper and Sally

CONTENTS

ACKNOWLEDGMENTS

I want to thank the following individuals who in a variety of ways made this book possible: Kathy Orr, Marian Higgins, Eddy, Melissa, and Sally Wickram, Jane Higgins, Marie Nichols, Mary Ann Bush, C. H. Patterson, and Jim Garrett. I am grateful to my wife, Sally, and to my children, Melissa and Eddy, for their understanding during the extended period of time in which I was absorbed in this project, and to my research assistant, Kathy Orr, for her patience, hard work, and inspiration during the many months we worked together to bring this book to fruition. C. H. Patterson and J. Garrett have provided stimulating and supportive friendships. Finally, I want to express my appreciation to Jane Higgins and Marie Nichols for typing the manuscript and Mary Ann Bush for her research assistance. I also wish to thank the following publications and organizations for their permission to reprint material.

Academic Press Inc. for "Instructions and EMG Feedback in Systematic Desensitization" by I. Wickramasekera, *Behavior Therapy*, 1972, *3*(3), 460-465; "Phobias and Preparedness" by M. E. P. Seligman, *Behavior Therapy*, 1971, *2*, 307-320; "On Assertive Behavior: A Brief Note" by A. A. Lazarus, *Behavior Therapy*, 1973, *4*, 697-699; "The Role of Expectancy and Physiological Feedback in Fear Research: A Review with Special Reference to Subject Characteristics" by T. D. Borkovec, *Behavior Therapy*, 1973, *4*, 491-505; "Increasing Heterosexual Responsiveness in the Treatment of Sexual Deviation" by D. H. Barlow, *Behavior Therapy*, 1973, *4*(5), 655-671; and "Self-Regulation of Pain: The Use of Alpha-Feedback and Hypnotic Training for the Control of Chronic Pain" by R. Melzack and C. Perry, *Experimental Neurology*, 1975, *46*, 452-469.

The *American Journal of Clinical Hypnosis* for "Electromyographic Feedback Training and Tension Headache: Preliminary Observations" by I. Wickramasekera, *American Journal of Clinical Hypnosis*, 1972, *15*(2), 83-85; "An Eye-Roll Test for Hypnotizability" by H. Spiegel, *American Journal of Clinical Hypnosis*, 1972, *15*(1), 25-28; "Reinforcement and/or Transference in Hypnosis and Psychotherapy: A Hypothesis," I Wickram-

Pergamon Press Limited for "Temperature Feedback for the Control of Migraine" by I. Wickramasekera, *Journal of Behaviour Therapy and Experimental Psychiatry*, 1973, *4*, 343-345; "Teaching the Nonverbal Components of Assertive Training" by M. Serber, *Journal of Behaviour Therapy and Experimental Psychiatry*, 1972, *3*, 179-183; "Desensitization, Re-sensitization and Desensitization Again: A Preliminary Study" by I. Wickramasekera, *Journal of Behaviour Therapy and Experimental Psychiatry*, *1*, 257-262; "Combined Use of Imaginal and Interoceptive Stimuli in Desensitizing Fear of Heart Attacks" by J. B. Furst and A. Cooper, *Journal of Behaviour Therapy and Experimental Psychiatry*, 1970, *1*, 87-89; "Septal Stimulation for the Initiation of Heterosexual Behavior in a Homosexual Male" by C. E. Moan and R. G. Heath, *Journal of Behaviour Therapy and Experimental Psychiatry*, 1972, *3*, 23-30; "New Methods in the Behavioral Treatment of Sexual Dysfunction" by W. C. Lobitz and J. LoPiccolo, *Journal of Behaviour Therapy and Experimental Psychiatry*, 1972, *3*, 265-271; and "Olfactory Aversion Therapy for Homosexual Behavior" by C. E. Colson, *Journal of Behaviour Therapy and Experimental Psychiatry*, 1972, *3*, 185-187.

Psychology Today for "Fall Into Helplessness" by M. E. P. Seligman, *Psychology Today*, June 1973. Copyright © Ziff-Davis Publishing Company.

Psychophysiology for "Hypnotic Control of Peripheral Skin Temperature: A Case Report" by C. Maslach, G. Marshall, and P. G. Zimbardo, *Psychophysiology*, 1972, *9*(6), 600-605. Copyright © 1972 by The Society for Psychophysiological Research.

Psychosomatic Medicine for "Suppression of Penile Tumescence by Instrumental Conditioning" by R. C. Rosen, *Psychosomatic Medicine*, 1973, *35*(6), 509-514. Copyright © 1973 by the American Psychosomatic Society, Inc.

Psychotherapy: Theory, Research and Practice for "The Application of Learning Theory to the Treatment of a Case of Sexual Exhibitionism" by I. Wickramasekera, *Psychotherapy: Theory, Research and Practice*, 1968, *5*(2), 108-112, and "A Technique for Controlling a Certain Type of Sexual Exhibitionism" by I. Wickramasekera, *Psychotherapy: Theory, Research and Practice*, 1972, *9*(3), 207-210.

Science for "On Being Sane in Insane Places" by D. L. Rosenhan, *Science*, 19 January 1973, *179*, 250-258, and "Objective Assessment of Hypnotically-Induced Time Distortion" by P. G. Zimbardo, G Marshall, G. White, and C. Maslach, *Science*, 20 July 1973, *181*, 282-284. Copyright 1973 by the American Association for the Advancement of Science.

BIOFEEDBACK, BEHAVIOR THERAPY AND HYPNOSIS: AN OVERVIEW

Ian Wickramasekera

Implicit or explicit verbal instructions supported by consequences are among the primary tools for behavior control in the "unwashed" world. In academic psychology, we distinguish between verbal instruction, suggestibility (primary or secondary), hypnosis, psychotherapy, and propaganda. One common denominator of these behavior influence procedures is the manipulation of verbal events. These distinctions have had some heuristic value, but they have also encouraged provincialism in conceptualization and investigation of the conditions for the verbal control of behavior. I propose that one basis for usefully distinguishing between verbal influence procedures is the degree of perceived involuntariness and subjective involvement with the verbal events. One of the major concerns of this book is to delineate ways in which biofeedback, behavior therapy, and hypnosis have contributed to the explanation and the arrangement of conditions to increase subjective involvement with words. These conditions have been most extensively studied with "patient" populations.

I accept the reality of "patient" and "therapist" roles. These roles, when wisely used, can facilitate the process of behavior change by providing rationales and opportunities to intervene with "clinically" significant behaviors. These roles also support science by providing rationales for placing people in situations (hospitals, consulting rooms, etc.) in which even primitively controlled observation and isolation of independent variables becomes a possibility. They also increase the probability of effective intervention by creating environments which reduce "noise" and which permit a maximum mobilization of the active ingredients for behavior change. These roles also may be abused, as the article by Rosenhan illustrates.

The stress on words in this approach is not to deny that preverbal or incohate events do not profoundly control behavior, but to recognize that once responses have been labeled, a primitive but fairly reliable technology for the manipulation of perception and behavior becomes available. It is premature and beyond the scope of this book to attempt an explanation of *how* verbal events come to acquire control, and be controlled, by autonomic and motor responses. The observation of psychopathology illustrates these complex interactions. (I am indebted to Dr. A. Ellis for his insistence on the central role of cognition in the explanation and control of psychopathology. He was for many years "a voice in the wilderness." At a recent meeting of A.P.A., I had the distinct pleasure of introducing him as "a man whose time has come.")

This book is a primitive initial step in illustrating how a variety of apparently unrelated conditions (besides reason and logic) can be arranged to potentiate the cognitive control of behavior. Recently, several methodologically sophisticated investigators in the behavior therapy area have launched a series of studies into the cognitive control of behavior. But I have as yet found little in their work of a conceptual nature that adds power to the cognitive control of behavior, beyond careful research on the seminal proposals of Dr. A. Ellis. There is another movement in behavior therapy which has sought to incorporate cognition into behavior therapy by simply placing the word "covert" in front of the constructs reinforcement, punishment, avoidance, and so on. It appears to me that it is highly unlikely that this approach by itself will advance our ability to reliably and powerfully control private events. This simplistic approach to forcing a marriage between operant conditioning and cognitive learning ignores the richness of investigative effort, which has collected around the construct, cognition. It is time we settled down to the hard multidisciplinary (psychophysiology, social psychology, psychotherapy, neurophysiology, etc.) work of identifying the variety of internal and external conditions that potentiate the verbal control of behavior. It is my hope that this book will illuminate even fragmentarily some promising areas in which more sophisticated clinicians and methodologists will begin pecking.

I realize that I may be accused of insensitivity to ethical issues. In an early paper, "Goals and Some Methods in Psychotherapy" (reprinted in this book), I struggled with what appeared to me to be one of the central ethical issues: the implications of coercive behavior technologies for our models of "mental health." For example, it may turn out that the use of manipulative techniques is inherently incompatible with the production of a "free" intelligent and creative person. But, in a sense, this is an empirical issue around which much hard data have yet not collected. Additionally, the technology is still imprecise, relatively unreliable, and unevenly strong. As manipulators of behavior, we are generally innocent of doing anything in our professional lives that is reliably effective with patients, unless we are among that small group of skilled clinical magicians. As manipulators of behavior, behavior therapists are more vocal and visible. They have not yet attained the superior manipulative skill of the psychotherapist, who has convinced his patient and even himself that he only helps people "grow" and that he does not inflict his goals and his values on his patients. The greatest advances in behavior control will come only when we have an effective and reliable technology to influence perception, values, and belief systems. Meanwhile, in the words of T. S. Eliot, it may be "better to do evil than to do nothing."

Section I

Biofeedback

What Is Biofeedback? What Are Its Clinical Implications?

Ian Wickramasekera

B iofeedback is a training procedure which enables a person to, within biological limits, alter physiological and bio-electrical events occurring within his or her skin. The essential features of biofeedback training are (1) continuous and accurate monitoring of the physiological response to be altered; (2) immediate feedback to the subject of changes in the response; (3) motivation to alter the response. Some of the biological responses that have been altered to date include EEG responses (alpha and theta), blood pressure, heart rate, muscle tension, salivation, urine formation, gastric motility, blood flow, and skin temperature (Barber et al., 1972; Wickramasekera, 1974a). The mechanism of such alterations in man is not clear as yet, but it has been assumed to be learning.

In the process of learning physiological self-control, it appears that certain reliable positive psychological changes (alterations of consciousness) occur in the trainee. Some of the verbally reported psychological alterations of consciousness include feelings of floating, lightness, expansion, euphoria, dreamy states, tranquility states, and feelings of competence. It is important to critically examine these verbal reports of alterations in consciousness with respect to physiological etiology (Grossberg, 1972). If these alterations of mood and emotion prove to be subjectively valid, and amenable to reliable elicitation by perhaps "demand characteristic" operations (Orne, 1959), there is no reason why the clinician should not explore the use of these procedures to induce positive affective changes in patients. Biofeedback technology may provide an alternative to present methods of inducing emotional changes. Currently, psychotropic drugs are the primary clinical method of altering mood, perception, and emotion, but their effects appear to be lacking in *specificity*, and they are not entirely free of side effects. Perhaps biofeedback technology will eventually provide a method of altering emotions that is relatively specific, free of serious side effects, and ideal for some patients. If biofeedback can provide an effective and reliable set of tools to induce positive emotions, then it may also have more general motivational applications. The identification through biofeedback studies of the pattern of psychophysiological changes that occur during spontaneously occurring motivational episodes and the specification of the situational and cognitive determinants of these psychophysiological changes may make it possible to elicit and sustain motivated behavior more reliably.

The informational feedback variable appears, under certain as yet unspecifiable conditions, to lock into a primitive competency drive, which feeds back into the learning process and sets in motion a powerful and accelerating motivational cycle. This motivational cycle appears not only to enhance the specific response being learned but also to mobilize the other adaptive resources of the person in a new and challenging way. Biofeedback research has important future contributions to make to the specification of the conditions for motivated behavior in man.

Clinical application of biofeedback technology requires that the physiological and psychological changes be capable of reliable elicitation, be generalizable from the training situation to the patient's natural habitat (home, school, office), be of sufficient magnitude to be clinically useful, be durable, and finally that the induced changes be relatively free of serious side effects. A reliable technology for producing large magnitude physiological changes is still in the future. But it appears likely that more careful attention to the literature of operant conditioning, cybernetics, and human skill learning (Fleishman, 1966) may generate hypotheses and techniques that will increase our ability to make clinical applications. The article by Blanchard et al. included in this section illustrates how the problem of producing large magnitude heart rate changes can be approached using a fine-grained and flexible shaping procedure. For example, the authors started out by requiring a five-BPM increase over baseline level and held that criterion constant for a twenty-minute experimental trial. They found that the use of this constant criterion was analogous at times to placing the subject on extinction. Therefore, they shifted to a *variable criterion* of reinforcement which was adjusted on a minute-by-minute basis and which maximized the contact with the reinforcement contingency (money). The variable criterion procedure was found to be significantly more effective. The investigators speculate that an even finer unit of analysis (beat-by-beat), which would require computer assistance, may enhance the procedure even further.

Biofeedback training also appears to have some similarities to skill learning and cognitive learning literatures. Hence, it might also be useful to pay attention to some of the parameters of acquisition that have been found to be important in those literatures. For example, massed versus spaced practice should be investigated in relation to the acquisition function in biofeedback training. Biofeedback research should also focus on other dimensions of skill learning including strength, endurance, steadiness, precision, and reaction time (Fleishman, 1966). The optimal conditions for discrimination learning with minimal or weak cues also deserves attention. In advanced stages of biofeedback training, systematic discrimination and attention training focused on proprioceptive and interoceptive cues may shift the focus of relevant feedback away from the instrument to the organism's own feedback system.

The simplistic view that biofeedback is operant conditioning of covert responses is incompletely supported by careful and extensive observation of human subjects. Discontinuity in the process of acquisition and the large individual differences that human subjects demonstrate suggest that a more complex form of learning is involved. It has, however, been politically prudent to regard it as a form of operant conditioning so that psychologists cannot be accused of practicing medicine. Realistically, it appears that a form of self-control more complicated than conventional operant learning is involved. Attention to the literature on cybernetics may have much heuristic value as neurophysiological knowledge increases. Clearly, several aspects of control theory appear to be relevant to this new type of learning.

Several recent reports taken together appear to indicate that instructional variables or verbal manipulations (conceptualized as demand characteristics, advanced organizers, subject or experimenter expectations, or hypnotic suggestions, etc.) can potentiate biofeedback effects (Wickramasekera, 1975; Melzack, 1975; Mandel, 1975; Walsh, 1974). The patient's expectations can be naturalistically structured through the use of selected "software" (e.g., selected articles on biofeedback from the mass media) and his suggestibility positively mobilized to support specific learning effects. These instructional-cognitive manipulations can vary on an implicit-explicit dimension, all the way from subtle implicit demand characteristics to an explicit standardized role induction interview or hypnotic induction with profound organismic involvement (Sarbin and Coe, 1972).

Clinically, we have found it effective in cases where the patient has either a religious-mystical (e.g., Quaker, Buddhist, Catholic, etc.) or literary background to interphase biofeedback training with this cultural history. This can be done before and during training by sensitively exploring commonalities between the goals and techniques of biofeedback and the above cultural traditions. The verbal explorations are next brought to a focus and crystallized by an appropriate phrase, or paradox (for example, at the still point of the turning world—time past and time future, allow but a little consciousness—only through time time is conquered—in my end is my beginning) that has personal meaning for the patient and which appears to accelerate his biofeedback learning. Such phrases also appear to succinctly package the meaning and importance of his therapy in a way that can be conveniently and unobtrusively carried into all corners of his life. The potency of this motivational manipulation probably stems from the synergistic operation of biofeedback learning and the mobilization of deep emotionally toned universal cultural strivings. Hence, what could very easily be perceived as the silly, dull task of moving a needle or turning off a tone becomes a challenging and illuminated experience which mobilizes the whole patient in new ways.

An impediment to clinical application of biofeedback is unreliability in the transfer of training. One approach to the problem of the transfer of training from clinic to natural habitat is to conduct the training in the natural habitat or to phase training into it. Attention to the literature on stimulus control of operant behavior may also be helpful in arranging natural environments that support the psychophysiological changes induced in the laboratory or clinic. The design of living and working conditions that promote anti-stress behavior is another future direction for behavioral engineering. Careful attention to the psychology of colors and shapes and the incorporation into living space of discriminative stimuli for anti-stress behavior, may support biofeedback learning. Future advances in electronics and marketing may make training in natural contexts possible by reducing the cost and size of biofeedback instruments, and by the production of more reliable and sturdy instruments which can be telemetrically monitored and regulated. These peripheral support systems can facilitate the transfer of learning but their effects can be potentiated very greatly by central changes (changes in belief systems) which selectively sensitize the perceptual process and bias the interpretation of observations in directions that are supportive of the new visceral learning. Significant progress with the transfer of training awaits the development of a powerful and reliable technology to alter belief systems. A combination of central and peripheral interventions may increase the probability of the transfer of learning from consulting room to natural habitat.

It is critical to the clinical application of biofeedback to determine whether or not there are individual differences in the ability to learn visceral control and as importantly to construct scales to identify and measure these differences. (The existence of such individual differences has limited the clinical utility of hypnosis). If, for example, variables like expectancy, and so forth are implicated in individual differences, then it may be worthwhile trying to circumvent them by arranging for subtle but powerful demand characteristics operations instructionally, situationally, and in terms of clinical procedures. Careful attention should also be paid to the credibility of the instructions and the clinical procedures (Orne, 1970) if demand characteristics effects are to be maximized. The data reported in the biofeedback studies printed in this book do not equally reveal the large and significant individual differences which emerge in routine biofeedback training in clinical and experimental settings. At least two of the studies (Roberts et al., 1973, Wickramasekera, 1973b) demonstrate these individual differences. The study by Roberts et al. with normal subjects clearly shows large individual differences among subjects in their ability to demonstrate voluntary control of skin temperature and this observation is confirmed by Wickramasekera with a clinical sample (migraine patients). A recent study (Stephens, et al., 1975) implicated a subject variable "ego strength" as measured by the M.M.P.I. with individual differences in biofeedback performance. We have hypothesized that up to a point hypnotizability as measured by Stanford Scales is positively correlated with biofeedback learning skill.

It is likely that certain limitations exist for the clinical application of biofeedback. Stressful environments and lifestyles may be incompatible with the cognitive control of autonomic functions, as well as the production of low-arousal states. This may be particularly true during the early phases of the acquisition curve. Chronically high-arousal levels maintained in some occupational lifestyles (e.g. sales) over several years may cause structural changes requiring surgical or chemical intervention. Learning-based procedures like biofeedback are most likely to be effective if used early, prophylactically, in the course of such a disturbance before irreversible structural changes have occurred. Biofeedback training may not, in certain instances, be transferable to inherently stressful natural habitats. Hence, a patient with a turbulent lifestyle may need not only to learn cognitive control of an autonomic function, but he should also be influenced into changing his lifestyle or more specifically, his values or priorities. Hence, a total treatment package for such a patient may have at least two principal components— one, cognitive regulation of autonomic function; and two, alteration of lifestyle and values. It is unlikely that without some cognitive restructuring (priority alterations) durable changes in autonomic functioning can be maintained. The wise "Guru" in Zen, Yoga, or Christian Meditation not only provides his student with a technique but also a credible mythology or philosophy of life, an intellectual system that restructures priorities or values in a manner consistent with the new technology. It is with regard to the latter component that hypnosis may prove to be most useful (Wickramasekera, 1971). Hypnotic procedures appear to provide promising tools to alter the values of hypnotizable and motivated subjects. A study by Wickramasekera demonstrated that it was possible to alter temporarily a value as basic and general as money in such patients (hypnotizable and motivated). It is one of the primary hypotheses of this book that verbal-instructional interventions are potentiated within the hypnotic interpersonal context. This hypothesis will be clarified and documented later.

Travis (1973) and Wickramasekera (1973a) found that the psychological concomitants of biofeedback-induced physiological changes (EEG and EMG) may not always be positive in nature and entirely free of side effects. Travis (1973) found that about 52% of his subjects (N=22) in an alpha enhancement situation found the experience "neutral or unpleasant." Wickramasekera found that an EMG-feedback training and relaxation procedure for tension headache was reliably associated with the onset of a recurrent nightmare that was so distressing to his patient that relaxation feedback training had to be terminated. The particular patient was generally disturbed but had insisted on circumscribed treatment only for his headache. Orne and Paskewitz (1974) have shown that it is possible to have sympathetic arousal, verbally reported anxiety, and concurrently to show abundant alpha density in the biofeedback situation. These preliminary observations illustrate the relevance of individual differences to biofeedback training and suggest the importance of a more sophisticated approach to clinical applications. The need for systematic clinical trials which are broadly observed and carefully monitored over long periods is illustrated by the studies cited above.

Biofeedback appears to provide a promising tool which may become an effective, reliable, and objective method in monitoring and eventually altering private events. Several studies included in the biofeedback section deal with highly private or subjective events—pain, fear (anxiety), and sexual pleasure. These subjective events have objective (physiological) correlates. These studies illustrate how the biofeedback method operates by monitoring the objective (physiological) correlate, and eventually through the alteration of the objective correlate, also alters the subjective experience (e.g., pain, fear, pleasure).

Pain has both psychological and physiological components. The psychological determinants of pain perception include meaning, anxiety, and suggestion. The articles by Melzack and Wickramasekera on arthritic pain illustrate how the impact of the informational feedback variable can be potentiated by suggestion or hypnosis. In fact it is the primary purpose of this book to identify variables (e.g. low arousal states, informational feedback, subject characteristics, situational and procedural variables, etc.) that potentiate verbal instructions (the things people say to themselves and the things that are said to them).

The studies of headache pain (Wickramasekera, 1972a; 1973a, b) demonstrate that both the intensity and duration of pain can be altered by changing the physiological correlate (EMG or temperature) appropriate to the specific headache syndrome. Muscular tension headaches appear to respond to EMG-feedback training and migraine (vascular headache) appears to respond to temperature feedback training. Hence, there appears to be some specificity as to the type of subjective event (type of pain) which will respond to which objective (EMG or temperature) manipulation. If this specificity of effect on muscular and vascular syndromes is replicated with improved controls, it will be an event without many precedents in the therapeutic behavioral literature.

But clinical observation indicates that for *some* individuals the correlation between verbal, physiological, and behavioral measures may be very low. For example the verbal report data may indicate a rapid decline in pain, but the EMG level may remain unchanged or the converse may be observed. This lack of congruence between response systems has previously been recognized in certain clinical dissociative symptoms, hypnosis, and more recently in behavior therapy for phobias. This type of observation was probably the basis for Freud's concept of the "unconcious" and it illustrates his clinical acumen .

Fear is another private event, which appears to be modifiable by biofeedback used either alone (Garrett and Silver, 1974) or as an adjunctive procedure to systematic desensitization (Wickramasekera, 1972, 1974b). The physiological correlates of fear selected for alteration in the above studies are EMG, EKG, and EEG (Alpha) responses. In certain chronic fears it may be important to directly alter central events (verbal definition or pre-verbal perception of a situation) because the peripheral concomitants may have become insignificant or not detectable, as in some animal studies of traumatic avoidance learning, which incidentally also demonstrate this uncoupling between motor and visceral response systems. There may be certain brain states, as operationally defined by the EEG (feedback training to increase theta density), which increase the probability of the recall of pre-verbal events and also potentiate the verbal-instructional redefinition and disruption of phobic responding.

Sexual pleasure is another highly private event which in the male has a reliable physiological correlate (penile erection). The study by Rosen (included in this section) demonstrates that erection may be suppressed to an effective stimulus, but the "private" correlate of penile suppression is not clear. It is also important to recognize that the private (psychological) and public (physiological) mechanisms of penile erection and suppression may be quite different. This study may be regarded as demonstrating how a combination of self instruction and feedback can inhibit a reflex or respond-ent behavior.

It appears that biofeedback is a promising technique but it is important to recognize that its effectiveness for clinical purposes remains to be established. There are as yet no double-blind, well-controlled studies with long-term (5-10 years) follow-ups which demonstrate specific effects. The long term follow-ups are particularly important with chronic conditions that show spontaneous fluctuations over time. Chronic symptoms are generally presented for treatment during acute episodes and the spontane-ous remission hypothesis is still a viable one in this field. It is assumed that the procedures used are "operant conditioning," to which they bear some superficial similarities and the *informational feedback* variable is the critical variable. Other uncontrolled variables may include subject expectations, experimenter expectations, interpersonal or relationship variables (empathy, warmth, etc.), motivation and incentives, inevitably increasing suggestibility in the biofeedback training situation (Wickramasekera 1971, 1974), and baseline individual differences in readiness to learn biological self control.

Biofeedback procedures with human subjects are particularly suscepti-ble to "placebo" effects (Wickramasekera 1974), and the fourth part of this book covers an approach to defining the mechanism of the "placebo" effect and predicting and controlling it so that this powerful but unreliable effect can be domesticated and reliably harnessed, rather than eliminated from a total specific treatment package.

We do not know the types of patients and symptoms that respond most readily to biofeedback. We need to know if the most effective strategy of intervention is to focus on specific symptoms (e.g. frontalis and occipitalis tension) or on more general response systems (EEG responses). A recent study (Schwartz, 1972) of self control of heart rate and blood pressure indicates that training a *pattern* of responses as opposed to *discrete* responses was very reliably associated with rapid acquisition and positive subjective states (relaxation and calm). If biofeedback training were to focus on a single response system or a pattern of responses, it might be useful to determine in advance diagnostically the psychophysiological stress profile of the patient. It has been shown (Lacey, 1967) that individuals generate unique and fairly reliable profiles (EKG, EMG, EEG, GSR, respiration, etc.) of response to stress across situations. The focus of intervention should probably zero in on the most responsive system or the point at which homeostatic central regulation appears to be weakest and the probability of clinical breakdown greatest. There also appears to be some clinical consensus that the response system with the most abundant cortical projections (e.g. EMG) is the most rapidly educable. Hence, biofeedback learning for stress management should probably begin with the most easily educable response system (e.g. EMG) and proceed next to the "high risk" (as determined by clinical symptoms or psychophysiological stress profile) response system (e.g. heart rate and/or blood pressure pattern training). We need to know the optimal conditions for training, e.g. should patients be treated intensively on an inpatient basis or bi-weekly on an outpatient basis? Where symptomatic relief itself is inadequate to maintain training efforts, what other reinforcement contingency may be manipulated? What reinforcements (social or concrete in what situations are most effective with which types of patients? How may pretreatment motivational instructions, the relationship variables (Truax and Mitchell, 1971), attraction to the therapist, and suggestion techniques be used to potentiate the "specific" effects of biofeedback? How should these variables be matched with patient or subject characteristics?

The early excitement about EEG biofeedback is dissipating in the face of more sophisticated analyses of the early studies. It is becoming clear that we need more basic science research in this field before we can plan clinical applications. The current clinical utility of EEG biofeedback may be restricted to the study of the behavioral correlates of visual events (Mulholland, 1966), vigilance training (Beatty et al., 1974), hypnogogic imagery (theta), and epilepsy management (Sterman et al., 1974). The epilepsy work involves laborious training of the sensorimotor rhythm (12-14HZ). This work may be reinterpreted in terms of immobility training. In fact, we have clinically observed, during EMG frontalis training for headache and phobic symptoms, that unexpectedly seizure activity also declines. Controlled comparative studies will tell us if the more economic EMG procedure produces results that are clinically comparable to the more complicated and expensive EEG procedure.

There is currently some concern because animal investigations of visceral learning are not replicating in expected ways (Miller and Dworkin, 1973). This should not discourage clinical human investigations at this point. Issues like the validity of the cognitive and somatic mediation hypotheses are not immediately relevant to clinical practice because the clinician is concerned with helping his patient *control,* not necessarily *condition,* his autonomic (Katkin and Murray, 1968) and central nervous system (Paskewitz and Orne, 1973).

The study of soft phenomena (fantasy, emotions, etc.) with hardware may expand the frontiers of inner space, and ironically it may turn out that the hard-headed behavioristic methodology may make major contributions to the study of "private" or subjective events.

Biofeedback training may contribute to the modification of hypnotizability, and it appears that changes in suggestibility are an inevitable concomitant of effective biofeedback (low arousal) training (Wickramasekera, 1971, 1974). Experimentally it may be impossible to separate the effects of informational feedback from suggestibility in clinical biofeedback studies because the informational properties (as opposed to incentive properties) of reinforcing events may be inseparably confounded with self instructional (suggestibility) variables.

In summary it is worth saying that there is a freshness, idealism, and simplicity of approach in clinical biofeedback which is reminiscent of behavior therapy in the early 60s. In fact, the biofeedback movement appears to be acquiring its own set of high priests, disciples, followers, and even a lunatic fringe. It is becoming the "respectable and scientific" cutting edge of a more general social movement that has utopian goals and resonates with profound and broadly based human visions. The popularity of biofeedback may also have to do with the paranoid spirit of our times ("self-control" is becoming a sacred word) and the "electronic-scientific" packaging with which biofeedback is associated in the popular mind. Exaggerated and naive claims for biofeedback and some dubious ethical procedures in currently marketing clinical applications may cause revulsion in sophisticated clinicians, hence, postponing the date when biofeedback technology will take its place among other tools in the clinician's armamentarium. Eventually the field of experimental biofeedback may be assimilated into the general body of psychophysiology. But before it does, it will have major implications for the training of future clinical psychologists. The investigation of altered states of consciousness with reliable biofeedback procedures and other tools may contribute to the understanding of psychotic states and greater caution in labeling "psychotic" people who may have spontaneously experienced or inadvertently self-induced such altered states. The self-fulfilling consequences such labels have are better appreciated today. The clinical psychologist of the twenty-first century will know as much about psychophysiology and altered states of consciousness as the psychologist of today knows about learning and psychodynamics. In a very real sense biofeedback has brought the body back into clinical psychology. It has provided the behaviorist with hardware and procedures with which to study private events. It has given the clinical psychologist a rationale for "touching" patients. The range of biological knowledge required to do informed biofeedback research or to intelligently and more specifically treat functional syndromes (e.g. headache, ulcer, cardiovascular dysfunctions, etc.) will cause increasing convergence between medical and psychological education. Biofeedback, behavior therapy, and the "new" hypnosis promise to clinically oriented behavioral scientists' interventions which may provide a degree of specificity lacking in current psychiatric therapies like E.C.T., psychotropic drugs, and psycho-surgery (Valenstein, 1973)

References

Barber, T.X. et al. (Eds). *Biofeedback and self-control.* Chicago: Aldine, 1972.

Beatty, J.; Greenberg, A.; Deibler, N.P. & Hanlon, J.F. Operant control of occipital theta rhythm affects performance in a radar monitoring task. *Science,* 1974, 183: 871-873.

Blanchard, E.B.; Scott, R.W.; Young, L.D. & Edmundson, E. The unit of measurement in behavioral approach to clinical cardiac control. Unpublished paper, 1974.

Fleishman, E.A. Human abilities and the acquisition of skill. In E.A. Bilodeau (Ed.), *Acquisition of skill.* New York: Academic Press, 1966.

Garrett, B.C. & Silver, M.P. The use of EMG and alpha biofeedback to relieve test anxiety in college students. Unpublished paper, 1974.

Grossberg, J.M. Brain wave feedback experiments and the concept of mental mechanisms. *Behavior Therapy and Experimental Psychiatry,* 1972, 3: 245-251.

Katkin, E.S. & Murray, E.M. Instrumental conditioning of autonomically mediated behavior. *Psychological Bulletin,* 1968, 70: 52-60.

Lacey, J.I. Somatic response patterning and stress: Some revisions of activation theory. In M.W. Appley & R. Trumbull (Eds.), *Psychological Stress.* Issues in research. New York: Appleton, 1967. Pp. 14-42.

Mandel, A.R. Biofeedback, hypnosis and heart rate control. Paper presented at A.P.A., Chicago, 1975.

Melzack, R. Self regulation of pain. *Experimental Neurology,* 1975, 46: 452-469.

Miller, N.E. & Dworkin, B.R. Visceral learning. In P.A. Obrist et al. (Eds.), *Contemporary trends in cardiovascular psychophysiology.* Chicago: Aldine-Atherton, 1973.

Mulholland, T. & Evans, C.R. Oculomotor function and alpha activation cycle. *Nature,* 1966, 211: 1278-1279.

Orne, M.T. The demand characteristics of an experimental design and their implications. Paper presented at A.P.A., Cincinnati, 1959.

Orne, M.T. Hypnosis, motivation and the ecological validity of the psychological experiment. In W.J. Arnold & M.M. Page (Eds), *Nebraska Symposium on Motivation.* Lincoln: University of Nebraska Press, 1970.

Orne, M.T. & Paskewitz, D.A. Aversive situational effects on alpha feedback training. *Science,* 1974, 186: 458-460.

Paskewitz, D. & Orne, M.T. Visual effects of alpha feedback training. *Science,* 1973, 181: 409.

Roberts, A.H.; Kewman, D.G. & MacDonald, H. Voluntary control of skin temperature: Unilateral changes using hypnosis and feedback. *Journal of Abnormal Psychology,* 1973, 82 (1): 163-168.

Sarbin, T.R. & Coe, W.C. *Hypnosis, a social psychological analysis of influence communication.* New York: Holt, Rhinehart and Winston, 1972.

Schwartz, G.E. Voluntary control of human cardiovascular integration and differentiation through feedback and reward. *Science,* 1972, 175: 90-93.

Sterman, M.B.; MacDonald, L.R. & Stone, R.K. Biofeedback training of the sensorimotor electroencephalogram rhythm in man: Effects on epilepsy. *Epilepsia,* 1974, 15: 395-416.

Stevens, J.H.; Harris, A.H.; Brady, J.V. & Schaffer, J.W. Psychological and physiological variables associated with large magnitude voluntary heart rate changes. *Psychophysiology,* 1975, 12 (4): 381-387.

Travis, T. Subjective aspects of the alpha enhancement situation. Unpublished report, 1973.

Truax, C.B. & Mitchell, K.M. Research on certain therapist interpersonal skills in relation to process and outcome. In A.E. Bergin & S.L. Garfield (Eds.), *Handbook of psychotherapy and behavior change.* New York: Wiley, 1971.

Valenstein, E. *Brain Control.* New York: Wiley, 1973.

Walsh, D.H. Interactive effects of alpha feedback and instructional set on subjective state. *Psychophysiology,* 1974, 11 (4): 428-435.

Wickramasekera, I. Effects of hypnosis and task motivational instructions in attempting to influence the voluntary self-deprivation of money. *Journal of Personality and Social Psychology,* 1971, 19: 311-314.

Wickramasekera, I. Effects of EMG feedback training on susceptibility to hypnosis: Preliminary observations. *Proceedings, 79th Annual Convention of the American Psychological Association, 1971.* Pp. 783-784.

Wickramasekera, I. EMG feedback training and tension headache: Preliminary observations. *American Journal of Clinical Hypnosis,* 1972, 15: 83-85. (a)

Wickramasekera, I. Instructions and EMG feedback in systematic desensitization: A case report. *Behavior Therapy,* 1972, 3: 460-465. (b)

Wickramasekera, I. On the apparent intrusion of a recurring nightmare into an EMG feedback training procedure. Unpublished paper, 1973. (a)

Wickramasekera, I. Temperature feedback for the control of migraine. *Behavior Therapy and Experimental Psychiatry,* 1973, 4: 343-345. (b)

Wickramasekera, I. Heart rate feedback and the control of cardiac neurosis. *Journal of Abnormal Psychology,* 1974, 00, 570 500.

Wickramasekera, I.; Truong, X.T.; Bush, M. & Orr, C. A case study of arthritic pain. Unpublished paper, 1975.

Part I

PAIN

Electromyographic Feedback Training and Tension Headache: Preliminary Observations

Ian Wickramasekera
University of Illinois
College of Medicine
Peoria

Sustained contraction of the scalp and neck muscles appears to be associated with tension headache (Ostfeld, 1962; Wolff, 1963). Electromyographic (EMG) feedback seems useful in the induction of muscular relaxation (Budzynski & Stoyva, 1969, Green, Walters, Green & Murphy, 1969). Budzynski, Stoyva and Adler (1970) described an EMG instrument and feedback training procedure which appeared to reduce both the intensity and frequency of tension headache. Their report was a collection of case studies and lacked several experimental controls. The purpose of the present study was to attempt to replicate their observations with more control, while retaining the merits of the case study method.

Method

Instrumentation: EMG Feedback System

The purpose of this instrument is to enable the S to monitor his muscle tension by means of an analog information feedback system. The S hears a tone with a frequency proportional to the EMG activity in the relevant muscle group. The feedback tone tracks the changing EMG level of the muscle. Three surface electrodes are applied either to the forearm extensor one inch below the elbow, or to the frontalis in such a way that the center electrode is centered on the forehead about one inch above the eyebrows. The instrument is constructed so that there is a maximum of 20K unbalanced electrode resistance and a maximum of 30K resistance to ground for each

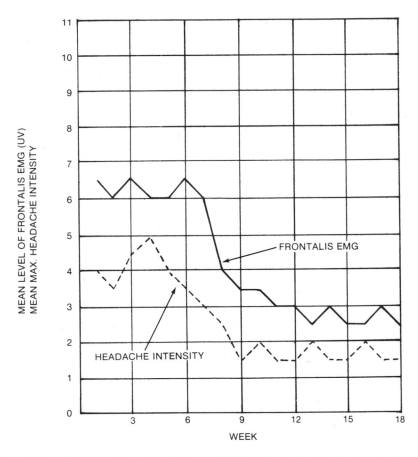

FIGURE 1. Headache Intensity and Frontalis EMG Over Time. (0-3 weeks is baseline: 3-6 weeks is noncontingent feedback; 6-18 weeks is contingent feedback)

active electrode. The instrument is constructed to eliminate the EKG, EEG, and "noise" artifacts.

The S is instructed to keep the tone low by relaxing the relevant muscle group. As the S improves this control, the loop gain of the feedback system is increased, thus requiring him to maintain a lower EMG level in order to hear a low tone. The response of muscle relaxation is shaped by increasing the difficulty of the task in three steps (three sensitivity settings, *i.e.,* low, medium, high). Brief visual feedback was provided only in the first session of training with the use of a meter unit calibrated in microamps. The microvolt level, sensitivity setting, and meter readout were interrelated. For example, for an *S* to hold a meter reading of 26 while the sensitivity control is increased from low to medium to high, the *S* must drop microvolt level from 5.8 to 4.1 to 3.7.

Procedure

Five female *S*s diagnosed by neurologists as chronic (6-20 years) tension headache cases, were accepted for the following medical and psychological procedures: (a) Psychological testing (M.M.P.I., SIISS Forms A (pretested prior to EMG feedback training) and B (posttested after EMG feedback training). (b) Complete physical examination by consulting internist, EEG, and examination by consulting neurologist. (c) Next, the patients were given

FIGURE 2. Headache Activity Over Time. (0-3 weeks is baseline; 3-6 weeks is noncontingent feedback; 6-18 weeks is contingent feedback)

charts on which they were required to keep an accurate record of the intensity and frequency of all headache activity. They were also instructed to cease taking any medication prescribed for their headaches till the conclusion of the study. (d) There was an initial three-week observation period to determine base rates of headache activity. (e) At the end of the three-week baseline period, Ss were oriented and instructed (for ten minutes) in the use of the EMG-feedback training procedure. The instruction was conducted with "true" or contingent EMG auditory feedback. (f) Next the patients received six sessions of "false" or noncontingent EMG auditory feedback training over a three-week period. Each session lasted 30 minutes. Patients did not know they were receiving "false" feedback, hence the study was single blind. The "false" auditory EMG feedback was not randomly generated and hence possibly frustrative in nature. After the orientation period, the EMG console was placed on a table behind the Ss chair. The earphones which delivered the auditory feedback were disconnected without the Ss knowledge from the EMG console and connected to a recorder that delivered taped auditory EMG feedback from the actual first six sessions of a S successfully trained to relax with "true" or contingent feedback. Hence during the control period, Ss received a pattern of feedback which had the appearance of reality and progress, because the feedback tone declined over time. But the decline was unrelated to anything that the S did or did not do during the control period. Informal postexperimental inquiry revealed that the Ss believed that they were receiving "true" feedback from their own frontalis and that they had improved in their relaxation skills. Ss continued to keep the record of their headache activity during the "false" feedback period. (g) At the end of the "false" feedback period, all patients received six sessions of EMG auditory feedback training with "true" or contingent feedback for another three weeks. Each contingent feedback training session was identical in length (30 minutes) to the previous noncontingent training sessions.

Results

Inspection of the records of all patients appear to indicate no significant difference in the frequency and intensity of headache activity between the baseline period and the noncontingent ("false") EMG feedback period. But there appears to be for all patients significant differences in both intensity and frequency of headache activity between the baseline period and the contingent feedback period. The significant differences in headache activity between the noncontingent and contingent feedback period appears to suggest that the observed differences were probably not a function of placebo efforts *(e.g.,* attention, impressive instrumentation, etc.) These preliminary data seem to suggest that contingent EMG auditory feedback training may be a promising method of reducing the frequency and intensity of tension headache.

References

Budzynski, T.H. & Stoyva, J.M. An instrument for producing deep muscle relaxation by means for analog information feedback. *Journal of Applied Behavior Analysis,* 1969, 2, 231-237.

Budzynski, T.H., Stoyva, J.M. & Adler, C. Feedback induced muscle application to tension headache. *Journal of Behavior Therapy and Experimental Psychiatry,* 1970, 1, 205-211.

Green, E.E., Walters, E.D., Green, A.M. & Murphy, G. Feedback technique for deep relaxation. *Psychophysiology,* 1969, 6, 372-377.

Ostfeld, A.M. *The common headache syndromes biochemistry, pathophysiology, therapy.* Springfield, Illinois: Thomas, 1969.

Wolff, H.G. *Headache and other pain.* New York: Oxford University Press, 1963.

Note: This study was partly supported by a grant from the A.S.C.H. Research Foundation.

The Application of Verbal Instructions and EMG Feedback Training to the Management of Tension Headache: Preliminary Observations

Ian Wickramasekera
University of Illinois
College of Medicine
Peoria

Sustained contraction of the scalp and neck muscles appears to be associated with tension headache.[1,2] Electromyographic (EMG) feedback seems useful in the induction of muscular relaxation.[3,4] Budzynski, Stoyva and Adler,[5] described an EMG instrument and feedback training procedure which appeared to reduce both the intensity and frequency of tension headache and in two subsequent studies,[6,7] we were able to replicate these observations. In a previous paper,[8] it was hypothesized that a combination of verbal instructions and response contingent EMG feedback would enhance the effectiveness of systematic desensitization training. The purpose of the present study was to attempt to note clinically the effects of first verbal relaxation instructions and later EMG feedback training on tension headache.

Relaxation Training Procedures

A. Verbal Relaxation instructions were taken verbatim from Wolpe and Lazurus[9] and administered individually to each patient by the present writer on 3 consecutive days of muscular relaxation training. Each training session was about 40 minutes in duration.

B. EMG Feedback Training and Instrumentation

The purpose of this instrument is to enable the subject to monitor his muscle tension by means of an analog information feedback system. The subject hears a tone with a frequency proportional to the EMG activity in the relevant muscle group. The feedback tone tracks the changing EMG level of the muscle. Three surface electrodes are applied to the frontalis in such a way that the center electrode is centered on the forehead about one inch above the eyebrows. The instrument is constructed (for additional technical details, see the manual of this commercially available instrument) so that there is a maximum of 20K unbalanced electrode resistance and a maximum of 30K resistance to ground for each active electrode. The instrument is constructed to eliminate the EKG, EEG, and "noise" artifacts.

The subject is instructed to keep the tone low by relaxing the relevant muscle group. As the subject improves his control, the loop gain of the feedback system is increased, thus requiring him to maintain a lower EMG level in order to hear a low tone. The response of muscle relaxation is shaped by increasing the difficulty of the task in three steps (3 sensitivity settings, i.e., low, medium, high). Brief visual feedback was provided only in the first session of training with the use of a meter unit calibrated in microamps. The microvolt level, sensitivity setting, and meter readout are interrelated. For example, for a subject to hold a meter reading of 26 while the sensitivity control is increased from low to medium to high, the subject must drop microvolt level from 5.8 to 4.1 to 3.7.

Procedure

Five female subjects diagnosed by neurologists as chronic (6-20 years) and almost daily tension headache cases, were accepted for the following medical and psychological procedures: 1. Psychological testing (M.M.P.I.), Stanford Hypnotic Susceptibility Scale forms A (pretested prior to EMG feedback training) and B (posttested after EMG feedback training). 2. Complete physical by consulting internist, EEG and examination by consulting neurologist. 3. Next, patients were given charts on which they were required to keep during the duration of the study an accurate record of the intensity and frequency of all headache activity. 4. There was an initial observation period to determine base rate headache activity and frontalis EMG (averaged over 10 minutes of observation). 5. At the end of the 3-week baseline period, subjects were seen on 3 consecutive days by the present writer for muscular relaxation training with the Wolpe and Lazarus[9] verbal instructions. After each verbal training session (40 minutes), frontalis EMG was monitored for 10 minutes. After the formal verbal training period, patients were required to come into the clinic and practice relaxation thrice each week, during the second and third weeks of relaxation with verbal instruction. EMG-monitoring of each patient occurred for 10 minutes after each relaxation practice session. 6. After 3 weeks relaxation practice with verbal instructions, subjects were instructed (for 10 minutes) in the use of the EMG feedback training procedure. The instruction was conducted with contingent EMG auditory feedback training for another 3 weeks. Each feedback training session was identical in length (40 minutes) and subjects were instructed to practice relaxation, combining what they had learned (subjective physical feedback sensation of deep relaxation e.g., heaviness, lightness, numbness, tingling, etc.) from both verbal instructions and feedback training. Frontalis EMG was monitored during the last 10 minutes of the feedback training period. 7. After EMG feedback training was completed, patients continued to record the frequency and intensity of headache activity and also came thrice a week for a 10-minute session of frontalis EMG monitoring for another 9 weeks. Patients were instructed to continue to practice relaxation at home at least twice a week even after the EMG feedback training was completed.

Results

Inspection of the records of all patients appeared to suggest a decline in the frequency and intensity of headache activity after the baseline period.

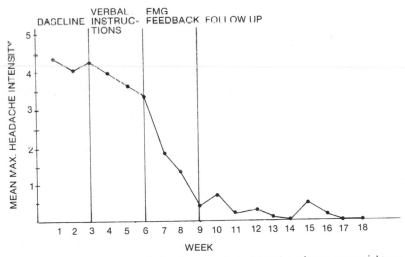

FIGURE 1. Mean maximum headache levels per week for 5 female patients over an eighteen-week period

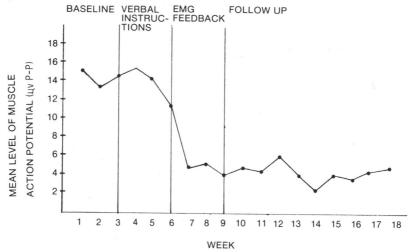

Figure 2. Mean frontalis EMG levels for 5 female patients over an eighteen-week period

The decline in the frequency and intensity of headache activity seems even more dramatic for 4 of the 5 patients and after the EMG feedback period. The small size of the sample and the confounding of the effects of verbal instructions and EMG feedback training made it difficult to draw conclusions and generalize from this data. Nevertheless, clinical impression and the more dramatic decline in frontalis EMG associated with the feedback training procedure appears to suggest that the addition of response contingent EMG feedback training results in a more specific and powerful procedure for the clinical management of tension headache. Further factorial studies should separate out the effects of verbal instructions and EMG feedback training on tension headache and also study the interaction effects of the procedures. In order to control for "placebo effects" and experimenter bias, this should be repeated with noncontingent but nonfrustrating EMG feedback[10] and a "blind experimenter."

References

1. Ostfeld AM: The common headache syndromes: biochemistry, pathophysiology, therapy. (New York: Grune & Stratton, 1962).

2. Wolff HG: Headache and other pain. (New York: Oxford University Press, 1963)

3. Budzynski TH, Stoyva JM: An instrument for producing deep muscle relaxation by means of analog information feedback. *J App Beh Anal* 2:231-237, 1969.

4. Green EE, Walters ED, Green AM, Murphy G: Feedback technique for deep relaxation. *Psychophysiol* 6:372-377, 1969.

5. Budzynski TH, Stoyva JM, Adler C: Feedback induced muscle application to tension headache. *J Beh Ther Exper Psychia* 1:205-211, 1970.

6. Wickramasekera I: Effects of EMG feedback on tension headaches. In Barber TX, et al: Biofeedback and self control. (Chicago: Aldine-Atherton, Inc., 1973).

7. Pope BK, Wickramasekera I: Relaxation and electromyographic feedback training and tension headache. Unpublished, 1972.

8. Wickramasekera I: Instructions and EMG feedback in systematic desensitization: a case report. *Beh Ther* 3:460-465, 1972.

9. Wolpe J, Lazarus AA: Behavior therapy techniques. (New York: Pergamon Press, 1966).

10. Wickramasekera I: The effects of EMG feedback training on susceptibility to hypnosis: preliminary observations. In Stoyva J, et al: Biofeedback and self-control. (Chicago: Aldine, 1972).

11. Wickramasekera I: The effects of EMG feedback training on susceptibility to hypnosis. More preliminary observations. *J. Abnormal Psychology* (in press).

Temperature Feedback
for the Control of Migraine

Ian Wickramasekera
University of Illinois
College of Medicine
Peoria

The migraine headache syndrome (Wolff, 1963) is characterized by periodic headache pain, which begins unilaterally but may become generalized. The headache may be associated with nausea, photophobia, and vomiting, and may be preceded by scotomata, hemianopia and unilateral paresthesia. There is a high probability that other members of the patient's family (siblings or parents) have similar headaches. The headaches may start at any age but most frequently during adolescence. The headache is reported to be associated with "cold extremities" (Wolff, 1963, p. 676) and the pain is produced primarily by distension of cranial arteries.

Muscle contraction headache appears to respond favorably to EMG feedback training (Budzynski, Stoyva and Adler, 1969, Wickramasekera, 1973a, and Wickramasekera, 1973b) but the migraine syndrome is apparently unresponsive to this procedure. Sargent, Green and Walters (1972a,b) reported on the successful use of autogenic feedback training in the treatment of migraine and tension headaches. Their procedure basically consisted of the use of a "temperature trainer" which indicated the differential temperature between the mid-forehead and the right index finger. The subjects were also required to learn certain autogenic phrases (Schultz and Luthe, 1969). The patients were told to attempt to increase the temperature of their hand in comparison to their forehead. The investigators found that a positive response was always associated with warmth in the hands but no apparent change in head sensations.

Patients

The two patients described here were first treated with EMG feedback training without positive response, and later with the "temperature trainer" with success. M. (age 45 yr) had suffered from chronic daily headaches since adolescence. F. (age 46 yr) had suffered from headaches since about 30. Both were school teachers, and both had previously received psychotherapy and chemotherapy several times, and had been examined and treated at leading medical clinics, all without positive outcome. Both patients had become quite resentful and skeptical, particularly after the EMG feedback procedure was unsuccessful. It was probably only the intensity and frequency of their headaches and the ineffectiveness of the chemical analgesics that motivated the patients to try another feedback procedure. They clearly had other types of problems (such as poor interpersonal and marital relations) but they were unwilling to work on them.

With the EMG feedback training procedure we use (Wickramasekera, 1972), the male patient (M) had completed 16 EMG feedback sessions in the consulting room and had been requested to practice relaxation at home for about 20 min at least once a day. The female patient (F) had completed 18 feedback training sessions plus instructions to practice relaxation. In both there was only a slight reduction in the intensity of headache. The frequency of headache remained unchanged. The patients were told that another feedback training procedure for headaches was available but that we were uncertain about its effectiveness. Both were initially reluctant, but M reenlisted for training after a 2-month break and F reenlisted reluctantly after considering our offer for about 3 weeks.

Methods

Both patients had at the outset received careful screening on a variety of psychological and medical tests (including an EEG and skull X-rays) by a psychologist, an internist, and a consulting neurologist. The method we used was essentially that described by Sargent, Green and Walters (1972) omitting the autogenic phrases. The patients were simply told to try to concentrate on increasing the temperature of their hands while remaining seated on a large padded recliner in a comfortable consulting room. The same facilities had been used for the EMG feedback training. The "head" thermistor is connected to the center of the forehead and the hand thermistor to the middle finger of the dominant hand. It is important that the subject not move the dominant hand during training. The temperature trainer has a "shaping" feature which provides feedback at two levels of sensitivity (high and low). When the instrument is in the high sensitivity mode, very small changes in temperature are reflected on the meter readout unit (visual feedback). The patients practiced the handwarming skill both with and

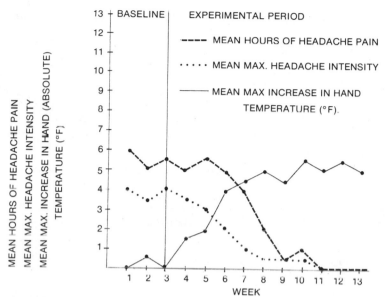

FIGURE 1. Data on F showing changes in headache duration, intensity and absolute hand temperature

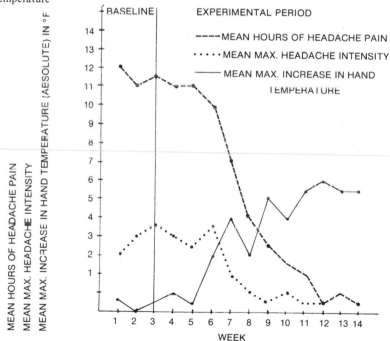

FIGURE 2. Data on M showing changes in headache duration, intensity and absolute hand temperature

without feedback in the clinic and in addition practiced at home without feedback.

Results

After another 3-week baseline period during which headache activity (frequency and intensity) was monitored and recorded, the temperature feedback training procedure was started. The temperature feedback data showed that the handwarming skill was acquired quite rapidly. It would be interesting to know if the rapid acquisition was related to the previous EMG feedback training. We have observed several migraine patients who did not receive prior EMG feedback training but who have also acquired the handwarming skill quite rapidly. Apparently the speed of acquisition of handwarming skill is generally greater than that of frontalis relaxation skill.

The frequency and intensity of the headache activity of these two patients appeared to decline as they increased their skill in warming their hands. During both the baseline and training periods there were no significant changes in consumption of analgesics. But at follow-up 3 months after training, both patients reported that they had reduced their consumption of analgesics to occasional aspirin for nonheadache-related events.

Discussion

This study confirms the earlier report of Sargent *et al.* that temperature feedback to increase warmth (and blood flow) in the extremities can be useful in the treatment of migraine headache. The main implication is that feedback training must be tailored to fit the type of headache—that is, temperature feedback is effective for migraine, but feedback-assisted muscle relaxation is not (though the latter seems useful for muscle contraction heachache). This observation supports the idea that temperature training in some way acts on the causal mechanism involved in migraine headache, rather than having some global placebo-suggestion effect. Also against interpreting the results as a placebo response is the fact that the two patients had been afflicted by the headaches for many years, and during that time exposed to a variety of other treatments without success.

If the ability to increase hand temperature is useful for aborting migraine headache pain, then it would be interesting to know if training migraine patients to reduce hand temperature would increase the probability of migraine attacks. It would be interesting to investigate this question. It is likely that influencing sympathetic nervous system function is the critical event and that increasing blood flow to the hands is simply a correlated event. If increasing blood flow to the hands were the critical event then it should be possible to induce or to abort migraine attacks by placing one's hands in buckets of water at suitable temperatures (e.g., to induce a migraine attack, use ice cold water and to abort a migraine attack use warm water). As far as I know nobody has conducted this experiment.

The biofeedback technique is a relatively direct procedure for studying the interaction of psychological and physiological responses. Biofeedback research may make many of the phenomena previously subsumed under "suggestion," "placebo," "hypnosis," etc. amenable to scientific methods of study. The application of the scientific method to the study of these phenomena may enable us to control and predict them and possibly eventually to increase their generality and power (Wickramasekera, 1972, 1973c). It is also possible that biofeedback may lead to a technology for creating more powerful and reliable placebos. Biofeedback training in general appears to involve aspects of both operant conditioning and skill learning (Woodworth and Schlosberg, 1961). Future double blind and factorial studies should investigate parameters which have been found to be relevant to these two bodies of literature (e.g. delay of reinforcement, massed, and distributed practice).

References

Budzynski T.H., Stoyva J.M. and Adler C. (1969) Feedback-Induced Muscle Relaxation: Application to Tension Headache, *J. Behav. Therapy & Exp. Psychiat.* **1,** 205-211.

Sargent J.D., Green E.E. and Walters E.D. (1972a) *Autogenic feedback training in a pilot study of migraine and tension headaches* (unpublished manuscript).

Sargent J.D., Green E.E. and Walters E.D. (1972b) *Preliminary report on the use of autogenic feedback training in the treatment of migraine and tension headaches* (unpublished manuscript).

Schultz J.H. and Luthe W. (1969) *Autogenic Therapy,* Vol I, Grune and Stratton, New York.

Wickramasekera I. (1972) The effects of EMG feedback training on susceptibility to hypnosis, *Biofeedback and Self Control* (Edited by Barber T.X. *et al.*), Aldine-Atherton, Chicago.

Wickramasekera I. (1973a) EMG feedback training and tension headache: Preliminary observations, *Biofeedback and Self Control* (Edited by Barber T.X. *et al.*), Aldine-Atherton, Chicago.

Wickramasekera I. (1973b) Instruction and EMG feedback training in tension headache, *Journal Headache* (in press).

Wickramasekera I. (1973c) Effects of EMG feedback training on susceptibility to hypnosis. More preliminary data, *J. Abnorm. Psychol.* (in press).

Wolf H.G. (1963) *Headache and Other Pain,* Oxford University Press, New York.

Woodworth R.S. and Schlosberg H. (1961) *Experimental Psychology,* Holt, Rinehart & Winston, New York.

Flow Chart and Commentary for Clinical Management of Headache Pain

Ian Wickramasekera

1. DIAGNOSTIC INTERVIEW

Etiologic, Associated or Precipitating Factors (Check and inquire)

A. Sustained muscle contraction of head, face, and neck *(tension headache)*.
B. Dialation of cranial arteries which sterile local inflammatory reaction (*migraine headache* patients appear to have very labile vascular systems).
C. *Organic diseases* and trauma of skull, brain, meninges, arteries, veins, eyes, nose, ears, and paranasal sinuses. (Was this checked?)
D. Essential hypertension. (Was this checked?)
E. Psychological factors (chronic depression, anxiety, perfectionism, rigidity, inhibited rage).
F. Allergies (seasonal or food), fatigue, loss of sleep, menstruation, bright lights, high humidity, high altitude, hunger (hypoglycemic reaction), foods and drugs that contain tyramine and certain other substances (for example, histamine, alcohol, oral contraceptives, hormonal therapy) inhaling nitrites and carbon monoxide.

Headache History (inquire and note)

A. How many *types* of headaches does the patient have? (For example, tension, migraine, cluster, sinus headaches, etc.)
B. *Onset* (age at onset, time of day or night, gradual or sudden, weekends, or vacations).
C. *Course* of headache (has become worse, improved, or stayed the same, periods of remission).
D. *Location* (unilateral, bilateral, generalized, focal, alternates sides).

E. *Frequency.* (Is the headache sporadic, daily, continuous, or seasonal?)

F. *Duration.* (Does the headache last for a few minutes, few hours, or a few days?)

G. *Type of pain.* (Is the pain dull, nagging, continuous, pulsating, throbbing, or deep and boring?)

H. *Prodromata* (warning signs), visual defects (blind spots, flashing lights, fortification spectra), hallucinations, ataxia, or vertigo present.

I. *Associated symptoms* (photophobia, nausea, vomiting, lacrimation, cranial tenderness, hypersensitivity to sound, nasal congestion, and anorexia).

J. *Sleep and sexual habits.* (Are there delays in falling asleep, frequent awakening or early awakening? Are primary or secondary orgasmic dysfunction or other sexual problems present?)

K. *Family history.* (Is there a positive family history of headaches with similar symptoms?)

L. *Previous physical and neurological examinations.* (What previous physical and neurological examinations have been done? What previous laboratory tests have been completed—skull x-rays, brain scan, EEG, spinal puncture, etc.?)

M. *Medications and response to them.* (What medications is the patient taking? Antidepressants (Elavil, Tofranil), ergotamine tartrate, reserpine, hormone therapy (menopause, birth control), any analgesic abuse?)

N. Collect headache activity data, EMG or temperature baseline

2. Structure Positive Expectations and Provide Advanced Organizers

A. Video tape of model patient

B. Reading from popular press (Time, Glamour, Readers' Digest)

3. Psychological Tests—MMPI, Eysenck, Protestant Ethic, Spiegal, SHSS A

4. Physiological Tests—EMG, GSR, heart rate, respiration, blood pressure, baseline and reaction to standardized stressors.

5. Physical Exam by Internist (M.D.) and consulting Neurologist (M.D.) and any indicated lab. tests (e.g. EEG, brain scan etc.) if omitted.

6. Relaxation Exercises and Cassette Tape

7. Feedback Training

A. Baseline (5 minutes)

B. +F.B. (15 minutes)

C. -F.B. (5 minutes)
D. +F.B. (15 minutes)
E. Stress Management (e.g. pressure, conflict)
F. Stress Scan
8. Repeat 7 above.

Commentary

    1. The causes of headache pain vary widely (for example, sustained muscle contraction, depression, food and seasonal allergies, essential arterial hypertension, vasodilation, infection and disease, tumors, hematomas, etc.). It is important to recognize correlated personality (anxiety, depression) and environmental (demanding work environments, loud sounds, poor ventilation, and inhalation of nitrites or carbon monoxide), variables which may precipitate or exacerbate the pain. Differential diagnosis of headache is facilitated by attention to the type of pain, age, and time (early morning or night, etc.) of onset of pain, the location of the pain, any associated physical symptoms (for example, nausea) or prodome and the presence of similar symptoms in other family members. The three-week baseline period can help the patient and therapist recognize more subtle environmental or intrapersonal factors that alter the probability of headache pain. Typically, *migraine* headaches start before the third decade of life, are unilateral on onset (may become bilateral or generalized), are episodic, may last three hours to four days, may show prodome, positive family history and association with menses in females. The pain of migraine is described as throbbing and severe. *Tension* headaches often begin later in life; the pain is bilateral and described as a "tight band" around the head. The pain may last for hours, days, weeks, or years. Family history and prodome are absent, sleep or sexual disturbances may be present. *Cluster* headaches start often at night, in men, in spring and in the fall. They may last a few minutes to several hours (rarely over four hours). The pain is described as burning severe and unilateral. The pain may present on alternate sides of the head. Cluster headaches occur in episodes or clusters. The location of the pain is frequently behind or around the eye. The cluster headache remits spontaneously and is associated on onset with elevated whole blood histamine level. The *headaches* which are caused by tumors, disease, or trauma to the head often begin in later life. These headaches often have a sudden onset. The pain is severe and continuous. Disturbances of the vision (diplopia, etc.) and mobility may be present. Comprehension may be impaired and diagnostic neurologic signs may be present.

    If chronic depression, secondary pain, or habituation to analgesics are present, prognosis for biofeedback as the sole intervention is poor. No behavioral scientist should accept a patient for biofeedback therapy for headache until careful medical evaluation (physical and neurological examination, plus appropriate laboratory tests) has been completed. A complete headache history is the best single diagnostic tool. An excellent delineation for clinicians of the headache syndromes and a description of how to take a headache history is to be found in Diamond and Dalessieo (1973). Personality changes secondary to chronic pain may be present and will require psychotherapeutic management (for example, the patient may have acquired feelings of bitterness and neglect by former friends and employers) if motivation for reduction of pain is to be mobilized and maintained. A pain habit (Fordyce et al., 1973) may be present and may require alteration of reinforcement (social and physical) contingencies. In some chronic pain disability cases the threat of immediate "return to work" should be reduced to stimulate motivation for recovery from pain. Generally with chronic pain cases it is better clinical strategy to establish broad positive goals (for example, more socialization, more vacations, more recreation, more and better sex life, etc.) which *indirectly* incorporate pain reduction, rather than to focus obsessively and narrowly on pain reduction. In some cases it may be necessary to explore alternative vocational plans and retraining opportunities.

2. Seeing a video tape of a model patient progressing through the headache management program and reading about the rationale and research of biofeedback can help structure positive expectations, teach the "biofeedback patient role" and mobilize motivation to participate actively in treatment. The reading material should be related to the patient's level of sophistication.

3. A battery of psychological tests are given more for their clinical research value than for any currently useful purpose. For example, I have hypothesized a positive correlation between the biofeedback skill and hypnotizability. It would also be useful to know in advance if high scores on the Protestant Ethic Scale identify people who have the self-discipline to participate in biofeedback.

4. The physiological tests are given to identify stress profiles for individual subjects. These profiles may become the basis for selecting specific response systems (the maximally reactive system) for future biofeedback training (e.g., simple mental arithmetic tests and the discharge of a cap gun can be used to induce experimental stress). A cardiovascular feedback measure is used if this system is most responsive to stress, demonstrating a "weak link" in central homeostatic regulation.

5. Patients should be accepted only on medical referral but if the above studies indicate the possibility of organic involvement, additional medical consultation should be required before starting biofeedback training.

6. Verbal relaxation exercises are taught "in vivo" to the patient over two contact sessions and concurrently an audio tape is cut of these verbal relaxation exercises. The patient is asked to practice these exercises at least twice a day.

7. Feedback training begins with electrodes placed on the frontalis, but the electrodes may be moved to easier locations (e.g. forearm extensor) if that location is found to be too difficult. If migraine type headache is suspected thermistors are placed on middle finger. Feedback training begins with 5 minutes of baseline (-F.B.) then proceeds to 15 minutes of contingent feedback training (+F.B.) and so on. The *stress management* procedure refers to the instruction to the patient to rehearse cognitively while still in the relaxed state events (e.g. conflict) that appear to be associated with the headache activity. The *Stress Scan* refers to the instruction to the patient to scan his body for any localized area of muscle contraction. Desensitization occurs more reliably at low arousal levels and detection of localized areas of tension is probably more acute at low arousal levels.

References

Dalessio, D. J. *Wolf's Headache and Other Head Pain.* New York: Oxford University Press, 1972.

Diamond, S., and Dalessio, D. J. *The Practicing Physician's Approach to Headache.* New York: Medcom Press, 1973.

Fordyce, W. E.; Fowler, R. S.; Lehmann, J. F.; DeLateur, B. J. Operant Conditioning in the Treatment of Chronic Pain. *Archives of Physical Medicine and Rehabilitation.* 1973, 54:399-408.

The Management of Rheumatoid Arthritic Pain: Preliminary Observations

Ian Wickramasekera
X. T. Truong
University of Illinois
College of Medicine.
Peoria

M. Bush and C. Orr
Bradley University
Peoria

R heumatoid arthritis remains one of the most disabling diseases of the skeletal system in terms of pain and crippling. The causative agent remains unknown and treatments are largely symptomatic and often inadequate in improving the patient's well-being or in limiting his disability. Nevertheless, it is a well-established fact that psychological factors can influence the course of as well as the patient's response to the disease (Hollander, 1966; King and Cobb, 1959; Cobb, et al., 1939; Patterson et al., 1943). Although more investigations are needed to determine the exact relationship between psychological factors and the pathogenesis of the disease, study of the effects of certain psychophysiological procedures on the patient's arthritic pain is of more immediate therapeutic relevance.

Pain has both psychological and physiological components. The psychological determinants of pain perception include tension, anxiety, and suggestion (Melzack, 1973). Headache pain has been reduced by EMG feedback training (Budzynski, Stoyva and Adler, 1969; Wickramasekera, 1973a, 1974a), and the hypothesized mechanism of reduction was the correlated decline in muscle tension. Pain may also be reduced through the mechanism of suggestion (Barber, 1969; Hilgard, 1969). Both logically and empirically there is reason to believe that biofeedback training can increase suggestibility. Logically the biofeedback training situation is similar to the sensory restriction (deprivation) situation, and there is evidence (Pena, 1963; Sanders and Rayher, 1968; Wickramasekera, 1969, 1970) that sensory restriction increases suggestibility. In fact, it is likely that the subject imposed (withdrawal of attention and focus on a single stimulus) sensory restriction that occurs in biofeedback will be more effective in increasing suggestibility than the type of externally imposed sensory restriction that occurs with the paraphernalia of sensory deprivation studies. Empirically several studies have demonstrated that both EMG and alpha biofeedback training are associated with increases in suggestibility (London, Hart and Lebovitz, 1968; Engstrom, London and Hart, 1970; Wickramasekera, 1971, 1973b), and in fact it has been hypothesized (Wickramasekera, 1974c) that any feedback procedure (EMG, temperature, heart rate) that induces a state of low arousal will increase suggestibility. This is not to imply that the *informational feedback variable* is unimportant in producing low arousal states but rather to suggest that its effects may be inevitably confounded with those of escalating suggestion in biofeedback training.

Positive instructions (relief from pain expectation) administered before and during the EMG feedback training might harness and direct the inevitable suggestibility elevation that occurs in low arousal states. Hence, the ingredient of positive suggestion may be added to that of informational feedback in the clinical situation to potentiate further the pain reduction package.

Patients

The patients in this study were volunteers, diagnosed by both their family physician and a physiatrist as rheumatoid arthritics, with severe joint pain, and were referred to this pilot project through the Arthritis Foundation. All subjects chosen for participation exhibited pain at least in one knee.

The first subject (M.H.) was a 30-year-old married female housewife who had reported pain in her knee for 15 years. Rheumatoid arthritis was diagnosed 1 year ago. The severity of the pain reportedly varied, being intensified by cold, motion, and carrying heavy objects. The subject had taken 8-10 tablets (300 mg) of aspirin per day for the last year and a half, on the instructions of her physician.

The second subject (D.P.), a 61-year-old married female housewife, was diagnosed as a rheumatoid arthritic 12 years ago. She reported that her pain was intensified by excessive walking. The subject, at the instruction of her physician, took from 10-12 tablets (300 mg) of aspirin per day. No other analgesics were used by either patient.

Apparatus

An EMG feedback instrument which provided both auditory and visual feedback was used to measure integrated skeletal muscle tension. The instrument was constructed to insure a maximum of 20K unbalanced electrode resistance and a maximum of 30K resistance to ground for each active electrode. The electrodes used were standard surface electrodes. The instrument is constructed to eliminate several artifacts (EEG, EKG) and to minimize "noise" if used correctly.

A metal stimulus calibrated in tenths of kilograms was used to apply known quantities of pressure to select locations around the patient's knee. The patient was instructed to report when she first perceived pain.

Procedure

The following is the flow chart of the study: (1) two *initial interviews;* first with the primary investigator, a psychologist, and the second, a medical interview with a consulting physiatrist; (2) a *battery of psychological tests* for possible future correlational study; (3) a *rationale* for the experiment was given verbally to each patient and all questions concerning experimentation were answered; (4) patients were given popular articles on biofeedback *(Time, Glamour,* etc.) to read and were instructed to feel free to ask any quesitons. This fourth step was primarily used to structure *positive* expectations in the subjects and create motivation for *active* participation; (5) all patients were instructed on how to keep daily charts of pain intensity and were told to do so throughout their participation in the project. All charts were checked at each meeting with the participant.

The second phase was the collection of baseline EMG data once a week by female research assistants. Baseline data was collected in three consecutive sessions; each session consisting of premeasures of the pain perception threshold as reported by the patient in response to stimulus pressure to the knee joint and baseline EMG data from the frontalis area.

The third phase consisted of training the patients once a week to monitor the muscle tension in the frontalis muscle by means of an analog information feedback system. Three surface electrodes were applied to the forehead; the middle electrode was at the center of the forehead approximately one inch above the eyebrows. The subject, equipped with earphones, heard a tone with a frequency proportional to the frontalis activity. The subject was then instructed to keep the tone at a low intensity by relaxing the specified muscle group. As the subject gained better control, the loop gain of the feedback system was increased, requiring that the subject maintain a lower EMG activity level to hear the tone. The response of muscle relaxation was then successively shaped by increasing the difficulty of the task by adjusting the sensitivity of the apparatus from low to medium and eventually to high. Pre and post measures of the pain perception threshold (K/pressure) were obtained before and after relaxation training.

The specific training procedure for each 30 minute session of frontalis relaxation consisted of 5 minutes of contingent feedback training interspersed with 2 minutes of verbal relaxation instruction (the autogenic phrases quiet, heavy, and warm, Schultz and Luthe, 1969). Thus, the subject received 5 minutes of contingent feedback (C.F.), 2 minutes of verbal relaxation (V.R.), 5 minutes of C.F., 2 minutes of V.R., and so on, for each 30 minute session.

Results

The results over a 26 week period for M.H. and a 28 week period for D.P. are shown in figs. 1 and 2. This period covers the winter and spring months when typically the pain is most marked, due to alterations in environmental humidity (Hollender, 1972). The mean level of frontalis activity during baseline for Subject 1 ranged from 5.0 to 6.8uV, and for Subject 2 from 9.8 to 20.6uV. Throughout the weeks of experimentation the frontalis level dropped gradually for both subjects, the first subject dropping to a low of 2.4uV (fig. 1) and the second to a low of 4.3uV (fig. 2).

The measures of perceived pain taken pre and post for each session are reported for both medial and lateral positions of the patella. Fig. 1 indicates that the subject (M.H.) consistently tolerated more pressure (K.) after the frontalis session than before. This data also shows that the pain threshold continued to decline during the experimental period. The data (Fig. 2) on pain perception for the second patient (D.P.) shows little overlap after the fifth session, indicating that the subject tolerated more pressure after the session than before.

The verbal report of subjective pain intensity shows in both cases a gradual decrease in the reported intensity of pain throughout the experimental period. Both subjects' anecdotal reports indicate more activities with less pain, since their participation in the project (e.g., bicycle riding, snow shoveling, driving long distances, dancing). The second subject also reported more restful sleep and a concurrent decline in blood pressure.

A record was also kept of the quantity of aspirin each subject took on a daily basis throughout experimentation. Subject 1 continued to take from 8 to 10 tablets of aspirin a day and Subject 2 from 10 to 12 per day. This pattern

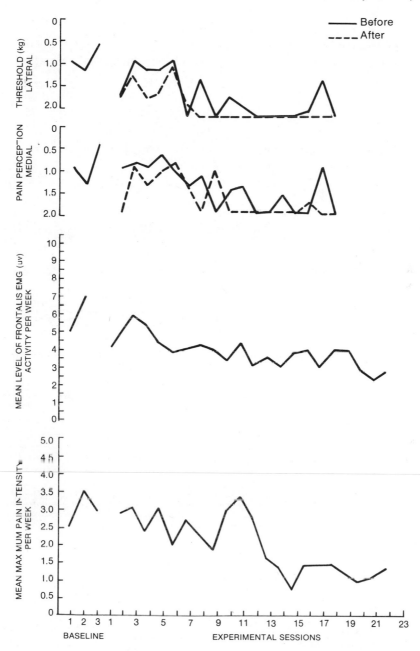

FIGURE 1.

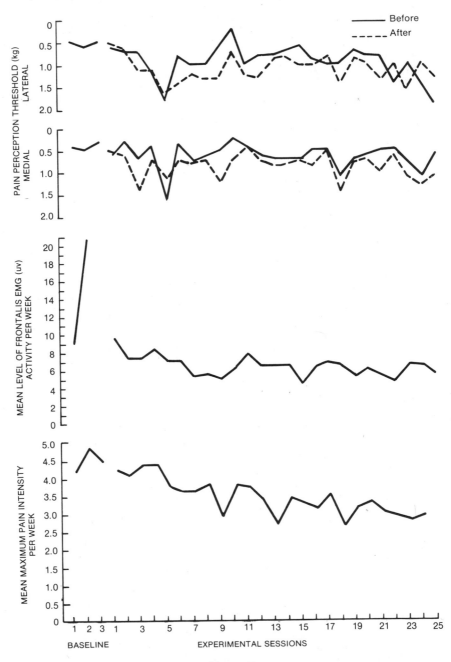

Figure 2.

of analgesic consumption was begun at the time the disease was diagnosed and was maintained at the instruction of the subjects' physicians, presumably to control inflammation. Our intervention was directed at the pain perception threshold, and hence we ignored the underlying disease process. Anecdotally the procedure appears also to have an impact on the disease process, and in the next phase of this investigation we plan to monitor both pain perception and the disease process.

Discussion

Before we chose the frontalis muscle as the source of EMG feedback, we tried to use other skeletal muscles in the vicinity of the involved joint, since, from pure clinical considerations, they could be expected to be quite active through such clinically observed signs as muscular splinting and spasms. However, we found that these muscles exhibited very erratic levels of activities that could not be used for feedback training with any stability.

This clinical trial arranged conditions to increase patients' relaxation skills and also to increase their suggestibility, thus confounding two related variables. No conclusions can be drawn from this study, but it appears to describe a promising set of procedures. At least 3 of the conditions arranged in this clinical trial are known to potentiate verbal instructions (suggestibility). These conditions are: (1) a credible rationale for the procedure (Borkovec and Nau, 1972; Caputo et al., 1973; McGlyn and McDonell, 1974; Diamond, 1974; Wickramasekera, 1974b); (2)structuring positive expectations (Diamond, 1974; Wickramasekera, 1974b; (3)EMG feedback assisted relaxation training procedures (Wickramasekera, 1971, 1973).

The above three conditions appear to potentiate the suggestion or "placebo effect" (Shapiro, 1971), and in this clinical trial we sought actively to direct and strengthen this powerful, but often unreliable, effect (Freud, 1959; Wickramasekera, this volume). It is hypothesized that the impact of other clinical methods can also be potentiated by paying careful attention to the conditions that increase suggestibility (Diamond, 1974; Wickramasekera, 1974 b).

References

Barber, T.S. *Hypnosis: A Scientific Approach.* New York: Von Nostrand Reinhold, 1969.

Budzynski, T.H., Stoyva, J.M., and Adler C. Feedback induced muscle relaxation: application to tension headache. *J. Behavior Therapy and Experimental Psychiatry,* 1969, *1*, 205-211.

Borkovec, T.D., and Nau, S.D. Credibility of analogue therapy rationales. *Journal of Behavior Therapy and Experimental Psychiatry,* 1972, *3*, 257-260.

Caputo, J.A.; Nau, S.D., and Borkovec, T.D. Credibility of therapy rationales and its effects on simulated anxiety reduction. Paper presented at Midwestern Psychological Association, Chicago, May 1973.

Cobb, S.; Bauer, W.; and Whiting, L. Environment factors in rheumotoid arthritis; study of the relationship between onset and exacerbation of arthritis and emotional and environmental factors. *Journal of the American Medical Association,* 1939, *113*, 668.

Diamond, M.J. Modification of Hypnotizability, A review. *Psychological Bulletin,* 1974, *81*, 180-198.

Engstrom, D.R., London, P., and Hart, J.T. EEG alpha feedback training and hypnotic susceptibility. *A.P.A., Proceedings,* 1970, *5*, 837-838.

Freud, S. *Collected Papers.* Vol. 1. New York: Basic Books, 1959.

Hollander, J.L. (Ed.) *Arthritis and Allied Conditions.* Philadelphia: Lea and Febiger, 1966.

Hilgard, E.R. Pain as a puzzle for psychology and physiology. *American Psychologist,* 1969, *24*, 103-113.

London, P., Hart, J., and Lebovitz, M. EEG alpha rhythms and hypnotic susceptibility. *Nature,* 1968, *219*, 71-72.

McGlynn, F.D., and McDonell, R.M. Subjective ratings of credibility following brief exposure to desensitization and pseudotherapy. *Behavior Research and Therapy,* 1974, *12*, 141-146.

Melzack, R. *The Puzzle of Pain.* New York: Basic Books, 1973.

Patterson, R.M., Craig, J.B., Waggner, R.W., and Freyberg, R.H. Studies of the relationship between emotional factors and rheumatoid arthritis. *American Journal of Psychiatry,* 1943, *99*, 775.

Pena, F. Perceptual isolation and hypnotic susceptibility. Unpublished doctoral dissertation, Washington State University, 1963.

Saunders, R.S., and Reyher, J. Sensory deprivation and the enhancement of hypnotic susceptibility. *Journal of Abnormal Psychology, 1969, 74,* 375-381.

Shapiro, A.P. Placebo effects in medicine, psychotherapy and psychoanalysis. In A.E. Bergin and S.L. Garfield (Eds.), *Handbook of Psychotherapy and Behavior Change: An Empirical Analysis.* New York: Wiley, 1971.

Wickramasekera, I. The effects of sensory restriction on susceptibility to hypnosis: a hypothesis, some preliminary data and theoretical speculation. *International Journal of Clinical and Experimental Hypnosis,* 1969, *17*, 217-224.

Wickramasekera, I. Effects of sensory restriction on susceptibility to hypnosis: a hypothesis and more preliminary data. *Journal of Abnormal Psychology*, 1970, *76*, 69-75.

Wickramasekera, I. Goals and some methods in psychotherapy: hypnosis and isolation. *American Journal of Clinical Hypnosis*, 1970, *13*, 95-100.

Wickramasekera, I. Effects of EMG feedback training on susceptibility to hypnosis: preliminary observations. *Proceedings of the 79th Annual Convention of A. P. A.*, 1971, *6*, 783-784 (summary).

Wickramasekera, I. The application of verbal instructions and EMG feedback training to the management of tension headache. preliminary observation: *Headache*, 1973, *13*, 74-76. (a)

Wickramasekera, I. The effects of EMG feedback training on hypnotic susceptibility: more preliminary data. *Journal of Abnormal Psychology*, 1973, *82*, 74-77. (b)

Wickramasekera, I. EMG feedback training and tension headache: preliminary observations. In N. E. Miller et al. (Eds.), *Biofeedback and Self-Control, 1973*. Chicago: Aldine, 1974. (a)

Wickramasekera, I. The modification of hypnotic behavior or extending the verbal control of complex human behavior. In F. Dengrove (Ed.), *Behavior Therapy and Hypnosis*. Springfield, Ill.: Charles Thomas, 1974. (b)

Wickramasekera, I. Heart rate feedback and the management of cardiac neurosis. *Journal of Abnormal Psychology*, 1974, *83*, 578-580 (c)

Self-Regulation of Pain: The Use of Alpha-Feedback and Hypnotic Training for the Control of Chronic Pain

Ronald Melzack and Campbell Perry

Departments of Psychology
McGill University and
Sir George Williams University
and the Lethbridge Rehabilitation
Center, Montreal
Quebec, Canada

Introduction

There is convincing evidence that pain perception is not simply a function of amount of physical damage alone. Rather, it is also determined by expectation, suggestion, level of anxiety, the meaning of the situation in which injury occurs, competing sensory stimuli and other psychological variables (9). It is therefore apparent that brain activities subserving these psychological processes play an essential role in determining the quality and intensity of perceived pain.

Alpha-feedback training methods (7) appear to provide an effective technique for the self-regulation of pain. Gannon and Sternbach (3) found that a subject who received prolonged alpha training was able to delay onset of migraine headaches by self-induction of an "alpha state," but was not able to modify the pain once it was underway. These observations are suggestive, and it is clear that a thorough study is needed. It is also apparent that alpha training can provide a "handle" on the general phenomenon of psychological (or cognitive) control of pain. Four variables, at least, can contribute to pain relief in the alpha-training procedure:

(a) Distraction of attention from a painful body site is known to be a mechanism of pain control in a variety of situations (14). Alpha training could teach people to distract themselves from pain by directing attention to different inner feelings and to a feedback signal (during training) which, because of its intermittent nature, is attention-demanding.

(b) Suggestion is known to affect pain experience (8). If alpha training is given with strong suggestion that the procedure will effectively diminish pain, these suggestive effects could be maximized by the use of hypnotic training procedures.

(c) The relaxation that accompanies an "alpha state" can produce a decrease in sensory inputs, such as those from muscles and viscera, which would reduce the general arousal level. This, in turn, would also lower the person's anxiety level (6), thereby diminishing the level of perceived pain (5).

(d) Finally, the development of a sense of control over pain is known to diminish the level of perceived pain (13). The knowledge that one is able to do something about pain, which is inherent in the alpha-training procedure, can bring about a marked reduction in the anxiety associated with pain, and, therefore, in the pain itself. (5).

The purpose of this study was to determine whether alpha training provides a suitable method for the control of pain of pathological origin. Our strategy has been to utilize alpha training in combination with hypnotic training and suggestion as a method of pain autoregulation, and to determine the relative contributions of each.

Methods

Subjects

Twenty-four patients, six males and 18 females, ranging in age from 28-70 yr (mean age of 48 yr), served as subjects in the experiment. They were outpatients who sought pain relief at two Montreal hospitals and were referred to this study by medical colleagues after consultation regarding their suitability. The pain syndromes and number of patients treated in each group are the following: back pain (10); peripheral nerve injury (4); cancer pain (3); arthritis (2); phantom limb and stump pain (2); post-traumatic pain (2); head pain (1).

The subjects were chosen on the basis of several criteria: (a) They suffered chronic pain of known somatic pathological origin, verified by thorough medical examination; many had persistent pain despite disc surgery, neurosurgical root or cord sections, or one or more standard physiotherapeutic methods. (b) They had continuous, unremitting pain, although it fluctuated in intensity. (c) The pain did not diminish significantly when the patient merely lay down and rested; indeed, many subjects stated that their pain often became worse when they were in a reclining position. (d) The subjects had to be English-speaking and demonstrate that they could understand and answer a Pain Questionnaire. (e) The patients had a normal EEG. (f) The pain could not be blocked completely by any analgesic or other drugs that they were taking. Patients that did not meet these criteria were rejected as prospective subjects. The subjects were randomly assigned to one of three groups: Group I (N = 12) received hypnotic training plus alpha training; Group II (N = 6) received hypnotic training alone; Group III (N = 6) received alpha training alone.

Hypnotic Training.

These instructions consisted of a sequence of items. They began with a set of extensive relaxation techniques, in which attention was focused upon relaxing each successive muscle group in turn and upon controlled breathing (6). They were followed by an adaptation of Hartland's Ego Strengthening Techniques (4) in which emphasis was placed upon feeling stronger and healthier, greater alertness and energy, less fatigue, less discouragement, a feeling of greater tranquility and of being able to overcome things that are ordinarily upsetting and worrying. The final portion consisted of suggestions that dealt with being able to think more clearly, to concentrate, to remember things, to be emotionally more calm, to be less tense both emotionally and physically, to be more self-confident and independent, and to be less fearful of failure. The duration of these instructions, which were specially prepared and taped for this study was about 20 min.[1]

Alpha Training

The instructions for alpha training consisted of strong, explicit suggestion that the alpha training would enable the subject to achieve control over pain. The subject was told that he would hear music when he produced alpha, and his aim should be to produce as much alpha as possible, thus keeping the music on; by this means he would learn to achieve a state that would enable him to control pain. The music feedback consisted of Bach flute music rearranged with a slight jazz beat.[2] This music was chosen because it was found to appeal to all who listened to it, regardless of musical tastes. All but

---

[1] Copies of the hypnotic training tape are available at cost from Dr. Campbell Perry, Sir George Williams University, Montreal.

[2] The recording used was: *Moe Kaufman Plays Bach*; GRT Recording Co., Record #9230-1008.

the first few subjects received cassettes of the music to play at home to help them practice the alpha training between sessions.

Apparatus.

The experiment was carried out in a shielded, sound-proof room which was furnished to resemble a comfortable sitting-room. After the electrodes were attached to the occipital and frontal scalp, the subjects lay on a comfortable reclining chair. EEG recordings were made using a Grass Model 8 Polygraph situated in an adjacent room. Specially constructed EEG integrators were used, with variable "windows" and digital read-out devices that registered the percentage of alpha for successive 100 second blocks. A Uher tape recorder was used to transmit the taped instructions or the music into the experimental room through a loudspeaker behind the subject's head. The room was dimly lit, yet there was enough light for the experimenter to observe the subject periodically via closed circuit television.

Procedure

All subjects, regardless of group, were told that they would be taught a technique, using electroencephalographic records, that would enable them to enter a "state" in which they would be better able to control their pain. For

TABLE 1

TRAINING PROCEDURES FOR THE SELF-REGULATION OF PAIN

Group	Type of session	No. of sessions
Group I	Baseline	2
	Hypnotic training	2
	Hypnotic training plus Alpha training	2
	Alpha training	6
	Practice	2
Group II	Baseline	2
	Hypnotic training	4
	Practice	2
Group III	Baseline	2
	Alpha training	8
	Practice	2

Groups I (alpa training plus Hypnotic training) and III (alpha training alone) this state was described as an "alpha state," while for Group II (hypnotic training alone) it was represented as an "hypnotic state."

The training methods consisted of the following component procedures (which are described below in detail): Baseline sessions; Training sessions (hypnotic training and/or alpha training); Practice sessions. Table 1 shows the sequence of these component procedures for each of the three groups. The sessions were scheduled at a rate of two or three per week, depending on the subject's available time.

Baseline Sessions.

There were two baseline sessions of approximately 1 hr each. During the first of these, the subjects were given, for about 30 min, a thorough description of the methods and aims of the study, and strong assurances that the procedure would diminish their pain. Their EEG was then recorded in the apparatus for 30 min. The second baseline session consisted of a shorter instruction period followed by the EEG recording period. Pain Questionnaires were administered before and after each session. These sessions provided baseline EEG data, against which later alpha levels could be compared. It was apparent from the Pain Questionnaires that many of the subjects felt better to some degree after the baseline sessions. Presumably this was because they had received strong suggestion that their pain would be relieved by the procedures, because they had obtained a sympathetic hearing of their pain problem, and because they were able to relax in a reclining chair with their eyes closed for a prolonged period of time. These sessions, then, should be considered as baseline-placebo sessions for pain control.

Training Sessions.

Each subject, on each training session, received the following: Pain Questionnaire; fitting of electrodes to the frontal and occipital scalp; first sessional baseline recording (10 min); the hypnotic instructions (20 min) and/or the alpha-feedback training (20 min) appropriate to the group; second sessional baseline recording (10 min); practice alpha-on without feedback (5 min; the subject was told to produce as much alpha as possible) and practice alpha-off (5 min; the subject was told to produce as little alpha as possible); removal of the electrodes; Pain Questionnaire. The duration of each training session, including Questionnaires, was approximately 2 hr for Group I and 1.0-1.5 hr for Groups II and III.

Group I received both the hypnotic training and the alpha training, whereas Groups II and III received portions of the same training procedures. Subjects in Group II listened to the taped recording of the hypnotic training instructions, and were told that these procedures would enable them to achieve control over their pain. They were also told that the EEG provides an index of relaxation, and that their EEG was being monitored to see how well they were doing. Subjects in Group III received alpha training with the instruction that learning to increase the amount of alpha would enable them to control their pain. Groups II and III received the same number of sessions of hypnotic instruction or alpha training as Group I (see Table 1), since the study sought to control for type of "treatment" rather than total number of sessions *per se.*

Practice Sessions.

Finally, for two sessions, the patients were told to practice the techniques they had learned in the training sessions in order to reduce their pain without benefit of feedback. As in all other sessions, the subjects were given a Pain Questionnaire at the beginning and end of each session.

Five subjects in Group I and one subject in Group III left the study before the training sessions were completed or before the practice sessions were begun. They left because of previously scheduled operations, illness, or the promise of immediate total pain relief by a local acupuncturist. If subjects left before completion of the training sessions, the data on the last two days of training or the mean data for all training days were used in the data analyses. This occurred only in subjects in Group I; one subject left after 7 training sessions, and three left after eight sessions. Subjects who did not participate in the practice sessions were excluded from the data analyses of the practice sessions only.

Pain Measurement.

The McGill Pain Questionnaire (11, 12) was used to measure the quality and intensity of pain perceived by the subject. The portion of the questionnaire relevant for this study is the list of words that describes the qualitative dimensions of pain. The classes and subclasses that comprise the qualitative "Pain Descriptor" list are shown in Table 2.

The McGill Pain Questionnaire has been shown (11) to provide valid, reliable scores which reflect the quality and intensity of clinical pain experienced by patients. The *Pain Rating Index* consists of the sum of the rank values of all the qualitative words chosen in selected subclasses. Thus the Pain Rating Index scores can be computed separately for the sensory or affective dimensions of pain, or for all the subclasses together. The latter score has been shown (11) to correlate highly with the intensity values designated on a 1-5 ordinal scale, but it is more sensitive to subtle, qualitative changes in perceived pain. Since the Pain Questionnaire was administered at the beginning and end of each session, it was possible to determine the differences between the pre- and post-session Pain Rating Index scores. These differences thus represent measures of pain relief produced by the procedures presented during each session.

In addition to the Pain Questionnaire data, tape-recorded information was obtained in the course of conversation at the beginning and end of each session. This information was concerned with each subject's general activity level, drug intake, and overall mood and response to treatment.

Alpha Measurement.

The occipital EEG was used for feedback and data analysis in all subjects. The EEG alpha data consisted of the % alpha in 100-sec blocks during each entire session. The 100-sec block which showed the highest % alpha was taken as an index of the % alpha output during each part of the procedure. It was found that the high point within a section of the procedure was highly correlated with the average alpha during the entire session, and thus appears to be a valid measure of overall alpha activity. The 100-sec block was chosen as the index of alpha output in order to eliminate artifacts from the computation, such as subjects dozing off for short periods.

In a preliminary study, verbal feedback of the % alpha emitted by the subject was provided every 5 min. Most subjects, however, complained that the interruption was disruptive and they reported difficulty resuming the "alpha state" or concentrating on the hypnotic instructions. They stated, moreover, that the % alpha meant little to them. Consequently, verbal feedback of % alpha was not given during the main study. The music feedback itself, plus assurances from the experimenter that they were progressing well, proved to be sufficient.

Because some subjects increased their % alpha output per session at a rapid rate, it was necessary, following the procedures of other investigators (3), to narrow their trigger "window" for the feedback period on subsequent sessions. This was done once only and it had the effect of challenging them to work harder to achieve maximum alpha output. It produced the problem, however, of comparing alpha output during the feedback periods at different sessions recorded at different trigger levels. This was overcome by using a correction factor which was based on a comparison of the percen-

TABLE 2
CLASSES AND SUBCLASSES OF PAIN DESCRIPTORS

Classes subclasses	Pain descriptors	Rank value	Classes subclasses	Pain descriptors	Rank value
Sensory			Affective		
Temporal	Flickering	1	Tension	Tiring	1
	Quivering	2		Exhausting	2
	Pulsing	3			
	Throbbing	4	Autonomic	Sickening	1
	Beating	5		Suffocating	2
	Pounding	6			
			Fear	Fearful	1
Spatial	Jumping	1		Frightful	2
	Flashing	2		Terrifying	3
	Shooting	3			
			Punishment	Punishing	1
Punctate	Pricking	1		Gruelling	2
pressure	Boring	2		Cruel	3
	Drilling	3		Vicious	4
	Stabbing	4		Killing	5
	Lancinating	5			
			Affective- evaluative- sensory:		
Incisive	Sharp	1	miscellaneous	Wretched	1
pressure	Cutting	2		Blinding	2
	Lacerating	3			

Constrictive pressure	Pinching	1	Evaluative	Annoying	1
	Pressing	2		Troublesome	2
	Gnawing	3		Miserable	3
	Cramping	4		Intense	4
	Crushing	5		Unbearable	5
Traction pressure	Tugging	1	Supplementary Sensory: spatial-pressure	Spreading	1
	Pulling	2		Radiating	2
	Wrenching	3		Penetrating	3
				Piercing	4
Thermal	Hot	1	Sensory: pressure-dullness	Tight	1
	Burning	2		Numb	2
	Scalding	3		Drawing	3
	Searing	4		Squeezing	4
				Tearing	5
Brightness	Tingling	1	Sensory: thermal	Cool	1
	Itchy	2		Cold	2
	Smarting	3		Freezing	3
	Stinging	4			
Dullness	Dull	1	Affective	Nagging	1
	Score	2		Nauseating	2
	Hurting	3		Agonizing	3
	Aching	4		Dreadful	4
	Heavy	5		Torturing	5
Sensory: miscellaneous	Tender	1			
	Taut	2			
	Rasping	3			
	Splitting	4			

tages of alpha output during two successive 100-sec blocks, one with the old trigger level and the other with the new one.

Results

Pain Questionnaire Data.

The Pain Questionnaire was administered at the beginning and end of each baseline, training, and practice session. The data are summarized in Tables 3 and 4.

Table 3 shows the mean percent decreases in the various Pain Rating Index scores for the baseline and all training Sessions for Groups I, II and III. It is apparent that the training procedures used in Group I produced larger mean decreases in Pain Rating Index scores than those produced during baseline-placebo sessions. Sign tests show that the p values are statistically significant for all Pain Rating Index scores. In contrast, the hypnotic training alone (Group II) and the alpha training alone (Group III) failed to produce changes that are statistically larger than those produced during the baseline sessions.

The largest net percent change on any measure was the decrease in the affective dimension of pain in Group I, although there were smaller, significant decreases in the sensory dimension and in the overall Pain Rating Index based on all words. It should be noted that the decreases based on all words during baseline sessions for Groups I, II and III vary from 16% (Group I) to 10% (Group III). In order to rule out the possibility of experimenter bias in the allocation of subjects to any particular group, the percent decreases during the baseline sessions for all three groups were compared. No significant differences between groups were found.

For convenience, Table 3 does not include data comparing pain decreases during the final practice sessions with those during the initial baseline sessions. In all cases, these levels fell below statistical significance. Nevertheless, the percentages of subjects who achieved pain decreases during practice sessions (Table 4) were impressive, although not statistically significant.

Table 4 shows the mean percent decreases in the Pain Rating Index based on pre- and post-session Questionnaires during the last two training sessions. This analysis was carried out to evaluate improvement toward the end of the series of training sessions, where the effects of training could be expected to be optimal. Statistical analysis of the differences between the baseline and the last two training sessions, using the t test, shows that

TABLE 3

MEAN PERCENT (%) DECREASES IN THE PAIN RATING INDEX
BASED ON PRE- AND POST-SESSION PAIN QUESTIONNAIRES PRESENTED
DURING THE BASELINE (B) AND ALL TRAINING (T) SESSIONS FOR GROUPS I, II, AND III

Category of Pain Rating Index	Group I—hypnotic training plus alpha training (N = 12)			Group II—hypnotic training alone (N = 6)			Group III—alpha training alone (N = 6)		
	Baseline (B)	Training (T)	ρ T > B	Baseline (B)	Training (T)	ρ T > B	Baseline (B)	Training (T)	ρ T > B
Sensory									
Mean[a]	14%	33%	0.02	11%	21%	NS[b]	10%	12%	NS
Range[a]	$(33^- - 70\%)$	$(3^- - 77\%)$		$(12^- - 45^+\%)$	$(19^- - 53\%)$		$(0 - 15\%)$	$(2^+ - 30^+\%)$	
Affective									
Mean[a]	8%	48%	0.03	29%	32%	NS	18%	15%	NS
Range[a]	$(200^- - 100^+\%)$	$(13^- - 85\%)$		$(12^- - 80^+\%)$	$(13^- - 75\%)$		$(0 - 60\%)$	$(0 - 57\%)$	
All descriptors									
Mean[a]	16%	34%	0.02	14%	23%	NS	10%	9%	NS
Range[a]	$(28^- - 81\%)$	$(9^+ - 6^-\%)$		$(17^- - 57\%)$	$(20^- - 55\%)$		$(4^+ - 30\%)$	$(9^+ - 23^+\%)$	

[a] A minus sign represents a pain increase
[b] NS: not statistically significant.

TABLE 4

MEAN PERCENT (%) DECREASES IN THE PAIN RATING INDEX
BASED ON PRE- AND POST-SESSION PAIN QUESTIONNAIRES PRESENTED
DURING THE BASELINE (B), THE LAST TWO TRAINING (T), AND
THE PRACTICE (P) SESSIONS FOR GROUPS I, II, AND III

	Group I—hypnotic training plus alpha training			Group II—hypnotic training alone			Group III—alpha training alone		
	Baseline (B)	Training (T)	Practice (P)	Baseline (B)	Training (T)	Practice (P)	Baseline (B)	Training (T)	Practice (P)
All descriptors									
Mean[a]	16%	36%	36%	14%	22%	45%	10%	-4%	17%
Range[a]	$(28^- - 81^+\%)$	$(20^- - 75^+\%)$	$(3^+ - 80^+\%)$	$(0 - 57^+\%)$	$(39^- - 057^+\%)$	$(12^+ - 100^+\%)$	$(5^+ - 30^+\%)$	$(40^- - 12^+\%)$	$(20^- - 54^+\%)$
% Subjects reporting pain decrease > 33%	25%	58%	57%	17%	50%	60%	0%	0%	33%
p value, $T > B$		0.03			NS			NS	
p value, $P > B$			NS[b]			NS			NS

[a] A minus sign represents a pain increase.
[b] NS: not statistically significant.

significant decreases in pain were produced only in Group I. Further analysis of the data (Table 4) indicates that 58% of the subjects in Group I experienced a decrease in pain of 33% or more during the last two training sessions, while 50% of the subjects in Group II and none of the subjects in Group III showed comparable levels of pain decrease.

The placebo effects—such as relaxation, suggestion, and the anticipation of pain relief—provided by the baseline sessions indicate the extent to which these effects contribute to the pain relief produced by the training procedures. The net differences between training and baseline sessions in the percentages of subjects who showed a pain decrease of 33% or more is 33% for Groups I and II, with mean decreases in the Pain Rating Index of 20% and 8% respectively. None of the subjects in Group III showed a pain decrease greater than 33% and, indeed, there was a slight increase in the mean PRI for the group. A subject-by-subject analysis of the differences between training and baseline sessions further indicates the powerful contribution of placebo effects to the overall effects of the training procedures. In Group I, 25% showed a net pain decrease of 33% or more, and 50% showed a net decrease of 20% or more. From Group II, the percentages of subjects who showed net decreases larger than 33% and 20% are 17% and 50% respectively. None of the subjects in Group III showed a net pain decrease greater than 20%.

Seven subjects in Group I carried out the practice sessions after completion of the training sessions. Four of the seven subjects (57%) showed a pain decrease of 33% or greater, compared with three out of five subjects (60%) in Group II who achieved comparable pain reduction. Compared to baseline-placebo sessions, however, only two subjects in Group I (29%), and two subjects in Group II (40%) showed more than 33% pain reduction. One subject in Group III (17%) showed more than 33% pain reduction compared to baseline sessions.

All the data, taken together, show that, for Group I, significantly greater decreases in all Pain Rating Index scores were produced during training sessions than during baseline sessions. Although none of the mean percent changes in pain produced in Groups II and III were large enough to achieve statistical significance, it is noteworthy that the effects were larger in Group II (hypnotic training alone) than in Group III (alpha training alone). Furthermore, almost identical percentages of the subjects in Group II as in Group I showed a pain reduction of 33% or more. Indeed, there was no significant difference between Groups I and II in terms of the number of subjects who diminished their pain by 33% or more, whereas Group III achieved less pain reduction than either of the other two groups (Fisher Exact Probability test; $p=0.05$).

TABLE 5

PERCENTAGE (%) OF SUBJECTS SHOWING INCREASES IN EEG ALPHA RHYTHM AND MEAN PERCENT ALPHA INCREASES ACROSS THE BASELINE AND LAST TWO TRAINING SESSIONS, AND WITHIN THE LAST TWO TRAINING SESSIONS

	Group I— hypnotic training plus alpha training	Group II— hypnotic training alone	Group III— alpha training alone
Across sessions			
Alpha-feedback period > baseline sessions			
% Subjects	82%	60%	50%
Mean Increase	13%	14%	13%
Range	2%–37%	6%–25%	4%–17%
Practice-on period > baseline sessions			
% Subjects	88%	80%	33%
Mean Increase	23%	11%	13%
Range	9%–39%	5%–32%	8%–22%

Within Training Sessions

Alpha-feedback period > first sessional baseline

% Subjects	27%	60%	100%
Mean	15%	14%	13%
Range	5%-21%	1%-25%	5%-21%

Second sessional baseline > first sessional baseline

% Subjects	36%	50%	83%
Mean	10%	13%	16%
Range	3%-16%	8%-18%	8%-33%

Practice-on period > first sessional baseline

% Subjects	50%	40%	83%
Mean	8%	13%	18%
Range	3%-20%	5%-21%	10%-23%

Practice-on > practice-off

% Subjects	88%	80%	50%
Mean	8%	9%	9%
Range	1%-31%	7%-10%	7%-12%

Alpha Training.

Analysis of the EEG alpha data for the last two training sessions shows that the subjects in Groups I and III learned to increase their EEG alpha output. However, the data (Table 5) reveal a surprising difference. The EEG alpha data may be compared across sessions (comparison of Training with Baseline sessions), or within sessions (comparison of the Training and the first Baseline periods of each session). It is apparent, in Table 5, that Group I shows larger increases in EEG alpha output in cross-session comparisons, while Group III shows larger increases in within-session comparisons. Since both methods of analysis are valid, the data show that subjects in both groups learned to increase their EEG alpha output. A relevant observation here is that the subjects in Group I showed a higher percent alpha on the last two sessional baselines compared with the baseline sessions, while subjects in Group III showed a decreased percent alpha when the same comparison was made. Although the subjects in Group II did not receive alpha training, the increases in percent alpha while they practiced the hypnotic-training procedure are shown in Table 5 and indicate that they increased their EEG alpha output to levels that compare favorably with the subjects that actually received alpha training.

In a portion of the training procedure, the subjects were asked to practice alpha or hypnotic training in the absence of feedback (Pr-on). Of 18 subjects in the three groups who provided reliable, artifact-free data, 13 produced increased alpha, four produced less alpha, and one showed no change. Using a sign test, the effect is significant at the 0.025 level. A further analysis is the comparison between Pr-on and Pr-off (the subjects were asked *not* to produce alpha). For this comparison, serial effects were avoided by reversing the order of Pr-on and Pr-off from one session to the next. In Group I, the subjects produced more alpha during the Pr-on than during the Pr-off condition; although the net difference is small, it is consistent (p 0.025). The difference is not significant in Group III.

While the data indicate that increases in alpha occurred in the majority of subjects, from small to substantial amounts, the fact that Group II (hypnotic training alone) showed comparable alpha increases suggests that these alpha increases can be obtained by means other than alpha training.

Duration of Relief.

An important feature of the effect of the treatment is that the duration of relief outlasted each training session by several hours (1-4 hr) in seven of the 12 subjects, and by 15-30 min in three. The subjects also reported even longer indirect changes. Several indicated that they slept better, were happier, and went to parties or met friends, which they had not done for years. There appeared to be a carry-over effect as a result of the procedure: pain relief for several hours in some; a happier, more confident mood in others.

Drug Intake.

Nine of the subjects in Group I took large quantities of analgesic drugs. On their own initiative, during the training sessions, three of these subjects decreased their drug intake by 30%, and one by 50%. Two others reported that they decreased their drug intake but could not provide a definite figure. Three subjects reported no change in drug intake.

Interview Follow-Up Data

Eleven subjects, distributed through the three groups, were interviewed 4-6 mo after completion of training. It was found that all those who obtained relief in the training sessions continued to practice hypnotic training or alpha training regularly or from time to time when their pain became unbearable. They further reported that they were able to reduce the pain to bearable levels by means of the procedures. Many of these subjects kept their cassettes of the music tapes, and stated that they utilized them as part of their home practice to control their pain.

Discussion

The data show that alpha training can produce a marked reduction in severe clinical pain, but only if it is accompanied by hypnotic training, which emphasizes "ego strengthening" and "progressive relaxation" techniques, and by placebo effects, which include distraction, suggestion, and the diminished anxiety due to anticipation of pain relief. No one of these contributions, taken alone, produces a significant effect. All three together provide a useful method of pain control in patients suffering severe pain which cannot be brought under control by other methods. The effect of the combined procedures is impressive: a substantial number of patients (58%) reported a significant reduction in pain (by 33% or greater). The alpha training alone had the smallest effect on the pain. The hypnotic suggestion had a larger effect, although it was not statistically significant. The effects with both procedures are statistically significant compared to the baseline-placebo effects. The effect of all three contributions (alpha training and hypnotic training, plus placebo effects) may be considered to be sufficiently large to comprise a useful clinical tool when other conventional procedures fail. An important additional observation is the fact that about half the subjects that received the combined procedures reduced their drug intake by substantial amounts during the training sessions.

Two points merit special consideration. First, three workman-compensation cases were included in Group I, and all three showed a resistance to admitting being helped. The magnitudes of the pain decreases during training sessions in these patients were among the lowest in the entire group. The proportion of people helped by the procedure, therefore, might be even higher than that indicated by the data, although 58% nevertheless remains a substantial proportion. Secondly, a decrease in pain by 33% represents a considerable success in view of the nature of the pain suffered by these patients. The majority had severe, chronic pain for years that was not diminished by several operations, neurosurgery on the spinal roots or spinal cord, prolonged physiotherapy, psychotherapy, or drugs. A decrease by 33%, therefore, is a substantial improvement in cases that had in many instances been labelled as hopeless.

It is reasonable to assume, on the basis of the data, that the alpha-feedback training procedure plays a role in the control of pain. However, the data indicate that the increase in EEG alpha is not the critical variable in pain relief; all three groups showed comparable increases in EEG alpha during the training sessions, but Groups I and II showed substantial pain relief while Group III did not. It is concluded, therefore, that the contribution of the alpha training procedure to pain relief is *not* due to increased EEG alpha as such but, rather, to the distraction of attention, suggestion, relaxation, and sense of control over pain which are an integral part of the procedure.

The data show that the practice sessions, in which the subjects attempted to diminish their pain without alpha-feedback or the hypnotic training tape, failed to provide relief at statistically significant levels, although 57% of the subjects in Group I and 60% of those in Group II were able to reduce their pain by 33% or more. While these percentages are impressive, the fact that statistical significance was not achieved further indicates the importance of *all the contributions of the training procedures in combination* in producing substantial pain relief.

The powerful contribution of the placebo effects, demonstrated in the comparisons between the training and baseline-placebo sessions, is not surprising. Approximately half of the effectiveness of powerful analgesic compounds—ranging from aspirin to morphine—are known (1, 2) to be attributable to placebo effects. Evans (2) has shown that a placebo's effectiveness is directly proportional to the apparent effectiveness of the active analgesic agent that doctor and patient believe they are using. The present study suggests that this relationship between placebo and pharmacological analgesic also holds true for other pain-relieving methods, such as the combination of alpha-feedback and hypnotic training.

The magnitude of the contribution of the hypnotic-training procedure developed for this study is strikingly high. Although the effects did not achieve statistical significance, it is apparent that the hypnotic training comprises a major contribution to the pain relief. Group II hypnotic alone) does not differ statistically from Group I in terms of the proportion of subjects that achieve substantial pain relief, but both differ significantly from Group III (alpha training alone). This result needs to be taken in conjunction with the finding that only subjects in Group I showed a mean percent decrease during training sessions that significantly exceeded the amount of pain relief achieved during baseline-placebo sessions. These two sets of data suggest that both techniques help a substantial number of subjects to reduce pain but that alpha training with hypnotic training leads to quantitatively greater pain decreases. The number of hours spent in training to reduce pain does not appear to be the crucial variable that determines the amounts of pain relief obtained in the present study, since the hypnosis-alone group did substantially better than the alpha-alone group even though the latter group received approximately twice as many hours in training.

The data show that Group I exhibits larger alpha increases when compared to the baseline sessions (across sessions), while Group III exhibits larger increases when compared to the sessional baseline segment (*within sessions*). It is possible that Group I subjects achieved significant degrees of pain relief so that, by the last two training sessions, they began the sessions in a relaxed state, anticipating relief, and therefore already producing considerable alpha. During subsequent training, they learned to raise the alpha to some extent, but it was not significantly higher than the sessional baseline levels although it was very much higher than the alpha levels in the first baseline sessions. Group III subjects, on the other hand, achieved little or no pain relief, and anticipated little relief at the beginning of the last two training sessions. Their alpha level was in fact lower than the initial baseline levels when their anticipation of relief was high. During training, therefore, they learned to raise their alpha levels well above the sessional baselines, but the final level achieved was not sufficiently higher than the initial baseline sessions. This speculation does not explain every detail of the alpha increases that were produced, but it suggests in a broad way why different results are obtained using across-session and within-session analyses.

This study resembles an earlier study by Melzack, Weisz and Sprague (13) which showed that intense auditory input together with strong suggestion that it diminishes pain produced significant increases in pain tolerance levels; in contrast, the auditory input alone or the strong suggestion alone had no effect. This in no way diminishes the importance of the auditory input. Rather it indicates that it must be accompanied by other contributions if it is to have an effect on pain. Similarly, the alpha-feedback contribution to the pain relief observed in Group I is not diminished in importance by the fact that hypnotic training may have to accompany it in order to reduce chronic pain.

It is clear that the effects of the combined procedures are not obtained in all patients, and the degree of pain relief is variable. It is important, nevertheless, to recognize that *some* people have achieved substantial pain relief which, though not total, is sufficient to make life more bearable, more productive, and happier. It is a fundamental fact in the field of pain that some patients will suffer pain for the rest of their lives. In such cases, the most effective therapy may be to teach them to live with their pain, to carry on productive lives in spite of it (10). In the present study, it is clear that alpha training alone has little effect on pain but has substantial effects when it is combined with hypnotic training and placebo contributions. The three contributions in combinaton may have dramatic effects in some patients. One effect does not detract from the others. Instead the data show that multiple approaches are more effective than each alone in treating pain which, it is now known (9), has multiple, interacting determinants.

Notes

1. Copies of the hypnotic training tape are available at cost from Dr. Campbell Perry, Sir George Williams University, Montreal.
2. The recording used was: *Moe Kaufman Plays Bach*, GRT Recording Co., Record #9230-1008.

References

1. Beecher, H.K. 1959. "Measurement of Subjective Responses: Quantitative Effects of Drugs." Oxford Univ. Press, New York.

2. Evans, F.J. 1974. The placebo response in pain reduction, pp. 289-296. In "Advances in Neurology, Vol. 4: International Symposium on Pain." J.J Bonica [Ed.]. Raven Press, New York.

3. Gannon, L., and R.A. Sternbach. 1971. Alpha enhancement as a treatment for pain: a case study. J. Behav. Ther. Exp. Psychiat. 2: 209-213.

4. Hartland, J. 1971. Further observations on the use of ego-strengthening techniques. Amer. J. Clin. Hypnosis 14: 1-8.

5. Hill, H.E., C.H. Kornetsky, H.G. Flanary, and A. Wikler. 1952. Effects of anxiety and morphine on discrimination of intensities of painful stimuli. J. Clin. Invest. 31: 473-480.

6. Jacobson, E. 1938. "Progressive Relaxation." Chicago Univ. Press, Chicago.

7. Kamiya, J. 1972. Conscious control of brain waves. In "Readings in Psychology Today." CRM Books, Del Mar, Cal.

8. McGlashan, T.H., F.J. Evans, and M.T. Orne. 1969. The nature of hypnotic analgesia and placebo response to experimental pain. Psychosom. Med. 31: 227-246.

9. Melzack, R. 1973. "The Puzzle of Pain." Basic Books, New York.

10. Melzack, R. 1974. Psychological concepts and methods for the control of pain, pp. 275-280. In "Advances in Neurology, Vol. 4: International Symposium on Pain." J.J. Bonica [Ed.]. Raven Press, New York.

11. Melzack, R. 1975. A questionnaire for the measurement of pain. In preparation.

12. Melzack, R., and W.S. Torgerson. 1971. On the language of pain. Anesthesiology 34: 50-59.

13. Melzack, R., A.Z. Weisz, and L.T. Sprague. 1963. Stratagems for controlling pain: contributions of auditory stimulation and suggestion. Exp. Neurol. 8: 239-247.

14. Morgenstern, F.S. 1964. The effects of sensory input and concentration on post-amputation phantom limb pain. J. Neurol. Neurosurg. Psychiatry 27: 58-65.

This study was supported by the Advanced Research Projects Agency of the Department of Defense and monitored by the Office of Naval Research under Contract No. N00014-70-C-0350. We are grateful to Elliott Dainow and Stephen Southmayd for their outstanding assistance in carrying out these studies. We also appreciate the technical assistance of Mary Ellen Jeans, Jacques Perras, Paul Taenzer and Joseph Vanagas, and the generous cooperation of Dr. Maurice Dongier at the Allan Memorial Institute, McGill University, and Dr. Serge Bikadoroff and the Lethbridge Rehabilitation Center, Montreal.

Part 2

ANXIETY

On the Apparent Intrusion of a Recurring Nightmare into an EMG Feedback Training Procedure

Ian Wickramasekera,
University of Illinois
College of Medicine
Peoria

MG-feedback training appears to be a promising approach to the symptomatic control of muscle contraction headache (Budzynski, Stoyva and Adler, 1970; Wickramasekera, 1972, 1973). This paper describes the verbally reported intrusion of a recurrent nightmare into the waking relaxation practice sessions of a patient in treatment (with EMG feedback) for chronic and continuous headache pain.

The biofeedback method (Barber et al., 1972) is currently being explored by research workers in the symptomatic treatment of a wide variety of clinical conditions, for example, migraine headache, muscle contraction headache, epilepsy, stomach ulcers, essential hypertension, and so forth. In addition, the instrumentation is unfortunately too readily available to the general public on a commercial basis. To date, no significant unpleasant side effects have been reported by human subjects when the biofeedback procedure was used for symptomatic treatment of clinical problems. The biofeedback training procedure has been associated with verbal reports of altered subjective experiences (e.g., floating sensation, euphoria, well-being, anxiety episodes, etc.) But it is too soon to conclude that the manipulation of the independent variable (e.g., alpha density in alpha feedback training) is responsible for the reported changes in subjective experience (e.g., feeling of euphoria). Controlled exploration of other interpretations, including a demand characteristic (Orne and Scheibe, 1964) hypothesis, need to be attempted. Miller has noted that some of his rats, reinforced with intercranial stimulation, decelerated their heart rates to the extent that they died. It is improbable that an intelligent human subject would behave like Miller's rats though clinically we encounter some people who appear to behave self-destructively for a "turn-on" (e.g., chronic drug users, enthusiasts of dangerous sports, etc).

In an etymological sense, the word "nightmare" relates to the belief that the phenomenon is caused by a demon pressing down on the sleeper's chest. Recurrent nightmares are regarded by psychotherapists as having dynamic significance and indicative of significant personal conflicts. Regarded from a psychophysiological viewpoint, nightmares seem to occur during arousal from slow wave sleep (stages III or IV sleep) and are never reported as associated with the rapid-eye-movement dreaming state (Broughton, 1968).

Patient

The patient's headache had been diagnosed as muscle contraction headache at the Mayo Clinic approximately one year prior to his first contact with the present therapist. The patient, Sam, is a 48-year-old, white, married male who has suffered from chronic headache pain since late adolescence. It appears that his headaches have grown slowly but progressively more intense and longer over the years, so that at the time of his contact with me, he had continuous chronic headache activity which varied only in intensity. The variations of intensity appear to be a function of environmental and intrapersonal stress; (for example, public speaking, visits to his mother, prolonged driving, conflicts in committee meetings, electioneering during a strike, etc.). The patient had been tried on a variety of medications by several neurologists without positive response but was currently and had been for about three years on a fixed dosage of Etrafon (3 per day), Fiorinal (3 per day) and Empirin (12-14 per day). He claimed that while the medication did not abolish continuous headache pain, it kept it within bearable limits. Patient is an ambitious and driving man who has risen to state level positions in his professional and church life. Patient appears perfectionistic in his professional and religious life and is in many ways a respected member of his community and the fundamentalist religious group he belongs to. His wife is a teacher and apparently a "placid" individual. Patient has four children, two of them black girls who were adopted at infancy. Patient reported that these children have posed problems in the white neighborhood and churches in which his family has been raised.

The patient had previously been in psychotherapy on several occasions but apparently without symptomatic relief of headache pain. He was extremely critical of his previous psychotherapists and physicians and he appeared, at least in the consulting room, to be the type of critical, cold, perfectionistic individual with whom it would be difficult to establish a working relationship. In his first interview with me, he reported that he was an "orphan" and an adopted only child, who ever since late childhood has had a recurrent nightmare which occurs about three or four times a year.

In this nightmare he is either surrounded or chased by "little green monsters" who "scream, holler, and point accusatory fingers at him." The patient claims that he can never comprehend what they are saying but they appear to be accusing him of something. He did not want to speculate on what he was being accused of. He reported very vivid memories of the orphanage and these memories clearly had some private significance for him, but he was unwilling to elaborate on the topic.

Patient completed the Life History Questionnaire, M.M.P.I., and was interviewed in some depth during our first session. In the second session, since he was eager to begin feedback training, the EMG feedback system was explained to him and he was connected to the instrument for thirty minutes for adaptation purposes and to secure baseline data. Three surface electrodes were placed on the frontalis and patient sat quietly in a recliner. His baseline EMG activity was unusually high and did not decline significantly even at the end of the thirty minutes. The S hears a tone with a frequency proportional to the EMG activity in the relevant muscle group. The feedback tone tracks the changing EMG level of the muscle. Three surface electrodes are applied to the frontalis in such a way that the center electrode is centered on the forehead about one inch above the eyebrows. This electrode placement picks up EMG activity from several facial muscles including the frontalis. The instrument is constructed so that there is a maximum of 20K unbalanced electrode resistance and a maximum of 30K resistance to ground for each active electrode. The instrument is constructed to eliminate the EKG, EEG, and "noise" artifacts.

In the third session, the patient began EMG-auditory feedback training with the instrument in the low sensitivity mode. He was instructed to try to reduce the frequency of the feedback tone and the corresponding EMG signal. The patient was instructed to practice relaxation training (without the feedback instrument) at least twice a day between sessions in his home. He was seen by me twice a week and practiced EMG-feedback induced relaxation training at each session. Each relaxation practice session in my office was divided into two blocks of time (thirty minutes with EMG feedback and fifteen minutes without EMG feedback). Patient appeared to be highly motivated to learn to relax and seemed deeply involved in the practice sessions. At first he reported that trying to relax seemed to increase the intensity of his headache pain. I responded to this statement by urging him not to try so hard but simply "to lie back, let go, and enjoy himself." These instructions appeared to change his attitude in some way because he no longer complained of increased headache pain after practice sessions.

As the relaxation training procedure approached the 14th EMG feedback session, the patient began to report a noticeable decline in the intensity of his headache pain after and between practice sessions. He also inquired about reducing the quantity of analgesics he was consuming. Because of his previous skeptical manner, I decided to take a cautious and skeptical attitude myself toward his reported "progress" and suggested that it was too soon to conclude that the procedure was helping him, even his daily headache activity chart clearly indicated a reduction in the intensity of headache pain. I suggested that he was possibly deluding himself. He opened the 17th session of therapy by stating again that his headaches were less intense than before and added that it was becoming easier all the time for him to experience the "floating feeling" that accompanied relaxation. He stated that he could sit in a regular chair in his living room and induce the floating, light feeling at will. I urged him to experiment with inducing this feeling for brief periods in situations in which he typically felt stress. His practice sessions in the office with EMG monitoring clearly indicated that he could drop the EMG activity of his frontalis to less than 3 microvolts rapidly, typically within two minutes, and on command. He apparently was developing considerable skill at producing low-level frontalis EMG signals and was also reporting that subjective feelings of lightness, floating, and limpness in his body during the relaxation periods were becoming increasingly pronounced. The patient opened the 18th session by stating that when he reached home after his previous therapy session, there was a fire engine parked in front of his house. The officers on duty told him that there had been a fire in one of his daughters' bedrooms and that they suspected that the fire had been started by a member of his household. This was the first time since the initial diagnostic session that the patient had offered any significant information about his family life. He added that the police had insisted that the family present itself for therapy at the Community Mental Health Center and that the daughters be treated for "pyromania." He stated that he has taken the girls for "treatment" but that he had expressed his unwillingness to participate in family therapy. He reported that the last few days were so unstable that he had been unable to practice his relaxation as faithfully as he had done before. I did not comment on his remarks except to request clarification of the reasons for his unwillingness to participate in family therapy at the Mental Health Center. The substance of his responses was focused in terms of his unwillingness to participate in therapist's attempt to "pry into his personal life" which according to him was "none of their business because they are supposed to be treating my daughters." At the conclusion of this verbal interchange, the patient suggested that we go ahead with the EMG feedback training, and I connected him to the instrument reluctantly because he seemed agitated. Within eight minutes he seemed settled and his frontalis EMG signal was less than 4 microvolts. After he had been at that level for approximately two minutes, he seemed to become agitated and suddenly opened his eyes, sat up and seemed quite frightened. I inquired what was happening and he stated that his previous frightening nightmare had begun to seep into his mind in vivid detail as soon as he began to have the "floating sensation." He stated it scared him because he felt that he was not asleep even though his eyes were closed. He was unwilling to try relaxing again and, since the hour was late, the session was terminated. Two days before his next appointment he telephoned me to complain that over "eighty percent" of the times he had attempted to induce the floating feeling at home, the nightmare would "hit" at precisely the moment the floating sensation began. He stated that he was too frightened even to attempt the relaxation at home. I suggested that we explore the phenomenon and his reaction to it at our next session.

He opened the next (19th) session by stating that he was thoroughly frightened by what was happening because he had attempted to practice relaxation twice since his last telephone conversation with me, but on the first occasion the nightmare had intruded and on the second occasion he was too agitated to relax. Also, it is worth noting that his headache activity chart indicated that the intensity of his headache activity had returned to the pretreatment baseline level. After he had talked about his fear of the nightmare, I suggested that one strategy for dealing with his fear of the nightmare was to attempt to desensitize it systematically (the procedure was explained in detail) with a counter conditioning stimulus other than relaxation (e.g., physical aggression directed on a punching bag).

I also told him that since the EMG-feedback training procedure may have increased his susceptibility to hypnosis (Wickramasekera, 1971, 1973), the meaning of the nightmare and its aversive properties could probably be explored and reduced with hypnotherapy. I inquired if the recent upheaval in his family situation and the social problems with his daughters had any bearing on his nightmare activity. He flatly denied any connection and rejected both alternative approaches (systematic desensitization and hypnotherapy) and elected to terminate treatment.

At no time during treatment prior to the 18th EMG feedback training session did this patient report any nightmare activity. After the 18th EMG feedback training session, "nightmare" activity became a high probability event whenever he attempted to practice his previous relaxation skill. A telephone call follow-up done eight months after termination of treatment indicated that his headache activity had returned to pretreatment baseline levels both in terms of intensity and frequency. A call to his personal physician confirmed that he continues to refill his prescriptions. Patient reports that since termination he has not used the relaxation skill he acquired and that the frequency of his nightmare activity is about what it was before he came to see me.

Discussion

The above observations generate some interesting theoretical speculations. Freudian theory and symptom substitution hypothesis caution against isolated symptomatic treatment. It may be hypothesized that an inherent homeostatic mechanism reacted self-protectively to halt "superficial" symptomatic treatment.

An alternative explanation may begin by noting that the probability of entry into the hypnotic state is increased by biofeedback training procedures (Engstrom, London, and Hart, 1970; Wickramasekera, 1971, 1973). These procedures train the subject to shut off voluntarily sensory input thus producing a condition of reduced sensory responsivity to external stimulation which is similar to sleep, but also increases the probability of attention to internal events, which facilitates hypnosis. It is known that as frontalis EMG levels approach 3 microvolts, low voltage theta appears in the EEG. Theta has been correlated with the onset of hypnogogic images and primary process material. Psychoanalytic theory predicts (Gill and Brenman, 1959) that under the above conditions, the efficiency of some ego functions will be reduced, hypnotizability will be increased, and that there will be an increased probability of access to primary process materials including previous memories. In the hypnotic state, hypnotic dreams occur which are similar but in some important respects unlike (Levitt and Chapman, 1972) night dreams. It may be hypothesized that Sam was entering the hypnotic state during relaxation practice and due to some unknown but reliable situational cue or some intrapersonal set was simply recalling in vivid detail a sleep-related nightmare.

Psychophysiologically, nightmares have been observed to occur during arousal from slow wave sleep (stages III and IV) and are never associated with the REM state (Broughton, 1968). It seems highly unlikely that this patient was awaking from slow wave sleep during the onset of his "nightmare." Snyder and Scott (1972) stress the importance of defining sleep in terms of both behavioral and EEG data. No EEG data was available in this case. But studies of sleeping subjects indicate that a drop in EMG activity in the head and neck is associated with the onset of dream activity (Aarons, 1968). It would be interesting to know if with some people the induction of low EMG levels in the head (with EMG feedback) would increase the probability of dream activity independent of sleep states. At least for this patient there appeared to be a reliable relationship between an experimental procedure and "nightmare" activity. If his experimentally-induced "nightmare" was as identical as he maintained with the more naturally occurring sleep-related phenomena, an important question arises. Are there conditions other than arousal from slow wave sleep under which nightmares may occur? REM activity has been reported to be unrelated to nightmare activity. If a nightmare is a type of dream, it is worth noting that recent speculation about the conditions under which dreams occur do not associate dreaming as tightly with REM sleep as was previously thought, but consider the REM state as a unique biological state in its own right which simply happens to be conducive to the recall of dream activity (Snyder and Scott, 1972).

Psychodynamically, it is worth noting that the most salient characteristic of the "little green monsters" was that they were "alien." The patient described himself as an "orphan" and reported feeling "different" from other kids during his childhood. It is tempting to infer that in a sense he may have felt like an alien. The patient recalled that his stepmother pampered and overindulged him. His stepmother may have sensed the patient's feeling of being different from other boys and may have attempted to make it up to him with her overindulgence. It is possible that the special treatment may only have reinforced the patient's feeling of being different and alien.

A theme of guilt appears to be manifested in his nightmare, in that he is being accused of something he can never hear in his sleep. It is possible that the patient was irrationally blaming himself for being an orphan, different and alien. The pampering by his stepmother probably produced jealousy and anger in his stepfather, who the patient remembers as ignoring him and fighting with his stepmother. The patient felt that his stepfather avoided him and, in fact, he finally abandoned the patient and his mother. Sam's realization that his presence was a source of conflict to his parents may have reinforced his feeling of guilt. It may be that he blamed himself for his mother's abandonment by his stepfather and for the break-up of their marriage.

In terms of current precipitating factors, it is possible that the patient felt that his black daughters were aliens in the white neighborhood in which he chose to live. He stated in the initial diagnostic period that their presence had caused many embarrassing incidents for the family. The incident with the fire may have brought the patient at some level of consciousness in touch with his black daughters' sense of alienation, frustration, and rage with their predicament. His unconscious reasons for adopting the black girls may have included a need to expiate his own irrational guilt about being an orphan and an alien, and a need to prove his own freedom from prejudice of "aliens" (like his mother had done before him, even to the point of breaking up with her husband), even at the expense of compulsively inflicting his own childhood feeling of being different and an alien on two black girls.

References

Aarons, L. Diurnal variations of muscle action potentials and word associations related to psychological orientation. *Psychophysiology,* 1968, *5,* 77-91.

Barber, T. X.; DiCara, L. V.; Kamiya, J.; Miller, N. E.; Shapiro, D.; & Stoyva, J. (Eds.). *Biofeedback and Self Control.* Chicago: Aldine-Atherton, 1971.

Broughton, R. J. Sleep disorders: Disorders of arousal. *Science.* 1968, *159,* 1070-1078.

Budzynski, T. H.; Stoyva, J. M.; & Adler, C. Feedback-induced muscle relaxation: Application to tension headache. *Journal of Behavior Therapy and Experimental Psychiatry,* 1970, *1,* 205-211.

Engstrom, D. R.; London, P. & Hart, J. T. EEG alpha feedback training and hypnotic susceptibility. *Proceedings of the 78th Annual Convention of the American Psychological Association,* 1970, *5,* 837-838.

Gill, M. M. & Brenman, M. *Hypnosis and Related States: Psychoanalytic Studies in Repression.* New York: International Universities Press, 1959.

Levitt, E. & Chapman, H. Hypnosis as a research method. In Fromm, E. & Shor, R. E. (Eds.) *Hypnosis. Research Developments and Perspectives.* Chicago: Aldine, 1972.

Orne, M. T. & Scheibe, K. E. The contribution of nondeprivation factors to the production of sensory deprivation effects. *Journal of Abnormal and Social Psychology,* 1964, *68,* 8-12.

Snyder, F. & Scott, J. The psychophysiology of sleep. In Greenfield, N. S. & Sternbach, R. A. (Eds.), *Handbook of Psychophysiology.* New York: Holt, Rinehart and Winston, 1972.

Wickramasekera, I. Effects of EMG feedback training on susceptibility to hypnosis: Preliminary observations. *Proceedings of the 79th Annual Convention of American Psychological Association,* 1971, 783-784.

Wickramasekera, I. Electromyographic feedback training and tension headache: Preliminary observations. *American Journal of Clinical Hypnosis,* 1972, *15,* 83-85.

Wickramasekera, I. The effects of EMG feedback training on hypnotic susceptibility. More preliminary data. *Journal of Abnormal Psychology,* 1973, *82,* 74-77. (a)

Wickramasekera, I. Instructions and EMG feedback in tension headache. *Headache,* 1973, *13* (2), 74-76. (b)

Instructions and EMG Feedback in Systematic Desensitization: A Case Report

Ian Wickramasekera
University of Illinois
College of Medicine
Peoria

B andura (1969) suggests that the effectiveness of reinforcement procedures may be enhanced by verbal instructions. The following case study appears to illustrate a clinical demonstration of the above hypotheses. The amount of time available for treatment of this patient was only 21 days and the amount of time the therapist could spend with her was limited to three sessions.

The patient, a 42-year-old white divorced female, the mother of seven children, reported an unhappy marriage for 22 years to a man she described as alcoholic. On welfare for many years, she had been compelled by the State to attend school for the previous four years to prepare for the General Education Development (GED) Examination, but was scared to take any examinations including those administered in school. The prospect of a public examination like the GED terrified her and she had previously withdrawn on three occasions from taking the test. She reported that, as an adolescent, she had dropped out of school in the 7th grade because of her fear of examinations. The patient's current teachers reported that she was a bright student and stated that, if she could overcome her fears, they felt certain that she would pass the examination. I was contacted three weeks prior to the scheduled GED examination and requested to help in overcoming her "examination phobia."

The patient was scheduled for an initial diagnostic interview and testing. She reported extreme fear of school or employment related tests and claimed that, before examinations, invariably she would have severe headaches, upset stomach, nausea, and feel weak and shaky. She had lost several employment opportunities because of her fears. We administered the Stanford Hypnotic Susceptibility Scale (SHSS) Form A to the patient to determine the extent to which her behavior could be controlled by verbal stimuli, and she was given a standardized set of simple written instructions for systematic desensitization, the technique itself, and its rationale. She was told that she would have to do most of the treatment herself because of the proximity of the examination and the shortage of therapist time. Arrangements were also made for her to observe a standard video tape used to orient all patients to desensitization. The tape described and demonstrated the treatment components (relaxation training, hierarchy construction, and desensitization proper) and showed the movement of a real patient through relaxation training and desensitization with electromyographic feedback (Budzynski and Stoyva, 1969; Leaf and Gardner, 1971; Wickramasekera, 1971b). The patient was told that only two more sessions were available with the present therapist, and that the second session would be used to respond to any questions which arose from reading the instruction sheet and viewing the video tape. The third session would be used to help her construct hierarchies and get her started with desensitization. The sessions with the present therapist varied between 60 to 90 min.

The patient's second visit to the clinic was scheduled for the next day. She met with the present therapist to discuss her reactions to the written instructions and the video tape on systematic desensitization. The use of the EMG feedback instrument[1] was demonstrated to her and she started relaxation training with the EMG electrodes on the frontalis with a feedback tone proportional in frequency to the EMG level. In general, electrical activity in this area is generated not only by the frontalis and corrugator muscles but also the eye, jaw, throat, and tongue muscles. The patient is instructed to keep the tone as low as possible by relaxing, and as she approximates a low tone the loop gain of the

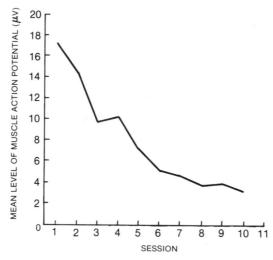

FIGURE 1. Mean frontalis EMG levels over ten sessions of relaxation training with auditory feedback.

---

[1]Commercially available feedback system manufactured by Mr. J. Picchiottino, Box 1459, Boulder, CO 80302. Electrode placement and other procedures followed specifically the instructions described in the manual. Technical details as to sensitivity equivalents, feedback loop, resistance between electrodes, etc., may be found in the manual. The instrument if correctly used is constructed to eliminate the EEG, EKG, and "noise" artifacts.

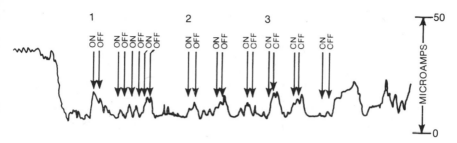

FIGURE 2. Section of paper from Rustrack Recorder showing changing EMG levels during systematic desensitization. The numbers 1, 2 and 3 refer to the points at which each of the first three scenes from the patient hierarchy was initially introduced to the relaxed patient. The expressions "on" and "off" refer to verbal instructions to the relaxed patient to commence to terminate scene visualization. Paper speed, 8 in./hr.

feedback system is increased, thus requiring her to reach a lower EMG level to hear a low tone. The response of relaxation is thus shaped through three adjustments in the sensitivity (low, medium, and high) of the system. It is easy with auditory feedback to observe and demonstrate to the patient the consequences of relaxing these muscles.

The patient was next introduced to my assistant (a married female high school graduate, who volunteers 4 hr. each day to the clinic) who supplements the EMG feedback training with three consecutive training sessions of verbal instructions in muscular relaxation (Wolpe and Lazarus, 1968). The training with verbal instructions preceded the EMG feedback training. The patient was also required to come to the clinic daily to practice for 30 min. with the EMG feedback device, and to practice relaxation at home for 30 min. daily. In a matter-of-fact manner she was told that the EMG unit enabled us to detect and record how much relaxation practice she was doing at home. She started her EMG feedback training on the low sensitivity level of the instrument and progressively worked up to the high sensitivity level. Her performance with feedback was monitored by my assistant at 5-min. intervals. Her performance was recorded from the meter readout unit. When the patient was reporting subjective feelings of numbness and tingling in her body in the relaxed state and when she could also keep the EMG feedback at a low level on the high sensitivity setting, she was judged to be ready for desensitization. The verbal report of this and other patients indicates that ability to maintain a "blank mind" is associated with very low frontalis EMG levels.

My assistant then gave the patient several hierarchies of previous patients with similar fears of examinations and asked her to use them to construct her own hierarchy. After the patient had completed the relaxation training and constructed her own hierarchy, which consisted of 20 cards on which the events leading up to and during the examination were briefly described in her own words, she was requested to memorize the contents of these notecards. During the desensitization proper, the patient was connected to the EMG unit and it was set at the high sensitivity level. The meter unit was disconnected from the EMG console and an especially adapted recorder (Rustrack Model 288 FIA, with silently operating feature) was connected to the EMG unit. (Of course a recorder like the Rustrack can only record gross patterns of electrical activity.) The patient was told to terminate scene visualization whenever the feedback tone increased markedly and not to start visualization again until the feedback had declined notably. The therapist presented verbally the first three scenes to the patient and, because the recorder was tracking the EMG signal, we were able to observe the EMG events associated with the verbal presentation by the therapist of the first three aversive events from the patient's hierarchy.

The data appear to suggest that instructing the patient to start cognitive rehearsal of an aversive event in the relaxed state is associated with an increase in the EMG signal and that instructing the patient to terminate cognitive rehearsal of the event is associated with a decline in the EMG signal. It also appears, in general, that repeating the cognitive rehearsal is associated with less arousal on each presentation. Because of the exploratory and pilot nature of this study, it is difficult to be certain that the changes in the EMG data were exclusively a function of cognitive rehearsal, as impressionistically they appeared to be. Supposedly close conformity to the instructions in the EMG manual should reduce the probability of artifacts.

After the therapist had desensitized the patient to the first three scenes, he withdrew. The patient continued the desensitization, drawing on the scenes she had memorized from her hierarchy. Presumably, she used the auditory feedback to monitor changes in her level of relaxation and to determine when to "switch on and off" the cognitive rehearsal of aversive events from her hierarchy. Hence, the last 17 scenes were desensitized by the patient in the clinic with auditory EMG feedback.

Results

The patient reported that the examination came upon her while three scenes still remained to be desensitized, but apparently she had obtained sufficient benefit from the procedure to go ahead and take the examination and pass it with only mild feelings of anxiety. After the examination was completed, she desensitized the last three scenes with EMG feedback. Soon afterward the patient had to take several civil service and employment examinations, which she approached with increasing confidence and on which she did exceptionally well. She reported that none of the previous unpleasant symptoms connected with examinations occurred.

Discussion

Intuitively, it seems that verbal instructions currently provide the most economic, precise, and elegant means of controlling complex human behavior. The identification of conditions and procedures (Wickramasekera, 1969, 1970a,b, 1971a,b) which will reliably increase the verbal stimulus control of behavior is a salient task. Suggestibility scales (e.g., Stanford Hypnotic Suggestibility Scales, Barber Suggestibility Scale) appear to provide a rough estimate of current or baseline responsivity to verbal stimuli under standard conditions. Our patient's score on the SHSS scale was 4, which indicates only a moderate degree of suggestibility or responsivity to verbal instructions. Barber's (1970) research indicates that relaxation instructions are one of the significant antecedent variables which increase suggestibility, and one of the effective functions of relaxation training in systematic desensitization may be regarded as a type of "setting event" (Kantor, 1959) that increases the subject's responsivity to verbal instructions (Wickramasekera, 1971b). The relaxed state may reduce the "noise" or interference in the system (Nakamura and Broen, 1965) thereby increasing the impact of any new sensory– verbal input. A recent study (Chapman and Feather, 1971) supports our hypothesis (Wickramasekera, 1971b) that relaxation increases sensitivity and attention to phobic imagery. Hence, at least one important way in which muscular relaxation may contribute to systematic desensitization is through sharpening the patient's focus of attention on the verbally presented conditioned stimuli (scene from hierarchy) and thereby increasing the probability that the conditioned response will be elicited. But the graded nature of the elicitation process maintains the arousal within tolerable limits, allowing extinction rather than the rare phenomenon of "resensitization" (Wickramasekera, 1970c) to occur. Clinically, it appears that, unless the conditioned response to the phobic stimulus can be elicited, it will be impossible to extinguish it in the consulting room. The conditioned response may, of course, be also elicited by "in vivo" procedures. Relaxation then appears to be a procedure that facilitates the effective manipulation of central events (cognition) and their autonomic concomitants, in a manner that is relatively independent of peripheral stimulation by real objects. Hence, one of the contributions of relaxation to systematic desensitization appears to be that it fairly reliably enhances the subjective reality of cognitive events and confers on them a measure of clarity and impact which is typically encountered only during "in vivo" stimulation.[2]

The above case illustrates how a combination of apparently effective procedures and strategies may facilitate the treatment of the motivated patient. Clinical experience appears to suggest that certain clear procedures were notable in her rehabilitation one, giving the patient responsibility appears to be an important strategy. This responsibility was conveyed behaviorally by limiting the therapist's involvement, assigning specific tasks to the patient and setting or working with a deadline for the cut off of treatment (Goldstein, Heller, and Sechrest, 1966). Showing (videotape)

---

[2]What is required now is an experiment in which a phobic stimulus is presented verbally to the same patient in a "relaxed state" (as defined by verbal report and psychophysiological measures) and later in a nonrelaxed state. We predict that the same verbal stimulus will, in general, have greater subjective reality when the patient is in a "relaxed state."

and telling (spoken and written instructions) the patient "how" she can participate in her own treatment enables her to translate her own motivation into a specific set of therapy relevant behaviors which both behaviorally define her commitment to intervene in her own life and which coincidentally also propels her treatment forward. The use of written instructions and videotape conceptualized as "advanced organizers" (Ausubel, 1963) for therapeutic learning has been previously suggested (Goldstein, Heller, and Sechrest, 1966; Goldstein, 1971). The use of informational feedback devices seems particularly relevant to work with motivated subjects (O'Brien and Azrin, 1970). The use of videotape and feedback instruments, etc., may provide for the potentiation of any latent "placebo effects" inherent in a treatment situation. Finally, and perhaps most importantly, the availability of the desensitization technique itself gives a sense of coherence, direction and plausibility to the therapeutic interventions.

References

Ausubel, D.P. The psychology of meaningful verbal learning. New York: Grune and Stratton, 1963.

Bandura, A. Principles of behavior modification. New York: Holt, Rinehart and Winston, 1969.

Budzynski, T.H., & Stoyva, J.M. An instrument for producing deep muscle relaxation by means of analog information feedback. *Journal of Applied Behavior Analysis*, 1969, *2*, 231—237.

Chapman, C.R., & Feather, B.W. Sensitivity to phobic imagery: A sensory decision theory analysis. *Behaviour Research and Therapy*, 1971, *9*, 161—168.

Goldstein, A.P., Heller, K., & Sechrest, L.B. Psychotherapy and the psychology of behavior change. New York: Wiley, 1966.

Goldstein, A.P. Psychotherapeutic attraction. New York: Pergamon Press, 1966.

Kantor, J.R. Interbehavioral Psychology. Bloomington, Indiana: Principia Press, 1959.

Leaf, W.B., & Gardner, K.R. A simplified electromyograph feedback apparatus for relaxation training. *Journal of Behavior Therapy and Experimental Psychiatry*, 1971, *2*, 39—43.

Nakamura, C.Y., & Broen, W.E. Further study of the effects of low drive states on competing responses. *Journal of Experimental Psychology*, 1965, *70*, 434—436.

O'Brien, F., & Azrin, N.H. Behavioral engineering: control of posture by informational feedback. *Journal of Applied Behavioral Analysis*, 1970, *3*, 235 240.

Wickramasekera, I. The effects of sensory restriction of susceptibility to hypnosis: A hypothesis, some preliminary data, and theoretical speculation. *International Journal of Clinical and Experimental Hypnosis*, 1969, *17*, 217—224.

Wickramasekera, I. The effects of "hypnosis" and a control procedure on verbal conditioning. Paper presented at the meeting of the American Psychological Association, Miami, September, 1970. (a)

Wickeramsekera, I. The effects of sensory restrictions on susceptibility to hypnosis: A hypothesis and more preliminary data. *Journal of Abnormal Psychology*, 1970, *715*, 68—72. (b)

Wickramasekera, I. Desensitization, resensitization and desensitization again: A preliminary study. *Journal of Behavior Therapy and Experimental Psychiatry*, 1970, *1*, 257—262. (c)

Wickramasekera, I. The effects of "hypnosis" and task motivational instructions in attempting to influence the voluntary self deprivation of money. *Journal of Personality and Social Psychology*, 1971, *19*, 311—314.(a)

Wickramasekera, I. The effects of EMG Feedback training on susceptibility to hypnosis: Preliminary observations. Paper presented at American Psychological Association, Washington, DC, September, 1971. (b)

Wolpe, J., & Lazarus, A.A. Behavior therapy techniques. New York: Pergamon Press, 1966.

Flow Chart and Commentary for Management of Systematic Desensitization

Ian Wickramasekera

1. Clinical Interview, therapeutic alliance, and rapport establishment.
2. Diagnostic Testing MMPI, Eysenck, Fear Survey Schedule, Spiegel, EMG, heart rate, GSR. Baseline.
3. Rationale and Literature on S.D. and Biofeedback presented (Handouts plus video tape).
4. A. Construct Stress Hierarchy
   B. Monitor Frontalis EMG before and at the end of session for 3 minutes.
   C. Relaxation Training I
   D. Cut Cassette Tape I
   E. Home Practice Twice a Day
5. A. Monitor Frontalis EMG before and at the end of session for 3 minutes.
   B. Relaxation Training II
   C. Cut Cassette Tape II
6. Practice with EMG auditory feedback 4-6 sessions connected to recorder.
7. A. Check Frontalis EMG - S.D. may start at 4uV
   B. Patient Memorizes and self presents 4 events from hierarchy at each session.
   C. Uses auditory feedback to monitor tension level. (Presentation and withdrawal contingent on tone.)
   D. Terminates with visualizing in low arousal state coping actively and comfortably with 4 events.
   E. Discussion of low and high points of session with therapist.
   F. Assign "in vivo" practice session
8. Review "in vivo" practice, feedback reports.
   Revision of hierarchy based on verbal report if necessary
   Repeat 7 A-E

Commentary

1.   The clinical interview seeks to identify areas of stress and the factors that precipitate or exacerbate them. It also seeks to understand the type of patient who has these areas of stress and pays attention to his values, life style, goals and his typical methods of coping with stress. Maladaptive ideas that cause and sustain stress are identified and challenged as in rational emotive therapy. The patient is hypnotically programmed to challenge these ideas in the natural habitat with post-hypnotic suggestion.

2.   A battery of psychological and physiological tests (EMG, heart rate, G.S.R., respiration) are given to all patients. The purpose of the physiological tests is to identify the individual patient's stress response profile when he is stimulated by standardized procedures (e.g. mental arithmetic, discharging cap gun, phobic material).

3.   Suitable articles from the popular press explaining systematic desensitization and biofeedback are read by the patient and his questions are answered. He also views a video tape of a model patient being desensitized. The aim is to mobilize "hope" and teach specifics of patient role.

4&5.   The situations that precipitate or exacerbate anxiety are identified and arranged on note cards hierarchically. The patient is taught verbal relaxation exercises "in vivo" in two sessions and an audio cassette tape is cut during the training sessions. Frontalis EMG is monitored before and at the end of each relaxation session. The patient is instructed to practice the relaxation exercises at least twice a day and he is told that his progress is being tracked on a recorder.

6.   The patient practices relaxation in the office with EMG feedback for 4-6 sessions while his progress is tracked on a one channel recorder.

7.   This feedback assisted training is continued until the patient can reach and maintain a low level of arousal (less than 4uV) from frontalis. At each session the patient memorizes and presents to himself while at a low level of arousal (4uV) no more than 4 events from his stress hierarchy. The changes in auditory feedback are used by the patient as an index of elicited stress. The event is rehearsed cognitively until there is very little disruption of the previously attained relaxation level. Then the next stress item from the hierarchy is self-presented from memory. The patient is asked to terminate each session with visualizing himself coping effectively and comfortably with each previously desensitized event. This type of cognitive rehearsal at a low level of arousal (typically the level of arousal drops progressively towards the tail end of the session and is frequently below 2.5uV at termination) appears to consolidate the desensitization process by establishing a broader attitudal and perceptual basis for the change.

All EMG changes during the session are monitored by a one channel EMG recorder. At the end of the session the patient and therapist discuss any problems or high points of the session and the patient is encouraged to reality test, in vivo up the point he desensitized himself. The patient report of reality testing is discussed and the stress hierarchy revised if necessary prior to repeating the previous procedure.

The Use of EMG and Alpha Biofeedback to Relieve Test Anxiety in College Students

B.L. Garrett and M.P. Silver
DePauw University, Indiana

T wo experiments were conducted to determine whether biofeedback training could be used to reduce test anxiety. In the first experiment, subjects trained to increase alpha production and to reduce frontalis muscle tension decreased significantly in test anxiety and increased significantly in class rank on exams, while controls did not. There was no effect on performance on tests given in the laboratory. In the second experiment an alpha group, an EMG group, and a group receiving both alpha and EMG training decreased significantly in test anxiety, while a no-contact control group and a group designed to control for placebo effects did not. The feedback techniques were equally effective in reducing test anxiety. There was no effect on semester grade point average.

The discovery that subjects could be trained to control various physiological variables typically noted as symptoms of anxiety has led to the hope that such training would be useful in treating anxious patients. This hope is strengthened by subjects' reports of a relaxed, pleasant state during training (Brown, 1970; Kamiya, 1968, 1969). Biofeedback has been used successfully to treat hypertension (Shapiro, Tursky, and Schwartz, 1971), migraine headache (Sargent, Green, and Walters, 1973), and tension headache (Budzynski, Stoyva and Adler, 1971), and as a preparation for desensitization (Wickramasekera, 1972). However, the speculation that biofeedback training could serve as a therapy for anxiety has been fostered primarily by reports in popular publications, and publication of firm evidence, either positive or negative, has been almost nonexistent (Meldman, 1973). The observation that ". . . an abundance of ideas coexists with a paucity of empirical data" seems a very apt one (Shapiro and Schwartz, 1972).

The following two experiments were intended to determine, under controlled conditions, whether biofeedback training could be used to reduce anxiety. Test anxiety was chosen to insure homogeneity of symptoms in the subjects and because of the availability of subjects and ease of measurement.

Experiment I
Method

Subjects

Subjects were thirty-six non-freshman college students who indicated interest in participating in research which might alleviate their test anxiety, and who scored in the upper two-thirds of 163 Introductory Psychology students on a test anxiety questionnaire. The questionnaire consisted of the ten items of the Debilitating Anxiety Scale (Alpert and Haber, 1960) and six items concerning physiological reactions to tests, such as illness and muscle tension. Both sets of questions discriminated well between individuals who separately reported interfering test anxiety and a willingness to participate in therapeutic research, and those who did not. The items were answered on a five-point scale.

Apparatus

A Grass Model 7B polygraph with a 7P5 AC preamplifier was used to amplify the EEG signal, which was filtered by a Krohn-Hite Model 3700 band pass filter. Digi-Bit (BRS-Foringer) logic modules turned on a Hunter 120A Klockounter and a 400 Hz feedback tone when alpha (8-13 Hz) EEG in excess of 21μ v occurred. Latency of the apparatus in detecting onset or termination of alpha was approximately .3 second. A Model PE-2 EMG feedback device (Bio-Feedback Systems, Boulder, Colorado), modified to include a second meter for data recording, was used to provide auditory and visual feedback of frontalis muscle tension.

Procedure

Subjects were given three tests expected to be sensitive to test anxiety and to show any changes in test-taking ability that might result from the relaxation training to follow. The first test was the Davis Reading Test (Davis and Davis, 1958), Form 1A, with a time limit of twenty minutes instead of the prescribed forty. The second test consisted of six block designs similar to the Kohs Block Designs in the Wechsler Adult Intelligence Scale (Wechsler, 1955), each design requiring all nine blocks. A subject's score was the time required to complete each design correctly. The final test was six sets of digits from the Wechsler Adult Intelligence Scale Digits Forward test, Trial I, beginning with the four-digit set and progressing to nine digits. These were presented by a tape recorder and written by the subjects. Total testing time was less than an hour. Following relaxation training, subjects were given alternate forms of the tests, including Form 1B of the Davis Reading Test, six similar block designs, and Trial II of the Digits Forward test, again beginning with the four-digit set. An attempt was made to induce stress by telling the subjects that they would be paid $1.50 for average performance on the tests and proportionately more or less for higher or lower performance.

The test scores were used to form eighteen matched pairs of subjects and the members of each pair were randomly assigned to an experimental or a control group. Members of the experimental group were scheduled for training sessions, while control subjects were informed that a sufficient number of subjects had been randomly selected for training and that they would not be needed except for testing later to establish norms for the tests. Experimental subjects were paid $1.60 per training session.

On entering the laboratory, the subject was seated in a small, dimly lighted room adjacent to the experimenter's room. Half the subjects began with alpha training and half started with EMG training. EEG electrode placement was frontal-occipital with an earlobe ground; all electrodes were on the right side of the head. Resistances were 5000 ohms or less. The EMG electrodes were one inch above the brow and two inches to the sides of the nasion, with the ground electrode centered between the recording electrodes. Each subject indicated that he was not subject to fainting, dizziness, or seizures and had not required psychotherapy during the past four years. One subject was eliminated due to this requirement.

Alpha subjects were given a brief explanation of alpha EEG, cautioned against smoking or drinking coffee during the half-hour preceding training, and asked to report any use of drugs. They were instructed to relax, blank the mind, and drift without thinking about anything in particular. These specific instructions were intended to speed training by reducing the initial experimenting and the frustration likely to occur with uninstructed subjects. While the emphasis on a relaxed state could have a contaminating effect on subjective reports called for at the end of training, it seemed necessary to indicate to the somewhat skeptical subjects that the training was relevant to their test anxiety. Each alpha training session consisted of eight five-minute periods; at the end of each period, the number of seconds during which alpha was produced was recorded and related to the subject via an intercom, and the subject was permitted to stretch and change position. It was necessary to increase the sensitivity of the alpha detection apparatus (to detect alpha of 19 μ v or greater) for two subjects with low-amplitude alpha and to decrease the sensitivity (to detect alpha of 23 μ v or greater) for one subject whose alpha was of high amplitude. Subjects began training with their eyes closed unless they produced alpha 50% of the time or more with their eyes closed; all subjects were able to produce appreciable amounts of alpha with their eyes open by the end of training.

During EMG sessions, subjects were given instructions to relax the forehead muscles as well as the rest of the body and to attempt to verbalize any sensations that accompanied relaxation. Subjects were told they could concentrate on either the auditory feedback (clicks proportional in rate to tension, presented through earphones) or the visual feedback (meter) or both, and they could work with eyes open or closed. The subject's muscle tension was recorded in microvolts at 100-second intervals, and the subject was informed of his median score and given an opportunity to stretch or change position after every third interval. There were eight five-minute periods per session.

Each subject received two sessions on consecutive days with one variable, then two sessions on consecutive days with the other variable. A week later one session with each variable was given on two consecutive days, providing three sessions with each variable. Thirteen subjects received an additional session of EMG training and two received an additional alpha training session because their performance did not meet a 3.0 μ v EMG or 50% alpha criterion. No subject was dropped due to poor training performance, since it seemed desirable to test the usefulness of training with unselected subjects. To enhance generalization to nonlaboratory situations, subjects were given several nonfeedback periods during the latter sessions of training and were required to practice at home for 15 minutes on each training day. Records kept by the subjects indicated that they were, in general, faithful in their practice.

The experimental and the control subjects took the alternate forms of the performance tests two days following training. Training and testing were completed about ten days before final examinations. Immediately after training, the experimental subjects completed a nine-item questionnaire, answered on a five-point scale, regarding effects of the training on relaxation. All subjects repeated the test anxiety questionnaire soon after final examinations, with instructions to answer the items with regard to final examinations only.

Results

Training Measures

The experimental subjects increased from a mean alpha production of

64.13% of the time to a mean of 77.61%, an increase of 21.02% over the baseline. The mean EMG level dropped from 5.84 μ v to 3.49 μ v, a decrease of 40.24%.

On the posttraining questionnaire, 83% of the experimental subjects indicated they were more relaxed than usual during the training sessions, and that the relaxation was greater than they could have achieved without the training. The same number indicated they were more relaxed than usual outside the laboratory, and 78% said they were better able to relax when they desired. Only 56% believed they were better able to concentrate, study, or perform skilled tasks than before. Eighty-nine percent reported the practice sessions at home were relaxing. The mean score on the questionnaire differed significantly from the mean expected under the assumption of no effect of the training on relaxation (t=8.04, df=17, p < .0005).

In response to a request for comments, a few subjects reported they were less tense when studying and one said his insomnia had disappeared. One who had sought informal counseling prior to the study because she became ill before exams reported almost total remission of the symptom as well as lessened headaches ten months after training. Nine subjects reported greater relaxation during alpha training, four favored EMG training, and five rated them equally. The subjects who showed marked differences between the two typically experienced greater relaxation accompanying the variable on which they performed most successfully.

Performance Tests

Each subject's score on the performance tests was the sum of his standard scores on the three subtests. A difference was taken for each subject between his score on the posttraining test and his score on the pretraining test, and these scores were subjected to a one-way analysis of variance for repeated measures. The difference between the trained group and the untrained group did not reach significance (F=.14). Similar comparisons on the individual subtests did not yield significance.

Test Anxiety

The trained subjects showed a decrease in test anxiety scores from a mean of 50.11 (maximum possible score was 80) to a mean of 32.56, or a mean decrease of 17.55 points. The untrained subjects dropped from a mean of 47.89 to 47.27, a decrease of .62 points. All trained subjects indicated anxiety decreases; seven control subjects showed increases and two reported no change. A comparison of the groups using the Kruskal-

Wallis one-way analysis of variance by ranks showed the difference was significant $(x=17.62, df=1, p < .001)$.

Academic Performance

Since it was thought that any benefits from test-anxiety reduction would be more easily detected under the controlled conditions of the performance tests, subjects were selected and assigned to groups without regard to their academic records. To compare changes in course examination performance of the two groups, subjects who scored above the median on the first examinations in their respective Introductory Psychology classes were eliminated, since there was limited opportunity for improvement for them. The change in percentile rank (in their respective classes) from the first exam to the final exam was compared for the remaining nine experimental subjects and twelve control subjects. The trained group showed a mean increase of 9.97 percentile points, while the untrained subjects increased an average of 4.02 percentile points. All nine trained subjects showed improvement, while seven of the twelve untrained subjects improved. Comparison of the first-exam percentiles with the final exam percentiles using the Friedman two-way analysis of variance indicated that the experimental group improved significantly $(x^2=8.1, df=1, p < .01)$, and that the control group did not $(x^2=.355, p > .50)$. However, a Kruskal-Wallis analysis did not show a significant difference between the groups in amount of change in class rank $(x^2=1.06, df=1, p > .30)$.

To control for initial differences, seven pairs of subjects matched on first-exam percentile scores were selected from the ones involved in the preceding analysis. The mean increase for the trained group was 10.8 percentile points and for the untrained group was 3.54 percentile points; the trained subject improved more than the untrained subject in five of the seven pairs. Although these data appear more promising, the Friedman two-way analysis of variance by ranks did not approach significance $x^2=1.28, df=1, p > .20)$.

Discussion

The results of this experiment support previous findings that subjects feel more relaxed during alpha-EEG training and EMG-reduction training. This finding is extended by showing that the effect persists outside the laboratory, even during a period of several days without practice, and that the subjects feel they can control their level of relaxation.

The results also provide evidence that anxiety toward a specific situation can be reduced by biofeedback training. This conclusion is supported not only by the significant difference between the groups on the test anxiety questionnaire, but also by informal comments that tests are now less threatening and studying is less tension-producing.

Evidence of improved performance is lacking in the data from the performance tests. It is possible that the subjects were not under sufficient tension during the testing periods, although they indicated that the tests were demanding. The significant improvement in exam grades for the experimental subjects is encouraging, though the improvement was small and the difference in improvement between the groups was not significant. It should be noted that the majority of control subjects came from one class, and this may account for the difference between the groups.

The evidence, then, is for an improvement in the way test-anxious subjects feel during exams and, perhaps, an improvement in performance on examinations following training with biofeedback. It must be cautioned, however, that the possibility of a placebo effect in the test-anxiety results should not be overlooked.

Experiment II
Method

Subjects

Fifty subjects were selected from the Introductory Psychology classes on the basis of the following requirements: (a) a score on the previously described test anxiety questionnaire that was above the median of the 163 students tested in Experiment I; (b) a grade point average below the university median; (c) the subject's statement that anxiety interfered with his test performance and that he was interested in participating in potentially therapeutic research; (d) at least one semester of college experience prior to the study. The subjects were randomly assigned to five groups of ten each, with minor adjustments made to equate the groups on mean test anxiety score and mean grade point average. Experimental subjects were paid $10 each and control subjects received $1 for completing the test anxiety questionnaire at the end of the experiment.

Apparatus

The equipment used to measure alpha EEG and EMG was the same as that used in Experiment I.

Procedure

The purpose of this experiment was to determine whether the test anxiety reduction found in Experiment I could be replicated, if so, whether the reduction might be due to placebo effects, and whether alpha and EMG training differ in effectiveness. The five groups were randomly designated to receive training in alpha EEG production (Alpha group), muscle tension reduction (EMG group), the two combined (Both group), or relaxation training without feedback (Relax group), or to receive no training (Control group).

Two subjects who withdrew from the study due to lack of interest or time conflicts were replaced; one subject who became ill near the end of the experiment could not be replaced. Thus, each group contained ten subjects except the Both group, which had nine. Again, no subjects were dropped due to poor training performance. No subjects required adjustment of the alpha detection sensitivity in this experiment as before. It was not necessary to drop any subject on the basis of medical or psychological history.

Subjects received two training sessions per week on alternate weeks for a total of ten sessions. The Both group alternated between alpha and EMG training on different weeks, half beginning with alpha and half with EMG. The purpose in distributing training over a ten-week period was to give the subjects the opportunity to learn to use the relaxation techniques in testing situations. Subject comment in Experiment I suggested that anxiety reduction left some subjects without motivation to study.

The training procedure and instructions were essentially the same as in Experiment I. The Relax group received instructions similar to those of the feedback groups, including instructions to relax, blank the mind, and relax the muscles. No mention was made of feedback and all subjects were asked not to discuss the experiment with other students. Use of dummy feedback was decided against on the assumption that it would be better to have these control subjects engaged in activity similar to that of the feedback subjects, rather than to reinforce them for doing whatever they might be doing at the time. The Relax subjects were told that physiological recordings were being made, and electrodes were attached for each session. A break was given every five minutes as with the other groups. Time in alpha was recorded for half the Relax subjects and muscle tension for the other half during the first and last sessions of the experiment.

Subjects were encouraged to practice the relaxation techniques outside the laboratory, particularly during periods of tension. As before, several periods were given without feedback to reduce dependence on the instrumentation. During the last three sessions the light in the training room was gradually increased from dim to moderate to make it easier for the subjects to maintain relaxation under more typical conditions.

All subjects, including the Controls, completed the test anxiety questionnaire again within a week after training ended. The study was complete about five days before final examinations.

Results

Training Measures

The Alpha group increased from a mean of 59.60% to 79.39%, an increase of 33.21% of the baseline. The EMG group decreased from a mean of 4.46 μ v to 2.25 μ v, a decrease of 49.55%. The Both subjects showed an alpha increase from 41.76% to 60.49%, a 44.85% increase, and decreased in muscle tension from 5.73 μ v to 3.72 μ v, a decrease of 41.37%. The Relax subjects whose alpha production was monitored increased from 34.44% to 40.77%, an increase of 18.37%; the Relax subjects whose muscle tension was monitored decreased from 10.2 μ v to 5.98 μ v, a decrease of 41.37%.

While the EMG change in the Relax group is larger than might be expected, it should be noted that their terminal level was still poorer than those of the feedback groups. It appears that the Relax subjects were not equivalent to the feedback groups initially. However, since pretraining scores were not resting measures but were medians of the scores in periods 2-4 on the first day, the preferred interpretation is that the Relax group's instructions initially resulted in increased tension, as often occurs when one is told to relax. The scores of the Alpha and EMG groups were superior to the scores obtained in Experiment I, probably due to the extended training. The Both group was comparable to the experimental group in Experiment I in EMG scores, and had lower initial and terminal alpha scores. Procedural differences apparently do not account for the initial differences between the Both group and the other feedback groups. These group differences are not reflected in the test anxiety and academic performance measures.

A posttraining questionnaire containing six of the items used in Experiment I yielded essentially the same results as previously. Ninety-two percent of the subjects reported they were more relaxed during training than ordinary. Greater relaxation than usual outside the laboratory was indicated by 87% and greater ability to relax when desired was reported by 92%. Sixty-seven percent reported increased ability to concentrate, study, or perform skilled tasks, etc. The mean score on the questionnaire for each of the feedback groups differed from the expected at the .0005 level (t=9.71, 5.71, 11.15; df=9, 9, 8); the Relax group's mean was significant at the .005

level (t=4.65, df=9). The four groups did not differ significantly among themselves (F=1.35, df=3, 35, p > .25). In the Both group, five subjects indicated greater relaxation during alpha training sessions, three favored EMG training, and one indicated equal relaxation under the two conditions. Informal comments of the subjects were similar to those in Experiment I.

Test Anxiety

The group means on the test anxiety questionnaire changed in the following manner: Alpha, from 50.3 to 38.9, a decrease of 11.4 points; EMG, from 49.5 to 38.3, a decrease of 11.2; Both, from 51.44 to 41.44, a decrease of 10; Relax, from 50.9 to 41.9, a decrease of 9; Control, from 49 to 46, a decrease of 3. The pretraining test anxiety scores were compared with the posttraining scores for each group, using the Friedman two-way analysis of variance by ranks. The decreases for the Alpha group and the EMG group were each significant at the .02 level (x^2=6.4, df=1). The comparison for the Both group was significant at the .05 level (x^2=4.58). Neither the Relax group nor the Control group showed a significant decrease (x^2=1.6, p > .20). When the combined feedback groups were compared with the two combined control groups using the Kruskal-Wallis analysis, the difference was significant (x^2=5.05, df=1, p < .05).

Academic Performance

To assess any effects on course grades, the subjects' grade point averages (GPA) for the semester of the study were compared with their grade point averages for the preceding semester and with the grade point averages for the combined previous semesters. The mean differences between the posttraining GPA and the GPA for the preceding semester were: Alpha, -.2079; EMG, -.0497; Both, .2305; Relax, -.0597; Control, -.0557. The only group which showed improvement was the Both group; the change in GPA was not significant for that group (x^2=3.15, df=1, p > 10) nor for any of the others, according to Friedman's analyses.

The mean differences between GPA for the semester of the study and for all previous semesters were: Alpha, -.0402; EMG, -.0438; Both, .2634; Relax, .0236; Control, -.0335. The change in GPA that came nearest to significance was in the EEG group (x^2=3.6, p >.10), and that change was negative.

Discussion

Biofeedback training using the modified procedure of this experiment was at least as effective as in Experiment I. The posttraining questionnaire indicated that the training, in the judgment of the subjects, produced a state of relaxation and an increased ability to relax. No group was shown to be superior in this respect; in fact the relax condition produced almost as high scores as the feedback conditions, suggesting that practice in relaxation is as effective as biofeedback in producing a subjective relaxed state. The possibility of a placebo effect in the questionnaire data therefore exists; however, the positive response of the relax group to the training indicates that the relaxation practice served as an effective control procedure for placebo effects.

Although the reduction in test anxiety was less than in Experiment I, it was significant for each of the biofeedback groups and not for either of the two control groups, and the biofeedback groups differed significantly from the control groups. The fact that the Relax group experienced approximately as much relaxation effect as the feedback groups but underwent less reduction in test anxiety indicates that the test anxiety reduction in the biofeedback groups was not due to a placebo effect.

While in Experiment I, each subject showed a decrease in test anxiety, some in this study showed increases. Yet, in informal questioning of feedback and relax subjects following training, they invariably reported the training reduced their test anxiety, even when their questionnaire scores suggested the opposite. This may indicate a defect in the questionnaire; on the other hand, it may be due to the fact that the pretraining questionnaire was administered at the first of the semester, a minimum of six weeks after the subjects' last exams, and the posttraining questionnaire was given when subjects were beginning to feel the stress of preparing for final examinations.

The academic improvement found in Experiment I was not duplicated. The difference in method of measuring academic improvement may have been a factor, since performance would likely be more consistent within a course than between semesters, and changes would therefore be more readily detected. Then, too, since there are so many factors that influence grades, it may be impractical to look for academic changes resulting from anxiety reduction with small groups of subjects.

Conclusions

The evidence is consistent in indicating that biofeedback training to increase alpha EEG production and to reduce muscle tension can be used to alleviate test anxiety. Whether that reduction in test anxiety can ultimately result in improved grades was not determined. It should be cautioned that specific anxiety was studied here, and the results may or may not apply to general anxiety. Particularly, the routine manner of training used in these two experiments may not be appropriate with generally anxious subjects, and in fact may not be best with symptoms like test anxiety. In dealing with anxious individuals referred by the university counseling center, this laboratory has found it effective to adjust the training procedure to suit the subject; this includes selection of the biofeedback variable or variables to be used, switching from one variable to another at an advantageous time, and postsession interviewing. These two studies do, however, indicate the potential for biofeedback training in dealing with some forms of anxiety.

References

Alpert, Richard, and Haber, Ralph Norman. Anxiety in academic achievement situations. *Journal of Abnormal and Social Psychology*, 1960, *61*, 207-215.

Brown, Barbara B. Recognition of aspects of consciousness through association with EEG alpha activity represented by a light signal. *Psychophysiology*, 1970, *6*, 442-452.

Budzynski, Thomas H., Stoyva, Johann M. and Adler, Charles. Feedback-induced muscle relaxation: Application to tension headache. *Journal of Behavior Therapy and Experimental Psychiatry*, 1970, *1*, 205-211.

Davis, Frederick B. and Davis, Charlotte Croon. *Davis Reading Test, Series 1*. New York: The Psychological Corporation, 1958.

Kamiya, Joseph. Conscious control of brain waves. *Psychology Today*, 1968, *1* (11), 56-60.

Kamiya, Joseph. Operant control of the EEG alpha rhythm and some of its reported effects on consciousness. In: C. Tart (ed.), *Altered States of Consciousness*. New York: Wiley, 1969.

Meldman, M.J. The alpha sonic inhibition of anxiety. *The Journal of Biofeedback*, 1973, *1*, 9-15.

Sargent, Joseph D., Green, Elmer E. and Walters, Dale E. Preliminary report on the use of autogenic feedback training in the treatment of migraine and tension headaches. *Psychosomatic Medicine*, 1973, *35*, 129-135.

Shapiro, David and Schwartz, Gary E. Biofeedback and visceral learning: Clinical applications. *Seminars in Psychiatry*, 1972, *4*, 171-184.

Shapiro, David, Tursky, Bernard, and Schwartz, Gary E. Decreased systolic blood pressure through operant conditioning techniques in patients with essential hypertension, *Science*, 1971, *173*, 740-742.

Wechsler, David. *Wechsler Adult Intelligence Scale*. New York: The Psychological Corporation, 1955.

Wickramasekera, Ian. Instructions and EMG feedback in systematic desensitization: A case report. *Behavior Therapy*, 1972, *3*, 460-465.

Note: The research reported here was supported by the Spencer Foundation, Chicago, Ill.

Heart Rate Feedback and the Control of Cardiac Neurosis

Ian Wickramasekera
University of Illinois
College of Medicine
Peoria

In previous studies it has been shown that biofeedback procedures can facilitate the desensitization of examination phobia (Wickramasekera, 1972) and headache pain (Budzynski, Stoyva and Adler, 1970; Wickramasekera, 1973 a, c, 1974). It appears that any procedure that focuses on an internal response (e.g., EMG, temperature, etc.) and provides a reliable means of modifying the response can be used to cultivate a state of low arousal (Wickramasekera, 1974). In the present study, heart rate feedback was used at first to cultivate a state of low arousal and later to alter the patient's cognitions about his cardiac function. The induction of low-arousal states appears to increase the probability of altering cognitive and attitudinal variables (Wickramasekera, 1973 b).

The patient was a 55-year-old, white, married male, the sales manager of a large urban real estate firm. One afternoon, five years ago, the patient had experienced shortness of breath and palpitation while mowing grass. The patient panicked and was taken to the emergency room of the local general hospital. The physical examination and tests were negative. Since that initial incident, there have been over twenty-five similar panics, trips to the emergency room and negative physical findings. The patient states that the primary symptoms that trigger these incidents are (1) a noticeable increase in his heart rate, (2) shortness of breath, (3) feeling of passing out. These sensations and his reactions to them had in the past five years seriously disrupted his job performance. His hypersensitivity to his cardiac function (he anticipated that even slight changes in his heart rate would trigger shortness of breath and fainting), limited his sales activities, which in turn made him feel like excess baggage to his employer. He was becoming hypersensitive to even minimal indications of impatience, or rejection from fellow salesmen, his boss, or customers. His preoccupation with his health, cardiac function (consultation with many different cardiologists and leading medical clinics), mild paranoid tendencies, and fear of being left alone were placing a severe strain on his marriage. He also avoided sexual relations for fear of another "heart attack." His wife had liked and admired the aggressive, risk-taking, independent man he had been prior to his cardiac neurosis. Her clear rejection and resentment of his dependency hurt his feelings and convinced him that he was unwanted both at work and at home. When he came to see me, he felt quite alone, angry, and bitter. He was sporadically deeply depressed, and he felt that his wilting self-confidence was obvious to others around him at work.

The patient had previously been treated ineffectively with hypnosis, psychotherapy, and chemotherapy by two psychiatrists, several medical specialists, and two nationally prominent medical clinics.

After the clinical diagnostic interview, the following psychological tests were administered: (1) The Spiegel Eye Roll Test of hypnotic susceptibility was administered by the present writer. The Spiegel test is a very brief clinical screening procedure which predicts hypnotizability. Scores on the test range from 0-5. The patient scored a 5 on the test which indicated a superior hypnotic susceptibility. (2) The MMPI was administered and found to be elevated above 70 T) on scales HS, D, Hy, Pd, Pa, Pt, and Sc. The greatest elevation was on the neurotic triad with a peak on D. After the diagnostic interview and psychological testing, the patient was told that his unravelling self-confidence and other symptoms (preoccupation with his health, depression, anxiety, suspiciousness, anger, etc.) were based on his belief and feeling that his cardiac function was outside his control and unreliable. It was pointed out that all the medical evidence indicated that his cardiac function was normal and reliable but that I recognized that he was unable to accept this finding completely. I added that it seemed to me that his previous self-confidence and business success were based on his independence and his ability to control the consequences of his behaviors. I concluded by saying that it appeared as if his present neurosis was based on his feeling of helplessness insofar as his heart was concerned.

The specific treatment proposed involved three steps (1) reading several popular articles on biofeedback, self-control, and their clinical applications. The purpose of this step was to structure the patient's expectations, to motivate him, and to prepare him to participate actively in his treatment. (2) Learning how to relax by slowing down his heart rate with biofeedback (heart-rate feedback) instrumentation. (3) Learning to speed up his heart rate and confronting the consequences of such acceleration.

Before the onset of therapy, I predicted that his symptoms might become worse before they got better, but that these passing setbacks would not detract from eventual victory over his fear and the reclaiming of his self-confidence. If he participated actively in his treatment, he would be taking control of his life again, and arresting the slide that had destroyed his self-confidence.

Specific Treatment Procedure

The patient was seen once a week for thirty minutes. He was connected to a cardiotachometer (Abbott cardiotachometer), which had a visual digital feedback capability. The cardiotachometer was also connected to a recorder. The patient was seated on a comfortable recliner with his eyes open and instructed to attempt to reduce his heart rate. The actual relaxation-feedback session was typically about fifteen to twenty minutes (it took about ten minutes to connect the subject and check the instrument). No verbal relaxation instructions of any type (muscular, autogenic, or hypnotic) were given to the patient. He was simply told to use the visual heart rate feedback to do more of whatever appeared to reduce his heart rate and relax his body. After about six sessions, the patient appeared to be able to lower his heart rate rapidly and reliably while on the recliner connected to the instrument.

The second procedure involved asking the patient to prepare twenty note cards on which he described briefly and vividly incidents or anticipated incidents involving palpitation, respiratory dysfunction, and syncope. The patient arranged and presented to himself (in imagination) these cards in graduated order. He was instructed to monitor his heart rate and to switch off the scene if it increased noticeably (10 beats per minute over baseline) for more than approximately sixty seconds. The cognitive operations were performed while relaxed on the same recliner and connected to the instruments.

The third and final procedure involved having the therapist flood (verbally) the patient while he monitored his heart rate. This was done by the present therapist with an elaborated form of the last four items from his aversive hierarchy. The four items had previously been desensitized by the patient with the biofeedback-assisted desensitization procedure. The patient-administered desensitization was arranged to precede the flooding intervention because clinically this patient strongly resembled the type of patient in whom resensitization (Wickramasekera, 1970) and deterioration effects can be demonstrated if a gradual approach is not used and if brief (rather than extended) exposure to aversive cues is used. It became clear to the patient, especially during the flooding that though his heart rate rose (range of 15-35 BPM) for remarkably long periods, he did not pass out, which was what he feared most. After the verbal flooding procedure, several stressful stimuli and exercises were presented (e.g., a cap gun discharged at 20, 15, 10, 5, then 2 feet from him, large books dropped unexpectedly, patient was instructed to breathe deep and hard for about twenty seconds). During these *in vivo* procedures, the patient's heart rate rose dramatically for transient periods but no panic or fainting occurred. Between these *in vivo* procedures, the patient practiced his relaxation with cardiac feedback and rapidly and reliably returned his heart rate to normal levels.

Treatment was terminated after sixteen sessions, and at the time of termination, the clinical picture had altered dramatically. The patient had been free of anxiety episodes for nearly two months. He had become more aggressive and risk taking in the work situation (as he had been prior to the onset of his symptoms). His relationship with his wife had improved and he had resumed sexual intercourse with her on a weekly basis. A separate interview with the patient's wife confirmed the patient's report of progress.

Follow-up sessions conducted six and twelve months later in which the patient and his wife were interviewed separately indicate that he has not had any anxiety episodes since the termination of treatment, and that his general vocational and marital adjustment have continued to improve.

Discussion

This case history illustrates an approach to managing cardiac neurosis in patients who, on the Spiegel Scale, appear highly hypnotizable. The following seemed to be the effective operations: (1) mobilizing the patient's hopes and faith (through the biofeedback reading); (2) structuring his expectations positively by selecting an intervention which had high-face validity and was immediately relevant to the patient's chronic fear (heart attack); (3) extending voluntary control into an area in which the patient was previously helpless; (4) arranging for the elicitation and extinction of distressing and probably poorly discriminated visceral sensations. It is possible but unlikely (because of chronic nature of problem and numerous prior interventions) that the above interventions were irrelevant to his recovery.

References

Budzynski, T., Stoyva, J., and Adler, C. Feedback-induced muscle relaxation: Application to tension headache. *Journal of Behavior Therapy and Experimental Psychiatry,* 1970, *1,* 205-211.

Wickramasekera, I. Desensitization, resensitization and desensitization again. *Journal of Behavior Therapy and Experimental Psychiatry,* 1970, *1,* 257-262.

Wickramasekera, I. Instructions and EMG feedback in systematic desensitization: A case report. *Behavior Therapy,* 1972, *13,* 460-465.

Wickramasekera, I. Application of verbal instructions and EMG feedback training to the management of tension headache: Preliminary observations. *Headache,* 1973, *13* (2), 74-76. (a)

Wickramasekera, I. Effects of EMG feedback on hypnotic susceptibility: More preliminary data. *Journal of Abnormal Psychology,* 1973, *82,* 74-77. (b)

Wickramasekera, I. EMG Feedback training and tension headache: Preliminary observations. In N.E. Miller, J. Stoyva, T.X. Barber, L. Dicara, J. Kamiya, and D. Shapiro (Eds.), *Biofeedback and Self Control* Chicago: Aldine-Atherton, 1973. (c)

Wickramasekera, I. Temperature feedback for the control of migraine. *Behavior Therapy and Experimental Psychiatry,* 1974, *4,* 343-345.

Part 3

CONTROL OR CONDITIONING

The Unit of Measurement in Behavioral Approaches to Clinical Cardiac Control[1]

Edward B. Blanchard,
Robert W. Scott,
Larry D. Young
and Eileen Edmundson
University of Mississippi
Medical Center, Mississippi

This paper presents the results of research efforts aimed at developing behavioral procedures, based on operant conditioning principles, to achieve clinically significant changes in heart rate (HR). That human HR can be controlled through the application of reinforcement and/or biofeedback procedures is well-established (Blanchard & Young, in press). However, for the most part, the magnitude of change obtained has been small, in the range of 1 to 6 beats per minute (BPM), and the length of experimental trial relatively short, usually about one minute. This was the state of research in this area when the studies described below began.

Since then two studies have been published which report large magnitude changes in HR: Headrick, Feather, and Wells (1971) achieved consistent increases in HR of 30 BPM in a single subject run for many trials; the length of trial was only one minute, however. More recently, Stephens, Harris, and Brady (1972) reported on four Ss, all of whom showed large magnitude changes in HR in one or both directions for trials varying in length from 5 to 60 minutes. In this latter study, the changes were obtained within the session rather than being maintained over several days, and no attention seems to have been paid to establishing a stable baseline.

1. This research was supported in part by a grant from the National Heart and Lung Institute, 1RO1HL14906-01.

For a procedure to have true clinical relevance, it must be able to produce large-scale changes in HR which are maintained over both relatively long experimental trials, and more importantly, over several experimental sessions or days. This paper presents three single-subject experiments aimed at developing such a procedure and shows how in the developmental process, considerations of the unit of measurement or analysis played a major part in improving the efficacy and efficiency of the procedure.

Ogden Lindsley[2], among others, has described the importance of the unit of measurement in the experimental analysis of behavior. Lindsley has advocated, "slicing the behavior as thin as possible" or using units of measurement that yield high rates of response and choosing behaviors that occur at a high rate in order to maximize the number of trials on which the behavior may be reinforced. Moreover, such a tactic tends to maintain the interest of both subject and experimenter. An example would be charting bites taken by an obese subject because this response occurs at a high rate as opposed to charting breaking of the diet which might occur only once a day.

Experiment 1

Method

The first experiment was an analogue study involving a normal male college student, 20 years old, whose HR was accelerated. The subject was a paid volunteer.

Apparatus S was comfortably seated in a reclining chair in an air-conditioned, sound-attenuated room. Facing him was a television set and a pair of running time meters which accumulated seconds of correct response, i.e., S's HR at or above the criterion HR. S received 1¢ per 10 seconds of correct response. The meters were electronically coupled via a Schmitt trigger to a Grass Model 7 polygraph on which S's EKG and HR were recorded from Lead II. Various other counters and timers were used to record Ss HR on a minute-to-minute basis.

Procedure Several aspects of the procedure were common to all of the experiments reported in this paper. Ss were asked to relax and not to try to exert control of the clocks of muscle tension or altering their respiration rate. All sessions lasted 40 minutes; the first 20 minutes were an "adaptation"

---

2. Ogden Lindsley, personal communication, 1970.

period during which *S*'s HR was recorded while he sat quietly in the experimental room. The last 20 minutes comprised the "experimental" trial during which the various experimental procedures described below were employed. Sessions were held at the rate of one per day.

The first condition employed consisted of the non-contingent presentation of television (NCTV) during the 20-minute experimental trials. In addition to establishing a baseline HR, this condition also served as a control for the effect on HR of the *S*'s focusing his attention. This baseline condition was terminated when *S*1's HR stabilized. For purposes of this study, a stable HR was defined as less than 10% variability (that is, the HR value for any one trial was within +5% of the mean HR for the three trials) in *S*'s HR across three consecutive trials.

During the second condition, the operation of the clocks and the reinforcement contingency were explained to *S* as was the fact that they were under the control of his internal bodily processes. The criterion HR which *S* had to achieve in order to receive reinforcement was set at 5 BPM above his baseline level and was held constant throughout the 20-minute experimental trial, hence the term "constant criterion" (CC). After *S*'s average HR for the entire 20-minute trial, that is, the total number of beats for the trial divided by 20, remained at or above this criterion for three consecutive trials, the criterion was raised another five BPM. This procedure was continued until *S*'s HR was stable at a rate of 20% greater than his baseline HR.

The third condition was the same as the first, that is, television was again presented noncontingently. This condition was included to determine the extent of the reversal of HR when the contingency was removed.

Results

The outcome data for this experiment are shown in Figure 1. *S*1's average HR during the baseline condition was 47 BPM. Over 26 trials of shaping and contingent reinforcement, his HR was increased to an average of 63 BPM over the final six trials. In the third condition (return to baseline), *S*1's HR returned essentially to its baseline level, averaging 50 BPM for the final three trials.

Although all decisions as to changes in the criterion HR in the shaping procedure were made on the basis of the overall HR for the 20-minute trial, data were collected for the HR on a minute-to-minute basis. In Figures 2-5 are shown minute-to-minute plots of HR for four trials, number 2, 5, 10, and 12, respectively. Examination of the results in terms of this *different unit of analysis* led to some interesting findings.

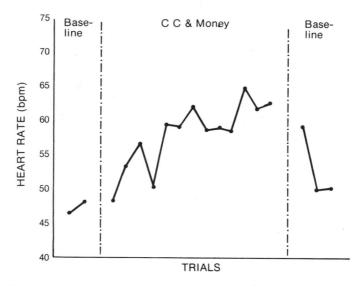

Figure 1. Mean heart rate for Subject 1 for all conditions of the experiment.

The results in Figure 2 show that during the baseline trials, $S1$'s HR was well-adapted to the experimental situation and continued at the adaptation level with the introduction of a novel, but meaningful, visual stimulus.

In Figure 3 the results are presented for a trial in which success was achieved, that is, $S1$'s HR during the experimental trial met the criterion level which is indicated on the figure.

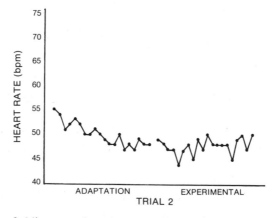

Figure 2. Minute-to-minute heart rate for Subject 1 for a baseline trial.

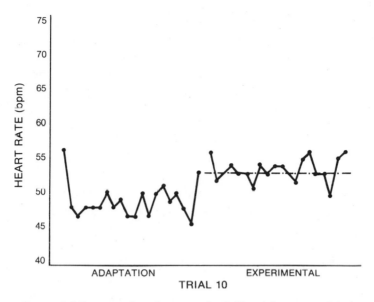

FIGURE 3. Minute-to-minute heart rate for Subject 1 for a successful trial.

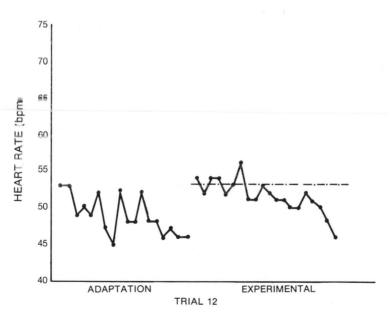

FIGURE 4. Minute-to-minute heart rate for Subject 1 for an initially successful trial.

It is clear that S1's HR has accelerated from the adaptation level to meet the criterion, but that no further acceleration was present during the trial.

Figure 4 shows a trial on which S1's HR initially accelerated to meet the criterion but then gradually decreased during the trial. Because the criterion for reinforcement was held constant for the entire trial, there was no way to try to intervene in this process.

Finally, in Figure 5, the results for an unsuccessful trial are presented. In this trial, there is still the initial surge in HR toward the criterion which was present in nearly all of the experimental trials. However, in this instance, because of the level of the criterion, S1 never reached the criterion and thus never received any reinforcement. This failure of the subject to receive any reinforcement for the entire trial, is analogous to his being put on extinction.

Discussion

The findings described above, which resulted from using a different level of analysis of the data, led to a search for a better, and more flexible, shaping procedure. Several features seemed desirable, based on our results: (1) the procedure should capitalize on the initial surge toward the criterion which Ss typically showed; (2) it should allow for decreases as shown in Figure 4 and be able to intervene in them; (3) it should constantly challenge the subject.

After several attempts at developing such a strategy, the shaping procedure described in the next experiment was developed. Its essence was

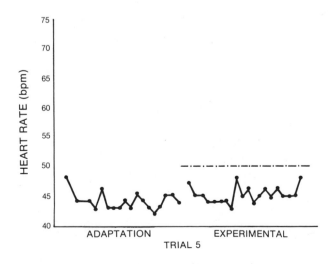

FIGURE 5. Minute-to-minute heart rate for Subject 1 for an unsuccessful trial.

the use of a *variable criterion* (VC) changed on a minute-to-minute basis so as to maximize the contact with the reinforcement contingency which the subject experienced.

Experiment 2

The second experiment was also an analogue study involving a normal female college student, 19 years old, whose HR was accelerated. The subject was a paid volunteer. The same apparatus was used with this *S* as in Experiment 1.

Procedure

In this experiment, sessions were conducted in the same manner as in Experiment 1. Also the same baseline procedure was used, noncontingent television. The second condition consisted of a *variable criterion* shaping procedure in which the criterion HR which *S2* had to emit to receive reinforcement was changed on a minute-to-minute basis in accordance with an established set of rules.[3] The final condition was a return to baseline conditions to complete the experimental analysis.

Results

The average HR for the 20-minute experimental trials is presented in two-day blocks in Figure 6 for *S2*. In conditions for which there were only three trials, the two plotted points represent the average of trials one and two and of trials two and three.

S2's baseline HR was 57 BPM. In six trials during condition two, the variable criterion procedure resulted in a rise of 30 BPM to an average of 87 BPM for the final three trials. In the reversal, nine trials were necessary for *S2* to return to her resting HR level and show stability.

In Figure 7 is shown the minute-to-minute HR data for the second conditioning trial, trial No. 6. Attention is called to the continued acceleration that HR showed throughout the trial, in contrast to the surge and decline (Figure 4) or surge and stability (Figure 3) achieved with the constant criterion procedure in Experiment 1.

Discussion

The results of Experiment 2 indicate that the variable criterion shaping procedure is more efficient than the constant criterion procedure.

---

3. A detailed set of instructions may be obtained on request from the first author.

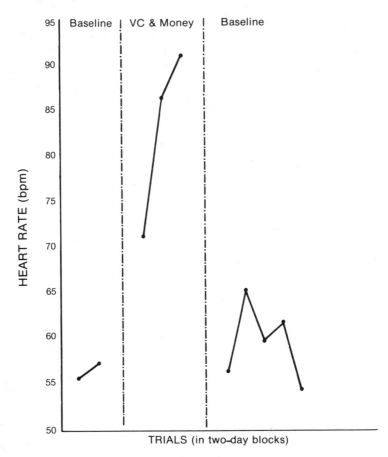

Figure 6. Mean heart rate for Subject 2 for all conditions of the experiment.

Moreover, they highlight the advantages of changing the unit of analysis in developing the procedure and certainly confirm the importance of the unit of analysis.

The results S2 achieved are comparable to the best results reported in the literature to date in terms of magnitude of change of HR and length of the experimental trial. In a sense, they surpass any previous results since the increase in HR did come from a stable baseline and was maintained over three successive trials (days).

In spite of the fact that these results are fairly impressive, it must be remembered that the experiments are analogue studies. The real test of the

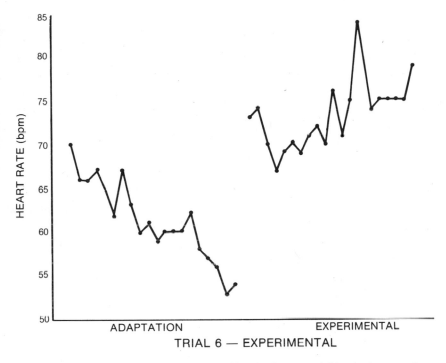

FIGURE 7. Minute-to-minute heart rate for Subject 2 using the variable criterion procedure.

efficacy of a procedure comes in an experiment with a clinical patient in which an abnormally high HR is decelerated. The experiment to be described next provides such a test and also an indirect comparison of the two shaping procedures.

Experiment 3

Method

Subject The subject for this experiment (*S*3) was a 46-year-old male referred by the Department of Cardiology; he had a 20-year history of tachycardia and had not been able to work for 14 months prior to beginning the experiment. He was receiving partial Social Security disability benefits because of his condition.

Procedure The procedures used here were a mixture of those used in the first two experiments but with some notable differences: (1) *S*3's HR was being decelerated; (2) since he was taking part as a form of treatment, he was told about the nature of the response whereas S1 and S2 were not.

The first condition was a baseline condition during which S3 watched commercial television programs during the experimental trial. Condition 2 was an attempt to decelerate S3's HR using the constant criterion procedure. In the third condition, the variable criterion shaping procedure was introduced. Finally, condition 4 represented a return to baseline conditions. Money was used as a reinforcer in both conditions 2 and 3.

Results

The average HR for the 20-minute experimental trial is presented in two-day blocks. S3's baseline HR was 88 BPM. Introduction of the constant criterion shaping procedure for 26 trials led to essentially no change.

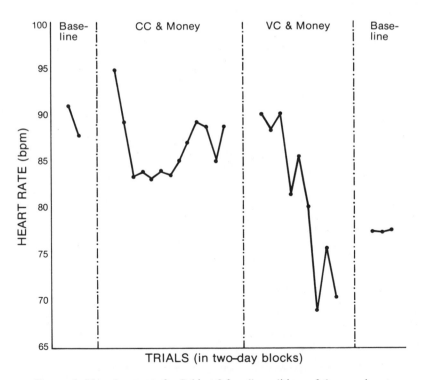

FIGURE 8. Mean heart rate for Subject 3 for all conditions of the experiment.

In condition 3, 18 trials with the variable criterion shaping procedure led to a dramatic reduction in *S*3's HR to the normal range, a drop of 16 BPM. His average HR for the final six trials was 72 BPM.

During the return to baseline in condition 4, *S*3's HR stabilized at 77 BPM. For clinical reasons, no further reversal was attempted. It should be noted, however, that his IIR during this condition did not overlap with his HR for the final six trials of condition 3.

Discussion

The results of Experiment 3 provide additional evidence for the improvement in efficacy and efficiency achieved through the variable criterion procedure. Moreover, the changes achieved constitute the first reported clinical application of biofeedback procedures in the area of HR. A major role in discovering the problems with the CC procedure and in developing the VC procedure was played by the unit of analysis. Changing from considering the entire 20-minute trial as a whole to viewing the behavior on a minute-to minute basis had decided advantages.

One could speculate that additional improvement might be possible if the data were considered on a beat-to-beat basis and that the criterion be altered on such a basis. In order to go to this finer level of analysis, a computer will probably be needed, but such an idea does seem to warrant exploration.

An exciting clinical aspect of our work is the apparent resistance of a *S*'s IIR, once decelerated, to return to its previous high, pathological level. In an earlier study (Peters, Scott, and Gillespie, 1971) involving the deceleration of IIR in a tachycardia patient, there was little acceleration of HR during the extinction phase. In fact, a large number of trials was necessary to condition *S*'s IIR back to his baseline level. For *S*3, this same resistance to extinction of a decelerated HR was noted. Since this was a clinical case, no attempt was made to obtain a return to his elevated baseline rate. This apparent resistance to extinction of a HR decelerated to the normal range does have clinical implication that a high degree of durability may be available from this procedure.

One final observation from our data is worth noting. In *S*s whose HR was decelerated in both this study (*S*3) and in a previous study (Peters et al., 1971), there were preexperimental complaints of being "anxious, tense, or nervous." There was a decrease in these verbalizations concurrent with the deceleration of HR. Furthermore, there were other anecdotal data relating to clinical improvement: $S3$, whose verbal report of feeling less anxious coincided with the middle of the VC shaping procedure (condition 3), actively sought and obtained employment toward the end of treatment. This was his first gainful employment in over 16 months and came in spite of his already receiving Social Security disability benefits. For the clinical subject in the earlier study, there were reports from the ward of improved behavior, and a decrease in tricophilic behavior which had previously been observed at a high rate.

Thus the procedures for changing HR seem to have decided psychological as well as physiological benefits when successfully applied, and successful application seems to depend on the proper unit of analysis.

References

Blanchard, E. B., & Young, L. D. Self-control of cardiac functioning: A promise as yet unfulfilled. *Psychological Bulletin* (in press).

Headrick, M. W., Feather, B. W., & Wells, D. T. Unidirectional and large magnitude heart rate changes with augmented sensory feedback. *Psychophysiology,* 1971, *8,* 132-148.

Peters, R. D., Scott, R. W., & Gillespie, W. J. The use of television as a reinforcer in the operant acceleration and deceleration of heart rate. Paper presented to the 79th annual convention, American Psychological Association, 1971.

Stephens, J. H., Harris, A. H., & Brady, J. V. Large magnitude heart rate changes in subjects instructed to change their heart rates and given exteroceptive feedback. *Psychophysiology,* 1972, *9,* 283-285.

Voluntary Control of Skin Temperature: Unilateral Changes Using Hypnosis and Feedback

Alan H. Roberts
University of Minnesota, Minneapolis

Donald G. Kewman and
Hugh Macdonald
Stanford University, Stanford

The recent work of Miller (1969) and his associates has demonstrated that glandular and visceral responses in animals can be modified by instrumental learning procedures without the mediation of skeletal responses. Using curare to control skeletal responses, he noted that it was apparently easier for paralyzed than unparalyzed animals to learn. He suggested that therapeutic training in humans might be enhanced by using hypnotic suggestion to increase learning and the transfer of training. Maslach, Marshall, and Zimbardo (1972) reported an exploratory study testing this hypothesis.

The purpose of this article is to demonstrate that subjects can learn to control voluntarily the skin temperature of one hand relative to the other, a task more specific and more difficult than simply raising or lowering skin temperature. This task was chosen because of its potential for producing differences of a magnitude that might have practical value and application. Some reports of attempts to control temperature by means of hypnotic suggestion or other means (Chapman, Goodell, & Wolff, 1959; Green, Green, & Walters, 1970; Hadfield, 1920; Luria, 1969; Maslach et al., 1972) suggested that large changes in skin temperature are possible. It is important to demonstrate that autonomic functions in man can be brought under cognitive volitional control and also that the magnitude of the changes are large enough to account for the psychosomatic symptoms observed in clinical settings.

Method

Subjects

A select group of four female and two male university students, ages 20-24 years, served as subjects. Five subjects were able to pass all items of Form C of the Stanford Hypnotic Susceptibility Scale (Weitzenhoffer & Hilgard, 1962). They had received extensive hypnotic training and experience prior to this experiment. One (Subject 5), while having minimum prior hypnotic experience, was able to pass all but one item of Form C. Only two (Subjects 4 and 6) smoked cigarettes. All but Subject 4 and Subject 6 had some practice and experience in meditation; Subject 1 and Subject 2 were currently practicing meditation exercises during the period this experiment was conducted.

Procedure

Each subject received from five to nine individual one-hour training sessions (see Table 1). During early training sessions a cold pad was placed on one hand and a warm pad was placed on the other hand for a few minutes; then the subject was asked to maintain the difference between the two hands after pads were removed. During these early training sessions, skin temperature was monitored as described later, but no feedback information was provided to subjects. Additional training sessions provided feedback to subjects and were similar to later experimental sessions. Data from these training sessions were not analyzed. Hypnosis was used during training as described below for experimental sessions.

Following training sessions, each subject individually participated in three consecutive experimental sessions with from one to four days intervening between each session. The subject was seated in a comfortable chair in a room of about 22.5° centigrade, and apparatus was hooked up and calibrated. Skin temperature was recorded on a Grass Model-7 Polygraph with two 10,000-ohm Fenwall Uni-curve Interchangeable Curve-matched Thermistors taped to the pad of the subject's middle finger on the left and right hands. The resistance of each thermistor was recorded independently on Grass low-level dc Model-7P1 preamplifiers in skin resistance mode. The two signals were then compared, their difference amplified five times and recorded on a fourth channel with a thermistor located near but not touching the subject's hands.

The compared signal was fed to a combined voltage-controlled oscillator and voltage-controlled "volume control" producing a tone that changed frequency and moved from one earphone to the other in a stereo headset. Thus, as the right hand became warmer relative to the left, the frequency of the tone increased, and the tone moved toward the right earphone. As the left hand became warmer relative to the right, the frequency of the tone decreased and it moved toward the left earphone.

Each subject underwent a 10-minute hypnotic induction followed by a 5-minute period of rest and relaxation. Hypnotic induction procedures were individualized for each subject, but the length of the induction was 10 minutes for all subjects. The feedback signal was then started, and the subject was instructed as follows via an intercom from the separate monitoring room where the experimenter remained following induction:

For the next several minutes, left [right] hand and finger are cold and right [left] hand and finger are warm. Left [right] is cold and right [left] is warm Left [right] finger cold, right [left] finger warm. Left [right] cold, right [left] warm. Tone to the right [left] side and up [down] in pitch.

This was followed by eight minutes without interruption by the experimenter, and then the instruction was repeated for the opposite hand. This was again followed by eight uninterrupted minutes, a third reversal of instruction, and another eight uninterrupted minutes. The feedback signal was then turned off and the subject was instructed to rest, relax, equalize the temperature of both hands, and make both hands comfortable. Finally the hypnotic trance was removed.

The hand chosen to start was different for each subject for each session, and subjects alternated between two experimenters in a predetermined balanced design. Thus, over three sessions, each subject was asked to perform nine consecutive simultaneous alternations in skin temperature.

In order to determine whether the response, once learned, could occur without external feedback or other external reinforcing stimuli, and to demonstrate further the independence of the response from other environ-environmental stimuli such as physical setting or room temperature, Subject 1 and Subject 2 participated in two additional experimental sessions. The format of these sessions was identical to that previously described except that subjects were tested in a specially designed constant temperature room in the Laboratory of Dermatology at the Stanford Medical Center.

Room temperature was set about 28° centigrade. Copper constantan thermocouples were taped to identical sites on the fingers as described previously. Skin temperatures and room temperature were monitored by a Honeywell recording system that printed temperatures directly in degrees centigrade. No feedback of any kind was provided during these sessions, but experimenters and instructions were alternated as previously described providing data from six consecutive simultaneous alternations over the two sessions. Following the completion of all experimental sessions, subjects wrote responses to a number of open-ended questions concerning previous hypnotic experience, general background and experience, subjective impressions and ratings of experimental training, and general reactions.

Results

Skin Temperature Changes

Data were analyzed at 25-second intervals during each eight-minute trial providing 19 data points for each subject. Results are shown for each subject separately in Table 1 and Figure 1 for right- and left-hand trials combined. Differences in hand temperature at the beginning of each trial were equated to a base line of zero. Mean changes in skin temperature from this base line, with negative scores indicating changes in the wrong direction, were compared to a hypothetical mean of zero change using t tests. Subjects 1, 2, 3, and 4 each showed statistically reliable changes in the correct direction for each of the nineteen 25-second intervals separately, averaged across the nine experimental trials.

Subject 5 (who had only five training sessions) showed significant changes ($p < .05$ or better) on each of the first eight 25-second intervals but not for the remaining 11 data points. This suggests that he was able to change his skin temperature in the correct direction initially when asked to do so but was unable to maintain the change during the entire eight-minute trial.

Subject 6 showed no significant differences for any of the 19 individual data points in this analysis. However, the overall results for all six subjects combined were significant for each data point analyzed separately as well as for the overall t, which was 14.63 ($df = 5, p < .001$).

Table 1 also shows that Subject 1 produced maximum temperature

TABLE 1

SEX, NUMBER OF TRAINING TRIALS PRIOR TO EXPERIMENTAL TRIALS, MAXIMUM TEMPERATURE DIFFERENCE ATTAINED ON ANY ONE EXPERIMENTAL TRIAL, AND MAXIMUM OF MEAN TEMPERATURE DIFFERENCES ATTAINED DURING ALL TRIALS FOR NINE EXPERIMENTAL TRIALS WITH FEEDBACK

(N = 6) AND SIX EXPERIMENTAL TRIALS WITHOUT FEEDBACK (N = 2)

Subject number	Sex	Training trials	Maximum temperature difference, any one of nine trials with feedback	Maximum temperature difference, any one of six trials without feedback*	Maximum of mean temperature differences for nine trials with feedback		Maximum of mean temperature differences for six trials without feedback	
					M	SD	M	SD
1	F	8	5.6	9.2	2.96	1.84	4.92	3.17
2	F	8	2.8	3.7	2.12	.58	2.37	1.14
3	F	5	2.5	—	1.97	.57	—	—
4	M	9	2.4	—	.99	.71	—	—
5	M	5	1.9	—	.37	.26	—	—
6	F	8	1.5	—	.18	.76	—	—

*In degrees centigrade.

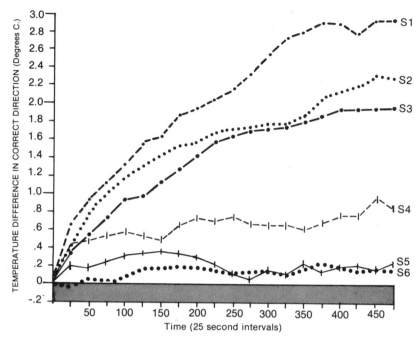

FIGURE 1. Mean temperature difference in the correct (specified) direction for nine alternating trials over three sessions with feedback. (Each subject is shown separately (*N*=6).)

differences as high as 5.6° centigrade in this part of the experiment, and the maximum of her average temperature difference was 2.96° centigrade. Subjects 2, 3, and 4, while producing smaller maximum temperature changes, were less variable in their performance than Subject 1. Across nine trials, average change from base temperature in the correct direction in one hand ranged from 0% to 10%. Changes from basal temperature were as high as 28% on individual trials.

Data from "right-hand warm" trials and "left-hand warm" trials were also analyzed separately. In this analysis the standard deviation was computed from the average of each of the 19 data points for all sessions combined so that $N = 19$ for each subject. The results are shown in Table 2. For left-hand warm trials, all subjects showed significant changes from zero in the correct direction beyond the .005 level of confidence. For right-hand warm trials, all showed significant changes from zero in the correct direction beyond the .0005 level of confidence except Subject 6, whose mean was .05 degrees centigrade in the direction opposite that requested.

When the differences attained in left-hand warm and right-hand warm

TABLE 2

AVERAGE TEMPERATURE CHANGE IN THE CORRECT DIRECTION FOR
RIGHT-HAND WARM AND LEFT-HAND WARM TRIALS SEPARATELY

Subject	Trial					
	Left-hand warm			Right-hand warm		
	M	*SD*	*t*	*M*	*SD*	*t*
1	1.60	.87	8.05	2.53	.66	16.65
2	1.54	.46	14.72	1.64	.46	15.50
3	1.58	.50	13.65	1.32	.52	11.02
4	.61	.19	13.85	.70	.16	19.60
5	.14	.17	3.45	.32	.12	12.02
6	.25	.12	8.75	−.05	.09	−2.32

Note. With 18 *df*, $p < .05$ when $t = 1.73$ and $p < .01$ when $t = 2.55$ (one tailed).

trials were compared, the mean of the differences was .12, which is not significant. However, the overall mean for the left-hand trials of .95 is significantly different from zero at the .025 level of confidence ($t = 3.34$, $df = 5$), and the mean of 1.07 for the right-hand trials is also significantly different from zero at the .025 level ($t = 2.78$, $df = 5$).

When Subject 1 and Subject 2 were evaluated for six additional alternating trials in the temperature-controlled room without feedback, they performed even better than previously. The results are shown in Table 1 and Figure 2. In these trials, data were recorded at 60-second intervals for the same eight-minute trials as described previously. Subject 1 attained a maximum temperature difference of 9.2° centigrade on one trial and Subject 2 a maximum difference of 3.7° centigrade. The maximum of the mean temperature differences for the six trials was 4.92 for Subject 1 and 2.37 for Subject 2.

Response Patterns

To determine the response patterns of each subject, temperatures of the right and left hands were averaged for each of the 19 data points for "left-warm" and "right-warm" trials separately during the nine experimental trials. The results were graphed, and inspection of the objective data

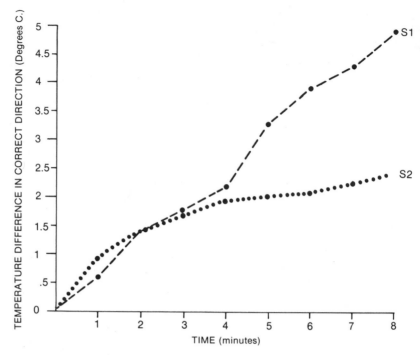

Figure 2. Mean temperature difference in the correct (specified) direction for six alternating trials over two sessions without feedback. (Each subject is shown separately (N=2).)

shows that different subjects used different response patterns to accomplish the results. These included making both hands colder (or warmer) but at different rates, holding one hand constant while raising or lowering the temperature of the other, or diverging the temperature of the two hands. This raises the possibility that different physiological processes may be involved in response patterns. It should be noted, also, that all subjects were able to change the temperatures of their hands significantly, but not always differentially.

Subjective Reports and Observations

One of the most notable aspects of this experiment was the apparent high degree of motivation and involvement of subjects. Appointments were all kept and on time. When the experiment was completed, subjects held a surprise party for one experimenter who was leaving (a happening we suspect is rare in experimental psychology). All subjects reported the experiment to be a helpful and valuable experience to them, and subjects who achieved the least control spontaneously expressed a wish to have learned more.

All six subjects reported hallucinating the effect of changing skin temperatures at some times during the experiment. During training trials, subjects would report temperature changes occurring when objective polygraph data showed no changes. On a few occasions some subjects reported that the feedback tone changed in the appropriate direction when, in fact, it had not.

All subjects reported that hypnosis helped, but only Subject 6 felt that it was necessary. Subject 2 felt that some altered state of consciousness, but not necessarily hypnosis, was necessary.

There appeared some relationship between reported depth of hypnotic trance and the ability to control skin temperature. Asked to rate average depth of hypnotic trance on a 5-point scale from "awake" to "very deep," Subject 1 and Subject 2 reported "very deep" (depth well beyond that required to complete successfully all items on Form C of the Stanford Scale), Subject 3 reported "deep" (depth required to complete all items on Form C), Subject 4 reported "moderate" (depth required to complete most of the items on Form C), and Subject 5 reported "light" (depth required to complete a few items on Form C). The exception to this pattern is Subject 6 who reported "very deep" along with Subject 1 and Subject 2.

Subjects were asked what they would say if they had to explain to someone else how they might control their skin temperature. Responses to this question were not consistent across subjects, and it is our impression that these written explanations were not particularly helpful in explaining what subjects did to produce the effect. However, the more successful subjects reported that they were able to communicate *with each other* concerning what they did and what they experienced (cf. Tart, 1972), although there is no independent evidence to support these reports.

Discussion

The data from this experiment unequivocally demonstrate that some individuals are capable of achieving a high degree of voluntary control over the autonomic processes involved in peripheral skin temperature regulation. There were, however, significant individual differences in terms of ability of learn, rate of learning, and the magnitude of control that could be achieved. Further experimental work will be needed in order to determine the degree to which learning ability is related to physiological, motivational, and personality variables.

The data from the present experiment do not clarify the physiological mechanisms responsible for the control of skin temperature. However, following the completion of the experimental work described in this article, A. H. Sacks and E. Glenn Tickner of the Palo Alto Research Foundation provided apparatus and helped collect some preliminary data. During a separate special session, the temperature of Subject 1 was monitored as previously while blood flow was recorded over the volar digital artery (at the ring finger) using an ultrasonic flow meter and transcutaneous probe. When the subject decreased temperature in the monitored hand, blood flow was almost completely cut off except during the suppressed arterial pulse. When the subject increased temperature in the hand, an accelerated pulse and blood flow was detected. Since different subjects use different response patterns, the possibility remains that different physiological processes are involved across subjects.

This study also confounds the variables of hypnosis and auditory feedback so that it is not clear whether hypnosis is a necessary adjunct to learning or promotes the learning process. Maslach et al. (1972) and others indicate that the effects described can be demonstrated with hypnosis and without external feedback, and the data in this study provide strong support for their findings. Miller (1969) and others, on the other hand, suggest that autonomic control can be learned with feedback and without hypnosis. Our own view, as yet unsupported by experimental evidence, is that the *ability* to alter one's state of consciousness (Hilgard, 1969; Tart, 1972), together with associated motivational and training variables, will be among the more critical variables in predicting the ability to control voluntarily autonomic processes, while hypnosis per se may not be necessary.

What seems clear is that some individuals can achieve a high degree of voluntary control over the autonomic process involved in regulating peripheral skin temperature. The control appears to be of sufficient magnitude to make possible the therapeutic management of certain psychosomatic disorders, some circulatory disorders (e.g., Raynaud's disease, migraine headache), or other disorders that might be helped by localized changes in blood flow (e.g., burns, arthritis). As suggested by Miller (1969), the data increase the likelihood that at least some psychosomatic reactions are learned and can be modified.

References

Chapman, L. F., Goodell, H., & Wolff, H. G. Increased intlamatory reaction induced by central nervous system activity. *Transactions of the Association of American Physicians*, 1959, **72**, 84-109.

Green, E. E., Green, A. M., & Walters, E. D. *Progress of cybernetics; Proceedings of the International Congress of Cybernetics, London, 1969*. London: Gordon and Breach, 1970.

Hadfield, J. A. The influence of suggestion on body temperature. *Lancet*, 1920, **2**, 68-69.

Hilgard, E. R. Altered states of awareness. *Journal of Nervous and Mental Disease*, 1969, **149**, 68-79.

Luria, A. R. *The mind of a mnemonist*. New York: Discus Books, 1969.

Maslach, C., Marshall, G., & Zimbardo, P. Hypnotic control of peripheral skin temperature: A case report. *Psychophysiology*, 1972, **9**, 600-605.

Miller, N. E. Learning of visceral and glandular responses. *Science*, 1969, **163**, 434-445.

Tart, C. T. States of consciousness and state-specific sciences *Science*, 1972, **176**, 1203-1210.

Weitzenhoffer, A. M., & Hilgard, E. R. *Stanford Hypnotic Susceptibility Scale, Form C*. Palo Alto, Calif.: Consulting Psychologists Press, 1962.

Note: This study was supported by National Institute of Mental Health Grant 03859 to Ernest R. Hilgard, and Social and Rehabilitation Services Grant 16-P-56810.

Effects of Electromyographic Feedback on Hypnotic Susceptibility: More Preliminary Data

Ian Wickramasekera
University of Illinois
College of Medicine
Peoria

Relaxation instructions seem to be one of the independent variables that increase suggestibility (Barber, 1969). There is a growing recognition (Bandura, 1969) that verbal instructions and cognitive factors can significantly add to the power of reinforcement variables. It seems likely that a combination of verbal instructions and response-contingent feedback will be more effective in deepening muscular relaxation than verbal instructions alone.

Electromyographic (EMG) feedback seems useful in the induction of muscular relaxation (Budzynski & Stoyva, 1969; Green, Walter, Green, & Murphy, 1969). Further, EMG feedback-induced muscle relaxation appears to increase suggestibility (Wickramasekera, 1972).

The purpose of this double-blind study was to determine if taped verbal relaxation instructions and response-contingent EMG feedback training would increase suggestibility or hypnotic susceptibility over that obtained with instructions and false or noncontingent feedback. The specific hypothesis tested was that 10 sessions of relaxation practice with response-contingent EMG feedback would result in a greater increase in hypnotic susceptibility as measured by the Stanford Hypnotic Susceptibility Scale, Forms A and B (SHSS:A, SHSS:B), of Weitzenhoffer and Hilgard (1959) than would relaxation instructions and non contingent feedback.

Method

Subjects

The subjects were 12 white undergraduate males between the ages of 18 and 22 who volunteered for a study of "relaxation training and hypnosis." Those who admitted to a history of psychiatric problems were excluded.

Design and Procedure

Subjects were pretested by a research assistant with Form A of the SHSS. After pretesting, subjects were randomly assigned to either a control (false feedback) or an experimental (accurate feedback) group. After the intervening EMG feedback treatment was administered by the author, the subjects were posttested by the previous research assistant who was blind as to which treatment group (control or experimental) the subject had been in. Hence, both subjects and hypnotist were blind as to feedback conditions.

After assignment to treatment groups, all subjects listened to the same set of taped instructions, which stated that they would be trained to relax deeply and that the EMG auditory feedback would facilitate this training process. The taped instructions followed closely those in the manual that accompany the portable EMG feedback apparatus. It included a simple explanation of the feedback system as basically an information system. The sequence of EMG feedback training and practice of tension-releasing cycling started with both auditory and visual feedback at the lowest sensitivity threshold, with electrodes placed on the forearm. After an initial 10-minute orientation period, all subjects received only auditory feedback. As the subject demonstrated progress by keeping the feedback at a low level (< 4 microvolts), the sensitivity was raised successively to the medium and high ranges and held there until the subject could reach the previous criteria at these sensitivity levels. A final plateau was reached in forearm training, and the subject could maintain a low level (< 4 microvolts) of feedback on high sensitivity. The electrodes were then attached to the area of the frontalis muscle of the forehead, and the previous training sequence (e.g., low to high sensitivity) was run. Both experimental and control subjects were reminded by the same taped instructions at the start of each training session to watch for and become familiar with the response-produced proprioceptive cue (heaviness, tingling, and numbness) of deep relaxation.

Procedures with control subjects differed from those with experimental subjects only with respect to the following conditions: *(a)* control subjects received false or noncontingent EMG feedback; *(b)* no changes in the sensitivity levels were made for control subjects (controls had no knowledge of this); and *(c)* the electrodes were moved from forearm to forehead for all control subjects at the start of the fourth session of training.

Feedback training consisted of ten 30-minute sessions. The subjects were seated on a large padded recliner during all procedures. After terminating his tenth training session, each subject was immediately retested with SHSS:B. All procedures were conducted individually. Posttesting with SHSS:B was done by the research assistant who was blind as to which subjects received the contingent EMG feedback. The entire study was done in the experimenter's office at a mental health clinic, and experimenters attempted to restrict their verbal contact with subjects to the taped instructions for feedback training and standardized hypnotic procedures. During the orientation period (first 10 minutes of first session), all subjects (control and experimental) were given both visual and auditory "true" or response-contingent EMG feedback. After the orientation, the EMG console and visual feedback were placed on a table behind the subject's chair. The earphones of control subjects were disconnected without their knowledge from the EMG console and connected to a recorder that delivered taped auditory EMG feedback from the actual first 10 relaxation training sessions of a psychiatric patient bearing "true" or response-contingent auditory EMG feedback. Hence, controls did not receive random feedback which would be frustrative but a pattern of feedback which had the appearance of progress because the feedback tone declined over time. But the decline or pattern of improvement was unrelated to anything the control subject actually did. Informal postexperimental inquiry indicated that the controls believed they were receiving accurate feedback and that they had improved substantially in their relaxation skills.

Results

Not all experimental subjects reached the preestablished criterion of relaxation training, but all approximated it at the end of the tenth session of training. None of the control subjects even approximated the criterion for forehead muscle relaxation. This is surprising since all control subjects stated verbally that they felt they had learned to relax deeply, and none of them stated that they suspected the feedback was inaccurate.

Pretest and posttest scores for each experimental and control subject

TABLE 1

**PRETEST AND POSTTEST SCORES ON THE
STANFORD HYPNOTIC SUSCEPTIBILITY SCALE**

	Experimental				Control		
Subject	Pretest	Posttest	Difference	Subject	Pretest	Posttest	Difference
1	5	9	4	7	4	6	2
2	8	10	2	8	6	3	—3
3	2	8	6	9	6	6	0
4	2	11	9	10	2	3	1
5	6	11	5	11	6	7	1
6	6	12	6	12	6	6	0

appear in Table 1. A Mann-Whitney test of the difference between the posttest scores of the experimental and control groups yielded a significant difference in the hypothesized direction (p = .001). A similar analysis yielded a nonsignificant difference between pretest scores. Hence, the experimental subjects who practiced relaxation with both the benefits of instructions and contingent feedback appeared to increase in suggestibility more than the control subjects who received only the benefits of verbal instructions with their relaxation practice.

Discussion

The very small size and select nature of the sample necessitates caution in drawing conclusions and generalizing from these data. However, this study replicates previous findings (Wickramasekera, 1972) on identical subjects. EMG feedback-induced relaxation training appears at least to increase hypnotic susceptibility of young college males. It is important to determine next what aspects of the training procedure contribute to this enhancement.

Since relaxation instructions have been found to contribute to suggestibility (Barber, 1969), it is probable that delivering these instructions more effectively will enhance suggestibility. It may be hypothesized that relaxation increases suggestibility or response to verbal instructions through the mechanism of improved attention to verbal stimuli. The training procedure may teach the subject to reduce the "noise" within his body. About 50% of body mass is skeletal muscle, and restricting the "noise" from this source may enhance suggestibility by improving the subject's capacity to attend to verbal instructions. To test this hypothesis, it is necessary to demonstrate that subjects in the contingent feedback group were in fact more muscularly relaxed than subjects in the false feedback group. It has previously been shown that *external* sensory restriction increases hypnotic susceptibility (Wickramasekera, 1969, 1970a), and it is at least possible that *internal* sensory restriction (reducing the internal "noise") may also increase the impact of verbal instructions (hypnotic test suggestions).

It may be argued that the critical variable in the study was subject expectancies rather than relaxation, that is, that control subjects did not perceive the experiment like experimental subjects. Identical instructions, procedures, and instrumentation were used with both controls and experimentals. Covertly, inaccurate feedback was substituted for accurate feedback in the control treatment. But the inaccurate feedback was designed in such a way that over time it appeared to parallel the subjective experience of the control subjects. The decline of the feedback tone in the control group appears to be generally correlated over time with subjects' relaxation efforts, but the correlation was not perfect. Hence by positively but noncontingently reinforcing the relaxation efforts, we appeared to create the illusion of improvement in relaxation skills, whereas, in fact, we may have only strengthened some subjective unknown responses of a "superstitious" (Skinner, 1953) nature. That this attempt to manipulate the subjective experience of the controls was generally effective was evidenced clinically by the spirited manner and sense of participation with which the control subjects approached the feedback training sessions and the feelings of gratitude they appeared to express for training in deep relaxation. None of the control subjects spontaneously questioned the veracity of the feedback tone. Other research in verbal conditioning indicates it is useless to infer "awareness" of response—reinforcement contingency or the lack of it—from subjects' verbal responses to progressively more suggestive interview questions (Bandura, 1969) with at best unreliable procedures (Weinstein & Lawson, 1963). It may be speculated further that it was some other variable that was the critical one. However, we are left with the fact that significant changes in a relatively stable dependent variable, hypnotizability (Hilgard, 1965), appear to have been demonstrated with standardized measure of the variable. This was done first in the context of a single-blind study (Wickramasekera, 1972) and has been reported now in a double-blind study. Furthermore, these changes appear to be a function of a relatively objective and simple training procedure.

The foregoing results lead to some clinically relevant speculations. It has been hypothesized (Wickramasekera, 1970b) that the primary value of hypnotic susceptibility scales in psychotherapy and behavior modification is that they indicate the extent to which the behavior of an individual may be controlled by verbal stimuli. Intuitively, it seems that verbal instructions provide the most economic, precise, and elegant means available today for controlling complex human behavior. Empirically, however, it seems that verbal methods of control are effective with only a relatively small proportion of the total population subjected to a verbal influence procedure like psychotherapy. Investigations with hypnotic susceptibility scales seem to reveal that there are significant individual differences in that particular type of susceptibility to control by verbal instructions which is called suggestibility.

The clinician even more than the research scientist is concerned in his everyday work with the prediction and verbal control of the behavior of specific individuals. Hypnotic research seems to reveal that for certain individuals, under certain conditions, the verbal control of behavior can be extended beyond "base-line" levels (Barber, 1969), and that for many people control may be extended even further with the use of certain prehypnotic procedures (Pena, 1963; Sanders & Reyher, 1969; Wickramasekera, 1969, 1970a).

Clinicians are concerned with altering complex human behavior, and their effectiveness may be increased if methods can be found to increase the efficacy, reliability, and generality with which verbal control can be exerted on behavior. Sensory restriction (Pena, 1963; Sanders & Reyher, 1969; Wickramasekera, 1969, 1970a) and apparently "relaxation" training (which seems more complex than was previously thought) are procedures which, for reasons that are still unclear, appear to facilitate the verbal control of behavior.

If the establishment of a voluntarily induced relaxed state is found to increase susceptibility to control by verbal stimuli or hypnotizability, then EMG training may become a useful adjunct to a wide variety of psychological treatment techniques. Clinically, it seems that a major subgoal in relaxation training is to induce in the patient the subjective feeling of "letting go," which when it occurs seems to increase the malleability of behavior. Subjectively, the experience of "trust" and "letting go" appear very similar, even though these subjective responses may be shaped up or elicited by procedures, for example, "core conditions" (Truax & Carkhuff, 1965) versus EMG feedback, which are objectively dissimilar. The development of reliable and effective procedures for altering or shaping subjective responses (private events) will contribute saliently to a reliable and powerful technology of behavior control. The importance of this subjective feeling of "letting go" has previously been recognized in more esoteric fields (e.g., Yoga, Zen, and religious conversion) and is currently coming into increasing recognition in the investigation of altered "states of consciousness" induced by a variety of agents (e.g., alpha and theta feedback training, LSD, and EMG feedback training).

References

Bandura, A. *Principles of behavior modification.* New York: Holt, Rinehart & Winston, 1969.

Barber, T. X. *Hypnosis: A scientific approach.* New York: Van Nostrand Reinhold, 1969.

Budzynski, T. H., & Stoyva, J. M. An instrument for producing deep muscle relaxation by means of analog information feedback. *Journal of Applied Behavior Analysis,* 1969, **2,** 231-237.

Green, E. E., Walter, E. D., Green, A. M., & Murphy, G. Feedback technique for deep relaxation. *Psychophysiology,* 1969, **6,** 372-377.

Hilgard, E. R. *Hypnotic susceptibility.* New York: Harcourt, Brace & World, 1965.

Pena, F. Perceptual isolation and hypnotic susceptibility. Unpublished doctoral dissertation, Washington State University, 1963.

Sanders, R. S., & Reyher, J. Sensory deprivation and the enhancement of hypnotic susceptibility. *Journal of Abnormal Psychology,* 1969, **74,** 375-381.

Skinner, B. R. *Science and human behavior.* New York: Macmillan, 1953.

Truax, C. B., & Carkhuff, R. R. Experimental manipulation of therapeutic conditions. *Journal of Consulting Psychology,* 1965, **29,** 119-129.

Weinstein, W. K., & Lawson, R. The effect of experimentally induced "awareness" upon performance in a free operant verbal conditioning and on subsequent test of "awareness." *Journal of Psychology,* 1963, **56,** 203-211.

Weitzenhoffer, A. M., & Hilgard, E. R. *Stanford Hypnotic Susceptibility Scale, Forms A and B.* Palo Alto, Calif.: Consulting Psychologists Press, 1959.

Wickramasekera, I. The effects of sensory restriction on susceptibility to hypnosis: A hypothesis and some preliminary data. *International Journal of Clinical and Experimental Hypnosis,* 1969, **17,** 217-224.

Wickramasekera, I. Effects of sensory restriction on susceptibility to hypnosis: A hypothesis and more preliminary data. *Journal of Abnormal Psychology,* 1970, **76,** 69-75. (a)

Wickramasekera, I. The effect of "hypnosis" and a control procedure of verbal conditioning. Paper presented at the meeting of the American Psychological Association, Miami, September 1970. (b)

Wickramasekera, I. Effects of EMG feedback training on susceptibility to hypnosis: Preliminary observations. In J. Stoyva et al. (Eds.), *Bio-feedback and self-control.* Chicago: Aldine-Atherton, 1971.

Suppression of Penile Tumescence by Instrumental Conditioning

Raymond C. Rosen
Department of Psychiatry
Rutgers Medical School
Piscataway, N. J.

Penile tumescence in the human male is directly facilitated by parasympathetic vasodilator fibers [*nervi erigentes*] from the sacral cord (1,2,3). Regardless of the source of stimulation, engorgement of the *corpus spongiosum* and *corpora cavernosa* results from this parasympathetically mediated expansion of the arterial lumina. The central role of the autonomic nervous system has led previous researchers to assert that penile tumescence is a totally involuntary response, subject only to reflexive control (4). This conceptualization has greatly influenced etiological accounts as well as treatment approaches to tumescence disorders (5).

Recent research has indicated, however, that some degree of voluntary control of tumescence might be possible (6,7). In these studies it appeared that instructed subjects were able to enhance or suppress voluntarily tumescence in the presence or absence of visual erotica.

To the extent that tumescence might be subject to voluntary control under certain conditions, it follows that instrumental contingencies could be important in the development and maintenance of the response. Fine differentiation of visceral behavior is possible through instrumental conditioning (8,9), and penile tumescence, being readily detectable, might be particularly susceptible to external contingencies. While changes in heart rate or blood pressure would typically pass unnoticed, penile tumescence in an "inappropriate" social situation could elicit immediate reinforcement, either positive or negative. It is hypothesized, therefore, that such contingencies could play an important role in developing the specificity of control apparent in the normal adult male.

The present study was conducted to ascertain the possible effects of contingent feedback on the suppression of elicited tumescence. Specifically, an attempt was made to demonstrate that, under controlled laboratory conditions, an instrumental conditioning procedure could produce substantial suppression of tumescence in normal male volunteers. The effects of such a procedure might have important implications for our understanding of the development of control of tumescence in both normal and disordered males.

Method

The laboratory measurement of penile tumescence is readily achieved through the use of a mercury strain-gauge (Parks Electronics) which reflects changes in penile diameter as an approximately linear function of resistance changes in the mercury column within the strain-gauge (10). By defining the criterion of tumescence onset (an increase in penile diameter of approximately 0.5 mm from the flaccid state), it is possible to establish the conditions for the presentation of immediate contingent feedback to the subject. This feedback (a dim red light projected into the darkened experimental chamber) was automatically triggered by a voltage discriminator circuit preset at the criterion strain-gauge level.

The subjects were forty males without any history of sexual dysfunction (undergraduate volunteers who took part in the experiment for academic credit). They were seated in a sound- and temperature-controlled room, where the details of the experiment were explained. Subjects were told that the purpose of the experiment was to determine the effects of erotic stimulation under different conditions. Subjects were encouraged to tell friends that the experiment involved listening to "sexy" tapes, without going into any further details, "so as not to spoil it for them!" As a result, a large source of volunteers was obtained, none of whom appeared to have any preconceptions, other than that they would be sexually aroused by the experiment.

Subjects were instructed to place the strain-gauge around the shaft of the penis, just below the coronal ridge, after the experimenter had left the room. This strain-gauge formed one leg of a Wheatstone bridge circuit (Parks Model 270 Plethysmograph Wheatstone Bridge), which allowed voltage changes to be displayed on a Beckman Type R Dynograph. Figure 1 illustrates the penile volume and finger pulse volume polygraph recordings.

Samples of pulse volume from the finger were obtained from 12 of the subjects. These data were obtained by means of a strain-gauge circuit similar to the penile strain-gauge, but AC coupled to the polygraph. Recording and programming of the experiment were conducted from an adjacent room.

In order to elicit penile tumescence, a series of erotic passages were extracted from popular pornography and tape-recorded in the form of ten-minute segments by a female narrator. The erotic tape-recordings used in the experiment were shown in earlier pilot research reliably to elicit sizable tumescence in the subject population.

For each of the four experimental sessions, subjects were presented with a different ten-minute passage (randomly selected) through Grason Stadler Model TDH earphones. Prior to the onset of the erotic narration, a three-minute period of quiet instrumental music was presented, during which time the diameter of the flaccid penis was assessed, and defined as the subject's basal level for that session. Strain-gauge expansion during the subsequent ten minutes of erotic stimulus presentation was reflected as mm polygraph pen deflection above the resting level. Strain-gauge calibration was checked before experimental sessions by means of a standard aluminum cylinder.

The experiment was divided into two phases: a baseline session and three subsequent treatment sessions. During the baseline (pretreatment) session, all subjects listened to one of the erotic passages while physiological measures were recorded. This session was intended to indicate the tumescence produced prior to treatment.

After this session, subjects were randomly divided into four groups (N=10): (i) *The Contingent Feedback* group was instructed to suppress their erections by turning off a red light which was projected into the experimental room whenever the subject's tumescence exceeded 0.5 mm diameter increase from the basal level. (ii) The *Yoked Feedback* group received similar instructions, but were presented with nonveridical (yoked) feedback. Yoking was achieved through the use of a tape-recording of the feedback record of each of the Contingent Feedback subjects, which was then used to trigger the feedback projection for each of the Yoked Feedback subjects. This meant that the yoked controls received the same order and duration of feedback, but *noncontingently*. The purpose of this Yoked group was to control for the possible intrinsically inhibiting effect of the feedback light irrespective of the contingency. (iii) The *Instructions Only* group were instructed to attempt to suppress tumescence in the presence of the erotic stimulus material. However, they were not provided with any form of prosthetic feedback. In fact, the feedback light was disconnected for this and the following group. (iv) The *No Treatment*

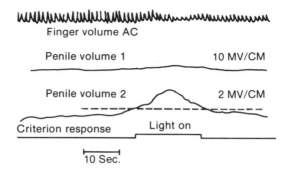

FIGURE 1. Representative portion of the polygraph record from a Contigent Feedback subject. Penile tumescence is displayed on two separate channels (one at a lower gain in order to maintain the full range of the response within the channel). The dashed line across the high gain penile channel indicates the level of the voltage discriminatory switch setting. Whenever penile diameter exceeds this criterion, the marker (lower channel) indicates the duration of the response. Also shown is the finger blood volume record (upper channel) which was recorded from 12 subjects.

Control group received repeated presentations of the erotic material without any inhibition instructions or external feedback. This group was included as a control for possible habituation effects. Subjects in all four groups had available normal tactile feedback from underclothing, skin contact with other body parts, etc.

Subjects in the suppression groups (i, ii, and iii) were all instructed to refrain from any manual suppression of tumescence. Moreover, they were instructed to attend to the tape-recordings as closely as possible as they would subsequently be tested on the content. Random assignment of subjects to experimental groups, and standardization of experimental instructions were used to minimize experimenter bias.

All sessions were spaced approximately one week apart. Postsession questionnaires were administered after the pretreatment, first and last treatment sessions. These questionnaires were designed to ascertain the subject's awareness of the experimental contingencies, as well as their subjective response to the procedure. Debriefing was conducted after the final (fourth) session.

Results

The most direct measure of the effectiveness of the contingency is the amount of time that the subject's tumescence exceeded the experimental criterion. In order to compare group differences, the mean percentage time above criterion for each group was computed. If a subject's tumescence exceeded the criterion for the entire session, that subject would therefore receive a score of 100% for that session. A subject who had attained complete suppression of tumescence would receive a score of 0% for the session. Figure 2 indicates these time above criterion data for each of the four experimental sessions (including the initial base-line session).

A one-way analysis of variance on the pretreatment data shows that there were no systematic differences between the groups prior to treatment, i.e., that the groups had in fact been randomly assigned. A two-way analysis of variance (11) of the data from four groups over all four experimental sessions shows that the main effect for groups was significant ($p < 0.005$), as well as the groups X sessions interaction effect ($p < 0.05$).

A planned comparison of the differences between group means indicates that the Contingent Feedback group was the only group that showed a significant ($p < 0.01$) suppression effect over the three treatment sessions. The No Treatment Control group showed no evidence of an habituation effect. Review of individual records suggested different suppression approaches in the contingent feedback group: (i) After exceeding the criterion a number of times early in the training sessions, some subjects were able to maintain a relatively constant below criterion response for

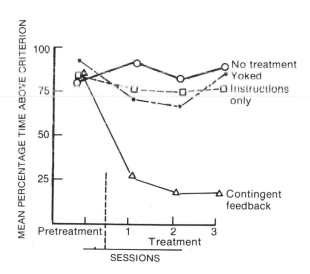

FIGURE 2. Average time above criterion (0.5 mm penile diameter increase from flaccid level) of the four groups over the four experimental sessions. Each point on the graph represents the mean time above criterion for ten subjects in one experimental session.

most of the sessions. (ii) Other subjects appeared to use the feedback light to maintain their response at just about criterion level. One subject received as many as 15 feedback presentations in one session.

Finger pulse volume data from twelve of the subjects was analyzed with respect to rate and amplitude. While there was no significant difference between the feedback and no-feedback groups in terms of the overall finger pulse amplitude or rate scores, there appeared to be a suggestive, but not statistically significant negative correlation ($r = -0.37$) between penile diameter increase and pulse rate changes: as subjects' penile diameter increased, their pulse rates tended to decrease. However, as the actual pulse rates showed relatively minor changes (2-5 beats/min), and the correlation is rather small, this finding should be cautiously interpreted.

In attempting to assess whether successful suppression of tumescence was associated with decreased attention to the content of the erotic material, the postsession questionnaires were also designed to elicit subjective reactions to the experimental procedure. Subjects were required to answer a number of questions concerning the content of the passages. No significant differences in recall scores emerged. Although subjects in the control conditions tended to rate themselves as having been less successful during the suppression phase, there was no evidence that the yoked subjects doubted the veridicality of the feedback. Moreover, there did not appear to be any systematic pattern of suppression strategies described by subjects (almost half the subjects reported some form of muscular or mental tension, while the remainder attempted to relax in some way).

One final questionnaire finding of note was that subjects appeared to be able to rate reasonably accurately the extent to which they had been successful in inhibiting their tumescence during the session. That is, subjective ratings of suppression correlated significantly ($p < 0.01$) with actual strain-gauge scores.

Discussion

The data from this experiment suggest that if normal male volunteers are provided with precise immediate feedback as soon as their tumescence exceeds a certain criterion, they are able to learn a remarkable degree of control with respect to that criterion. Moreover, results of the control groups suggest that the suppression obtained is not attributable to any of the nonspecific experimental factors. Nor can the results be accounted for solely on the basis of attentional differences between the groups.

It has been demonstrated in animals (12) as well as humans (13) that remarkable specificity of function of the autonomic nervous system can be achieved through instrumental conditioning. The results obtained in this study suggest that penile tumescence, as a parasympathetically mediated response, is particularly susceptible to suppression as a function of external contingencies.

Although this study was conducted on normal subjects in a laboratory situation, tentative clinical inferences can be drawn from the results. Masters and Johnson (5, p. 196) have stated that "Erections develop just as involuntarily and with just as little effort as breathing." On the other hand, the results of this study suggest that instrumental contingencies could control tumescence in a manner analogous to the control of somatic behavior. This suggests an alternative etiological formulation in certain cases of psychogenic impotence.

It would also appear feasible to extend such instrumental conditioning techniques to the treatment of certain disorders. If, for example, penile tumescence is elicited in the presence of socially unacceptable stimuli (fetishism), a contingent feedback procedure similar to that used in this study might be sufficient to enable the individual to suppress tumescence when necessary. This might prove a more effective, as well as a more humane alternative to current aversion therapy procedures (14, 15).

Summary

Penile tumescence has been widely regarded as an involuntary response, susceptible only to reflexive control. The present study was designed to investigate the possible modification of penile tumescence by instrumental conditioning procedures.

Penile tumescence in this experiment was elicited by erotic tape-recorded passages of approximately 10-minutes' duration. Forty normal male volunteers were randomly divided into four experimental conditions, which included a contingent feedback group, a yoked control, an instructions only, and a no treatment group. All subjects received one pretreatment and three treatment sessions.

Highly significant suppression of tumescence was obtained as a result of the contingent feedback procedure. None of the control groups demonstrated this effect, indicating that the instrumental conditioning procedure is particularly effective in modifying this response. Postsession questionnaires did not provide any evidence for specific patterns of somatic or cognitive mediation. Finger pulse volume data collected is suggestive of a correlation between tumescence suppression and direct parasympathetic (vagal) control.

These data suggest that instrumental contingencies might play an important role in the development of control of penile tumescence in the human male. This notion could have implications for etiological formulations of certain potency disorders, as well as behavioral therapies for such disorders.

References

1. Learmonth JR: A contribution to the neurophysiology of the urinary bladder. Brain 54:147—176, 1931

2. Weiss HD: The physiology of human penile erection. Ann Intern Med 76:793—799, 1972

3. Katchadourian HA, Lunde DT: Fundamentals of Human Sexuality. New York, Holt, Rinehart and Winston, 1972

4. Masters WH, Johnson VE: Human Sexual Response. Boston, Little Brown, 1966

5. Masters WH, Johnson VE: Human Sexual Inadequacy. Boston, Little Brown, 1970

6. Laws DR, Rubin HB: Instructional control of an autonomic sexual response. Appl Behav Anal 2:93—99, 1969

7. Henson DE, Rubin HB: Voluntary control of eroticism. Appl Behav Anal 4:37—44, 1971

8. Shapiro D, Tursky B, Schwartz GE: Differentiation of heart rate and systolic blood pressure in man by operant conditioning. Psychosom Med 32:417—423, 1970

9. Schwartz GE: Voluntary control of human cardiovascular integration and differentiation through feedback and reward. Science 175:90—93, 1972

10. Zuckerman M: Physiological measures of sexual arousal in the human. Psychol Bull 75:297—329, 1971

11. Winer BJ: Statistical Principles in Experimental Design. New York, McGraw-Hill, 1962

12. Miller NE: Learning of visceral and glandular responses. Science 163:434—445, 1969

13. Katkin ES, Murray EN: Instrumental conditioning of autonomically mediated behavior: Theoretical and methodological issues Psychol Bull 70:52—68, 1968

14. Feldman MP: Aversion therapy for sexual deviations: A critical review Psychol Bull 65:65—79, 1966

15. Rachman S, Teasdale J: Aversion Therapy and Behavior Disorders: An Analysis. Coral Gables, University of Miami Press, 1969.

Note: This research was supported in part by funds from Office of Education Grant 2-700041(509).

Section II

Behavior Therapy

Behavior Therapy Instructional Variables, Situational Variables and Subject Characteristics

Ian Wickramasekera

Behavior Therapy

Behavior therapy is supposed to represent the application of the principles and techniques of laboratory psychology to the clinical situation. If such a relationship between laboratory and clinic exists today, it is clearly strained and superficial (Buchwald and Young, 1969; Wilkins, 1971; Locke, 1971). The most promising and creative behavioral therapy techniques (e.g., systematic desensitization and its variants) are at best only superficially analogous to similar procedures in the animal laboratory. But in a more general sense, laboratory studies of human and animal behavior have inspired behavior therapists to challenge the "superstitions" (Skinner, 1953) of dynamic clinical lore. The attempts of behavior therapists to subject their treatment procedures to even primitively controlled observation is a hopeful sign. Behavior therapists' attempts to study relatively specific and operationally definable dependent variables (symptoms or verbal, motor, and visceral changes) and to manipulate experimentally specific antecedents (instructional sets, relaxation, graded approach, etc.) and consequences (incentives, informational feedback, aversive stimuli) have advanced psychotherapy outcome research.

In behavior therapy, there is a serious attempt to apply the scientific method to the phenomena of behavioral deficit and deviance. The word "deviance" is used in a statistical rather than in a prescriptive (ethical) sense. The hypotheses and techniques of behavior therapy have been applied to the alteration of cognitive, visceral, and motor responses of neurotics, mental defectives, psychotics, and normals. The primary focus in behavior therapy has been on behavior in a "public" (observable) sense and on the physiological and verbal correlates of changes in motor behavior. Behavior therapists have also attempted to design clinical interventions based on laboratory information about the optimal conditions for the acquisition, maintenance, and extinction of responses. The Skinnerians have generally paid little explicit, formal, and direct attention to the alteration of private events (cognitions, feelings, and physiological changes). But ironically, behavior therapists appear to be doing more to advance the scientific study of private events than "insight"-oriented psychotherapists. Their analytic, operational, and quantitative approach has led to several important serendipitous discoveries (e.g., the reactive effects of self-monitoring, the low correlations between verbal, motor, and visceral responses, and so forth). Behavior therapists appear to have derived the original inspiration for their rebellion from Watson, Skinner, and Hull, but it appears that their everyday practice is frequently concerned with the topics that preoccupied arch-introspectionists like Titchener. While it may appear a subversive suggestion, it is at least possible that today the work of Wundt, Titchener, and Fechner is more relevant in many respects to the current clinical practice of behavior therapy than the volumes of Skinner.

Instructional Variables,
Situational Variables and
Subject Characteristics

The bulk of the available evidence appears to indicate that situational variables exert powerful effects on complex human behavior (Mischel, 1973; Peterson, 1968). Instructional variables effectively packaged and conveyed can also exert precise, powerful, and reliable effects on complex human behavior (Goldstein, 1962; Wickramasekera, 1973b; Meichenbaum, 1973; Barber, 1969). The learning-reinforcement history and the nervous system a subject brings add a third dimension (subject characteristics) which, if carefully specified operationally and in terms of individual differences, may increase our ability to control and predict complex behavior. Specific subject characteristics (e.g., hypnotizability, degree of socialization, physiological lability, and response stereotypy, assertiveness, etc.) when considered in relation to specific instructional and situational variables, may increase our ability to control and predict accurately some types (e.g., phobic and sexual) of complex human behavior.

Instructing a person to observe accurately, track, and record a given segment of his behavior is useful from both diagnostic and intervention standpoints (McFall, 1970; Johnson and White, 1971). Truax and Mitchell, 1971 describe a complex self-observation procedure which they call "self-exploration," which consists of introspectively searching for relationships between immediate or past feelings, and situational antecedents, concomitants or consequences. They have attempted to specify in measureable terms (with rating scales of known reliability and validity) the interpersonal conditions under which the probability of this patient activity (self-exploration) may be increased or decreased. Patient self-exploration appears to be reliably associated with a wide range of patient benefits including symptomatic relief. The level of patient self-exploration may be increased or decreased by contingently manipulating powerful therapist-dispensed social reinforcers like accurate empathy or warmth (Truax and Mitchell, 1971).

Diagnostically, the self-observation procedure (introspective or extrospective) gives the patient a concrete way of participating actively in his treatment through self-diagnosis. Through self-observation, the patient may discover or become aware of unexpected contingencies between his symptoms and internal (emotions, thoughts, moods, sensations, etc.) or external (discriminative or eliciting stimuli) environmental events. In terms of intervention, self-observation and specific instructional sets have been found to decelerate behavior under conditions where the monitored behavior was aversive to the subject (McFall, 1970). Johnson and White (1971) point out the very act of self-observation appears to increase the frequency of a valued response. Hence, baselines derived from self-observation may be reactive measures. The specific instructional sets given the subject may affect the frequency of the response by cognitively arranging aversive or reinforcing consequences. For example, McFall's (1970) data show that instructing a subject to record the frequency with which he *resisted* the temptation to smoke is associated with a dramatic decline in the frequency of smoking. In a therapeutic program, the effects of self-observation alone may be only temporary (McFall and Hammen, 1971; Mahoney, Maura and Wade, in press). But in combination with strong and highly credible therapeutic rationale (Orne, 1970), a self-monitoring procedure may temporarily slow down several high-frequency behaviors (e.g., smoking, eating, hair pulling, compulsive rituals, etc.) and create an optimistic patient orientation that can be strengthened with more specifically effective interventions (e.g., arranging response-reinforcement contingencies in natural habitat, response prevention, contact desensitization, etc.)

The article by Orne and Scheibe (1964) included in this book is a classic demonstration of effective and credible structuring of explicit and implicit expectations (demand characteristics) through instructional and situational manipulations. This study demonstrated that nearly all the bizarre phenomena of sensory deprivation can be elicited in subjects, with powerful preexperimental structuring of expectancies and without the actual use of sensory deprivation chambers and other paraphernalia. The experimental subjects' expectancies were structured by context cues (experiment conducted in a psychiatric hospital, medical history taken, medical release form signed, tray containing drugs and medical instruments prominently displayed and labeled "emergency tray") and verbal instructions (to report unusual feelings, imagery, hallucinations, and to press panic button in case of emergency to secure medical assistance). Experimental subjects reported and demonstrated a significantly larger number of unusual phenomena (perceptual aberrations, intellectual dullness, anxiety, and spatial disorientation) than control subjects who were subjected to the same physical conditions but were structured to expect nothing unusual. The article illustrates the profound effects which instructional-situational arrangements can have on verbal, affective, and motor responses in man. In terms of experimental design, it implies that "demand characteristics" may compete with the other independent variables as an explanation of the results of an experiment (changes in dependent variables).

In clinical practice, the credible structuring of the patient's expectations by suitable pretherapy reading (e.g., an article in *Time* about the promise of biofeedback), therapeutically planned remarks "dropped," (Haley, 1967) or "asides" from secretaries and others may facilitate the patient's receptivity to therapy and/or attraction (Goldstein, 1971) to a specific therapist or intervention (e.g., systematic desensitization, hypnosis, etc.). It also appears that instructing a patient prior to therapy on how to participate most productively increases the probability of a positive outcome (Strupp and Bloxom, 1973). This verbal instruction may be delivered in written form, a role-induction interview, or a film. The verbal instruction attempts to indoctrinate good patient behaviors (e.g., expressing personal feelings; talking about problems can be helpful; patient should take responsibility to implement change; change takes time, no "cures" but only more effective ways of coping).

The article by Rosehan (1973) in this section illustrates the major effects that an institutional-instructional context can have on the perceptions and judgments of even highly trained professionals when they are confronted by eight pseudopatients. A specific situation (a hospital context) can create a powerful bias in clinical judgment in favor of redefining the "normal" in terms of pathology. The study by Rosehan indicates that the tendency to err on the side of caution and label a healthy person "sick" can have serious personal, legal, social, and vocational consequences. It appears that professional conclusions drawn about the behavior of eight normal people were strongly influenced by expectations about the context of observation. The normal behavior of the patient had to be "fake" because the patient was seen in a psychiatric hospital setting. The situational control of patient emotions and behaviors is also well-illustrated by the depersonalizing effects (e.g., hopelessness, anonymity, helplessness) of institutional socialization. In summary, it appears then that situational factors can, under certain conditions, control complex clinical judgments, and that such judgments can have self-fulfilling consequences (patients will eventually become depressed or apathetic).

In the first article by Seligman (1973) printed in this book, the author states that in the situation of inescapable aversion or trauma, an organism learns that it cannot control consequences or that it is helpless. Initially, it may demonstrate anxiety and tension, but as it learns that aversive consequences are independent of its action, it no longer struggles but submits passively. Seligman (1973) draws several parallels between the learned helpless paradigm and clinical depression which have diagnostic, intervention, and preventative implications. From Seligman's analysis, it appears that anxiety may precede depression and may be the first and more adaptive response to stress.

Patients, particularly institutionalized ones, and children have little or no control over their social and physical environments. In a more general sense, our fears and our hopes (e.g., affectional and sexual) exert strong control over our behavior. An article by Mahoney and Thoresen (1972) illustrates how a person can arrange an environment that strengthens his valued behaviors and weakens his maladaptive behaviors through the use of stimulus control of reinforcement, and punishment procedures. Mahoney and Thoresen suggest that self-regulation is based on knowledge of what variables control one's behavior, (both in terms of antecedents and consequences) and an effective set of interventions to alter these variables or one's reaction to them. They cite the incident with the bewitching Sirens encountered in the travels of Odysseus as a classic example of self-control through environmental manipulation. To control the behavior of his oarsmen, Odysseus filled their ears with beeswax, and to regulate his own behavior, he arranged to be tied to a mast instructing them in advance not to release him under any circumstances. The enhancement of self-control is a remedy for the learned helplessness described by Seligman (1973) which may cause some clinical depressions. The arrangement of a motivating environment and the structuring of the patient's expectations with careful attention to the optimal conditions for instructional manipulations (Wickramasekera, 1973 a, b), can provide a context for effective clinical alteration of fear and sexual arousal.

Fear Arousal

It is assumed in behavior therapy that phobias are analogous to experimentally-established, conditioned-avoidance responses (Eysenck and Rachman, 1965), and Mowrer's (1947) two-factor theory of avoidance behavior is said to explain the acquisition of phobias. A recent review (Herrnstein, 1969) of the experimental evidence on avoidance conditioning challenges the validity of Mowrer's (1947) two-factor theory. Another recent review (Costello, 1970) found salient dissimilarities between clinical phobias and conditioned-avoidance responses. Costello suggests that clinical phobias grow out of failure to develop coping behaviors in situations which are in some ways attractive. The above considerations and clinical observation cast some doubt on the animal avoidance-conditioning model as an adequate description of the acquisition of clinical phobias. But this does not mean that strategies for reducing phobic behavior based on the avoidance model are inapplicable to some clinical phobias.

Dissatisfaction with the avoidance model has lead Eysenck (1969) to propose an alternative "incubation" theory of phobias in which elicitation of the conditioned responses themselves are reinforcing and in which repeated presentation of the unreinforced conditioned stimulus leads to the increase rather than decrease of anxiety. Such a theory, under conditions of high arousal, would predict the rare "sensitization" phenomena clinically demonstrated by Wickramasekera (1970) with a highly suggestible obsessive-compulsive patient. In the above case study included in this book, three separate sets of symptoms (weight loss, frequency of sexual intercourse, and frequency of "paranoid" behaviors) were decreased, increased, and decreased again by altering the usual desensitization procedure. The alteration instituted during the middle phase of treatment consisted of brief massed presentation of aversive images in the absence of patient relaxation. Hence, in the above case study, the subject was his own control and desensitization, sensitization, and desensitization again were administered. Paul (1969) demonstrated a similar "sensitization" phenomenon with physiological measures by using stressful images and by omitting formal relaxation training or hypnosis. Some animal literature (Reed, 1974; Baum, 1970) also suggests that a brief aversive conditioned stimulus presentation will also cause sensitization if a counter conditioning stimulus (e.g., positive intracranial stimulation) is omitted. In summary, it appears that under the following conditions, sensitization can be demonstrated: (1) brief exposure to aversive stimulus without time to adapt to it; (2) highly suggestible patients or people who can demonstrate rapid instructional-cognitive control of visceral responses; (3) highly anxious patients (high-drive level) who typically demonstrate a high level of spontaneous autonomic activity and who habituate slowly (Mathews, 1971). The latter two subject characteristics imply that the incidence of phobias may differ between individuals and types of individuals. Clinically, these subjective features may determine the preponderant location (verbal, motor and/or visceral response systems) of the phobic responses. The above considerations alone appear to suggest that it is poor clinical diagnosis and intervention strategy to assume that all phobias are homogeneous or alike.

One of the reasons it has not been possible to generalize from the analogue desensitization studies to clinical subjects is that the diagnostic criterion measures (behavioral avoidance tests and verbal reports) in the analogue studies have labeled people "phobic" who are less phobic than clinical patients. The diagnostic and outcome measures used in analogue studies have been questioned (Bernstein and Paul, 1971) and have recently (Bernstein and Nietzel, 1973) been shown empirically to be subject to contaminating effects of situational influences (demand characteristics, etc.). The analogue studies (Wilkins, 1971; Kazdin, 1973) have demonstrated that a variety of situational, instructional, and other variables can facilitate the extinction of subclinical phobias and fears (e.g., spiders, snakes, public speaking, test anxiety). These variables include instructions, expectations, and context cues (demand characteristics), social reinforcement, informational feedback, and attentional shifts. These alone may be useful but insufficient conditions to extinguish clinical phobias. But when used in combination with more clinically relevant variables like relaxation training (low sympathetic arousal and a "noise" free head), these instructional-informational variables may be potentiated in two ways. First, it has been shown in the hypnotic literature (Barber, 1969) that relaxation potentiates verbal instructions. Second, the type of patient who "idles" high (high level of spontaneous autonomic activity) habituates very slowly (Lader et al., 1967), and Lader and Mathews (1968) have suggested that relaxation may be one method of lowering the level at which the patient "idles."

The second article by Seligman (1971) offers some logical and empirical documentation for distinguishing between types of phobias. This distinction appears to illuminate the etiology of some clinical phobias. He states that some clinical phobias are highly "prepared" instances of classical conditioning. Prepared fears are characterized by the following features: (1) one trial or very rapid acquisition; (2) selectivity and possible survival value for the species; (3) they are noncognitive and are not reliably extinguished by information and logic; (4) they do not respond to typical laboratory extinction procedures (nonreinforced presentation of conditioned stimuli). Seligman's position questions the generality of the laws of learning and introduces the notion of a species' specific preparation for learning. He has also suggested that there may be some ways of thinking in which humans are particularly prepared to engage. It is possible that some fears may be acquired on the basis of prepared self-instruction (the things a person says to himself about a situation or object), and this notion is not very far from the "irrational ideas" of Ellis (1962) and the racial unconscious of Jung (1953).

Prepared learning and thinking may be operationally defined in terms of the number of trials to acquisition and extinction. Guisto, Caincross, and King (1971) indicate that adrenalin secretion is reliably associated with reflexive or innate fear responses but has less clearly been shown to be associated with learned responses motivated by fear. This finding lends support to the notion that prepared fears which may involve "innate" fear behavior (e.g., trembling, urination, or defecation) may have a larger biochemical or visceral component than nonprepared fears. Clinically, the above observations and speculations imply that in certain phobias it may be imperative to go directly and with major emphasis to visceral responses and sensations (the physiological response component) that are associated with the phobia. The articles by Furst and Cooper (1970) and Wickramasekera (1974a) illustrate that approach. In both case studies, cardiac neurosis was the target symptom. The neurosis was associated with specific distressing visceral and physical sensations and responses. These sensations and responses were elicited by *in vivo* procedures. For example, Wickramasekera (1974a) trained his patient to increase his heart rate with feedback, to breathe deeply and rapidly (to induce dizziness, numbness) and to confront unexpected stress (cap gun discharged unexpectedly). These interventions were conducted in a gradual manner, in an atmosphere of safety, and in the context of heart-rate, feedback-induced relaxation between *in vivo* stimulations. Furst and Cooper (1970) likewise prescribed a set of exercises (scissoring and tensing arms) which either partially or totally replicated the physical sensations (pain in chest, increased heart rate) which typically triggered the panic reaction. These sensations and responses appear to trigger catastrophising cognitive appraisal (Ellis, 1962), which probably increases the epinephrine excretion and sets in motion a positive feedback cycle which results in panic. Eliciting the physical and visceral sensations in a context of safety reduces the probability of negative cognitive appraisal (catastrophic tendency) and the other consequences that generate panic.

The conditioned avoidance model is probably inadequate to explain the mechanism of all phobias. But it has been politically useful because it has legitimized clinical experimentation and inspired empirical research into a variety of creative behavior therapy techniques (e.g., desensitization and its variants, implosion, induced anxiety). Effective intervention with the above techniques, supposedly derived from learning theory, does not prove that the phobia was originally acquired in the manner described by the learning model. In the long run, a variety of effective treatment interventions that are reliably effective with specific types of phobias or anxieties may illuminate the etiology of subsets of phobias. It may turn out that some types of phobias are instances of prepared learning while other types of phobias are instances of nonprepared learning. The specific mechanisms of phobic acquisition may include modeling, classical conditioning, self-instruction (Meichenbaum, 1973; Ellis, 1962) and even instrumental conditioning (note the biofeedback literature). In instances of prepared learning, good clinical strategy would direct attention first to the physiological concomitants of the phobia. Eventually, we may even identify which of the variables effective in reducing phobic behavior (e.g., instructions-suggestions, social reinforcement, relaxation, graded exposure, assertive responses, anger expression, and feedback) are best suited to which type of phobia with which type of subject.

Phobic behavior is composed of at least three interconnected response systems (verbal, motor, and physiological) which are poorly intercorrelated (Lang, 1969) and which change at different rates (Mathews, 1971). In the classification of phobias and anxieties, there appears to be large and significant individual differences in the relative degree of dysfunction of specific response system components. For example, in one case, most of the phobic dysfunction may be focused in the verbal dimension. Clearer diagnostic specification of these relevant subject characteristics may make more informed clinical comparisons with analogue subjects possible. For example, a few clinical phobias and most analogue phobias may require no more than a verbal redefinition of the phobic experience. There is also a need for interventions that systematically alter every dysfunctional response component (verbal, motor, visceral) in a phobia and do so economically. It is known that the verbal instructions given to certain suggestible patients and the verbal inferences (statements they make to themselves) they make about a treatment situation or procedure appear to alter all three response systems (verbal, motor, visceral) and do so very rapidly (Shapiro, 1971). I hypothesize that identifying the conditions under which the impact of verbal events may be generally and reliably increased is one promising road to discovering a single intervention (verbal instructions) which has a reliably powerful impact on all three response systems involved in phobic behavior; in other words, one precise, brief, reliable, and powerful central intervention (verbal instruction) that alters all peripheral response systems (motor and visceral) in phobic behavior. The clinical hypnosis literature is replete with instances of phobias treated in one session with hypnosis, but these patients typically relapse (Wolpe, Salter and Reyna, 1964).

The reasons for the rapid and high response-relapse rates have never been systematically investigated. The behavior therapists have implied conditioning explanations of the high relapse rates, but cognitive explanations involving attribution theory, effort, and so forth are also possible. The very rapid, almost effortless, symptomatic relief that sometimes comes from hypnosis may create a posttreatment credibility gap in the patient that unravels his therapeutic, perceptual, and cognitive redefinition of the situation and produces the consequent symptomatic relapse. In some cases, it appears that instructional hypnotic interventions can lead to more permanent "cures" if combined with credible rationales for the effectiveness of hypnosis and with a laborious (on patient's part) effort, manipulation, which strengthens the rationale for the "cure."

An affirmative verbal relabeling of a fearful situation by the patient and the instigation by the therapist of an aggressive approach in the patient towards a fearful predicament, can cause a dramatic decline in phobic sensitivity. Assertive training is basically training in personal risk-taking and can be an effective adjunct to a desensitization procedure. The cognitive relabeling of a situation and assertive training are most effective if conducted by someone to whom the patient is attracted (Goldstein, 1971), who is accurately empathic (Truax and Mitchell, 1971), and warm (Morris and Suckerman, 1974), who is confident and exudes positive expectations (Goldstein, 1962). In an article included in this book, Lazarus (1973) points out that self-assertion includes the following salient components: (1) the ability to express negative feelings; (2) the ability to say no; (3) the ability to ask for favors and to make requests; (4) the ability to initiate, sustain, and terminate general conversations; (5) the ability to express positive feelings (e.g., tenderness, love, warmth). The essence of self-assertion appears to be an expansion of the zone of personal risk-taking, and the development of skill and comfort in risk-taking.

Sexual Arousal

The words *deviation* and *deviant* will be used in this discussion in a strictly descriptive (statistical) and not prescriptive sense. A sexual deviation is a statistically infrequent form of predominantly operant behavior which has subjectively pleasant antecedents, concomitants, and consequences. A sexual *dysfunction* (Masters and Johnson 1970) in its most critical aspect is respondent behavior (vaginismus, premature ejaculation, impotence, and so forth) which can have subjectively aversive antecedents and consequences. A second way in which a sexual deviation is clinically separable from a sexual dysfunction is with respect to motivation. In most adult sexual deviants, there is seldom intrinsic motivation to change, but in the case of adult sexual dysfunction, there is nearly always strong intrinsic motivation for change. A third way in which a sexual deviation is different from a dysfunction pertains to cultural relativity. What is sexually deviant is defined mainly by time, culture, and social class. For example, in the time of Plato in the upper social classes of Greece, homosexuality was valued behavior. A sexual dysfunction is biologically unadaptive behavior, and secondary impotence is probably not valued behavior in any culture.

Individuals whose sexual behavior is deviant (e.g. homosexual) may be nondeviant in all other aspects of their behavior, and if they are well-adjusted, their family background appears indistinguishable from well-adjusted heterosexuals (Seligman, 1974). Hence, sexual deviants are probably not a homogeneous group with respect to personality features. If such cross-situational behavioral consistencies exist, they are probably a function of membership in a nonpreferred minority group, which elicits aversive social, personal, legal, and vocational consequences. But there are probably large and significant individual differences in the ways in which individual sexual deviants manage these aversive consequences. If such aversive consequences are managed by recourse to duplicity, then guilt may follow, accompanied by conflict and anxiety; then formidable barriers arise to self-respect and self-worth. Reductions in the aversive legal and vocational consequences of identification with a minority form of sexual behavior may reduce the external discomforts confronted by individual sexual deviants, but unless the culture as a whole comes to value such forms of sexual behavior, it remains improbable that sexual deviants will not continue to undervalue themselves as people. Membership in a deviant (minority) group can have positive consequences if the deviant behavior is valued by the culture (e.g., superior intelligence, artistic ability, and so forth.)

Clinical experience indicates that there are probably six specific diagnostic dimensions that require attention in the evaluation and effective management of sexual deviations. Management in this instance does not necessarily imply changing sexual orientation but may imply increasing the individual's comfort with a given sexual orientation. The following six dimensions of arousal and behavioral functioning deserve clinical attention: (1) Identification of the objects of sexual arousal and the availability of a technology for the acquisition of new sexual arousal patterns to replace deviant ones (should the patient request such a service). The acquisition of new sexual arousal patterns may remain within a given sex (e.g., female children to female adults (Wickramasekera, 1968)) or may involve the development of heterosexual arousal in a homosexual male (Barlow, 1973). (2) Gender role deviation refers to the degree to which an individual's psychological gender deviates from his anatomical gender. In the extreme case of transexuality, an anatomical male may have the gender identity of a female. (3) A technology for the reliable suppression and eventual extinction of deviant sexual arousal, if the individual chooses to eliminate it for reasons of comfort or security from his behavior repertoire. (4) Aversive emotions (guilt, fear, anxiety, inferiority feelings, shame, hostility) may inhibit sexual arousal and behavior with a given sexual object (e.g., females). (5) Overlearned smooth social-sexual skills and information which increase the probability of reinforcing consequences in interpersonal relations. (6) Vocational counseling and guidance towards a sub community which can provide support systems.

A Technology for the Identification and Acquisition of New Sexual Arousal Patterns

The development of diagnostic tools to identify and measure sexual arousal and interest is still in an exploratory state (Zukerman, 1971). A variety of tools have been proposed (e.g., G.S.R., heart rate, respiration, pupillary response, blood pressure, penile erections, EEG-contingent negative variation (CNV), biochemical measures) to detect and quantify sexual arousal. Blood pressure and penile erection appear to date to be the most promising measures demonstrating reliable and graded reactions (Zukerman, 1972). Barlow (1973) in an article included in this book reviews a variety of methods for increasing heterosexual arousal in homosexual males and concludes that increasing heterosexual arousal in homosexuals may be more important in the prognosis for reversing homosexuality than reducing deviant arousal.

Two recent case studies, one of orgasmic reconditioning (Marquis, 1970), and the other of septal stimulation (Moan and Heath, 1972), demonstrate primitive clinical procedures to create new sexual arousal patterns. The methods are roughly analogous to classical conditioning, because temporal contiguity between response and U.C.S. is supposed to be important to them. The article by Moan and Heath (1972) in this section describes a promising but loosely linked (between behaviors and septal stimulation) procedure which eventually may be refined to manipulate reliably sexual arousal patterns. An operant fading method is described by Barlow (1973), and it appears to be a promising and researchable method for creating sexual arousal. An attractive female slide is faded into a very attractive male slide while penile circumference changes are monitored. The images are superimposed on one another. An adjustable transformer increases the brightness of the female slide, resulting in a simultaneous decrease in the brightness of the male slide. The female image is faded into the male image contingent on the subject maintaining 75 percent of a full erection.

Barlow (1973) observes that aversive conditioning procedures to suppress homosexual arousal alone are associated with paradoxical heterosexual arousal. This observation is not easily predictable from conditioning theory. The article by Hallam, Rachman, and Falkowski (1972) suggests that the effects of electrical aversion therapy may be even partially mediated cognitively, illustrating the possible role of cognitive-attitudinal factors in the acquisition, maintenance, and extinction of deviant sexual arousal. The nature of the sexual cognitions and images that are associated with autonomic arousal and ejaculation may have important prognostic implications for the clinical management of a sexual reorientation procedure. In an article, Evans (1968) has shown that deviant masturbatory fantasy can undo the effect of a sexual reorientation program. Clinical experience indicates that specific arousal and masturbatory techniques (e.g., masturbation on one's stomach) in the male, may impede full erection and vaginal penetration by fostering ejaculation without erection.

Gender Deviations

Sexual arousal probably includes, in addition to autonomic components, cognitive and motor features which are relevant to "gender identity" (Money and Ehrhardt, 1973). The cognitive values (esthetic vs. athletic) and the skeletal (aggressive vs. passive) role behaviors contribute importantly to the definition of an individual's sexual gender identity (Constantinople, 1973). Clinically, it appears that homosexuals can be distributed on a continuum in terms of their gender identity. It appears that some homosexuals think, feel, and behave like heterosexual males, and their gender identity is basically masculine. On the opposite end are homosexuals who think of themselves as women, who feel feminine, and who behave like females (walk, talk, sit, and so forth). Most homosexuals are probably distributed somewhere between these polarities. It is probable that effeminate ways of thinking, feeling, and acting seriously influence the autonomic aspects of sexual arousal patterns. To alter an established sexual arousal pattern, it may be necessary to influence effeminate motor and cognitive activities and personal values. Recent logical and empirical analyses (Constantinople, 1973; Bem, 1974) suggest that masculinity-feminity may not be bipolar phenomena but may in fact be multidimensional; multidimensional in the sense of being composed of subtraits (e.g. conventionality, passivity, analytical, aggressive) which are present in the same individual under different conditions. In other words, some individuals rather than being strongly sex-typed, may be androgynous or able to emit both masculine and feminine behaviors depending on the situational appropriateness of the various behaviors. In the case of the intelligent adult who has attained a sense of identity, androgyny may be a highly adaptive behavior.

Gender roles appear to be learned very early in life (Money and Ehrhardt, 1973) on an observational and instrumental basis. In primitive societies, gender roles are more clearly defined for men and women and frequently do not overlap. In modern societies, the recent blurring and overlapping of social roles and styles for males and females may pose greater challenges and strains in the acquisition of sexual gender identity. These challenges may be particularly overwhelming for children of limited intelligence (or learning ability) and children who are constitutionally predisposed to excessive autonomic arousal (Eysenck, 1960). It appears to be important to know what implications the blurring of social roles will have on sexual behavior in the future and on institutions like the family.

Extinction of "Deviant"
Sexual Arousal Patterns

The nature of the masturbatory fantasy used by the patient is often quite critical to the acquisition, maintenance, and extinction of deviant sexual patterns. Evans (1968) has shown that the patient's use of deviant masturbatory fantasy has clear implications for the aversion therapy treatment of sexual exhibitionism. Treatment required more sessions, and the probability of relapse was greater if the patient used deviant masturbatory fantasy during and after treatment. Many methods have been advocated to suppress and eventually extinguish deviant sexual arousal (e.g., covert sensitization, electrical aversion therapy, chemical aversion therapy). The suppression of deviant sexual arousal may be unnecessary in most instances if an effective program of adaptive sexual arousal is in progress. Sometimes to reduce the interfering effects of deviant arousal and to reduce the probability of acting out and consequent legal action which will remove the patient from the sexual reorientation program, it may be necessary to consider suppressing deviant sexual arousal. The article by Wilson and Davison (1969) suggests that certain types of aversive stimuli may be more appropriate to certain response systems than electric shock. Basically, they suggest attention to the topographical nature of stimuli and not simply to functional considerations. The article by Colson (1972) suggests associating a cheap and simple noxious olfactory stimulus with homosexual arousal to inhibit deviant sexual arousal. Inhibiting deviant sexual arousal may be more desirable if it is only one component in a larger intervention package which includes attention to the extinction of heterosexual anxieties and shaping of heterosexual skills (Birk et al., 1971).

A major limitation on all consulting-room procedures that seek to inhibit deviant sexual arousal is the unreliable transfer of the inhibition from the consulting room to the natural habitat of the patient, where the experimental aversive contingency is not in effect. This is probably the strongest practical objection to the popular "electrical" aversion therapies (Feldman and MacCulloch (1971). Clinically and empirically, (Azarin and Holz, 1966) it appears that inhibition of arousal will be most effective if the aversive consequences are delivered early rather than later in a deviant behavioral sequence (e.g., if the aversive consequences are elicited no sooner, the thought of acting out deviantly occurs) Installing the aversion within the patient, at a location where the response-punishment contingency cannot be dismantled by the patient, and arranging for the delivery of the aversion each time a deviant response occurs, may increase the probability of the reliable inhibition of deviant sexual arousal. Wickramasekera (1972, 1974b) describes a procedure (aversive-behavior-rehearsal) to inhibit deviant sexual behavior which makes environmental arrangements to generate intense aversion and to attach the aversion to internal cues (interoceptive conditioning). The procedure appears to install the aversion inside the patient and outside his control. It appears also to inhibit deviant behavior reliably and early in the sequence of behavioral arousal. The aversive-behavior-rehearsal procedure which has been independently replicated (Serber, 1970; Reitz and Keil, 1971; Stevenson and Jones, 1972) appears to have only limited applicability. It seems to be analogous to a natural but accelerated socialization procedure. The impressive reliability with which the installed contingency transfers to the natural habitat fits nicely with predictions from Miller's (1964) conflict-displacement theory which predicts a flatter gradient of generalization if aversion is attached to internal cues. The procedure may simply be a tool to identify highly motivated patients and may be without any specific effectiveness. Clinical experience and some psychophysiological data indicate that while the procedure does in fact identify highly motivated patients, it additionally has powerful specific psychophysiological effects on them. The procedure actively operates the verbal, visceral, and motor response systems of the patient. Hence, if there are any specific effects, they may be explained along alternative lines including cognitive dissonance (voluntary participation increases dissonance), satiation, aversive conditioning, self-disclosure, and so forth. Our current clinical trials examine the hypothesis that the procedure has no specific effects itself but is an effective tool in selecting highly motivated subjects who will respond to any intervention or any comparable intervention. Preliminary data do not support the above hypothesis. Our preliminary psychophysiological data (heart rate, G.S.R., respiration) on the concomitants of the procedure are clear-cut and supportive of our initial hypothesis that the procedure may involve interoceptive conditioning (Wickramasekera, 1972). But the motivational hypothesis deserves further attention, and we are attempting to manipulate "motivation" by arranging to restrict the patient's choices to jail or our aversive procedure. The active participation of the patient may be the only significant variable because after the behavioral trap ("voluntary" commitment to procedure) is entered, the aversive consequences for high-anxiety, morally inhibited subjects may follow automatically from environmental arrangements. In terms of Eysenck's model, it appears that neurotic introverts will profit most from the above treatment.

Inhibitory Aversive Emotions

Aversive emotions (anxiety, inferiority feelings, shame, guilt, hostility) may inhibit sexual arousal to a given sexual object (e.g., adult females) and may also reduce the probability of behavioral (motor) exploration with such sexual objects. Often the patient may not have recognized and accurately labeled the emotions he feels in the presence of threatening sexual objects. For example, a feeling of mild anxiety in close relationships with the opposite sex may over the years have been mislabeled "boredom" and "restlessness." The patient may have rationalized a fear of intimate contact as a lack of interest. Hence, the withdrawal from females is rationalized as a value choice (e.g., girls don't turn me on, religious scruples, and so forth) which may eventually become a self-fulfilling prophecy. The article by Wickramasekera (1968) illustrates a case in which fear appears to have been rationalized as a religious scruple. Extinction of the fear (by systematic desensitization) and the shaping (through reinforcement) of progressively more intimate sexual behaviors resulted in an increased frequency of sexual approach to adult females and a corresponding decline in sexual approach to adolescent females. The shaping procedure used was similar to the "sensate focus" method described by Masters and Johnson (1970) which also increases comfort in sexual situations, encourages exploratory sexual behavior, and is an *in vivo* procedure to desensitize performance anxiety. The procedure described by Wickramasekera (1968) has many advantages because it begins cognitively but phases into a concurrent physical dimension. Once initiated, the procedure transfers well to the natural habitat, permitting both respondents (emotions like guilt, shame, and fear to extinguish in both parties) and operants (heterosexual cognitions and skills to be reinforced by powerful primary sexual reinforcement) to change slowly while concurrently a credible cognitive rationale for the behavior changes in both parties is elaborated by the therapist using the comments and emerging values of the couple.

Aversive emotions (e.g., performance anxiety) may cause specific sexual dysfunctions (e.g., premature ejaculation, secondary impotence, and so forth.) The sexual dysfunction discourages heterosexual approach behaviors, or if intercourse is attempted and fails, the individual prematurely exits the competitive heterosexual scene and may resort to homosexuality where he or she may play a "safe" passive role. That person may henceforth refuse the risk of competitive heterosexual relationships. Sexual dysfunctions of recent onset are probably most effectively and economically managed with hypnosis and with a combination of concrete desensitizing and ego-building suggestions. Chronic sexual dysfunctions probably require more systematic and extended procedures like those described by Masters and Johnson (1970).

Articles by Marston (1968) and one by Meichenbaum (1973) imply that the effective management of private events and self-instructional sets can have important effects on overt behavior. In the context of a relationship in which the patient is attracted to the therapist (Goldstein, 1971) and an authoritative transference exists, information, inspirational exhortative instructions, and a credible rationale (Orne, 1970) may be powerful tools to encourage personal risk-taking and redefine a situation cognitively so that aversive respondents are reduced if not eliminated. The article by LoPiccolo and Lobitz (1972) illustrates how a therapist who is an attractive authority-figure may use discriminating self-disclosure and judicious modeling as powerful disinhibiting or anxiety-extinguishing tools to give "permission" for creative sexual exploration. In cases where aversive emotions continue to induce inhibitions, in spite of informational, instructional, modeling and self-disclosure manipulations, systematic desensitization and sometimes implosion may be necessary, for example, in the case of a young adult who persists in feeling guilty before or after heterosexual intercourse or an adult homosexual who continues to feel personal shame before or after a homosexual act. These aversive emotions, because they frequently block or terminate relationships, inhibit the emergence of more complex social intercourse which can be important for self-esteem, and the erection of social support systems.

Aversive emotions like rage and hostility, which inhibit relaxed and giving interpersonal and sexual communication, are probably best managed in group psychotherapy (Birk et al., 1971) or with Gestalt alternate role-taking procedures (Perls, 1969). In cases where the hostility is chronic because of inadequate self-assertion skills (failure to say no, unwillingness to make reasonable requests, failure to stand up for legitimate rights, etc.) a program of assertive training for both verbal and nonverbal behavior components may be necessary (Serber, 1972). Serber points out in his article that self-assertion is conveyed on at least two dimensions—verbal and nonverbal. Previously, attention has been paid mostly to self-assertive verbalization. Serber (1972) notes that the nonverbal dimension also conveys much information about one's assertive behavior both to oneself and to others and requires specific training exercises. He points out that the following variables may need specific training to increase assertive behavior and to convey a confident image: (1) voice volume; (2) eye contact; (3) fluency of speech; (4) facial expression; (5) body posture; (6) distance from speaker; (7) hand and arm gestures.

Overlearned, Smooth
Social-Sexual Skills

Other components that are important to the implementation of sexual arousal in a social context are skill and information. Appropriate social-sexual skills that are smooth and overlearned increase the probability of social and sexual reinforcement in interpersonal relations. An important aspect of these skills includes both the ability to express anger and the ability to express love. Lazarus (1973) demonstrates in the article printed in this book that self-assertion and interpersonal risk-taking include both the ability to express rage and the willingness to make oneself vulnerable in reaching out with tenderness to others in both verbal and nonverbal dimensions.

Because of inhibitory anxiety, lack of information, or the lack of practice, an individual may have significant deficits in socially relevant operants. As a consequence, he or she may act and feel clumsy, awkward, and inept in intimate, social, or sexual situations. Discriminating therapist self-disclosure and either role-playing or live therapist-modeling (e.g., arrange a double date with a patient) can facilitate the emergence of relevant social-sexual skills. Information on how, when, where, and from whom to ask for dates can often significantly alter the probability of reinforcement when date-seeking behavior is still a low probability response for a specific patient. The above heterosexual information and skills are typically acquired during adolescence through the natural socialization process, but heterosexual avoidance may result in large deficits in these salient social skills for some individuals.

Vocation Counseling and Guidance
Towards a Sub Community

There are many homosexuals who do not want to alter their sexual arousal patterns, but who seek to become more comfortable with their homosexual orientation. It is a challenge to be both homosexual and comfortable. Homosexual behavior in most of the United States can have serious legal, vocational, social, and familial consequences for the individual, apart from any personal guilt or shame he or she may feel. Hence, a large component of the personal fear, anxiety, guilt, or shame with which many homosexuals live may be reality-based and culturally engineered to discourage a nonpreferred and unpopular form of sexual expression. Consequently, homosexual behavior has to be emitted covertly or the individual has to risk loss of employment, social ostracism (rejection by family and many heterosexual friends), and possible prosecution. Social institutions and procedures are arranged to provide incentives like security, stability, and continuity (e.g. marriage, contracts and property settlements, adoption privileges) to heterosexual relationships and no such incentive systems exist to encourage homosexual relationships. The individual homosexual in the greater portion of the United States is indirectly forced into a life of duplicity because he or she cannot risk exposure. Duplicity provides the ideal conditions for the acquisition of guilt, shame, and anxiety.

Certain vocational avenues (e.g., the arts, higher education and some skilled trades) which are relatively few in number, are more tolerant of overt homosexual behavior than the rest of the world of work. Realistic vocational counseling and guidance towards such employment may reduce the probability of external strains in the case of some homosexuals. Intuitively and clinically, the acquisition of self-respect and self-acceptance appears to be importantly related to the availability of at least one small subcommunity in which the individual can be himself or act authentically, at least in a personal-sexual sense, in other words, a place and a set of people where he can be known as a homosexual but still be accepted and valued for his other social and personal skills and competencies. Over the span of life and the transient crises in everyday living, such a place and a set of people can be a "support system" that makes the difference between mental "health" and mental "illness," a sanctuary in which a man is seen first as a person and only second as a homosexual. Hence, the therapist should have the information necessary to guide a homosexual towards such a support system where he may validate his worth as a person and where he may find employment relatively free of grave risks.

References

Azarin, N. H., & Holz, W. C. Punishment. In W. K. Honig (Ed.), *Operant behavior, areas of research and application.* New York: Appleton-Century Crofts, 1966.

Barber, T. X. *Hypnosis—A scientific approach.* New York: Von Nostrand Reinhold, 1969.

Barlow, D. Increasing heterosexual responsiveness in the treatment of sexual deviation. *Behavior Therapy,* 1973, *4* (5), 655-671.

Baum, M. Extinction of avoidance responding through response prevention (flooding). *Psychological Bulletin,* 1970, *74,* 276-284.

Bem, S. L. The measurement of psychological androgyny. *Journal of Consulting and Clinical Psychology,*1974, *42,* 155-162.

Bernstein, D. A., & Nietzel, M. T. Procedural variation in behavioral avoidance tests. *Journal of Consulting and Clinical Psychology,* 1973, *41,* 165-174.

Bernstein, D. A., & Paul, G. L. Some comments on therapy analogue research with small animal "phobias." *Journal of Behavior Therapy and Experimental Psychiatry,* 1971, *2,* 225-237.

Birk, L., Huddleston, W., Miller, E., & Cohler, B. Avoidance conditioning for homosexuality. *Archives of General Psychiatry,* 1971, *25,* 314-325.

Buchwald, A., & Young, R. D. Some comments on the foundation of behavior therapy. In C. M. Franks (Ed.), *Behavior therapy appraisal and status.* New York: McGraw-Hill, 1969.

Colson, C. E. Olfactory aversion therapy for homosexual behavior. *Journal of Behavior Therapy and Experimental Psychiatry,* 1972, *3,* 185-187.

Constantinople, A. Masculinity-femininity: An exception to a famous dictum? *Psychological Bulletin, 1973, 80,* 389-407.

Costello, C. G. Dissimilarities between conditioned avoidance responses and phobias. *Psychological Review,* 1970, *7* (3), 250-254.

Ellis, A. *Reason and emotion in psychotherapy.* New York: Lyle Stuart, 1962.

Evans, D. R., Masturbatory fantasy and sexual deviation, *Behavior Research and Therapy,* 1968, *6,* 17-19.

Eysenck, H. J. A theory of the incubation of anxiety/fear responses. *Behavior research and therapy,* 1968, *6,* 309-321.

Eysenck, H. J. & Rachman, S. *The causes and the cures of neurosis.* London: Routledge and Kegan Paul, 1965.

Feldman, M. P., & MacCulloch, M. J. *Homosexual behavior: Therapy and assessment.* Elmsford, N.Y.: Pergamon, 1971.

Furst, J. B., & Cooper, A. Combined use of imaginal and introceptive stimuli desensitizing fear of heart attack. *Journal of Behavior Therapy and Experimental Psychiatry,* 1970, *1,* 87-89.

Goldstein, A. P. *Therapist patient expectancies in psychotherapy.* Elmsford, N.Y.: Pergamon, 1962.

Goldstein, A. P. *Psychotherapeutic attraction.* Elmsford, N.Y.: Pergamon, 1971.

Goldstein, A. P. *Structured learning theory toward a psychotherapy for the poor.* New York: Academic Press, 1973.

Guisto, F. L., Caincross, K., & King, M. G. Hormonal influences on fear-motivated responses. *Psychological Bulletin,* 1971, 75 (6), 432-444.

Haley, J. *Advanced techniques of hypnosis and therapy. Selected papers of Milton H. Erickson.* New York: Grune and Stratton, 1967.

Hallam, R., Rachman, S., & Falkowski, W. Subjective, attitudinal and physiological effects of electrical aversion therapy. *Behavior Research and Therapy,* 1972, *10,* 1-13.

Hernstein, R. J. Method and theory in the study of avoidance. *Psychological Review,* 1969, *76,* 49-69.

Johnson, S. M., & White, G. Self-observation as an agent of behavioral change. *Behavior Therapy,* 1971, *2* (4), 488-497.

Jung, C. G. *Collected works.* London: Routledge and Kegan Paul, 1953

Kazdin, A. E. The effects of suggestion and pre-testing on avoidance reduction in fearful subjects. *Journal of Behavior Therapy and Experimental Psychiatry,* 1973, *4,* 213-221.

Lader, M. H., Gelder, M. G., & Marks, I. Palmar conductance measures as predictors of response to desensitization. *Journal of Psychosomatic Research,* 1967, *11,* 283-290.

Lader, M. H., & Mathews, A. M. A physiological model of phobic anxiety and desensitization. *Behavior Therapy and Research,* 1968, *6,* 411-421.

Lang, P. J. The mechanics of desensitization and the laboratory study of human fear. In C. Franks (Ed.), *Behavior Therapy: Appraisal and Status.* New York: McGraw-Hill, 1969.

Lazarus, A. On assertive behavior: A brief note. *Behavior Therapy,* 1973, *4,* 697-699.

Locke, E. A. Is behavior therapy behavioristic? *Psychological Bulletin,* 1971, 76, 5, 318-327.

LoPiccolo, W. C., & Lobitz, J. New methods in the behavioral treatment of sexual dysfunction. *Behavior Therapy and Experimental Psychiatry,* 1972, *3,* 265-271.

MacFall, R. M. The effects of self-monitoring on normal smoking behavior. *Journal of Consulting and Clinical Psychology,* 1970, *35,* 135-142.

MacFall, R. M., & Hammen, C. C. Motivation, structure, and self monitoring: The role of nonspecific factors in smoking reduction. *Journal of Consulting and Clinical Psychology,* 1971, *37,* 80-86.

Mahoney, M. J., Moura, N. G. M., & Wade, J. C. The relative efficacy of self reward, self punishment and self monitoring techniques for weight loss. *Journal of Consulting and Clinical Psychology,* in press.

Mahoney, M. J., & Thoresen, C. E., Behavioral self-control: Power to the person. Unpublished manuscript, Stanford University, 1972.

Marquis, J. N. Orgasmic reconditioning: Changing sexual object choice through controlling masturbatory fantasies. *Journal of Behavior Therapy and Experimental Psychiatry,* 1970, *1,* 263-271.

Marston, A. Dealing with low self-confidence. *Educational Research,* 1968, *10,* 134-138.

Masters, W. H., & Johnson, V. E. *Human Sexual Inadequacy,* Boston: Little, Brown, 1970.

Mathews, A. Psychophysiological approaches to the investigation of desensitization and related procedures. *Psychological Bulletin,* 1971, *76,* 73-91.

Meichenbaum, D. H. Cognitive factors in behavior modification: Modifying what clients say to themselves. In C. M. Franks & G. T. Wilson, (Eds.), *Annual Review of Behavior Therapy,* New York: Brunner-Mazel, 1973.

Miller, N. E. Some implications of modern behavior theory for personality change and psychotherapy. In D. Byrne and P. Worchel (Eds.), *Personality Change.* New York: Wiley, 1964.

Miller, N. E., & Murray, E. J. Displacement and conflict: Learnable drive as a basis for the steeper gradient of avoidance than of conflict. *Journal of Experimental Psychology,* 1952, *43,* 227-231.

Mischel, W. On the empirical dilemmas of psychodynamic approaches: Issues and alternatives. *Journal of Abnormal Psychology,* 1973, *82,* 335-344.

Morris, R. J., & Suckerman, K. R. Therapist warmth as a factor in automated systematic desensitization. *Journal of Consulting and Clinical Psychology,* 1974, *42,* 244-250.

Moan, C. E., & Heath, R. G. Septal stimulation for the initiation of heterosexual behavior in a homosexual male. *Behavior Therapy and Experimental Psychiatry,* 1972, *3,* 23-30.

Money, J., & Ehrhardt, A. A. *Man and Woman, Boy and Girl.* Baltimore: John Hopkins Press, 1973.

Mowrer, O. H. On the dual nature of learning: A re-interpretation of "conditioning" and "problem solving." *Harvard Educational Review,* 1947, *17,* 102-148.

Orne, M. T. Hypnosis, motivation and the ecological validity of the psychological experiment. In W. J. Arnold and M. M. Page (Eds.), *Nebraska Symposium on Motivation,* Lincoln: University of Nebraska Press, 1970.

Orne, M. T., & Scheibe, K. E. The contribution of nondeprivation factors in the production of sensory deprivation effects. *Journal of Abnormal Social Psychology,* 1964, *68,* 3-12.

Paul, G. L. Physiological effects of relaxation training and hypnotic suggestion. *Journal of Abnormal Psychology,* 1969, *74,* 425-437.

Perls, F. *Gestalt Therapy Verbatim.* Lafayette, Ca.: Real People Press, 1969.

Peterson, D. R. *The Clinical Study of Social Behavior.* New York: Appleton-Century Crofts, 1968.

Reed, L. Efficient deconditioning of avoidance: III. Unpublished paper, Physiological Psychology Laboratory, Bradley University, Peoria, Ill., 1974.

Reitz, W. E. & Keil, W. E. Behavioral treatment of an exhibitionist. *Behavior Therapy and Experimental Psychiatry,* 1971, *2,* 67-69.

Rosehan, D. L. On being sane in insane places. *Science,* 1973, *179,* 250-258.

Seligman, M. E. P. Fall into helplessness. *Psychology Today,* 1973, *7,* 43-48.

Seligman, M. E. P. Phobias and preparedness. *Behavior Therapy,* 1971, *2,* 307-320.

Seligman, W. A., Parental background of male homosexuals and heterosexuals. *Archives of Sexual Behavior,* 1974, *3,* (1), 1-18.

Serber, M. Shame aversion therapy. *Behavior Therapy and Experimental Psychiatry.* 1970, *1,* 213-215.

Serber, M. Teaching the nonverbal components of assertive training. *Journal of Behavior Therapy and Experimental Psychiatry,* 1972, *3,* 179-183.

Shapiro, A. Placebo effects in medicine, psychotherapy, and psychoanalysis. In A. E. Bergin, & S. L. Garfield, (Eds.), *Handbook of Psychotherapy and Behavior Change.* New York: Wiley, 1971.

Skinner, B. F. *Science and human behavior.* New York: Macmillan, 1953.

Strupp, H. H., & Bloxom, A. L. Preparing lower-class patients for group psychotherapy. *Journal of Consulting and Clinical Psychology.* 1973, *41*, 373-384.

Stevenson, J., & Jones I. H. Behavior therapy techniques for exhibitionism, *Archives of General Psychiatry.* 1972, *27*, 239-241.

Truax, C. B., & Mitchell, K. M. Research on certain therapist interpersonal skills in relation to process and outcome. In A. E. Bergin, & S. L. Garfield, (Eds), *Handbook of Psychotherapy and Behavior Change.* New York: Wiley, 1971.

Wickramasekera, I. Sexual exhibitionism: The application of learning theory to the treatment of a case of sexual exhibitionism. *Psychotherapy: Theory, Research, and Practice,* 1968, *5* (2), 108-112.

Wickramasekera, I. Desensitization, re-sensitization and desensitization again. *Behavior Therapy and Experimental Psychiatry,* 1970, *1*, 257-262.

Wickramasekera, I. A brief (2 sessions) technique for controlling a certain type of sexual exhibitionism. *Psychotherapy, Research and Practice.* 1972, *9*, 207-210.

Wickramasekera, I. Verbal instructions, hypnosis and behavior change. Unpublished paper. 1973. (a)

Wickramasekera, I. The modification of hypnotic behavior. Unpublished paper, 1973. (b)

Wickramasekera, I. Heart rate feedback and the control of cardiac neurosis. *Journal of Abnormal Psychology,* 1974, *83*, 578-580. (a)

Wickramasekera, I. "In vivo" aversive behavior rehearsal (I-V-ABR) and vicarious aversive behavior rehearsal (V-ABR) for sexual exhibitionism. *Biofeedback, Behavior Therapy and Hypnosis,* unpublished paper, 1974, (b)

Wilkins, W. Desensitization: Social and cognitive factors underlying the effectiveness of Wolpe's procedure. *Psychological Bulletin,* 1971, *76*, 311-317.

Wilson, G. T., & Davison, G. Aversion technique in behavior therapy. *Journal of Consulting and Clinical Psychology.* 1969, *33*, 327-329.

Wolpe, J., et al. *The conditioning therapies.* New York: Holt, Rinehart & Winston, 1964.

Zukerman, M. Physiological measures of sexual arousal in the human. *Psychological Bulletin,* 1971, *75*, 297-329.

Part I

THE MANAGEMENT OF AVERSIVE AROUSAL

The Contribution of Nondeprivation Factors in the Production of Sensory Deprivation Effects: The Psychology of the "Panic Button"

Martin T. Orne
Harvard Medical School, Boston
Karl E. Scheibe
University of California, Berkeley

It seems reasonable to view the subject in a psychological experiment as a social as well as an experimental animal. To do so, however, makes necessary a distinction between that part of the subject's behavior which is a function of the experimental variable under analysis and that part which is tied to his perception of the experiment as a social situation.

To support this view, Orne (1959b) has shown that subjects in hypnosis experiments behave in a way that is largely congruent with their preconceptions of hypnosis. Orne (1959a; 1962), in developing the concept of "demand characteristics," has also suggested that the results of many psychological experiments are liable to be biased by those cues, both implicit and explicit, that communicate to the subject what is expected of him in the experimental situation.

The results of any experiment involving human subjects are seen to include at least two distinct components. The first, which may be called the true experimental effect, is entirely contingent upon the antecedence of the independent variable. The second is induced by the social cues that attend the experimental situation and is unrelated to the independent variable. An analogy may aptly be drawn to the distinction between "real" and "placebo" effects in pharmacological research, where it is first necessary to discern the extent and direction of the placebo component before a meaningful conclusion can be drawn about the real effect.

Research findings on sensory deprivation are likely to be subject to the kind of bias here described. Little attempt has been made to separate those aspects of the reactions to sensory deprivation actually due to the diminution of sensory input from those due to the matrix of social cues surrounding the experimental situation.

Since the first studies at McGill University in 1951, there have been many attempts to delineate and account for the effects of prolonged sensory deprivation. Experimental techniques have been devised to reduce insofar as possible all forms of external stimulation. The McGill research employed a sound-damped cubicle: the subject rests on a soft bed, wearing translucent goggles over his eyes and cardboard gauntlets over his forearms and hands (Bexton, Heron, & Scott, 1954). Another technique involves placing normal subjects in tank-type respirators, so that movement is restricted and external sources of stimulation are rendered fairly homogeneous (Leiderman, Mendelson, Wexler, & Solomon, 1958). A third technique consists of prolonged total immersion in a tank of water at body temperature, with the subject using a face mask for breathing (Lilly, 1956). With a very few exceptions (Vernon & McGill, 1957; Zubek, Sansom, & Prysiazniuk, 1960) these procedures have produced significant changes in behavior, usually in the form of a decrement in psychological efficiency.

Bexton et al. (1954) report a general cognitive deterioration under the McGill conditions. Deprivation subjects showed decrements on a number of pre- and postisolation cognitive tasks. Subjects reported an intenseness of visual imagery, an inability to concentrate, and spatial and temporal disorientation. Scott, Bexton, Heron, and Doane (1959) and Doane, Mahatoo, Heron, and Scott (1959) provide further evidence on several more testing instruments, including some of the perceptual-motor variety. The findings of Vernon, McGill, Gulick, and Candland (1961) have been less striking, but the general tenor of their conclusions is the same. Likewise, studies by Zubek et al. (1960) and Zubek, Pushkar, Sansom, and Gowing (1961) show an impairment of mental functioning along the lines noted above. A remark by Hebb (1958) perhaps best epitomizes the

---

*One notable exception is the work of Jackson (1960; Jackson & Kelly, 1962) who explored the role of "indirect suggestion" in the production of sensory deprivation effects.

findings of these studies: "Without physical pain, without drugs, the personality can be badly deformed simply by modifying the perceptual environment [p. 110]."

An alternative view of these data would be that at least in part the dramatic effects could be a function of the demand characteristics of the experimental situation. Thus, the cues in the experimental procedure itself would communicate to the subject the behavior expected of him.

There is evidence in an experiment by Kandel, Myers, and Murphy (1958) that preparing a subject for probable hallucinations significantly affects the frequency of hallucinations. This preparation was accomplished by verbal instructions. However, such devices as "panic buttons" in experiments (Vernon et al., 1961; Zubek et al., 1961) are in a sense eloquent "instructions." The use of such a device increases the subject's expectation that something intolerable may occur, and, with it, the likelihood of a bad experience.

Indeed, it is possible to refer to many potential role cues of greater or lesser subtlety. In an experiment by Freedman, Grunebaum, and Greenblatt (1961), subjects were required to sign a forbidding release form prior to participation. Psychiatric screenings have been commonly used to single out individuals who might be harmed by an experiment, and physical examinations have been given to make sure of the subject's ability to withstand experimental stress. Even the existence of such experimental accouterments as observation mirrors and microphones has a potential cue value. As one of our own subjects remarked, "If you didn't expect to see or hear something unusual, why were you looking and listening?"

It should be made clear that the experiment to be described was *not* designed to test any hypothesis about the *nature* of sensory deprivation. Rather it was aimed at calling attention to a set of variables which must be considered in evaluating that phenomenon. The postulate that certain cues increase the likelihood of occurrence of a predicted effect is easily converted into an empirical question: If the cues attending the typical sensory deprivation experiment are retained *while no sensory deprivation takes place,* is it still possible to produce effects similar to those produced in such an experiment?

Method

Subjects

Subjects were recruited for "a psychological experiment in Meaning Deprivation" through the placement services of colleges and universities in the Boston area. Each subject was paid $2 an hour plus transportation costs. In order to correspond more closely with the practice in most previous sensory deprivation experiments, only male college students ranging in age from 18 to 25 were used. Subjects were excluded who had previously participated in sensory deprivation experiments or who were too familiar with sensory deprivation experiment results.* Twenty subjects in all took part; each was assigned alternately to the experimental and control groups, with 10 subjects comprising each group.

Procedure for Experimental Group

All subjects who called to volunteer were told that the experimental session would last an indefinite period of time, and that in order for the subject to participate, it would be necessary for him to reserve an entire day or entire evening. He was also told that the experiment was to be performed at a psychiatric hospital.

When the subject arrived there he was greeted by the experimenter, dressed in a white medical coat. Prior to giving instructions, the experimenter asked the subject briefly about his medical history, asked him whether he had a history of dizziness, or fainting spells, and so on. An aura of great seriousness and importance was maintained throughout this introductory period. As a prop to reinforce the subject's notion that great caution was necessary in the experiment, a tray of drugs and medical instruments, labeled "Emergency Tray" was in full view. No direct reference was ever made to this tray unless the subject asked, and then he was told that this was one of the precautionary measures taken for the experiment, and that he had nothing to worry about.

At the conclusion of the introductory remarks, the following set of instructions, a composite of the instructions used in other sensory deprivation experiments, was read to the subject:

" The experiment for which you have volunteered has as its object the determination of the psychological consequences of a special kind of deprivation procedure.

"There are three parts to the experiment: Testing Period I, the Experimental Deprivation Condition, and Testing Period II. You will receive special instructions in the testing periods.

---

*Four subjects were thus eliminated. One further subject was dropped because he was not only unable to perform two of the pretests—one involving a reversible figure and the other a mirror tracing task—but had great difficulty even in understanding the instructions.

"During the deprivation period, which will last an undisclosed length of time, you will have an optional task involving adding numbers, the full instructions for which will be explained once we enter the chamber.

"While you are in the chamber, you will be under constant observation. Also, there will be a microphone through which anything you might say will be recorded. It is important that you report your experiences freely and completely. You are not expected to talk a great deal, but you should report any visual imagery, fantasies, special or unusual feelings, difficulties in concentration, hallucinations, feelings of disorientation, or the like. Such experiences are not unusual under the conditions to which you are to be subjected.

"If at any time you feel very discomforted, you may obtain release immediately by pressing the button which I will show you once we enter the chamber (by knocking on the window for control subjects). Do not hesitate to use this button if the situation becomes difficult (this sentence deleted for control subjects). However, try to stick it out if you can.

"Should you feel upset, or should anything untoward develop, a physician is immediately at hand (this sentence deleted for control subjects).

"Remember, I should like you to pay special attention to any special visual or other sensations, or feelings of disorientation, and to report these experiences as they happen.

"Do you have any questions?"

At the conclusion of the instructions, questions were answered if at all possible by referring to portions of the written instructions. The subject was then asked to sign a release form that was almost identical in detail with the one used by Freedman et al. (1961). It was worded so as to relieve the Massachusetts Mental Health Center and all affiliated organizations and personnel from legal responsibility for consequences of the experiment. All experimental subjects signed the form, although some were a little reluctant to do so.

Next, the subjects' blood pressure and pulse count were recorded. These measures were also taken for control subjects, who were told, however, that it was being done only because it was part of the procedure for experimental subjects. After this, subjects were given the pretest battery to be described below. At the conclusion of the battery they were allowed to go to the bathroom, after which they were accompanied by the experimenter to the "isolation chamber."

The isolation chamber was a quiet room 6 X 7 X 8 feet in dimension. It was furnished simply with a large oak desk and two comfortable chairs. Beige drapes covered a small, shaded window above the desk, but the room was amply lighted by a circular fluorescent fixture. One wall was fitted with a 2 X 4 foot observation mirror, the function of which was explained to the subject upon entering.

On the desk were a number of objects: a thermos of ice water, a glass, and a sandwich; a microphone; a stack of approximately 2,000 sheets of paper containing numbers; a red pushbutton mounted on a board and labeled "Emergency Alarm."

In the instruction period the subject was informed that the food and water were for his convenience, and that he could partake of them at any time. He was told further that the microphone was sensitive enough to pick up anything said in the room, and that he should comment upon the experience whenever he felt so inclined.

Each sheet of paper containing numbers was made up of eight columns of single random digits. The subject was told that, as an optional task, he could add the adjacent digits in the columns, and record the sum in the space between them. It was made clear to him that he might do as much or as little of this task as he pleased, and that he did not have to do it at all if he did not want to. He was instructed, however, to confine his use of paper and pencil to the prescribed optional activity. In addition, he was requested to remain awake throughout the period, but was assured that if he really became sleepy, it was permissible to go to sleep.

The subject was finally informed that by pressing the pushbutton, which was shown to activate a loud alarm, he would obtain release from the experiment.

Upon completing the instructions, the experimenter asked the subject if everything was clear to him; if it was, the experimenter left, audibly locking the door behind him.

The room, it should be pointed out, could hardly be construed as a sensory deprivation environment. Voices and footsteps could be heard from other parts of the building, and at various times the sound of automobiles, airplanes, and the chirping of birds outside were clearly audible. The room was well lighted and large enough for the subject to move about freely; movements were not prohibited by the instructions.

After the subject had been in the room for exactly 4 hours, the experimenter returned to carry out an interview of the type to be described below, and to run the subject again through the testing procedure: his blood pressure and pulse were rechecked; he was asked for further comments or questions at the conclusion, paid for his services, and released after he had promised not to relate details of the experiment to others. The entire procedure from the time the subject arrived to the time he left generally took 6 hours.

Procedure for Control Group

Control subjects were treated in exactly the same manner as experimental subjects except for the following particulars. First, when greeting the subject, the experimenter wore business clothes and acted in a less officious manner. The testing room, or office, was not equipped with an emergency tray, nor was the medical history interview conducted. In lieu of this, the subject was told that he was part of a control group for a sensory deprivation experiment. The usual conditions of such an experiment—translucent goggles, white noise, arm gauntlets, soft bed, and restriction of activity—were described to the subject. He was informed that he would be given exactly the same tests and receive the same instructions, with minor modifications, that experimental sensory deprivation subjects received. He was told that it was necessary to place him in the same chamber for the same period of time, so that the effects of the more restrictive sensory deprivation conditions could be differentiated from the effects of simply being left alone in a room for a period of time. He was urged to report his experiences freely and completely, and was told that recordings were being made of all his comments. After these introductory remarks, the same set of instructions was read to the control subject as was read to the experimental meaning deprivation subject (with the modifications noted in the section on procedure for the experimental group).

The cubicle was outfitted in exactly the same way, except that there was no "Emergency Alarm." Control subjects were told that if they wanted to gain release they could do so by knocking on the window.

The postexperimental treatment was the same for both groups, except that the experimenter wore a white coat for the experimental subjects.

Tests and Criteria

Several criteria were used in the selection of tests. First, the choice was made from among the approximately 75 tests that have been used by previous investigators of sensory deprivation. Second, only those tests were considered which were reported as positive indicators of sensory deprivation; that is, the results of which were significantly different for control and experimental groups. From the 25 tests that met these criteria,

10 were selected on the basis of ease and speed of administration, ease and objectivity of scoring, and availability of testing materials. Tests of both cognitive and perceptual abilities were included. Whenever possible, exactly the same tests were used as were used by previous investigators. In some cases approximations were necessary because of a lack of adequate descriptions in the reports or the uniqueness of a test. The battery which emerged was as follows. Tests are listed in order of administration. Unless otherwise noted, tests were given in exactly the same way before and after isolation.

Mirror Tracing. Subjects were instructed to trace a line around the .25-inch border of a six pointed star on a conventional mirror-drawing apparatus. The score was the number of times the traced line went out of the border. Vernon et al. (1961) found a significant decrement in the performance of this task after deprivation.

Spatial Orientation. Subjects were asked to draw a figure in response to specific commands, without seeing the paper on which they drew. For this purpose, a mirror drawing shield without the mirror was used. Instructions were as follows:

"Draw a line three inches to your left and stop. Now 90 degrees to the right of the direction you were moving, draw a line two inches and stop. Now 90 degrees to the right again, draw a line three inches and stop. Now 90 degrees to the left, draw a line three inches and stop. Now 90 degrees to the right, draw a line two inches and stop. Now 90 degrees to the right again, draw a line one inch and stop. Finally, draw a line back to your original starting position."

Figures were scored for both linear and angular deviation from the figure thus described. Doane et al. (1959) found experimental subjects exhibited significantly more angular deviation on this task, while linear deviation was apparently not scored. Linear deviation scores were included in the present experiment with the expectation that experimental subjects would also do worse on this aspect of spatial orientation.

Word Recognition. Subjects were given 90 seconds to study a list of 20 words that had been taken from words classified as AA (highest) frequency in the Thorndike–Lorge (1944) tabulation. Immediately at the conclusion of this period, subjects were instructed to circle, on a list of 70 words of similar frequency, as many of the original 20 as they recognized. After isolation, the recognition test was administered without additional opportunity for study. The score was the number of correct recognitions. This procedure was adapted from that of Zubek et al. (1960), who found significantly poorer recognition scores for experimental subjects.

Reversible Figure. Subjects were instructed to press a counter key every time there was a shift in a reversible figure. A 4 X 6 inch reproduction of the reversible staircase figure was used for this test. The score was the number of alternations in 1 minute. Significantly faster alternation cycles were found for experimental subjects by Freedman et al. (1961) and by Freedman and Greenblatt (1961).

The Digit-Symbol subtest of the Wechsler Adult Intelligence Scale. Standard administration and scoring procedures were used. Scott et al. (1959) and Davis, McCourt, and Solomon (1960) found a significant superiority in accuracy of control subjects in this task.

MacQuarrie–Morris Test of Mechanical Ability. Standard administration and scoring procedures were used. Zubek et al. (1960) and Vernon et al. (1961) found decrements for sensory deprivation subjects on motor coordination tasks very closely related to this test.

Simple Form perception. Six simple geometrical forms, completely regular, were cut from black construction paper and pasted on 10 X 10 inch neutral gray cards. These forms were: a plus sign, two parallel lines, a circle, a single straight line, an equilateral triangle, and a square. The cards were held one at a time in front of the viewer, at a distance of 12 feet. In the pretesting, subjects were asked to describe what they saw on the cards, and to note any irregularities. In the posttesting, the following instructions, identical to those used by Freedman and Greenblatt (1961), were given:

> I am going to show you some simple charts [cards], and I would like to have you tell me what each one looks like to you—not what you think it really is, but what it looks like subjectively.

Scores were obtained by subtracting the number of distortions reported in prestesting from the number reported in posttesting. No more than a single distortion was counted for each card. This test was given immediately after the subjects emerged from isolation, in congruence with the Freedman and Greenblatt procedure. These investigators found significantly more simple form distortions in experimental than in control subjects.

Size Constancy. Fifteen light gray circular disks of graduated diameter were pasted on a large sheet of dark gray cardboard and shown, from a distance of 12 feet, to the subjects who were asked to estimate which disk most approximated in size the standard disk, mounted on a similar background, and held 2 feet from the eyes. Scores were assigned in terms of the number and direction of step deviations from the standard. Doane et al. (1959) report that the subjects tend to see figures larger after deprivation. This test was pulled out of order and given right after the simple form perception test when the subject came out of the isolation chamber. This is in accord with the procedures of Doane et al. and also of Freedman and Greenblatt (1961).

Spiral Aftereffect. An 8-inch Archimedes' spiral rotating at about 40 rpm was viewed at a distance of 3 feet for 90 seconds. At a signal from the experimenter, the subject shifted his vision to an identical spiral which was stationary. Subjects were instructed to say "stop" upon cessation of the movement aftereffect thus induced. The score was the number of seconds that the effect persisted. Doane et al. (1959) report a greater duration of this effect after isolation.

Logical Deductions. Subtest 3 of the Watson-Glazer Appraisal of Critical Thinking was administered after isolation only. Standard administration and scoring procedures were used. Goldberger and Holt (1958) found that the performance of sensory deprivation subjects on this test was significantly poorer than was that of controls.

The postisolation interview was conducted in exactly the same manner for all subjects. The experimenter first called upon the subject to express, at whatever length was agreeable to him, the general nature of his experience, his feelings, thoughts, and so forth. After these comments, the experimenter asked him to estimate the time he had spent in isolation and to make an affective evaluation of the experience; the experimenter questioned the subject on the presence of anxiety, of temporal or spatial disorientation, of distortions of perception, or of perceptions of doubtful origin; finally the experimenter asked the subject to elaborate upon some of the subject's opening remarks. The information gained in this interview, together with the notes made on visual observations of the subject and recording of his spontaneous remarks, was used in forming general clinical evaluations of his behavior in the experimental situation.

Results

In Table 1 is presented summary information on the battery of 10 tests. The table includes determinations of statistical significance. Note the multiple methods of scoring for a few of the measures.

Although the preexperimental performances of the experimental and control groups were not significantly different, the analysis of covariance technique was used to take into account any systematic influence of initial values on the postexperimental comparisons. For comparisons without preexperimental components, simple *t* tests were used. In one instance the plotting of the data appeared so grossly abnormal that the distribution-free Mann-Whitney *U* test was used on difference scores. One-tailed statistical probabilities are reported (except for the one statistically insignificant instance of a mean difference in the direction opposite prediction, that is, Word Recognition). Since this report is concerned with a critical appraisal of factors involved in prior findings rather than an initial setting-forth of evidence, the 10% confidence level was selected as an appropriate alpha.

It can be observed that 6 of the 14 criteria achieve statistical significance. Note again that the mean differences of 13 of the 14 criteria are in the direction predicted.

A Mann-Whitney *U* test was performed on the summation ranks of all the 14 measures as a convenient method for summarizing the overall differences. The one-tailed probability which emerges is $p = .001$, a clear demonstration of expected effects.

Subjects' Reports and the Experimenter's Clinical Impressions

That expected differences exist between the groups is further demonstrated in Table 2, which shows for each subject the number and kind of sensory deprivation "symptom" observed or reported. Following is a brief elaboration of the criteria in the column headings. An analysis of the data reported in Table 2 indicates that experimental subjects exhibited a significantly greater number of sensory deprivation "symptoms" than did control subjects ($p=.01$, one-tailed, Man-Whitney *U* test).

Perceptual aberrations. Various reports of unusual perceptions or imaginal activity were obtained, both in subjects' spontaneous remarks and in the interview. Some examples are: "the walls of the room are starting to waver"; "the objects on the desk are becoming animated and moving about"; "the lighting in the room is growing gradually dimmer and yellower"; "the buzzing of the fluorescent light is growing alternately louder and softer, so that at times it sounds like a jackhammer"; "there are multicolored spots on the wall"; and "the numbers on the number sheets are blurring and assuming various inkblot forms." None of these experiences was especially upsetting to the subjects, nor did they appear in most cases to be more than mildly compelling. An exception is the one experi-

TABLE 1
SUMMARY AND ANALYSIS OF 10 TESTS FOR CONTROL AND EXPERIMENTAL GROUPS

Test and group	Pretest M	Posttest M	Difference statistic
Mirror Tracing (errors)			
Experimental	28.1	19.7	$F = 1.67$[a]
Control	35.8	15.2	
Spatial Orientation			
Angular deviation			
Experimental	45.7	53.9	$F = .25$[a]
Control	52.5	59.1	
Linear deviation			
Experimental	5.3	5.4	$F = 3.34*$
Control	6.4	5.7	
Word Recognition (N correct)			
Experimental	17.3	15.6	$t = .50$
Control	15.2	12.3	
Reversible Figure (rate per minute)			
Experimental	29.0	35.0	$F = 1.54$[a]
Control	20.1	25.0	
Digit Symbol (N correct)			
Experimental	98.2	109.9	$F = .05$[a]
Control	99.2	111.9	
Mechanical Ability			
Tapping speed (N completed)			
Experimental	33.9	32.2	$F = 2.26$
Control	32.9	35.0	

Table I Continued

Tracing speed (N completed)			
Experimental	55.6	52.3	$F = 4.57$*
Control	53.1	58.4	
Visual pursuit (N completed)			
Experimental	5.7	8.9	$F = .22$[a]
Control	5.7	9.2	
Simple Forms (N increment distortions)			
Experimental	—	3.1	$U = 19$**
Control	—	0.8	
Size Constancy (change in steps)			
Experimental	—	0.6	$t = 1.03$[a]
Control	—	0.0	
Spiral Aftereffect			
Duration, seconds			
Experimental	24.4	27.1	$F = .99$[a]
Control	15.6	16.1	
Absolute change			
Experimental	—	7.0	$t = 3.38$***
Control	—	2.7	
Logical Deduction (N correct)			
Experimental	—	20.3	$t = 1.64$
Control	—	22.1	

Note.—F = adjusted postexperimental scores, analysis of covariance; t = t tests, U = Mann-Whitney U test, where plot of data appeared grossly abnormal.

[a] Indicates differences between groups were in predicted direction.

*p = .05 one-tailed

**p = .01m, one-tailed.

***p = .001, nondirectional measure.

TABLE 2

OCCURRENCE OF SENSORY DEPRIVATION SYMPTOMS IN CONTROL AND EXPERIMENTAL SUBJECTS

Subject and group	Perceptual aberrations	Intellectual dullness	Affectively unpleasant	Anxiety fears	Spatial disorientation	Restlessness	Irritability	Total number of symptoms
Experimental								
E1	X	X	O	O	X	O	O	3
E2	X	O	X	X	X	X	X	6
E3	O	X	X	X	O	X	O	4
E4	X	X	X	X	X	O	O	5
E5	X	X	X	X	X	X	X	7
E6	O	X	X	X	X	X	X	6
E7	O	O	O	O	O	O	X	1
E8	X	O	O	O	O	O	O	1
E9	X	X	X	X	X	X	X	7
E10	X	X	O	X	X	X	X	6

TABLE 2 CONTINUED

Control								
C_1	O	O	O	O	O	O	O	0
C_2	X	O	O	X	O	O	O	2
C_3	O	O	O	O	O	O	O	0
C_4	O	O	X	O	X	O	O	0
C_5	X	O	O	X	O	X	O	5
C_6	O	O	O	O	O	O	X	0
C_7	X	O	O	X	O	O	X	3
C_8	O	O	O	O	O	O	O	1
C_9	O	O	O	O	O	O	X	0
C_{10}	X	X	X	X	X	X	X	7
Summary and significance								
Frequency Experimental	7	8	6	6	6	7	6	
Frequency Control	4	1	2	4	2	2	3	
Fisher exact p	.11	<.01	.06	.33	.06	<.05	.35	

Note.—See text for discussion of categories.
Mean positive entries: Experimental group, 4.5; Control group, 1.8.
$U = 16.5$, $p = .01$, one-tailed.

mental subject who terminated by pressing the panic button, and who gave "disorganization of senses" as one of his reasons for ending the experiment.

Intellectual dullness. Generally, this refers to a report by the subject that he experienced marked difficulty in concentration. Typically, those who complained of this said that there was little difficulty at first, but that after about half the period they became unable, even with considerable effort, to think for more than a few seconds on any serious topic. Also included in this category are reports of "blank periods" when the subject could not remember thinking of anything, and which he characterized as being extremely vague and abstract.

Affectively unpleasant. In the interview, subjects were asked to make an overall evaluation of the pleasantness or unpleasantness of the experience. Reports ranged from extremely unpleasant to extremely pleasant. Positive entries in this column indicate a report of mildly unpleasant or worse.

Anxiety or fears. Positive entries in this column denote a report of thoughts of being forgotten, or of being inadvertently left in the room for a long time, or of being trapped while the building burned down. Several subjects reported claustrophobic anxiety.

Spatial disorientation. Included here are reports of the relative dimensions of the room seeming to change, or of the size of the subject in relation to the room seeming to change, or more general comments of confusion or amnesia regarding the location of the room in the building or of the building in the city.

Restlessness. Ratings of restlessness were based on reports by some subjects that they began wondering whether the experiment was worth the money, entertaining semihostile thoughts regarding the experimenter, or having serious impulses to end the experiment. Usually, the reports indicated that such irritability was rather short-lived and not serious, and none of the subjects was overtly hostile to the experimenter upon completion of the experiment.

It will be noted in Table 2 that there are two apparent reversals in each group. An example of these is the final subject in the control group who was in fact quite upset by the experience, and terminated it by knocking on the window 3 minutes before the end of the 4-hour period. Excepting these two reversals, however, the resulting clinical impressions for the two groups were distinct and consistent.

The control group subject typically started his isolation period by inspecting the room, looking through the drawers in the desk, then settling in one of the chairs, and beginning to add the numbers. After this, the pattern of activity would generally consist of long periods of repose interspersed with moderate amounts of activity on the serial additions. These subjects gave the impression, while in the chamber, of being in every way relaxed and in a pleasant frame of mind. The rate of verbalization was lower for control than for experimental subjects; typically there was but a single rather long comment at the beginning telling the experimenter how the subject intended to occupy his time while in the chamber.

In marked contrast to the repose of the controls was the general behavior of the experimental subjects. They usually began the experiment in much the same way as controls: inspection followed by some adding of numbers. But, after the first hour there would ensue a marked restlessness, a decrease in the performance of serial additions, frequent comments of displeasure at some aspect of the experience, or remarks indicating concern over lack of time sense. Occasionally experimental subjects would try to sleep, but with little success. Some exercised, while others undertook an intense and minute inspection of the room. Viewed in relation to the controls, these subjects gave an impression of almost being tortured. While the control group seemed to alternate between quiet contemplation and work with numbers, experimental subjects seemed to fluctuate between periods of unpleasant restlessness and abstract, vague periods of total inactivity.

Discussion

These findings demonstrate that subjects' behavior can be differentially manipulated by altering the implicit and explicit cues in the experimental situation, and further that subjects may react to social cues, or demand characteristics, in such a way as to confound experimental results.

In the light of our findings, it would seem plausible to suggest that an important confounding variable may be present in much of the reported sensory deprivation research. (Our data yield no evidence, of course, regarding the effect of actual restriction of sensory input. It is possible that many aspects of the reported phenomena in sensory deprivation studies *are* due to the restriction of sensory input.) Our data emphasize the need for further research to determine the actual extent to which the reported "sensory deprivation phenomena" are related to the decrement of sensory input.

In any experiment, the subject's reaction may be viewed as resulting from both the actual treatment (restriction of sensory input by means of gauntlets, goggles, special chambers, etc.) and the social situation created by the setting in which the experiment is conducted, the instructions used, and the cue characteristics of the treatment operations themselves. For example, in our particular experiment the treatment was not that of sensory deprivation, but, rather, of 4-hour isolation. At the same time, the situation (demand characteristics) was deliberately varied for the control and the experimental groups. We interpret our data to mean that four hours of isolation coupled with differing sets of demand characteristics yield different experimental results.

The demonstrated effectiveness of demand characteristics in this or any experiment is not taken to indicate that subjects openly and willfully cooperate with the experimenter. Rather, it is likely that social cues can determine the subject's actual experience in the situation. There is reason to believe that the subjects in the Meaning Deprivation experimental condition actually did experience considerable discomfort. The demand characteristics communicated to the subjects that they would feel discomfort despite any efforts to forestall discomfort. It must be remembered that in order for this communication to be effective, the treatment conditions must be such that they might reasonably be expected to produce just those effects suggested by the pre-experimental cues. This is to say that treatment conditions in themselves communicate crucial social cues and that these are assimilated with the other social cues in the experimental setting to form the demand characteristics of the particular experiment. If both these components of demand characteristics consistently provide an expectation of discomfort and a decrement in performance, then it is likely that the subject's experience as well as his behavior will be constrained by these demands: A distinction is to be made between behavior constrained in this fashion and conscious cooperation (Sarbin, 1950).

The main difficulty in designing definitive sensory deprivation experiments is the inevitable close relationship between the alterations in the physical environment that are necessary to decrease sensory input and the demand characteristics communicated by their use. In order to create the treatment of sensory deprivation, goggles, gauntlets, and various other devices have to be employed. Their use provides obvious cues as to how the subject is expected to behave in the situation.

These considerations suggest that a feasible approach would be to utilize conditions of maximal deprivation while varying the demand characteristics. It is possible to structure the situation so that different groups perceive the restriction as a means to a variety of experimental purposes. It is not possible to eliminate demand characteristics, but they can be varied with relative ease. Cues provided by the deprivation manipulations themselves must remain fairly constant, but the other cues can be systematically varied, thereby creating a variety of totally distinct sets of demand characteristics for different groups. Such studies would go far toward clarifying the actual effects of reduced sensory input.

References

Bexton, W. H., Heron, W., & Scott, T. H. Effects of decreased variation in the sensory environment. *Canad. J. Psychol.*, 1954, *8*, 70-77.

Davis, J. M., McCourt, W. F., & Solomon, P. Effect of visual stimulation on hallucinations and other mental experience during sensory deprivation. *Amer. J. Psychiat.*, 1960, *116*, 889-892.

Doane, B. K. Mahatoo, W., Heron, W., & Scott, T. H. Changes in perceptual function after isolation. *Canad. J. Psychol.*, 1959, *13*, 210-219.

Freedman, S. J., & Greenblatt, M. Studies in human isolation: I. Perceptual findings. *U. S. Armed Forces Med. J.*, 1961, *11*, 1330-1348.

Freedman, S. J., Grunebaum, H. U., & Greenblatt, M. Perceptual and cognitive changes in sensory deprivation. In P. Solomon et al. (Eds.), *Sensory deprivation: A symposium held at Harvard Medical School.* Cambridge: Harvard Univer. Press, 1961. Pp. 58-71.

Goldberger, L., & Holt, R. R. Experimental interference with reality contact (perceptual isolation): Method and group results. *J. Nerv. Ment. Dis.*, 1958, *127*, 99-112.

Hebb, D. O. The motivating effects of exteroceptive stimulation. *Amer. Psychologist*, 1958, *13*, 109-113.

Jackson, C. W. An exploratory study of the role of suggestion in research on sensory deprivation. Unpublished doctoral dissertation, University of Michigan, 1960.

Jackson, C. W., & Kelly, E. L. Influence of suggestion and subjects' prior knowledge in research on sensory deprivation. *Science*, 1962, *135*, 211-212.

Kandel, E. J., Myers, T. I., & Murphy, D. B. Influence of prior verbalization and instructions on visual sensations reported under conditions of reduced sensory input. *Amer. Psychologist*, 1958, *13*, 334. (Abstract)

Leiderman, P. H., Mendelson, J. N., Wexler, D., & Solomon, P. Sensory deprivation: Clinical aspects *A.M.A. Arch. Intern. Med.*, 1958, *101*, 389-396.

Lilly, J. C. Mental effects of reduction of ordinary levels of physical stimuli on intact, healthy persons. *Psychiat. Res. Rep.*, 1956, *5*, 1-9.

Orne, M. T. The demand characteristics of an experimental design and their implications. Paper read at American Psychological Association, Cincinnati, September 1959. (a)

Orne, M. T. The nature of hypnosis: Artifact and essence. *J. Abnorm. Soc. Psychol.*, 1959, *58*, 277-299. (b)

Orne, M. T. On the social psychology of the psychological experiment: With particular reference to demand characteristics and their implications. *Amer. Psychologist*, 1962, *17*, 776-783.

Sarbin, T. R. Contributions to role-taking theory: I. Hypnotic behavior. *Psychol. Rev.*, 1950, *57*, 255-270.

Scott, T. H., Bexton, W. H., Heron, W., & Doane, B. K. Cognitive effects of perceptual isolation. *Canad. J. Psychol.,* 1959, *13,* 200-209.

Thorndike, E. L., & Lorge, I. *The teacher's word book of 30,000 words.* New York: Teachers College, Columbia University, Bureau of Publications, 1944.

Vernon, J. A., & McGill, T. E. The effect of sensory deprivation upon rote learning. *Amer. J. Psychol.,* 1957, *70,* 637-639.

Vernon, J. A., McGill, T. E., Gulick, W. L., & Candland, D. K. The effect of human isolation upon some perceptual and motor skills. In P. Solomon et al. (Eds.), *Sensory deprivation: A symposium held at Harvard Medical School.* Cambridge: Harvard Univer. Press, 1961. Pp. 41-57.

Zubek, J. P., Pushkar, Dolores, Sansom, Wilma, & Growing, J. Perceptual changes after prolonged sensory isolation (darkness and silence). *Canad. J. Psychol.,* 1961, *15,* 83-100.

Zubek, J. P., Sansom, Wilma, & Prysiazniuk, A. Intellectual changes during prolonged perceptual isolation (darkness and silence). *Canad. J. Psychol.,* 1960, *14,* 233-243.

Note: This study was supported in part by Contract AF 49(638)-728 from the Air Force Office of Scientific Research and in part by Public Health Research Grant M-3369, National Institute of Mental Health, United States Public Health Service.

We would like to thank Ronald Shor for his help in the analysis of the data and in the exposition of our findings. We are grateful also to Donald N. O'Connell, Emily C. Orne, and M. Brewster Smith for their many valuable suggestions and comments.

On Being Sane
in Insane Places

D. L. Rosenhan
Stanford University, Stanford

If sanity and insanity exist, how shall we know them?
The question is neither capricious nor itself insane. However much we
may be personally convinced that we can tell the normal from the
abnormal, the evidence is simply not compelling. It is commonplace, for
example, to read about murder trials wherein eminent psychiatrists for the
defense are contradicted by equally eminent psychiatrists for the prosecution on the matter of the defendant's sanity. More generally, there are a great
deal of conflicting data on the reliability, utility, and meaning of such terms
as "sanity," "insanity," "mental illness," and schizophrenia" (1). Finally, as
early as 1934, Benedict suggested that normality and abnormality are not
universal (2). What is viewed as normal in one culture may be seen as quite
aberrant in another. Thus, notions of normality and abnormality may not be
quite as accurate as people believe they are.

To raise questions regarding normality and abnormality is in no way
to question the fact that some behaviors are deviant or odd. Murder is
deviant. So, too, are hallucinations. Nor does raining such questions deny
the existence of the personal anguish that is often associated with "mental
illness." Anxiety and depression exist. Psychological suffering exists. But
normality and abnormality, sanity and insanity, and the diagnoses that
flow from them may be less substantive than many believe them to be.

At its heart, the question of whether the sane can be distinguished
from the insane (and whether degrees of insanity can be distinguished from
each other) is a simple matter: do the salient characteristics that lead to
diagnoses reside in the patients themselves or in the environments and
contexts in which observers find them? From Bleuler, through Kretchmer,
through the formulators of the recently revised *Diagnostic and Statistical
Manual* of the American Psychiatric Association, the belief has been
strong that patients present symptoms, that those symptoms can be
categorized, and, implicitly, that the sane are distinguishable from the
insane. More recently, however, this belief has been questioned. Based in

part on theoretical and anthropological considerations, but also on philosophical, legal, and therapeutic ones, the view has grown that psychological categorization of mental illness is useless at best and downright harmful, misleading and pejorative at worst. Psychiatric diagnoses, in this view, are in the minds of the observers and are not valid summaries of characteristics displayed by the observed *(3-5)*.

Gains can be made in deciding which of these is more nearly accurate by getting normal people (that is, people who do not have, and have never suffered, symptoms of serious psychiatric disorders) admitted to psychiatric hospitals and then determining whether they were discovered to be sane and, if so, how. If the sanity of such pseudopatients were always detected, there would be prima facie evidence that a sane individual can be distinguished from the insane context in which he is found. Normality (and presumably abnormality) is distinct enough that it can be recognized wherever it occurs, for it is carried within the person. If, on the other hand, the sanity of the pseudopatients were never discovered, serious difficulties would arise for those who support traditional modes of psychiatric diagnosis. Given that the hospital staff was not incompetent, that the pseudopatient had been behaving as sanely as he had been outside of the hospital, and that it had never been previously suggested that he belonged in a psychiatric hospital, such an unlikely outcome would support the view that psychiatric diagnosis betrays little about the patient but much about the environment in which an observer finds him.

This article describes such an experiment. Eight sane people gained secret admission to 12 different hospitals *(6)*. Their diagnostic experiences constitute the data of the first part of this article; the remainder is devoted to a description of their experiences in psychiatric institutions. Too few psychiatrists and psychologists, even those who have worked in such hospitals, know what the experience is like. They rarely talk about it with former patients, perhaps because they distrust information coming from the previously insane. Those who have worked in psychiatric hospitals are likely to have adapted so thoroughly to the settings that they are insensitive to the impact of that experience. And while there have been occasional reports of researchers who submitted themselves to psychiatric hospitalization *(7)*, these researchers have commonly remained in the hospitals for short periods of time, often with the knowledge of the hospital staff. It is difficult to know the extent to which they were treated like patients or like research colleagues. Nevertheless, their reports about the inside of the psychiatric hospital have been valuable. This article extends those efforts.

Pseudopatients and Their Settings

The eight pseudopatients were a varied group. One was a psychology graduate student in his twenties. The remaining seven were older and "established." Among them were three psychologists, a pediatrician, a psychiatrist, a painter, and a housewife. Three pseudopatients were women, five were men. All of them employed pseudonyms, lest their alleged diagnoses embarrass them later. Those who were in mental health professions alleged another occupation in order to avoid the special attentions that might be accorded by staff, as a matter of courtesy or caution, to ailing colleagues *(8)*. With the exception of myself (I was the first pseudopatient and my presence was known to the hospital administrator and chief psychologist and, so far as I can tell, to them alone), the presence of pseudopatients and the nature of the research program was not known to the hospital staffs *(9)*.

The settings were similarly varied. In order to generalize the findings, admission into a variety of hospitals·was sought. The 12 hospitals in the sample were located in five different states on the East and West coasts. Some were old and shabby, some were quite new. Some were research-oriented, others not. Some had good staff-patient ratios, others were quite understaffed. Only one was a strictly private hospital. All of the others were supported by state or federal funds or, in one instance, by university funds.

After calling the hospital for an appointment, the pseudopatient arrived at the admissions office complaining that he had been hearing voices. Asked what the voices said, he replied that they were often unclear, but as far as he could tell they said "empty," "hollow," and "thud." The voices were unfamiliar and were of the same sex as the pseudopatient. The choice of these symptoms was occasioned by their apparent similarity to existential symptoms. Such symptoms are alleged to arise from painful concerns about the perceived meaninglessness of one's life. It is as if the hallucinating person were saying, "My life is empty and hollow." The choice of these symptoms was also determined by the *absence* of a single report of existential psychoses in the literature.

Beyond alleging the symptoms and falsifying name, vocation, and employment, no further alterations of person, history, or circumstances were made. The significant events of the pseudopatient's life history were presented as they had actually occurred. Relationships with parents and siblings, with spouse and children, with people at work and in school, consistent with the aforementioned exceptions, were described as they were or had been. Frustrations and upsets were described along with joys and satisfactions. These facts are important to remember. If anything, they strongly biased the subsequent results in favor of detecting sanity, since none of their histories or current behaviors was seriously pathological in any way.

Immediately upon admission to the psychiatric ward, the pseudopatient ceased simulating *any* symptoms of abnormality. In some cases, there was a brief period of mild nervousness and anxiety, since none of the pseudopatients really believed that they would be admitted so easily. Indeed, their shared fear was that they would be immediately exposed as frauds and greatly embarrassed. Moreover, many of them had never visited a psychiatric ward; even those who had, nevertheless had some genuine fears about what might happen to them. Their nervousness, then, was quite appropriate to the novelty of the hospital setting, and it abated rapidly.

Apart from that short-lived nervousness, the pseudopatient behaved on the ward as he "normally" behaved. The pseudopatient spoke to patients and staff as he might ordinarily. Because there is uncommonly little to do on a psychiatric ward, he attempted to engage others in conversation. When asked by staff how he was feeling, he indicated that he was fine, that he no longer experienced symptoms. He responded to instructions from attendants, to calls for medication (which was not swallowed), and to dining-hall instructions. Beyond such activities as were available to him on the admissions ward, he spent his time writing down his observations about the ward, its patients, and the staff. Initially these notes were written "secretly," but as it soon became clear that no one much cared, they were subsequently written on standard tablets of paper in such public places as the dayroom. No secret was made of these activities.

The pseudopatient, very much as a true psychiatric patient, entered a hospital with no foreknowledge of when he would be discharged. Each was told that he would have to get out by his own devices, essentially by convincing the staff that he was sane. The psychological stresses associated with hospitalization were considerable, and all but one of the pseudopatients desired to be discharged almost immediately after being admitted. They were, therefore, motivated not only to behave sanely, but to be paragons of cooperation. That their behavior was in no way disruptive is confirmed by nursing reports, which have been obtained on most of the patients. These reports uniformly indicate that the patients were "friendly," "cooperative," and "exhibited no abnormal indications."

The Normal Are Not Detectably Sane

Despite their public "show" of sanity, the pseudopatients were never detected. Admitted, except in one case, with a diagnosis of schizophrenia *(10)*, each was discharged with a diagnosis of schizophrenia "in remission." The label "in remission" should in no way be dismissed as a formality, for at no time during any hospitalization had any question been raised about any pseudopatient's simulation. Nor are there any indications in the hospital records that the pseudopatient's status was suspect. Rather, the evidence is strong that, once labeled schizophrenic, the pseudopatient was stuck with that label. If the pseudopatient was to be discharged, he must naturally be "in remission"; but he was not sane, nor, in the institution's view, had he ever been sane.

The uniform failure to recognize sanity cannot be attributed to the quality of the hospitals, for, although there were considerable variations among them, several are considered excellent. Nor can it be alleged that there was simply not enough time to observe the pseudopatients. Length of hospitalization ranged from 7 to 52 days, with an average of 19 days. The pseudopatients were not, in fact, carefully observed, but this failure clearly speaks more to traditions within psychiatric hospitals than to lack of opportunity.

Finally, it cannot be said that the failure to recognize the pseudopatients' sanity was due to the fact that they were not behaving sanely. While there was clearly some tension present in all of them, their daily visitors could detect no serious behavioral consequences—nor, indeed, could other patients. It was quite common for the patients to "detect" the pseudopatients' sanity. During the first three hospitalizations, when accurate counts were kept, 35 of a total of 118 patients on the admissions ward voiced their suspicions, some vigorously. "You're not crazy. You're a journalist or a professor [referring to the continual note-taking]. You're checking up on the hospital." While most of the patients were reassured by the pseudopatient's insistence that he had been sick before he came in but was fine now, some continued to believe that the pseudopatient was sane throughout his hospitalization *(11)*. The fact that the patients often recognized normality when staff did not raises important questions.

Failure to detect sanity during the course of hospitalization may be due to the fact that physicians operate with a strong bias toward what statisticians call the type 2 error *(5)*. This is to say that physicians are more inclined to call a healthy person sick (a false positive, type 2) than a sick person healthy (a false negative, type 1). The reasons for this are not hard to find: it is clearly more dangerous to misdiagnose illness than health. Better to err on the side of caution, to suspect illness even among the healthy.

But what holds for medicine does not hold equally well for psychiatry. Medical illnesses, while unfortunate, are not commonly pejorative. Psychiatric diagnoses, on the contrary, carry with them personal, legal, and social stigmas *(12)*. It was therefore important to see whether the tendency toward diagnosing the sane insane could be reversed. The following experiment was arranged at a research and teaching hospital whose staff had heard these findings but doubted that such an error could occur in their hospital. The staff was informed that at some time during the following 3 months, one or more pseudopatients would attempt to be admitted into the psychiatric hospital. Each staff member was asked to rate each patient who presented himself at admissions or on the ward according to the likelihood that the patient was a pseudopatient. A 10-point scale was used, with a 1 and 2 reflecting high confidence that the patient was a pseudopatient.

Judgments were obtained on 193 patients who were admitted for psychiatric treatment. All staff who had had sustained contact with or primary responsibility for the patient—attendants, nurses, psychiatrists, physicians, and psychologists—were asked to make judgments. Forty-one patients were alleged, with high confidence, to be pseudopatients by at least one member of the staff. Twenty-three were considered suspect by at least one psychiatrist. Nineteen were suspected by one psychiatrist *and* one other staff member. Actually, no genuine pseudopatient (at least from my group) presented himself during this period.

The experiment is instructive. It indicates that the tendency to designate sane people as insane can be reversed when the stakes (in this case, prestige and diagnostic acumen) are high. But what can be said of the 19 people who were suspected of being "sane" by one psychiatrist and another staff member? Were these people truly "sane," or was it rather the case that in the course of avoiding the type 2 error the staff tended to make more errors of the first sort—calling the crazy "sane"? There is no way of knowing. But one thing is certain: any diagnostic process that lends itself so readily to massive errors of this sort cannot be a very reliable one.

The Stickiness of Psychodiagnostic Labels

Beyond the tendency to call the healthy sick—a tendency that accounts better for diagnostic behavior on admission than it does for such behavior after a lengthy period of exposure—the data speak to the massive role of labeling in psychiatric assessment. Having once been labeled schizophrenic, there is nothing the pseudopatient can do to overcome the tag. The tag profoundly colors others' perceptions of him and his behavior.

From one viewpoint, these data are hardly surprising, for it has long been known that elements are given meaning by the context in which they occur. Gestalt psychology made this point vigorously, and Asch *(13)* demonstrated that there are "central" personality traits (such as "warm" versus "cold") which are so powerful that they markedly color the meaning of other information in forming an impression of a given personality *(14)*. "Insane," "schizophrenic," "manic-depressive," and "crazy" are probably among the most powerful of such central traits. Once a person is designated abnormal, all of his other behaviors and characteristics are colored by that label. Indeed, that label is so powerful that many of the pseudopatients' normal behaviors were overlooked entirely or profoundly misinterpreted. Some examples may clarify this issue.

Earlier I indicated that there were no changes in the pseudopatient's personal history and current status beyond those of name, employment, and where necessary, vocation. Otherwise, a veridical description of personal history and circumstances was offered. Those circumstances were not psychotic. How were they made consonant with the diagnosis of psychosis? Or were those diagnoses modified in such a way as to bring them into accord with the circumstances of the pseudopatients's life, as described by him?

As far as I can determine, diagnoses were in no way affected by the relative health of the circumstances of a pseudopatient's life. Rather, the reverse occurred: the perception of his circumstances was shaped entirely by the diagnosis. A clear example of such translation is found in the case of a pseudopatient who had had a close relationship with his mother but was rather remote from his father during his early childhood. During adolescence and beyond, however, his father became a close friend, while his relationship with his mother cooled. His present relationship with his wife was characteristically close and warm. Apart from occasional angry exchanges, friction was minimal. The children had rarely been spanked. Surely there is nothing especially pathological about such a history. Indeed, many readers may see a similar pattern in their own experiences, with no markedly deleterious consequences. Observe, however, how such a history was translated in the psychopathological context, this from the case summary prepared after the patient was discharged.

> This white 39-year-old male . . . manifests a long history of considerable ambivalence in close relationships, which begins in early childhood. A warm relationship with his mother cools during his adolescence. A distant relationship to his father is described as becoming very intense. Affective stability is absent. His attempts to control emotionality with his wife and children are punctuated by angry outbursts and, in the case of the children, spankings. And while he says that he has several good friends, one senses considerable ambivalence embedded in those relationships also. . . .

The facts of the case were unintentionally distorted by the staff to achieve consistency with a popular theory of the dynamics of a schizophrenic reaction (15). Nothing of an ambivalent nature had been described in relations with parents, spouse, or friends. To the extent that ambivalence could be inferred, it was probably not greater than is found in all human relationships. It is true the pseudopatient's relationships with his parents changed over time, but in the ordinary context that would hardly be remarkable—indeed, it might very well be expected. Clearly, the meaning ascribed to his verbalizations (that is, ambivalence, affective instability) was determined by the diagnosis: schizophrenia. An entirely different meaning would have been ascribed if it were known that the man was "normal."

All pseudopatients took extensive notes publicly. Under ordinary circumstances, such behavior would have raised questions in the minds of observers, as, in fact, it did among patients. Indeed, it seemed so certain that the notes would elicit suspicion that elaborate precautions were taken to remove them from the ward each day. But the precautions proved needless. The closest any staff member came to questioning these notes occurred when one pseudopatient asked his physician what kind of medication he was receiving and began to write down the response. "You needn't write it," he was told gently. "If you have trouble remembering, just ask me again."

If no questions were asked of the pseudopatients, how was their writing interpreted? Nursing records for three patients indicate that the writing was seen as an aspect of their pathological behavior. "Patient engages in writing behavior" was the daily nursing comment on one of the pseudopatients who was never questioned about his writing. Given that the patient is in the hospital, he must be psychologically disturbed. And given that he is disturbed, continuous writing must be a behavioral manifestation of that disturbance, perhaps a subset of the compulsive behaviors that are sometimes correlated with schizophrenia.

One tacit characteristic of psychiatric diagnosis is that it locates the sources of aberration within the individual and only rarely within the complex of stimuli that surrounds him. Consequently, behaviors that are stimulated by the environment are commonly misattributed to the patient's disorder. For example, one kindly nurse found a pseudopatient pacing the long hospital corridors. "Nervous, Mr. X?" she asked. "No, bored," he said.

The notes kept by pseudopatients are full of patient behaviors that were misinterpreted by well-intentioned staff. Often enough, a patient would go "berserk" because he had, wittingly or unwittingly, been mistreated by, say, an attendant. A nurse coming upon the scene would rarely inquire even cursorily into the environmental stimuli of the patient's behavior. Rather, she assumed that his upset derived from his pathology, not from his present interactions with other staff members. Occasionally, the staff might assume that the patient's family (especially when they had recently visited) or other patients had stimulated the outburst. But never were the staff found to assume that one of themselves or the structure of the hospital had anything to do with a patient's behavior. One psychiatrist pointed to a group of patients who were sitting outside the cafeteria entrance half an hour before lunchtime. To a group of young residents he indicated that such behavior was characteristic of the oral-acquisitive nature of the syndrome. It seemed not to occur to him that there were very few things to anticipate in a psychiatric hospital besides eating.

A psychiatric label has a life and an influence of its own. Once the impression has been formed that the patient is schizophrenic, the expectation is that he will continue to be schizophrenic. When a sufficient amount of time has passed, during which the patient has done nothing bizarre, he is considered to be in remission and available for discharge. But the label endures beyond discharge, with the unconfirmed expectation that he will behave as a schizophrenic again. Such labels, conferred by mental health professionals, are as influential on the patient as they are on his relatives and friends, and it should not surprise anyone that the diagnosis acts on all of them as a self-fulfilling prophecy. Eventually, the patient himself accepts the diagnosis, with all of its surplus meanings and expectations, and behaves accordingly *(5)*.

The inferences to be made from these matters are quite simple. Much as Zigler and Phillips have demonstrated that there is enormous overlap in the symptoms presented by patients who have been variously diagnosed *(16)*, so there is enormous overlap in the behaviors of the sane and the insane. The sane are not "sane" all of the time. We lose our tempers "for no good reason." We are occasionally depressed or anxious, again for no good reason. And we may find it difficult to get along with one or another person—again for no reason that we can specify. Similarly, the insane are not always insane. Indeed, it was the impression of the pseudopatients while living with them that they were sane for long periods of time—that the bizarre behaviors upon which their diagnoses were allegedly predicated constituted only a small fraction of their total behavior. If it makes no sense to label ourselves permanently depressed on the basis of an occasional depression, then it takes better evidence than is presently available to label all patients insane or schizophrenic on the basis of bizarre behaviors or cognitions. It seems more useful, as Mischel *(17)* has pointed out, to limit our discussions to *behaviors,* the stimuli that provoke them, and their correlates.

It is not known why powerful impressions of personality traits, such as "crazy" or "insane," arise. Conceivably, when the origins of and stimuli that give rise to a behavior are remote or unknown, or when the behavior strikes us as immutable, trait labels regarding the *behaver* arise. When, on the other hand, the origins and stimuli are known and available, discourse is limited to the behavior itself. Thus, I may hallucinate because I am sleeping, or I may hallucinate because I have ingested a peculiar drug. These are termed sleep-induced hallucinations, or dreams, and drug-induced hallucinations, respectively. But when the stimuli to my hallucinations are unknown, that is called craziness, or schizophrenia—as if that inference were somehow as illuminating as the others.

The Experience of
Psychiatric Hospitalization

The term "mental illness" is of recent origin. It was coined by people who were humane in their inclinations and who wanted very much to raise the station of (and the public's sympathies toward) the psychologically disturbed from that of witches and "crazies" to one that was akin to the physically ill. And they were at least partially successful, for the treatment of the mentally ill *has* improved considerably over the years. But while treatment has improved, it is doubtful that people really regard the mentally ill in the same way that they view the physically ill. A broken leg is something one recovers from, but mental illness allegedly endures forever *(18)*. A broken leg does not threaten the observer, but a crazy schizophrenic? There is by now a host of evidence that attitudes toward the mentally ill are characterized by fear, hostility, aloofness, suspicion, and dread *(19)*. The mentally ill are society's lepers.

That such attitudes infect the general population is perhaps not surprising, only upsetting. But that they affect the professionals—attendants, nurses, physicians, psychologists, and social workers—who treat and deal with the mentally ill is more disconcerting, both because such attitudes are self-evidently pernicious and because they are unwitting. Most mental health professionals would insist that they are sympathetic toward the mentally ill, that they are neither avoidant nor hostile. But it is more likely that an exquisite ambivalence characterizes their relations with psychiatric patients, such that their avowed impulses are only part of their entire attitude. Negative attitudes are there too and can easily be detected. Such attitudes should not surprise us. They are the natural offspring of the labels patients wear and the places in which they are found.

Consider the structure of the typical psychiatric hospital. Staff and patients are strictly segregated. Staff have their own living space, including their dining facilities, bathrooms, and assembly places. The glassed quarters that contain the professional staff, which the pseudopatients came to call "the cage," sit out on every dayroom. The staff emerge primarily for caretaking purposes—to give medication, to conduct a therapy or group meeting, to instruct or reprimand a patient. Otherwise, staff keep to themselves, almost as if the disorder that afflicts their charges is somehow catching.

So much is patient-staff segregation the rule that, for four public hospitals in which an attempt was made to measure the degree to which staff and patients mingle, it was necessary to use "time out of the staff cage" as the operational measure. While it was not the case that all time spent out of the cage was spent mingling with patients (attendants, for example, would occasionally emerge to watch television in the dayroom), it was the only way in which one could gather reliable data on time for measuring.

The average amount of time spent by attendants outside of the cage was 11.3 percent (range, 3 to 52 percent). This figure does not represent only time spent mingling with patients, but also includes time spent on such chores as folding laundry, supervising patients while they shave, directing ward clean-up, and sending patients to off-ward activities. It was the relatively rare attendant who spent time talking with patients or playing games with them. It proved impossible to obtain a "percent mingling time" for nurses, since the amount of time they spent out of the cage was too brief. Rather, we counted instances of emergence from the cage. On the average, daytime nurses emerged from the cage 11.5 times per shift, including instances when they left the ward entirely (range, 4 to 39 times). Late afternoon and night nurses were even less available, emerging on the average 9.4 times per shift (range, 4 to 41 times). Data on early morning nurses, who arrived usually after midnight and departed at 8 a.m., are not available because patients were asleep during most of this period.

Physicians, especially psychiatrists, were even less available. They were rarely seen on the wards. Quite commonly, they would be seen only when they arrived and departed, with the remaining time being spent in their offices or in the cage. On the average, physicians emerged on the ward 6.7 times per day (range, 1 to 17 times). It proved difficult to make an accurate estimate in this regard, since physicians often maintained hours that allowed them to come and go at different times.

The hierarchical organization of the psychiatric hospital has been commented on before (20), but the latent meaning of that kind of organization is worth noting again. Those with the most power have least to do with patients, and those with the least power are most involved with them. Recall, however, that the acquisition of role-appropriate behaviors occurs mainly through the observation of others, with the most powerful having the most influence. Consequently, it is understandable that attendants not only spend more time with patients than do any other members of the staff—that is required by their station in the hierarchy—but also, insofar as they learn from their superiors' behavior, spend as little time with patients as they can. Attendants are seen mainly in the cage, which is where the models, the action, and the power are.

I turn now to a different set of studies, these dealing with staff response to patient-initiated contact. It has long been known that the amount of time a person spends with you can be an index of your significance to him. If he initiates and maintains eye contact, there is reason to believe that he is considering your requests and needs. If he pauses to chat or actually stops and talks, there is added reason to infer that he is individuating you. In four hospitals, the pseudopatient approached the staff member with a request which took the following form: "Pardon me, Mr. [or Dr. or Mrs.] X, could you tell me when I will be eligible for grounds privileges?" (or ". . . when I will be presented at the staff meeting?" or ". . . when I am likely to be discharged?"). While the content of the question varied according to the appropriateness of the target and the pseudopatient's (apparent) current needs, the form was always a courteous and relevant request for information. Care was taken never to approach a particular member of the staff more than once a day, lest the staff member become suspicious or irritated. In examining these data, remember that the behavior of the pseudopatients was neither bizarre nor disruptive. One could indeed engage in good coversation with them.

The data for these experiments are shown in Table 1, separately for physicians (column 1) and for nurses and attendants (column 2). Minor differences between these four institutions were overwhelmed by the degree to which staff avoided continuing contacts that patients had initiated. By far, their most common response consisted of either a brief response to the question, offered while they were "on the move" and with head averted, or no reponse at all.

The encounter frequently took the following bizarre form: (pseudo-patient) "Pardon me, Dr. X. Could you tell me when I am eligible for grounds privileges?" (physician) "Good morning, Dave. How are you today?" (Moves off without waiting for a response.)

It is instructive to compare these data with data recently obtained at Stanford University. It has been alleged that large and eminent universities are characterized by faculty who are so busy that they have no time for students. For this comparison, a young lady approached individual faculty members who seemed to be walking purposefully to some meeting or teaching engagement and asked them the following six questions.

1) "Pardon me, could you direct me to Encina Hall?" (at the medical school: ". . . to the Clinical Research Center?").

2) "Do you know where Fish Annex is?" (there is no Fish Annex at Stanford).

3) "Do you teach here?"

4) "How does one apply for admission to the college?" (at the medical school: ". . . to the medical school?").

5) "Is it difficult to get in?"

6) "Is there financial aid?"

Without exception, as can be seen in Table 1 (column 3), all of the questions were answered. No matter how rushed they were, all respondents not only maintained eye contact, but stopped to talk. Indeed, many of the respondents went out of their way to direct or take the questioner to the office she was seeking, to try to locate "Fish Annex," or to discuss with her the possibilities of being admitted to the university.

Similar data, also shown in Table 1 (columns 4, 5, and 6), were obtained in the hospital. Here too, the young lady came prepared with six questions. After the first question, however, she remarked to 18 of her respondents (column 4), "I'm looking for a psychiatrist," and to 15 others (column 5), "I'm looking for an internist." Ten other respondents received no inserted comment (column 6). The general degree of cooperative responses is considerably higher for these university groups than it was for

TABLE 1. SELF-INITIATED CONTACT BY PSEUDOPATIENTS WITH PSYCHIATRISTS AND NURSES AND ATTENDANTS, COMPARED TO CONTACT WITH OTHER GROUPS.

Contact	Psychiatric hospitals		University campus (nonmedical)	University medical center		
					Physicians	
	(1) Psychiatrists	(2) Nurses and attendants	(3) Faculty	(4) "Looking for a psychiatrist"	(5) "Looking for an internist"	(6) No additional comment
Responses						
Moves on, head averted (%)	71	88	0	0	0	0
Makes eye contact (%)	23	10	0	11	0	0
Pauses and chats (%)	2	2	0	11	0	10
Stops and talks (%)	4	0.5	100	78	100	90
Mean number of questions answered (out of 6)	*	*	6	3.8	4.8	4.5
Respondents (No.)	13	47	14	18	15	10
Attempts (No.)	185	1283	14	18	15	10

*Not applicable.

pseudopatients in psychiatric hospitals. Even so, differences are apparent within the medical school setting. Once having indicated that she was looking for a psychiatrist, the degree of cooperation elicited was less than when she sought an internist.

Powerlessness and Depersonalization

Eye contact and verbal contact reflect concern and individuation; their absence, avoidance and depersonalization. The data I have presented do not do justice to the rich daily encounters that grew up around matters of depersonalization and avoidance. I have records of patients who were beaten by staff for the sin of having initiated verbal contact. During my own experience, for example, one patient was beaten in the presence of other patients for having approached an attendant and told him, "I like you." Occasionally, punishment meted out to patients for misdemeanors seemed so excessive that it could not be justified by the most radical interpretations of psychiatric canon. Nevertheless, they appeared to go unquestioned. Tempers were often short. A patient who had not heard a call for medication would be roundly excoriated, and the morning attendants would often wake patients with, "Come on, you m-----f-----s, out of bed!"

Neither anecdotal nor "hard" data can convey the overwhelming sense of powerlessness which invades the individual as he is continually exposed to the depersonalization of the psychiatric hospital. It hardly matters *which* psychiatric hospital—the excellent public ones and the very plush private hospital were better than the rural and shabby ones in this regard, but, again, the features that psychiatric hospitals had in common overwhelmed by far their apparent differences.

Powerlessness was evident everywhere. The patient is deprived of many of his legal rights by dint of his psychiatric commitment *(21)*. He is shorn of credibility by virtue of his psychiatric label. His freedom of movement is restricted. He cannot initiate contact with the staff, but may only respond to such overtures as they make. Personal privacy is minimal. Patient quarters and possessions can be entered and examined by any staff member, for whatever reason. His personal history and anguish is available to any staff member (often including the "grey lady" and "candy striper" volunteer) who chooses to read his folder, regardless of their therapeutic relationship to him. His personal hygiene and waste evacuation are often monitored. The water closets may have no doors.

At times, depersonalization reached such proportions that pseudopatients had the sense that they were invisible, or at least unworthy of account. Upon being admitted, I and other pseudopatients took the initial physical examinations in a semipublic room, where staff members went about their own business as if we were not there.

On the ward, attendants delivered verbal and occasionally serious physical abuse to patients in the presence of other observing patients, some of whom (the pseudopatients) were writing it all down. Abusive behavior, on the other hand, terminated quite abruptly when other staff members were known to be coming. Staff are credible witnesses. Patients are not.

A nurse unbuttoned her uniform to adjust her brassiere in the presence of an entire ward of viewing men. One did not have the sense that she was being seductive. Rather, she didn't notice us. A group of staff persons might point to a patient in the dayroom and discuss him animatedly, as if he were not there.

One illuminating instance of depersonalization and invisibility occurred with regard to medications. All told, the pseudopatients were administered nearly 2100 pills, including Elavil, Stelazine, Compazine, and Thorazine, to name but a few. (That such a variety of medications should have been adminstered to patients presenting identical symptoms is itself worthy of note.) Only two were swallowed. The rest were either pocketed or deposited in the toilet. The pseudopatients were not alone in this. Although I have no precise records on how many patients rejected their medications, the pseudopatients frequently found the medications of other patients in the toilet before they deposited their own. As long as they were cooperative, their behavior and the pseudopatients' own in this matter, as in other important matters, went unnoticed throughout.

Reactions to such depersonalization among pseudopatients were intense. Although they had come to the hospital as participant observers and were fully aware that they did not "belong," they nevertheless found themselves caught up in and fighting the process of depersonalization. Some examples: a graduate student in psychology asked his wife to bring his textbooks to the hospital so he could "catch up on his homework"—this despite the elaborate precautions taken to conceal his professional association. The same student, who had trained for quite some time to get into the hospital, and who had looked forward to the experience, "remembered" some drag races that he had wanted to see on the weekend and insisted that he be discharged by that time. Another pseudopatient attempted a romance with 'a nurse. Subsequently, he informed the staff that he was applying for admission to graduate school in psychology and was very likely to be admitted, since a graduate professor was one of his regular hospital visitors. The same person began to engage in psychotherapy with other patients—all of this as a way of becoming a person in an impersonal environment.

The Sources of Depersonalization

What are the origins of depersonalization? I have already mentioned two. First are attitudes held by all of us toward the mentally ill—including those who treat them—attitudes characterized by fear, distrust, and horrible expectations on the one hand, and benevolent intentions on the other. Our ambivalence leads, in this instance as in others, to avoidance.

Second, and not entirely separate, the hierarchical structure of the psychiatric hospital facilitates depersonalization. Those who are at the top have least to do with patients, and their behavior inspires the rest of the staff. Average daily contact with psychiatrists, psychologists, residents, and physicians combined ranged from 3.9 to 25.1 minutes, with an overall mean of 6.8 (six pseudopatients over a total of 129 days of hospitalization). Included in this average are time spent in the admissions interview, ward meetings in the presence of a senior staff member, group and individual psychotherapy contacts, case presentation conferences, and discharge meetings. Clearly, patients do not spend much time in interpersonal contact with doctoral staff. And doctoral staff serve as models for nurses and attendants.

There are probably other sources. Psychiatric installations are presently in serious financial straits. Staff shortages are pervasive, staff time at a premium. Something has to give, and that something is patient contact. Yet, while financial stresses are realities, too much can be made of them. I have the impression that the psychological forces that result in depersonalization are much stronger than the fiscal ones and that the addition of more staff would not correspondingly improve patient care in this regard. The incidence of staff meetings and the enormous amount of record-keeping on patients, for example, have not been as substantially reduced as has patient contact. Priorities exist, even during hard times. Patient contact is not a significant priority in the traditional psychiatric hospital, and fiscal pressures do not account for this. Avoidance and depersonalization may.

Heavy reliance upon psychotropic medication tacitly contributes to depersonalization by convincing staff that treatment is indeed being conducted and that further patient contact may not be necessary. Even here, however, caution needs to be exercised in understanding the role of psychotropic drugs. If patients were powerful rather than powerless, if they were viewed as interesting individuals rather than diagnostic entities, if they were socially significant rather than social lepers, if their anguish truly and wholly compelled our sympathies and concerns, would we not *seek* contact with them, despite the availability of medications? Perhaps for the pleasure of it all?

The Consequences of Labeling and Depersonalization

Whenever the ratio of what is known to what needs to be known approaches zero, we tend to invent "knowledge" and assume that we understand more than we actually do. We seem unable to acknowledge that we simply don't know. The needs for diagnosis and remediation of behavioral and emotional problems are enormous. But rather than acknowledge that we are just embarking on understanding, we continue to label patients "schizophrenic," "manic-depressive," and "insane," as if in those words we had captured the essence of understanding. The facts of the matter are that we have known for a long time that diagnoses are often not useful or reliable, but we have nevertheless continued to use them. We now know that we cannot distinguish insanity from sanity. It is depressing to consider how that information will be used.

Not merely depressing, but frightening. How many people, one wonders, are sane but not recognized as such in our psychiatric institutions? How many have been needlessly stripped of their privileges of citizenship, from the right to vote and drive to that of handling their own accounts? How many have feigned insanity in order to avoid the criminal consequences of their behavior, and, conversely, how many would rather stand trial than live interminably in a psychiatric hospital—but are wrongly thought to be mentally ill? How many have been stigmatized by well-intentioned, but nevertheless erroneous, diagnoses? On the last point, recall again that a "type 2 error" in psychiatric diagnosis does not have the same consequences it does in medical diagnosis. A diagnosis of cancer that has been found to be in error is cause for celebration. But psychiatric diagnoses are rarely found to be in error. The label sticks, a mark of inadequacy forever.

Finally, how many patients might be "sane" outside the psychiatric hospital but seem insane in it—not because craziness resides in them, as it were, but because they are responding to a bizarre setting, one that may be unique to institutions which harbor nether people? Goffman *(4)* calls the process of socialization to such institutions "mortification"—an apt metaphor that includes the processes of depersonalization that have been described here. And while it is impossible to know whether the pseudopatients' responses to these processes are characteristic of all inmates—they were, after all, not real patients—it is difficult to believe that these processes of socialization to a psychiatric hospital provide useful attitudes or habits of response for living in the "real world."

Summary and Conclusions

It is clear that we cannot distinguish the sane from the insane in psychiatric hospitals. The hospital itself imposes a special environment in which the meanings of behavior can easily be misunderstood. The consequences to patients hospitalized in such an environment—the powerlessness, depersonalization, segregation, mortification, and self-labeling—seem undoubtedly counter-therapeutic.

I do not, even now, understand this problem well enough to perceive solutions. But two matters seem to have some promise. The first concerns the proliferation of community mental health facilities, of crisis intervention centers, of the human potential movement, and of behavior therapies that, for all of their own problems, tend to avoid psychiatric labels, to focus on specific problems and behaviors, and to retain the individual in a relatively nonpejorative environment. Clearly, to the extent that we refrain from sending the distressed to insane places, our impressions of them are less likely to be distorted. (The risk of distorted perceptions, it seems to me, is always present, since we are much more sensitive to an individual's behaviors and verbalizations than we are to the subtle contextual stimuli that often promote them. At issue here is a matter of magnitude. And, as I have shown, the magnitude of distortion is exceedingly high in the extreme context that is a psychiatric hospital.)

The second matter that might prove promising speaks to the need to increase the sensitivity of mental health workers and researchers to the *Catch 22* position of psychiatric patients. Simply reading materials in this area will be of help to some such workers and researchers. For others, directly experiencing the impact of psychiatric hospitalization will be of enormous use. Clearly, further research into the social psychology of such total institutions will both facilitate treatment and deepen understanding.

I and the other pseudopatients in the psychiatric setting had distinctly negative reactions. We do not pretend to describe the subjective experiences of true patients. Theirs may be different from ours, particularly with the passage of time and the necessary process of adaptation to one's environment. But we can and do speak to the relatively more objective indices of treatment within the hospital. It could be a mistake, and a very unfortunate one, to consider that what happened to us derived from malice or stupidity on the part of the staff. Quite the contrary, our overwhelming impression of them was of people who really cared, who were committed, and who were uncommonly intelligent. Where they failed, as they sometimes did painfully, it would be more accurate to attribute those failures to the environment in which they, too, found themselves than to personal callousness. Their perceptions and behavior were controlled by the situation, rather than being motivated by a malicious disposition. In a more benign environment, one that was less attached to global diagnosis, their behaviors and judgments might have been more benign and effective.

References and Notes

1. P. Ash, *J. Abnorm. Soc. Psyhol. 44*, 272 (1949); A. T. Beck, *Amer. J. Psychiat. 119*, 210 (1962); A. T. Boisen, *Psychiatry 2*, 233 (1938); N. Kreitman, *J. Ment. Sci. 107*, 876 (1961); N. Kreitman, P. Sainsbury, J. Morrisey, J. Towers, J. Scrivener, *ibid.*, p. 887; H. O. Schmitt and C. P. Fonda, *J. Abnorm. Soc. Psychol. 52*, 262 (1956); W. Seeman, *J. Nerv. Ment. Dis. 118*, 541 (1953). For an analysis of these artifacts and summaries of the disputes, see J. Zubin, *Annu. Rev. Psychol. 18*, 373 (1967); L. Phillips and J. G. Draguns, *ibid. 22*, 447 (1971).

2. R. Benedict, *J. Gen. Psychol. 10*, 59 (1934).

3. See in this regard H. Becker, *Outsiders: Studies in the Sociology of Deviance* (Free Press, New York, 1963); B. M. Braginsky, D. D. Braginsky, K. Ring, *Methods of Madness: The Mental Hospital as a Last Resort* (Holt, Rinehart & Winston, New York, 1969); G. M. Crocetti and P. V. Lemkau, *Amer. Sociol. Rev. 30*, 577 (1965); E. Goffman, *Behavior in Public Places* (Free Press, New York, 1964); R. D. Laing, *The Divided Self: A Study of Sanity and Madness* (Quadrangle, Chicago, 1960); D. L. Phillips, *Amer. Sociol. Rev. 28*, 963 (1963); T. R. Sarbin, *Psychol. Today 6*, 18 (1972); E. Schur, *Amer. J. Sociol. 75*, 309 (1969); T. Szasz, *Law, Liberty and Psychiatry* (Macmillan, New York, 1963); *The Myth of Mental Illness: Foundations of a Theory of Mental Illness* (Hoeber-Harper, New York, 1963). For a critique of some of these views, see W. R. Gove, *Amer. Sociol. Rev. 35*, 873 (1970).

4. E. Goffman, *Asylums* (Doubleday, Garden City, N.Y., 1961).

5. T. J. Scheff, *Being Mentally Ill: A Sociological Theory* (Aldine, Chicago, 1966).

6. Data from a ninth pseudopatient are not incorporated in this report because, although his sanity went undetected, he falsified aspects of his personal history, including his marital status and parental relationships. His experimental behaviors therefore were not identical to those of the other pseudopatients.

7. A. Barry, *Bellevue Is a State of Mind* (Harcourt Brace Jovanovich, New York, 1971); I. Belknap, *Human Problems of a State Mental Hospital* (McGraw-Hill, New York, 1956); W. Caudill, F. C. Redlich, H. R. Gilmore, E. B. Brody, *Amer. J. Orthopsychiat. 22*, 314 (1952); A. R. Goldman, R. H. Bohr, T. A. Steinberg, *Prof. Psychol. 1*, 427 (1970); unauthored, *Roche Report 1* (No. 13), 8 (1971).

8. Beyond the personal difficulties that the pseudopatient is likely to experience in the hospital, there are legal and social ones that, combined, require considerable attention before entry. For example, once admitted to a psychiatric institution, it is difficult, if not impossible, to be discharged on short notice, state law to the contrary notwithstanding. I was not sensitive to these difficulties at the outset of the project, nor to the personal and situational emergencies that can arise, but later a writ of habeas corpus was prepared for each of the entering pseudopatients and an attorney was kept "on call" during every hospitalization. I am grateful to John Kaplan and Robert Bartels for legal advice and assistance in these matters.

9. However distateful such concealment is, it was a necessary first step to examining these questions. Without concealment, there would have been no way to know how valid these experiences were; nor was there any way of knowing whether whatever detections occurred were a tribute to the diagnostic acumen of the staff or to the hospital's rumor network. Obviously, since my concerns are general ones that cut across individual hospitals and staffs, I have respected their anonymity and have eliminated clues that might lead to their identification.

10. Interestingly, of the 12 admissions, 11 were diagnosed as schizophrenic and one, with the indentical symptomatology, as manic-depressive psychosis. This diagnosis has a more favorable prognosis, and it was given by the only private hospital in our sample. On the relations between social class and psychiatric diagnosis, see A. deB. Hollingshead and F. C. Redlich, *Social Class and Mental Illness: A Community Study* (Wiley, New York, 1958).

11. It is possible, of course, that patients have quite broad latitudes in diagnosis and therefore are inclined to call many people sane, even those whose behavior is patently aberrant. However, although we have no hard data on this matter, it was our distinct impression that this was not the case. In many instances, patients not only singled us out for attention, but came to imitate our behaviors and styles.

12. J. Cumming and E. Cumming, *Community Ment. Health 1,* 135 (1965); A. Farina and K. Ring, *J. Abnorm. Psychol. 70,* 47 (1965); H. E. Freeman and O. G. Simmons, *The Mental Patient Comes Home* (Wiley, New York, 1963); W. G. Johannsen, *Ment. Hygiene 53,* 218 (1969); A. S. Linsky, *Soc. Psychiat. 5,* 166 (1970).

13. S. E. Asch, *J. Abnorm. Soc. Psychol. 41,* 258 (1946); *Social Psychology* (Prentice-Hall, New York, 1952).

14. See also I. N. Mensh and J. Wishner, *J. Personality 16,* 188 (1947); J. Wishner, *Psychol. Rev. 67,* 96 (1960); J. S. Bruner and R. Tagiuri, in *Handbook of Social Psychology,* G. Lindzey, Ed. (Addison-Wesley, Cambridge, Mass., 1954), vol. 2, pp. 634-654; J. S. Bruner, D. Shapiro, R. Tagiuri, in *Person Perception and Interpersonal Behavior,* R. Tagiuri and L. Petrullo, Eds. (Stanford Univ. Press, Stanford, Calif., 1958), pp. 277-288.

15. For an example of a similar self-fulfilling prophecy, in this instance dealing with the "central" trait of intelligence, see R. Rosenthal and L. Jacobson, *Pygmalion in the Classroom* (Holt, Rinehart & Winston, New York, 1968).

16. E. Zigler and L. Phillips, *J. Abnorm. Soc. Psychol. 63,* 69 (1961). See also R. K. Freudenberg and J. P. Robertson, *A.M.A. Arch. Neurol. Psychiatr. 76,* 14 (1956).

17. W. Mischel, *Personality and Assessment* (Wiley, New York, 1968).

18. The most recent and unfortunate instance of this tenet is that of Senator Thomas Eagleton.

19. T. R. Sarbin and J. C. Mancuso, *J. Clin. Consult. Psychol. 35,* 159 (1970); T. R. Sarbin, *ibid. 31,* 447, (1967); J. C. Nunnally, Jr., *Popular Conceptions of Mental Health* (Holt, Rinehart & Winston, New York, 1961).

20. A. H. Stanton and M. S. Schwartz, *The Mental Hospital: A Study of Institutional Participation in Psychiatric Illness and Treatment* (Basic, New York, 1954).

21. D. B. Wexler and S. E. Scoville, *Ariz. Law Rev. 13,* 1 (1971).

Fall Into Helplessness

Martin E. P. Seligman
University of Pennsylvania
Philadelphia

D
epression is the common cold of psychopathology, at once familiar and mysterious. Most of us have suffered depression in the wake of some traumatic event—some terrible loss—in our lives. Most of these depressions, like the common cold, run their course in time.

Serious forms of depression afflict from four to eight million Americans. Many of these depressive Americans will recover. Some of them won't; they'll just give up, becoming like T. S. Eliot's hollow men, a ". . . shape without form, shade without color. Paralyzed force, gesture without motion . . ." Many of those who are hospitalized will simply turn their heads to the wall. Others, at least one out of 200, will take their own lives. Yet we know there are some individuals who *never* succumb to depression, no matter how great their loss.

The *Wall Street Journal* has called depression the "disease of the '70s," and perhaps it is part of the character of our times. It is not a new malady, however. Physicians have been describing depression since the days of Hippocrates; he called it melancholia. The 2,500 years since Hippocrates have added little to our knowledge of the cure and prevention of depression. Our ignorance is due not to lack of research on the problem, but, I believe, to a lack of clearly defined and focused theory. Without a theory to organize what is known about the symptoms and cause, predictions about the cure and prevention of depression are, at best, haphazard.

A Cogent Theory

I think such a theory is possible, and my belief is based on the phenomenon known as "learned helplessness." [See "For Helplessness: Can We Immunize the Weak?," by Martin E. P. Seligman, PT, June 1969.] There are considerable parallels between the behaviors that define learned helplessness and the major symptoms of depression. In addition, the types of events that set off depression parallel the events that set off learned helplessness. I believe that cure for depression occurs when the individual comes to believe that he is not helpless and that an individual's susceptibility to depression depends on the success or failure of his previous experience with controlling his environment.

So the focus of my theory is that if the symptoms of learned helplessness and depression are equivalent, then what we have learned experimentally about the cause, cure and prevention of learned helplessness can be applied to depression.

Inescapable Shock

A few years ago, Steven F. Maier, J. Bruce Overmier and I stumbled onto the behavioral phenomenon of learned helplessness while we were using dogs and traumatic shock to test a particular learning theory. We had strapped dogs into a Pavlovian harness and given them electric shock—traumatic, but not physically damaging. Later the dogs were put into a two-compartment shuttlebox where they were supposed to learn to escape shock by jumping across the barrier separating the compartments.

A nonshocked, experimentally naïve dog, when placed in a shuttlebox, typically behaves in the following way: at the onset of the first electric shock, the dog defecates, urinates, howls, and runs around frantically until it accidentally scrambles over the barrier and escapes the shock. On the next trial, the dog, running and howling, crosses the barrier more quickly. This pattern continues until the dog learns to avoid shock altogether.

But our dogs were not naive. While in a harness from which they could not escape, they had already experienced shock over which they had no control. That is, nothing they did or did not do affected their receipt of shock. When placed in the shuttlebox, these dogs reacted at first in much the same manner as a naive dog, but not for long. The dogs soon stopped running and howling, settled down and took the shock, whining quietly. Typically, the dog did not cross the barrier and escape. Instead, it seemed to give up. On succeeding trials, the dog made virtually no attempts to get away. It passively took as much shock as was given.

After testing alternative hypotheses, we developed the theory that it was not trauma per se (electric shock) that interfered with the dog's adaptive responding. Rather, it was the experience of having *no control* over the trauma. We have found that if animals can control shock by any response—be it an active or a passive one—they do not later become helpless. Only those animals who receive uncontrollable shock will later give up. The experience in the harness had taught the dog that its responses did not pay, that his actions did not matter. We concluded that the dogs in our experiments had learned that they were helpless.

Our learned-helplessness hypothesis has been tested and confirmed in many ways with both animal and human subjects. Tests with human beings revealed dramatic parallels between the behavior of subjects who have learned helplessness and the major symptoms exhibited by depressed individuals.

Reactive Depression

Depression, like most clinical labels, embraces a whole family of disorders. As a label it is probably no more discriminating than "disease of the skin," which describes both acne and cancer. The word "depressed" as a behavioral description explicitly denotes a reduction or depression in responding. The reactive depressions, the focus of this article, are most common. As distinguished from process depression, reactive depression is set off by some external event, is probably not hormonally based, does not cycle regularly in time, and does not have a genetic history. The kind of depression experienced by manic-depressives is process depression.

Some of the events that may set off reactive depression are familiar to each of us: death, loss, rejection by or separation from loved ones; physical disease, failure in work or school, financial setback, and growing old. There are a host of others, or course, but those capture the flavor. I suggest that what all these experiences have in common—what depression is—is the belief in one's own helplessness.

Goodies From the Sky

Many clinicians have reported an increasing pervasiveness of depression among college students. Since this is a generation that has been raised with more reinforcers—more sex, more intellectual stimulation, more buying power, more cars, more music, etc.—than any previous generation, why should they be depressed? Yet the occurrence of reinforcers in our affluent society is so independent of the actions of the children who receive them, the goodies might as well have fallen from the sky. And perhaps that is our answer. Rewards as well as punishments that come independently of one's own effort can be depressing.

We can mention "success" depression in this context. When an individual finally reaches a goal after years of striving, such as getting a Ph.D. or becoming company president, depression often ensues. Even the disciplined astronaut, hero of his nation and the world, can become depressed after he has returned from walking on the Moon.

From a learned-helplessness viewpoint, success depression may occur because reinforcers are no longer contingent on present responding. After years of goal-directed activity, a person now gets his reinforcers because of who he *is* rather than because of what he is *doing*. Perhaps this explains the number of beautiful women who become depressed and attempt suicide. They receive abundant positive reinforcers not for what they do but for how they look.

Symptoms in Common

Consider the parallels between depression and learned helplessness: the most prominent symptom of depression, passivity, is also the central symptom of learned helplessness. Joseph Mendels describes the slowdown in responding associated with depression:

> . . .Loss of interest, decrease in energy, inability to accomplish tasks, difficulty in concentration, and the erosion of motivation and ambition all combine to impair efficient functioning. For many depressives the first signs of illness are in the area of their increasing inability to cope with their work and responsibility. . .

Aaron T. Beck describes "paralysis of the will" as a striking characteristic of depression:

> In severe cases, there often is complete paralysis of the will. The patient has no desire to do anything, even those things which are essential to life. Consequently, he may be relatively immobile unless prodded or pushed into activity by others. It is sometimes necessary to pull the patient out of bed, wash, dress and feed him . . .

Experiments in learned helplessness have produced passivity in many kinds of animals, even the lowly cockroach, and in human subjects. Donald Hiroto subjected college students to loud noise. He used three groups: group one could not escape hearing the loud noise; group two heard the loud noise but could turn it off by pressing a button; group three heard no noise.

In the second part of the experiment, Hiroto presented the students with a finger shuttlebox. Moving one's fingers back and forth across the shuttlebox turned off the loud noise. The students in group two, who had previously learned to silence the noise by pushing a button, and those in group three, who had no experience with the loud noise, readily learned to move their finger across the shuttlebox to control the noise. But the students in group one, whose previous attempts to turn off the noise had been futile, now merely sat with their hands in the shuttlebox, passively accepting the loud noise. They had learned that they were helpless.

Hiroto also found out that "externals" [see "External Control and Internal Control," by Julian B. Rotter, *Psychology Today,* June 1971] were more susceptible to learned helplessness than "internals." Externals are persons who believe that reinforcement comes from outside themselves; they believe in luck. Internals believe that their own actions control reinforcement.

Born Losers

Depressed patients not only make fewer responses, but they are "set" to interpret their own responses, when they do make them, as failures or as doomed to failure. Each of them bears an invisible tattoo. "I'm a Born Loser." Beck considers this negative cognitive set to be the primary characteristic of depression:

> . . . The depressed patient is peculiarly sensitive to any impediments to his goal-directed activity. An obstacle is regarded as an impossible barrier, difficulty in dealing with a problem is interpreted as a total failure. His cognitive response to a problem or difficulty is likely to be an idea such as 'I'm licked.' 'I'll never be able to do this,' or 'I'm blocked no matter what I do'. . .

This cognitive set crops up repeatedly in experiments with depressives. Alfred S. Friedman observed that although a patient was performing adequately during a test, the patient would occasionally reiterate his original protest of "I can't do it," "I don't know how," etc. This is also our experience in testing depressed patients.

Negative cognitive set crops up in both depression and learned helplessness. When testing students, William Miller, David Klein and I found that depression and learned helplessness produced the same difficulty in seeing that responding is successful. We found that depressed individuals view their skilled actions very much as if they were in a chance situation. Their depression is not a general form of pessimism about the world, but pessimism that is specific to their own actions. In animal behavior this is demonstrated by associative retardation: animals don't catch on even though they make a response that turns off shock; they have difficulty in learning what responses produce relief.

Maier and I found in separate experiments, that normal aggressiveness and competitiveness become deficient in the subjects who have succumbed to learned helplessness. In competition, these animals lose out to animals who have learned that they control the effects of their responses. Further, they do not fight back when attacked.

Depressed individuals, similarly, are usually less agressive and competitive than nondepressed individuals. The behavior of depressed patients is depleted of hostility and even their dreams are less hostile. This symptom forms the basis for the Freudian view of depression. Freud claimed that the hostility of depressed people was directed inward toward themselves rather than outward. Be this as it may, the *symptom* corresponds to the depleted aggression and competitiveness of helpless dogs and rats.

The Balm of Time

Depression also often dissipates with time. When a man's wife dies, he may be depressed for several days, several months, or even several years. But time usually heals. One of the most tragic aspects of suicide is that if the person could have waited for a few weeks, the depression might well have lifted.

Time is also an important variable in learned helplessness. Overmier and I found that the day after they received one session of inescapable shock, dogs behaved helplessly in the shuttlebox. However, if two days elapsed between the inescapable shock and testing, the dogs were not helpless; their helplessness, like the widower's depression, had run its course. Unfortunately, helplessness does not always respond so well to the elixir of time. We found that multiple sessions of inescapable shock made the animals' learned helplessness virtually irreversible. We also found that

TABLE 1

	Learned Helplessness	Depression
SYMPTOMS	1. passivity 2. difficulty learning that responses produce relief 3. lack of aggression 4. dissipates in time 5. weight loss and undereating. anorexia, sexual deficits (?) 6. norepinephrine depletion 7. ulcers and stress	1. passivity 2. negative cognitive set 3. introjected hostility 4. time course 5. loss of libido 6. norepinephrine depletion 7. ulcers (?) and stress 8. feelings of helplessness
CAUSE	learning that responding and reinforcement are independent	belief that responding is useless
CURE	1. directive therapy: forced exposure to responding producing reinforcement 2. electroconvulsive shock 3. pharmacological agents (?) 4. time	1. recovery of belief that responding produces reinforcement 2. electroconvulsive shock (?) 3. pharmacological agents (?) 4. time
PREVENTION	inoculation with mastery over reinforcement	inoculation (?)

animals that had been reared from birth in our laboratories with a limited history of controlling reinforcers also failed to recover from learned helplessness over time.

Often when we are depressed, we lose our appetites and our zest for life. Jay M. Weiss, Neal E. Miller and their colleagues at Rockefeller University found that rats that had received inescapable shock lost weight and ate less than rats who had been able to escape from shock. In addition, the brains of the rats subjected to inescapable shock are depleted of norepinephrine, an important transmitter substance in the central nervous system. Joseph J. Schildkraut and Seymour S. Kety have suggested that the cause of depression may be a deficiency of norepinephrine at receptor sites in the brain. This is because reserpine, a drug that depletes norepinephrine, among other things, produces depression in man. Moreover, antidepressant drugs increase the brain's supply of norepinephrine. Therefore, there may be a chemical similarity between depression and learned helplessness.

Weiss found that rats subjected to uncontrollable shock got more stomach ulcers than rats receiving no shock or shock they could control.

No one has done a study of ulcers in depression, so we don't know if human experience will correspond to ulceration in helpless rats. However, anxiety and agitation are sometimes seen along with depression. It is my speculation, however, that anxiety persists as long as the depressed person believes there might still be something he can do to extract himself from his dilemma. When he finally comes to believe that no response will work, depression wholly displaces anxiety.

The Chances for Cure

As arrayed above, there are considerable parallels between the behaviors which define learned helplessness and the major symptoms of depression. We have also seen that the cause of learned helplessness and reactive depression is similar: both occur when important events are out of control. Let me now speculate about the possibility of curing both.

In our animal experiments, we knew that only when the dog learned to escape the shock, only when it learned that it could control its environment, would a cure for its learned helplessness be found.

At first, we could not persuade the dog to move to the other side of the box, not even by dropping meat there when the dog was hungry. As a last resort, we forcibly dragged the dog across the barrier on a leash. After much dragging, the dog caught on and eventually was able to escape the shock on its own. Recovery from helplessness was complete and lasting for each animal. We can say with confidence that so far only "directive therapy"—forcing the animal to see that it can succeed by responding—works reliably in curing learned helplessness. However, T.R. Dorworth has recently found that electroconvulsive shock breaks up helplessness in dogs. Electroconvulsive shock is often used as a therapy for depression and it seems to be effective about 60 percent of the time.

Although we do not know how to cure depression, there are therapies that alleviate it, and they are consonant with the learned helplessness approach. Successful therapy occurs when the patient believes that his responses produce gratification, that he is an effective human being.

Against the Grain

In an Alabama hospital, for instance, E. S. Taulbee and H. W. Wright have created an "antidepression room." They seat a severely depressed patient in the room and then abuse him in a simple manner. He is told to sand a block of wood, then is reprimanded because he is sanding against the grain of the wood. After he switches to sanding *with* the grain, he is reprimanded for sanding with the grain. The abuse continues until the depressed patient gets angry. He is then promptly led out of the room with apologies. His outburst, and its immediate effect on the person abusing him, breaks up his depression. From the helplessness viewpoint, the patient is forced to vent his anger, one of the most powerful responses people have for controlling others. When anger is dragged out of him, he is powerfully reinforced.

Other methods reported to be effective against depression involve the patient's relearning that he controls reinforcers.

Expressing strong emotions is a therapy that seems to help depressed patients, as self-assertion does. In assertive training, the patient rehearses asserting himself and then puts into practice the responses he has learned that bring him social reinforcers.

Morita therapy puts patients in bed for about a week to "sensitize them to reinforcement." Then the patients progress from light to heavy to complicated work [see "Morita Therapy," by Takehisa Kora and Kenshiro Ohara, *Psychology Today,* March 1973].

The Lift of Success

Other forms of graded-task assignments also have been effective. Elaine P. Burgess first had her patients perform some simple task, such as making a telephone call. As the task requirements increased, the patient was reinforced by the therapist for successfully completing each task. Burgess emphasized how crucial it is in the graded-task treatment that the patient succeed.

Using a similar form of graded-task assignment, Aaron Beck, Dean Schuyler, Peter Brill and I began by asking patients to read a short paragraph aloud. Finally, we could get severely depressed patients to give extemporaneous speeches, with a noticeable lifting of their depression. What one patient said was illuminating: "You know, I used to be a debater in high school and I had forgotten how good I was."

Finally, there is the age-old strategy adopted by individuals to dispel their own minor depressions: doing work that is difficult but gratifying. There is no better way to see that one's responses are still effective. It is crucial to succeed. Merely starting and giving up only makes things worse.

Dramatic successes in medicine have come more frequently from prevention than from treatment, and I would hazard a guess that inoculation and immunization have saved more lives than cure. Surprisingly, psychotherapy is almost exclusively limited to curative procedures, and preventive procedures rarely play an explicit role.

In studies of dogs and rats we have found that behavioral immunization prevents learned helplessness. Dogs that first receive experience in mastering shock do not become helpless after experiencing subsequent inescapable shock. Dogs that are deprived of natural opportunities to control their own rewards in their development are more vulnerable to helplessness than naturally immunized dogs.

The Masterful Life

Even less is known about the prevention of depression than about its cure. We can only speculate on this, but the data on immunization against learned helplessness guide our speculations. The life histories of those individuals who are particularly resistant to depression or who are resilient from depression may have been filled with mastery. Persons who have had extensive experience in controlling and manipulating the sources of reinforcement in their lives may see the future optimistically. A life without mastery may produce vulnerability to depression. Adults who lost their parents when they were children are unusually susceptible to depression and suicide.

A word of caution is in order. While it may be possible to immunize people against debilitating depression by giving them a history of control over reinforcers, it may be possible to get too much of a good thing. The person who has met only success may be highly susceptible to depression when he faces a loss. One is reminded, for example, of the stock market crash of 1929: it was not the low-income people who jumped to their deaths, but those who had been "super-successful" and suddenly faced gross defeat.

One can also look at successful therapy as preventative. After all, therapy usually does not focus just on undoing past problems. It also should arm the patient against future depressions. Perhaps therapy for depression would be more successful if it explicitly aimed at providing the patient with a wide repertoire of coping responses. He could use these responses in future situations where he finds his usual reactions do not control his reinforcements. Finally, we can speculate about child rearing. What kind of experiences can best protect our children against the debilitating effects of helplessness and depression? A tentative answer follows from the learned helplessness view of depression: to see oneself as an effective human being may require a childhood filled with powerful synchronies between responding and its consequences.

Phobias and Preparedness

Martin E. P. Seligman
University of Pennsylvania
Philadelphia

Behavior therapists have proposed a plausible learning alternative to the psychoanalytic view of phobias. This paper examines some inadequacies of the learning model and suggests a way of accounting for phobias which combines the biological and learning points of view. Ironically, what emerges somewhat resembles the psychoanalytic view, and it may help to reconstruct notions like symbolism.

Wolpe and Rachman (1961) have clearly stated the case for a learning theory interpretation of phobias. They examined Freud's classic "Little Hans" case (1909), and proposed an alternative approach. To refresh the reader's memory, Little Hans was a 5-year-old boy who developed a horse phobia. Freud interpreted the fear of horses as an outcome of the Oedipal conflict; Hans desired his mother sexually, wished his father out of the way, and, fearing his father's retribution (castration), displaced the fear onto horses. Wolpe and Rachman effectively criticized Freud's use of evidence, taking him to task for focusing only on material from Hans which confirmed the interpretation while disregarding his explicit rejections of the interpretation. Wolpe and Rachman's exposé of the looseness of psychoanalytic argument and evidence is perhaps as clearheaded a critique of analytic inference as exists in the literature. They also outlined a learning theory view of little Han's phobia. What little Hans was afraid of, in their view, was not his father, but horses. To quote their interpretation:

> In brief, phobias are regarded as conditioned anxiety (fear) reactions. *Any* "neutral" stimulus, simple or complex, that happens to make an impact on an individual at about the time that a fear reaction is evoked, acquires the ability to evoke fear subsequently. If the fear at the original conditioning situation is of high intensity or if the conditioning is many times repeated, the conditioned fear will show the persistence that is characteristic of *neurotic* fear; and there will be generalization of fear reactions to stimuli resembling the conditioned stimulus.
>
> Hans, we are told, was a sensitive child who "was never unmoved if someone wept in his presence" and long before the phobia developed became "uneasy on seeing horses in the merry-go-round being beaten" (p. 254). It is our

contention that the incident to which Freud refers as merely the exciting cause of Han's phobia was in fact the cause of the entire disorder. Hans actually says, "No. I only got it (the phobia) then. When the horse in the bus fell down, it gave me such a fright, really! That was when I got the nonsense" (p. 192). The father says, "All of this was confirmed by my wife, as well as the fact that the anxiety broke out immediately afterwards" (p. 193).

Horses became phobic via Hans via classical conditioning because he saw horses at the same time as being frightened. Such a view has much *prima facie* plausibility. The conditioning of fear has been demonstrated repeatedly in the laboratory both in humans and animals. Watson and Rayner (1919) paired a startling noise with a white rat to "Little Albert," and Albert became afraid of rats, rabbits, and other furry objects. The classical conditioning of fear was subsequently brought into the animal laboratory by Estes and Skinner (1941), and the literature on it is now truly voluminous (e.g., Campbell & Church, 1969; Brush, 1971).

Further impetus for learning interpretation of the cause of phobias comes from the dramatic success which behavior therapists have had in breaking up phobias using learning techniques (e.g., Wolpe & Lazarus, 1969). Phobias can be "extinguished" by counterconditioning relaxation to representations of phobic stimulus. If phobias can be extinguished by techniques developed in the learning laboratory, this suggests, but by no means proves, that they were originally acquired by such learning.

There are some salient problems with the learning interpretation of phobias which seem related to inadequacies of theories of learning themselves. These difficulties also crop up in learning accounts of other forms of human psychopathology, but we shall discuss only phobias here.

The first problem is that phobias do not extinguish under conventional procedures which reliably extinguish classically conditioned fear in the laboratory. When an individual with a cat phobia imagines a cat or comes across a cat, he is exposed to an extinction *procedure*. By the learning account, the cat (CS) was once paired with some fear-evoking trauma, unconditioned stimulus (UCS), and as a consequence, the cat became an elicitor of fear. *When the cat is presented without the original UCS, the association should diminish.* But it is commonplace that exposure to the phobic stimulus or brooding about the phobic object does not diminish fear and may even enhance it. It will not do to say that the cat itself became a UCS, because this is merely a restatement of the problem. Why should cats become UCS's when paired with trauma, and not tones which are paired with shock in the laboratory?

There is a common misconception among clinicians about the

extinction of conditioned fear in the laboratory, and it is worthwhile examining the evidence at some length. The misconception arises from a careless interpretation of the avoidance learning literature, a leap from the fact that avoidance responding does not extinguish to the mistaken inference that conditioned fear does not extinguish.

In a typical laboratory avoidance procedure, an animal is exposed to the following contingencies: (1) some CS such as a tone is paired with strong electric shock (UCS). Such pairing causes the classical conditioning of fear to the tone. (2) If the animal responds, e.g., by running to the other side of the shuttle box after the shock comes on, both the shock and the tone terminate. This instrumental escape response is reinforced by the termination of the painful shock, possibly by the termination of the fear-evoking CS and also by the nonoccurrence of shock. Which of these reinforcements is more effective is in dispute (e.g., Rescorla & Solomon, 1967; Herrnstein, 1969; Bolles, 1970), but is irrelevant for the present discussion. It is well-documented that, once an animal begins avoiding reliably, if the shock is now disconnected (a so-called extinction procedure) the animal will contine to respond, not infrequently outlasting the experimenter's patience (e.g., Solomon, Kamin, & Wynne, 1953; Seligman & Campbell, 1965). What many have inferred from this, however, is that fear once learned does not extinguish. But it does not follow from failure of avoidance to extinguish that classical conditioning of fear does not extinguish. Notice that, as the contingencies are arranged, if the animal avoids on every trial (i.e., responds to the tone and terminates it before the shock would have appeared) it is not exposed to the fact that the tone no longer predicts shock. That is to say: an extinction of avoidance procedure does not necessarily entail an extinction of classically conditioned fear procedure. It turns out that, if the avoidance response is prevented, thus forcibly exposing the animal to the fact that tone is no longer followed by shock, avoidance readily extinguishes (for an extensive review, see Baum, 1970). Avoidance extinguishes after blocking because fear is extinguished, since the subject is exposed to the CS, no longer predicting the UCS. Avoidance fails to extinguish before blocking because the response is continually reinforced by shock prevention and by CS termination. The animal has no way of "finding out" that shock would not have occurred if he had not responded. If the animal continues to respond every time, disconnecting the shock is the experimenter's secret. Moreover, if an instrumental avoidance paradigm is not used, so that fear is conditioned without an instrumental contingency, the fear extinguishes to the CS. This is true of both behavioral indexes of fear (e.g., Wagner, Siegel, & Fein, 1967) as well as physiological (e.g., Black, Carlson, & Solomon, 1962). In fact, this is such common knowledge among people working in these fields that not much systematic study of it has been published, rather it is assumed in their procedures. For example, after fear has been classically conditioned, the effects of the CS are commonly tested only for the first few trials of extinction. After that, the CS soon becomes impotent (e.g., Rescorla & LoLordo, 1967; Kamin, 1965).

Although the weight of evidence indicates extinction of conditioned fear, sophisticated readers may be aware of the paradoxical "Napalkov" (1963) effect (see also Eysenck, 1968). It is observed that occasionally fear is actually enhanced during presentation of the CS unreinforced by shock (Rohrbaugh & Riccio, 1970). There seems to be no ready explanation for the conditions under which this relatively rare phenomenon occurs; but it will hardly do as a refuge for those who want to hold that it explains the failure of phobias to extinguish. First, because the most common observation is monotonically decreasing fear in extinction, and second, because extinction probably sets in after a few trials of paradoxical enhancement (Rohrbaugh & Riccio, 1970).

There is one way out and that is to claim that phobias involve avoidance and so do not extinguish because they are analogous to laboratory avoidance (Eysenck & Rachman, 1965). So, e.g., when Freud's notorious Little Hans thinks of horses, he also performs some avoidance response which he believes prevents the real UCS, and he never finds out that horses are no longer paired with the unconditionally frightening event. By avoiding, he never exposes himself to the fact that the CS is no longer paired with the UCS and the CR remains. This way out is unpalatable because it postulates on unobservable avoidance response in the absence of independent evidence for such a process. Incidentally, this avoidance formulation should not be confused with a very real avoidance component in phobias: that people go to great lengths to avoid the phobic object—but this is an example of avoiding the CS, not of being exposed to the CS and avoiding the UCS. For example, a woman afraid of heights will actively avoid getting herself into a situation in which she is very far off the ground. In such a case, fear of heights should remain, since she cannot be exposed to heights no longer paired with the original UCS. Our concern is not with cases in which the person successfully avoids any exposure to the CS and, therefore, avoids exposure to the extinction contingency, but rather with those individuals who are exposed to the CS when it is no longer paired with UCS. The problem we are tackling is that phobics actually exposed to the CS do not extinguish, and avoidance of the CS is irrelevant to this problem. For example, a spider phobic individual will think about spiders, see pictures of spiders, and even actually see spiders. All of these situations constitute exposure to the CS (more or less) no longer paired with the original UCS. Yet it is commonplace that such inadvertant exposures rarely weaken, and may even strengthen, the phobia.

Before leaving the difference in extinguishability of phobias and laboratory conditioned fear, we should mention another difference. Implicit in the general process learning view of phobias is the assumption that they can be learned in one trial: It must be enough for one traumatic experience paired with a CS to produce a phobia. One-trial conditioning of fear is the exception, not the rule, in laboratory fear conditioning. The conditioning of fear commonly takes between three and six trials (e.g., Kamin, 1969; Seligman, 1968). If extremely traumatic UCSs are used, such as fear of imminent death (Campbell, Sanderson, & Laverty, 1964), one-trial conditioning can be obtained. But let us keep in mind that fear conditioning in the laboratory is only rarely full-blown in one trial, but for phobias it should be commonplace.

In summary, one difficulty for the behavior therapy view of phobias is that they are hard to extinguish, while the alleged laboratory model of classically conditioned fear extinguishes readily. A homier way of making the same point is to say that phobias are irrational. Telling a phobic, however persuasively, that cats (CS) won't do him any harm, or showing him that the UCS doesn't occur when cats are around is rarely effective. Showing an animal that the CS no longer predicts the UCS usually results in extinction (Black, 1959). The "laws" of fear conditioning (Rescorla & Solomon, 1967) look very much like expectations: CSs that are paired with shock become fearful and stop being fearful when they predict no shock. Conditioned and differential inhibitors, CSs that predict the absence of shock, become active inhibitors of fear (Rescorla, 1970). Very long CSs which end in shock inhibit fear at their outset and evoke fear at their termination (Rescorla, 1968; Seligman & Meyer, 1970). We shall later try to account for the noncognitive nature of phobias, their inextinguishability, and their one-trial acquisition.

Before doing so, let us look at another neglected property of phobias which is difficult to model by ordinary classical conditioning of fear. According to Pavlov's view of conditioning, the choice of CS is a matter of indifference. "Any natural phenomenon chosen at will may be converted into a conditioned stimulus . . . any visual stimulus, any desired sound, any odor and the stimulation of any part of the skin" (Pavlov, 1928, p. 86). This is the heart of the general process view of learning and, by this widely held view, any CS which happens to be associated with trauma should become phobic. But a neglected fact about phobias is that, by and large, they comprise a relatively nonarbitrary and limited set of objects: agoraphobia, fear of specific animals, insect phobias, fear of heights, and fear of the dark, etc. All these are relatively common phobias. And only rarely, if ever, do we have pajama phobias, grass phobias, electric-outlet phobias, hammer phobias, even though these things are likely to be associated with trauma in our world. The set of potentially phobic events may be nonarbitrary: events related to the survival of the human species through the long course of evolution (see Marks, 970, pp. 63-68, for a clearheaded discussion of the nonarbitrariness of phobic stimuli).

What is it about phobias that makes them (1) selective, (2) so resistant to extinction, (3) irrational, and (4) capable of being learned in one trial? *Phobias are highly prepared to be learned by humans, and, like other highly prepared relationships, they are selective and resistant to extinction, learned even with degraded input, and probably are noncognitive.* Phobias may be instances of classically conditioned fear, but not unprepared conditioned fear such as a tone paired with shock. Rather, they are instances of prepared conditioning of fear. So phobias can indeed be modelled by a "simple learning process," but one needs to modify general process learning theory to do it. The modification, argued at length elsewhere (Seligman, 1970; Seligman & Hager, in press) may be summarized as follows:

Since the time of Pavlov and Thorndike, the laws of learning have been formulated using arbitrary sets of events, such as a click paired with meat powder for dogs, and the pressing of levers for flour pellets in rats. At the base of such endeavors is the premise that the laws found would be general from one set of events to another. Arbitrarily chosen relationships were at a premium, since the laws that emerged should be uncontaminated by the idiosyncratic past experience that the animal brings to the situation or by the biological characteristics of his particular species. However, one danger in such a strategy is that the laws so found would be peculiar to arbitrary events arbitrarily concatenated. This danger is particularly acute when one realizes that animals and humans do a great deal of learning about contingencies which their species has faced for eons. Not only do birds learn to turn wheels for grain, which their ancestors never did, but they also *learn* to migrate away from the North Star in the fall (Emlen, 1970b) a contingency their ancestors faced before them. Not only do humans learn to fear crossing busy streets, but also to fear the dark. All this learning may not be the same.

A dimension of preparedness has been operationally defined:

> ". . . confront an organism with a CS paired with UCS or with a response which produces an outcome. Depending on the specifics, the organism can be either prepared, unprepared, or contraprepared for learning about the events. The relative preparedness of an organism for learning about a situation is defined by the amount of input (e.g., numbers of trials, pairings, bits of information, etc.) which must occur before that output (responses, acts, repertoire, etc.), which is construed as evidence of acquisition, reliably occurs. It does not matter how input or output are specified, as long as that specification can be used consistently for all points on the continuum. Thus, using the preparedness dimension is independent of whether one happens to be an S-R theorist, a cognitive theorist, an information processing theorist, an ethologist, or what have you. Let us illustrate how one can place an experimental situation at various points on the continuum for classical conditioning. If the organism makes the indicated response consistently from the very first presentation of the CS on, such "learning" represents a clear case of instinctive responding, the extreme of the prepared end of the dimension. If the organism makes the response consistently after only a few pairings, it is somewhat prepared. If the response emerges only after many pairings, the organism is unprepared. If acquisition occurs only after very many pairings or does not occur at all, the organism is said to be contraprepared. The number of pairings is the measure that makes the dimension a continuum, and implicit in this dimension is the notion that "learning" and "instinct" are continuous. Typically ethologists have studied situations from the prepared side of the dimension, while general process learning theorists have largely restricted themselves to the unprepared region. The contraprepared part of the dimension has been largely uninvestigated, or at least unpublished" (Seligman, p 408, 1970)

By now, it has been well-documented that some contingencies are learned about much more readily than others. In virtually every major paradigm that learning theorists have used, some contingencies are learned with highly degraded input (one trial, long delay of reinforcement) while others are learned only painstakingly. A few examples follow.

Many readers have probably acquired some taste aversion after being sick to their stomachs. Garcia and associates (for review, see Garcia, McGowan, & Green, 1971) have found that this is a prepared form of classical conditioning. Rats learn to associate tastes, rather than external cues like lights, with nausea, and they can learn this in one trial even with a several hour delay between the taste and the illness. Pairing a light with foot shock, on the other hand, takes several trials to acquire and can bridge a delay of only a few seconds. Note that this prepared learning reflects a real contingency which rodents have faced through the course of evolution: tastes are paired with poisoning, and the effects of poisons do not usually begin immediately. Such prepared learning gives a selective advantage.

In the realm of instrumental learning, Brown and Jenkins (1968) showed that pigeons learn to peck a lighted key which is paired with grain, even though pecking the key has no effect on grain. Yet rats learn only by trial and error to press a bar for food and only if bar-pressing produces food. In avoidance learning, birds have a great deal of trouble learning to peck a key to prevent shock, but can learn to hop up (Emlen, 1970a) or fly away (Bedford & Anger, 1967) to avoid shock. Rats have trouble learning to bar press to avoid, but learn to jump up to avoid in one trial (Baum, 1966). In discrimination learning, dogs learn readily to go to the left rather than to the right, if the cues which tell them which way to go are in different places, but can't learn if the cues differ in quality, rather than place. Conversely they can learn to put their paw up or keep it down if the cues differ in quality, but not if they differ in location (Dobrzecka, Szwejkowska, & Konorski, 1966). Seligman (1970) and Seligman and Hager (in press) discuss many other examples of prepared, unprepared, and contraprepared learning. The upshot of these examples is that learning itself may be quite different depending on how prepared the organism is for the particular contingency he confronts.

We can now return to phobias: The difficulty that learning theory has in modeling phobias by the classical conditioning of fear does not result from phobias' being phenomena *sui generis,* but, rather, results because the conditioning used as a model was unprepared rather than prepared conditioning. Prepared learning provides a better fit with phobias than unprepared learning because we have reason to believe that it (1) can be acquired in one trial; (2) is selective; (3) is resistant to extinction; and (4) may be noncognitive. Let us now look at the evidence that leads in this direction.

In the first place, prepared classical conditioning by definition occurs in one or a very few trials. It is defined as conditioning that occurs with minimal or even degraded input. Like phobias, the contingencies around which prepared learning revolves are not arbitrary, but rather those that may have been intimately involved in the survival of the species. Prepared learning is highly selective: When a rat becomes ill, taste aversion develops but not aversions to the sound and sights that were also contiguous with illness. When grain is presented, pigeons peck at lighted keys, but do not step on treadles or turn wheels. When chaffinches develop, they learn the song of their species, and ignore the similar songs of other species (Marler, 1970). Reevaluate Watson's classical experiment with Little Albert. Furry things, like rats and rabbits, became aversive to Little Albert, but Watson and Rayner themselves probably did not. Maybe this experiment really is a more adequate model of human phobias than fear conditioning in the rat. Conditioning occurred in two trials, making it operationally prepared and it was also selective. Bregman (1934), probably aware of the difficulty of making children afraid of scissors and electric outlets, repeated the Little Albert experiment using common household CS like curtains and blocks instead of furry things. She got no fear conditioning at all. Furthermore, English (1929) did not get fear conditioning to a wooden duck, even after many pairings with a startling noise.

Aside from being selective, Watson and Rayner's prepared fear conditioning does not extinguish readily. Special procedures, such as counter-conditioning (Jones, 1924) are necessary to produce remission of fear. It seems likely that prepared learning like phobic learning is highly resistant to extinction. Garcia's taste aversions are somewhat persistent, even though the animal must drink the fluid to survive. Rozin's (1967) taste aversions persisted even after his rats were restored to health. Wild rats, who become poisoned on a new taste, will often starve to death before eating other new flavors (Rzoska, 1953). Human taste aversions are also resistant to change—they may dissipate in time, rather than with trials of unreinforced exposure. Other forms of prepared learning, unlike unprepared learning, are highly resistant to extinction. Williams and Williams (1969) made the "auto-shaped" key-pecking of pigeons counterproductive pecking the lighted key was no longer independent of grain presentation, it actually *prevented* grain. The pigeons pecked anyway. Stimbert (1970) trained rats to make the correct choice in a maze either using another rat as the cue or with masking tape, over the course the cue rat had traversed as the cue. The "rat" cue was learned readily (prepared), whereas the masking tape cue was learned painstakingly (unprepared). The cue rat did not lose his cuing ability even after 150 trials in which food was no longer presented, but the masking tape cue extinguished in 20 trials. Seligman, Ives, Ames, and Mineka (1970) conditioned drinking in rats by pairing a compound CS with thirst-inducing NaCl-procaine, When mild thirst was part of the CS, conditioning did not extinguish; but if mild thirst were not part of the CS, conditioning occurred and extinguished rapidly.

Thus, if phobias are seen as prepared classical conditioning, their one-trial acquisition, their selectivity, and their persistence may follow. The "irrationality" of phobias is also compatible with what data exists on prepared classical conditioning. Seligman (1970) suggested that unprepared contingencies are learned and extinguish cognitively, i.e., by such mechanisms as expectations, intentions, beliefs, or attention, while unprepared associations are learned more primitively or noncognitively. Prepared associations may be the blind association that Pavlov and Thorndike had thought they were studying, whereas they wound up working on the laws of unprepared learning or expectancies.

The noncognitive nature of prepared associations is illustrated by at least one observation: Knowing that the stomach flu and not the sauce Béarnaise caused the vomiting does not inhibit the aversion to the sauce. In addition, there are several experiments which suggest that, unlike unprepared conditioning, prepared conditioning is not readily modified by information. When unprepared CSs such as tones are paired with shock, information plays a large role in learning. Kamin (1969) has demonstrated that, when tone is paired with shock and then both tone and light are paired with shock, no fear conditioning occurs to the light. Prior conditioning with tone "blocks" the rat's learning that the redundant light also predicts shock. Kalat and Rozin (in press) repeated the blocking study with the more prepared contingency of taste and illness. The redundant CS was *not* blocked in their studies, indicating that taste-nausea conditioning may be primitive and noncognitive. Garcia, Kovner, and Green (1970) reported a related finding. Rats learned to avoid shock with taste as the discriminative stimulus in a shuttle box. When tested in the home cage, no aversion to taste was found. When the rats had the taste as a stimulus for illness, however, aversion was total even in the home cage. In the taste-shock contingency, taste merely becomes a *cue* for shock in the shuttlebox. But when taste predicts illness, the taste aversion is full-blown even though the rat is in a different place. The taste may actually take on some qualities of the illness. Finally, Roll and Smith (in press) demonstrated that taste aversion could occur even when the rat was anesthetized, and Nachman (1970) reported that electroconvulsive shock, which eliminates fear conditioning, did not eliminate the memory of taste aversion.

Human phobias are similar. Showing or telling a phobic that cats are not going to hurt him is rarely effective. *Phobic* fear is by definition not readily inhibited by rational means. Rather, one needs to resort to special procedures, such as the counterconditioning employed in systematic desensitization. We do not yet know much about how to get rid of prepared associations like taste-illness, imprinting, and auto-shaping, although we know that mere extinction is not very effective. Might counterconditioning be an effective procedure in these cases? At any rate, we may now be in the position to develop a fruitful animal model of phobias, and discover how best to produce extinction; for we can do fear conditioning not with a tone or light, as is usual, but with more CSs such as the picture and sound of snakes or hawks paired with shock for a rat. It would not be surprising to find one trial fear conditioning and great resistance to extinction. Such experiments would allow us to explore the ways of getting rid of fear, and might suggest new therapeutic techniques with phobias.

There is one subtlety to the form of the argument which should be underlined. It is not argued that no phobia about objects of modern technology exists, or that all phobias are noncognitive. People sometimes talk themselves into phobias. There are airplane phobias and fears of electric shock. The preparedness view is not disconfirmed by isolated examples: it points to the fact that the great majority of phobias are about objects of natural importance to the survival of the species. It does not deny that other phobias are possible, it only claims that they should be less frequent, since they are less prepared.

In some ways, we have come full circle. We began by concurring in the rejection of the psychoanalytic interpretation of phobias, e.g., that horses were fearful to Little Hans because they symbolized his father's retribution. We modified the learning reconstruction of phobias by suggesting a modification of general process learning theory. Phobias, in our view, are not instances of unprepared fear conditioning, but of prepared fear conditioning. Nonarbitrary stimuli seem particularly ready to become phobic objects for human beings and this may also be true of "soteria," the opposite number from phobias (e.g., Linus' blanket). Particular CSs are readily conditioned to particular UCSs. Perhaps this is a way of reconstructing symbolism. Is it possible that there really is something to horses and wolves, etc., that makes them highly associable with certain kinds of traumas, perhaps even sexual ones? Does anyone have a lamb phobia? This is testable. When Little Hans acquired his phobia, there were not only horses around, but other things, such as his nurse or a bus and yet these did not become phobic objects. Why only horses? If children were given horses and blackboards, both paired with anxiety-arousal, would they learn readily to be afraid of horses but not of blackboards?

So, for a biologically-oriented learning theorist, to what can the notion of symbolism amount? A is symbolic of B, if and only if human beings are prepared, in the sense defined, to learn that A is associated with B. If humans can acquire with A the properties of B after only minimal input, then it is meaningful to say that A is symbolic of B.

Even more speculatively, does preparedness range beyond simple symbolic associations? Are there ways of thinking in which humans are particularly prepared to engage, as Lenneberg (1967) has argued for language and cognition? If association, causal inference, and forms of cognition are prepared, are there stories that man is prepared to formulate and accept? If so, a meaningful version of the racial unconscious lurks close behind.

References

Baum, M. Rapid extinction of an avoidance response following a period of response prevention. *Psychological Reports*, 1966, *18*, 59-64.

Baum, M. Extinction of avoidance responding through response prevention (flooding). *Psychological Bulletin*, 1970, *74*, 276-284.

Bedford, J., & Anger, D. Flight as an avoidance response in pigeons. Paper presented at the meeting of the Psychonomic Society, St. Louis, Mo., October, 1967.

Black, A. H. The extinction of avoidance responding under curare. *Journal of Comparative and Physiological Psychology*, 1958, *51*, 519-524.

Black, A. H., Carlson, N. J., & Solomon, R. I. Exploratory studies of the conditioning of autonomic responses in curarized dogs. *Psychological Monographs*, 1962, 1-31, Whole number 548.

Bolles, R. Species-specific defense reactions and avoidance learning. *Psychological Review*, 1970, *77*, 32-48.

Bregman, E. An attempt to modify the emotional attitude of infants by the conditioned response technique. *Journal of Genetic Psychology*, 1934, *45*, 169-198.

Brown, P., & Jenkins, H. Autoshaping of the pigeon's key peck. *Journal of the Experimental Analysis of Behavior*, 1968, *11*, 1-8.

Brush, R. R. (ed.) *Aversive conditioning and learning.* New York: Academic Press, 1971.

Campbell, B. A. & Church, R. M. *Punishment and aversive behavior.* New York: Appleton-Century-Crofts, 1969.

Campbell, D., Sanderson, R. E., & Laverty, S. G. Characteristics of a conditioned response in human subjects during extinction trials following a simple traumatic conditioning trial. *Journal of Abnormal and Social Psychology*, 1964, *68*, 627-639.

Dobrzecka, C., Szwejkowska, G. & Konorski, J. Qualitive versus directional cues in two forms of differentiation. *Science*, 1966, *153*, 87-89.

Emlen, S. The influence of magnetic information on the orientation of the indigo bunting *(Passerina Cyanea). Animal Behavior*, 1970a, *18*, 215-224.

Emlen, S. Celestial rotation: its importance in the development of migratory orientation. *Science*, 1970b, *170*, 1198-1201.

English, H. B. Three cases of the "conditioned fear response." *Journal of Abnormal and Social Psychology*, 1929, *34*, 221-225.

Estes, W. K., & Skinner, B. F. Some quantitative properties of anxiety. *Journal of Experimental Psychology*, 1941, *29*, 390-400.

Eysenck, H. J. A theory of the incubation of anxiety/fear response. *Behavior Research and Therapy*, 1968, *6*, 309-321.

Eysenck, H. J., & Rachman, S. *The causes and cures of neurosis.* London: Routledge and Kegan Paul, 1965.

Freud, S. The analysis of a phobia in a five-year old boy. (1909). In *Collected Papers*, Vol. 3. London: Hogarth, 1950.

Garcia, J., Kovner, R., & Green, K. Cue properties of flavors in avoidance. *Psychonomic Science*, 1970, *20*, 313-314.

Garcia, J., McGowan, B., & Green, K. Sensory quality and integration: constraints on conditioning? In A. H. Black & W. F. Prokasy (Eds.), *Classical conditioning*. New York: Appleton Century-Crofts, 1971, in press.

Herrnstein, R. J. Method and theory in the study of avoidance. *Psychological Review*, 1969, *76*, 49-69.

Jones, M. C. The elimination of children's fears. *Journal of Experimental Psychology*, 1924, *7*, 383-390.

Kalat, J., & Rozin, P. You can lead a rat to poison but you can't make him think. In M. E. P. Seligman & J. Hager. *The biological boundaries of learning*. New York: Appleton-Century-Crofts, in press.

Kamin, L. J. Temporal and intensity characteristics of the conditioned stimulus. In W. Prokasy (Ed.), *Classical conditioning*. New York: Appleton-Century-Crofts, 1965. Pp. 279-290.

Kamin, L. J. Predictability, surprise, attention, and conditioning. In B. A. Campbell and R. M. Church (Eds.), *Punishment and aversive behavior*. New York: Appleton-Century-Crofts, 1969. Pp. 317-332.

Lenneberg, E. *The biological foundations of language*. New York: Wiley, 1967.

Marks, I. *Fears and phobias*. New York: Academic Press, 1970.

Marler, P. A comparative approach to vocal learning. *Journal of Comparative and Physiological Psychology*. Monograph, 1970, *71*, 1-25.

Nachman, M. Limited effects of electroconvulsive shock on memory of taste stimulation. *Journal of Comparative and Physiological Psychology*, 1970, *73*, 31-37.

Napalkov, A. V. Information process of the brain. In N. Wener and J. G. Sefade (Eds.), *Progress of brain research, nerve, brain, and memory models*. 1963, Vol. 2, 59-69. New York: American Elsevier.

Pavlov, I. P. *Lectures on conditioned reflexes*. New York: International Publishers, 1928.

Rescorla, R. A. Inhibition of delay in Pavlovian fear conditioning. *Journal of Comparative and Physiological Psychology*, 1967, *64*, 114-120.

Rescorla, R. A. Pavlovian conditioned inhibition. *Psychological Bulletin*, 1969, *72*, 77-94.

Rescorla, R. A., & LoLordo, V. M. Inhibition of avoidance behavior. *Journal of Comparative and Physiological Psychology*, 1965, *59*, 406-412.

Rescorla, R. A., & Solomon, R. L. Two process learning theory: relations between Pavlovian conditioning and instrumental learning. *Psychological Review*, 1967, *74*, 151-182.

Roll, D., & Smith, J. Conditioned taste aversion in anesthetized rats. In M. E. P. Seligman and J. Hager. *Biological boundaries of learning*. New York: Appleton-Century-Crofts, in press.

Rohrbaugh, M., & Riccio, D. Paradoxical enhancement of learned fear. *Journal of Abnormal Psychology*, 1970, *75*, 210-216.

Rozin, P. Specific aversions as components of specific hungers. *Journal of Comparative and Physiological Psychology*, 1967, *64*, 237-242.

Rozin, P., & Kalat, J. Adaptive specializations in learning and memory. In M. E. P. Seligman and J. Hager *Biological boundaries of learning.* New York: Appleton-Century-Crofts, in press.

Rzoska, J. Bait shyness, a study in rat behaviour. *British Journal of Animal Behaviour,* 1953, *1,* 128-135

Seligman, M. E. P. Chronic fear produced by unpredictable electric shock. *Journal of Comparative and Physiological Psychology,* 1968, *66,* 402-411.

Seligman, M. E. P. On the generality of the laws of learning. *Psychological Review,* 1970, *77,* 406-418.

Seligman, M. E. P., & Campbell, B. A. Effect of intensity and duration of punishment on extinction of an avoidance response. *Journal of Comparative and Physiological Psychology,* 1965, *59,* 295-297.

Seligman, M. E. P., & Hager, J. *Biological boundaries of learning.* New York: Appleton-Century-Crofts, in press.

Seligman, M. E. P., Ives, C. I., Ames, H., & Mineka, S. Conditioned drinking and its failure to extinguish: Avoidance, preparedness or functional autonomy? *Journal of Comparative and Physiological Psychology,* 1970, *71,* 411-419.

Seligman, M. E. P., & Meyer, B. Chronic fear and ulcers in rats as a function of the unpredictability of safety. *Journal of Comparative and Physiological Psychology,* 1970, *73,* 202-208.

Solomon, R. L., Kamin, L. J., & Wynne, I. C. Traumatic avoidance learning; the outcomes of serveral extinction procedures with dogs. *Journal of Abnormal and Social Psychology,* 1953, *48,* 291.

Stimbert, V. A comparison of learning based on social or nonsocial discriminative stimuli. *Psychonomic Science,* 1970, *20,* 185-186.

Wagner, A. R., Siegel, L. S., & Fein, G. G. Extinction of conditioned fear as a function of percentage of reinforcement. *Journal of Comparative and Physiological Psychology,* 1967, *63,* 160-164.

Watson, J. B., & Rayner, R. Conditioned emotional reactions. *Journal of Experimental Psychology,* 1920, *3,* 1-14.

Williams, D. R., & Williams, H. Auto-maintenance in the pigeon: sustained pecking despite contingent nonreinforcement. *Journal of the Experimental Analysis of Behavior,* 1969, *12,* 511-520.

Wolpe, J., & Lazarus, A. *The practice of behavior therapy.* London: Pergamon, 1969.

Wolpe, J., & Rachman, S. Psychoanalytic evidence: A critique of Freud's case of Little Hans. *Journal of Nervous and Mental Diseases,* 1960, *130,* 198-220.

Note: This study was supported by PHS grant MH19604 to the author.

On Assertive Behavior: A Brief Note

Arnold A. Lazarus
University College
Rutgers University
New Brunswick, N. J.

The main components of assertive (or emotionally expressive) behaviors may be divided into four separate and specific response patterns: the ability to say "no"; the ability to ask for favors or to make requests; the ability to express positive and negative feelings; the ability to initiate, continue, and terminate general conversations.

People who are deficient in "assertive behavior" will display incapacities in one or more of the abovementioned areas. An excellent assessment procedure for determining whether or not a client requires "assertive training" is to inquire under what specific conditions he is inclined to accede to unreasonable demands, is unable to make reasonable requests, fails to express his feelings, and feels socially and interpersonally inhibited or at a loss for words. Each area requires specific retraining because (in my experience) the degree of generalization or transfer from one assertive area to another is very slight. Thus, a client may learn to say "no!" and stand up for his rights, but he may remain deficient in asking for favors or in expressing positive feelings.

Effective interpersonal functioning in our society seems to require competence in the various areas alluded to above. Since Salter (1949) emphasized the importance of "excitation" (emotional freedom) and Wolpe (1958) described "assertive training," the literature on behavior therapy has burgeoned with accounts of verbal, nonverbal, individual and group procedures for promoting these so-called "assertive behaviors." As mentioned elsewhere (Lazarus, 1971), it is unfortunate that the bulk of these reports tends to place undue emphasis upon the ability to contradict and verbally attack other people. While these authors may have been influenced by Wolpe's (1958, 1969) emphasis on "aggressive, anger-expressing behavior," it cannot be overemphasized that there is little to be gained (and perhaps much to be lost) from the acquisition of abrasive and obnoxious interpersonal behaviors in the guise of "assertive training."

Numerous manuscripts describe the precise ways in which people are being programmed to mete out punishment, to deal with their intimates as adversaries, to ignore the needs of others, and to make a fetish of gaining the upper hand. Individual and group maneuvers range from "shout training" to hostile nonverbal gestures intended to make other people feel ill at ease. While there are undoubtedly some interpersonal situations where these hostile tactics pay emotional dividends, is it not far more effective to educate people in applying the obvious and subtle nuances of *positive reinforcement?* Time spent teaching people how to emit forthright expressions of love, adoration, affection, appreciation, and the specific verbal and nonverbal facets of compassion, tenderness, warmth and other positive feelings often undermines the need for anger responses and righteous indignation.

Perhaps a personal vignette will place this brief note into perspective. Recently, while shopping for shirts, I was served by an extremely surly and unobliging salesman. He was brusque and most unhelpful. I found myself feeling progressively irritated by his manner. Now what would be an adaptive assertive response under these circumstances? Should I personally upbraid him? Should I employ a oneupmanship tactic and hint that a visit to a dermatologist might do wonders for his acne? Should I report him to the manager?

Each of the foregoing responses represents an attack, with or without justification. It is in fact poor psychology, for aggressive behaviors often serve to escalate counteraggressive and defensive responses. Instead of attacking him, I simply said: "You seem to be having a hell of a bad day. Is something wrong?" He responded by informing me that his wife was in the hospital and that he was anxious about her. I expressed my sympathy and inquired whether he would care to tell me what was ailing her. She had undergone an emergency appendectomy the previous day and still had a fever. I managed to make some reasuring comments about modern sugical techniques and broad-spectrum antibiotics. He appeared immensely relieved and his entire demeanor changed immediately. I left the store ten minutes later with my shirts and with a good feeling that my "assertive behavior" had brought comfort to a fellow human being while enabling me to obtain the exact merchandise that I was seeking.

References

Lazarus, A A *Behavior therapy and beyond.* New York: McGraw-Hill, 1971.

Salter, A. *Conditioned reflex therapy.* New York: Farrar Strauss, 1949.

Wolpe, J. *Psychotherapy by reciprocal inhibition.* Stanford: Stanford University Press, 1958.

Wolpe, J. *The practice of behavior therapy.* New York. Pergamon Press, 1969.

Teaching the Nonverbal Components of Assertive Training

Michael Serber
Atascadero State Hospital
Atascadero, California

M ost published and verbal reports dealing with assertive training concentrate primarily on the explicit verbal message. This is also true of a recently published book on assertive training (Alberti and Emmons, 1970).

Unfortunately, a most important aspect of assertive training, the paralinguistic component—how the message is delivered—has not had its fair share of attention and has been left mostly to chance, apart from some pilot studies of limited scope (Ivey, 1968). A number of independent researchers evaluating the importance of nonverbal communication have found that in many situations the nonverbal messages are perceived as more important than the verbal by the subject (Mehrabian, 1968; Mehrabian and Ferris, 1967). In reality, it is much simpler to instruct a client to "tell off her husband" than to work out the details of an appropriate, effective message. Any experienced clinician is well aware of the fact that what ineffective persons often lack is not knowledge or courage but a command of style. Lack of style can be behaviorally defined as the inability to master appropriate nonverbal, as well as verbal, components of behavior.

To define functionally what is or is not appropriate, I am guided by what is accepted in general social usage—people don't shout during moments of tenderness, don't smile when angry, don't stand eight feet away from friends when carrying on an intimate conversation, and speak fluently when they desire something. The number of individuals who say the right thing the wrong way is legion. This figures prominently in the folk humor of our culture. Some neo-Freudian therapists, such as the Gestalt therapists and transactional analysts have regarded the style of a person's communication as the object of insight and the source of therapeutic change (Berne, 1964; Perls, Hefferline and Goodman, 1951).

Wilhelm Reich in his book, *Character Analysis* (1949), vividly describes the paralinguistic behaviors or styles of communication exhibited by some of his patients. Fritz Perls, a patient of Reich's, who developed Gestalt therapy (very much in vogue during the 60's) extensively employed Reichian character analysis to give his patients, individually or in groups, direct feedback about "the way" in which they said or did things. More recently, Marshall McLuhan (1964) has made much of the idea that the way people do things is what they do, or in his words "the medium is the message."

All of the so-called humanistic schools of psychology, even when they address themselves to identifying and describing a behavior, do little to teach alternative behaviors. The assumption among "nondirective" psychotherapists is that once a patient understands or feels his "character" or the "game" he plays, he will be free to adopt more appropriate behavior. My departure from this position is that understanding, whether defined in cognitive or emotional terms, is in itself not adequate for achieving longstanding or significant behavioral change. To define the behavior in need of change is only a preliminary step which has to be followed by specific instruction, modeling, role-playing and the behavioral rehearsal of alternative behavior. It is also necessary to separate out the significant nonverbal components of a total pattern and shape each one separately. In sharp contrast to traditional psychotherapeutic strategies, the behavioral approach avoids the emotional confrontation of a patient regarding behavior for which he has not developed any alternatives (Laws and Serber, 1971). Emotional confrontation may only result in raising the anxiety level of the patient, even to the point that it markedly diminishes his learning capacity.

Behavior therapy has available to it the technology necessary to shape nonverbal behavior. Information giving, modeling, role-playing, and behavior rehearsal coupled with audiovisual feedback comprise an adequate armamentarium.

The Selection of Nonverbal Behaviors to be Taught

As in the teaching of verbal behavior, the elements that are considered most important for communication are selected, giving priority to those whose shaping is likely to contribute most significantly to the end product which I call "a total socially meaningful behavior." The selection of elements depends on the requirements of the training situation. For example, telephoning an employer is simpler than telling him face-to-face that he has been unfair. In the phone conversation, eye contact, facial expression, body expression and distance from the person with whom one is interacting are unimportant—in contrast to face-to-face confrontation.

I have found it useful to break down nonverbal behavior into the following specifics:

1. Loudness of voice
2. Fluency of spoken words
3. Eye contact
4. Facial expression
5. Body expression
6. Distance from person with whom one is interacting

Loudness and fluency are vocal features that are not dependent upon the content of the verbal message. Fluency in fact may be completely at odds with the explicit message, yet if fluency is lacking from a message, the overall impact of what is said is greatly diminished.

Some of the six variables listed are easily measurable—loudness of voice, fluency, distance from the other person, eye contact—but body and facial expression defy simple measurement. They can, in fact, be measured, but by complex techniques that are time-consuming and unnecessary for clinical work (Ekman, Friesen and Taussig, 1969). In fact, all of the variables mentioned can be satisfactorily assessed by a clinician or behavioral rater with adequate experience in working with this kind of behavior. In a study evaluating the effects of assertive training, behavioral raters were employed to rate the "softer" variables such as body expression and facial expression (Laws and Serber, 1971). The raters were trained by the use of prepared videotaped models of body and facial expression appropriate to the social settings concerned.

It may not be necessary for the clinician to rate every training session, but the fact that the variables to be shaped can be objectified makes the trainer sensitive to the fact that objective behavioral assessment could become a regular part of the overall assessment.

The Shaping of a Nonverbal Variable

The conditions most favorable for the training of nonverbal behaviors are:

1. A clearly defined situation
2. Concentration upon a limited number of nonverbal variables
3. Audiovisual feedback

I have been employing a half-inch videotape recorder and camera with a 5:1 zoom lens, and a 12-inch television monitor. The entire outfit is kept on a small cart which can easily be rolled from room to room. No auxiliary lights are necessary if room lighting is bright enough for reading and without excessive contrast.

To begin working with a nonverbal behavior, it is necessary to choose a situation which can be repeated *in toto* or in part for several trials without any significant alteration. An example of such a situation would be the following: a trainee is told, "You have just met a prospective employer who is sitting behind his desk. He will act sympathetically toward you—smile, ask supporting questions, etc. It is your task in three minutes to begin a conversation with him and try to impress him with your qualifications for a (specific) job." The role of the employer is played by the therapist or an assistant. The patient's effort is videotaped and the most deficient element in his behavior usually selected first for modification. I have found it a good general rule to work with only one nonverbal variable at a time. For example, in the audiovisual replay of the situation, it may be impossible to hear the voice of the trainee. Then our first purpose will be to shape the loudness factor.

The patient is shown a replay of his roleplaying and informed which verbal variable is in need of modification. The appropriate behavior is then modeled for him. The modeling usually has to be repeated many times, and each time the trainee approximates it to the best of his ability. After several trials, each followed by videotape feedback, the patient shows progress for which he is positively reinforced by praise and given further instruction through modeling and role-playing. The attention to a particular nonverbal variable continues until significant improvement has been achieved. One may then move on to another variable.

It is common, when observing patients carrying out sample behaviors, to find that some nonverbal variables are already satisfactory, while others are grossly deficient. The patient who has an overall deficiency is the one who needs the most careful and concentrated work, with smaller improvements expected of him and with much positive reinforcement for each advance that he makes.

The "softer" nonverbal behaviors, such as body and facial expression require more role-playing skill on the part of the trainer, with clear explanations and explicit modeling. Specially trained models are highly desirable. They should have been through a systematic course based on the Stanislavsky system so as to be able to give training in a wide range of expressive behaviors (Stanislavsky, 1936).

If one is not in a position to measure kinesics, it is especially important to have a well-defined picture of the behavior required. A number of nonverbal techniques can be employed to develop body and facial expression. One helpful technique I have labeled the "silent movie." The trainee is told to use only his face and body to express his feelings and thoughts. He is requested to perform a timed sample exercise (2-3 minutes) in a stated situation, without any vocalization. This "silent movie" is then modeled for the trainee, and usually, after several trials, both facial and body expression may become more mobile and appropriate.

A frequent problem, distinct from lack of facial or body expression (immobility), is inappropriateness of facial or body expression. We frequently see a person delivering verbal invective with a smile on his face, or a rigid or cold individual speaking words of affection and endearment. Usually both verbal and nonverbal behaviors are in need of modification in these people, and a major goal of nonverbal training is establishing a unity of verbal and nonverbal behavior which will lead to increased effectiveness of communication. I am not suggesting that the explicit verbal repertoire be sacrificed in favor of "paralinguistic" training. The explicit message must continue to receive its necessary attention and modification.

I have made no mention of generalization of training from one behavioral variable to another. It is certainly present and obvious in sequential videotaped training sessions; but assessment of generalization has not yet been undertaken.

A Case Study

The patient, a 21-year-old male, had marked difficulty carrying on a conversation and communicating his desires to other patients and staff. He affected a silly grimace whenever he spoke to anyone. He had particular difficulty in standing up for himself, as the grin belied whatever annoyance he was trying to express verbally.

A 3-minute role-playing situation was constructed requiring the patient to deny some unjust charges. He had formulated what he was going to say and was told that the other role-player in the situation would disagree with him but he was to insist that he was unjustly accused. The entire sequence was videotaped and an assessment of the tape was made immediately after the role-playing.

The assessment was as follows:

1. *Loudness of voice.* The patient could easily be heard 12 feet away from where he was standing, though he was not shouting. Loudness was satisfactory.

2. *Facial expression* was inappropriate. When the patient was

telling how wronged he had been, he persistently grinned and the expression on his face never changed.

3. *Body expression.* The patient's body was not rigid, and he used his arms and trunk appropriately.

4. *Eye contact.* Fifteen-second spot rating on the videotape revealed the patient to be staring at the floor in over 80 per cent of the spot checks.

5. *Fluency.* The patient repeated many words and syllables within each sentence. There were many pauses of over 4 seconds between words and the speech was not rhythmic.

The behavior first singled out for modification was the chronic grin. The grin was described for him, a video replay was shown demonstrating its omnipresence, and the modelling of an alternative expression was demonstrated to him. He was requested to concentrate only on modifying this one aspect of his behavior (the grin) during the first working session. Modeling was frequently repeated, followed by his own attempt and then videotape feedback. The silent movie technique was especially helpful, the patient being required to convey his message mainly through facial expression. He began to display scowling, frowning, and looking serious which were quite new to his repertoire. After a 45-minute session devoted to his facial expression, he carried out a 3-minute total interaction with almost no sign of a grin. The patient was advised to practice his newly acquired nonverbal behavior in his interactions with other patients and staff, and told to return for another training session in four days.

During the second training session, the new facial expressions he had learned were reinforced and his lack of eye contact was tackled. The appropriate behavior was modeled and the patient role-played it in several situations. He approximated the model perfectly after 15 minutes of training. The rest of the session (30 minutes) involved work on verbal fluency. The patient was made aware of his pauses between words, lack of rhythm, and repetition of syllables and words. Each fluency problem was worked on individually until the patient's behavior approximated the model to a high degree. A metronome proved of great value in training rhythmicity, as well as giving ongoing feedback as to pauses within sentences. The patient also used a tape-recorder to practice alone between training sessions. In two weeks, the overall fluency increased markedly.

One session was then devoted to integrating all the nonverbal behaviors which the patient had recently learned. Training had taken three weeks and a total of five 45-minute sessions with diligent practice between sessions. His interpersonal communication improved so much that staff and other patients were taking him seriously when he voiced his desires and displeasures.

References

Alberti R.E. and Emmons M.L. (1970) *Your Perfect Right—a Guide to Assertive Behavior,* Impact, S.L.O.

Berne E. (1964) *Games People Play,* Grove Press, N.Y.

Ekman P., Friessen W.V. and Taussig T. (1969) VID-R and scan: tools and methods in the analysis of facial expression and body movements (Edited by Gerbner G., Holsti O., Knippendorff K., Paisley W. and Stone P.), *Content Analysis,* Wiley, N.Y.

Perls F., Hefferline R.F., Goodman P. (1951) *Gestalt Therapy,* Dell, N.Y.

Ivey A.E., Normington C.J., Miller D., Morrill W.H. (1968) Microcounseling and Attending Behavior, *Jl. Counseling Psychol. 15,* 1-12, No. 5, part 2, monog.

Laws R. and Serber M. (1971) *Measurement and Evaluation of Assertive Training.* Paper presented at the meeting of the Association for Advancement of Behavior Therapy, Washington D.C.; September 1971.

Reich W. (1949) *Character Analysis,* Orgone Institute Press, N.Y.

Mehrabian A. and Ferris S.R. (1967) Inference of attitudes from non-verbal communication in two channels, *J. Consulting Psychol. 31,* 248-252.

Mehrabian A. (1968) Relationship of attitude to seated posture orientation and distance, *J. Personality Soc. Psychol. 10,* 26-30.

McLuhan M. (1964) *Understanding Media,* Signet Classics, N.Y.

Stanislavsky C. (1936) *An Actor Prepares,* Theater Arts, New York.

Desensitization, Re-Sensitization and Desensitization Again: A Preliminary Study

Ian Wickramasekera

University of Illinois
College of Medicine
Peoria

This paper describes the apparently successful desensitization, re-sensitization and repeat desensitization of a case of obsessive-compulsive sexual behavior. The typical procedure for isolating effective treatment variables is the group comparison. An alternative approach is to attempt an intra-subject replication. The intra-subject replication can provide a demonstration of the functional relationship between antecedent and consequent variables. Comparing the procedures Sidman (1960, p. 85) notes, "Intra-subject and to a lesser extent intra-group replication provides a unique demonstration of a technique's reliability."

Background Information

The patient, Mr. C., a 41-year-old, white, married male, was referred to our clinic by his family doctor for the treatment of "obsessive thoughts of a sexual nature which are disturbing his marriage and which threaten his employment." The subject *(S)* had been married for 17 years and employed on the present job for 12 years.

S attributed the onset of his symptoms to the discovery (in the form of love letters) of his wife's infidelity, 6 months prior to his first contact with the present therapist. His symptoms had apparently not responded to various medications prescribed by physicians. The primary presenting symptoms were restlessness, insomnia, sporadic crying and extended outbursts of verbal abuse (bitch, whore, etc.) focused on his wife. In addition, he had lost weight (approximately 30 lb), was demanding and attempting sexual intercourse with his wife several times a day (range 1-7) and was extremely suspicious of her. He appeared to have an "uncontrollable urge" to drop whatever he was doing several times a day and rush home to "check" on her, remind her of her infidelity, and have intercourse. The frequency of these unscheduled visits home was such that his employer was threatening to discharge him.

The patient's wife admitted that she had been "unfaithful" (several sexual contacts with the same man in motels and in her own home) for a period of approximately 4 months, but insisted that after her husband had discovered her infidelity and "exploded," all contacts (verbal and nonverbal) with her lover had ceased. She claimed that her marriage had been in a "rut" and that she did not "really love" the man she had been involved with. She said that she was sorry for the pain she had cost her husband and had attempted unsuccessfully to make it up to him in the last 6 months. But she claimed that his sexual preoccupations, abuse of her, loss of weight, and unauthorized absences from work had only increased. She stated that she believed he wanted to continue to punish her.

The patient stated that since the onset of his symptoms, his wife had improved her housekeeping, quit work, and was more attentive to him as a wife. *S* stated that he wanted to be hypnotized so that he could "forget" his wife's infidelity and no longer be "possessed" by it. He stated that thoughts of his wife in different "positions" and "places" with her lover were what was "driving him crazy."

Method

Formulation of treatment plan

"Psycho-dynamically" a sado-masochistic interaction between husband and wife seemed the central problem. The patient's compulsive sexuality and his wife's need to atone seemed to be reinforcing their complementary role enactments (Kelly, 1955).

The treatment plan was to desensitize the respondent consequences of the patient's obsessive thoughts (operants) and to guide his thoughts toward a rationale or "insight" for giving up his symptoms, no longer to leave him vulnerable to future recurrences of infidelity. An attempt was also made to help the patient find some "meaning" in his present suffering. Specifically, he was encouraged to see his present symptoms as having contributed to some degree to the revitalizing of his marriage.

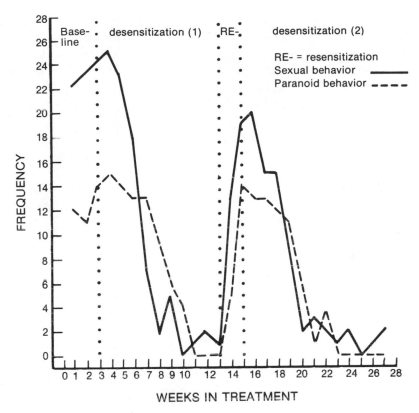

FIGURE 1. Frequency of paranoid and sexual behaviors per week in treatment.

Preliminary procedures

The background information having been gathered in an intensive (2 hour) interview with S and his wife, separately and together, S was told that it would be 3 weeks before his next appointment. He was instructed to start keeping a careful record each Friday evening of his weight till treatment was terminated, and arrangements were made to weigh him on each visit to the clinic. In the course of a private interview with S's wife, she was instructed immediately to start observing and recording two types of information about her husband's behavior: (1) The frequency of all his visits home on working days between 8 a.m. and 5 p.m. (excluding the regular return home from work at the end of the working day). This class of observations would be an index of paranoid behaviors. (2) The frequency

of his attempts at sexual intercourse (partial or total removal of his pants
with statement of sexual interest) with her each week. These observations
would be an index of sexual behaviors. Careful observing and accurate
recording were stressed and she was told to make every attempt to ensure
that her husband did not know she was collecting these data. The decision
was made to monitor these two areas (paranoid and sexual) of behavior in
addition to his weight, because they seemed more amenable to objective
specification than other symptoms and because they were very disruptive
to his life.

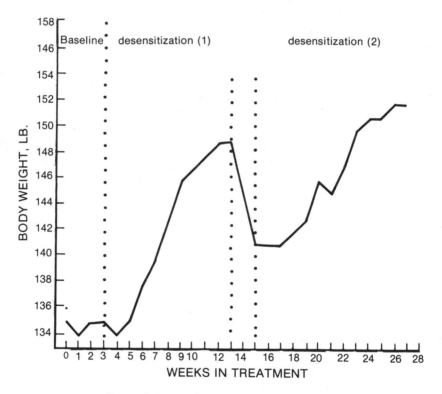

FIGURE 2. Body weight per week in treatment.

In terms of Figures 1 and 2, the initial intensive interview occurred at
"0 weeks in treatment." After the 3 weeks' baseline period, the Stanford
Hypnotic Susceptibility Scale (SHSS) Form A, was administered to
measure the S's current hypnotic susceptibility, since he had requested
hypnotic treatment in the initial interview. His score on the SHSS was low
(2) and the clinical impression was that he was resisting "induction." After

the administration of the SHSS, the *S* was told that the present therapist suspected that his "resistance" to hypnosis was based on the fear that through hypnosis the memory of his wife's infidelity would be erased and that would leave him vulnerable to similar infidelities in the future. He was told that there was an "unpleasant" procedure involving sensory restriction (Wickramasekera, 1969, 1970) which might reduce his "resistance to hypnosis," but an alternative "pleasant" method called "desensitization" which did not involve hypnosis was also available for treating him. He was told that desensitization would "drain the pain out of his memories but leave them fresh and clear." The desensitization procedure was described briefly and presented as being "non-hypnotic." He was told to think about these alternatives (sensory restriction and hypnosis, or desensitization) and make a decision before the next session.

First desensitization

In the next session ("4 weeks in treatment" according to Figures 1 and 2) the patient requested the desensitization treatment and hierarchy construction and desensitization was begun. The total hierarchy consisted of 48 scenes. The least aversive scene (1) was seeing himself at home lying on the couch listening to his wife cooking in the kitchen. The most aversive was (48) seeing Mrs. C. indulging in an "unnatural act" of sex with her lover on *S*'s own bed.

Each scene was put on a separate note card (total 48 cards) and very infrequently changed in order or content during treatment. Relaxation training was given both in the office and by means of a taped set of relaxation instructions recorded on a cassette tape. The portable recorder and tape were rented to *S* for a sum of $10.00 per week (not included in regular fee per treatment session). The major purposes of the recorder rental procedure were to motivate speedy acquisition of the relaxation skill and to increase the probability of the practice of relaxation in the patient's natural habitat.

Sessions were one week apart. Each session was 55 to 60 minutes. The only departure from the standard desensitization procedure (Wolpe, 1969) was that during the entire treatment (desensitization and re-sensitization) the patient was told to keep his eyes open and concentrate on the empty white wall in front of him.

Re-sensitization

An attempt was made to re-sensitize the patient in the 13th and 14th session of treatment.

Wolpe (1958) observed and Wolpe (1969, p. 127) specifically states that "exposure and prolonged exposure in particular to a very disturbing scene can seriously increase phobic sensitivity." Though an "obsession" may be different in many respects from a phobia, the present treatment procedure was based on the assumption that they had similar "respondent" (excessive autonomic arousal) consequences. From an ethical point of view there appeared to be no problem, since there was no solid evidence that "re-sensitization" was even possible with the procedure to be described below.

Re-sensitization consisted of telling the patient that "a slightly different but improved method will be used today. Please signal any discomfort or anxiety you feel in the usual way but continue to imagine the scene until I tell you to stop imagining it." When the desensitization procedure was terminated, there remained 30 scenes which had not been presented. All 30 of these scenes were presented in rapid succession during the attempted re-sensitization procedure (sessions 13 and 14). During re-sensitization whenever the patient signalled anxiety (with left forefinger) the presentation was continued for 1½ minutes from the time the signal was observed. The re-sensitization sessions were approximately equal in length (55-60 minutes) to the regular desensitization sessions.

Second desensitization

Standard desensitization was resumed at the 15th session and continued until the 28th. Sessions were again one week apart, except that the 19th and 20th were 5 weeks apart.

Results

The "baseline" was presented to the patient as a waiting period. During the baseline there was no verbal or other contact between the subject and the therapist. Both S and his wife called in their reports to a secretary, who recorded and plotted the data they reported. Figure 1 shows that paranoid and sexual behavior increased somewhat during this period. Figure 2 indicates that the patient's weight remained fairly stable. During the first desensitization period (scenes 1-18) the paranoid and sexual behaviors declined steadily over time while the patient's weight increased. Associated impressionistic clinical features included good rapport and lack of resistance in the treatment situation. S's symptoms seemed to respond so rapidly that the therapist was genuinely skeptical about the existence of a functional relationship between the desensitization procedure and the symptomatic changes. The hypotheses of "spontaneous recovery" and/or a "placebo" effect seemed more likely.

During the re-sensitization period (scenes 19-48) the paranoid and sexual behaviors increased in frequency and the patient's weight declined. Clinically, the patient seemed more agitated and depressed during the 14th and particularly the 15th session of treatment. The therapist continued to try to maintain rapport by being-sympathetic and attentive. Before the 15th session, the patient's wife called the clinic and insisted on speaking to the therapist. She seemed extremely agitated and insisted that he was getting worse. She stated he had come home intoxicated twice, was eating less and not sleeping (lying in bed awake and sporadically abusing her and demanding intercourse). The therapist tried to be sympathetic and stated that all he could do was to continue to try to "find out what was wrong with the patient." When the patient came in for the 15th session, he seemed more agitated than ever before and was even "hostile." He spontaneously stated, "Doc, last time you threw too much at me, you hit me with a sledge-hammer." The therapist's response was to accept the patient's "insight" and to suggest that we "slow down and back up" to the previous procedure.

In the 15th session systematic desensitization was restarted 10 scenes down from where it had been stopped in the first desensitization phase. It was subsequently continued to scene 48. During this phase of desensitization, the patient's paranoid and sexual behaviors again declined in frequency and his weight began to increase steadily till termination. Clinically the patient also appeared to improve in terms of rapport and seemed more calm and optimistic about his future. Desensitization was completed in the 24th week in treatment.

Three additional sessions were spent mainly guiding the patient's thinking towards a rationale for his previous "suffering" and reinforcing the view that through his symptoms his marriage had been "enriched" and salvaged from the "rut it was in." An intensive follow-up with a structured interview with the wife and husband 6 months after termination indicated that there had been no reactivation of the previous symptoms nor had new symptoms developed.

Discussion

Since the patient's obsessive thoughts were not directly observable (a covert symptom), three apparently correlated aspects of his problem were monitored. In the final analysis, the relationship between the obsessive thoughts and his overt symptoms is only inferential. The two behavioral measures (paranoid and sexual) could be specified relatively objectively but the accuracy with which the patient's wife observed and recorded these behaviors is unknown. Diagnostically it appears that the patient's problem was of the "acute" type that is known often to "remit spontaneously." But the observation that the symptoms could be manipulated up and down suggests the attainment of a measure of stimulus control over these symptomatic responses. How many reversals are necessary with clinical problems of this type is a question which has both statistical and ethical implications. It seems that the results of "implosive therapy" (Stampfl and Levis, 1968), and practical considerations have discouraged previous attempts to determine if the "re-sensitization" could be produced in the manner implied by Wolpe (1969).

One may doubt the generality of the phenomena demonstrated in this case study. But as Sidman (1960) notes, "Once we find that repeated manipulation of a variable produces consistent behavioral changes in a single organism, a failure to get consistent inter-subject replication simply points the way to a more intensive functional investigation." Parametric studies of the variable in question should then be undertaken.

The re-sensitization procedure described in this paper seems relevant to what Eysenck (1968) has called the "Napalkov phenomenon" which he describes as "an increment in the CR over a period of time when the CS is applied once or a number of times, but without reinforcement." Normally this procedure would give rise to extinction. Eysenck suggests that his concept of incubation, "increments in the CR after several evocations of the unreinforced CS," is necessary to account for certain phenomena in the formation of neuroses and for the effects of "aversion therapy." From his formulation of "incubation," Eysenck derives two parameters. These are strength of the UCR and score elevation on "neuroticism—anxiety— emotionality inventories." It would be interesting to see the results of further studies of "re-sensitization" with better controls and outcome measures along the parametric dimensions suggested by Eysenck.

Clinicians have anecdotally reported that *in vivo* re-sensitization occurs, but there does not appear to be any previous empirical demonstration in the literature of specific re-sensitization with a non-*in vivo* or imagination—relaxation procedure. The use of a desensitization—re-sensitization— desensitization design appears to be a promising approach to the validation and more intensive study of "active process variables" in systematic desensitization.

References

Eysenck H.J. (1968) A theory of the incubation of anxiety/fear responses, *Behav. Res. & Therapy 6*, 309-321.

Kelly G.A. (1955) *The Psychology of Personal Constructs.* W.W. Norton and Co., New York.

Sidman M. (1960) *Tactics of Scientific Research.* Basic Books, New York.

Stampfl T.G. and Levis D.J. (1968) Implosive therapy—a behavioral therapy, *Behav. Res. & Therapy 6*, 31-36.

Wolpe J. (1968) *Psychotherapy by Reciprocal Inhibition.* Stanford University Press, Stanford.

Wolpe J. (1969) *The Practice of Behavior Therapy,* Pergamon Press, New York.

Wickramasekera I. (1969) The effects of sensory restriction on susceptibility to hypnosis, a hypotheses and some preliminary data, *Int. J. of Exp. Hypnos. 17*, 217-224.

Wickramasekera I. (1970) The effects of sensory restriction on susceptibility to hypnosis: a hypothesis and more preliminary data, *J. Abnorm. Psychol. 75*, 68-72.

Combined Use of Imaginal and Interoceptive Stimuli in Desensitizing Fear of Heart Attacks

J.B. Furst and A. Cooper
Albert Einstein
College of Medicine
Department of Psychiatry
New York City

I n a high percentage of cases, a patient's phobic anxiety appears to be triggered by stimuli which emanate from a situation or source external to the patient's body. But in certain cases, the phobia appears to be triggered off by a complex series of events which includes stimuli arising from both outside and inside the patient's body. The sequence appears to be: perception of the feared event or situation→anxiety→bodily changes consequent to increased tension → perception and misinterpretation of these changes ▸ acute anxiety (the phobic response).

The following case illustrates a method of duplicating interoceptive stimuli for people suffering from fears of heart attack.

Case Report

Mrs. X was a 44-year-old housewife living with her husband and three children ranging from 3 to 14 years of age. She had never had any psychiatric treatment. She had functioned well in life and had no psychiatric symptoms except a fear of thunderstorms lasting many years. Two years previously, the fear had got much worse; it had generalized to cloudy days, rainy days, radio predictions of possible storms, and even to fireworks and the sound of airplane jet motors or hot-rod cars. It had also generalized to the time of the year when thunderstorms were likely, so that all spring, summer, and fall she was in a continuous state of anxiety and was confined to her home in cloudy or stormy weather or whenever the radio predicted a chance of storm even in the next 24 hours. During thunderstorms, she required constant companionship.

In the summer before treatment began, she had one day during a storm experienced some palpitation and shortness of breath, causing an immediate panic about having a heart attack. She had heart examinations, including EKG tests—all negative—on three separate occasions but she no longer felt able to do her housework as energetically as before. If she became slightly winded, or felt an extra-systole, she became anxious and would stop work and lie down for a time.

On examination, her physical condition was good and her mental status was negative except for the anxieties noted above. Our diagnosis was psychoneurosis, phobic reaction, and systematic desensitization was decided upon.

The patient relaxed and visualized and in 23 sessions was successfully desensitized to all aspects of thunderstorms and associated weather phenomena. During the course of this desensitization, in the week preceding the 14th session, she found herself menstruating and especially tense. During the 14th session the therapist evidently failed to note a rise in tension from one scene presentation to the next, nor did the patient herself signal it. Suddenly she experienced a sinking sensation in her chest and next she was experiencing a full-blown anxiety attack concerning her heart. Desensitization was interrupted and the patient was allowed to get up and walk around since she could not sit still without extreme effort. The attack eventually yielded to various measures, including a tranquilizer.

It was decided to interrupt the thunderstorm hierarchy and do a desensitization to the heart attack syndrome. The first hierarchy was one of *words*—lowest item being "Heartbeat" and highest being "Heart Attack." Next, she was desensitized to various *thoughts* about her heart and chest. A low item was "I have an ache in my chest"; a high item was "I have a pain over my heart." She was next desensitized to a hierarchy of *memories* of various feelings, ranging from imagining a "sensation" in her chest up to items such as pains, heart poundings, breathlessness, etc. Items were imagined singly and then in pairs, until finally the full combination of feelings was visualized.

We then duplicated in actuality the hierarchy of disturbing physical feelings. The patient was relaxed as usual in a semi-reclining position. The procedure was to interrupt the relaxation with a physical procedure which either mimicked or actually caused the feared sensation. As soon as she reported feeling any trace of the sensation, she was instructed to stop the procedure, relax again, and breathe normally. This immediately caused the disappearance of the sensation. In subsequent trials, the sensation was held for longer periods of time until it was clear that she could experience it without anxiety.

The feeling of needing air was produced simply by having her hold her breath for increasing lengths of time. Breathlessness was duplicated by having her perform fast breathing. The sensation of tension and vague pain in the chest, one of the most anxiety-causing stimuli, was duplicated as follows: She was asked to sit up and hold her arms rigidly straight out in front of her. She then scissored her arms, crossing them at the elbows so that they were approximately at a 60 degree-angle to each other. The therapist then grasped her wrists and scissored the arms a little more, instructing her to resist the movement. This maneuver immediately created a definite sense of tension in her chest, the amount of tension being controllable by the force and duration of the scissoring.

The extremely feared sensation of stiffness and pain in the left chest and arm was reproduced by having the patient, from a sitting position, extend the left arm rigidly forward and upward until the fist was at the level of the top of the head and vertically above the right shoulder. The therapist then pushed downward and medially on the outstretched, stiffened arm and the patient was instructed to resist any movement. This maneuver immediately produced pain and tension in the left pectoral and shoulder-girdle muscles, which was either quite similar to, or identical with, the fearful sensations the patient had experienced. These sensations were produced in a sub-hierarchy ranging from mild intensity and short duration to high intensity and longer duration.

The sensation of "nervousness in the chest" was obtained by having the patient sit slightly slumped over and engage in fast, deliberately tremulous breathing. This maneuver was first modeled by the therapist and them imitated by the patient.

The experience of heart pounding and lightheadedness was reproduced by having the patient exhale, hold her breath till it became uncomfortable, and then take several rapid breaths. The sensations produced in this manner ceased as soon as the patient returned to normal breathing. After several repetitions, the patient could experience the extrasystoles with no feeling of anxiety whatsoever.

The heart attack hierarchy was completed in seven sessions, of which the last two were used mainly for the *in vivo* maneuvers. Following this, the patient reported on immediate improvement in her ability to do housework and undergo exercise-related breathlessness, without fear. We then resumed work on the thunderstorm hierarchy, one session being used to review items previously desensitized. There appeared to have been no loss of the previously attained desensitization and the full hierarchy was completed uneventfully in seven more sessions.

She went through the storm season without experiencing a return of the severe panic or any fear related to the sensations previously associated with the idea of heart attack. She did experience anxiety of moderate intensity during one very prolonged and extremely violent thunderstorm within a month of ending treatment. During this anxiety she noticed that her heart was pounding for a moment, but did not experience any fear.

The patient practiced muscular relaxation at home, kept reviewing items from the hierarchies and remained comfortable during the stormy season. At follow-up, 11 months later, she remained symptom-free and had not developed any other signs of neurosis.

The Role of Expectancy and Physiological Feedback in Fear Research: A Review with Special Reference to Subject Characteristics

Thomas D. Borkovec
Department of Psychology
University of Iowa
Iowa City

Review of the expectancy literature in fear research indicates that a subject characteristic of intensity of fear is related to whether demand characteristic effects confound treatment effects. Review of physiological feedback studies suggests the potentially important role of physiological cues in maintaining and/or modifying fear behavior. Together, the two areas indicate that more research effort should be devoted to (a) the interaction of motoric, verbal, and physiological components of fear and (b) the role of individual differences, particularly at the physiological level, in those components and their modification.

Increased attention has been recently devoted to the effects of expectancy and physiological feedback in analogue fear studies. Expectancy manipulations operationally involve administration of therapy procedures with vs. without therapeutic instructions. Physiological feedback studies focus on the effects of amplified physiological signals (real or false) or the effects of actual manipulation of general arousal on fear behavior. Both of these research approaches will be viewed here as involving the manipulation of discriminative stimuli in the fearful subject's experimental environment which set the occasion for certain subsequent verbal and motoric behavior in that environment. The purpose of the present paper is to review and relate the relevant studies in these seemingly separate areas and to draw implications for outcome research with special reference to subject characteristic factors.

Expectancy

Wilkins (in press) has correctly cautioned researchers to avoid the circularity involved in positing an internal "expectancy" construct as an explanation of behavior or behavioral change. This problem can be overcome by viewing expectancy manipulations (presence or absence of therapeutic instructions) as discriminative stimuli or demand characteristics (Orne, 1959; Bernstein, in press) influencing posttest fear behavior. That is, implicit or explicit communication is made to the subjects in the therapeutic instruction conditions that the posttest is an assessment of the successfulness of the therapy sessions in *changing* their fear behavior (high demand for improved overt behavior), while subjects in the nontherapeutic condition are given no suggestions that they are to display posttest behavior different from their pretest behavior (low demand for improved behavior).

TABLE 1
PLACEBO AND CROSSED EXPECTANCY DESIGNS

	High demand for improved behavior	"Active" treatment effects	Low demand for improved behavior
(1) Treatment with nontherapeutic instructions		X	X
(2) Treatment with therapeutic instructions	X	X	
(3) Placebo with therapeutic instructions	X		
(4) Placebo with nontherapeutic instructions			X

The traditional control for such nonspecific therapy factors has been the use of placebo conditions. The complementary nature of the crossed expectancy design to the placebo control is seen in Table 1. The usual comparison has been between the treatment and placebo conditions, both of which are presented as effective therapeutic procedures (e.g., Paul, 1966). Both conditions are assumed to equate expectancy (an assumption that has been recently questioned by Baker and Kahn (1972) and Borkovec and Nau (in press)) and the critical difference is presumably the treatment component alone. If treatment is found to be superior to placebo on outcome measures, the conclusion is usually drawn that something "active" in the treatment itself was the cause of the improvement. A crossed expectancy factor, on the other hand, allows *identical* matching of treatment conditions on the active treatment procedure and attempts to vary only the subject's "expectancy" about the effect the procedure is presumed to have on his subsequent behavior. The choice of either design is, of course, a matter of the aim of the investigation: efficacy of a treatment procedure vs. the contribution of therapeutic suggestion to a treatment procedure. But two additional implications may follow from the crossed expectancy design: (a) A treatment procedure which produces improvement greater than a placebo condition, regardless of expectancy instructions, is indeed a powerful modification technique and includes some active ingredient separate from demand effects. (b) A treatment procedure which produces improvement greater than a placebo condition only under therapeutic instructions may be a powerful technique, but its effectiveness resides either in the power of its face validity to the subject or in the interaction of its face validity and its active ingredients. That active ingredients can interact with expectancy conditions has been demonstrated even in drug research (e.g., Dinnerstein and Halm, 1970).

While the above discussion indicates the potentially important role that the crossed expectancy factor can play in coming to conclusions about the active ingredients of treatment procedures, the data thus far collected employing this design have been equivocal. Ten of these studies (McGlynn, Mealiea, & Nawas, 1969; McGlynn & Mapp, 1970; McGlynn & Williams, 1970; Lomont & Brock, 1971; McGlynn, 1971; McGlynn, Reynolds, & Linder, 1971a; McGlynn, Reynolds, & Linder, 1971b; Howlett & Nawas, 1972; McGlynn, 1972; McGlynn, Gaynor, & Phur, 1972) have demonstrated that systematic desensitization is equally effective with or without therapeutic instructions, while nine others (Efran & Marcia, 1967; Leitenberg, Agras, Barlow, & Oliveau, 1969; Marcia, Rubin, & Efran, 1969; Oliveau, Agras, Leitenberg, Moore, & Wright, 1969; Parrino, 1971; Borkovec, 1972; Miller, 1972; Persely & Leventhal, 1972; Rappaport, 1972) found therapeutic expectancy superior to nontherapeutic expectancy within therapy conditions (including desensitization, implosion, and operant shaping).

In one attempt to eliminate the confusion, McGlynn, Reynolds, and Linder (1971b) tested the hypothesis that the timing of the therapeutic instructions (pre-treatment instructions alone vs. pre- plus intra-treatment instructions) was the major determinant in demonstrating the expectancy effect. They found no difference between these two therapeutic desensitization conditions and neither differed from a non-therapeutic desensitization group, while all three conditions showed greater improvement than pseudo-desensitization and no-treatment groups. The discrepant data remained unexplained.

While other procedural variations may have contributed to the contradictory results in the expectancy literature (Davison & Wilson 1973; Wilkins, in press), it is proposed that the subject characteristic differences may also play an important role. Bernstein (in press) has argued that the influence of demand characteristics can be reduced if investigators are careful to select truly phobic subjects for their research. This would suggest that perhaps the contradictory results among the expectancy studies reflect a greater proportion of more fearful subjects in studies failing to demonstrate the expectancy effect. As seen in Table 2, a review of the selection criteria employed in the expectancy studies supports this notion. Studies failing to find an expectancy effect employed only those subjects who reported the highest level of fear on their respective self-report scales; studies demonstrating expectancy effects allowed a range of fear report within their scales. Secondly, with one exception (Miller, 1972), the latter studies employed a less stringent behavioral selection criterion. Finally, in three of the studies using less stringent selection criteria and favoring the expectancy effect (Leitenberg et al., 1969; Oliveau et al., 1969; Parrino, 1971), subjects had several exposures to the actual feared object during the course of treatment. As Lomont and Brock (1971) have suggested, the demand for showing improvement during these exposures was clearly greater for subjects in the therapeutic condition ("these exposures are to assess your progress") than for those in non-therapeutic condition ("these exposures are to refresh your memory"). It is known from other research that mere repeated exposure results in increased improvement (Rachman, 1966; Borkovec & Craighead, 1971) and that therapeutic suggestions of improvement produce significantly greater approach change than simple repeated exposure (Borkovec, 1973).

The above review of expectancy studies suggests the following hypothesis: External demand characteristics for improved overt behavior in outcome studies have a greater effect on low, fearful subjects than on high, fearful subjects *within* the analogue phobic population. This hypothesis implies that many analogue outcome studies (those using some

TABLE 2
CROSSED EXPECTANCY FACTOR STUDIES DEMONSTRATING AND FAILING TO DEMONSTRATE EXPECTANCY EFFECTS AND THEIR SELF-REPORT AND BEHAVIORAL SUBJECT SELECTION CRITERIA

	Subject selection criteria	
Studies demonstrating an expectancy effect	Self-report [a]	Behavioral [b] approach
Efran & Marcia, 1967	"very much afraid or terror" (6 or 7 on a 7-pt. scale)	bare hand
Leitenberg *et al.*, 1969	"definitely tense, extremely tense, or terror" (3, 4, or 5 on a 5-pt. scale)	bare hand
Marcia *et al.*, 1969	"very much afraid or terror" (6 or 7 on a 7-pt. scale)	bare hand
Oliveau *et al.*, 1969	"definitely tense, extremely tense, or terror" (3, 4, or 5 on a 5-pt. scale)	bare hand
Parrino, 1971	"much fear, very much fear, or terror" (5, 6, or 7 on a 7-pt. scale)	bare hand
Borkovec, 1972	"much fear, very much fear, or terror" (5, 6, or 7 on a 7-pt. scale)	bare hand
Miller, 1972	"fearful"	lift object briefly
Persely & Leventhal, 1972	"very much afraid or terror" (6 or 7 on a 7-pt. scale)	bare hand
Rappaport, 1972	"much fear, very much fear, or terror" (5, 6 or 7 on a 7-pt. scale)	no pretest
Studies demonstrating no expectancy effect		
McGlynn *et al.*, 1969	"intense fear" [c]	gloved hand
McGlynn & Mapp, 1970	"intense fear" [c]	gloved hand
McGlynn & Williams, 1970	"intense fear" [c]	10-in. wooden pointer
Howlett & Nawas, 1972	reported inability to touch object with gloved hand	12-in. wooden pointer
Lomont & Brock, 1971	"terror" (7 on a 7-pt. scale)	approach no closer than 3 ft
McGlynn, 1971	"intense fear" [c]	gloved hand
McGlynn *et al.*, 1971a	"intense fear" [c]	gloved hand
McGlynn, *et al.*, 1971b	"intense fear" [c]	gloved hand
McGlynn, 1972	"intense fear" [c]	gloved hand
McGlynn *et al.*, 1972	"intense fear" [c]	gloved hand

[a] *S* was excluded from participation if he reported less fear than indicated.
[b] *S* was excluded from participation if he touched object as indicated.
[c] 7 on a 7-pt. scale.

or all low, phobic subjects) may primarily reflect a demand effect (in agreement with Bernstein & Paul, 1971) or a demand by subject characteristic interaction effect. How the investigator defines intensity of fear, then, becomes an extremely important decision which may influence the extent and direction of the effects which his treatment and extra-treatment variables will have on outcome.

Physiological Feedback

While verbal, overt behavioral, and cognitive aspects are often included in behavioral definitions of anxiety, the physiological component has long held an important position (e.g., Wolpe, 1958; Speilberger, 1966; Paul, 1969; Mathews, 1971). The role of physiological responses to be stressed here is somewhat similar, functionally, to the role of expectancy manipulations presented above. As a response-produced stimulus, physiological reactions may serve as discriminative cues for subsequent verbal, behavioral, and cognitive responses. Stampfl and Levis (1969) have indicated the importance of including interoceptive stimuli as part of the CS complex in the implosive treatment of anxiety, while recent case studies (Everaerd, 1970; Furst & Cooper, 1970) suggest that such cues may be the crucial component in the maintenance, and the efficient elimination, of some types of neurotic disturbances. Most of the experimental evidence for the importance of internal cuing and its influence on emotional behavior come from studies presenting physiological feedback (false or real) during treatment or test conditions, or from studies directly manipulating arousal level prior to testing. The use of real autonomic feedback has been reported effective in modifying autonomic functioning in experimental subjects (Brener & Hothersall, 1966; Lang, Stroufe, & Hastings, 1967; Budzynski & Stoyva, 1969; Green, Walters, Green, & Murphy, 1969; Grim, 1971) and clinical patients (Jacobs & Felton, 1969; Budzynski, Stoyva, & Adler, 1970). Such studies are suggestive of the potential effect that a subject's internal responding may have on subsequent behavior, if the subject is made aware of such feedback through amplified signals. Much of the remaining research has stemmed from the work of Schachter and his co-workers (Schachter & Singer, 1962; Schachter & Wheeler, 1962; Schachter, 1964; Nisbett & Schachter, 1966). The theory of emotion based on their research suggests that nonspecific arousal interacts with environmental cues in determining overt emotional behavior. Thus, a subject will label a feeling state as a particular emotion depending on the environmental cues available to him when he cannot identify the source of the arousal.

False Feedback Manipulations

Koenig and Del Castillo (1969) demonstrated the potentially important role of the physiological cues in maintaining fear responses. Awareness of the onset of extinction trials in an aversive conditioning paradigm was shown to facilitate extinction of conditioned GSR, while false feedback indicating continued emotional responsivity to the CS-retarded GSR extinction in both aware and non-aware conditions. Similarly, Wilkins (1971a) found that false feedback can influence the emotionality of a subject's interpretation of environmental stimuli. Presented with ambiguous auditory messages, subjects receiving high arousal feedback reported more emotional interpretations of the messages than subjects receiving low arousal feedback.

In the area of fear reduction, Valins and Ray (1967) produced approach improvements in snake phobics by manipulating heart rate feedback during slide presentation of feared stimuli. Both Sushinsky and Bootzin (1970) and Gaupp, Stern, and Galbraith (1972) failed to replicate this effect, but both studies in an appropriate effort of control included a problematical behavioral pretest. First, this may have guaranteed more fearful subjects who, given the expectancy literature discussed above, are less susceptible to demand effects. Secondly, during a pretest snake exposure, subjects will experience fear (physiological cues, avoidance, etc.) prior to the weaker exposure (slides of snakes). Despite the use of the treatment task and false feedback to demonstrate to the subject that she is not fearful, a subject may respond more in accord with her own past experience with the *in vivo* situation than with an experimenter's feedback devices and tasks (Bandura, 1969; Davison & Wilson, in press), if there is no reason for the subject to believe that her pretest reaction is likely to change as a consequence of the experimental task. This was indeed the case, since in both studies subjects were run under non-therapeutic (low demand) instructions. Within-group analysis in the Gaupp *et al.* (1972) study demonstrated, incidentally, the possible importance of actual feedback: subjects showing EKG decreases over slide presentations displayed greater posttest approach than subjects showing no change or increases in EKG. A third attempted replication of the Valins and Ray (1967) experiment was also unsuccessful. Kent, Wilson, and Nelson (1972), pointing to the use of money incentives for increased approach in the Valins and Ray study, used a "conventional" approach posttest and failed to find significant differences between experimental and control groups (although the differences were apparently in the Valins and Ray direction). The discrepancy appears to be between the use of high (money) vs. low demand posttests.

Taken together, the above studies suggest that false feedback may modify fear behavior in low fearful subjects if pretest experience does not mitigate the effects of the feedback stimulus and if posttesting is done under conditions high in demand for improved overt behavior. Borkovec and Glasgow (in press) recently obtained data partially supporting this hypothesis. Fearful subjects were randomly assigned to a Solomon four-groups design (pretest vs. no-pretest and heart-rate feedback vs. nonfeedback during snake-slide presentation). Posttesting was performed under high demand instructions. As predicted, non-pretested subjects receiving heart-rate feedback displayed greater posttest approach than non-pretested subjects receiving the same signals described as electronic noise. No differences were found between feedback and non-feedback groups who had been exposed to a pretest. Additionally, actual heart-rate during slide presentation was greater in the pretested groups than the non-pretested groups across feedback conditions, suggesting a mitigating influence of actual feedback on false feedback effects.

Finally, in a snake-fear study assessing the interaction of demand characteristics (suggested improvement vs. no suggested improvement instructions) and false feedback (heart rate increasing vs. decreasing during posttest), Borkovec (in press) found pulse rate reductions over testings only under the condition of strong demand and increasing feedback. Approach behavior was complexly determined by an interaction of feedback and subject characteristics, and is discussed later.

Arousal Manipulations

Aside from the correlational evidence in Gaupp *et al.* (1972) and Borkovec and Glasgow (in press) only three experimental studies have assessed the influence of what might be considered direct manipulation of real feedback on subsequent phobic behavior. In the first, Anthony and Duerfeldt (1970) presented half of their subjects with training task exposures to the feared stimulus involving minimal tension. Subjects in this condition were asked to repeatedly move the feared object to "their point of slightest tension." The other half of the subjects were asked to move the object to "their point of maximum tension, all the tension you can stand." The latter group showed significantly less approach improvement than the former on the posttest. In the second study (Rimm, Kennedy, Miller, &

Tchida, 1971), subjects underwent drive-induction (threat of snake exposure, threat of shock, or frustration), drive-reduction (relaxation or music), or no-task control conditions. The relaxation group displayed significantly greater approach than the three drive-induction groups and greater approach than the music group, while the control condition was significantly different from snake threat and frustration conditions. Given that posttesting was performed under low demand conditions (no implications that drive tasks were expected to influence approach), the main difference among the groups was the presence or absence of physiological arousal cues during the immediately following posttest exposure. Low arousal subjects displayed the greatest approach, despite the fact that all but one of the arousal manipulations occurred under a context irrelevant to the phobic stimulus. Finally, Borkovec (1972) demonstrated that both systematic desensitization and implosive therapy successfully reduced physiological arousal responses to phobic stimulus exposure, but only those subjects receiving therapeutic instructions within those therapy groups displayed increased approach. Hypothetically, modified internal cues were thus discriminative of increased approach only when instructional sets resulted in labelling internal cue change as indicative of improvement.

Earlier, it was concluded that external demand for improved overt behavior has a greater affect on low, fearful subjects than on high, fearful subjects. Given the physiological feedback research, two corollary hypotheses can be offered: (a) External demand cue manipulation will affect fear behavior to the extent that actual, internal physiological cues are absent. Subjects for whom the physiological component is very strong will be little affected by demand cues suggesting improvement; physiological cues will maintain fear behavior until such cues and/or their functional relationships with subsequent behaviors are changed. (b) Actual physiological cue manipulation will reduce (or maintain) fear behavior in the presence of external demand cues discriminative of non-fear (or fear) behavior.

Implications

Two commonsense and related implications follow from these hypotheses yet little research effort has been addressed to them. The first implication is that human behavior involves a complex set of somewhat separate, but certainly interacting, response systems. The separateness of verbal, motoric and physiological indices of fear is seen in the typically low intercorrelations (Lang, 1968), and the evidence that solely changing verbal behavior (Hart, 1966; Suinn, Jorgensen, Stewart, & McGuirk, 1971), verbal associations (Hekmat & Vanian, 1971), or motor behavior (Leitenberg *et al.,* 1971) can produce fear reduction. Of greater importance and veridicality to human behavior, however, is the potential interaction of the three response systems. Intercorrelation may be low due to different lag time of change in the different systems (Mathews, 1971). And the fact that desirable change can occur from treatment of any isolated system suggests only that therapy packages should be developed which systematically modify every response system involved, in the most efficient and efficacious way (Lang, 1968). Unfortunately, little research had been directly aimed at untangling the interacting effects of the three response systems on each other, although the evidence of their potential interaction is clear (Wilkins, 1971b).

The second implication involves the importance of individual differences in fear behavior and its maintaining conditions. Given the various response systems (verbal, cognitive, motoric, and physiological) and their interrelationships, it can be reasonably suggested that individuals differ in terms of which response system or systems play the primary, functional role in the fear response and/or how those systems interrelate. The remainder of this discussion will be devoted to individual differences at the physiological level.

Bernstein and Paul (1971) strongly state that "it is incumbent upon E to employ as Ss only persons who can be shown to display significant and therefore clinically relevant increases in physiological arousal and cognitive distress (i.e., anxiety) as a result of the presence of the presumed eliciting stimulus object." Yet subjects in most analogue studies are matched on behavioral avoidance and equated on self-report indices of fear. This leaves physiological reactivity, rarely assessed or controlled. Almost all analogue studies, then, employ phobic selection criteria which in no way directly tap a response system considered of major importance in the definition of anxiety. Oddly enough in many studies, physiological measurement is absent even from posttest improvement indices, even though the treatment techniques often assessed (e.g., systematic desensitization, implosive therapy) depend to some extent on classical autonomic conditioning paradigms for their theoretical underpinnings. Thus, despite elaborate matching and random assignment procedures, it is quite likely that some studies incorporate few subjects for whom physiological reactivity and internal cues are functionally important in their fear behavior. Even with an equal sampling of high and low reactivity subjects, there is little guarantee that random assignment (with usually small *n*) equates treatment groups within a study on this potentially important variable.

If the physiological component of fear behavior is important and if selection criteria of many studies ignore this factor, resulting inevitably in either poor representation of such responses or lack of information about its representation, then what is to be said about the results of such studies? What type of underlying extinction or counterconditioning principle can be tested if a treatment technique primarily designed to modify a particular response system is applied to subjects for whom that response system is functionally irrelevant? It is not suprising that manipulations such as reinforcement, modeling, demand characteristics, placebo, repeated testing, etc., produce significant changes in approach behavior. Such effects can be expected if one assumes that avoidance behavior and reports of fear can be established and/or maintained by reinforcement, modeling, demand characteristics, suggestion, and lack of opportunity to behave toward the "feared" object. To reiterate the two hypotheses, in the absence of strong physiological cues, other response systems are more easily modified via external stimuli; in the presence of strong physiological cues, such cues need to be modified before other external manipulations can efficiently influence other response systems.

One study (Borkovec, in press) directly addressed the issue of individual differences in physiological reactivity and their influence on changes in approach behavior. Analogue snake-phobic subjects strong vs. weak in actual reactivity and strong vs. weak in self-reported autonomic activity were exposed to repeated testing under various suggestion and physiological feedback conditions. The absence of strong internal cues, as defined by actual reactivity, was found to be related to approach change in two separate studies. Two of eight groups in the second study showed discrepant results, one due to high pretest performance. The second group, however, involving subjects strong in both perceived and actual reactivity prior to posttest displayed surprisingly superior posttest approach. Correlated with its approach improvement was this group's substantial pulse rate reduction at posttest. While no cause-and-effect conclusion can be drawn, this result does similarly lead to the hypothesis that in the presence of strong internal cues (subjects strong in both perceived and actual reactivity), such cues need to be modified before other cues (e.g., suggested improvement) can affect approach behavior.

Three other recent studies lend further support to the importance of individual differences in physiological reactivity and their relation to outcome in analogue research. Lang, Melamed, and Hart (1970) report a finding which strongly suggests that subjects for whom the physiological component of the fear response appears important respond best under desensitization therapy. Specifically, greater outcome improvement was found among subjects displaying high heart rates during reportedly fearful scenes and greater heart rate decrease over repeated presentations of scenes. Subjects not as autonomically responsive and not reporting fear correlated with responsivity showed less fear reduction at posttest.

Grim (1971) found that muscle tension increased state anxiety among subjects initially low in self-reported anxiety but decreased anxiety among initially high-anxiety subjects. Further, real physiological (respiration) feedback facilitated decreases in anxiety among all relaxing subjects except those with initial, low anxiety scores.

Finally, Farmer and Wright (1971) tested the anxiety-inhibiting effects of muscle relaxation as a function of individual differences in muscle tension as measured by Fisher and Cleveland's (1958) body image Barrier scores. In a typical analogue snake-phobia study, high and low Barrier subjects received desensitization-with-relaxation, desensitization-with-muscle-tension, or no treatment. Relaxation was found to reduce successfully fear in both subject groups, but to a greater extent among high Barrier subjects, while only low Barrier subjects showed improvement under muscle-tension conditions. The authors suggest that the most efficient elimination of conditioned anxiety would be achieved by inhibiting a subject's maximum physiological response system.

The present paper, of course, would propose that the most efficient elimination of fear behavior would be achieved by modifying that response system or systems most functionally involved in the behavior, be it physiological or otherwise. The effectiveness of desensitization and implosive therapy techniques may in part be due to the extinction of conditioned autonomic responses. That active ingredient will be important to the extent that that response system is functionally important to the subject's fear behavior, i.e., with high physiological reaction (high phobic) subjects. But, considering fear behavior as involving a set of interacting response systems, such changes are, necessarily, only part of the explanation. Elimination of physiological cues, however, formerly maintaining the fear behavior and mitigating the effects of external stimuli, allows the opportunity for the other response systems to be influenced by therapeutic context or other external demand characteristics. Thus, all the variables listed by Wilkins (1971b) as contributing to desensitization effectiveness (i.e., expectancy, therapist reinforcement, information feedback, controlled attention shifts, and exposure to contingencies of non-avoidant behavior) are indeed important to the extent that they modify cognitive, self-report, and overt behavioral response systems. These variables may account for most of the changes in studies employing typical analogue phobic subjects. In studies of intensely fearful subjects, on the other hand, modification of internal cues may often be necessary before manipulation of other variables will influence remaining response systems.

References

Anthony, R.M., & Duerfeldt, P.H. The effect of tension level and contingent reinforcement on fear reduction. *Behavior Therapy,* 1970, *1,* 445-464.

Baker, B.L., & Kahn, M. A reply to "Critique of 'Treatment of insomnia by relaxation training': Relaxation Training, Rogerian Therapy, or demand characteristics." *Journal of Abnormal Psychology,* 1972, *79,* 94-96.

Bandura, A. *Principles of behavior modification.* New York: Holt, Rinehart and Winston, 1969.

Bernstein, D. A. Behavioral fear assessment: anxiety or artifact? In H. Adams & P. Unikel (Eds.), *Issues and trends in behavior therapy.* Springfield: Charles C. Thomas, in press.

Bernstein, D.A., & Paul, G.L. Some comments on therapy analogue research with small animal "phobias." *Journal of Behavior Therapy and Experimental Psychiatry,* 1971, *2,* 225-237.

Borkovec, T.D. Effects of expectancy on the outcome of systematic desensitization and implosive treatments for analogue fear. *Behavior Therapy,* 1972, *3,* 29-40.

Borkovec, T.D. The effects of instructional suggestion and physiological cues on analogue fear. *Behavior Therapy,* 1973, *4,* 185-192.

Borkovec, T.D., & Craighead, W.E. The comparison of two methods of assessing fear and avoidance behavior. *Behaviour Research and Therapy,* 1971, *9,* 285-291.

Borkovec, T.D., & Glasgow, R.E. Boundary conditions of false heart-rate feedback effects on avoidance behavior: a resolution of discrepant results. *Behaviour Research and Therapy,* in press.

Borkovec, T.D., & Nau, S.D. Credibility of analogue therapy rationales. *Journal of Behavior Therapy and Experimental Psychiatry,* in press.

Brener, J., & Hothersall, D. Heart rate control under conditions of augmented sensory feedback. *Psychophysiology,* 1966, *3,* 23-28.

Budzynski, T.H., & Stoyva, J.M. An instrument for producing deep muscle relaxation by means of analogue information feedback. *Journal of Applied Behavior Analysis,* 1969, *2,* 231-237.

Budzynski, T., Stoyva, J., & Adler, C. Feedback-induced muscle relaxation: application to tension headache. *Journal of Behavior Therapy and Experimental Psychiatry,* 1970, *1,* 205-211.

Davison, G.C., & Wilson, G.T. Processes of fear-reduction in systematic desensitization: cognitive and social reinforcement factors in humans. *Behavior Therapy,* 1973, *4,* 1-21.

Dinnerstein, A.J., & Halm, J. Modification of placebo effects by means of drugs: effects of aspirin and placebos on self-rated moods. *Journal of Abnormal Psychology,* 1970, *75,* 308-314.

Efran, J.S., & Marcia, J.E. Treatment of fears by expectancy manipulation: An exploratory investigation. *Proceedings of the 75th Annual Convention of the American Psychological Association,* 1967, *2,* 239-240.

Everaerd, W.T. Reading as the counterconditioning agent in a cardiac neurosis. *Journal of Behavior Therapy and Experimental Psychiatry,* 1970, *1,* 165-167.

Farmer, R.G., & Wright, J.M. Muscular reactivity and systematic desensitization, *Behavior Therapy,* 1972, *2,* 1-10.

Fisher, S., & Cleveland, S.E. *Body image and personality.* Princeton: Van Nostrand, 1958.

Furst, J.B., & Cooper, A. Combined use of imaginal and interoceptive stimuli in desensitizing fear of heart attacks. *Journal of Behavior Therapy and Experimental Psychiatry,* 1970, *1,* 87-89.

Gaupp, L.A., Stern, R.M., & Galbraith, G.G. False heart-rate feedback and reciprocal inhibition by aversive relief in the treatment of snake avoidance behavior. *Behavior Therapy,* 1972, *3,* 7-20.

Green, E.E., Walters, E.D., Green, A.M., & Murphy, G. Feedback technique for deep relaxation. *Psychophysiology,* 1969, *6,* 271-277.

Grim, P.F. Anxiety change produced by self-induced muscle tension and by relaxation with respiration feedback. *Behavior Therapy,* 1971, *2,* 11-17.

Hart, J.D. Fear reduction as a function of the assumption and success of a therapeutic role. Unpublished master's thesis, University of Wisconsin, 1966.

Hekmat, H., & Vanian, D. Behavior modification through covert sematic desensitization. *Journal of Consulating and Clinical Psychology,* 1971, *36,* 248-251.

Howlett, S.C., & Nawas, M.M. Exposure to aversive imagery and suggestion in systematic desensitization. In Rubin, R.D., Fensterheim, H., Lazarus, A.A., & Franks, C.M. (Eds.), *Advances in behavior therapy.* New York: Academic Press, 1971. Pp. 123-135.

Jacobs, A., & Felton, G.S. Visual feedback of myoelectric output to facilitate muscle relaxation in normal persons and patients with neck injuries. *Archives of Physical and Medical Rehabilitation,* 1969, *50,* 34-39.

Kent, R.N., Wilson, G.T., & Nelson, R. Effects of false heart-rate feedback on avoidance behavior: an investigation of "cognitive desensitization." *Behavior Therapy,* 1972, *3,* 1-6.

Koenig, K.P., & Del Castillo, D. False feedback and longevity of the conditioned GSR during extinction: some implications for aversion therapy. *Journal of Abnormal Psychology,* 1969, *74,* 505-510.

Lang, P.J. Fear reduction and fear behavior: problems in treating a construct. In J.M. Shlien (Ed.), *Research in psychotherapy.* American Psychological Association, Washington, D.C., 1968. Pp. 90-102.

Lang, P.J., Melamed, B.G., & Hart, J. A psychophysiological analysis of fear modification using an automated desensitization procedure. *Journal of Abnormal Psychology,* 1970, *76,* 220-234.

Lang, P.J., Stroufe, L.A., & Hastings, J.E. Effects of feedback and instructional set on the control of cardiac-rate variability. *Journal of Experimental Psychology,* 1967, *75,* 425-430.

Leitenberg, H., Agras, W.S., Barlow, D.H., & Oliveau, D.C. Contribution of selective positive reinforcement and therapeutic instructions to systematic desensitization. *Journal of Abnormal Psychology,* 1969, *74,* 113-118.

Leitenberg, H., Agras, S., Butz, R., & Wincze, J. Relationship between heart rate and behavioral change during the treatment of phobias. *Journal of Abnormal Psychology,* 1971, *78,* 59-68.

Lomont, J.F., & Brock, L. Cognitive factors in systematic desensitization. *Behavior Research and Therapy,* 1971, *9,* 187-195.

Marcia, J.E., Rubin, B.M., & Efran, J.S. Systematic desensitization: Expectancy change or counterconditioning. *Journal of Abnormal Psychology,* 1969, *74,* 382-387.

Mathews, A.M. Psychophysiological approaches to the investigation of desensitization and related procedures. *Psychological Bulletin,* 1971, *76,* 73-91.

McGlynn, F.D. Experimental desensitization following three types of instructions. *Behaviour Research and Therapy,* 1971, *9,* 367-369.

McGlynn, F.D., Mealiea, W.L., & Nawas, M.M. Systematic desensitization of snake-avoidance under two conditions of suggestion. *Psychological Reports,* 1969, *25,* 220-222.

McGlynn, F.D., & Mapp, R.H. Systematic desensitization of snake-avoidance following three types of suggestion. *Behavior Research and Therapy,* 1970, *8,* 197-201.

McGlynn, F.D., & Williams, C.W. Systematic desensitization of snake-avoidance under three conditions of suggestion. *Journal of Behavior Therapy and Experimental Psychiatry,* 1970, *1,* 97-101.

McGlynn, F.D., Reynolds, E.J., & Linder, L.H. Experimental desensitization following therapeutically-oriented and physiologically-oriented instructions. *Journal of Behavior Therapy and Experimental Psychiatry,* 1971a, *2,* 13-18.

McGlynn, F.D., Reynolds, E.J., & Linder, L.H. Systematic desensitization with pretreatment and intra-treatment therapeutic instructions. *Behavior Research and Therapy,* 1971b, *9,* 57-64.

McGlynn, F.D. Systematic desensitization under two conditions of induced expectancy. *Behaviour Research and Therapy,* 1972, *10,* 229-234.

McGlynn, F.D., Gaynor, R., & Phur, J. Experimental desensitization of snake-avoidance after an instructional manipulation. *Journal of Clinical Psychology,* 1972, *28,* 224-227.

Miller, S.B. The contribution of therapeutic instructions to systematic desensitization. *Behaviour Research and Therapy,* 1972, *10,* 159-170.

Nisbett, R.E., & Schachter, S. Cognitive manipulation of pain. *Journal of Experimental Social Psychology,* 1966, *2,* 227-236.

Oliveau, D.C., Agras, W.S., Leitenberg, H., Moore, R.C., & Wright, E.D. Systematic desensitization, therapeutically-oriented instructions and selective positive reinforcement. *Behaviour Research and Therapy,* 1969, *7,* 27-34.

Orne, M.T. On the social psychology of the psychological experiment: with particular reference to demand characteristics and their implications. Symposium paper presented at American Psychological Association Convention, New York, 1961.

Parrino, J.J. Effect of pretherapy information on learning in psychotherapy. *Journal of Abnormal Psychology,* 1971, *77,* 17-24.

Paul, G.L. *Insight vs. desensitization in psychotherapy.* Stanford: Stanford University Press, 1966.

Paul, G.L. Physiological effects of relaxation training and hypnotic suggestion. *Journal of Abnormal Psychology,* 1969, *74,* 425-437.

Persely, G., & Leventhal, D. B. The effects of therapeutically-oriented instructions and of the pairing of anxiety imagery and relaxation in systematic desensitization. *Behavior Therapy*, 1972, *3*, 417-424.

Rachman, S. Studies in desensitization. III. Speed of generalization. *Behaviour Research and Therapy*, 1966, *4*, 7-15.

Rappaport, H. The modification of avoidance behavior: Expectancy, autonomic reactivity, and verbal report. *Journal of Consulting and Clinical Psychology*, 1972, *39*, 404-414.

Rimm, D.C., Kennedy, T.D., Miller, H.L., & Tchida, G.R. Experimentally manipulated drive level and avoidance behavior. *Journal of Abnormal Psychology*, 1971, *78*, 43 48.

Schachter, S. The interaction of cognitive and physiological determinants of emotional state. In L. Berkowitz (Ed.), *Advances in experimental social psychology*, Vol. 1, New York: Academic Press, 1964. Pp. 49-80.

Schachter, S., & Singer, J. E. Cognitive, social, and physiological determinants of emotional state. *Psychological Review*, 1962, *69*, 379-399.

Schachter, S., & Wheeler, L. Epinephrine, chlorpromazine and amusement. *Journal of Abnormal and Social Psychology*, 1962, *65*, 121-128.

Spielberger, C.D. Theory and research on anxiety. In C.D. Spielberger (Ed.), *Anxiety and behavior*. New York: Academic Press, 1966. Pp. 3-20.

Stampfl, T.G., & Levis, D.J. Learning theory: an aid to dynamic therapeutic practice. In L.D. Eron and R. Callahan (Eds.), *Relationship of theory to practice in psychotherapy*. Chicago: Aldine, 1969. Pp. 85-114.

Suinn, R.M., Jorgensen, G.T., Stewart, S.T., & McGuirk, F.D. Fears as attitudes: experimental reduction of fear through reinforcement. *Journal of Abnormal Psychology*, 1971, *78*, 272-279.

Sushinsky, L.W., & Bootzin, R.R. Cognitive desensitization as a model of systematic desensitization. *Behaviour Research and Therapy*, 1970, *8*, 29-34.

Valins, S., & Ray, A.A. Effects of cognitive desensitization on avoidance behavior. *Journal of Personality and Social Psychology*, 1967, *4*, 400-408.

Wilkins, W. Perceptual distortion to account for arousal. *Journal of Abnormal Psychology*, 1971a, *78*, 252-265.

Wilkins, W. Desensitization: social and cognitive factors underlying the effectiveness of Wolpe's procedure. *Psychological Bulletin*, 1971b, *76*, 311-317.

Wilkins, W. Expectancy of therapeutic gain: an empirical and conceptual critique. *Journal of Consulting and Clinical Psychology*, in press.

Wolpe, J. *Psychotherapy by reciprocal inhibition*. Stanford: Stanford University Press, 1958.

Expectancy in the Behavioral Management of Fear

Ian Wickramasekera
Peoria School of Medicine
University of Illinois College of Medicine
Peoria

Patient expectation can powerfully influence the outcome of both physiological (medical) and psychological interventions (Shapiro, 1971). This variable has been labeled expectancy, but the specific mechanism of its operation in altering maladaptive motor and visceral behavior has not been specified. A recent review (Hilgard and Hilgard, 1975) of a large number of controlled studies indicates that the expectation or placebo variable tends to be about 50% as effective as a genuine analgesic (e.g., morphine) in the control of primarily organic pain (e.g., post-surgical)

Several efforts have been made in the Behavior Therapy Literature, with mixed results, to document the effectiveness of the expectancy variable (Wilkins, 1973; Borkovec, 1973). Only about half of the studies have found a significant expectancy effect. Efforts to resolve this paradox within Behavior Therapy have taken many forms including the following: a denial of the reality of the effect, calling the issue a semantic problem; conceptualizing it as an epiphenomenon; and attempting to specify the conditions (high physiological fear component) under which the effect will *not* be observed (Borkovec, 1973).

The clear medical evidence for an expectancy effect and the confused state of the behavioral literature in regard to the same effect suggest that the methodologically sophisticated behavioral researchers may be impeded by the incomplete nature of their clinical sophistication. Sophisticated clinicians have always recognized that a basic property of the powerful expectancy effect was its unreliability. I pointed this out previously (Wickramasekera, 1969, 1970) with the following quotation from Freud:

In the first place, let me remind you that psychotherapy is in no way a modern method of healing. . . . In Lowenfeld's instructive work *(Lehrbuch der gesamten Psychotherapie)* many of the methods of primitive and ancient medical science are described. The majority of them must be classed under the head of psychotherapy; in order to effect a cure a condition of "expectant faith" was induced in sick persons. . . . We have learned to use the word "suggestion" for this phenomenon, and Mobius has taught us that the unreliability which we deplore in so many of our therapeutic measures may be traced back actually to the disturbing influence of this very powerful factor. . . . It is disadvantageous, however, to leave entirely in the hands of the patient what the mental factor in your treatment of him shall be. In this way it is uncontrollable; it can neither be measured nor intensified. Is it not then a justifiable endeavour on the part of a physician to seek to control this factor, to use it with a purpose, and to direct and strengthen it? This and nothing else is what scientific psychotherapy proposes [pp. 250-251]

Unreliability of the expectancy effect in the therapy context can mean one or more of the following:

1. There are large and significant individual differences in the extent to which the expectancy variable will be effective in changing behavior. I hypothesize that the above differences are at least partly related to neurophysiological differences (which are genetically transmitted or acquired prior to late adolescence) in the direct instructional (verbal) control of motor and visceral behavior. This variable has been most systematically investigated under the rubric individual differences in "hypnotizability," and refers to what the subject says to himself or what is said to him. The distinction between primary and secondary suggestibility is ignored in this analysis.

2. Intra-subject reliability of instructional (verbal) control of behavior will oscillate within limits, depending on at least one or more of the following factors:

a. The extent and depth to which the instructional intervention is perceived by the subject to intrude into his life style and to militate against or enhance his behavioral and phantasy priorities.

b. The extent to which the intervention is perceived as episodic (Orne, 1965) or as likely to have durable consequences. In the hypnosis literature one is struck by the high reliability in hypnotic performance in the laboratory situation (which is a relatively non-intrusive episodic transaction which is potentially insulatable from life by the special "research subject" role) and by the greater oscillations in hypnotic performance in the clinical treatment situation even in subjects of high measured hypnotizability.

c. The character of the specific subject's unique and relatively stable profile of hypnotizability. This means that a given subject will show a profile of response to instructional intervention, for example, poor response to psychomotor test suggestions, good response to cognitive items, and superior response to auditory but not visual hallucinations. Different instructional interventions (e.g., visually or cognitively loaded) will differentially effect separate but stable response systems. The recently, well-documented dissociations (poor coupling) between verbal, motor, and visceral response systems (Lang, 1971) probably provided the observational basis for the Freudian concept of "unconscious" behavior, and appear relevant to this dimension of individual difference. It is likely that careful attention to an individual's unique and relatively stable psychophysiological profile (Lacey, 1967) will further increase the precision of instructional interventions.

    d. The nature of the transaction between patient and therapist with regard to the extent to which "attraction"—positive transference or negative transference—aspects predominate. Another determinant of the patient's response may be the degree of prior deprivation or satiation of social approval. It appears that changes in this variable cannot be simply attributed to general sensory deprivation, general drive level, or cue properties of verbal approval (Eisenberger, 1970). In one-shot or short-term relationships most of the quality of some patients' perceptions (in high credibility clinical situations) are projectively generated, but in medium to long term relationships, reality factors may begin to intrude into all patients' perceptions. Accurate identification and management of these components will support the instructional control of behavior.

    e. The face validity or credibility (Borkovec and Nau, 1972) of the intervention and of the therapist is a major factor in securing initial compliance with instructional control and in insuring the active participation of the patient with the change process.

    f. The effectiveness of the instructional delivery system. Intrinsic properties of the delivery system and some "setting events" (Kantor, 1959) can increase the accuracy and reliability of instructional impact.

    1. Barber (1969) has shown that the response to test suggestions is enhanced by (A.) a "forceful" rather than a lackadasical tone of voice and (B.) by prior, verbal instructions to relax.

    2. A personal delivery system (Paul and Trimble 1970) may be for some subjects more effective than an impersonal or automated system (e.g., taped recorded relaxation, systematic desensitization, or implosion versus therapist delivered treatments).

    3. Volume and fluency of the delivery system may influence the degree of impact. The degree of eye contact and distance from the subject prior to and during the delivery may influence the intensity of instructional impact (Serber, 1972).

    4. The amount of pre-therapy training (role induction) in covert or overt manipulations that increase the vividity of phantasy involvement.

(Specific techniques to implement phantasy involvement and procedures 5, 6, and 7 are discussed later in the article entitled "The Modification of Hypnotic Behavior").

5. The amount of patient prior training and experience with interpersonal "risk taking" behavior and the therapist's skill in arranging the conditions for "trust." Trust training may be defined as increasing the rate of the patient's participatory behavior (in fantasy and behaviorally) and reducing the rate of his critical analytic pedestrian scanning of the instructional content and behavior of the therapist.

6. Subjecting the patient to prior or concurrent sensory restriction appears to enhance instructional control of behavior (Pena, 1963; Wickramasekera, 1969, 1970; Sanders and Reyher, 1969). The prior or concurrent ingestion by the patient of some psychedelic drugs also appears to enhance the instructional control of behavior (Barber, 1970). The systematic and judicious use of modest quantities of "spirits" in the consulting room may in certain cases be an appropriate adjunct to initially enhance psychotherapeutic rapport.

7. Training the patient to rapidly reach low levels of arousal (a hypnogogic state) also appears to enhance the direct instructional control of visceral and other behaviors. This training has been shown to be effective with biofeedback procedures used to increase alpha density (Engstrom, et al., 1970) and to reduce EMG levels (Wickramasekera, 1971, 1973).

Some Hypothetical Mechanisms in the Instructional Change of Behavior

1. In some instances cognitive change (instructionally induced) will produce in some subjects immediate and direct changes in visceral (inhibit aversive arousal) and motor (induce compulsive motor approach behavior) response systems. Most of these changes will probably be short lived if not supported by the counterconditioning and/or extinction mechanisms in the natural habitat.

2. Cognitive changes instructionally induced may not directly alter visceral or motor response systems, but may create a cognitive set favorable to the operation of the conditioning mechanisms of extinction and/or counterconditioning in the natural habitat, a psychophysiological pattern (e.g. a low arousal profile) that increases the probability of habituation or extinction.

a. Positive cognitive relabeling may increase the probability of positive affect when in contact "in vivo" with the aversive object or situation. The apparent non-specific character of visceral arousal in emotion leaves room for cognitive manipulations (Schachter and Singer, 1962). A positive affective post-hypnotic suggestion can be given to a highly hypnotizable subject to temporarily place the subject in contact with a phobic object. Reality testing can enable the conditioning mechanisms of extinction and/or counterconditioning to operate on behavior.

3. Positive expectations may increase the probability that the patient will actively participate with the total treatment package, for example, the subject is more likely to do his homework and to actively attend to the therapist and participate with the interventions in the consulting room. Positive expectations may orient the subject to selectively, more sensitively, and continually scan his behavior for evidence of "progress" and to inhibit counterevidence as he makes his way through his natural habitat. In other words, the perceptual discrimination mechanism may be involved. The perceptual mechanism may be altered in a way that increases the probability of reality testing and facilitates the impact of the conditioning mechanisms of extinction and counterconditioning.

4. If the expectation is positive and participation with the treatment intervention is voluntary, then dissonance theory (Festinger, 1957) predicts that the patient is more likely to stay longer in the phobic situation allowing the specific conditioning mechanisms (extinction or counterconditioning) more time to operate on the phobia.

In conclusion, the confusion in the behavior therapy literature in regard to the expectancy variable may be reduced by (1) attending to individual differences in instructional control of behavior ("hypnotizability"), for example, matching subjects for high or low hypnotizability, and (2) using procedures that increase the power and reliability of instructional manipulations, because before the elusive expectancy variable can be analytically studied, it has to be generated more reliably and at uniformly higher power levels.

The medical literature and to a much greater extent the behavioral literature have failed to attend to the above mulit-dimensional aspects of the powerful placebo or expectancy effect. Hypnotizability as measured by standardized tests is an essential but incomplete approach to creating a powerful and reliable technology of instructional control. The next frontier in this technology will come with careful specification of the syntax (forms) of the language (Bandler and Grinder, 1975) of behavior change and its relationship to the psychophysiological profile of the individual. In the words of Gregory Bateson, "What happens when messages in digital mode are flung at an analog thinker?"

References

Bandler, R. and Grinder, J., *The Structure of Magic*. Palo Alto, Calif.: Science and Behavior Books, n.d.

Barber, T. X., *Hypnosis, A Scientific Approach*. New York: Van Nostrand, 1969.

Barber, T.X., *LSD, Marihuana, Yoga and Hypnosis*. Chicago: Aldine, 1970.

Bateson, G., "Introduction." In Bandler, R., and Grinder, J. *The Structure of Magic*, Palo Alto, Calif.: Science and Behavior Books, 1975.

Borkovec, T., The role of expectancy and physiological feedback in fear research: A review with special reference to subject characteristics. *Behavior Therapy*, 1973, 4, 491-505.

Borkovec, T., and Nau, S. D.,.Credibility of analogue therapy rationales, *Journal of Behavior Therapy and Experimental Psychiatry* 1972, 3, 257-260.

Engstrom, D. R., London, P., and Hart, J. T., EEG alpha feedback training and hypnotic susceptability. *Proceedings A.P.A.* 1970, 5, 837-838.

Eisenberger, R. Is there a deprivation-satiation function for social approval? *Psychological Bulletin* 1970, 74, 255-275.

Festinger, K., *A Theory of Cognitive Dissonance*. New York: Harper and Row, 1957.

Hilgard, E. R., and Hilgard, J. R., *Hypnosis in the Relief of Pain*. Los Altos, Calif.: William Kaufmann, 1975.

Kantor, J. R., *Interbehavioral Psychology*. Bloomington, Ind.: Principia Press, 1959.

Lacey, J. I., Somatic response patterning and stress: Some revisions of activation theory. In M. H. Appley and R. Trumball, (Eds.) *Psychological Stress Issues in Research*. New York: Appleton, Crofts, 1967.

Lang, P. J., The application of psychophysiological methods to the study of psychotherapy and behavior modification. In A. E. Bergin and S. G. Garfield (Eds.) *Handbook of Psychotherapy and Behavior Change*, New York: John Wiley, 1971.

Orne, M. T., and Shor, E., *The Nature of Hypnosis*. New York: Holt, Rinehart and Winston, 1965

Paul, G. L. and Trimble, R. W., Recorded vs "live" relaxation training and hypnotic suggestion: Comparative effectiveness for reducing arousal and inhibiting stress response. *Behavior Therapy* 1, 285-302.

Pena, F., Perceptual isolation and hypnotic susceptibility. Unpublished doctoral dissertation, Washington State University, 1963.

Sanders, R. S., and Reyher, J., Sensory deprivation and enhancement of hypnotic susceptibility. *Journal of Abnormal Psychology*, 1969, 74, 375-381.

Schachter, S., and Singer, J. E., Cognitive, social and physiological determinants of emotional state. *Psychological Review*, 1962, 69, 379-399.

Serber, M., Teaching the non-verbal components of assertive training. *Journal of Behavior Therapy and Exp. Psychiatry* 1972, 3, 179-183.

Shapiro, A., Placebo effects in medicine, psychotherapy and psychoanalysis. In A. Bergin and S. Garfield, (Eds.) *Handbook of Psychotherapy and Behavior Change.* New York: Wiley, 1971.

Wickramasekera, I., The effects of sensory restriction on susceptibility to hypnosis. *International Journal of Clinical and Experimental Hypnosis,* 1969, 17, 217-227.

Wickramasekera, I., Effects of sensory restriction on susceptibility to hypnosis. *Journal of Abnormal Psychology,* 1970, 76, 69-75.

Wickramasekera, I., Effects of EMG feedback training on susceptibility to hypnosis. *Proceedings of the 79 Annual Convention of the American Psychological Association* (Summary) 1971, 6, 783-784.

Wickramasekera, I., Effects of EMG feedback on hypnotic susceptibility: More preliminary data. *Journal of Abnormal Psychology* 1973, 82, 1, 74-77.

Wilkins, W., Expectancy of therapeutic gain: An empirical and conceptual critique. *Journal of Consulting and Clinical Psychology.* 1973, 40, 69-77.

Part 2

THE
MANAGEMENT
OF SEXUAL
AROUSAL

The Application of Learning Theory to the Management of a Case of Sexual Exhibitionism

Ian Wickramasekera
Peoria School of Medicine
University of Illinois
College of Medicine
Peoria

This case history describes the apparently successful treatment of a patient who had been an exhibitionist for more than five years. The particular techniques combined desensitization and the shaping of a response incompatible with anxiety.

History

The patient, a 23-year-old, white, single man, was referred to our clinic by the dean of his university because he had been apprehended by the local police for sexual exhibitionism. The police agreed not to press charges if the student would secure treatment.

The patient's parents occupy very prominent places in the social and religious life of the community. In high school and at the time of treatment, the patient was an A student, very active in athletics, and prominent in the social life of the campus.

The examining psychiatrist diagnosed the patient as sociopathic personality disturbance and noted in his report that the prognosis for behavior change was poor in view of the fact that the patient had a history of exhibitionism dating back to his 13th year.

The patient had shared a room with his two younger sisters during his early childhood and had a problem controlling his masturbation in adolescence. His earliest recollection of overt sexual exhibitionism was standing unzipped in the shadows of a barn whose doors overlooked a highway. In the ensuing years, the patient continued to exhibit himself on the average about once a month at windows and while driving his car in strange towns. Complaints had been either "hushed up" or explained away on the basis of indiscretions. Careful questioning revealed that the preferred sexual object was a young (age 8-14 years) immature female. The patient had gone "steady" twice in his life, but had dated many different girls briefly. At the time of the arrest, he had been engaged for two years and was shortly to be married. His fiancée was a senior in a different college and she was apparently quite religiously-oriented.

Pre-treatment Status of Response

Starting about two months prior to his arrest, the patient had begun to expose himself more frequently and in many *more* locations (outside junior high schools, in public libraries, in stores, while driving his car close to the sidewalk at traffic lights and stop signs, etc.). Previously he had exposed himself only at his window and while driving his car with his pants open through strange towns. Now he was exposing himself consistently in at least seven additional physical locations.

The rate of the response had also increased. Previously he had no recollection of ever exceeding one or two exposures a month, but in the two months prior to the arrest, he had at times exposed himself as many as ten times per week.

He also reported that he was restless most of the time, unable to concentrate, and generally "jumpy." He noted that he was considering postponing his approaching marriage due to his "poor health."

Until the time of the arrest, the patient had been able to keep all knowledge of his exhibitionism carefully concealed from his fiancée. Physical contact between them had never gone beyond kissing and holding hands. In fact, he admitted that in all his heterosexual experience he had never touched a female's genitals, though on one occasion he had lightly fondled a girl's breasts through her blouse. The patient firmly asserted that his avoidance of all sexual contact was exclusively due to religious scruples. He denied homosexual contact of any type, either in childhood or adolescence. His masturbatory fantasies, which were exclusively heterosexual, always stopped short of actual sexual intercourse.

The patient reported that in the past when the impulse to expose himself arose but the location was "dangerous," he would seek relief in solitary masturbation. However, he added that more recently masturbation seemed less pleasant to him.

On the basis of the above information, the following diagnostic hypotheses were formulated: (1) The patient was fearful of sexual contact with adult females and specifically of vaginal contact. (2) The alternative masturbatory response was becoming progressively less reinforcing. (3) The religious scruples were rationalizations.

Theoretical Views of the Etiology of Exhibitionism

Psychoanalytic theory asserts that the exhibitionistic response is a defense against castration anxiety. Castration anxiety is among other things traced to the vagina dentata hypothesis (Fenichel, 1963), which may suggest a vaginal phobia. In terms of a two-factor learning theory, this would imply that certain stimulus configurations (young females in this case), typically elicit anxiety and the performance of the exhibitionistic instrumental response in their presence is anxiety-reducing. The act of self-exposure and the perception of his intact penis has somehow acquired the ability to reduce this drive (anxiety). But the exhibitionistic response probably persists because young females lose their aversive properties, and since the exhibitionistic response is a form of solution learning, it comes to be increasingly maintained by sexual drive reduction. Hence, a response originally acquired on the basis of anxiety reduction may come to be increasingly maintained by sexual drive reduction.

Behavior Modification Plan

Two approaches seemed open, but the second one seemed to have more long term merits.

I. Contingencies could be manipulated to restore even temporarily the reinforcing properties of the masturbatory response. The prediction would be that as masturbation increased in frequency, the more "dangerous" exhibitionistic response would decrease in frequency.

II. An alternative approach would attempt to shift the sexual approach responses from young females to adult females and to increase the amount of associated reinforcement from mere exposure to actual physical contact and intercourse with adult females. The first step in remediation then would be to associate "relaxed" rather than "agitated" responses with the sexual stimuli of adult females. The next step would be to set up contingencies in which the patient's sexual approach responses toward adult females would have a high probability of reinforcement.

Preparation of Patient for Treatment

After the psychological testing was completed and a comprehensive picture assembled of the patient's current life space, a meeting was scheduled to explain the treatment plan to the patient and to secure his consent to implement it. In a matter-of-fact manner, it was explained to the patient that had he been born in a different time or into a different sex, he could probably have continued to practice exhibitionism and live a productive and profitable life (e.g., as a burlesque artist). But that at the present time and in the present location, the penalties for self-exposure were severe, as the patient had found out (he had been asked to drop out of school till "cured.") The therapist then told the patient that he believed that the patient's lack of sexual experience with adult females was due to the patient's fear of sexual contact wth adult females. This fear, he pointed out, had led to a legally prohibited means of sexual expression. The therapist also remarked that he considered the patient's talk about religious scruples rather flimsy camouflage. Initially the patient responded with anger to these observations and vigorously repeated his claim to religious scruples. The therapist then explained that the primary goals of the treatment, should he agree to accept them, would be to desensitize (principle was explained) his fear of sexual contact with adult females and to shape his sexual responses more in the direction of heterosexual intercourse. The therapist predicted that when the patient started having heterosexual intercourse, he would lose interest in his potentially dangerous exhibitionist behavior. The therapist pointed out that the active participation of the patient's fiancée would be vitally important to the treatment procedure. The therapist stressed the fact that since the patient was engaged to be married, the conventional social prohibitions against premarital intercourse were somewhat more relaxed. But he also emphasized the fact that the proposed treatment procedure was purely experimental, even though it seemed to make good sense. The patient and the therapist also discussed the fact that with the use of conventional treatment procedures, the prognosis for recovery was poor and the duration of treatment was indefinite. The patient was also told that if he would prefer to undertake conventional treatment, arrangements could be made for such services either in the present clinic or with a private practitioner. He was then given the names of several private practitioners and directed to go home and think further about this choice. The patient was strongly encouraged to discuss in confidence with his minister his present predicament and the choice he had between the lesser of two imperfect solutions. He was also requested to discuss the treatment plan with his fiancée (who for the first time had learned about his sexual deviation after his arrest.)

A few days later, the patient indicated that he was willing to take the experimental treatment and an appointment was scheduled with him and his fiancée. The patient's fiancée felt that before treatment commenced she should marry the patient. This inclincation was strongly discouraged by the therapist on two grounds: (1) The treatment was purely experimental and there was no guarantee that it would succeed. (2) There was a possibility that should the treatment succeed, the present basis of their mutual attraction would dissolve and that the patient would develop a wider interest in females.

Initially the patient's fiancée raised numerous objections to the second part of the treatment plan on both religious grounds and the possibility of pregnancy. The therapist admitted that there were serious moral issues involved here. He noted that the discovery of the patient's problems did not seem to have disrupted her plans to marry the patient and she apparently still loved him and was eager to assist with his social rehabilitation. At the close of the interview, both the patient and his fiancée tentatively agreed to try the experimental treatment plan.

Treatment Techniques

The first step in the treatment plan was to train the patient in relaxation and this was largely accomplished with the use of a tape and relaxation instructions. From here on, the desensitization procedure described by Wolpe (1958) was used consistently. Instruction in the tensing and relaxing of his muscles were also recorded on a tape the patient purchased and the tape was used as a guide to his practice of relaxation at home. The relaxation training period took approximately three one-hour sessions. But between clinic sessions, the patient engaged in distributed practice of these exercises 1 to 1½ hours daily. Even after the desensitization proper had begun, the patient continued to practice muscular relaxation at home.

The construction of the anxiety hierarchy provided additional evidence of the patient's aversion for the sexual stimuli of adult females. For example, one of his homework assignments was to construct in rough form a hierarchy starting with strictly social contact between himself and adult females and terminating in sexual contact. He was also required to construct a similar hierarchy for young females. The scenes covering social contact with adult females were on the average 25 words long, but those covering sexual contact with adult females were on the average only 3 words long. During hierarchy refinement, the patient appeared to be sweating and restless as the sexual imagery of adult females was approximated.

As the desensitization procedure approached its middle phase (in the 7th session) it was decided to start the shaping of an additional response incompatible with the anxiety evoked by the sexual stimuli of adult females. The patient was assigned selected readings with progressively more heterosexual erotic content (care was taken to avoid material containing reference to young females). This was perceived as the first step in shaping bolder heterosexual approach responses to adult females. For example, the first step was reading a lightly sexually-toned passage from Steinbeck for five minutes in the sixth session. After he had completed reading it, he was reinforced with verbal approval "very good," "fine," etc., and a smile. These reading sessions were seldom in excess of ten minutes and he typically read two to three passages with continuous reinforcement ("very good," "fine," etc.). At the termination of this technique in the 12th session, he was reading passages from books like *Fanny Hill* and did not seem to need verbal reinforcement to keep up this type of reading at home. Previously he had reported being unable to read even moderately heterosexual erotic content for presumably religious reasons. The purpose of this step was to direct his mediating responses (verbal behaviors or thoughts, etc.) into the area of the sexual stimuli of adult females.

The next step was to set up a series of trips with his fiancée to both neighboring towns and to distant large towns for recreational purposes (ball games, plays, movies, zoos, etc.) and these were scheduled towards the terminal phase of the desensitization procedure. The first of these trips was scheduled in between the 12th and 13th session of treatment. Before each trip, the couple was explicitly told how far petting behavior should go and strictly forbidden to go beyond the prescribed points. These points were fondling of breasts, stomach, legs, thighs, and finally genital areas. Before these trips were scheduled, the therapist explained to the subject's finacée the rationale of the treatment and the importance of consistently and clearly reinforcing his limited sexual approach responses. For example, on the first trip the patient was explicitly restricted to kissing and fondling of his fiancée's breasts. These restrictions on the extent of sexual responses were generally reduced as he continued to report greater comfort and feelings of competency in his sexual relationship. After the initial stages of this shaping procedure, both the patient and his fiancee began to take an active interest in the treatment.

As the desensitization and shaping proceeded concurrently, the patient spontaneously reported a phasing-out of his impulse to exhibit himself and his exhibitionistic ruminations. However, at least on two occasions during the initial stages of treatment (between the 2nd and 4th sessions), the patient reported that while returning home from a distant town where he had searched fruitlessly for employment, he had driven a number of blocks with his pants unzipped. On both occasions the exposures had occurred in areas where young females were at play.

During the 14th session of the treatment phase, the therapist recommended that the patient move out of his parents' home and attempt to support himself independently. This recommendation was made because it was the therapist's judgment that the patient's parents and particularly his mother were reinforcing what seemed to be his dependent attitudes. When this recommendation was first made in the 2nd session of treatment it was ignored, but when it was repeated in the 14th session of treatment, it was quickly implemented.

Termination

Treatment was terminated after the 18th session. At this time the patient and his fiancée reported a very satisfactory sexual relationship between them. According to the patient's report at termination, he had not exposed himself since the 4th session of treatment (a period of approximately 2½ months). The frequency of his sexual relationships with his fiancée had risen from nearly zero to a mean of two relationships (mainly petting and coitus) per week. There was no evidence of "symptom substitution," even though a deliberate effort was made to look for it in the final interview. There were no indications of homosexual preoccupations or other deviant preoccupations. The patient reported an increased ability to concentrate and freedom from the pre-treatment restlessness. Also both he and his fiancée reported their relationship was "deeper and more real" to them now. At termination, the patient had secured employment and was making tentative plans to complete his education and get married.

Follow-up

In the first follow-up six months after treatment, the patient and his fiancée were separately asked: 1. Has there been any recurrence at all of self-exposure? 2. (a) Have you had any new disturbing thoughts, feelings, or motor responses? (b) Have you re-experienced any old disturbing behaviors of the above type? 3. How frequent and satisfying is your present sexual relationship? 4. How often do you have thoughts and feelings about self-exposure? The patient responded to the first and second questions in the negative. He reported that his sexual relationships with his fiancée have increased to a mean of about three intimacies a week since the termination of treatment (this was confirmed independently by his fiancée) and he described their relationship as "extremely" satisfying. In response to the 4th question, he stated that just after the termination of treatment, he had sporadically had thoughts and feelings about self-exposure and particularly at times when he felt "low." But recently these thoughts and feelings had become "very infrequent."

The patient's fiancée, to the extent she could, confirmed his descriptions. They were to be married very shortly.

In an identical follow-up procedure, ten months after termination (the patient had now married his fiancée) both persons' responses were substantially the same as four months previously. The only difference was that the patient could not recall any thoughts or impulses to self-exposure in the last four months.

Conclusions

The unique feature of this treatment consisted in that the extinction of the anxiety associated with the sexual stimuli of adult females was accomplished by training the patient in not merely one but two responses incompatible with anxiety. The sexual stimuli of adult females were paired with relaxation responses and sexual approach responses. The interference theory of extinction (Kimble 1961) would seem to predict more lasting extinction under such conditions. The brevity of the treatment was probably due to at least three factors. One, the treatment procedure involved the manipulation of very powerful reinforcement contingencies (sexual stimuli). Two, the desensitization procedure was run nearly *concurrently* with shaping of an incompatible response (heterosexual approach responses). Three, it is our experience (Wickramasekera, 1967) that changes in cognitive and affective responses are most effectively induced by first changing the patient's motor responses. The self-evident nature of the patient's changed motor behavior may increase his feeling of "hope" and reduce his resistance to cognitive manipulations. Hence, treatment may be accelerated by a snowballing "placebo" effect.

Nearly all published studies of the behavioral treatment of sexual deviations up to date have used one form or another of "aversion therapy" (Feldman, 1966). These have been either "punishment" (Azrin and Holz,

1966) or avoidance-conditioning procedures. The present study suggests that sexual deviations may also be treated through the shaping and positive reinforcement procedures. This study illustrates an alternative approach which may have some merit, but the lack of proper controls makes it impossible to draw any conclusions from the data.

It seems relatively inefficient to provide "insight" into a patient's insecurities and immaturities till we have been able to set up contingencies of reinforcement that help patients to emit more mature behavior and secure reinforcement for it. After "symptomatic recovery" has been induced, any sort of plausible rationale (Freudian, existential, Adlerian, R.T., etc.) of the etiology of the disturbance, which will hopefully function to prevent further unadaptive learning, may be explored with the patient, particularly if the therapist feels an obligation to "explain" and the patient a need to "understand how it all got started in the first place." But the matter of etiology would seem peripheral to the immediate problem of behavior modification.

References

Azrin, N. H. & Holz, W. C. Punishment. In Honig, W. K. (Ed.), *Operant Behavior, Areas of Research and Application.* New York: Appleton-Century Crofts, 1966.

Ellis, A. *Reason and Emotion in Psychotherapy.* New York, Lyle Stuart, 1963.

Feldman, M. P. Aversion Therapy in Sexual Deviations. *Psychological Bulletin,* 1966, *65,* 65-78.

Fenichel, Otto. *The Psychoanalytic Theory of Neurosis.* London: Routledge and Kegan Paul, 1963.

Kimble, G. A. *Conditioning and Learning.* New York: Appleton-Century-Crofts, 1961.

Krasner, L. & Ullmann, L. P. (Eds.). *Research in behavior modification.* New York: Holt, Rinehart & Winston, 1965.

Mensh, Ivan N. Psychopathic Conditions, Addictions and Sexual Deviations. In Wolman (Ed.) *Handbook of Clinical Psychology.* New York: McGraw Hill, 1965.

Wickramasekera, I. The Use of Some Learning Theory Derived Techniques in the Treatment of Paranoid Schizophrenia. *Psychotherapy, Theory, Research and Practice.* 1967, *4,* 22-26.

Wolberg, L. R. *The Technique of Psychotherapy.* New York: Grune and Stratton, 1957.

Wolpe, J. *Psychotherapy by Reciprocal Inhibition.* Stanford, Calif.: Stanford Unversity Press, 1958.

Increasing Heterosexual Responsiveness in the Treatment of Sexual Deviation

David H. Barlow

Department of Psychiatry
University of Mississippi
Medical Center
Jackson

D espite wide agreement that avoidance of heterosexuality is a major component in the genesis and maintenance of sexual deviation, the development of therapeutic procedures to increase heterosexual responsiveness has been largely neglected in favor of aversion therapy to suppress deviant responsiveness. Therapeutic procedures that have been employed to increase heterosexual responsiveness include: aversion relief techniques in which relief from an aversive stimulus is paired with heterosexual stimuli; "systematic desensitization procedures" in which heterosexual avoidance is desensitized either in imagination or in the real situation; social retraining where heterosexual skills are directly encouraged and taught; or pairing techniques in which sexual arousal is elicited and associated with heterosexual stimuli. Clinical and experimental evidence for the effectiveness of these procedures, as well as some newly developed techniques which cannot be classified in the above categories, is evaluated and the relationship of these procedures to aversion therapy in the treatment of sexual deviation is discussed.

A strikingly similar viewpoint on homosexual behavior and to some extent deviant sexual behavior in general is held by psychoanalytic and behavioral theorists. This view emphasizes the importance of fear of or avoidance of heterosexuality in the genesis and maintenance of such behavior. Analysts such as Rado (1949), Ovesey, Gaylin, and Hendin (1963), and Bieber, Bieber, Dain, Dince, Drellich, Grand, Grundlach,

Kremer, Wilber, and Bieber (1963), and behaviorists such as Wolpe (1969), Ramsey and Van Velzen (1968), and Feldman and MacCulloch (1971), view heterosexual fear and avoidance as major determinants of homosexuality. In addition, both Ovesey *et al.* (1963) and Stevenson and Wolpe (1960) speak of the necessity of increasing more appropriate and assertive heterosocial behaviors in the treatment of sexual deviation.

Despite these views, aversion therapy aimed at eliminating sexual deviation is increasingly advocated as the treatment of choice (Barlow, 1972), due in part to the growing application of the experimental behavioral sciences to the clinic and in part to the relative success of this technique (MacCulloch & Feldman, 1967; Feldman & MacCulloch, 1971) compared to psychoanalytic psychotherapy (Bieber *et al.*, 1963). In a period of 10 years, seven series of cases containing at least ten patients (Freund, 1960; Feldman & MacCulloch, 1965; MacCulloch & Feldman, 1967; Bancroft, 1969; Gelder & Marks, 1969; Evans, 1968; Morganstern, Pierce, & Rees, 1965; Fookes, 1968) and four controlled outcome studies (McConaghy, 1969; Bancroft, 1970; Birk, Huddleston, Miller, & Cohler, 1971; Feldman & MacCulloch, 1971) have reported on the effectiveness of aversion therapy for sexual deviation.

The emphasis on aversion therapy suggests that most clinicians are ignoring a second treatment goal in sexual deviation, that of increasing heterosexual responsiveness. This attitude is exemplified by Bond and Evans (1967) who state "It is probable that if they can abstain from their deviant behavior for a sufficient period of time, normal outlets for the control of sexual arousal will develop" (p. 1162). The potential dangers of this are obvious. As West (1968) points out "Aversion therapy may cause some patients to undertake heterosexual experiments who otherwise might not have done so, but it will leave others impotent and frustrated and in a worse state than they were before" (p.260).

Findings from two recent studies support earlier theories on the importance of heterosexual responsiveness in the treatment of sexual deviation. Feldman and MacCulloch (1971), in a large, controlled study comparing aversion therapy and psychotherapy, report that the most important predictor of success in treatment is prior heterosexual experience. Of those patients with prior heterosexual experience, fully 80% improved while only 20% with no prior heterosexual experience improved. These results are similar to those of Bieber *et al.* (1963), who reported that 50% of those homosexuals who were bisexual at the time of treatment became exclusively heterosexual, while only 18% of those who were exclusively homosexual at the time of treatment (but may have had heterosexual experiences earlier) became heterosexual.

In this same vein, an important finding was recently reported by Bancroft (1970) who divided homosexuals who had received either aversion therapy directed at homosexual responsiveness or systematic desensitization to heterosexual themes into clinically improved and unimproved at a follow-up. Those patients who improved had demonstrated significantly greater increases in heterosexual arousal as measured by penile circumference changes and positive heterosexual attitudes during treatment irrespective of mode of treatment. Decreases in homosexual arousal and attitude during treatment occurred equally in both improved and unimproved groups, and were not related to clinical outcome. Although the overall percentage of success was not high, the implication is that when success is achieved, increasing heterosexual responsiveness, by whatever technique, is a more important factor in treatment than decreasing homosexual responsiveness. To the extent that clinical judgments of improvement are valid, these correlational findings suggest the necessity of discovering effective techniques to increase heterosexual responsiveness.

Although clinicians employing aversion therapy emphasize the suppression of deviant arousal, many of these therapies include procedures intended to increase heterosexual arousal. Since these procedures are most often embedded in aversive therapy, it is difficult to determine if they are clinically effective. Furthermore, most case studies and series of cases systematically measure and report only changes in deviant behavior.

On the other hand, a few recent case studies (Kraft, 1967; Huff, 1970) report successful treatment of sexual deviation through the exclusive use of techniques designed to increase heterosexual responsiveness resulting in these single cases in declines in reports of homosexual responsiveness as well as increases in heterosexual responsiveness. These observations, as well as those of Bancroft (1970), raise the possibility that when these techniques are tacked onto aversion therapy they may contribute more to a successful outcome than reports emphasizing aversion therapy would indicate.

This paper critically examines the evidence for the effectiveness of such techniques. These procedures will be classified into four categories, based on similarities in practice or common theoretical underpinnings: aversion relief; systematic desensitization procedures; social retraining, and pairing. Other techniques which do not fit into these four categories, comprise a fifth category.

Aversion Relief

Aversion relief treatment involves pairing a heterosexual stimulus with relief from a noxious stimulus. This technique has been widely utilized to increase heterosexual responsiveness, probably because it is very convenient to apply in conjunction with aversion therapy. The use of an aversive stimulus insures that a period of relief following the termination of that stimulus will occur. It is, therefore, easy to pair a heterosexual stimulus with the relief. Because of this, aversion relief has always been used in conjunction with aversion therapy.

Aversion relief was first used in treating sexual deviation by Thorpe, Schmidt, Brown, and Castell (1964) who treated three homosexuals, one transvestite, and one fetish. The aversion therapy procedure consisted of projecting, on a screen, a number of words (up to 23) connoting deviant experiences. Shock accompanied each presentation. The last word in the series, however, described "normal" activities, such as "heterosexual" and signified the end of the shock session. Thorpe *et al.* reported that "tremendous relief" was experienced at this time and, presumably, this word became associated with that relief. Following treatment, all patients reported some increased heterosexual interest, although no measure of this was taken and no follow-up reported. Thorpe *et al.* speculated that this procedure worked either by inhibiting heterosexual anxiety, or positively reinforcing heterosexual approach behavior.

In the numerous case studies and series of cases since this report, the heterosexual "relief" stimulus has taken two forms, verbal, usually words or phrases depicting heterosexual interest such as "intercourse" (Gaupp, Stern, & Ratliff, 1971) or pictorial such as slides of nude females (Larson, 1970). Most case studies anecdotally report increases in heterosexual responsiveness.

The aversion therapy and aversion relief procedure devised by Feldman and MacCulloch (1965) is perhaps the best known and has been applied to the largest number of cases; a total of 78 through 1971. The authors state that the goal of the aversion relief procedure is to reduce "heterosexual anxiety."

In a controlled study comparing two groups of homosexuals, each receiving a form of aversion therapy with an aversion relief component, with a third group receiving psychotherapy (Feldman & MacCulloch, 1971), heterosexual interest, as measured by an attitude scale, increased initially in all three groups with no difference among groups. Because the purpose of the experiment was to compare the effects of these therapies on homosexual interest rather than heterosexual interest, experimental design considerations made further comparison of heterosexual interest among the three groups at follow-ups impossible.

McConaghy (1969) compared electrical aversion therapy containing an aversion relief paradigm with chemical aversion therapy which contained no element designed to increase heterosexual behavior in two groups of homosexuals. Subjective reports of heterosexual desire and relations two weeks after treatment revealed no significant difference between the group receiving aversion therapy with aversion relief and the group receiving aversion therapy in which no attempt was made to increase heterosexual interest.

Solyom and Miller (1965) applied aversion relief to six homosexuals while continually monitoring a physiological response, in this case finger plethysmograph, to heterosexual stimuli. Although they noted a "trend" to greater plethysmograph response to female pictures, when the individual data are examined, only two patients showed increased responding to female pictures over treatment, while three showed decreased responding. This result is further confused by the fact that the two patients who showed increased responding to females did not report any increased heterosexual interest or behavior.

In the only series to assess heterosexual interest continually by means of a valid objective measure, penile circumference change, Abel, Levis, and Clancy (1970) administered aversion therapy to five nonhomosexual deviates by shocking verbalization of the deviant acts at different points in the chain of behavior. After the initial series of shocks, verbalizing a sequence of heterosexual behavior was associated with relief from shock. The results one week after treatment indicate that heterosexual arousal dropped somewhat, although at an eight-week follow-up heterosexual arousal was higher than baseline levels. Thus, aversion relief had no immediate effect.

In view of the well-documented observation that heterosexual responsiveness increases during aversion therapy in the absence of any attempt to accomplish this goal (Bancroft, 1969; Gelder & Marks, 1969; Barlow, Leitenberg, & Agras, 1969), all clinical reports that aversion relief is effective are suspect since aversion relief has never been used in the absence of aversion therapy to isolate treatment effects.

Currently, then, there is no evidence that aversion relief increases heterosexual responsiveness. Furthermore, the stated goals of aversion relief differ from therapist to therapist; but, if the specific goal of aversion relief is to reduce heterosexual anxiety (Feldman & MacCulloch, 1971) there is no experimental evidence anywhere in the literature that aversion relief does, in fact, reduce anxiety, heterosexual or otherwise, in humans.

It is revealing that in the empirical field of behavior modification, the use of a therapeutic technique has now been reported in the literature on approximately 150 cases and continues to be employed clinically without any evidence that it is effective.

Systematic Desensitization Techniques

Although the mechanism of action is not clear, (Agras, Leitenberg, Barlow, Curtis, Edwards, & Wright, 1971) systematic desensitization, either in imagination or *in vivo* aims at eliminating fear or anxiety associated with heterosexual behavior. This approach is most consistent with the various theories on the genesis and maintenance of homosexual behavior mentioned above, and is further buttressed by two surveys.

Bieber *et al.* (1963) noted that 70 of the 106 patients in his survey reported fear or aversion to female genitalia. Ramsay and Van Velzen (1968) collected questionnaires from 25 homosexuals, 24 heterosexuals, and 17 bisexuals. The answers to a series of questions indicated that homosexuals are not merely indifferent to heterosexual situations, but have strong negative emotional feelings concerning them, much as many heterosexuals find homosexual practices aversive.

Recently Freund, Langevin, Cibiri, and Zajac (1973) documented that homosexuals and heterosexuals both react negatively to nude slides of the nonpreferred sex on attitudinal and penile response measures.

The use of desensitization, or a close variant, has been reported in conjunction with aversion therapy in four instances. In a large series containing 15 homosexuals, 7 exhibitionists, and 5 fetishistic transvestites, Fookes (1968) paired relaxing music with heterosexual slides after a course of electrical aversion. Fookes reported that this variant of desensitization produced increases in heterosexual behavior in some patients. Levin, Hirsch, Shugar, and Kapche (1968) also reported success in desensitizing a homosexual using the standard desensitization in imagination procedure in conjunction with aversion therapy. Using systematic desensitization in the real situation, Cooper (1963) successfully treated a fetish by chemical aversion and by instructing the patient to lie in bed naked with his wife until he felt comfortable and to attempt small steps progressively leading to sexual intercourse only when he felt no anxiety when engaging in the previous step. Gray (1970) used a similar procedure in conjunction with covert sensitization for treatment of a homosexual.

Unlike aversion relief, desensitization has been used in the absence of aversion therapy. Kraft, in several reports (1967a,b; 1969a,b), suggests that decreasing heterosexual anxiety alone may be sufficient not only to increase heterosexual behavior, but to eliminate homosexual behavior, and reports that in several cases of homosexuality (1967a,b) desensitization in imagination apparently accomplished this goal. Huff (1970) and LoPiccolo (1971) also reported increases in heterosexual responsiveness after desensitizing homosexuals in imagination although LoPiccolo's patient began engaging in the target behavior before he was desensitized!

Successful desensitization in the real situation, in the absence of aversion therapy, has been reported by DiScipio (1968) with a homosexual, and Wickramasekera (1968) with an exhibitionist, although DiScipio's patient later relapsed.

Whatever the therapeutic mechanism of action, systematic desensitization in the real situation offers the naive patient the advantage of learning the intricacies of sexual approach behavior first hand from a cooperative partner.

The only attempt to evaluate the efficacy of systematic desensitization in treating sexual deviation was reported by Bancroft (1970) who treated two groups of 15 homosexuals each. One group received systematic desensitization in imagination to heterosexual themes, the second group was treated by electrical aversion therapy. No difference was noted between groups either after treatment or at six-month follow-up on reports of homosexual or heterosexual behavior or sexual arousal as measured by penile circumference change. However, when changes from beginning of treatment to the follow-up are examined within groups, both treatments increased heterosexual arousal, as measured by penile circumference change, immediately after treatment, with aversion (surprisingly) increasing heterosexual arousal slightly but not significantly more than the systematic desensitization. Only aversion, however, significantly reduced homosexual arousal immediately after treatment.

Bancroft then dichotomized the groups into improved and unimproved, based on the *reports of behavior* at a six-month follow-up and found that *during treatment,* reduction of homosexual arousal occurred in both the improved and unimproved groups, but that significant increases in heterosexual arousal occurred only in the improved group. This suggests that development of heterosexual responsiveness, whether through systematic desensitization or through aversion, is the prerequisite for clinical improvement and that aversion therapy may work not because it decreases homosexual responsiveness but, paradoxically, because it increases heterosexual responsiveness. However, all conclusions are tentative since the study did not include a placebo control or a no-treatment control. Thus, the relatively modest therapeutic results (only 5 out of the original 15 were rated as much improved or improved after treatment in the systematic desensitization group) could be due to placebo factors or the passage of time.

Thus, there is no experimental evidence that desensitization procedures increase heterosexual responsiveness. However, the clinical reports of success in the absence of aversion therapy would justify further investigation of these techniques.

Social Retraining

Another approach is assertive training, or a variant, behavior rehearsal. Essentially, these procedures teach new social skills to those patients who, because of avoidance or behavioral deficiencies, are unable to function effectively in heterosocial situations. In one of the first reports, using this approach exclusively, Stevenson and Wolpe (1960) taught three sexual deviates to be more assertive. This resulted not only in the establishment or strengthening of social and sexual aspects of heterosexual behavior based on the patients' report, but also eliminated most deviant behavior. Edwards (1972) reported that a similar procedure was successful with a pedophilic.

As part of a comprehensive treatment program including aversion therapy, Cautela and Wisocki (1969) provided behavior rehearsals with a female to teach correct social and assertive behavior to six homosexuals who then reported increases in heterosexual responsiveness.

The establishment of adequate social behavior would seem to be a necessary precursor to sexual behavior. This approach is similar to techniques that Salter (1949) and Ellis (1956, 1959) use, in which homosexual activity is largely ignored and the patient is taught in the first instance to be more assertive, and second, is given instructions and encouragement on appropriate heterosocial and heterosexual behavior. Ellis (1956) reports 75% of a series of 40 homosexuals were improved. Improvement is not defined, however, and there is reason to believe that homosexual behavior had not diminished in the series. No follow-up is reported.

Although exact procedures are seldom reported, other clinicians practicing inidvidual psychotherapy (Ovesey *et al.,* 1963) or group psychotherapy (Birk, Miller, & Cohler, 1970) describe the teaching of assertiveness and more effective heterosexual approach behavior during the course of therapy. It is possible that this aspect of therapy accounts for reports of success using this approach. In view of the seeming importance of teaching appropriate heterosocial behavior, it is surprising that no research at all has been reported in this area.

Pairing

Another grouping of techniques shares a common basic procedure in which elicited sexual arousal is paired with heterosexual stimuli for the purpose of increasing heterosexual arousal. When close attention is paid to timing relationships, the procedure is sometimes called classical conditioning. In other reports it is called counterconditioning, or pairing. When masturbation is used to produce sexual arousal, the procedure has been called masturbatory conditioning or orgasmic reconditioning.

Although the notion that sexual arousal patterns are learned through association is not new (Binet, 1888; Dollard & Miller, 1950), several analogue studies have recently verified this hypothesis. Both Lovibond (1963) and Wood and Obrist (1968) conditioned autonomic responses to neutral stimuli that were repeatedly paired with sexual arousal. McConaghy (1970) paired erotic slides with geometrical configurations and produced penile circumference changes to the configurations in 10 heterosexual and 15 homosexual subjects.

In a somewhat closer approach to the clinical situation, Rachman (1966) paired a slide picturing a pair of women's boots with slides of nude females and obtained increases in penile circumference to the boots in three volunteer, normal subjects, and later replicated these findings with five additional subjects (Rachman & Hodgson, 1968). These procedures were termed classical conditioning.

Early attempts at applying the principles of classical conditioning or pairing to clinical populations were made using hormonal injections to elicit sexual arousal (Freund, 1960; James, 1962). Freund (1960) was the first to attempt this in his pioneering report of the treatment of a series of male homosexuals. After a course of aversion therapy, 10 mg of testosterone propinate were injected and approximately seven hours later pictures of nude or seminude women were shown to the patient. Results are reported for 47 patients. Forty and four-tenths percent made a "heterosexual adjustment" immediately following treatment. This percentage dropped to 25.5% after 3 years. Unfortunately, it is not clear whether the "adjustment" was due to a drop in homosexual behavior, a rise in heterosexual behavior, or both, and there is no evidence that the hormone treatment increased heterosexual responsiveness.

In another physiological approach, Moan and Heath (1972) reported increased heterosexual responding in a homosexual after pairing heterosexual stimuli and behavior with septal stimulation.

In a procedure close to that employed by Rachman (1966), Beech, Watts, and Poole (1971) increased heterosexual arousal to mature females in a heterosexual pedophilic by pairing sexual arousal elicited by pictures of young females with slides of increasingly older females. Interest in young girls spontaneously declined although no aversion was used.

Several case studies have reported pairing sexual arousal produced by masturbation with heterosexual stimuli in the treatment of homosexuality (Thorpe, Schmidt, & Castell, 1963; Marquis, 1970; Annon, 1971), sado-masochism (Davison, 1968; Mees, 1966; Marquis, 1970), voyeurism (Jackson, 1969), and heterosexual pedophilia (Annon, 1971). In most cases, subjects are instructed to masturbate to a series of pictures or fantasies which progressively approximates the desired heterosexual activity.

Evidence for the efficacy of masturbatory conditioning does not go beyond the case study level. In only one case (Jackson, 1969) has this procedure been the sole therapeutic technique. However, it is interesting to note that pairing masturbatory arousal with various fantasies has been hypothesized to play an important role in the etiology of specific deviant sexual preferences. McGuire, Carlisle, and Young (1965) suggested that deviates have some critical first sexual experience with a person or object which need not be sexually arousing at the time, but later provides a fantasy for masturbation. Historical evidence for the process is presented in a series of 45 deviates by McGuire *et al.* (1965) and in a second series reported by Evans (1968). Thus, altering masturbatory fantasy may be the most direct and efficient method of changing sexual preferences and deserves further investigation.

In one series of single-case experiments, the pairing procedure has been experimentally analyzed (Herman, Barlow, & Agras, in press). In this experiment the principles of classical conditioning were closely followed. Three exclusive male homosexuals chose slides or movies of males as unconditioned stimuli (UCS) and a female slide as the conditioned stimulus (CS). The experimental design consisted of backward pairing, classical conditioning, backward pairing, and classical conditioning once more. During backward pairing none of the three subjects showed any increase in heterosexual responsiveness as measured by penile changes to female slides and scores on attitude scales. During classical conditioning, two subjects showed sharp increases in heterosexual arousal although one subject first required alteration of the temporal relationship of the CS and UCS. This arousal dropped somewhat after a return to the control phase and returned during the last classical conditioning phase. Homosexual responsiveness decreased to near zero for one subject but remained high for the second subject. The third subject demonstrated no clinically useful change during classical conditioning despite the presence of an adequate response to the UCS.

These studies suggest that classical conditioning is capable of increasing heterosexual arousal in homosexual patients. However, in all cases occasional procedural difficulties in temporal relationships between the CS and UCS and the maintenance of an adequate response to the UCS were noted. Furthermore, clinical follow-ups revealed that the two subjects who improved had difficulty in implementing their new-found heterosexual arousal, due to deficits in social skills.

This experimental evidence, along with evidence from analogue studies, suggests that the various airing procedures are therapeutically useful. Future research should determine the extent of their usefulness and the advantages and disadvantages of different methods of eliciting sexual arousal.

Other Procedures

Several techniques have recently been reported which do not easily fit in the previous categories. Two of these procedures are based on operant methodology, a third employs intensive exposure to heterosexual stimuli.

Shaping. In case reports by Quinn, Harbison, and McAllister (1970) and Harbison, Quinn, and McAllister (1970) attempts were made to increase penile response to heterosexual stimuli through selective positive reinforcement, a technique better known as shaping, in two cases of homosexuality. After a course of aversion therapy, the patients were fluid deprived and then reinforced with a drink of lime juice for longer heterosexual fantasies and/or progressively greater increases in penile circumference to slides of a nude female. Penile responses increased over the course of treatment as did the heterosexual score on an attitude scale. The homosexual score on the attitude scale also declined over pretreatment values. No report of behavior was given.

Fading. A second "operant" approach concentrates on introducing or "fading in" heterosexual stimuli during periods of sexual arousal in an effort to change stimulus control of sexual responsiveness. This technique has been investigated in a series of three contolled, single case experiments with homosexuals (Barlow & Agras, in press). In this procedure, one male and one female slide were superimposed on one another. Through the use of an adjustable transformer, an increase in the brightness of the female slide resulted in a simultaneous decrease in the brightness of the male slide. During treatment the female stimuli was faded in contingent on the subject maintaining 75% of a full erection as measured by a strain gauge device through a series of 20 steps ranging from 100% male brightness to 100% female brightness. The experimental design consisted of fading, a control procedure where fading was reversed or stopped, following by a return to fading.

The first homosexual completed the fading procedure in that he became sexually aroused to the female slide alone in six sessions. This arousal generalized to female slides in separate measurement sessions and to reports of behavior. In a control phase, when fading was reversed, heterosexual arousal and reports of behavior dropped considerably. When the female slide was faded in once more, heterosexual arousal increased. Homosexual responsiveness remained high throughout the experiment.

In the second experiment heterosexual arousal rose during the initial fading, continued rising, but then dropped sharply during a control phase in which fading was stopped at the half-way point and the slides shown separately, and rose once again when fading was reintroduced. Again, homosexual arousal remained high but had dropped sharply after termination, *without* therapeutic attempts to accomplish this goal, at follow-ups of 1 and 3 months. This experimental procedure and result was replicated on a third homosexual.

Although these experiments suggest that a fading procedure is effective in instigating new patterns of sexual arousal, clinical assessments following treatment indicated that the first two subjects needed training in heterosocial skills to implement their newly acquired arousal.

Exposure. One final technique to increase heterosexual responsiveness (Herman, Barlow, & Agras, 1971; Herman, 1971) involved exposing homosexuals to high-intensity movies of a nude, seductive female. This technique was experimentally analyzed in three single cases with two homosexuals and a pedophilic.

The procedure was straightforward. An 8-mm movie of a nude, seductive female was shown daily for 10 minutes. During the control phase a movie of a nude, seductive male was shown accompanied by a therapeutic rationale. The third phase consisted of a return to the female exposure condition.

In all subjects, exposure to the female film increased heterosexual arousal. During the homosexual film, heterosexual arousal dropped for all subjects and rose once again when the heterosexual film was reintroduced. All subjects reported generalization to fantasies and behavior outside of treatment. Homosexual arousal had earlier been decreased in one subject through aversion therapy. In other subjects, homosexual arousal did not decrease during treatment. Follow-ups of from three months to one year revealed that two subjects had difficulty in heterosexual relations, despite continued arousal, due to deficient social skills.

Although the experimental analysis isolates exposure as responsible for changes in patterns of sexual arousal, the mechanism of action is not clear. The authors consider that this process may be similar to the "flooding" or "implosion" treatment of fear (Stampfl & Lewis, 1967) which is consistent with the notion that heterophobia is a major component of sexual deviation. Another possibility is that it provides the subjects with new fantasy material which is then associated with sexual arousal outside treatment.

Concluding Comments

In view of the long-standing agreement among therapists on the importance of instigating heterosexual behavior, it is surprising how little research has been done. Thus the plethora of techniques described in this paper are more often based on assumption and hypothesis rather than evidence of effectiveness, although several different approaches do show promise.

Furthermore, these techniques often have different goals. For instance, systematic desensitization in the first instance is directed at reducing heterosexual "anxiety." Pairing procedures or fading techniques, on the other hand, are designed to instigate heterosexual arousal while social retraining aims to teach adequate heterosocial skills. Many clinicians have concentrated on one of the above goals implicitly assuming that other appropriate behavior will follow. There is clinical evidence from our lab (Herman, 1971) and others (Annon, 1971) that an increase in heterosexual arousal is not always followed by acquisition of the necessary social skills to implement the arousal. On the other hand, many clinical anecdotes note that decreasing heterosexual anxiety or increasing heterosocial skills does not result in increased arousal. This suggests that heterosexual responsiveness is not a unitary concept, but actually consists of several distinct behavioral components. If this is the case, some combination of the above techniques such as a pairing procedure or fading techniques to instigate heterosexual arousal and social training to build heterosocial skills may constitute the most effective approach to the problem. Some patients may require intervention in only one area. There is an immediate need for a precise delineation of the various behavioral components constituting heterosexual responsiveness, and for the development of reliable and valid measurement devices to assess the extent of deficiencies in each component so that the appropriate technique or combination of techniques can be administered.

Finally, the relationship of aversion therapy and procedures to increase heterosexual responsiveness in the treatment of sexual deviation is not clear. Some evidence now exists suggesting that aversion therapy may not be necessary. In several cases where heterosexual responsiveness was increased without therapeutic attempts to suppress deviant responsiveness, deviant responses declined anyway, either during treatment (Kraft, 1967; Herman, 1971) or immediately after treatment (Barlow & Agras, in press). Since the ready use of aversive techniques has precluded this type of observation in most cases to date, more information is needed on the generality of this phenomenon and the patient variables which may predict its occurrence. Similarly, the observation noted independently by several investigators that aversive techniques alone set the occasion for rises in heterosexual responsiveness (Bancroft, 1971; Gelder & Marks, 1969; Barlow, Leitenberg, & Agras, 1969) is a paradoxical and puzzling phenomenon worthy of further investigation. This finding is reminiscent of side effects noted when aversive techniques are applied to disruptive behavior in children and psychotic adults. In these cases, socially appropriate behavior appears concurrent with deceleration of disruptive behavior and in the absence of any positive contingencies (Sajwaj & Risley, in press; Wahler, Sperling, Thomas, Teeter, & Luper, 1970). If this phenomenon is verified by future clinical research, then variables responsible for this effect should be isolated and arranged to maximize therapeutic benefit.

References

Abel, G., Levis, D., & Clancy, J. Aversion therapy applied to taped sequences of deviate behavior in exhibitionism and other sexual deviation: A preliminary report. *Journal of Behavior Therapy and Experimental Psychiatry,* 1970, *1,* 59-60.

Agras, W. S., Leitenberg, H., Barlow, D. H., Curtis, N. A., Edwards, J., & Wright, D. The role of relaxation in systematic desensitization. *Archives of General Psychiatry,* 1971, *25,* 511-514.

Annon, J. S. The extension of learning principles to the analysis and treatment of sexual problems. *Dissertation Abstracts International,* 1971, *32(6-B),* 3627.

Bancroft, J. Aversion therapy of homosexuality: A pilot study of 10 cases. *British Journal of Psychiatry,* 1969, *115,* 1417-1431.

Bancroft, J. A comparative study of aversion and desensitization in the treatment of homosexuality. In L. E. Burns and J. L. Worsley (Eds.), *Behaviour therapy in the 1970's.* Bristol: Wright, 1970. Pp. 12-33.

Bancroft, J. The application of psychophysiological measures to the assessment and modification of sexual behavior. *Behaviour Research and Therapy,* 1971, *9,* 119-130.

Barlow, D. H. Aversive procedures. In W. S. Agras (Ed.). *Behavior modification: principles and clinical applications.* Boston: Little, Brown, 1972. Pp. 87-125.

Barlow, D. H., Leitenberg, H., & Agras, W. S. The experimental control of sexual deviation through manipulation of the noxious scene in covert sensitization. *Journal of Abnormal Psychology,* 1969, *74,* 596-601.

Barlow, D. H., & Agras, W. S. Fading to increase heterosexual responsiveness in homosexuals. *Journal of Applied Behavior Analysis,* in press.

Beech, H. R., Watts, F., & Poole, A. D. Classical conditioning of sexual deviation: A preliminary note. *Behavior Therapy,* 1971, *2,* 400-402.

Beiber, B., Bieber, I., Dain, H. J., Dince, P. R., Drellich, M. G., Grundlach, H. G., Grundlach, R. H., Kremer, Malvina W., Wilber, Cornelia B., & Bieber, T. D. *Homosexuality.* New York: Basic Books, 1963.

Binet, A. *Etudes de psychologie experimentale.* Paris, 1888.

Birk, L., Miller, E., & Cohler, B. Group psychotherapy for homosexual men by male-female cotherapists. *Acta Psychiatrica Scandinavica,* Supplementum *218,* 1970, 9-36.

Birk, L., Huddleston, W., Miller, E., & Cohler, B. Avoidance conditioning for homosexuality. *Archives of General Psychiatry,* 1971, *25,* 314-323.

Bond, I., & Evans, D. Avoidance therapy: Its use in two cases of underwear fetishism. *Canadian Medical Association Journal,* 1967, *96,* 1160-1162.

Cautela, J. R., & Wisocki, P. A. The use of male and female therapists in the treatment of homosexual behavior. In R. Rubin and C. Franks (Eds.), *Advances in behavior therapy,* 1968. New York: Academic Press, 1969. Pp. 165-174.

Cooper, A. A. A case of fetishism and impotence treated by behavior therapy. *British Journal of Psychiatry*, 1963, *109*, 649-652.

Davison, G. C. Elimination of a sadistic fantasy by a client-controlled counterconditioning technique: A case study. *Journal of Abnormal Psychology*, 1968, *73*, 84-90.

DiScipio, W. Modified progressive desensitization and homosexuality. *British Journal of Medical Psychology*, 1968, *41*, 267-272.

Dollard, J., & Miller, N. E. *Personality and psychotherapy*. New York: McGraw-Hill, 1950.

Edwards, N. B. Case conference: Assertive training in a case of homosexual pedophilia. *Journal of Behavior Therapy and Experimental Psychiatry*, 1972, *3*, 55-63.

Ellis, A. The effectiveness of psychotherapy with individuals who have severe homosexual problems. *Journal of Consulting Psychology*, 1956, *20*, 58-60.

Ellis, A. A homosexual treated with rational psychotherapy. *Journal of Clinical Psychology*, 1959, *15*, 338-343.

Evans, D. R. Masturbatory fantasy and sexual deviation. *Behaviour Research and Therapy*, 1968, *6*, 17-19.

Feldman, M. P., & MacCulloch, M. J. The application of anticipatory avoidance learning to the treatment of homosexuality. I. Theory, technique, and preliminary results. *Behaviour Research and Therapy*, 1965, *2*, 165.

Feldman, M. P., & MacCulloch, M. J. *Homosexual behaviour: Theory and assessment*. Oxford, Pergamon Press, Ltd., 1971.

Fookes, B. H. Some experiences in the use of aversion therapy in male homosexuality, exhibitionism, and fetishism-transvestism. *British Journal of Psychiatry*, 1968, *115*, 339-341.

Freund, K. Some problems in the treatment of homosexuality. In Eysenck, H. J. (Ed.), *Behavior therapy and the neuroses*. London: Pergamon Press, 1960. Pp. 312-326.

Freund, K., Langevin, R., Cibiri, S., & Zajac, Y. Heterosexual aversion in homosexual males. *British Journal of Psychiatry*, 1973, *122*, 163.

Gaupp, L. A., Stern, R. M., & Ratliff, R. G. The use of aversion-relief procedures in the treatment of a case of voyeurism. *Behavior Therapy*, 1971, *2*, 585-588.

Gelder, M. G., & Marks, I. M. Aversion treatment in transvestism and transsexualism. In R. Green (Ed.), *Transsexualism and sex reassignment*. Baltimore: Johns Hopkins Press, 1969. Pp. 383-413.

Gray, J. J. Case conference: Behavior therapy in a patient with homosexual fantasies and heterosexual anxiety. *Journal of Behavior Therapy and Experimental Psychiatry*, 1970, *1*, 225-232.

Harbison, J., Quinn, J., & McAllister, H. The positive conditioning of heterosexual behavior. Paper presented to Conference on Behavior Modification, Dublin, 1970.

Herman, S. H. An experimental analysis of two methods of increasing heterosexual arousal in homosexuals. Unpublished doctoral dissertation, University of Mississippi, 1971.

Herman, S. H., Barlow, D. H., & Agras, W. S. Exposure to heterosexual stimuli: An effective variable in treating homosexuality? *Proceedings of the American Psychological Association 79th Annual Convention*. Washington, DC: American Psychological Association, 1971, 699-700.

Herman, S. H., Barlow, D. H., & Agras, W. S. An experimental analysis of classical conditioning as a method of increasing heterosexual arousal in homosexuals. *Behavior Therapy* (in press).

Huff, F. The desensitization of a homosexual. *Behaviour Research and Therapy,* 1970, *8,* 99-102.

Jackson, B. A case of voyeurism treated by counter-conditioning. *Behaviour Research and Therapy,* 1969, *7,* 133-134.

James, B. Case of homosexuality treated by aversion therapy. *British Medical Journal,* 1962, *1,* 768-770.

Kraft, T. A case of homosexuality treated by systematic desensitization. *American Journal of Psychotherapy,* 1967a, *21,* 815-821.

Kraft, T. Behavior therapy and the treatment of sexual perversions. *Psychotherapy and Psychosomatics,* 1967b, *15,* 351-357.

Kraft, T. Desensitization and the treatment of sexual disorders. *The Journal of Sex Research,* 1969a, *5,* 130-134.

Kraft, T. Treatment for sexual perversions. *Behaviour Research and Therapy,* 1969b, *7,* 215.

Larson, D. An adaptation of the Feldman and MacCulloch approach to treatment of homosexuality by the application of anticipatory avoidance learning. *Behaviour Research and Therapy,* 1970, *8,* 209-210.

Levin, S., Hirsch, I., Shugar, G., & Kapche, R. Treatment of homosexuality and heterosexual anxiety with avoidance conditioning and systematic desensitization: Data and case report. *Psychotherapy: Theory, Research and Practice,* 1968, *5,* 160-168.

LoPiccolo, J. Case study: Systematic desensitization of homosexuality. *Behavior Therapy,* 1971, *2,* 394-399.

Lovibond, S. H. Conceptual thinking, personality, and conditioning. *British Journal of Social Clinical Psychology,* 1963, *2,* 100-111.

MacCulloch, M. J., & Feldman, M. P. Aversion therapy in the management of 43 homosexuals. *British Medical Journal,* 1967, *2,* 594-597.

Marquis, J. N. Orgasmic reconditioning: Changing sexual object choice through controlling masturbation fantasies. *Journal of Behavior Therapy and Experimental Psychiatry,* 1970, *1,* 263-271.

McConaghy, N. Subjective and penile plethysmograph responses following aversion relief and apomorphine aversion therapy for homosexual impulses. *British Journal of Psychiatry,* 1969, *115,* 723-730.

McConaghy, N. Penile response conditioning and its relationship to aversion therapy in homosexuals. *Behavior Therapy,* 1970, *1,* 213-221.

McGuire, R. J., Carlisle, J. M., & Young, B. G. Sexual deviations as conditioned behavior. *Behaviour Research and Therapy,* 1965, *2,* 185-190.

Mees, H. L. Sadistic fantasies modified by aversive conditioning and substitution: A case study. *Behaviour Research and Therapy,* 1966, *4,* 317-320.

Moan, C. E., & Heath, R. G. Septal stimulation for the initiation of heterosexual behavior in a homosexual male. *Journal of Behavior Therapy and Experimental Psychiatry,* 1972, *3,* 23-30.

Morgenstern, F. S., Pearce, J. P., & Rees, L. Predicting the outcome of behavior therapy by psychological tests. *Behaviour Research and Therapy*, 1965, *2*, 191-200.

Ovesey, L., Gaylin, W., & Hendin, H. Psychotherapy of male homosexuality. *Archives of General Psychiatry*, 1963, *9*, 19-31.

Quinn, J., Harbison, J., & McAllister, H. An attempt to shape human penile responses. *Behaviour Research and Therapy*, 1970, *8*, 213-216.

Rachman, S. Sexual fetishism: An experimental analogue. *The Psychological Record*, 1966, *16*, 293-296.

Rachman, S., & Hodgson, R. J. Experimentally induced "sexual fetishism": Replication and development. *The Psychological Record*, 1968, *18*, 25-27.

Rado, S. An adaptational view of sexual behavior. In P. Hoch and J. Zubin (Eds.), *Psychosexual development in health and disease*. New York: Grune and Stratton, 1949.

Ramsey, R. W., & Van Velzen, V. Behaviour therapy for sexual perversions. *Behaviour Research and Therapy*, 1968, *6*, 17-19.

Sajwaj, T. E., & Risley, T. R. Punishment techniques in behavior modification. *Journal of Applied Behavior Analysis* (in press).

Salter, A. *Conditioned reflex therapy*. New York: Farrar, Strauss, 1949. Republished: New York: Capricorn Books, 1961.

Solyom, L., & Miller, S. A differential conditioning procedure as the initial phase of behavior therapy of homosexuality. *Behaviour Research and Therapy*, 1965, *3*, 147-160.

Stampfl, T. G., & Levis, D. J. Essentials of implosive therapy: a learning theory based on psychodynamic behavioral therapy. *Journal of Abnormal Psychology*, 1967, *72*, 496-503.

Stevenson, I., & Wolpe, J. Recovery from sexual deviation through overcoming nonsexual neurotic responses. *American Journal of Psychiatry*, 1960, *116*, 789.

Thorpe, J., Schmidt, E., Brown, P., & Castell, D. Aversion-relief therapy: A new method for general application. *Behaviour Research and Therapy*, 1964, *2*, 71-82.

Thorpe, J., Schmidt, E., & Castell, D. A comparison of positive and negative (aversive) conditioning in the treatment of homosexuality. *Behaviour Research and Therapy*, 1963, *1*, 357-362.

Wahler, R. G., Sperling, K. A., Thomas, M. R., Teeter, N. C., & Luper, H. L. Modification of childhood stuttering: Some response-response relationships. *Journal of Experimental Child Psychology*, 1970, *9*, 411-428.

West, D. J. *Homosexuality*. 3rd Edition. London: Penguin Books, 1968.

Wickramasekera, I. The application of learning theory to the treatment of a case of sexual exhibitionism. *Psychotherapy: Theory, Research, and Practice*, 1968, *5*, 108-112.

Wood, D., & Obrist, P. Minimal and maximal sensory intake and exercises as unconditioned stimuli in human heart-rate conditioning. *Journal of Experimental Psychology*, 1968., *76*, 254-262.

Wolpe, J. *The practice of behavior therapy*. New York: Pergamon Press, 1969.

Note: Preparation of this manuscript was supported by National Institute of Mental Health Grant MH-20258.

Septal Stimulation for the Initiation of Heterosexual Behavior in a Homosexual Male

Charles E. Moan and
Robert G. Heath
Department of Psychiatry and Neurology
Tulane University School of Medicine
New Orleans

P leasure has long been known to be a primary reinforcing condition for acquiring and establishing behavior in animals and man. They develop the particular responses that are followed by states of pleasure. The knowledge that these states can be important positive reinforcers has led to significant applications in psychotherapy, as witness the large number of studies reporting the effectiveness of various operational forms of pleasure in altering or "counterconditioning" undesired human behaviors. Over the past several years, considerable interest has also fastened on the fact that a pleasurable response can be induced by direct activation of the brain and raised hopes that this might be applied to the treatment of disordered human behavior.

In 1952, at a symposium on depth electrode studies in animals and man, investigators at Tulane University School of Medicine first described 26 patients' pleasurable responses to stimulation of specific deep regions of the brain, initially observed with electrical stimulation to septal region (Heath, 1954). Subsequently, techniques were developed for intracranial self-stimulation and the study of what appeared to be reward and aversive areas of the brain in animals (Olds, 1960; Olds, 1962; Olds and Milner, 1954; Olds and Olds, 1964). These were incorporated and modified by the Tulane researchers in human studies, enabling them to extend their scope to man (Bishop *et al.,* 1963; Heath, 1954, 1963, 1964; Heath and Guerrero-

Figueroa, 1968). Following an initial observation that there were pleasurable experiences accompanying electrical stimulation of the deep structures of the brain, they found that there were positive and negative reinforcing properties of such stimulation and that there were effective stimulus parameters and brain "reward" areas in man. In particular, they found that stimulation of the septal area consistently resulted in a pleasurable response and frequently induced an associated sexual motive state. Considering the findings of these investigations, it seemed logical to employ pleasure-yielding septal stimulation as a treatment modality for facilitating the initiation, development, and demonstration of new and adaptive behaviors. The purpose of this study, therefore, was to explore the possibility of using it to bring about heterosexual behavior in a fixed, overt homosexual male. This was but one phase of the therapeutic program undertaken to deal with the complex symptomatology of this individual who had consistently failed to respond to other treatment approaches and was a most serious suicidal risk.

Case History

Background

Patient B-19 is a 24-year-old single, white male of unremarkable gestation and birth whose immediate family consists of parents, age 55, and a sister, 19. The father, described by the patient as a tyrannical, abusive, and demanding individual given to excessive drinking and episodic anger and violence, reportedly considers his son to be a deeply disappointing young man who was a failure and coward during childhood and adolescence. The mother is characterized as an extremely withdrawn, rigid, and emotionally controlled woman, whose embrace B-19 cannot recall. Rather, she serves to mediate between him and his father, is given to excessive complaining about her surroundings and circumstances and consistently approaches the patient for solutions to her marital conflicts. In contrast, he reports considerable affection for his sister, with whom he states he can share his confidences, anxieties, and disappointments.

The educational background of B-19 is characterized by nine major residential and school changes and by the early manifestation of behavioral and disciplinary problems which resulted in three expulsions from school and two examinations by child specialists by age 11. From first grade on, he consistently experienced difficulties in interacting with other boys and actively sought to avoid contact and competition with them, while becoming increasingly aggressive and punitive toward his female peers. These behaviors resulted in his being teased, picked on, and ostracized by his classmates. In desperation, he was sent to an all-male parochial school where he experienced further rejection and isolation and turned to individual pursuits, interests, and reveries. High school began with a psychiatric referral because of an inability to get along with his peers and increasingly poor grades. He dropped out after 3 years and took a part-time job as a stock clerk before military enlistment, which resulted in a psychiatric discharge after 1 month due to "homosexual tendencies." Seven months were then spent working in a factory followed by 2 years as a "drifter" travelling idly around the country, engaging in numerous homosexual relationships and being supported financially by homosexual partners.

Symptomatology

The patient exhibits a distinct preoccupation with his body image and is given to extreme somatization characterized by multiple vague and fluctuating complaints regarding suspected changes in facial dimensions, loss of libido and hormone imbalance, agitation and fatigability, and various conditions of discomfort in his head. In addition to these hypochondriacal traits, he demonstrates considerable paranoid ideation, which often exceeds the limits of reality. Such thinking is highlighted by a marked fear of the future, a dramatic dread of inflicted physical pain, a daily expectation of dying and deliberate avoidance of people, especially men. Hypersensitive to criticism and unreasonably self-conscious in public, he feels sealed off and alienated from society in general. Paradoxically, however, he cannot tolerate being ignored and is generally disdainful, arrogant, and grandiose in his presentation of knowledge and expresses hostility for gaining attention and recognition. Regarding the discomforts of these conditions, he conceives of himself as a "special" person who will be rewarded by God for the endurance of present hardships. The extent of his paranoia fluctuates situationally, but is often of true psychotic proportion.

B-19 is also distinguished by marked apathy, chronic boredom, lack of motivation to achieve, and deep sense of being ineffectual, inadequate, worthless, and inferior. He avoids making any plans, has no meaningful feelings for others, and complains of having no talents worth mention. He is a severe procrastinator, gives up easily, and obsesses on his personal problems to the point of incapacitation. Depression and suicidal rumination are reportedly his daily companions. Further, he feels that he will never find happiness or peace of mind and that his lack of masculinity and intellectual power cause him to want to end his life. Complaints are also present of an alteration in his ability to experience pleasure, where he states that he is bored by everything and left constantly blasé. Having initially turned to alcohol, drugs, and sexual acting out for pleasure and stimulation, drugs no longer produce a high or euphoria and he gets no "kick" out of sex—"not even masturbation." He does have a three-year history of drug abuse, which ran a course punctuated by alcohol, amphetamines, barbiturates, major and minor tranquilizers, the sniffing of chemical agents and solvents, marijuana, and nutmeg. Addiction and preference were for amphetamines, which gave him a "lift," confidence, energy and elation. With continued usage, however, alcohol and drugs, even in greater frequency and dosage, failed to produce the desired effects and resulted in severe depression and a state he referred to as "brain pollution."

For the past 5 years he has exhibited fixed, overt homosexual behavior but has never in his life experienced heterosexual relations of any kind. He prefers to be the dominant individual in anal intercourse, with fellatio being tolerated but not necessarily sought. He is most attracted to and jealous of handsome, well-built and -dressed, intelligent, and masculine men; though, he is far more comfortable when lovemaking is with effeminate males. Those with whom he has had sexual relations over any consistent period of time have been several years older than he and characteristically of marginal emotional stability. He describes himself as having been "sexually precocious," experiencing erotic feelings toward his sister when bathed together as children, having begun "wet dreams" at age 5 or 6 (which he elaborates as a sense of pleasurable relief when he wet the bed), and having very actively indulged in masturbation since age 12 (still a preferred behavior). Homosexual encounters began at this time, as well as wide reading in the area of sexual deviations and perversions. There has never been an active interest in females, though he admits that he is somewhat aroused by pictures of women in various degrading and pitiable positions. In no way does the patient himself physically manifest effeminate mannerisms, gestures or movements.

Hospitalizations, Evaluations and
Examinations

Following two previous psychiatric hospitalizations of approximately 5 months each and initiated by suicidal depressions, B-19 was examined and admitted to the Tulane Service of the Department of Psychiatry of

Charity Hospital of New Orleans. Physical and neurological examinations were within normal limits, as were the results of urinalyses and blood chemical determinations. Psychological evaluation indicated bright normal intellectual functioning (WAIS Verbal Score 118, Performance Score 104, Full Scale Score 113) and an unusually hypersensitive and obessive-compulsive individual who experiences chronic depression of a degree which leaves him functionally disorganized, confused, discontented, and bitter. His tolerance for frustration is extremely low, and he responds quickly with suspicion, anger, impatience, querulousness, and vindictiveness. Psychiatric examination indicated that the symptom complex exhibited by the patient was consistent with temporal lobe epilepsy. Conventional scalp EEGs showed an abnormality characterized by bitemporal slow-wave activity, maximal on the left. Paroxysmal delta activity also appeared over the right temporal region, with Chlorolose activation. Pneumoencephalogram was normal.

Technical Procedure and
Apparatus

Operative procedure and stereotaxic implantation of electrodes followed techniques previously described (Heath *et al.*, 1968). The patient was under general anesthesia, with visualization of the ventricular system by air and pantopaque. Stainless steel Teflon-insulated electrodes 0.003 in. diameter, each with three to six leads separated by 2 mm, were implanted into the following brain regions: right mid septal, right hippocampus, left and right amygdalae, right anterior hypothalamus, right posterior ventral lateral thalamus, left caudate nucleus, and at two subcortical sites within the left lobe of the cerebellum. Cortical leads were placed under the dura sites in the left and right frontal regions, left and right parietal areas, and right temporal region. Triple-lead silver ball polyvinyl chloride acetate-insulated electrodes were implanted into the left anterior and left posterior septal region. The silver ball contact points were 0.5 mm in diameter, each 2 mm apart. Intracerebral cannulae were implanted into the septal region bilaterally and into the hippocampus (Heath and de Balbian Verster, 1961; Heath and Founds, 1960).

EEG recordings were obtained on two Grass Model VI electroencephalographs, one 12-channel and one 8-channel, synchronized by the use of a time code generator. EEGs from various sites indicated that all artifacts due to anesthesia and brain trauma incurred at operation had disappeared 3 weeks after surgery. At this time B-19's responses to passive electrical stimuli (Heath, 1954) delivered to all deep brain sites where electrodes had been implanted were carefully examined and indicated that only stimulation of the septal region resulted in a pleasurable experience, with stimulation of other sites being either neutral or aversive. The range of stimulation was 0.5-7.5 mA. The present study, being but one part of an overall treatment program and dealing with the effects of the pleasure responses upon behavior, concerns only those electrodes implanted in the septal areas specified.

A later phase of the treatment procedure involved equipping the patient with a three-button self-stimulating transistorized device (Bishop *et al.* 1963, Heath, 1963; Heath, 1964) attached to electrodes in the septal region and permitting him to stimulate any of the sites *ad lib.* Each depression of a button delivered a 1-sec stimulus whose count was automatically registered.

Treatment Program

The present procedure was but one phase of the total therapeutic program for this patient and was consistently coordinated with his attitude and disposition, his physical and emotional well-being, and the requirements of other aspects of treatment. Although this, at times, resulted in a weakening of experimental design, attention to the overall welfare of the patient was justifiably placed before exploratory investigation and analysis.

Initiation of the procedure took place 3 months following surgery for electrode implantation and 4 weeks after the determination of the parameters of subjectively pleasurable septal stimulation. At this time, B-19 viewed a 15-min 8 mm. "stag" film featuring sexual intercourse and related activities between a male and female. There was continuous EEG recording of the patient, as well as observation through a two-way mirror. He showed no obvious verbal or gestural response during the presentation but was highly resentful, angry, and unwilling to respond at its conclusion. Base rate (pre-film) EEG indicated the presence of tension and hyperalertness prior to viewing, reflected by low voltage, low amplitude activity. No significant changes in EEG were apparent during the time the patient watched the film; but high amplitude alpha activity was noted at the end of the session, indicating some relaxation because the movie was over. There were no focal changes seen during this procedure. Detailed EEG findings throughout the entire treatment program are reported elsewhere (Heath, 1971).

A program involving both passive (other-induced) and self-stimulation of the septal region was begun the following day. A summary of the stimulation sessions is presented in Table 1. During and following the initial three periods of passive stimulation, B-19 exhibited an improved mood, smiled frequently, stated that he could think more clearly, and reported a sense of generalized muscle relaxation. He likened these responses to the pleasurable states he had sought and experienced through the use of amphetamines. Moreover, he reported an associated state of sexual motivation. EEGs obtained between periods of stimulation were unremarkable.

On the next two occasions the patient was allowed free access to the buttons of the self-stimulator which activated the left anterior and right mid-septal leads. While activation of both resulted in reports of positive and pleasant experiences, mid-septal stiumlation was obviously preferred over anterior at a ratio of 2.3 : 1 (Table 1). During these sessions, B-19 stimulated himself to a point that, both behaviorally and introspectively, he was

TABLE 1.
SUMMARY OF SEPTAL STIMULATIONS IN PATIENT B-19

Stimulation Day	Type of Stimulation	Locus	Stimulus Magnitude	Stimulus Duration	Self-Stimulations
1	Passive	Rt. Mid-Sept.	2 mA	2 min	—
3	Passive	Lt. Ant-Sept.	6 mA	8 min	—
7	Passive	Lt. Ant-Sept.	3-7•5 mA	5 min	—
8	Self	Lt. Ant-Sept.	7•5 mA	3 hr 5 min	350
		Rt. Mid-Sept.	2•3 mA	3 hr 5 min	850
9	Self	Lt. Ant-Sept.	7•5 mA	3 hr 30 min	432
		Rt. Mid-Sept.	2•3 mA	3 hr 30 min	927
17	Passive	Lt. Ant- and Rt. Mid-Sept.	0•5 mA	1 min	—
		Lt. Ant- and Lt. Post-Sept.	4•25 mA	1•5 min	—
		Lt. Ant-Sept.	3•25 mA	1 min	—
		Lt. Post-Sept.	2•25-2•50 mA	1 min	—
18	Self	Rt. Mid-Sept.	0•5 mA	3 hr	134
		Lt. Ant- and Lt. Post-Sept.	0•5 mA	3 hr	58
		Lt. Ant- and Lt. Post-Sept.	0•5 mA	3 hr	69
21	Passive	Rt. Mid-Sept.	1-1•5 mA	20 sec	—

experiencing an almost overwhelming euphoria and elation and had to be disconnected, despite his vigorous protests. His post stimulation EEGs were unremarkable. Over the next 4 days there was no septal stimulation, either passive or self—, because of an intervening weekend and other of the patient's commitments. However, during this time B-19 did show a notable improvement in disposition and behavior, was less recalcitrant and more cooperative both at the laboratory and his hospital ward, and reported increasing interest in female personnel and feelings of sexual arousal with a compulsion to masturbate. The next afternoon he agreed without reluctance to re-view the stag film and during its showing became sexually aroused, had an erection, and masturbated to orgasm. At the conclusion of this session the patient stated that he "felt great" and was highly pleased with himself. EEG immediately before the movie was not unusual; and no specific activity was later present to be linked with any events during the film. The behavior of the patient over the ensuing 4 days showed increased self-satisfaction, preoccupation with sex, and a continued growing interest in women. At this time, and throughout all phases of the present procedure, no attempt was made to instigate any formal psychotherapeutic program. The patient was, however, given encouragement and support in the development of heterosexual interest and was directly counseled when he solicited information regarding sexual technique and behavior.

Stimulation was resumed with passive activation of various combinations of electrodes at several sites within the septal region (Table 1). It resulted in the patient reporting feelings of alertness, elation and being quite "high." Consequent self-stimulation through other septal electrode combinations (Table 1) produced an experience of warmth, a flushing sensation, and sexual arousal.

At this time, the patient was maintaining an active interest in females, culminating in an expressed desire to attempt heterosexual activity in the near future. Therefore, arrangements were made for a 21-year-old prostitute to spend 2 hours with him in a laboratory specially prepared to afford complete privacy. B-19 was receptive to the plan, and the woman agreed after being apprised of the circumstances. On the afternoon of their meeting, the patient's electrodes were attached to the encephalograph via an extension cord for increased mobility, and recordings were obtained for 45 minutes, with an interruption for delivery of passive stimulation of the septal region for 20 seconds (Table 1). B-19 was then introduced to the prostitute, and EEGs were obtained throughout his relationship with her (Heath, 1971).

Separate interviews with the patient and the prostitute provided information about their time spent together. Both reported that B-19 was initially anxious and reluctant when they were left alone, though his apprehension gradually subsided. The first hour of the session was essentially spent in conversation about the patient's experiences with drugs, his homosexuality, and his personal shortcomings, and negative qualities. Such material was seemingly presented as a defense on his part against progressing too far too quickly. During this time, his partner was most accepting and reassuring and gradually moved closer to him in an attempt to arouse his interest in her. He responded by trying to avoid eye contact, but at no time did he move away or express a desire to discontinue. She proceeded to remove her dress, but not her underclothing. B-19 did not respond with any advance though he did report feelings of interest and sexual arousal. As the second hour began, she relates that his attitude took an even more positive shift to which she reacted by removing her bra and panties and lying down next to him. Then, in a patient and supportive manner, she encouraged him to spend some time in a manual exploration and examination of her body, directing him to areas which were particularly sensitive and assisting him in the initial manipulation of her genitalia and breasts. At times, the patient would ask questions and seek reinforcement regarding his performance and progress, to which she would respond directly and informatively. After about 20 minutes of such interaction, she begun to mount him, and though he was somewhat reticent he did achieve penetration. Active intercourse followed during which she had an orgasm that he was apparently able to sense. He became very excited at this and suggested that they turn over in order that he might assume the initiative. In this position he often paused to delay orgasm and to increase the duration of the pleasurable experience. Then, despite the milieu and the encumbrance of the electrode wires, he successfully ejaculated. Subsequently, he expressed how much he had enjoyed her and how he hoped that he would have sex with her again in the near future.

During this session, EEG recordings from the deep leads (Heath, 1971) indicated that delta waves appeared at several of these sites as sexual arousal increased and that immediately prior to orgasm striking changes in recordings from septal leads occurred resembling epilepti-form discharge. These changes were characterized by spike and slow wave activity with considerable numbers of superimposed fast frequencies. This pattern was essentially unchanged at the moment of orgasm. However, shortly after its onset the recordings were overwhelmed by the effects of movement; and, although it was impossible to separate the meaningful from the artifact, septal seizural activity seemed to endure throughout the orgastic response. Such data emphasize the relationship between activity in the septal region and a pleasure reaction.

Current Status

For nearly 11 months following termination of the treatment program described, the patient has been receiving counseling on a regular basis at the outpatient clinic of a community mental health center and returning to the Tulane Department of Psychiatry for periodic progress reports. He has held various part-time jobs and been tentatively approved for vocational rehabilitation job training. While he looks and is apparently functioning better, he still has a complaining disposition which does not permit him readily to admit his progress. However, he did meet and form a close sexual relationship with a married woman for almost 10 months. Their interactions consisted of sexual fore-play, oral-genital contact, mutual masturbatory activity, and intromission during which he refrained from orgasm because the girl insisted that he withdraw and complete ejaculation extravaginally. Being married she was somewhat fearful and guilty about intercourse and the uncertainty of the relationship. This circumstance led to an increasingly untenable situation, so that they finally stopped seeing one another. He reports that homosexual behavior occurred only twice, when he needed money and "hustling" was a quick way to get it when he was out of work. However, he states that such acting out was not intended to be a replacement for sex with females, which he indicates he is definitely motivated to continue. There will be further contact with the patient in the future to assess his progress and to assist him when he encounters obstacles or setbacks which he reportedly needs help in resolving.

Discussion and Implications

The purpose of the present study was to explore the potential of pleasure-yielding septal stimulation for facilitating the development of new behaviors—in specific, the initiation of heterosexuality in a homosexual male. The history of this individual prior to stimulation was highlighted by chronic, severe depression, a bitter and complaining disposition, gross interpersonal difficulties, fixed homosexual behavior, and increasing failure to experience pleasure. However, the septal stimulation procedure described resulted in an improved mood, self-confidence, generalized muscle relaxation, euphoria, elation, interpersonal warmth, tension release, and sexual arousal. The patient became progressively more invested in his treatment and increasingly more cooperative and self-satisfied. It was during subjectively pleasurable states such as these that he became sexually motivated and masturbated on viewing a heterosexual film and later participated in sexual intercourse with a female.

The desirable and pleasant conditions which B-19 experienced as a result of septal stimulation, and which reportedly lingered for considerable lengths of time, apparently produces a state or mood which facilitated his exposure to stimuli and situations previously antagonistic, anxiety-inducing, or negatively laden, and for which he had indifference, contempt, or revulsion. Moreover, the pleasurable states seemed clearly sufficient to counter his anxieties regarding heterosexuality and allow him to experience this totally new behavior, while gaining enough satisfaction from it.

Certainly, septal stimulation is a novel treatment for human psychological disorders, and requires continued investigation and elaboration. Of central interest in the case of B-19 was the effectiveness of pleasurable stimulation in the development of new and more adaptive sexual behavior. There was no attempt to eliminate the homosexuality through aversive stimulation of other areas of the brain. The success reported points toward future effective use of septal activation for reinforcing desired behavior and extinguishing undesired behavior. Because of the nature of the patient and the overall treatment plan in the present study, the pleasurable stimulation was not dependent on any given behavior. However, contingency programs could certainly be designed to use such pleasurable reinforcement most efficiently to alleviate or alter psychological distress. Plans for such treatment programs are under way by the Tulane staff and will be activated in the near future.

Further investigation of the applications of septal stimulation to psychotherapeutic endeavors might well be through using its resulting states of pleasure in variants of desensitization or other forms of counter-conditioning. Or, externally-controlled shaping of appropriate behaviors might be accomplished through using pleasure-yielding stimulation as a positive reinforcement for wanted responses. In addition, the use of the self-stimulator might be expanded, through careful design, to maintain new response styles and continuous reduction of feelings of tension, anxiety, or agitation. It is important to note, however, that implanting electrodes for septal stimulation has been undertaken only in patients who failed to show any response to any previous psychiatric treatment; and that it is not being recommended for cases that can be effectively dealt with in other ways. Also, septal stimulation requires considerably more investigation by other researchers to establish its function and possible application to such problems as chronic depressions, character disorders, anhedonia, and autistic, and other psychotic reactions.

Another target of research would be to identify chemical agents which might produce pleasure-yielding stimulation of the septal areas. Investigations already undertaken (Heath, 1971; Heath and Founds, 1960) have involved introducing acetylcholine or levarterenol bitartrate through intracerebral cannulae implanted in the septal region. This treatment induced strong feelings of pleasure and a sexual motive state in both a male and a female, resulting in repeated orgasms in the woman but not in the man. EEG recordings from the septal region during the sexual arousal were similar in these two patients. Continued study may lead to the identification of septally activating pleasure-inducing drugs that are administered orally or parenterally. Such drugs would conveniently elicit selected pleasurable responses for psycho-therapeutic use.

References

Bishop M. P., Elder S. T. and Heath R. G. (1963). Intracranial self-stimulation in man, *Science 140* (3565), 394-396.

Heath R. G. (Ed.) (1954) *Studies in Schizophrenia,* Harvard University Press, Cambridge, Mass. (The initial report of findings in 26 patients prepared with depth electrodes was made in 1952 at a meeting in New Orleans, Louisiana.)

Heath R. G. (1963) Electrical self-stimulation of the brain in man. *Am. J. Psychiat. 120* (6), 571-577.

Heath R. G. (Ed.) (1964) *The Role of Pleasure in Behavior,* Hoeber Medical Division, Harper and Row, New York

Heath R. G. (1971) Pleasure and brain activity in man: deep and surface electroencephalograms during orgasms, *J. Nerv. Ment. Dis.* (in press).

Heath R. G. and de Balbian Verster F. (1961) Effects of chemical stimulation to discrete brain areas, *Am. J. Psychiat. 117,* 980-990.

Heath R. G. and Founds W. L. (1960) A perfusion cannula for intracerebral microinjections, *Electroenceph. Clin. Neurophysiol. 12,* 930-932.

Heath R. G. and Guerrero—Figueroa R. (1968) Stimulation of the human brain, *Acta Neurol. Latinoamer. 14,* 116-124.

Heathe R. G., John S. B. and Fontana C. J. (1968) The pleasure responses: studies of stereotaxic techniics in patients, *Computers and Electronic Devices in Psychiatry* (Edited by N. Kline and E. Laska), Grune and Stratton, New York.

Olds J. (1960) Approach-avoidance dissociations in rat brains, *Am. J. Physiol. 199,* 965-968.

Olds J. (1962) Hypothalamic substrates of reward, *Physiol. Rev. 42,* 554-604.

Olds J. and Milner P. (1954) Positive reinforcement produced by electrical stimulation of septal area and other regions of rat brain, *J. Comp. Physiol. Psychol. 47,* 419-427.

Olds J. and Olds M. E. (1964) The mechanisms of voluntary behavior, *The Role of Pleasure in Behavior* (Edited by R. G. Heath), Hoeber Medical Division, Harper and Row, New York.

The Management of Premature Ejaculation*

Ian Wickramasekera
University of Illinois
College of Medicine
Peoria

Diagnosis

This is a sexual dysfunction in the male which is characterized by ejaculation prior to vaginal penetration or ejaculation within a few minutes or a few thrusts after penetration. The ejaculatory reflex is controlled mainly by the sympathetic division of the autonomic nervous system. Typically, the man ejaculates before his mate has been able to derive sexual satisfaction or has been able to reach orgasm. As Helen Kaplan (1974) has pointed out, the essential deficit in this syndrome is related not to *time* but to *function*. Central control of the ejaculatory mechanism has not been established, and the male is unable to tolerate high levels of sexual pleasure without ejaculating reflexively.

It is useful to distinguish between two types (Kaplan, 1974) of premature ejaculators. Type A is represented by the young man who has never had a history of good ejaculatory control and has had no problems with erection. Type B is represented by the older man with unreliable erectile function who has previously had a history of good ejaculatory control. Type B is frequently a precursor of secondary impotence.

Etiology

The Type B patient is more likely to need a neurological and/or a urological work-up because of the remote possibility of an organic etiology for the premature ejaculation.

---

*I want to express my gratitude to the staff of the Reproductive Biology Research Foundation, St. Louis, Missouri, for the instruction I received from them. They are, of course, not responsible for the opinions expressed in this article.

Psychological etiology commonly takes the form of a deficit in tolerance for high sustained levels of sexual excitement. This deficit is frequently compounded by the anticipation of failure to control ejaculation and a learned cognitive tendency to catastrophize about the meaning and consequences of failure (prematurity). Both cognitive components further increase the probability of aversive sympathetic arousal. Because the mechanism of ejaculation is primarily sympathetic, psychological (central stimulation) factors may further increase the probability of general sympathetic arousal and consequently ejaculation. In some cases sadistic feelings towards females have been inferred on the part of the man. Certainly many wives of premature ejaculators are angry, frustrated, and may relate destructively towards their husbands, but it is possible that these attitudes on the part of both male and female are secondary reactions to chronic sexual frustration and failure.

Personal and Social Consequences of Premature Ejaculation

The premature ejaculator develops feelings of guilt, shame, and futility within and around the sexual situation, because he fails his sexual partner very often. He also fails to develop a relaxed comfortable style of love making which can inhibit this aversive arousal during sex. The wife may verbally or nonverbally express frustration and anger. She may become demanding, avoid sex altogether, or step out on her husband. Because of the premature ejaculator's fear of failure, he may limit his social and physical contact with his wife, which the wife may interpret as "lack of love" or "coldness." She may become more demanding, feel unattractive, and believe that if he "really" loved her he would not avoid her and would be able to control his ejaculation. She may attempt to resolve the problem by "going on a diet," getting a new hair style or buying "sexy" clothes. The failure of the above interventions to resolve the prematurity will intensify her feelings of frustration, hostility or depression. The man in turn may develop profound feelings of inferiority and seek refuge in excessive alcohol, compulsive masturbation, work, TV (late show), or some other form of avoidance behavior, which creates secondary marital problems.

Therapy

1. It is important to explain firmly that the mechanism of ejaculation is involuntary and that wishing, wanting, and demanding are ineffective remedial procedures with the autonomic nervous system. This

information can immediately depressurize the marital unit and terminate the allocation of blame.

2. Explain that the *relationship* is the patient and that both parties may often have contributed to the dysfunction. These instructions tend to stop the assignment of blame. They reduce guilt and pressure in the relationship, and defuse many potential fights.

3. *Sensate Focus.* During this procedure, conducted in the nude with lights on, the couple **explore** each other's bodies nongenitally to the point that no threat or performance pressure remains in the sexual situation. Sexual intercourse is strictly prohibited. The exercise is structured to make "failure" impossible, because sexual intercourse is strictly forbidden during the initial phase. All physical goals (of ejaculation, erection, lubrication, etc.) are declared irrelevant; the only goals are psychological (e.g. fun, security, comfort, etc.).

The goal during the first part of the sensate focus (Masters and Johnson, 1970) is to mobilize the total sensuous (not sexual) potentials of the body and to promote feelings of comfort, security and relaxation in the sexual situation. The orientation should be towards "process" rather than "product" (physical goals, e.g. ejaculation, erection, lubrication). The patients should be encouraged to enjoy the process (hors d'oeuvres) and not rush for the meat (genitals). Patients should be encouraged to take the attitude of a gourmet rather than a glutton towards sex. The communication between the partners should be mainly in terms of "I language," with studious avoidance of "mind reading" or inferential speculation, for example, "I feel," "I want," "I think." Each person should state what he or she **feels** and **wants** and should be able to allow the same freedom to the other member of the marital unit. Instructionally, it should be made clear and credible that each person should take responsibility for his own sexual functioning, since nobody else can perform a *natural function* for another (e.g., "You do not expect anybody else to breathe or defecate for you."). It is important that each partner become an active participant, since the distance from cortex to crotch, which is only a few feet anatomically, can psychologically be expanded by some individuals to several light years. Some females need "permission" to move freely and make "noises" during sex. They need reassurance that they will not look vulgar to their husbands. The pleasure of most men is increased by such observations, but there may be a few men who will be threatened by such demonstrations. The couple should risk sharing vulnerabilities or expressing tender feelings, fears, and hurts. Each member of the marital unit should also "risk" assuming that his partner has already changed and that his partner will not deliberately hurt him. An attitude of

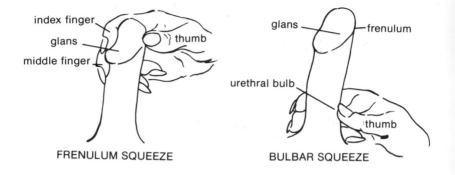

FRENULUM SQUEEZE   BULBAR SQUEEZE

Figure 1. Masters and Johnson's Squeeze Techniques

Figure 2. 1st Training Position for Ejaculatory Control

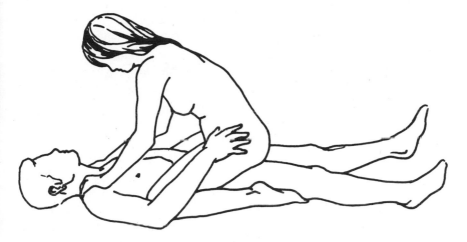

FIGURE 3. 2nd Training Position for Ejaculatory Control

FIGURE 4. 3rd Training Position for Ejaculatory Control

"therapeutic neutrality" should be maintained in which neither party *locks* the other into his or her past. The "I language" "vulnerability" and "neutrality" principles are critical and should be elaborated and checked at each session. These instructional and communicational principles are equally important to positive outcome as the behavioral exercises. They are essential conditions for reducing the probability of future symptomatic relapse. Behavioral (motor) procedures in the narrow sense, devoid of informational and instructional inputs, can quickly become empty rituals.

In the second stage of sensate focus, genital contact is incorporated into the procedure. The frenulum squeeze is first used extra vaginally (Figures 1 and 2) and later intra-vaginally (Figure 3) in the female superior position. The wife stimulates the penis to a point just prior to ejaculation and then squeezes its glans by placing her thumb on the frenulum and two fingers on top of the glans (Figure 1). The squeeze is applied strongly for three to four seconds until the male loses the urge to ejaculate. This procedure (alternation between stimulation and squeezing) is continued six or seven times during each session of first extra-vaginal and later intra-vaginal contact. Psychologically the premature ejaculator for the first time feels his sense of futility falling away from him and being replaced by a sense of security and self-control. The bulbar squeeze (Figure 1) may be substituted for the frenulum squeeze and may be used either extra- or intra-vaginally. The bulbar squeeze does not require disconnection of genitals. It is important to urge the female to apply strong pressure when using either squeeze and to reassure her that she will not hurt the male.

When the couple first moves to the female superior position (Figure 3), it is important that the female at first move in a non-demanding or gently stimulating manner. After the male can tolerate brisk intravaginal stimulation, the couple can be instructed to move to a side-by-side position (Figure 4). In the side-by-side position the couple should stop intercourse when the male feels he is approaching ejaculation and resume moving when this feeling has passed. Through this "stop-start" technique, the man will continue to develop increasing tolerance for high levels of sexual excitement. Finally, the couple is instructed to move to the male superior position and to continue to use the "stop-start" technique.

In some difficult cases where the male is still very anxious and fearful of failure, either prior or concurrent, "in vitro" (cognitive rehearsal in relaxed state of anxiety eliciting previous or anticipated sexual events) biofeedback or hypnotically assisted systematic desensitization is recommended. Drugs (phenothezine type) that inhibit sympathetic nervous system function can retard ejaculation, but probably do so by causing retrograde ejaculation (ejaculation emptied into bladder instead of urethra). The management of the condition with medication is probably subject to the limitations of state specific learning.

Prognosis.

The prognosis is excellent (98% positive outcome) for premature ejaculation managed by a competent and experienced therapist. The following complications arise infrequently, but can frustrate effective resolution.

Complications

1. The wife may complain that the procedure is too mechanical and may feel reluctant to participate. This complaint is sometimes genuine and not part of a covert agenda to sabotage effective resolution. The couple is told that complex spontaneous behaviors sometimes have to begin as mechanical and fragmentary exercises. One must master the alphabet before one can write poetry.

2. The wife may complain that all the sexual stimulation during ejaculatory control training leaves her very frustrated and angry. This is sometimes not a part of an agenda to sabotage treatment. If this is a genuine complaint, it can be dealt with by asking the husband to masturbate his wife to orgasm after the completion of each training session, or the wife may be given "permission" to masturbate herself to orgasm.

3. Infrequently one encounters a female who is a "ball buster," that is, a female who is demanding and critical even during sensate focus. The male may be dependent and hypersensitive to her moods and tends to take his own moods from her.

4. Some females appear to sabotage effective resolution because they covertly want to maintain the male's "crippled" sexual status. This desire to maintain the male's crippled sexual status appears related to a fear of abandonment, or to a fear that if the male becomes potent, the balance of power in the family may disturbed. Sometimes the wife's lack of respect for her husband is conveyed through her behavioral demonstrations of lack of confidence in his ability to resolve his premature ejaculation. The wife's attitude can become a self-fulfilling prophecy for a husband who is weak and dependent in his marital relationship, but who may be strong and aggressive in his professional life. Sex therapy is contraindicated for such couples till resolution of these more general insecurities has been managed by individual therapy or marriage counseling.

References

Kaplan, Helen. *The New Sex Therapy.* New York, Brunner/ Mazel, 1974.

Masters, W. H. and Johnson, V. E. *Human Sexual Inadequacy,* Boston: Little, Brown and Company, 1970.

The author wishes to thank the staff of the Reproductive Biology Research Foundation, St. Louis, Missouri, for the instruction and training he received there in 1973 and 1975.

New Methods in the Behavioral Treatment of Sexual Dysfunction

W. Charles Lobitz
and Joseph LoPiccolo
Psychology Clinic
University of Oregon
Eugene

Since 1969, the Sex Research Program at the University of Oregon Psychology Clinic has been treating couples for a variety of sexual dysfunctions. This program, directed by Joseph LoPiccolo, is part of a doctoral training program in clinical psychology and has involved the treatment of approximately 25 couples per year by a total of 16 different male—female co-therapy teams over the last 3 years. The program has had good success in treating sexual dysfunction by a behavioral approach. Within this approach, we have developed or adapted from others a number of new techniques for the treatment of sexual dysfunction. This paper describes some of these techniques and presents clinical examples and outcome statistics to document their effectiveness.

Background

The general behavioral model used is based on the procedures developed by Wolpe (1969), Hastings (1963), and Masters and Johnson (1970). In the absence of any physical pathology, sexual dysfunction is viewed as a learned phenomenon, maintained internally by performance anxiety and externally by a nonreinforcing environment, principally the partner. In addition, a lack of sexual skill, knowledge, and communication on the part of one or both partners contributes to the dysfunction.

Within this social learning model, the dysfunction is treated through training changes in the couple's sexual behavior. Both partners are involved in the therapy process. Treatment consists of 15 sessions in which a male—female co-therapy team plans tasks ("homework") to be carried out by the dysfunctioning couple between sessions. Performance anxiety in either the totally inorgasmic female or in the male with erectile failure is treated through *in vivo* graded exposure tasks following the systematic desensitization format developed by Wolpe (1969) and refined by Masters and Johnson (1970). Premature ejaculation is treated through a retraining program advocated by Semans (1956), as modified by the use of the "squeeze" technique (Masters and Johnson, 1970). In the case of all dysfunctions, intercourse is temporarily prohibited while the couple's repertoire of sexual behavior is rebuilt.

On the above framework, the Sex Research Program has developed several clinical innovations designed to facilitate changes in sexual behavior. These innovations fall into one of five classes: (1) Procedures designed to allow the therapists to obtain regular data on the clients' sexual behavior and to ensure that the clients carry out the "homework" assignments. (2) Procedures which enhance the clients' desire and arousal towards his or her partner. (3) Procedures which teach interpersonal sexual skills. (4) Procedures which disinhibit clients towards displaying their own sexual arousal and responsiveness. (5) Procedures designed to maintain treatment gains after therapy has ended.

Data on Clients'
Sexual Behavior

A hallmark of behavioral approaches to treatment has been the reliance on observable, quantifiable client behavior. Most problems which lend themselves to a behavioral approach (e.g., phobic or aggressive responses) are readily observable. Home observations of client behavior have become commonplace in behavioral assessment and intervention (e.g., Lewinsohn and Shaffer, 1971; Patterson, Ray and Shaw, 1968). However, for both ethical and practical reasons, neither home nor laboratory observations of client behavior are possible when treating sexual dysfunction. Yet, for our program, therapists must know exactly what the clients are doing and whether they are following the treatment procedures at home. Our clients are asked to be their own data collectors. On each day on which any sexual activity occurs, clients fill out a *daily record form* detailing their sexual behavior. For each activity, the client specifies its durations, numerical ratings of the pleasure and arousal that he obtained, and subjective comments about the activity. In addition, he specifies numerical ratings of the degree of pleasure and arousal which he perceived his partner to have obtained. Throughout treatment these daily records provide therapists with feedback. Using these data they tailor the program to the client's progress.

Client Motivation

While clients are generally motivated to carry out the program, including filling out daily record forms, at times they may find it difficult to follow the prescriptions. For example, they may be tired or busy with other activities and thus avoid engaging in the prescribed number of "homework" sessions. They may be tempted to break the prohibition on intercourse or to resist trying new sexual activities that the therapists prescribe. A *refundable penalty deposit* provides an incentive for following the program. At the beginning of treatment, the clients pay their full 15 session fee plus an equal amount as a penalty deposit. If the client does not violate any of the treatment rules, his deposit is refunded in full at the end of treatment. However, should a violation occur, 1/15th of the deposit is not refunded. On a second violation, another 2/15ths is forfeited, i.e., 3/15ths altogether. The progression continues arithmetically, so that for the fifth violation 5/15ths of the deposit is forfeited, using up the entire deposit. A sixth violation would cause the therapists to terminate treatment. Treatment rules are specified in a "penalty contract" which the clients sign at the beginning of therapy. Basically, the rules are that the clients must keep appointments, turn in the daily record forms prior to their appointment, and engage in only those sexual behaviors programmed for them by the therapists.

Although this procedure has not been systematically evaluated, the fact that more than one violation rarely occurs attests to its effectiveness in motivating the clients to follow the program rules. Over the last 19 cases treated, couples were fined an average of 0·7 times. No couple has been penalized more than three times. For some clients, the penalty deposit is a more effective motivator than for others. Younger couples, especially those in the counterculture for whom money is not a powerful reinforcer, are less apt to be influenced by the threat of losing their deposit. However, for older, middle-class couples, the penalty deposit provides a powerful motivation. For example, a successful certified public accountant resisted completing his assigned "homework" sessions with his wife, complaining that he had too much office work to do. Instead of cajoling her husband, the wife quietly reminded him of the penalty fee. A quick mental calculation convinced him that it was financially worthwhile to forego his office work in favor of the session with his wife.

Enhancing Clients' Arousal

A frequent aspect of sexual dysfunction is the inability of one or both clients to become sexually aroused by the partner. In cases of sexual deviations, other therapists (Davison, 1968; Marquis, 1970) have used a *classical conditioning* procedure during masturbation to condition arousal to appropriate sexual objects. We have adapted this to raise arousal levels in dysfunctional couples. The conditioning is accomplished either through masturbation or in sexual activity with the partner.

In masturbation, the client is instructed to focus on any erotic stimuli that are currently arousing. These stimuli may consist of literature, pictures, and/or fantasy. Within our program, stimulus materials have ranged from heterosexual erotic materials to homosexual fantasies. Once aroused, the client masturbates to orgasm. Just prior to orgasm, he switches his focus to fantasies of sexual activity with his partner. The unconditioned stimuli of previously arousing fantasies and materials and the unconditioned responses of sexual arousal and orgasm are, thus, paired with the presently neutral stimulus of sexual activity with the partner. On subsequent occasions, the client is instructed to switch to fantasies of the partner at earlier points in time, until fantasies of the partner become a conditioned stimulus for sexual arousal and the artificial stimuli previously used are no longer necessary. For clients who have difficulty in fantasizing their partner, we have supplied a Polaroid camera and instructed them to photograph their partner in sexual activity. They use these photographs in lieu of fantasy.

This same conditioning procedure is used in sexual activity with the partner as well as in masturbation. The client first fantasizes erotic scenes to become aroused and then switches his focus to the present reality of sexual activity with his partner. A case study detailing this procedure has been reported elsewhere (LoPiccolo, Stewart, and Watkins, 1972).

In the case of women who have never experienced orgasm from any source of physical stimulation, fantasy and erotic materials alone do not enhance the arousal level enough to produce orgasm. In such cases, *a nine-step masturbation program* has proven highly successful in producing the clients' first orgasm. The use of masturbation in treating frigidity has been reported previously (Ellis, 1960; Hastings, 1963). We have incorporated it as a systematic part of our treatment for primary orgasmic dysfunction. This program is based on evidence that more women can reach orgasm through masturbation than through any other means (Kinsey *et al.,* 1953), and that masturbation produces the most intense orgasms (Masters and Johnson, 1966). The nine steps follow a graduated approach model (Wolpe, 1969) to desensitize the client to masturbation. The details of the program have been described elsewhere (LoPiccolo and Lobitz, 1972, in press) but can be summarized as follows:

Step 1: The client is given the assignment to increase her self-awareness by examining her nude body and appreciating its beauty. She uses a hand mirror to examine her genitals and identify the various areas with the aid of diagrams in Hastings' book *Sexual Expression in Marriage* (1966). In addition she is started on a program of Kegel's (1952) exercises for increasing tone and vascularity of the pelvic musculature.

Step 2: The client is instructed to explore her genitals tactually as well as visually. To avoid performance anxiety, she is not given any expectation to become aroused at this point.

Step 3: Tactual and visual exploration are focused on locating sensitive areas that produce feelings of pleasure when stimulated.

Step 4: The client is told to concentrate on manual stimulation of identified pleasurable areas. At this point the female therapist discusses techniques of masturbation, including the use of a lubricant.

Step 5: If orgasm does not occur during Step 4, the client is told to increase the intensity and duration of masturbation. She is told to masturbate until "something happens" or until she becomes tired or sore.

Step 6: If orgasm is not reached during Step 5, we instruct the client to purchase a vibrator of the type sold in pharmacies for facial or body massage. In our most difficult case to date, three weeks of daily 45-minute vibrator sessions were required to produce orgasm.

Step 7: Once the client has achieved orgasm through masturbation, we introduce the husband to the procedure by having him observe her. This desensitizes her to displaying arousal and orgasm in his presence and also functions as an excellent learning experience for him.

Step 8: The husband manipulates his wife in the manner she has demonstrated in Step 7.

Step 9: Once orgasm has occurred in Step 8, we instruct the couple to engage in intercourse while the husband stimulates his wife's genitals, either manually or with a vibrator.

We currently also use heterosexual erotic pictures or literature to supplement the nine-step masturbation program. The efficacy of this combination was demonstrated fortuitously when three different women in the masturbation program saw a sexually explicit film at a local X-rated cinema. They each reported masturbating to their first orgasm shortly after having viewed the film.

Teaching Interpersonal
Sexual Skills

Most couples who seek treatment for sexual dysfunction have behavioral skill deficits. They may feel deep affection for each other, but have difficulty expressing their emotions, initiating and refusing sexual contact, and assertively communicating their likes and dislikes. We view these deficits not as emotional inhibitions, but primarily as a lack of social skill. These deficits are overcome in therapy sessions through therapist *modeling* and client *role-playing*. These techniques have achieved considerable efficacy in the treatment of social avoidance and other phobias (e.g., Bandura, 1971). We have directly adapted them to cases of sexual dysfunction.

In the Sex Research Program, these techniques are used to demonstrate appropriate initiation, refusal, and emotional assertion responses, and to allow the couple to practice these in a protected environment. They are then instructed to practice these skills at home as part of their intersession "homework" assignment. For example, a female client might complain that her husband initiates sexual activity in a crude, alienating manner, that he never displays his love for her, and that he does not engage in sexual behaviors that she finds arousing. In this case, a mutual failure is involved—the wife has not taught her husband what she desires. The therapy team models verbal initiation of sexual activity and verbal expression of tender emotions and has the clients practice these behaviors in the therapy session, while giving each other feedback about their performances.

Disinhibition of Sexuality

Role-playing is useful not only in skill training, but also as a disinhibitor of sexual responses. Hilliard (1960) has instructed inorgasmic women to feign orgasm to satisfy their partners. She reported that in many cases this pretense became a reality. Therapists in our own program have instructed inorgasmic women to role-play an orgasm, not to deceive their partner, but to disinhibit themselves about losing control and showing intense sexual arousal. Since the male partner is present when these instructions are given, deceit is avoided. This particular use of role-playing is analogous to Kelly's (1955) fixed-role therapy in which the client is asked to enact the role of someone different from himself. In sex therapy, the role is a different sexual response rather than an entire personality change.

Orgasmic roleplaying is useful at two points in therapy: first, for the woman who is highly aroused by masturbation but becomes apprehensive at the approaching orgasm and thus loses sexual arousal as stimulation continues; second, for the woman who masturbates to orgasm alone but cannot achieve it if her partner is present. In either case we instruct the couple to engage in the following procedure. During sexual activity at home, the woman is to role-play not just an orgasm, but a gross exaggeration of orgasm with violent convulsions and inarticulate screaming. Knowing that this orgasm is not real, the couple is free to make a game, even a parody of the response. We instruct them to repeat this until they pass from their initial anxiety and embarrassment to amusement and finally boredom with the procedure.

Orgasmic role-playing has been especially useful with intellectual, controlled clients who are ashamed and embarrassed about the muscular contractions and involuntary noises which accompany orgasm. In three cases where the women had been unable to reach orgasm despite the use of all our other treatment procedures, this technique led to their first orgasm.

Our most common stratagem for disinhibiting clients to sexual responses is *therapist self-disclosure*. In advocating self-disclosure, Jourard (1964) has emphasized therapist spontaneity during the session but has stated that one need not tell the client about one's life outside the therapy hour (p. 71). In the Sex Research Program, therapists do not only answer clients' questions, but also volunteer information about their own sexual behavior. Because the therapist has a respected position of authority in our culture, the therapists unashamedly discussing their own enjoyment of sexual activity is an acceptable and seemingly effective way of disinhibiting clients about their own sexuality. In particular, self-disclosure about masturbation and oral-genital sex facilitates change in the client's attitude towards these behaviors. However, self-disclosure should be withheld until the client has gotten to know the therapist. Premature self-disclosure may alienate some clients.

Another use of therapist self-disclosure has been in reducing clients' anxiety about their "abnormality" or "inadequacy" in having a sexual dysfunction. For example, one premature ejaculator, who had made considerable progress in therapy, was concerned that he would always have to rely on the squeeze technique as part of his lovemaking. The male therapist reassured him by saying that he also used the squeeze on occasion. The female therapist, who, in this instance was the male therapist's wife, reinforced the point by stating that she encouraged the squeeze as part of their sexual repertoire because it prolonged their lovemaking.

Maintaining Treatment Gains

Regardless of a treatment program's initial success, the proof of its efficacy is the degree to which clients can maintain their gains once therapy has ended. Our follow-up assessment 6 months after termination indicate that treatment gains have generally persisted.

This maintenance is due, in part, to *client participation in planning treatment* in the final therapy sessions. After 12 or 13 sessions of therapy, the clients have a good idea of the strategy behind their treatment. With the therapists' guidance, they now plan their own "homework" assignments for the next sessions. This prepares them to handle any problems which may arise after therapy has terminated. At the end of therapy, the clients write out a maintenance program of specific behaviors for the months following. At this time, they also make a list of the behaviors that contributed to their problem before treatment, how these have changed, and what they plan to do should the problems recur. The clients keep these lists.

Results

Over the past 3 years the Sex Research Program has experienced generally good results in the treatment of sexual dysfunction. Applying Masters and Johnson's (1970) criterion that the female partner be satisfied "in at least 50 per cent of their coital connections (p. 92)," our success rate is as follows: 13 out of 13 treated cases of female primary orgasmic dysfunction, six out of six premature ejaculation cases, four out of six erectile failure cases, three out of nine cases of secondary orgasmic dysfunction. However, with regard to the secondary orgasmic dysfunction cases, it should be noted that our three most recently treated cases are our three successes. These followed a major revision of our program for secondary orgasmic dysfunction, based on data from the first six cases. The data and the revisions are reported elsewhere (McGovern and Stewart, 1972).

To supplement Masters and Johnson's (1970) criterion for success, we have developed a measurement instrument, the Oregon Sex Inventory (LoPiccolo, 1972, Steger, 1972), for assessing pre- and post treatment changes in a couple's sexual functioning. Our success rate as reflected by the scales of this inventory equals or exceeds the rate on Masters and Johnson's (1970) criterion.

We think our success is due, in part, to the clinical innovations with which we supplement a "traditional" behavioral treatment program. Daily client records provide data on ongoing sexual behavior. A refundable penalty fee deposit heightens motivation. Fantasy and pornography, in combination with a nine-step masturbation program, enhance sexual responsiveness. Role-playing serves to impart social-sexual skills and to disinhibit female orgasm. Therapist self-disclosure reduces client inhibition and anxiety, and models an open acceptance of sexuality. To ensure the maintenance of therapy gains, clients plan their own treatment for the final stages and for the months following therapy.

Despite our generally good success rate, the separate effectiveness of each procedure needs to be investigated. In all of the cases treated, a combination of procedures has been used, thus precluding an evaluation of any particular technique's contribution. We are currently engaged in research to evaluate the components of our program.

References

Bandura A. (1971) Vicarious and self-reinforcement processes, *The Nature of Reinforcement* (Edited by Glaser.), Academic Press, New York.

Davison G. S. (1968) Elimination of a sadistic fantasy by a client-controlled counter-conditioning technique, *J. Abnorm. Psychol. 77*, 84-90.

Ellis A. (1960) *The Art and Science of Love*, Lyle Stuart, New York.

Hastings D. W. (1963) *Impotence and Frigidity*, Little, Brown, Boston.

Hastings D. W. (1966) *Sexual Expression in Marriage*, Bantam, New York.

Hilliard M. (1960) *A Woman Doctor Looks at Love and Life*, Permabook, New York.

Jourard S. M. (1964) *The Transparent Self*, D. Van Nostrand, Princeton, N.J.

Kelly G. A. (1955) *The Psychology of Personal Constructs*, Norton, New York.

Kegel A. H. (1952) Sexual functions of the pubococcygens muscle, *West. J. Sang. Obstet. Gynol. 60*, 521.

Kinsey A. C., Pomeroy W. B., Martin C. E. and Gebhard P. H. (1953) *Sexual Behavior in the Human Female*, W. B. Saunders, Philadelphia.

Lewinsohn P. M. and Shaffer M. (1971) Use of home observations as an integral part of the treatment of depression: Preliminary report and case studies, *J. Consult. Clin. Psychol. 37*, 87-94.

LoPiccolo J. (1972) "Scoring and Interpretation Manual for the Oregon Sex Inventory," Unpublished manuscript, University of Oregon.

LoPiccolo J. and Lobitz W. C. (1972) The role of masturbation in the treatment of sexual dysfunction, *Arch Sexual Behav.* (in press).

LoPiccolo J., Stewart R. and Watkins B. (1972) Case study: Treatment of erectile failure and ejaculatory incompetence with homosexual etiology, *J. Behav. Ther. & Exp. Psychiat. 3*, 233-236.

Marquis J. N. (1970) Orgasmic reconditioning: Changing sexual object choice through controlling masturbation fantasies, *J. Behav. Ther. & Exp. Psychiat. 1*, 263-271.

Masters W. H. and Johnson V. E. (1966) *Human Sexual Response*, Little, Brown, Boston.

Masters W. H. and Johnson V. E. (1970) *Human Sexual Inadequacy*, Little Brown. Boston.

McGovern K. B. and Steward R. C. (April, 1972) "The Secondary Orgasmic Dysfunctional Female: A Critical Analysis and Strategies for Treatment," Paper presented at the annual meeting of the Western Psychological Association, Portland, Oregon.

Patterson G. R., Ray R. S. and Shaw D. A. (1968) Direct intervention in the families of deviant children, *Oregon Research Institute Research Bulletin 8*, No. 9.

Semans J. (1956) Premature ejaculation: A new approach, *Sth. Med. J. 46*, 353-357.

Steger J. (April, 1972) "The Assessment of Sexual Function and Dysfunction," Paper presented at the annual meeting of the Western Psychological Association, Portland Oregon.

Wolpe J. (1969) *The Practice of Behavior Therapy,* Pergamon Press, New York.

Note: Preparation of this manuscript was supported in part by a grant from the University of Oregon Office of Scientific and Scholarly Research.

Masturbatory Fantasy and Sexual Deviation

D. R. Evans
Ontario Institute for
Studies in Education
Toronto

The hypothesis has been advanced that masturbation to deviant fantasy tends to increase the habit strength of sexual deviations. It is demonstrated that, of two groups of exhibitionists deconditioned with emotive imagery and aversive conditioning, the group with normal masturbatory fantasy deconditioned significantly faster than the group with deviant masturbatory fantasy. Prognosis and implications for therapy are briefly discussed. The importance of this variable is indicated by the observation that, of 52 sexual deviates, 41 (79 per cent) indicated deviant masturbatory fantasy in varying degrees.

Therapy based on learning theory postulates have increasingly gained acceptance and success in the treatment of deviant behaviour. Along with these therapeutic advances has come a new perspective on the aetiological factors leading to such behaviour. While the initial factors leading to an individual's inclination toward a specific sexual deviation can often be established, the factors maintaining the habit strength of such behavior between deviant incidents are not always clear.

McGuire, Carlisle, and Young (1965) have suggested that most theorists tend to support the hypothesis that one-trial learning from a crucial, but often accidental, sexual experience is sufficient to explain the habit strength of the sexually deviant behavior. They and others tend to disagree with the contention that an initial, overwhelming contact with a specific deviant activity can account for the development and maintenance of the behavior at such a high habit strength over a long period of time. In some cases, for instance, the deviant may only act out once a month and yet be beset by urges to do so almost daily.

McGuire, Carlisle, and Young (1965) have offered an alternate hypothesis, namely, that the initial deviant act is important only in as far as it supplies the fantasy, which is used during masturbation. Thus, each time the subject masturbates with the deviant activity as fantasy, the habit strength of the actual deviant behavior is increased. These authors, in their paper, suggest that, in any group of sexual deviates, a majority will be found who fit this pattern.

In agreement with McGuire, Carlisle, and Young (1965), it is felt that a direct test of this hypothesis would be to attempt to change a normal subject into a deviant by means of the appropriate masturbatory fantasy. However, as they point out, this would be unethical and thus, some other means of testing the hypothesis must be decided upon. One indirect test would be the relative ease with which subjects having normal and deviant masturbatory fantasies would decondition to their sexual deviation. The object of this paper then, is to investigate whether exhibitionists, who have normal masturbatory fantasy, may be deconditioned more rapidly than exhibitionists who have exhibitionistic masturbatory fantasy. The method of deconditioning in this study was a modification of that suggested by Feldman and MacCulloch (1964), in which images were used as the CS instead of pictures. The rationale for this approach has been reported in an earlier paper (Evans, 1967).

Method

The subjects in this study were ten exhibitionists referred by psychiatrists to a private Behavior Therapy Clinic in Toronto prior to January 30, 1967. Five subjects indicated that, between exhibitionistic activities, they masturbated with normal heterosexual fantasies. The other subjects reported that, between exhibitionistic activities, they masturbated to fantasies of exhibiting. The subjects in the normal fantasy group reported exhibiting an average of 2·4 times per month in the 6-month period prior to treatment. In this same time period, the five subjects in the exhibitionistic fantasy group exhibited an average of 2·7 times per month. An analysis of the differences in frequency of acting out for the two groups with the Mann Whitney U test, yielded a U of 5, for which $P=0·15$. Thus, it must be assumed that the frequency of acting out among the two groups is not different.

The apparatus consisted of a Kodak Carousel 35 mm automatic slide projector, model 800, with a foot-pedal remote control. The projector was modified so that it was an eighty-position rotary switch. Each pole of this switch was connected in series with a single pole single slide switch. This arrangement allowed the experimenter to select a slide position which would start a Hunter timer, and after a preselected delay, would put the subject in circuit with a Hunter shock stimulator. Shock at variable voltage levels was administered by means of finger electrodes attached to the subject's ring and index fingers.

Prior to treatment, each subject was asked to provide details of his exhibitionistic activities. From this data, image-provoking phrases were constructed for each subject. These were typed on white paper and photographed. The negative 35 mm film was used to make 2 x 2 in. slides for use in the Kodak Carousel projector. A bank of 100 slides of phrases depicting normal activities was also prepared for use with all subjects. Where appropriate to the subject's situation, the normal stimuli included phrases depicting normal heterosexual behavior.

Treatment was conducted in two connecting rooms with a communicating door, a one-way vision mirror and a rear projection screen. On one side of the partition was housed the apparatus, arranged so that the stimuli were projected on the screen. On the other side of the partition, the subject was seated in a reclining chair facing the screen. The foot pedal was placed so that the subject could conveniently advance the slides when he so wished.

During the first session, the subjects were seen by the psychiatrist and a full history was taken. Following this, they were interviewed by the psychologist or psychometrist and a list of deviant stimulus situations was constructed. These were then prepared according to the procedure noted above. The subjects were then treated once a week for ten weeks. In the next two months, the subjects were treated every two weeks, and then once a month as a follow-up.

At each session, the subjects were shown sixty image-producing slides, twenty of which were related to the deviant behavior, and forty of which were related to normal activities. The position of the phrases related to deviant activities was randomly determined for each subject in each session. Each deviant phrase was connected with the apparatus to produce shock after a short delay interval. Shock was terminated automatically when the subject advanced the projector to the next normal slide. The delay was randomly varied between 3 and 6 seconds during each session. Before viewing the slides, the subject was hooked up to the shock stimulator which was turned on and the shock level gradually increased. The subjects were instructed to depress the foot pedal when they could no longer tolerate the shock. This shock level was then used for the duration of the session. Thus, the subject could choose the shock level he wished, with the implicit assumption that he would voluntarily administer an aversive reinforcement.

The subjects were then told that they would see a series of slides of phrases on the screen and were asked to imagine as vividly as possible the situation suggested. They were told that they could go on to the next phrase by pressing the foot pedal. After each trial, the subjects were given checklists to cover the time period until their next appointment, on which they were asked to record each time they acted out, or had an urge to do so.

Results

The treatment procedure outlined, consisted of an initial block of 10 weekly trials and then booster sessions on a decreasing frequency over a 2 year period. As a result, follow-up criteria are dated from the time of admission of each subject.

All ten subjects had reached the 6-month point following treatment. The measure employed in this study is the number of weeks following the initiation of treatment, at which the subject reported no further acting out or urges to do so. For the normal fantasy group, the subjects reported this state after a median of 4 weeks with a range of 3—5 weeks, while the exhibitionistic fantasy group reported this state after a median of 24 weeks with a range of 4—24 weeks. An analysis of the difference between the two groups on this criterion, by means of the Mann Whitney U Test, yielded a U of two with a $P=0 032$. It was observed, then, that the deviant behavior in terms of acting out and urges to do so, was deconditioned more rapidly in the normal fantasy group.

Discussion

The results of this study support the hypothesis of McGuire, Carlisle, and Young (1965) that deviant masturbatory fantasy affects the habit strength of a subject's sexual deviation. It is of note that two of the subjects in the exhibitionistic fantasy group were still acting out at a reduced frequency at the 6-month follow-up criteria. On the other hand, all deviant activity had ceased in the normal fantasy group between 3 and 5 weeks following the initiation of treatment. These results underline the importance of masturbatory fantasy in sexual deviation.

McGuire, Carlisle, and Young (1965) suggested that, in any group of sexual deviates, over 50 percent will exhibit this phenomenon. Among a group of fifty-two sexual deviates, (16 homosexuals, 16 exhibitionists, 8 pedophiles, 5 voyeurs, 4 transvestites, and 3 fetishists), it was found that forty-one (79 per cent) reported the use of deviant fantasy while masturbating. The results of this study also suggest a poorer prognosis with deconditioning therapy with subjects in which deviant masturbatory fantasy is present. Therapists should consider more frequent and intensive sessions with subjects who report this activity.

References

Evans D. R. (1967) An exploratory study into the treatment of exhibitionism by means of emotive imagery and aversive conditioning. *Can. Psychol. 8,* 161.

Feldman M. P. and MacCulloch M. J. (1964) A systematic approach to the treatment of homosexuality. *Am. Psychiat. 121,* 167—171.

McGuire R. J., Carlisle J. M. and Young B. G. (1965) Sexual deviations as conditioned behaviour: A hypothesis. *Behav. Res. & Therapy 2,* 185-190.

Aversion Techniques in Behavior Therapy

G. Terence Wilson and Gerald C. Davison

State University of New York
at Stony Brook

An important issue in the use of aversion techniques concerns the nature of the noxious stimulus. Earlier versions of aversion treatment favored the use of chemically-produced aversion in the form of a nausea-producing drug. (cf. Lemere & Voegtlin, 1950). Current trends, however, almost exclusively emphasize electrical aversive stimulation. Rachman (1965) and Rachman and Teasdale (in press) detail the reasons which have dictated this shift to electrical noxious stimuli. At a practical level, the use of nausea-producing drugs results in an unpleasant and unsavory experience for client and clinical staff alike. At a more theoretical level, Eysenck and Rachman (1965) have suggested that these drugs act as central nervous system neural depressants, and thereby are likely to impede the conditionability of the client in accord with Eysenck's personality theory. Yet these factors are really secondary to the most cogent of Rachman and Teasdale's points, namely, the difficulty in adhering to the *traditional conditioning paradigm* (in both classical and anticipatory avoidance conditioning) when using chemical aversion. The crucial parameters here are temporal, that is, getting optimal interstimulus intervals; sequential, that is, having the CS precede the UCS; the frequency of repetition of CS-UCS pairings; and finally, precision in specifying the intensity and duration of the stimuli. Variable and fluctuating individual differences in reactions to emetic drugs virtually proscribe the precision required by the conditioning paradigm for successful application.

Given their premise of the traditional conditioning paradigm, Rachman and Teasdale's points are both well-taken and compelling. However, some recent findings from the physiological-psychology literature raise questions for current practices in aversion therapy, and suggest also some metatheoretical considerations for behavior therapy.

Garcia and his associates have recently demonstrated that the procedure of pairing a perceptible cue with an effective reinforcer does not lead automatically to effective associative learning. Rather, it seems that the cue must be "appropriate" for the consequences that ensue. Thus, Garcia and Koelling (1966) have shown that avoidance learning with gastrointestinal disturbances produced by ionizing radiation as the UCS readily transferred to a gustatory stimulus, but not to audiovisual and tactile stimuli. On the other hand, avoidance learning with electric shock as the UCS transferred to the audio-visual and tactile stimuli, but not to the gustatory stimulus. Garcia and Koelling (1967) reported the same differential effect following the injection of a drug. Garcia, McGowan, Ervin, and Koelling (1968) paired either flavor or size of food pellets as conditioned stimuli with either malaise induced by X-ray or electric shock as the UCS in four groups of rats. The combination of flavor and illness resulted in a significant conditioned decrease in food consumption, but that of size and illness did not. Conversely, the combination of size and pain produced an inhibition of eating while flavor and pain did not. The authors argue that since flavor is closely related to the chemical composition of food, natural selection would favor associative mechanisms relating flavor and olfaction to the aftereffects of ingestion; and they suggest how effective associative learning depends on central neural convergence of the paired afferent input.

These data appear to discredit the commonly made procedural prescription that, in the treatment of an alcoholic, for instance, shock be used to condition aversion to the sight, smell, and taste of alcohol, to exogenous as well as to endogenous stimuli. It seems that fear responses from a shock UCS may be conditioned only to nongustatory attributes of alcohol in our example, and not to the taste and/or smell of alcohol. Any radical change in these conditioned stimuli, such as could be produced by a different evironmental complex, could be expected to lead to the "spontaneous recovery" of the consumption of alcohol (Estes, 1955). The best strategy would seem to be to create a chemically-based aversion to the taste and/or smell of alcohol and not to the complex of visual, personal, and other stimuli defining the treatment situation.

Garcia, Ervin, Yorke, and Koelling (1967) and Revusky (1968) have extended this notion of the peculiar "appropriateness" of cues to reinforcers, finding that reinforcement can be delayed well beyond the time interval posited as mandatory for effective reinforcement by the traditional S-R model of associative learning. It will be recalled that one of the major arguments in favor of electrical aversion relates to the temporal control it allows.

Interestingly enough, Lazarus (1968) has independently and from a purely clinical standpoint expressed similar views. He reports the case of an alcoholic whose alcohol consumption remained recalcitrant to faradic shock but disappeared rapidly when a singularly foul-smelling admixture of smelling salts was substituted as the noxious UCS. He goes on to observe that whereas faradic shock seems "appropriate" when the concern is with visual and/or tactile stimuli, as would be the case in a handwashing compulsion, it may be inappropriate in handling overeating and alcoholic consumption. Of course, these and similar clinical observations (e.g., Cautela, 1967; Davison, 1968) are in line with Garcia's psychophysiological findings.

The foregoing raises also some interesting issues on the metatheoretical level. The learning-oriented behavior modification literature, especially the operant, emphasizes the overriding importance of *functional* definitions of problems in distinct contrast to *topographical* (e.g., Ferster, 1965; Staats & Staats, 1963). In the attempt to extrapolate from research with infrahumans to research with humans, learning theory-oriented behavior modifiers seem, on reflection, to have had little choice but to stress the functional to the virtual exclusion of the topographical, nay, physiological nature of stimuli and responses. Thus, one terms a response as topographically complex as "walking to the door" an "operant" if it can be shown to relate functionally to antecedent and consequent stimuli in the same fashion as more carefully delineated operants in the Skinner box. The same holds true for behavior therapy approaches which stress the classical conditioning paradigm: Pavlov (1928) himself proposed that "every imaginable phenomenon of the outer world affecting a specific receptive surface of the body may be converted into a CS [p. 88]."

The Garcia research obviously raises the serious question of this preoccupation with functional identities to the exclusion of the specific nature of the particular stimuli and responses within one's presumed conditioning paradigm. This work also illustrates most clearly the possible dangers inherent within a limited conception of "behavior modification" as deriving from "modern learning theory" or, more properly, learning principles. Familiarity with such psychophysiological work as Garcia's (inter alia) makes clear the desirability of expanding the field of behavior modification to include general experimental psychology as a whole (cf. Davison, in press).

References

Cautela, J. Covert sensitization. *Psychological Reports,* 1967, *20,* 459-468.

Davison, G. C. Elimination of a sadistic fantasy by a client-controlled counterconditioning technique: A case study. *Journal of Abnormal Psychology,* 1968, *73,* 84-90.

Davison, G. C. Appraisal of behavior modification techniques with adults in institutional settings. In C. M. Franks (Ed.), *Assessment and status of the behavioral therapies and associated developments.* New York: McGraw-Hill, in press.

Estes, W. K. Statistical theory of spontaneous recovery and regression. *Psychological Review,* 1955, *62,* 145-154.

Eysenck, H. J., & Rachman, S. *The causes and cures of neurosis.* London: Routledge & Kegan Paul, 1965.

Ferster, C. B. Classification of behavioral pathology. In L. Krasner & L. P. Ullmann (Eds.), *Research in behavior modification.* New York: Holt, 1965.

Garcia, J., Ervin, F. R., Yorke, C. H., & Koelling, R. A. Conditioning with delayed vitamin injections. *Science,* 1967, *155,* 716.

Garcia, J., & Koelling, R. A. Relation of cue to consequence in avoidance learning. *Psychonomic Science,* 1966, *4,* 123—124.

Garcia, J., & Koelling, R. A. A comparison of aversions induced by X-rays, toxins, and drugs in the rat. *Radiation Research,* 1967, *7,* 439.

Garcia, J., McGowan, B. K., Ervin, F. R., & Koelling, R. A. Cues: Their relative effectiveness as a function of the reinforcer. *Science,* 1968, *160,* 794—795.

Lazarus, A. A. Aversion therapy and sensory modalities: Clinical impressions. *Perceptual and Motor Skills,* 1968, *27,* 178.

Lemere, G., & Voegtlin, W. An evaluation of the aversion treatment of alcoholism. *Quarterly Journal for the Study of Alcoholism,* 1950, *11,* 199-204.

Pavlov, I. P. *Lectures on conditioned reflexes.* New York: International, 1928.

Rachman, S. Aversion therapy: Chemical or electrical? *Behaviour Research and Therapy,* 1965, *2,* 289-300.

Rachman, S., & Teasdale, J. D. Aversion therapy. In C. M. Franks (Ed.), *Assessment and status of the behavioral therapies and associated developments.* New York: McGraw-Hill, in press.

Revusky, S. H. Aversion to sucrose produced by contingent X-irradiation: Temporal and dosage parameters. *Journal of Comparative and Physiological Psychology,* 1968, *65,* 17-22.

Staats, A. W., & Staats, C. K. *Complex human behavior.* New York: Holt, 1963.

Olfactory Aversion Therapy for Homosexual Behavior

Charles E. Colson
Institute for Behavioral Services
Hinsdale, Illinois

The effectiveness of aversive counterconditioning procedures in the treatment of disorders involving inappropriate stimulus attachments—e.g., alcoholism and other addictions, homosexuality, fetishism, etc.—is well established (Bandura, 1969; Wolpe, 1969). The methods most often used in such treatment have been faradic stimulation, nauseous pharmacological agents, and symbolically induced feelings of nausea. Wolpe (1969) and Kennedy and Foreyt (1968) have reported using noxious-smelling substances to induce feelings of aversion in a clinical counterconditioning situation. Wolpe utilized a "vile-smelling solution" of asafetida; while Kennedy and Foreyt employed butyric acid gas which was introduced to the patient by means of a blower fan-and-stopcock delivery apparatus. In both instances, the behavior problem was over-eating. The present paper describes the application of noxious olfactory stimuli to the counterconditioning treatment of a case of homosexual behavior.

The patient, a 24-yr-old male graduate student who was actively bisexual (preferentially homosexual), had sought treatment for the purpose of "reapportioning" his sexual interests in order to preserve his marriage. In consultation with the patient, it was decided to try an aversive counterconditioning procedure directed toward thoughts about looking for male sexual partners, picking up men, and sexual activities with men. Because faradic stimulation apparatus was not readily available, and because the patient proved unable to identify stimuli which, on imagination, would produce any feelings of aversion, we attempted the use of several noxious olfactory stimuli to achieve the desired physical aversion.

Treatment

Phase I

The client was put into a relaxed state and instructed to recall and visualize a recent, very pleasurable sexual experience with another male and to *narrate* this encounter to the therapist. At various points in the narration, phials of dilute ammonium sulfide (odor of rotten eggs) and butyric acid (dirty athletic socks or underwear) and conventional "smelling salts" (aromatic ammonia) were held a few inches beneath the patient's nose and he was instructed to sniff, at the same time continuing his visualizing and narration. The noxious substance was then removed after an average exposure of 12 seconds, and the client was instructed to "think of nothing" or to visualize the therapist's words of relaxation for 30—40 seconds. He was then told to resume his narration, and the procedure was repeated.

After this conditioning session, which lasted less than 15 minutes, and during which the noxious aromas were introduced a total of seven times, the patient reported that he was surprised to realize that for the five days immediately following, he did not experience any urge to look for a male sexual partner. The first time he did look at a male with sexual interest (sixth day following treatment) he began to re-experience some of the choking sensations he had felt as a result of the ammonia vapors and subsequently he lost his incipient desire.

This one session provided the whole of the conditioning treatment. Two weeks later, when the academic year ended, the patient had had no homosexual contacts; and had not even gone to look for a male partner— which preceding the conditioning session he had been doing about three times a week. Although no aversion-relief or other differential conditioning procedure was employed (see Bandura, 1969, pp. 520—525), the aversion did not generalize to the patient's relations with his wife. Coitus continued at the rate of two or three times a week, equal to their best weeks before the conditioning session. The ending of the academic year precluded additional treatment sessions at that time.

One month after classes resumed in the fall, the patient returned for additional treatment for non-sexual difficulties he and his wife were experiencing. He reported that in spite of the fact that the aversion treatment had consisted of only one conditioning session, he had not engaged in any homosexual behavior for an entire month. Thereafter, he had gone looking for male sexual partners an average of once every 7—10 days. Actual homosexual contact had resulted from approximately half these attempts. (Previously, he had usually managed to secure a partner whenever he sought one.) This partial success in securing male partners might in part be attributable to what the patient described as the "half-hearted" way in which he looked for such partners. He described himself as not being displeased if his looking did not result in finding one.

After six sessions of marital counseling, the marriage had improved substantially but the patient's homosexual behavior remained about the same. The olfactory aversion therapy procedure was then resumed. (The reason for delaying its resumption was that the patient was not willing to give up his homosexual activities irrevocably until he was certain he would still have a wife to turn to.) A baseline record of all homosexually-oriented behavior was taken for a period of 2 weeks. In spite of the fact that the patient was trying diligently to "be good," he reported 11 occasions during the first week on which he had caught himself looking at males with sexual interest, thinking about going out looking, or becoming excited about the thought of looking for a male partner. During the second baseline week there were 16 such occurrences, including two instances of actually finding a partner and engaging in homosexual activities.

Phase II

The aversion therapy was resumed at this point. The procedure was identical to that employed in the previous conditioning session, except that this time the patient was instructed to recall and narrate the experience of finding himself in the vicinity of the library with nothing to do (a frequent reality) and of walking to the library with the intention of finding someone, entering the building, walking toward the restrooms, etc. Aversion was terminated when the patient indicated that he felt like leaving the library as quickly as possible and returning home. The next week the patient reported he had been able to walk past the library at times when he had nothing to do and not become sexually excited; and had been able to work successfully in the library without any ill effects. There were six occasions when he had briefly felt excited but at some distance from the library. Treatment therefore centered on imagining and relating the experience of being on campus and walking in the direction of the library while becoming progressively more excited. This time aversion was terminated at the patient indicating that he was turning around, walking away from the library, and returning home.

The following week, the patient reported that on one occasion he had the car at his disposal and nothing to do while his wife was out of town. He had become quite excited about the prospect of being able to look for males, whereupon he inhaled from an ammonia capsule he had with him. The excitement dissipated immediately, and he drove directly home and had a very productive day of studying.

At last report, it was 6 weeks since the patient actually went looking for a male sexual partner; and his homosexual thoughts during that time had consisted principally of observing his own reactions to situations that were previously exciting to him. He reported that on the two or three occasions when he had found himself becoming excited (again, usually in the vicinity of the library) merely thinking about the ammonia capsules would dissipate the excitement so that he could continue his work without interruption.

Discussion

For this patient, the aromatic ammonia ampules were the most effective of the noxious stimuli tried, perhaps because the other solutions were too dilute to be truly noxious. The corrosiveness of ammonium sulfide militates against its use in more concentrated solution. These ampules are quite safe, convenient, inexpensive, and readily obtainable from most pharmacies. The ammonia vapors are extremely pungent when held a few inches from the nose, yet they cannot be detected when held at arm's length. The odor disappears almost instantly upon withdrawal of the capsule, affording the therapist virtually perfect control over the onset, duration, intensity, and recovery time for the physical aversion produced. The ampules are quite portable, so that the patient may carry them with him, either to use as "boosters" or—after instruction in conditioning parameters—to extend the conditioning treatment *in vivo*. The patient in the present report did indeed do this, in particular, in those locations where he usually went to find male partners.)

The nature and extent of the effects resulting from the application and withdrawal of noxious olfactory stimuli for aversive counterconditioning argue strongly in favor of the investigation and clinical utilization of such procedures, especially in those instances in which the lack of sophisticated apparatus, the difficulties associated with the control of pharmacologically-induced aversion and its side-effects, or the inability of the patient vividly to imagine aversive stimuli, render the use of other procedures questionable or impossible.

References

Bandura A. (1969) *Principles of Behavior Modification,* Holt, Rinehart and Winston, New York.

Kennedy W. A. and Foreyt J. P. (1968) Control of eating behavior in an obese patient by avoidance conditioning, *Psychol. Rep. 22,* 571-576.

Wolpe J. (1969) *The Practice of Behavior Therapy,* Pergamon, New York.

Subjective, Attitudinal, and Physiological Effects of Electrical Aversion Therapy

R. Hallam,
S. Rachman and
W. Falkowski
Department of Psychology
Institute of Psychiatry
De Crespigny Park
London and
Maudsley and Bethlem
Royal Hospitals

In their analysis of aversion therapy, Rachman and Teasdale (1969) proposed that the chemical form of this therapy met sufficient criteria to be classed as a form of classical conditioning: "It seems clear that chemical aversion therapy falls into classical conditioning paradigm in which repeated association is made between the stimuli associated with the undesirable activity and an unconditioned nausea reaction provoked by an emetic" (p 29). Although they found little information about the psycho-physiological effects of treatment, it appears that many patients do exhibit subjective and gross physiological changes (nausea and vomiting, etc.) after chemical treatment. For the most part, these changes are compatible with a classical conditioning theory.

The evidence on electrical aversion therapy is, however, more difficult to interpret. A straightforward classical conditioning theory would run as follows. The repetition of the Cs→UCS sequence (i.e., deviant stimulus→shock) would lead to the growth of a conditioned response, such that, CS (deviant stimulus)→CR (pain/anxiety?).

Part of the problem is attributable to uncertainty about the expected nature of the CR. Do we expect patients treated by electrical aversion to experience pain when shown the CS (e.g., female clothing)? Clearly we do not; instead we would probably expect the patients to report anxiety rather than pain. In his classical paper on anxiety (Mowrer, 1938) actually described this emotional reaction as the conditioned pain response and certainly the two-factor theory of avoidance behavior leans heavily on the role of anxiety. The application of that theory to electrical aversion therapy appears to require that the patient develops anxiety to the CS. In all, it seems reasonable to expect that patients should report anxiety to the deviant stimuli after treatment. Further, it seems reasonable to expect to find evidence of conditioned psychophysiological reactions after treatment.

1. Plainly, if UCS (shock)→pain/anxiety plus GSR/cardiac changes,

2. then, CS (deviant stimulus)→UCS (Xn)

3. should lead to CS (deviant stimulus)→pain/anxiety plus GSR/cardiac change.

So, after treatment, patients should report anxiety and also display appropriate psycho-physiological changes in the presence of the deviant stimuli. As Rachman and Teasdale (1969) present the case, there is very little evidence of either effect and a suggestion that contrary results may be found (for example, Marks and Gelder's (1967) sexual cases reported indifference rather than anxiety).

In the present two studies we attempted to obtain information about some subjective consequences and physiological effects of electrical aversion therapy.

Part One—Subjective
Consequences During and After
Electrical Aversion Therapy

Sixteen patients were given a standardized interview within ten days of completing aversion therapy. Although the interviewer had not treated any of the patients himself, he was aware of the nature of their problem and the type of treatment administered. The subjective effects observed at the termination of treatment were supplemented by direct or indirect information regarding the patient's status at a four-month follow-up period. In roughly one-third of the cases, the follow-up information was obtained by the same interviewer and in the remaining cases the information was obtained indirectly from the therapist concerned or the official case-notes.

The subjective information was collected for purposes of general interest and also to determine whether or not these patients experienced an "aversion" after the treatment. We were also interested in the side-effects, if any, of the treatment; the subjective changes which occur during the period of treatment; the subjective status of the patients shortly after completion of treatment. With these questions in mind, we decided to collect information from patients who had two different types of problem and also, from two groups of patients with a similar problem but different social background and prognostic features. The three groups consisted of: (a) six middle-class alcoholic patients of stable background with a reasonably good prognosis; (b) five alcoholic patients from a lower socio-economic group with consistently less satisfactory work records and less stable family backgrounds whose prognosis was of course less promising; (c) the third group of five patients consisted of three homosexuals, one sadist and one fetishist.

Broadly speaking the therapeutic outcome for the three groups was as follows: in the middle-class alcoholic sample, five out of six patients were substantially improved at four months; in the class IV to V group of alcoholics, there were three out of five failures; two of the sexual cases were substantially improved at four months, two were outright failures, and the fifth was slightly improved.

While eight of the eleven alcoholic patients had some knowledge of aversion therapy prior to their treatment, none of the five sexual cases had any information on the subject prior to treatment. Only two of the eleven alcoholics had previously undergone aversion therapy (chemical) and both of these were successfully treated by the electrical method. Four of the eleven alcoholics and only one of the sexual cases stated that they expected the treatment to fail. In four out of five instances, their expectations were fulfilled. The remainder expressed an open-minded attitude towards the treatment and there were eight out of eleven successes in this group. This suggestion of an association between optimistic expectancy and therapeutic outcome might be worth exploring in more detail but it should be borne in mind that the pessimists were, with one exception, alcoholics who had been unsuccessfully treated in a variety of hospitals and with a variety of techniques prior to the present study.

The reported side-effects were few in number and mild in character. Twelve of the sixteen patients said that the treatment turned out to be far easier and less upsetting than they had anticipated. In the majority of cases, they ranked the aversion sessions as being less unpleasant than visits to the dentist. The great majority of the patients were not disturbed by receiving the electric shocks and in the sexual patients the most difficult part of the treatment was said to be the effort and concentration required to produce the requisite fantasies. Only one of the sixteen patients reported any measure of apprehension the night before each treatment session and only one of the eleven alcoholic patients experienced fear half-an-hour before the treatment sessions. In the sexual cases, however, three out of the five patients reported marked tension half-an-hour before treatment. During the treatment sessions, tension was experienced by six of the eleven alcoholics and four of the five sexual cases. In the sexual cases, all of the patients reported a feeling of relief and tiredness at the end of the session and similar feelings were reported by half of the alcoholics. In summary, the aversion treatment was surprisingly well-tolerated and few difficulties arose during and before sessions.

The subjective changes experienced throughout the entire treatment period were rather interesting and although consistent with the findings of Marks and Gelder (1967), they do cast a slightly different light on the question of whether or not a true aversion develops. First, the similarity. In the five sexual cases, only one patient expressed a dislike or distaste for the deviant stimulus. Three of the remaining four expressed indifference and the last patient showed no change and was in any case a therapeutic failure. In the good prognosis group of alcoholics, however, four of the six patients reported that the smell and taste of alcohol had altered in an unpleasant way. Three of them said that it was now repulsive and the fourth that the taste and smell had become bitter. All four of these patients were therapeutic successes and of the two remaining patients who reported no repulsion developing, one was a success and the other a failure. In this small subgroup of alcoholics treated by electrical aversion, a true aversion did develop and it appears to be related to therapeutic outcome. It should be noted that the type of treatment administered to these patients included sessions during which they were required to smell and taste a selection of alcoholic drinks. In the last group, consisting of five patients with poor prognosis, they were not permitted to taste alcohol during or between the treatment sessions. Two of the five patients reported a change in the smell of alcohol. One patient found the smell repulsive and the other said it had become mild. Two other patients said that they felt indifferent to alcohol but that the smell had not altered. The fifth patient reported no changes and was a therapeutic failure. The patient who experienced repulsion was a therapeutic success.

This qualitative evidence indicates that aversion therapy is capable of producing a true aversion. The reports of olfactory and gustatory aversion developing after electrical treatment are unexpected and therefore of particular interest. A more reasonable expectation and one which is indeed widely assumed, would be that patients who received electrical aversion therapy would develop a fear of the deviant stimuli. None of the patients, in any of the groups, reported feelings of fear or anxiety in the presence of the deviant stimuli. Instead of fear, we sometimes observe repulsion. None of the sexual cases developed fear or anxiety but three reported a decrease in interest or total indifference to the deviant stimulus.

The persistence of tempting fantasies concerning the deviant activity during the treatment period seems to be associated with therapeutic failure. Three of the four therapeutic failures in the alcoholic groups reported recurring fantasies of temptation during the treatment period. In the sexual patients, the two clear successes reported a decrease in tempting fantasies during the treatment and one of the two outright failures experienced an increase in fantasies of temptation. There was surprisingly little evidence of major changes in mood during the entire treatment period and these tended more often to be increases in irritability than depression (only two instances). Six of the sixteen patients reported the occurrence of mild disturbances of sleep during the treatment period and three of these had associated dreams of an unpleasant character.

At the completion of treatment, three of the four therapeutic failures in the alcoholic group reported that alcohol had retained its attraction. The patients who experienced repulsion during the course of the treatment period tended, with one exception, to retain this repulsion at the completion of treatment. In the alcoholic group there was very little evidence (one case only) of the development of avoidance of drinking places after treatment. In the sexual cases however, three out of five patients described what might be considered to be avoidance behavior when the treatment had been completed. Every patient was asked whether he had come into contact with the deviant stimulus or situation in the ten days posttreatment and most of them had done so. In only one case was there evidence of fear—a successfully treated alcoholic patient. During this immediate posttreatment period, eight of the eleven alcoholic patients experienced some desire to return to drinking but four of them managed to control the desire and were still abstinent at the four-month follow-up period. In the five sexual cases, the two patients who experienced a temptation to return to their deviant activity during this 10-day posttreatment period, were eventual therapeutic failures. The two failures experienced no change in the extent to which they were attracted to their deviant activity whereas all three of the successes had undergone a change in the attractiveness of deviant sexual activity. The successes also reported a considerable reduction in the amount of deviant fantasy time. In only one of the five sexual cases was there evidence of an undesirable mood change during this period—one patient experienced increased irritability. In summary, the evidence from this immediate posttreatment period suggests that the reappearance of a strong attraction towards or desire for the deviant activity during this early stage, is a sign of poor prognosis. The development and retention of repulsion or indifference is a sign of better prognosis but not a certain indication.

Contrary to expectation, the major subjective changes of therapeutic significance are those of repulsion or indifference and *not* fear or anxiety. In the sexual cases, some avoidance behavior was reported but there was little sign of this in the alcoholic cases.

Part Two—Physiological and
Attitudinal Changes After
Electrical Aversion Therapy
and/or General
Psychiatric Therapy

The operation of pairing an attractive deviant stimulus with a noxious stimulus conforms in many respects to the laboratory classical conditioning paradigm and it has been assumed that the resulting conditioned emotional reactions, such as anxiety or nausea, mediate attitudinal changes and avoidance behavior outside treatment. However, the literature on laboratory conditioned autonomic responses provides very little support for the view that CRs will persist any longer than a few trials after the UCS has been withdrawn, especially when the subject has been informed of the onset of extinction (see Rachman and Teasdale, 1969). This rapid extinction seems to be true of the conditioned GSR, (Grings and Lockhart, 1963), the eyeblink (Spence, 1966) and cardiac response (Chatterjee and Eriksen, 1962; Obrist *et al.,* 1969). Even when ten sessions of aversive conditioning, comprising 205 shock trials, have been administered, the GSR does not prove more resistant to extinction (Hallam, 1971); in this study, slight evidence for the development of a conditioned cardiac deceleration response was obtained. This response was retained on the first few trials of a retest series after a one-month interval.

Laboratory studies of aversive conditioning using *neutral* conditioned stimuli may not be relevant to aversion therapy in a psychiatric population. The following experiment was therefore conducted to test the hypothesis that, after electrical aversion therapy for alcoholism, (a) an attitude-change signifying aversion to the deviant activity will develop and (b) the autonomic response to the deviant stimuli used in treatment will change in the direction of increased responsivity.

Method

An aversion therapy group (n=10, 7 male, 3 female) was compared to a control group (n=8, 5 male, 3 female) which had not received aversion therapy. Assignment to groups was random. All 18 S's were in-patients with diagnosis of primary alcoholism, and they all received a wide spectrum of treatments including group therapy, A.A. meetings, drug therapy, and rehabilitation. They were drawn mainly from the higher socio-economic range. S's had been dry for two or more weeks before autonomic assessments were made and they were not allowed to drink during their stay on the ward.

Aversion therapy (15 sessions) consisted of two procedures (a) a slide of a bar, or bottles of alcohol, was projected onto a screen and shock was administered to the arm when the S signalled a fantasy of drinking in that situation; (b) shocks were given during the tasting, smelling, and seeing of several favored alcoholic drinks.

All patients were assessed before and after treatment (4—8 weeks later) to measure their autonomic responses to drinking stimuli and to meaningful stimuli unrelated to drinking. The assessment did not take place in the treatment environment and S's knew that they would not be shocked. In the pre-treatment session S's were questioned to find out their habitual pattern of drinking and four detailed fantasies of drinking situations were constructed and agreed upon. Four fantasies of equal vividness but unrelated to drinking were also obtained (e.g., work or pastime activities which were mainly pleasurable). S's also selected the five most attractive slides from a pool depicting bars and bottles of alcohol. Five neutral slides unrelated to drinking were also used in the assessment. They consisted of three views and two slides of paintings, a war scene and an abstract.

The purpose of the control group was to measure the influence of treatment per se on the response to drinking stimuli. Moreover, this group controls for the effect of retesting with the same stimuli and for the effects due to the passage of time. The aversion group had of course received many presentations of the slides and fantasies during treatment whereas the control group had not. Assuming that aversion therapy has a sensitizing effect on the response to drinking stimuli, the effects of repeated presentation should lead to habituation of the autonomic responses to the stimuli, which would reduce rather than enhance any experimental effect due to sensitization. However, in the aversion group, familiarity with drinking and neutral slides was equated by exposing the neutral slides for an equal length of time during aversion sessions (but, of course, not associated with shock).

The comparison between neutral and drinking stimuli tests for the presence of responses specific to alcohol-related stimuli, and also provides some indication of the effects of non-specific factors due to treatment, such as change in arousal level, general sensitizing effects, etc.

Apparatus

Subjects were tested in a partially sound-proofed, darkened room. Instructions were given via an intercom from an adjoining room which housed a Grass polygraph. Pulse volume was obtained from a photo-electric transducer attached to the ear. The signal was fed into a cardiota-chometer which provided a beat-by-beat record of heart-rate. Skin resistance was measured by passing a 20μ A current through two Ag/ag Cl electrodes attached to the palmar surface of two adjacent fingers.

Assessment procedure

Each subject was assessed before and after the completion of treatment. When the subjects had settled down with electrodes attached, descriptions of the eight fantasy stimuli were read out in a random order with an interval of 30—75 seconds between each one. Subjects had been instructed to press a signal button when they obtained a clear image and to maintain it until E said "right, stop," 15 seconds later. One practice fantasy was given initially. No more than two fantasies of the same type followed on consecutively. After fantasy recording, a mood scale was given (MAACL, Zuckerman, 1964) and then the ten slides were presented for a duration of 10 seconds each, randomized and spaced as above. Subjects were simply instructed to attend to the slides. The mood scale was then readministered after shock electrodes had been attached to assess the subject's reaction to shock. (N.B. subjects had been told explicitly that they would *not* be shocked to fantasies or slides.)

Data analysis

Heart rate response (HRR) to fantasies: Pre-stimulus measures were taken in a 20 second period prior to each description of the fantasy.

Responses were measured during instructions to obtain the fantasy (5 seconds), latency (5 seconds prior to subject's signal), fantasy (3 x 5 second periods) and a recovery period (4 x 5 second periods). Each subject's data consisted of the scores for each period averaged over the four fantasies. Highest and lowest HR readings (i.e., peak and trough HR) in each 5-second period were taken. These were punched onto paper-tape together with ten pre-stimulus HR readings for each fantasy (i.e., HR at 2 second intervals during the 20 second period). The data reduction, which was carried out by computer consisted initially of the conversion of all HR readings into inter-beat intervals (IBI in msecs.) The response scores (peak and trough measures in each 5 second period) were then expressed in terms of the mean and standard deviation of the 40 pre-stimulus IBI's (Mean=0, SD=100). Each subject's response data were therefore standardized according to his own HR level and HR variability. The correlations between these range-corrected responses and HR level and variability were later examined for initial-value effects over all subjects; they were not significant.

HRR to slides

HR was read off every second during 3 x 10 second periods (i.e., before, during, and after slide presentation). A range correction was made as above.

Skin resistance (SR)

Skin resistance was simply computed as a change score, using the highest R in the pre-stimulus period as the initial level, and the lowest R during instructions, fantasy, and fantasy recovery periods as post-stimulus scores. In the case of slides, the lowest R during and after slide presentation was subtracted from the highest R in the pre-stimulus period. "Recovery" scores were obtained by subtracting the highest R in the recovery period (20 seconds after the fantasy, or 10 seconds after the slide) from the highest R in the pre-stimulus periods. A square root transformation was applied to change-scores in order to normalize the distribution.

Measurement of attitude

Each of the 10 slides was rated on 7-point semantic differential scales before and after treatment. The following scales were used to measure hypothetical factors of general evaluation (good—bad, kind—cruel, attractive—unattractive,), taste (appetizing—repulsive, tasty—distasteful, pleasant—unpleasant,) anxiety (makes-me-calm—makes-me-anxious, alarming—relaxing) and danger (harmless—harmful, dangerous—safe).

Ratings were averaged for each factor over the five drinking and five neutral slides.

Results

Each dependent variable was subjected to a 3-way analysis of variance, i.e., groups (aversion vs. control) x stimuli (drinking vs. neutral) x trials (pre- vs. post-treatment).

Skin resistance

The analysis was carried out with eight subjects in each group as the SR records of two aversion subjects were spoilt. Although subjects responded to the fantasies and slides, there was no group or treatment effect for any of the measures. The only significant effect was an overall difference between stimuli in the fantasy recovery score (St, $F=6\cdot52, p < 0\cdot05$) which indicated that resistance level was slower to recover after drinking fantasies than after neutral fantasies.

Pre stimulus SR levels did not differ between groups, between stimuli or between pre- and posttreatment assessments.

Heart rate

The response scores in the three 5-second periods during the fantasy were averaged to obtain a single score as were the four fantasy recovery periods. The overall response to fantasies was HR acceleration which was reflected in both peak and trough measures of HR. None of the statistical effects involving interaction with groups were significant during the fantasy period. The only difference to emerge was a triple interaction in the latency period ($F=6\cdot76, p < 0\cdot05$) but this was not a treatment effect as it appeared to be due to the fact that control subjects gave a somewhat greater accelerative response to drinking stimuli in this period pre-treatment. Similarly, the overall response to slides during and after slide presentation did not differ between groups. (See Figure 1).

As in the skin resistance data, there were significant effects common to aversion and control subjects. Peak HR was significantly higher during the drinking fantasies than the neutral fantasies (St. (fantasy period), $F=4\cdot93, p < 0\cdot05$). In the case of the response to slides which was essentially decelerative, drinking slides elicited significantly less cardiac deceleration during slide presentation (St. $F=8\cdot14, p < 0\cdot02$). By far the most significant were the trials x stimuli interaction effects due to a loss of differentiation between neutral and drinking stimuli after treatment (See Figure 2). This interaction was

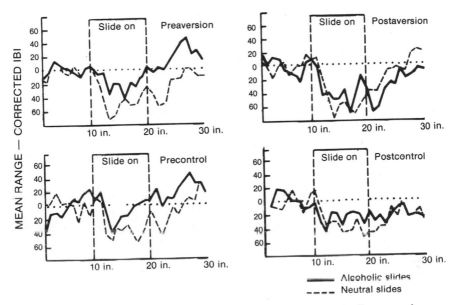

FIGURE 1. Cardiac response to slides in aversion (*n*=10) and control groups (*n*=8), expressed as second-by-second averages of each S's mean response to the 5 neutral and 5 alcoholic slides. Response measures were range-corrected IBI's (see text). A downward shift in the curve represents cardiac deceleration; max. change was approx. 2-3 beats per minute.

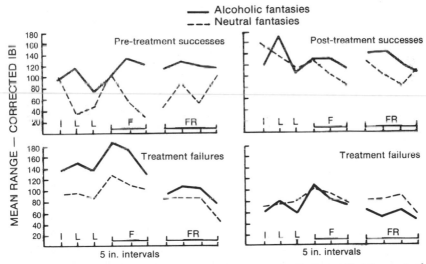

FIGURE 2. Peak cardiac response during instructions to fantasy (I), first and last 5 seconds of the latency period (L,L), fantasy (F), and fantasy recovery period (FR), expressed as mean range-corrected IBI's (see text). Maximum change (cardiac acceleration) was approx. 5 - 6 beats per minute.

significant during instructions to obtain the fantasy (trough HR F=11·38, $p<0·005$, peak HR F=6·06, $p<0·05$) and during the fantasy period only, (trough HR, F=19·15, $p<0·005$, peak HR F=6·08, $p<0·05$). The trials x stimulus interaction was also significant at the 10 percent level in the period after slide presentation (mean of 10 range-corrected IBI's).

Pre-stimulus measures of HR and HR variability did not differ between groups or stimuli. The only significant basal level effect was an increase in HR variablity after treatment (Trials, F=4·98, $p<0·05$). Image Latency: The time required to obtain the relevant imagery to alcoholic and to neutral stimuli, was assessed before and after treatment. The mean latencies proved to be surprisingly short—3 to 4 seconds—probably because they were being assessed in a no-shock condition, unlike a treatment session.

There is a suggestion of a slight change in image latency as a result of treatment. Irrespective of treatment type or outcome, the latencies to obtain alcoholic images increased slightly:

	Pretreatment (sec)	Posttreatment
Alcoholic	3.36	4.23
Neutral	4.05	3.53

F=4.04, $p<0.061$.

We found no evidence of increased latencies in the aversion-treated group or in the group of successfully treated aversion therapy patients. However, one of these successful cases showed a clearcut increase in latency after treatment.

Attitude change

Drinking slides were rated similarly by aversion and control subjects pre-treatment; that is, they were rated as slightly good, tasty, harmless, and relaxing. Ratings of neutral slides remained stable after treatment but drinking slides were rated as slightly bad (Tr x St, $p<0·005$), distasteful ($p<0·001$), anxiety-provoking ($p<0·05$), and dangerous ($p<0·005$) by all subjects (see Figure 3). There were, however, group differences in the taste factor; both neutral and drinking slides became more repugnant (distasteful) to the aversion group (Grp. x Tr, F=13.5, $p<0·005$) but the change was greater for the latter slides (Grp. x Tr x St, F=4·87, $p<0·05$). The aversion subjects also showed a relatively greater shift in the anxiety ratings of drinking and neutral slides combined (Grp. x Tr, $p<0·1$).

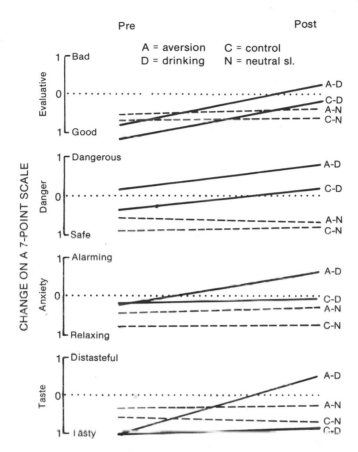

FIGURE 3. Overall change in attitude to the 5 drinking slides (unbroken line) and 5 neutral slides (dotted line) on four semantic factors, in aversion and control groups. The zero point represents neutrality on bipolar scales. The direction of change is given by adjectives taken from component scales of each factor.

Conclusion

Contrary to expectation, aversion therapy did not increase the size of autonomic responses to drinking stimuli. All subjects tended to respond differentially to alcoholic and nonalcoholic stimulation in both SR and HR but in the case of HR this difference was maximal *before* treatment, and it decreased significantly after treatment. Both aversion and control groups showed significant changes in attitude to drinking stimuli, indicating that drinking had become devalued and more dangerous. However, there was a difference on the taste factor: aversion subjects found the drinking slides more distasteful after treatment than controls.

Comparison between treatment
successes and failures

Four months after treatment, subjects were categorized as successes (complete abstinence or no serious bouts of drinking, $n=8$) and failures (frequent drinking, or serious bouts of drinking, $n=10$). The success group comprised 6/10 aversion subjects and 2/8 controls. A comparison between the HRR to fantasies in these two groups revealed significant differences in the peak HR scores during 'instructions to fantasy' and the 'fantasy period'. Successful patients did not appear to show the adaptation of the HRR to drinking fantasies which was observed in the failures: in fact, the response to both 'neutral' and 'drinking' fantasies was maintained or increased (fantasy instructions, Gr. x Tr, $F=4·9, p < 0·05$, fantasy period, Gr x Tr, $F=5·34, p < 0·05$) (See Figure 2).

In plain words, the main psychophysiological effect of any significance in this study is the distinction in heart rate responsivity between successes and failures, *irrespective of type of treatment*. Prior to treatment, all groups showed an increased heart rate to test stimuli, neutral and drink-related. When re-assessed after treatment, the failures no longer showed heart rate responsivity. The successes, on the other hand, continued to exhibit HR responsivity to both types of stimulus and they did not habituate to the test stimuli. This persisting sensitivity distinguishes the successes from the failures.

On the attitudes scales, the successful cases evidenced larger shifts in their ratings of drinking slides than did the failures. The difference was significant for general evaluative and anxiety factors (Gr x Tr x St., $F=4·52, p < 0·05$; $F=5·9, p < 0·05$, respectively). No differences were observed on the taste factor. Hence there is no direct relationship between the distaste, which developed in the aversion therapy group, and clinical outcome.

Discussion

Contrary to expectation, the aversion therapy group showed no evidence of having developed SRR's or HRR's conditioned to the alcoholic stimuli. Neither did we find evidence for the development of anxiety to these stimuli over and above the slight increase in ratings of the neutral stimuli. In view of the fact that there was a significant correlation between HRR (during all fantasies) and the subjective ratings of anxiety to slides ($r=0·54, p < 0·05$), it seems reasonable to have expected the heart-rate data to reveal conditioned anxiety had it been present. The only significant physiological data show a persisting heart-rate sensitivity to all stimuli, in successful cases irrespective of type of treatment.

The attitude data show that the aversion therapy group developed a repugnance (distaste) for drinking stimuli, but this did not predict clinical outcome. Successful cases, irrespective of treatment, showed significant increases in their anxiety about, and devaluation of, drinking.

In sum, the successful cases showed HR and attitudinal effects; the aversion therapy group developed repugnance for alcohol stimuli but no specific effects of clinical importance.

Conclusions

Combining the results of the two investigations, the practical implications are that electrical aversion therapy is well-tolerated and produces few desirable effects. Subjectively, it results in feelings of repugnance among most alcoholic patients treated by a particular method but the prognostic value of this change is uncertain. There are strong suggestions that if patients, alcoholic or sexual, do *not* report subjective or attitudinal shifts post-treatment, their clinical prognosis is poor.

On theoretical grounds, three changes were predicted from conditioning theory.

(1) After aversion therapy, subjects will display conditioned heart-rate responses to deviant stimuli.

(2) After aversion therapy, subjects will display conditioned galvanic skin responses to deviant stimuli.

(3) After aversion therapy, subjects will report anxiety towards deviant stimuli.

In practice, only the third expectation was fulfilled and at that, only partially. As noted earlier, we detected no psychophysiological effects specifically attributable to aversion therapy. The only specific effect of aversion therapy was the development of repugnance (aversion?) but this did not relate to successful treatment.

In a sense, the most interesting outcome of the investigations is to be found in the control-treatment group. The successful cases in this group shared with the aversion therapy successes, the only two clinically significant variables of change. The successful control cases also displayed persisting heart-rate sensitivity and the same attitudinal shifts on the evaluative and anxiety factors. In view of the content of the control treatment (group meetings, A.A. talks etc.) it is no surprise to find a change on the attitude scales of successful cases. The persisting heart rate responsivity of this group was not expected, however, and it suggests that if a general therapeutic improvement takes place, then the patient becomes (or remains?) physiologically sensitive to alcoholic stimuli. The replication of this finding in sexual cases would be most interesting.

What then are the theoretical consequences, if any, of our two investigations?

We failed in our attempt to find psychophysiological supporting evidence for the classical conditioning theory of electrical aversion therapy. The patients did not develop conditioned GSR's or HRR's to the alcoholic stimuli. The heightened HR sensitivity is not attributable to aversion therapy and this result is not predictable from the conditioning theory. Although we found little to comfort the proponents of conditioning theory, eager critics should not celebrate a premature mortality. We may have been searching in the wrong place or in the wrong manner and, moreover, one of us has a growing list of experiments which fail to confirm.

The subjective and attitudinal evidence provides no direct support for the conditioning theory but there are some crumbs of comfort. According to prediction, we observed an increase in deviant stimulus-produced anxiety after aversion treatment. However, this increase is extremely slight and worse, it appears in the control patients without undergoing aversion. This slight and non-specific increase in anxiety is consistent with the relative absence of avoidance behavior after treatment.

The only evidence of a change attributable specifically to aversion therapy is found in the development of a repulsion/aversion to drink. This distinguishes the A.T. group from the controls. In addition, the subjective investigation yielded similar evidence—in those patients whose aversion therapy sessions included the tasting of alcohol. Unfortunately the suggestion arising from the subjective study, that the development of a feeling of repulsion augurs well for clinical outcome, is not supported by the data from the control study. At present all we can state is that the development of a repulsion to the smell and taste of alcohol is fostered by electrical aversion treatment which incorporates shock trials administered during and after testing. The clinical consequences of such a repulsion are uncertain.

As far as the conditioning theory is concerned, the development of this taste/smell repulsion may prove to be a useful staring point—square one. For example, it could be reasoned that we should look for conditioned alimentary reactions rather than study electrodermal and cardiovascular activity. However, those people who feel that the conditioning theory should be abandoned may, with some justification, use our findings to advocate a cognitive approach.

In his enlightening account of aversive conditioning theory, Bandura (1969, p.426 ff.) discussed some of the contradictory evidence. In particular, he noted the independence of autonomic reactivity and avoidance behavior (e.g., avoidance behavior persists after the disappearance of autonomic responses; sympathectomized animals can acquire stable avoidance behavior). On the whole, our investigations have failed to produce supporting evidence for conditioning theory; on the contrary, they add to Bandura's list of examples illustrating the relative independence of autonomic responsiveness and successful avoidance behavior. Our successfully treated patients showed none of the expected autonomic changes and the single instance of autonomic responsiveness is of no clear significance.

In our investigations there is one major finding that seems to demand a cognitive explanation. The successful control cases, like the successful aversion cases, continued to show heightened heart rate responses after treatment. The only psychophysiological distinction between successes and failures, heart rate responsivity, can be obtained by attitude change therapy, group therapy etc. Furthermore, the fact that this heart rate responsivity is common to control and aversion successes, suggests that *success* may be attributable to the common therapeutic variables—namely, hospital in-patient care combined with group meetings, non-interpretive weekly sessions of psychotherapy and so on. Not exactly a radical proposition, it is true. It is, however, made somewhat more interesting by the fact that when it is successful, it is associated with psychophysiological responsivity. Generally, we have tended to assume that mediation works in one direction only. However, our findings provide another example of mediation from attitude change to physiological change.

Although our findings appear to favor a cognitive explanation of aversion therapy effects, the arguments described by Rachman and Teasdale (1969) are not superseded and their conclusion seems still to be apposite: "a purely cognitive explanation is as unsatisfactory as a purely non-cognitive explanation" (p. 117).

Finally, we would like to suggest that cognitive theorists are likely to find early joy if they concentrate on the treatment of alcoholism whereas conditioning theorists may do better with therapy for sexual disorders.

References

Bandura A. (1969) *Principles of Behavior Modification.* Holt, Rinehart and Winston, New York.

Chatterjee B. B. and Eriksen C. W. (1962) Cognitive factors in heart rate conditioning. *J. Exp. Psychol. 64,* 272-279.

Grings W. W. and Lockhart R. A. (1963) Effects of "anxiety-lessening" instructions and differential set development on the extinction of the G.S.R. *J. Exp. Psychol. 66,* 222-229.

Hallam R. S. (1971) The clinical significance of classical conditioning: an experimental investigation. Ph.D. dissertation, University of London.

Marks I. M. and Gelder M. G. (1967) Transvestism and fetishism: Clinical and psychological changes during faradic aversion. *Br. L. Psychiat. 113,* 711-729.

Mowrer O. H. (1939) A stimulus-response analysis of anxiety and its role as a reinforcing agent. *Psychol. Rev. 46,* 533-656.

Obrist P. A., Webb R. A. and Sutterer J. R. (1969) Heart rate and somatic changes during aversive conditioning and a simple reaction time task. *Psychophysiology 5,* 696-723.

Rachman S. and Teasdale J. (1969) *Aversion Therapy and Behaviour Disorders: an analysis.* Routledge, Kegan Paul, London.

Spence K. W. (1966) Cognitive and drive factors in the extinction of the conditioned eyeblink in human subjects. *Psychol. Rev. 73,* 445-458.

Zuckerman M., Lubin B., Vogel L. and Valerius E. (1964) Measurement of experimentally induced affects. *J. Consult. Psychol. 28,* 418-425.

Note: This research was supported, in part, by a grant from the Maudsley-Bethlem Hospital Research Fund.

A Technique for Controlling a Certain Type of Sexual Exhibitionism

Ian Wickramasekera
University of Illinois
College of Medicine
Peoria

The following paper describes a provisional experimental technique for the control of sexual exhibitionism. The technique is brief (2-4 sessions and the duration of each session is approximately 50-60 mins.) and relatively objective. It appears to be applicable only to a subset of sexual exhibitionists, for example, neurotic patients with high manifest anxiety, fundamentalist religious backgrounds, and strong motivation. It is our impression that even patients as select as those above cannot reliably control their impulse to exhibit themselves when involved in a conventional cognitively-focused psychotherapy. Procedures very similar to the present one have independently been developed and are reported to be highly effective (Serber 1970, Reitz & Keil 1971). The uniqueness of the present procedure resides in its incorporation of both cognitive and behavioral strategies, in a context of video feedback to increase the probability of a more complete (motoric, affective, and cognitive) and durable form of behavior change.

Observational and Speculative Origins of the Technique

In the last eight years we have experimented with several techniques of controlling sexual exhibitionism. For example, I have tried systematic desensitization and behavior-shaping procedures (Wickramasekera, 1968), hypnosis and certain Gestalt techniques, and more recently electric shock used as a straight punishment (Azrin & Holz, 1966) procedure. The technique or combination of techniques I selected was influenced by my diagnostic hypotheses concerning what had originally caused and more importantly what was currently maintaining the deviant behavior.

Aversion Therapy

Through clinical experimentation with electrical aversion, we stumbled on two interesting observations. (1) Aversive methods appear very quickly and reliably to inhibit (follow-ups ranging from 6 months to 3½ years) deviant sexual behavior in certain males. Clinically these males are recognizable, even though I know of no objectively validated and reliable method of identifying them. I speculated and Eysenck (1968) recently suggested that these are the types of patients who would demonstrate the "Napalkov phenomenon." This phenomenon refers to an increase in the magnitude of the CR when the CS is presented without the UCS. This procedure typically produces extinction but in some animals it has been shown to produce an increase of the conditioned emotional response (Rohrbaugh & Riccio, 1970). I have suggested (Wickramasekera, 1970), that the rare phenomenon of "resensitization" in systematic desensitization is probably related to the "Napalkov phenomenon." Resensitization appears to be associated with a rapid deterioration of the patient's symptoms and appears to be caused by high anxiety stimuli prematurely introduced into treatment. (2) We also noticed that, for the majority of sexual exhibitionists treated with aversion therapy, the behavioral rehearsal of their deviant act in the consulting room appeared to be far more aversive than the actual electrical aversion which was paired with this behavioral rehearsal.

The following is a description of the electrical aversion method we used. First, we required the patient to form a clear subjective image of the deviant act. When the image was clear, he was requested to raise his left forefinger and immediately an unpleasant electric shock was delivered to his leg. Typically after several such pairings, the patient will report an inability to form a subjective image of the deviant act. The treatment next shifts to an overt behavioral sequence. The deviant act is divided into ten parts. For example, behavior one may involve unzipping his pants and behavior ten may involve masturbation with full erection. So that in the second stage of the technique the patient was actually behaviorally, and not simply cognitively, rehearsing the deviant act in the consulting room. The aversive stimulus was first applied to only behavior ten. On the next day, if behavior ten could not be elicited with verbal instructions and persuasion, aversion was applied only to behavior nine, and so on down the chain to behavior one.

I found that persuading even highly motivated patients to go through the second part (behavior rehearsal) of the treatment sequence was extremely difficult. The patient became shaky, nauseous, reported headache, cramps, lightheadedness, and palpitations. This led me to wonder if rehearsing the deviant act in the consulting room was not more aversive to some patients than the electric shock itself. If the behavioral rehearsal of the deviant act in a clinical situation was highly aversive in itself, it seemed to have at least one major advantage over externally originating electrical aversion: the patient's active participation in generating within himself the aversive consequences. It would be interesting to know if such internally generated aversion, which probably involved interoceptive conditioning and visceral changes, would be less susceptible to discrimination learning. Currently discrimination appears to be the major factor reducing the generalization of the conditioned emotional response (Mowrer, 1938) from the consulting room to the patient's natural habitat.

Hypnotherapy

While experimenting with hypnotic techniques in controlling sexual exhibitionism, we made the following observations. Certain exhibitionists, it appeared, would frequently, spontaneously, and unknowingly enter a dissociated or trance-like state prior to an exhibitionistic episode and while in that altered state of consciousness (Tart, 1969) would cognitively rehearse the highlights of the anticipated episode several hours prior to the actual event. This cognitive rehearsal of the event within a presumed altered state of consciousness prior to its actual occurrence appeared to be a type of self-induced post-hypnotic suggestion. Also the deviant act itself is frequently described by this sub-set of exhibitionists as if it were enacted in a trance state. For example, it is enacted compulsively (or quasi-automatically), it is enacted with apparent reduced critical judgment (e.g., patient will use his own car with identifiable number plates, etc.), narrowed focus of attention, a partial or total amnesia and after completion of the act there is a subjective feeling of tension release or closure. There are clearly certain striking resemblances between the above subjective experience of certain exhibitionists and certain known parameters of hypnotic behavior in general (Hilgard, 1965) and post-hypnotic behavior in particular (Orne et al., 1968; Wickramasekera, 1971).

Clinically it seems that for a sub-set of exhibitionists the reinforcement properties of the behavior stem significantly from the secrecy, "privacy" and anonymity with which the deviant behaviors are enacted. It also appears that the deviant act is maintained by several very autistic, unverbalized fantasies, and primitive affects which require accidental contact with a certain type of female, in a certain environmental context to be potentiated. It would be interesting to know if the reinforcing consequences of the deviant behavior would alter and satiate if the act was repeatedly elicited under conditions identical to those prevailing in the natural context in which the deviation occurred, but altered in two ways. (1) Without the element of anonymity; (2) If the patient could be induced to attend, to verbalize, and to reflect on the thoughts and feelings which were passing through him as he enacted the deviant behavior. For example, if the patient were to expose himself to several women who were attractive to him but who knew who he was and to whom he would verbalize and talk about the thoughts and feelings that passed through him while he was engaged in the exhibitionistic act.

The above observations and speculations led me to abandon the use of electrical aversion and concentrate exclusively on arranging contingencies to maximize the internally generated aversion the patient experienced and to attempt to alter the "meaning" of the deviant behavior for the patient by changing the context and conditions under which it was enacted.

Description of Technique

The experimental treatment consisted of persuading the patient actually to rehearse the deviant sexual act in an environmental context as close as possible to that in which the deviation naturally occurred, and in the presence of at first one, then two, and finally three carefully selected (for convergence with his ideal deviant sexual object) females. The females make no comment but sit expressionlessly observing him and moving the focus of their attention on cue from me, from his penis to his eyes and to other parts of his body. The present therapist was always present guiding the procedures. The patient was told that the females knew his name and had read his case record. The females we used were primarily interns or trainees in psychology or social work. Only patients who were chronic offenders (from police records), who had not responded to conventional psychotherapy, and who volunteered for the treatment were accepted. They were carefully briefed as to what they would be expected to do, and informed that this method of treatment was purely experimental, but that it seemed quite promising compared to other long-term conventional interventions. The patient was also asked to sign a paper indicating that he understood that this was an experimental method of treatment. If the patient had a lawyer, the lawyer was also involved in making the decision to participate with this experimental method of treatment. To date we have used this intervention with six patients and none of them has appeared to need or be willing to go through the procedure more than four times. Each actual deviation rehearsal session has typically not exceeded 20 minutes. After the females were dismissed, I have spent 20 to 40 minutes encouraging the patient to verbalize any feelings, thoughts, and sensations he did not verbalize while enacting the deviation. Behavioral rehearsal appears to increase the probability of self-recognition of important private events (cognitions and emotions).

In using this procedure, we noticed that certain subjects appeared to dissociate or slip into a trance-like state while rehearsing the deviation in the clinic. To try to discourage this we adapted certain Gestalt therapy techniques which instruct the patient to conduct verbally and aloud an introspective dialogue between himself and his penis while enacting the deviation. We also encourage him to verbalize aloud the specific subjective feelings in his body while enacting the deviation, e.g., dry mouth and throat, weak legs, light head, speeding heart, pounding sensation in stomach, tightness in chest. In addition, we also invite him to verbalize aloud to himself and to the females his assumptions and his fantasies regarding what he thinks the females are feeling, seeing, and thinking about him. He is also invited to switch roles and having personified his penis to give it a voice so that it can verbalize aloud what it is feeling and thinking about him and the females who are observing it. I have found that this procedure, in addition to maintaining the anxiety at a high level, disrupts any fantasies of privacy and occasionally produces some very remarkable personal references and "insights" which patients report are very meaningful to them.

Recently we have begun to video tape the treatment (and encourage the females to ask him brief pointed questions; e.g., What are you thinking? What are you feeling?). These changes appear to increase the impact of the procedure. The following appear to be plausible reasons for the increased impact. (1) Several patients stated that viewing their deviant behavior on a TV screen with the therapist was even more aversive than actually engaging in it at the time it was taped. (2) Patients have suggested the video tape viewing and discussion be used as "boosters" if they would ever feel a weakening of self-control over the symptom in the future. (3) The video feedback may have an impact on patients who dissociate during behavior rehearsal in spite of the verbal and instructional interventions. (4) The thought that someone, somewhere, has a visual record of their deviant behavior may·be a sobering reflection and a potent deterrent to acting out exhibitionistic impulses. Finally, experimental studies indicate that informational feedback and self-confrontation appear to be potent tools with motivated subjects (O'Brien & Azrin, 1970). We have to date treated six exhibitionists with the method outlined above. Treatment to date has never exceeded four contact sessions with the clinic. None of the treated patients have reported, nor have we detected, a breakdown of self-control over the symptom (Table 1). Follow-up is maintained through the mail, on the telephone at monthly intervals, through probation officers and police records. It is of course possible that self-control over the symptom has broken down but has gone unreported and undetected by us.

TABLE 1

**LIST OF MALE SEXUAL EXHIBITIONISTS WHO
EXPERIENCED THE EXPERIMENTAL TREATMENT**

	Years Since Onset of Symptom	Age	Frequency of Deviation per Month	Experimental Treatment Sessions	Follow-up in Months
1	14	32	2-4	3	22 months
2	16	29	1-2	3	16 months
3	40	49	1-2	3	18 months
4	6	20	3-4	4	3 months
5	18	37	1-4	4	35 months
6	4	26	1-3	3	6 months

This technique is limited both in its scope and its applicability. But in view of the current status of thinking about psychotherapy, there is no reason to apologize for the limitations of the procedure. "This means a departure from old technique testing to new technique building and requires application of specific techniques to specific problems under controlled conditions of the type stipulated for experimental case studies and subsequent field trials (Bergin & Strupp, 1970, p. 21)." Empirically this procedure seems promising but why it is effective is still unclear. What, if any, are the effective ingredients in the procedure is also unclear. Recent investigations (Baum & Posner, 1971; Marks et al., in press) of the conditions under which "resensitization" or the enhancement of fear, occur may imply that many of my cognitive procedures are "superstitious" and that the only salient conditions for effective symptomatic control are: (1) High pre-treatment patient anxiety,·(2) Brief rather than extended exposure to the aversive aspects of the treatment procedure, the duration of the exposure being the critical factor. The effective implementation of the technique assumes a good and open relationship between patient and therapist that enables the therapist to lead the patient through a procedure that can be really quite harrowing to both of them.

References

Azrin, N. H., & Holz, W. C. Punishment. In W. K. Honiz (Ed.), *Operant behavior, areas of research and application.* New York: Appleton-Century-Crofts, 1966.

Baum, M., & Poser, E. G. Comparison of flooding procedures in animals and man. *Behavior Research and Therapy,* 1971, *9,* 249-254.

Bergin, A. E., & Strupp, H. H. New directions of psychotherapy research. *Journal of Abnormal Psychology,* 1970, *76,* 13-26.

Eysenck, H. J. A theory of the incubation of anxiety/fear responses. *Behavior Research and Therapy.* 1968, *6,* 309-321.

Hilgard, E. R. *Hypnotic susceptibility.* New York: Harcourt, Brace, and World, 1965.

Marks, I. M., Boulougouris, J. C., & Marset, P. Flooding and desensitization in the treatment of phobic patients. *British Journal of Psychiatry* (in press).

Mowrer, O. H. Preparatory set (expectancy)—a determinant in motivation and learning. *Psychology Review,* 1938, *45,* 62-91.

O'Brien, F., & Azrin, N. H. Behavioral engineering: control of posture by informational feedback. *Journal of Applied Behavior Analysis.* 1970. *3,* 235-240.

Orne, M. T., Sheehan, P. W., & Evans, F. J. Occurrence of posthypnotic behavior outside the experimental setting. *Journal of Personality and Social Psychology,* 1968, *9,* 189-196.

Reitz, W. E., & Keil, W. E. Behavioral treatment of an exhibitionist. *Behavior Therapy and Experimental Psychiatry,* 1971, *2,* 67-69.

Rohrbaugh, M., & Riccio, E. Paradoxical enhancement of learned fear. *Journal of Abnormal Psychology,* 1970, *75,* 210-216.

Serber, M. Shame aversion therapy. *Behavior Therapy and Experimental Psychiatry,* 1970, *1,* 213-215.

Tart, C. T. (Ed.), *Altered states of consciousness.* New York: John Wiley and Sons, 1969.

Wickramasekera, I. The application of learning theory to the treatment of a case of sexual exhibitionism. *Psychotherapy: Theory, Research and Practice,* 1968, *5*(2), 108-112.

Wickramasekera, I. Desensitization, re-sensitization and desensitization again. *Behavior Therapy and Experimental Psychiatry,* 1970, *1,* 257-262.

Wickramasekera, I. The effects of "hypnosis" and task motivational instruction in attempting to influence the voluntary self-deprivation of money. *Journal of Personality and Social Psychology,* 1971, *19,* 311-314.

Aversive Behavior Rehearsal for Sexual Exhibitionism

Ian Wickramasekera

University of Illinois
College of Medicine
Peoria

The aversive behavior rehearsal (ABR) technique is a specific technique for the management of chronic sexual exhibitionism. The "in vivo" ABR (I-V-ABR) makes an appointment for the patient to come into the clinic and expose himself at a specific time and place to people who know of him. The vicarious aversive behavior rehearsal (V-ABR) technique arranges for a chronic exhibitionist to observe via video tape the I-V-ABR treatment of a fellow exhibitionist. Twenty chronic exhibitionists have been treated within one to four sessions with the above methods and none has relapsed to date in follow-ups ranging up to seven years.

About one-third of all arrests for sexual offenses are for sexual exhibitionism, but the real incidence is probably higher since only a minority are arrested and come to trial. The rate of recidivism is quite high and 25 per cent of those appearing in court have previous convictions for the same offense.

In the past twelve years, I have experimented with a variety of techniques and combinations of techniques in searching for a reliable and brief method of symptomatic control of sexual exhibitionism. I have tried a variety of interventions including dynamically oriented psychotherapy, rational-emotive therapy, Gestalt therapy, hypnotherapy, systematic desensitization, operant shaping of heterosexual behavior (Wickramasekera, 1968), and aversive conditioning (shock). The ABR procedure was inspired by or incorporates apparently effective ingredients from the previous interventions.

The Aversive Behavior Rehearsal (ABR) technique (Wickramasekera, 1972) appears to be a specific technique for the management of chronic (repeated offenders as defined by police records) sexual exhibitionism in a specific subset of exhibitionists. The technique or a variant of it has been independently replicated by several investigators (Serber, 1970; Reitz & Keil, 1971; Stevenson & Jones, 1972).

In Vivo ABR (I-V-ABR) Procedure

The in vivo ABR procedure appears to be indicated for patients who are introverted, anxious, moralistic, and non-assertive. It is probably contra-indicated for the extroverted, sociopathic type of patient whose trait anxiety level is low.

The I-V-ABR procedure prescribes and elicits the patient's symptom (exhibitionism) under conditions which overlap substantially with the naturally occurring event but with certain critical alterations. (1) The "exposure" is deliberately planned by therapist and patient several weeks in advance and scheduled for a specific time and place. (2) The "exposure" is enacted under conditions of reduced anonymity. (3) During its enactment, the behavior is subjected by the patient and therapist to cognitive-verbal exploration of associated affect, bodily sensations, and fantasy. The goal is to elicit and demythologize any autistic fantasies that may mediate cognitively the exhibitionism in the natural habitat. Conditions are arranged to increase the probability that the patient will take a pedestrian, critical, and analytic view of what he is in fact doing during the act of "exposure," in a sense a form of discrimination training for response-produced stimuli (fantasy). It has been hypothesized (Wickramasekera, 1972) that at least for the subtest of exhibitionists discussed in this paper the enactment of sexual exhibitionism occurs under internal conditions of increased fantasy involvement (Sarbin and Coe, 1972) and reduced critical judgment (Hilgard, 1965). These patients show reduced critical judgment when they use public places, compulsively return to the same place with their car license plates clearly visible, and in numerous other ways temporarily ignore situational dangers. It appears that a cognitive shift from fantasy involvement to a critical pedestrian view may alter the future probability of exhibitionism under the internal conditions (moods of self-pity, boredom, anger, failure, etc.) and external conditions (warm weather, parks, girls in short skirts, etc.) which set the stage for exposure. In some respects the above intervention is equivalent to reducing the probability of "hypnotic" behavior under specific internal and external conditions which may operate as discriminative stimuli for hypnotic behavior as it has been conceptualized by some writers (Sarbin and Coe, 1972; Wickramasekera, 1974).

Vicarious ABR (V-ABR) Procedure

A recent variant of the ABR procedure is called Vicarious Aversive Behavior Rehearsal (V-ABR) and is based on instructing and situationally arranging for an exhibitionistic patient to observe a video tape of a real exhibitionist being processed "in vivo" through the ABR procedure. The symptomatic consequences of V-ABR appear to be similar to the "in vivo" ABR procedure, but our sample is still small (N = 4), and our follow-ups are inadequate (four to eleven months) to provide more than a tentative impression of a promising variant of ABR. The V-ABR procedure is probably indicated for the same type of patients who benefit from the "in vivo" ABR procedure, but who cannot be processed through the entire I-V-ABR for one or more of the following reasons: (1) deficient in the motivation necessary to go through the in vivo ABR; (2) medical contraindications which require that the patient be exempt from the severe stress of the I-V-ABR procedure (e.g., positive history of cardiovascular or CNS complications, angina pectoris, cardiac decompensation, hypertension, epilepsy, etc.); (3) patient with weak reality contact or marginal adjustment, or who is pre-psychotic or acutely disturbed. The V-ABR is offered only to those patients who have carefully considered and refused the "in vivo" ADR procedure or to those who, in the clinical judgment of the present therapist or his medical consultant, are likely to be hurt by the "in vivo" ABR.

Flow Chart of ABR Procedure

I. Initial diagnostic interview
   A. Collect following facts and formulate relationships
      1. First event (age, circumstances)
      2. Frequency (in remote and recent past, and in present)
      3. Locations
      4. Time of day or night
      5. Duration of episode
      6. Age and sex of observers (special features)
      7. Masturbation, ejaculation, associated rituals and fantasies
      8. Triggering events (e.g., conflict, failure, weather, female clothing, daydreams, and fantasies)
   B. 1. Present treatment plan and alternatives with prognosis
      2. Present intervention as research, not routine treatment
      3. State side effects, patient reads article on ABR
      4. State restriction on intercourse for three weeks following Procedures I and II

II. Psychological and psychophysiological tests
1. MMPI
2. Eysenck Personality Inventory
3. Taylor Manifest Anxiety Scale
4. Spiegel Eye Roll Test of Hypnotizability
5. SHSS Form A
6. Hypnosis Attitude Scale
7. Protestant Ethic Scale
8. Respiration
9. G.S.R. } Baseline and Response to
10. EMG } Standardized Stimuli
11. Heart Rate
III. Medical tests and physical examination (any contraindications?)
IV. Discuss treatment plan with significant others and lawyers;
read and sign consent for treatment and video tape forms
V. Procedure I (40 minutes of self-disclosure, intensive self-
exploration, and confrontation, of which approximately 20
minutes is actual physical exposure)
VI. Procedure II (40 minutes of intensive self-disclosure, self-
exploration, and confrontation, of which approximately 20
minutes is actual physical exposure)
VII. Follow up (three weeks later) with observation of video tape
of Procedure I while monitored psychophysiologically (heart
rate, EMG, GSR, respiration); retake MMPI
VIII. Follow ups at following intervals:
A. Three weeks after treatment (view neutral and aversive
video tapes)
B. Thereafter: 2, 6, 9, 12 months, then once each year

Components I-IV have diagnostic utility and also appear to potentiate certain active ingredients in the behavior influence process. These ingredients include self-disclosure, self-exploration, commitment, structuring of positive expectations, and giving the patient responsibility for making the technique work (demand characteristics), which have been empirically demonstrated to be effective variables in both the psychotherapy and the social psychological research literature (Strupp & Bergin, 1972; Goldstein, Heller & Sechrest, 1966).

Component I, section A, both elicits and shapes the patient's self-exploratory and self-monitoring behaviors from very specific topics (e.g., first events of exposure, age, etc.) to eventually a very general form of self-monitoring and self-exploration (identification of triggering events). At this more general level, the patient is attempting to relate the onset of his symptom to internal (e.g., conflict, failure, self-pity, boredom, etc.) and environmental events (the warm weather, specific location, length of women's skirts, types of female clothing, etc.). These antecedents appear to overlap between subjects to some extent, but are also highly idiosyncratic. The identification of these internal and external antecedents or triggering events is quite important in terms of helping the patient develop an "early warning" system for his post-therapy prophylactic use. Component I, section B, essentially involves selling the patient on the ABR technique but doing so in a cautious and ethical manner. For example, to create positive expectations the patient is now instructed to find and read a favorable review (*Human Behavior,* April 1973) written in non-technical terms of this intervention. Previously observed side effects are described (repeated nightmares, temporary anxiety or depression, secondary impotence) and the requirement of abstinence from sexual intercourse for three weeks after treatment is presented.

Components II and III are mainly intended to enable an eventual more precise and objective specification of the type of patient for whom this procedure is indicated or contraindicated. It has been hypothesized (Wickramasekera, 1972) that trait anxiety, hypnotizability, the degree of socialization, and autonomic lability are implicated in the probability of certain sexual deviations. In addition, the combination of extensive psychological, psychophysiological, and medical tests may create the therapeutic expectation in the patient that "grave and healing events" are about to occur. The psychophysiological tests currently involve: (a) a 20 to 15 minute adaptation period; (b) a 10 minute baseline period, (c) the discharge of a cap pistol from 3 feet behind the subject at about the level of his head; (d) instructions to solve simple mental arithmetic problems and to read aloud the titles of the books in the bookcase across the room from him; (3) instructions to the subject to visualize with his eyes closed a pleasant and relaxing scene (e.g., soaking in the bathtub, sipping a martini while relaxing by a fire, etc.); and (f) instructions to visualize with eyes closed the last time he was arrested for indecent exposure.

Component IV is the culmination of a series of progressively more tightly interlocking tacit behavioral commitments to change. It requires the patient to make a full disclosure of his deviation, its frequency and chronicity to significant others (parents, wife, etc.) and his lawyer. It also challenges *him* to persuade *them* of the wisdom of undergoing the ABR procedure, and in the process of doing so he appears to strengthen his own commitment. One patient has been lost to date at this point because his lawyer labeled the ABR procedure "insane" (which it probably is in some respects), and told the patient that if he cooperated with the video taping, he could expect to appear nude on the "Today Show" or "Huntley and Brinkley News." This component closes with the patient signing a release allowing me to video tape his naked body for the "advancement of science" and releasing me of all responsibility for possible negative consequences of the ABR procedure. He acknowledges on the release that the negative side effects have been carefully explained to him. Components I through IV may take as many as four to eight sessions (each session 50 minutes) to complete, depending on the individual patient's initial level of defensiveness and commitment.

In summary, the preliminary orientation and screening procedures carefully structure the patient's expectations in a positive direction, and increase his commitment to "public" (self-disclosure) living and socially appropriate risk taking and assertiveness.

It is conceivable that these interventions alone are sufficient to produce symptomatic control. This is an empirical question that can be answered by simply putting patients processed to this point on a waiting list and comparing their relapse rate with patients who additionally received the complete in vivo ABR processing.

Components V and VI involve approximately two 40-minute sessions of full self-disclosure, self-exploration, and self-confrontation in the presence of five mental health professionals (social workers, senior medical students, psychiatric nurses, psychology interns, etc.) in a large room with a one-way mirror and video taping of the entire proceedings. It is sometimes hinted at this point that there may be other authorized observers (e.g., referring probation officer, arresting law officer, etc.) on the other side of the mirror. A psychiatric nurse is included in the team in case of medical emergency, also a large, sturdy male video tape operator in case the patient becomes combative (which has not happened to date). I open the session in a kind, but grave, manner and become progressively more obnoxious and confronting as the session progresses. I begin by putting a series of rapid questions to the patient (Please state your name, age, address, marital status, occupation, children—names and ages, wife, religion, specific deviant sexual acts, associated rituals and locations, objects of exposure.)

The patient is instructed in the following number system (1, 2, 3) to cue specific acts of exposure and masturbation. The use of numbers appears more effective in securing compliance under stress than verbal requests. The patient is told, "When I say *one,* you will unzip your pants and underpants; when I say *two,* you will get a firm grip on your penis (use patient's own word for penis, e.g., cock); when I say *three,* you will start to masturbate ("jack-off," etc.)."

During and between exposures the patient is pointedly questioned by all the team members individually and requested to attend to different parts of his body or their legs, breasts, crotches, hips, etc. For example, he might be asked to respond to all or some of the following questions and instructions: What is your mood when you expose yourself? What triggers the mood? What do you see now as you look at' yourself in the mirror? Describe what you think we see as we look at you right now. What do you think we are feeling (thinking, etc.) as we look at you now? How do your hands feel? How does your head (legs, penis, stomach, etc.) feel? Give your penis a voice, let it talk to us. Tell us about the man you are in your public life. Tell us about your private life. What are your masturbatory fantasies? And so on.

During components V and VI, the patient is asked to disrobe and dress several times while he is encouraged to explore the relationship between his current feelings, and his moods ,prior to exposure, during exposure, and their relationship to antecedents, consequences, and immediate situational factors. He is frequently relieved to be asked to "zip up," or pull up his pants, but this relief is short lived because soon afterwards he is asked to disrobe again. At the close of the session, the patient is frequently in tears, trembling, weak, and nauseous.

I dismiss the team and change abruptly into a warm, kind, supportive figure, who wipes the patient's eyes and fetches him a drink of water. I sincerely and freely express my admiration for the courage and strength he demonstrated during the previous "hell," and I leave him in doubt for a few days as to whether another procedure will be required.

The primary contraindications for another procedure are massive sympathetic arousal during the first procedure, "insightful" verbalization with active patient participation, and any evidence of bizarre behavior during or after the procedure (very rare event). The primary indication for a second procedure is marginal arousal and "unauthorized" psychological escape behavior while physically present (disassociation). If a second procedure is scheduled, we begin by asking specific details about his cognitive, affective, and motor reactions during and after the first procedure, particularly, immediate and delayed reactions. The session continues with some variation on previous material, any new material, or loose ends from the previous session. To disrupt any persisting disassociation, team members approach him physically and ask him to describe physical details of other team members, their clothing or their bodies.

Results

The in vivo ABR procedure has been offered to twenty-five patients. Five have refused at the onset or have not completed the I-V-ABR or V-

ABR. Twenty patients have been treated with the ABR procedure to date. Sixteen with the in vivo ABR and four with the vicarious ABR. No patient treated with the ABR procedure has reported exposing himself nor have we detected any relapses up to date. All patients report having between one to four thoughts of exposure at least once in three months. But, the thoughts are brief and easily terminated. Approximately one-half of the patients report mild to severe anxiety when thoughts of exposure occur to them. The rest of the patients report a "neutral" feeling if thoughts of exposure occur to them. All patients report that the frequency of exposure fantasies is reduced dramatically since treatment and the quality and duration of the fantasies, if they occur at all, "feel" vastly different from the pre-treatment fantasies.

The follow-ups for the in vivo procedure range from three months to six years and nine months. The follow-ups for the vicarious ABR are too brief (range four months to eleven months) to attach much significance to them at this time. The follow-ups are based on four kinds of data: (1) Patients' verbal reports during the periodic individual interviews. The systematic follow-up interviews appear to be reactive measures, because many patients report that prior to their follow-up appointment, their anxiety level increases, and in fantasy the previous ABR procedure is reactivated in memory. It appears that these regular follow-up sessions strengthen the ABR procedure and should be regarded as part of it. Since these are patients' subjective verbal reports they are open to all the limitations associated with such sources of information. (2) Private interviews with significant others (wife, employers, parents, etc.) or telephone calls to them are used at the time of the patient's follow-up interview to check on the patient's verbal report. (3) Search of police records on indecent exposure in the three surrounding counties are used to verify the patient's verbal report. This procedure is recent and is still incompletely established. The law enforcement system appears responsive and supportive of this project, but their own records and those at a state-wide level are incomplete. (4) Recently we have begun to add a fourth evaluation component to our follow-up system. The patient has previously been shown the results of his video-physio evaluation procedure which occurs three weeks after treatment. This increases the credibility of the treatment effects. The routine psychophysiological testing (heart rate, GSR, respiration) of the patient during the periodic follow-up interview is presented to the patient as "to detect how much of the previous conditioning persists." Some patients perceive this new procedure as a "lie detector test," and this of course may contribute further to the inhibition of the deviant behavior. During this procedure the patient is instructed after a baseline to expose himself in fantasy and casually asked while still connected to the instrument the number of times he exposed himself since the last follow up.

TABLE 1

**CHARACTERISTICS OF MALE SEXUAL EXHIBITIONISTS
AND THEIR TREATMENTS.
I-V-ABR = "IN VIVO" AVERSIVE BEHAVIOR REHEARSAL
V-ABR = VICARIOUS AVERSIVE BEHAVIOR REHEARSAL**

Subject	Duration (in years)	Age	Frequency of Deviation per Month	Method	Number of Treatment Sessions	Follow-up in Months or Years
1	14	32	2 - 4	I-V-ABR	3	5 Years, 3 Months
2	16	29	1 - 2	I-V-ABR	3	4 Years, 3 Months
3	40	49	1 - 2	I-V-ABR	3	4 Years, 9 Months
4	6	20	3 - 4	I-V-ABR	4	4 Years, 6 Months
5	18	37	1 - 4	I-V-ABR	4	6 Years, 9 Months
6	4	26	1 - 3	I-V-ABR	3	4 Years, 11 Months
7	7	32	1 - 20	I-V-ABR	2	3 Years, 3 Months
8	12	30	1 - 3	I-V-ABR	2	3 Years, 5 Months
9	5	22	1	I-V-ABR	2	3 Years, 3 Months
10	25	50	1 - 7	I-V-ABR	2	3 Years, 2 Months
11	11	29	1 - 2	I-V-ABR	2	2 Years, 3 Months
12	4	22	1 - 4	I-V-ABR	2	17 Months
13	20	42	1 - 14	I-V-ABR	2	6 Months
14	7	23	1 - 2	I-V-ABR	2	9 Months
15	9	28	1 - 9	V-ABR	1	11 Months
16	13	29	1 - 3	V-ABR	1	8 Months
17	10	26	1 - 2	V-ABR	1	6 Months
18	12	36	2 - 4	V-ABR	1	4 Months
19	8	24	1 - 12	I-V-ABR	1	3 Months
20	10	29	1 - 12	I-V-ABR	1	3 Months

The in vivo ABR does appear to have some side effects which are observed between in vivo ABR procedures I and II or immediately after the treatment. These side effects include moderate to mild anxiety, tension, and depression, of one to four weeks' duration. One or more of these symptoms have been reported by all in vivo ABR patients. These symptoms seem to have disappeared in all cases after five weeks. Repeated nightmares in which the ABR procedure or a variant of it is rehearsed in sleep have been reported by three patients. Secondary impotence of brief

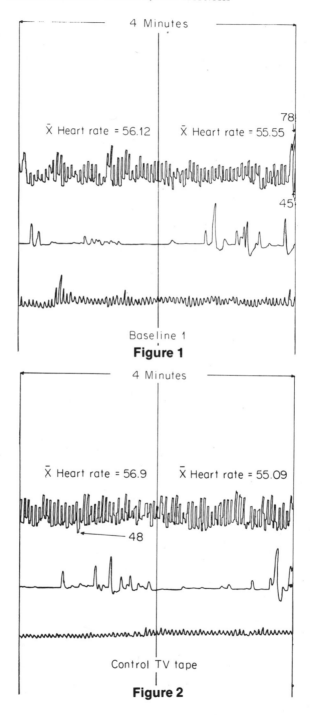

Figure 1

Figure 2

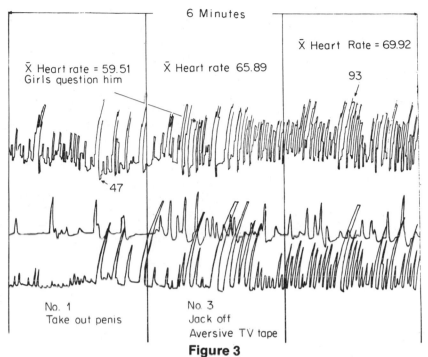

Figure 3

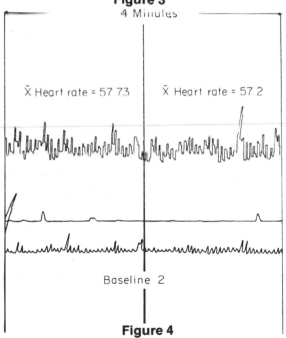

Figure 4

duration (two to four weeks) has been reported by three patients. Temporary loss of interest in sex has been reported by approximately ten in vivo ABR patients. All symptoms appear to have cleared up two months after treatment.

The secondary impotence has particularly concerned us; and in an attempt to reduce the future probability of it, we have introduced a prohibition against all sexual intercourse by patients for three weeks after in vivo ABR procedure I. The mechanism of erection is primarily parasympathetic, and hence a temporary state of massive sympathetic arousal (post-treatment anxiety and tension) is probably antagonistic to effective sexual functioning in the male patient. Residual anxiety has usually subsided by the third week after treatment. About one-half of the patients will disassociate (psychologically absent though physically present, or go some place else in their head) during procedure I and II to avoid the impact of the aversive reality that has been carefully arranged for them. They will not attend or become "numb" to the full concrete impact of the aversive reality. This probably natural response to stress has to be rapidly terminated in this context. This "unauthorized form of escape behavior" (Azarin & Holz, 1966) has been terminated by insisting forcefully that the patient describe the present physical reality (color of female's eyes, hair, shape of their breasts, legs, clothes, etc.), his own physical reactions, his current autistic fantasies, and his speculations about the thoughts and feelings behind the females' faces. I can usually subjectively estimate the intensity of the aversion generated by how severe is the exhaustion or tension headache I feel after the procedure. The procedure is really quite harrowing to all concerned.

To determine the psychophysiological consequences of being processed through the ABR procedure and being reminded of it (memory stimulated by observation of the video tape record of their treatment), the following instructional and situational arrangements are made: The patient is told to return to the therapist's office for "a test" approximately three weeks after the last in vivo ABR procedure. In the therapist's office the patient is connected to a physiograph (which is screened from the patient) while he sits quietly on a comfortable recliner. In front of the subject, approximately eight feet away, are two video tape monitors. The monitor above is programed to show a portion of the video tape (aversive tape) of the patient's treatment. The monitor below is programed to show a "neutral" or control tape (a portion of the initial diagnostic interview by the present therapist of the patient). After connection to the physiograph, the patient is given 20 minutes to adapt and "relax" in the situation. At the end of the adaptation period, the control tape is activated remotely by the present therapist and allowed to run for 8 minutes. After the control tape is turned off, the aversive tape is activated remotely and allowed to run also for 8 minutes. The subject has previously been instructed to observe both tapes carefully, but he is not informed about the content of the video tapes or the order in which they will be shown. After 8 minutes of exposure to the aversive tape, it is switched off, and the subject is simply instructed to relax for 10 minutes before he is disconnected from the physiograph, which has been monitoring and recording his heart rate (BPM), respiration, and GSR during the adaptation, observation, and relaxation periods.

FLOW CHART OF VIDEO-PHYSIOGRAPH ASSESSMENT PROCEDURE

1. Adaptation and baseline (20 minutes)
2. Control TV tape (8 minutes)
*3. Aversive TV tape (8 minutes)
4. Return to baseline (8 minutes)

The purpose of the control tape is to determine the psychophysiological consequences of simply orienting to and observing a video tape of oneself while connected to a physiograph. Simple inspection of the physiograph record during the exposure to control and aversive tape sequences indicates clear and significant differences in heart rate, GSR, and respiration. Statistical analyses were not done because they did not seem necessary in the case of the four records of this type we have collected to date with this psychophysiological evaluation procedure.

The figures show psychophysiological changes occurring in a white male adult during two baseline periods and while observing an aversive tape (a video tape of himself behaviorally rehearsing sexual exposure and masturbation in the presence of three females and two males). The upper trace is of heart rate (BPM), the middle trace of GSR, and the bottom trace is of respiration. Paper speed is six inches per minute. This patient's record was selected because he demonstrates physiological changes in all three response systems (heart rate, GSR, respiration). Not all subjects tested to date demonstrate clear changes in all three response systems. As implied by Lacey (1959), individual patients appear to show response profiles.

Discussion

Instructionally and situationally the ABR procedure arranges for the elicitation of strong aversive internal consequences (typically patients report or manifest one or more of the following before, during, or immediately after the procedure: trembling, nausea, lightheadedness, palpitations, weakness, cramps, butterflies in stomach, headaches, tightness in chest). "Voluntary" participation (Wickramasekera, 1971) ensures that the patient actively generates the aversive consequences in himself. The aversion is installed inside the subject and outside his control, so the aversive contingency cannot be easily dismantled by the patient, as for example with a portable and remotely controlled shock generator. It has been speculated (Wickramasekera, 1972) that the procedure may involve interoceptive conditioning, and this speculation appears to be reinforced by some theoretical and empirical data (Miller & Murray, 1952; Miller, 1949; Miller, 1964). Professor Neal Miller has suggested (personal communication, 1973) that if aversion is attached to internal cues, the gradient of generalization will be flatter. The above hypothesis may explain the apparently reliable transfer of the suppression of exhibitionism from the clinical situation to the patient's natural habitat.

It appears that if the ABR technique is continued over several sessions the patient will desensitize to the technique. Hence, treatment should cease with a brief "resensitization" (Wickramasekera, 1970).

Many exhibitionists are quiet, non-assertive, moralistic individuals, who take few risks in their "public" lives but become very daring figures during their "private" exhibitionistic episodes and fantasies. Their public image may be one of respectability, caution, reliability, and industry, whereas in their private feelings they are desperately bored, resentful, self-pitying individuals whose fantasies are defiant and dangerously exciting.

During procedures I and II, the patient frequently develops "insight" into this inconsistency between his public and private lives and is strongly encouraged to act in more adaptive risk taking and assertive ways (e.g., asking for a raise or promotion, speaking back to his wife, boss, or a peer, changing jobs, trying a love affair, etc.) in his public life. It appears likely that the inhibition of aggressive, sexual-novelty, and excitement needs increases episodically the probability of maladaptive expression (indecent exposure) of such deprivations.

At a theoretical level, several explanations of the reduction of exhibitionism are possible which have implications for empirical manipulations. But, first it is necessary to recognize that the technique is clearly overdetermined because it appears to incorporate several ingredients which have previously been shown to be or claimed to be effective ingredients in the psychotherapy, social psychological, and learning literatures. Its overdetermined features place it in the category of a broad spectrum behavior therapy approach to behavior management.

For example, the reduction of exhibitionism may be attributed to extinction or nonreinforcement of the private fantasies and exhibitionistic role behaviors in the clinical exposure situation (females do not react with shock or fear). Punishment (Azrin & Holz 1966) of the fantasies and exposure role behavior by the connection of aversive visceral consequences to internal cues should also be considered. "Insight" and "self-disclosure" (Mowrer 1964) may be said to explain the positive outcomes. Cognitive dissonance theory predicts maximum attitudinal change under conditions of voluntary participation, minimal reward, and maximum effort. All the above three ingredients are incorporated into the ABR procedure. Powerful demand characteristics structuring (Orne, 1970) may be said to explain the positive outcome. Credibility or face validity is an important property of a therapeutic procedure to a patient, and four exhibitionists have spontaneously told me that they had anticipated a technique like the ABR and wondered if it would help them.

At an even lower level of abstraction, it may be said that the treatment simply arranges for a series of events that identify highly motivated exhibitionists who would respond to any form of treatment. Hence, the results are due to some nonspecific placebo effect. Alternately, it may be said that the screening events are arranged to make the patient increasingly vulnerable to interpersonal influence, and that once such an orientation is established, the specific treatment technique is irrelevant. The treatment procedure involves several components, some of which may be effective and the others "superstitions." The technique is highly researchable and may be disassembled along several empirical dimensions (e.g., verbal instructions, situational arrangements, frequency and duration of treatments, etc.). For example, men may be substituted or included with women, or verbal instructions and patient self-exploration could be increased, reduced, or eliminated. The diagnostic screening could be eliminated or the diagnostic screening retained and the treatment procedures (I and II) eliminated. Another alternative would be to retain the diagnostic screening and replace the "exposure" procedure with an equally unpleasant aversive (shock) conditioning procedure. At a strictly empirical level, the above independent variables need to be manipulated and symptomatic outcome monitored over several years.

Currently, we are attempting to look rather grossly at the motivational hypothesis by attempting to narrow the patient's choice from three alternatives (1.psychotherapy; 2.threat of legal action; 3.ABR) to two alternatives (1.threat of legal action; 2.ABR) and finally to secure involuntary legal commitment to the ABR procedure. To secure the above purpose, to expand our follow-up net, and to secure more baseline data on this deviation, we are conducting exploratory negotiations both at local and state-wide levels (while protecting patient confidentiality) with law enforcement agencies and the courts.

We are also attempting to identify the psychological, behavioral, and psychophysiological subject characteristics that predict maximum response to this treatment procedure. The extensive diagnostic screening was initially intended eventually to improve prediction of positive outcomes with this procedure, but the zero relapse rate to date has frustrated this purpose. It is likely that as our sample increases we will detect relapses enabling us to look more closely at them and our techniques. Clinical impressions confirm the view that hypnotizability, the degree of socialization, religiosity, introversion, autonomic responsivity, and manifest anxiety are salient predictors of positive outcome with this procedure. Nearly all the exhibitionistic subjects we have screened to date and treated (either with V-ABR or in vivo ABR) have had most of these subject characteristics.

References

Azrin, N. H., & Holz, W. C. Punishment. In W. K. Honig (Ed.), *Operant behavior, areas of research and application*. New York: Appleton-Century-Crofts, 1966.

Goldstein, A. P.; Heller, K.; & Sechrest, L. B. *Psychotherapy and the psychology of behavior change*. New York: Wiley & Sons, 1966.

Hilgard, E. R. *Hypnotic susceptibility*. New York: Harcourt, Brace and World, 1965.

Lacey, J. I. Psychophysiological approaches to the evaluation of psychotherapeutic process and outcome. In E. A. Rubenstein and M. B. Parloff (Eds.), *Research in Psychotherapy*. Washington, D. C.: A. P. A., 1959.

Masters, W. H., & Masters, V. E. *Human sexual inadequacy*. Boston: Little Brown, 1970.

Miller, N. F., & Murray, E. J. Displacement and conflict: Learnable drive as a basis for the steeper gradient of avoidance than of conflict. *Journal of Experimental Psychology*, 1952, *43*, 227-231.

Miller, N. E. Liberalization of basic S-R concepts: Extension to conflict behavior, motivation and social learning. In S. Koch (Ed.), *Psychology: A study of a science*. New York: McGraw-Hill, 1959.

Miller, N. E. Some implications of modern behavior therapy for personality change and psychotherapy. In D. Byrne and P. Worchel (Eds.), *Personality change*. New York: Wiley, 1964.

Mowrer, O. H. *The new group therapy*. New Jersey: Van Nostrand, 1964.

Orne, M. T. Hypnosis, motivation and the ecological validity of the psychological experiment. In W. J. Arnold and M. M. Page (Eds.), *Nebraska Symposium on Motivation*. Lincoln: University of Nebraska Press, 1970.

Reitz, W. E., & Keil, W. E. Behavioral treatment of an exhibitionist. *Behavior Therapy and Experimental Psychiatry*, 1971, *2*, 67-69.

Sarbin, T. R. and Coe, W. C. *Hypnosis; A Social Psychological Analysis of Influence Communication*. Holt, Rinehart and Winston, New York, 1972.

Serber, M. Shame aversion therapy. *Behavior Therapy and Experimental Psychiatry*, 1970, *1*, 213-215.

Stevenson, J., & Jones, I. H. Behavior therapy techniques for exhibitionism. *Archives of General Psychiatry*, 1972, *27*, 239-241.

Strupp, H. H., & Bergin, A. E. Some empirical and conceptual bases for coordinated research in psychotherapy. *Changing frontiers in the science of psychotherapy*. Chicago: Aldine-Atherton, 1972.

Truax, C. B., & Carkhuff, R. *Toward effective counseling and psychotherapy*. Chicago: Aldine, 1967.

Wickramasekera, I. The application of learning theory to the treatment of a case of sexual exhibitionism. *Psychotherapy: Theory, Research and Practice*, 1968, *5*, 108-112.

Wickramasekera, I. Desensitization, resensitization and desensitization again. *Journal of Behavior Therapy and Experimental Psychiatry*, 1970, *1*, 257-262.

Wickramasekera, I. The effect of "hypnosis" and task motivational instruction in attempting to influence the voluntary self-deprivation of money. *Journal of Personality and Social Psychology*, 1971, *19*, 311-314.

Wickramasekera, I. A technique for controlling a certain type of sexual exhibitionism. *Psychotherapy: Theory, Research and Practice*, 1972, *9*, 207-210.

Wickramasekera, I. Effects of EMG feedback on hypnotic susceptibility. *Journal of Abnormal Psychology*. 1973, 82, 74-77.

The author wishes to express his thanks to Professor N.E. Miller of Rockefeller University for providing the reference on transfer of training.

Hypnosis

Verbal Instructions and Behavior Change

Ian Wickramasekera

University of Illinois
College of Medicine
Peoria

Instructions, suggestions and informational feedback are among the major tools of behavior therapy, hypnosis, and biofeedback. These tools are alike in that they involve verbal events occurring in the form of instructions given by a therapist to a patient, inferences that are made by patients, or self-instruction that patients administer to themselves. I make no distinction, in the final analysis, between instructions and hypnotic suggestions as Hilgard (1965) appears to do, because both may initiate hypnotic behavior under certain conditions. This section is concerned with *what* and *how* may internal and external conditions be arranged to potentiate verbal "instructions" or events. Verbal influence procedures include education, psychotherapy, and hypnosis. It appears that the degree of subjective involvement and the perceived involuntariness of the instructions are the definitive features of hypnotic behavior.

Hypnotic procedures constitute the oldest form of psychological treatment and in a sense contain, in unrefined form, all the psychologically effective ingredients necessary for inducing complex changes in human behavior (Wickramasekera, 1973a). The third section of this book outlines and attempts to document this assertion.

Today, hypnosis is best defined as a set of instructional-situational manipulations which have a high probability of success with an identifiable group of people (highly susceptible) under conditions of high motivation to participate. Hypnosis should be defined today in terms of a set of procedures, rather than as an explanation of dramatic behavioral changes caused by an as yet unidentified set of psychophysiological alterations (Barber, 1969). Laboratory studies show that hypnotic procedures involve certain verbal instructions (e.g., verbal definition of the situation as "hypnosis," sleep, relax instructions, concentrate, try instructions, it-is-easy-to-respond instructions, etc.) and situational arrangements which, with responsive subjects, can initiate profound and clinically significant changes. These changes vary all the way from changes in experimental pain tolerance (Hilgard, 1969; Barber, 1969) to quasi-automatic behaviors (Orne et al., 1968) and value alterations (Wickramasekera, 1971) that appear to be independent of their original situational determinants. For example, Orne et al. (1968) found that an established posthypnotic response could be reliably elicited, if the right posthypnotic stimulus were used by an individual other than the experimenter-hypnotist, even operating outside the experimental situation. Wickramasekera (1971) found that labeling a procedure "hypnosis" was effective in temporarily talking subjects out of accepting money for services rendered. The empirical results of the above studies are clearcut, but both studies pose some problems in inference and interpretation.

The determination of whether or not hypnotic behaviors are associated with a unique "state" or configuration of psychophysiological events is not an obstacle to routine clinical use of hypnotic technology with responsive patients. Spiegel (1972) describes a method that is objective, rapid, reliable, and fairly accurate to identify individual differences in response to hypnosis and which may also be used to induce hypnosis rapidly. But even more important, the last article (Wickramasekera, 1973c) of this book indicates that there are relatively objective, reliable, and promising procedures—laboratory-based—for increasing the hypnotic responsivity of initially resistant subjects. The extension to the clinic of these laboratory procedures that appear effective in minimizing the significance of individual differences will require validity tests in clinical settings and possibly adaptations for a clinical population.

Superior hypnotic subjects demonstrate dramatically the power of verbal instructions to control complex and clinically relevant human behavior. For example, controlled laboratory studies with superior hypnotic subjects (Hilgard, 1969, Barber, 1969) have supported the validity of the verbal-hypnotic control of pain in surgery and in chronic disease. Superior hypnotic subjects have, under controlled conditions, demonstrated the verbal control of other autonomic functions (Roberts et al., 1973, Maslach et al., 1972, Sarbin and Slagle, 1972) and as basic an aspect of orientation as the "sense of time" (Zimbardo et al., 1973). The article by Maslach et al. (1972), printed in the third section of this book, demonstrates that verbal instructions delivered to a superior hypnotic subject can have powerful, measurable, and specific effects on skin temperature. Another article (Zimbardo et al., 1973), also printed in the third section of this book, demonstrates that the sense of time of superior hypnotic subjects can be altered in precisely and objectively measurable ways. It is still unclear what components of the hypnotic procedure and/or subject behavior enables superior subjects to alter visceral responses and temporal orientation.

For operational purposes, it appears more fruitful to approach hypnosis not as an *explanation* of certain dramatic behavioral phenomena, but rather as an historically descriptive category for a set of researchable arrangements, which increase the probability of the verbal control of complex human behavior. More specifically this section identifies certain subject, experimenter, and procedural-situational variables that appear to potentiate the range and impact of verbal instructions.

These variables are drawn from a variety of fields (education, psychotherapy, psychophysiology, sleep research, physiological psychology,etc.) not directly related to hypnosis. The immediate prospects for behavior control through brain control (chemical, electrical or surgical) appear limited by reasons of economy, specificity, reliability, transferability (laboratory to natural habitat), and adaptibility to a changing environment (Valenstein, 1973). Potentiating verbal instructions appear at least in the short run to be the most promising approach to a technology of behavior control.

Converging Conditions

It is the primary hypothesis of this section that the hypnotic interpersonal situation is a model that appears to arrange for convergence and maximal interactive potentiation of a set of psychologically potent conditions that increase the probability of the *verbal control* of complex behavior. The relevant overlapping psychological conditions appear to be the following: (1) an initial "consent" or voluntary participation situation; (2) structuring of explicit and implicit expectations; (3) "transference" eliciting interpersonal arrangements; (4) social reinforcement and informational feedback; (5) manipulation of attention; (6) social and sensory restriction; (7) relaxation; and (8) "permission" to act "as if" or to ignore "conventional reality," an invitation to emit operants that can have respondent (autonomic) consequences, etc.

Verbally mediated social influence procedures (sermons, education, psychotherapy, biofeedback, transcendental meditation, advertising, etc.) and psychotherapy cults (Behavior Therapy, Primal Scream, Gestalt Therapy, etc.) stress one or more of the above conditions of verbal influence in their theory or technique. For example, Gestalt therapy uses condition 8 to promote "experiential" learning. Primal Scream practices appear to stress conditions 2, 3, 6, and 7 in either their priming of the patient or in therapy interventions. Psychoanalysis has stressed conditions 2, 3 and 6. Behavior therapy practices (not theory) stress conditions 2, 4, 5, 6, and 7. But it is hypnosis that appears to make most use, either concurrently or sequentially, of nearly all the conditions identified to date that potentiate verbal instructions. Hypnosis is probably, today, the only technology of social influence which enables us to match *in advance* subject and intervention properties. The matching approach appears to be the most promising strategy (Bergin and Strupp, 1972) to increase the probability of effective social influence. Brief primitive tests (Speigel, 1972) are available today that identify in advance individual differences in hypnotic responsivity. In addition, as Wickramasekera notes in this section, experimental hypnosis is developing a specific technology to minimize the practical significance of the individual differences or to increase hypnotic responsivity.

The conditions listed below are related but have been conceptually discriminated for research purposes in the learning, social-psychological, and clinical literature.

(1) A subject who voluntarily seeks a hypnotic experience is more responsive to operator influence than one who approaches hypnosis because of external pressure (e.g., high incentives, threats, etc.). An initial consent or "voluntary" participation situation increases the probability of more profound and complex hypnotic behaviors. The extensive hypnotic research with "coerced" volunteers supports the above contention (Hilgard, 1965). Studies have shown that subjects who volunteer freely for hypnosis generally emit more and complex hypnotic behavior than subjects "coerced" into volunteering for hypnosis studies. Cognitive dissonance theory predicts and finds that under conditions of high volition, the magnitude of the dissonance aroused will be larger (Brehm and Cohen, 1962, Festinger, 1957).

Brehm and Cohen (1962) provide an example of a farmer, who, at the start of the season, decides to plant tobacco rather than corn and later discovers that tobacco causes a deadly disease. Because the inconsistency created by growing a crop that had deadly effects could have been avoided, the farmer experiences dissonance. Greater dissonance arousal increases the probability of influence and opinion change. The psychological "feeling of freedom" may not be inconsistent with effectively determined behavior if instructionally human needs or priorities can be rearranged. People may "feel free" yet be effectively controlled if the focus of influence is not on a specific behavior but on the wants and values of the person.

An article by Wickramasekera (1971) shows how a priority as basic and generally relevant as money can be temporarily displaced downwards through a "clever" hypnotic instructional manipulation that temporarily rearranges the needs and priorities of superior hypnotic subjects. Subjects who previously had agreed to take money for participation in a study refused it after "recognizing" that a contribution to the progress of science was more important than cash. The behavior of the experimental subjects in this study was effectively determined, yet the subjects "felt" that they were "freely" choosing to reject the money.

The basic precondition for an effective social influence manipulation is an attentive, aroused, and active subject. These foundational elements can be used to shape the patient into participating actively in *changing his own behavior*. Without his participation, the change process moves very slowly, if at all. The business of securing the patient's participation with the effort to influence him is importantly related to the perceived attractiveness of the therapist, the treatment techniques, and the treatment goals. Once the patient's participation with the change process has begun, there can be strong facilitatory interactive effects between therapist, technique, and goal variables if the change process is effectively managed.

The literature on increasing psychotherapeutic attraction (Goldstein, 1971, 1973) and increasing hypnotic susceptibility (reviewed by Wickramasekera) illustrates further how subjects who do not initially cooperate with a social influence process may be shaped into participation by attentional, arousal, and activity (motor) manipulations. A reliable and effective technology for influencing "values" and participatory behavior may leave terms like "free choice" and "volition" without much practical content. On the other hand, terms like "resistance" refer with a paucity of heuristic value to real events that can bring the change process to a halt. The term "counter-control" (Davison, 1973) appears to have more heuristic value because it draws our attention to patient initiated behaviors that block or deflect the forms and sources of social influence. These specific obstructions or deflections have to be identified and defused without triggering increased counter-control behaviors. Further labels like "resistance" do not advance our knowledge of how to arrange conditions to increase the probability of subject participation with a social influence process. To label a patient "resistant" discourages creative efforts to motivate and prepare the patient for participating actively in a change process. The research on increasing hypnotizability, increasing psychotherapeutic attraction (Goldstein, 1971), and increasing readiness for psychotherapy (Truax et al., 1966, Hoehn-Saric et al., 1964, Strupp and Bloxom, 1973, Goldstein, 1973) suggests specific procedures to motivate and shape up responsive participation with a social influence process.

(2) Hypnotic procedures use instructions, assigned social roles,

and situational variables to structure explicitly and implicitly a subject's expectations. For example, the subject has previously learned and is instructed to expect unusual experiences. He is assigned an overtly passive role by the operator, and he is placed in a social situation in which *the observers expect* unusual behavior. Recent laboratory procedures to increase hypnotic susceptibility have found effective structuring of subject expectations a powerful independent variable, and the article by Wickramasekera on increasing hypnotizability, printed in this book, illustrates the techniques and aims in structuring expectations. The aim in structuring expectations is to inculcate positive attitudes towards hypnosis. This is achieved by defining hypnosis as a pleasant, interesting, and consent situation. Positive expectations about a subject's ability to respond may also be induced by unobtrusive types of "prompts," bogus personality test predictions, and the observation of superior hypnotic models who verbalize freely their subjective experiences. The paper by Wickramasekera on the modification of hypnotic susceptibility details these techniques.

The power of explicit or implicit expectations in work with human subjects has been repeatedly demonstrated in several areas, including the placebo response in the medical literature (Shapiro, 1971), the psychotherapeutic literature (Goldstein, 1962), the social-psychological literature (Rosenthal, 1966; Orne, 1970), and recently in the behavior therapy literature (Bernstein and Neitzel, 1973; Wilkins, 1971; Kazdin, 1973; Tori and Worell, 1973; Borkovec, 1973). Subject or patient expectations not only have been demonstrated to alter significantly affective, verbal, and behavioral responses, but also have been shown to produce clearcut physiological changes under autonomic control (Shapiro, 1971).

(3) In the hypnotic situation, there is an arrangement of conditions to elicit "transference" phenomena (Wickramasekera, 1970a), especially the authoritative and interpersonal attraction aspects of this phenomena. A consenting subject voluntarily enters a type of subtle behavioral trap in which discriminative stimuli are arranged to increase the probability that the subject will emit the core aspects of the many prior socially learned subordinate roles (teacher-*student*, doctor-*patient*, priest-*penitent*, parent-*child*, etc.), which are appropriate to such instructional situational arrangements. In other words, a social role is assigned the subject, which, if accepted by him, triggers a type of inner compulsion to enact expected behaviors which can increase in intensity as the rate of transactions and mutual reinforcements escalate and elaborate. Hence, an initially loose public, social contract (to follow hypnotic instructions) grows inevitably tighter and private if participation continues as a function of ongoing and subsequent interlocking tacit social contracts with the hypnotist. The increase in intensity of the involvement with the hypnotist may be a function

of many variables, including increasingly poor objective discriminations and more remote stimulus and response generalizations. Eventually the subject may be responding in a manner more appropriate to an early parent-child model characterized by the biological and psychological dependence of an immature child on a strong nurturing adult. This authoritative situation, regardless of how it is produced, increases the subject's responsivity to influence (Milgrim, 1963).

At the same time, a related but probably not entirely overlapping process occurs. The hypnotist comes to be regarded with increasing respect, awe and affection, because he appears to be expanding the subject's human potential. The subject may discover that he can experience a variety of interesting phenomena (e.g., hallucinations, cognitive inhibitions, analgesia) which he previously considered beyond his normal capacity. Hence, he may come to feel gratitude and interest in the operator. The interpersonal attraction literature (Goldstein, 1971) and the general psychotherapeutic literature (Gardner, 1964) both demonstrate that the patient's attraction to the therapist increases the probability of changing the patient's behavior.

In two articles printed in the third section of this book, Wickramasekera (1970a, b) points out that hypnosis appears to provide a convenient, natural and brief means of increasing interpersonal attraction by cultivating a subject's initial fascination with a procedure (hypnosis) or a person (the hypnotist). In the article on the effects of hypnosis on verbal conditioning, (Wickramasekera, 1970b) some empirical evidence is offered to support the above clinical observations. Hypnotic manipulations systematically develop the interpersonal attraction generating potential of the "consent" situation and the subtle behavioral trap that the hypnotic situation provides. Once a "transference" relationship has been established, characterized by "authority" and "love," a variety of psychological submechanisms are potentiated which have independently (Bergin and Strupp, 1972) been demonstrated to be effective in inducing behavior change. The specifiable mechanisms include identification, modeling, verbal persuasion, empathy, warmth, counterconditioning, extinction, discrimination, etc. In such a relationship over a long term, (e.g., as in romance or psychotherapy) not only is the subject's vulnerability to influence increased, but the hypnotist's vulnerability to patient influence also increases (e.g., the hypnotist may come to care and feel affection for the patient). This mutuality of influence enhancement probably operates as a built-in natural protection against the exploitation of the patient by the therapist. The effectiveness of this patient protective device can be reduced if the hypnotist can remain personally detached from his technical influence procedures. The ineffective management (e.g., poor timing of requests due to inadequate prior compliance shaping, sustained reinforcement deprivation of patient, etc.) of such complementary and supplementary role enactments can touch off a sequence of patient initiated "countercontrol" (Davison, 1973) procedures. Behavioral entry and participation with hypnotic procedures may be associated with progressively more temporary central, and autonomic nervous system changes (Ornstein, 1973; Sarbin and Slagle, 1972) which shift the focus of the enactments from the initial voluntary side of a continuum to the quasi-autonomic or involuntary tail of the continuum.

(4) Hypnotic procedures stress the role of *social reinforcement and informational* feedback. Informational feedback and social reinforcement have empirically been shown to be potent techniques in the behavior therapy literature (Murray and Jacobson, 1971; Agras et al., 1968, 1969; Leitenberg et al., 1968; Borkovec, 1973). Immediate informational feedback is the basic condition for any biofeedback training, and it has been demonstrated to be effective in altering central nervous system responses and visceral responses. Informational feedback has also been shown to be independently effective in inducing behavioral change (Lewisohn and Shaw, 1969; McFall, 1970). Informational feedback appears basic to all biological self regulation and may also be basic to behavioral organization and the prediction and control of complex human behavior (Powers, 1973).

The sophisticated hypnotist carefully observes and tracks the patient's nonverbal behavior. He feeds his observations back to the patient in a manner that gradually confirms the expectations he has structured for the patient, and the consequence is that the patient grows progressively more receptive to influence from the hypnotist. The hypnotist may suggest different physical sensations and provide prompts to initiate the experience. The immediate feedback and awareness of the prompted sensations may increase the patient's subjective involvement with the hypnotic procedures. A social learning analysis of the operations through which a skilled clinical hypnotist manipulates a subject's experience clearly demonstrates many of the procedures (prompting, fading, shaping, chaining, etc.) of operant conditioning technology (Sachs, 1971; Kidder, 1973).

In clinical hypnosis, social reinforcement is explicitly and implicitly used in a fairly contingent manner to shape participatory behaviors in hypnotic subjects. In two articles printed in the hypnosis section of this book, Wickramasekera (1970 a, b) suggests that there may be logical and empirical reasons for believing an operator's social reinforcer effectiveness is increased by a hypnotic induction and successful administration of test suggestions.

(5) In educational psychology (Lindgren, 1972; Thistlewaite, 1959) and the general literature on conditioning and learning (Kimble, 1961; Terrace, 1966) there is broad agreement that *attentional manipulations*

enhance learning. The manipulation of attention is operationalized by instructions to create conditions of social and sensory restriction. The subject is instructed to close his eyes and listen quietly (immobility). The hypnotist's voice becomes the major input from the external world. Hypnotic procedures deliberately manipulate *attention* in task relevant ways. The conditions may be arranged to produce either a state of diffuse attention (Hilgard, 1965) or a state of selective attention (Weitzenhoffer, 1969). If the clinical goal is diffuse attention, or a state of low arousal (to reduce anxiety or pain), then verbal instructions to relax and become drowsy and detached may be useful. If the clinical goal requires attention to a specific sensory or motor experience or event, then task motivational instructions (exhortative instructions to cooperate or try and reassurances that it is easy to respond) to produce a selectively attentive condition may be most useful. During hypnosis not only is attention typically more diffuse or selective (to the voice ot touch of the hypnotist), but also the rate of attentional shifts appear to markedly decelerate (Hilgard, 1965). Consequently a brain state characterized by a diffuse, sluggish, and undifferentiated attentional mechanism is produced by selective attention to the hypnotist's verbal instructions, a brain state devoid of many external constraints.

(6) The hypnotic procedure imposes social and sensory restriction on the patient (e.g., eyes closed, attend only to hypnotist's voice, restrict movement). Empirical studies in operant conditioning have shown that social deprivation may increase an experimenter's social reinforcer effectiveness and increase his ability to manipulate the patient's motivation with deprivation-satiation procedures (Eisenberger, 1970).

A variety of social-psychological studies have shown that sensory and social restriction procedures also increase the probability of behavior influence and susceptibility to propaganda (Goldstein, Heller, and Sechrest, 1966; Wickramasekera, 1970c; Suedfeld, 1969; Zubek, 1973). In fact, as an article by Wickramasekera (1970c) in the hypnosis section of this book demonstrates, increasing the level of prior social and sensory restriction increases the probability of hypnotic behavior.

Sleep (Foulkes, 1966) and altered states of consciousness research (Bertini, et al., 1969) taken together suggest that under conditions of extended social and sensory restriction the probability is increased of certain reliable EEG changes (e.g. high amplitude alpha and low voltage theta activity) which are conducive to sleep onset. During these sleep onset periods or "twilight states" (Budzynski, 1973) there are fairly reliable spontaneous reports of alterations in body image (swelling, floating, twirling, hallucinatory experiences and hypersuggestibility. It appears that for centuries hypnotists have unknowingly manipulated these naturally occurring phenomena to deepen and extend the power of verbal instructions.

(7) Mild somatic relaxation appears to increase the probability of

complex learning (Spence, 1956; Nakamura and Broen, 1965). The behavior therapy literature suggests that relaxation appears to facilitate both the "vividness and the autonomic effects of imagery" while at the same time facilitating the extinction of phobic responses (Mathews, 1971; Lipsitz and Gilner, 1974). Relaxation exercises (Wolpe and Lazarus, 1966) appear clinically to increase the probability of producing sustained positive affective (e.g., feelings of well being, euphoria, etc.) central nervous system states. It appears that the "relaxation response" (Benson, Beary and Carol, 1974) is mediated by the parasympathetic nervous system (Benson, Rosner, Marzetta, Klemchuk, 1974; Berry, Benson and Klumchuk, 1974) and involves the anterior hypothalamus. This positive affective-brain state may be similar to that elicited by positive intercranial stimulation (ICS) of the lateral hypothalamus and limbic system (Valenstein, 1973; Heath and Moan, 1972), which has been demonstrated to enhance reliably the extinction of strong conditioned avoidance responses (Hunsicker et al., 1973; Reid, Miller et al., 1973). Conditioned avoidance responses are incomplete experimental models of clinical phobias, but they appear to have some heuristic value.

It is probable that peripheral physical relaxation per se is not critical to the extinction of phobic responses in systematic desensitization (Rachman, 1968; Wolpin and Raines, 1966; Lader and Mathews, 1968). But physical relaxation may increase the probability of the critical positive central nervous system state, which clinically appears necessary for effective "in vitro" (in imagination) systematic desensitization. This positive affective brain state may be activated directly by ICS (Reid et al., 1973; Hunsicker, Nelson and Reid, 1973), or indirectly by relaxation exercises (Wolpe and Lazarus, 1966), positive hypnotic imagery (Lazarus and Ambrovitz, 1962), EMG and alpha biofeedback (Wickramasekera, 1972a; Garrett and Silver, 1973; Travis et al., 1973), and transcendental meditation (Wallace, 1970). It is also worth investigating the role of euphoria inducing chemicals on the extinction of phobic responses. For example, does morphine facilitate the extinction of conditioned avoidance responses in a response prevention paradigm? Morphine has been shown to potentiate the behavioral effects of ICS (Bush, 1974).

Relaxation instructions have been shown to be one of the effective antecedent conditions in eliciting hypnotic behavior (Barber, 1969), and hypnotic subjects appear to be more subjectively (verbal report) and objectively (EMG, GSR, heart rate, respiration) relaxed following a standardized hypnotic induction (Barber and Hahn, 1963; Paul, 1969). In fact, an article (Wickramasekera, 1973a) printed in the first part (Biofeedback) of this book demonstrates that prior relaxation training with EMG feedback increases the probability of hypnotic behavior. Hence, it appears that the relaxed condition associated with hypnosis may facilitate certain forms of complex human learning and a variety of other clinically relevant patient behaviors by creating an affectively positive and low "noise" brain state conducive to more effective stress management.

(8) The hypnotic roles of "operator" and "subject" temporarily suspend implicit subtle rules of social intercourse. It is this disinhibition of both operator and subject that legitimizes naked exhortative verbal influence procedures (between adults) from the operator and goal directed striving by the subject. Permission to act "as if" can have important informational (perceptual and cognitive) and psychophysiological consequences (Sarbin and Slagle, 1972). Several systems of behavior influence (Kelly, 1955; Mowrer, 1964; Perls, 1969) and one influential theory of hypnosis (Sarbin and Andersen, 1967) place primary emphasis on role playing and role involvement procedures. Role taking and profound role involvement can trigger fresh sensory experiences, emotions (due to the respondent consequences of operant behavior), and thoughts which can become the basis for major redefinition of chronic clinical problems and a new sense of perspective.

Verbal Mediation and Private Events

Behavioral engineers are confronted with two goals: one, the alteration of observable or public behavioral events; and two, alteration of private or not directly observable events (emotions, values, thoughts, perceptions). These important private events are verbally mediated. Probably partly because of verbal mediation, the technology for the modification of private events in man is far inferior, in terms of reliability, power, and precision, to the impressive control of overt behavior that can be demonstrated with animals (presumably lacking a verbal mediation system) in controlled environments. Since control of human behavior through physical environmental manipulations is not always feasible, the development of a powerful and reliable technology to manipulate the verbal mediation system may enhance the probability of controlling complex human behavior. Such a technology would specify the conditions under which verbal instructions precisely, reliably, and powerfully alter cognitive, somatic, and visceral events. The techniques and conditions arranged in clinical and experimental hypnosis are directly concerned with the instructional control of the verbal mediation system. The research on the interpersonal skills (Truax and Mitchell, 1971) of the therapist that facilitate "personality" change (Mischel, 1973) have focused on procedures and conditions (accurate empathy, warmth, self congruence, etc.) to improve the verbal control of behavior. Hypnosis research and psychotherapy process research are contributing to a technology focused on the alteration of public and private behaviors.

Parameters of Hypnosis Relevant to Behavior Change

Certain characteristics of hypnotic behavior appear to have special relevance to behavior control. (1) The *reduction of critical judgment* (Hilgard, 1965) which appears to characterize hypnotic behavior is peculiarly useful in the initiation of behavior change. Critical analytic thinking appears to limit subjective involvement and characterizes left cerebral hemispheric functioning (Galin and Ornstein, 1972). Inhibiting this mode of consciousness hypnotically lifts the obstacles to experimenting behaviorally with new roles and fresh perceptions, feelings, and cognitions. The disinhibition of right hemispheric functions, which are supposedly nonlinear, simultaneous, and intuitive (Sperry, 1964; Milner, 1971), may permit a fresh appraisal of therapeutic messages and experimentation with non-pedestrian ways of observing and processing experience. Clinical lore has always regarded an *experience* as more potent than an *explanation* in producing behavior change. Demythologizing and remythologizing the patient may initially require some loosening of existing perceptual and cognitive "filters," which lock experience and behavior into maladaptive coping techniques. It is, in fact, tempting to regard the Freudian technique of free association as a disguised residual hypnotic procedure to loosen cognitive soil prior to interpretative seeding. An article by Wickramasekera (1970d) printed in this section notes that many careful observers (Freud, 1959; Mowrer, 1964; Szasz, 1961) of psychopathology have either explicitly or implicitly stated that maladaptive values (behavioral priorities) support deviant behavior. Rigidly held values and attitudes that are incongruent with current life conditions can generate much intra- and interpersonal conflict and stress. In an article on the manipulation of monetary value, Wickramasekera (1971) suggests that the reduction of critical judgment within hypnosis appears to provide an ideal opportunity to initiate changes in therapeutically relevant values.

Clinically, it appears useful in generalizing value changes from consulting room to natural habitat to encourage the patient to meditate on appropriate religious or literary paradoxes (e.g., give to get, die to live, step back to step forward, lose to win, etc.) integrated into personalized clinical material. Paradoxes, because of their generality and their compelling poetic concreteness, appear to accommodate and to organize a wide variety of idiosyncratic experiences and promote acceptance of apparent inconsistencies. In a sense, they probably also operate as a buffer against the inevitable intermittent disconfirmation of expectancies in the corporeal world. It is worth noting that religious teachers like Christ and Buddha have also made sagacious use of them. In promoting the transfer of therapeutic learning from consulting room to natural habitat, hypnosis may have some value because instructions delivered within the experimental hypnotic situation appear to become independent of it (Orne, Sheehan and Evans, 1968). For example, Orne, Sheehan and Evans (1968) found that a post-hypnotic suggestion implanted in an experimental context was found to be elicitable in a nonexperimental situation (the reception area) by the experimenter's secretary.

(2) The total role involvement that can occur in superior hypnotic subjects has clear implications for *emotional arousal* and increasing the probability of behavior change. Religious and clinical lore (Wolpe, 1969; Freud, 1959) plus some laboratory data (Frank, 1961; Lang, 1971) stress the importance of emotional arousal and modification as preconditions for behavior change. The importance of relevant emotional arousal is widely recognized, both for symptomatic changes and specifically for the alteration of the respondently conditioned aspects of a symptom. A medium to deep level of hypnotic behavior nearly always is a multidimensional experience (having cognitive, affective and motoric components) and, hence, the potential of hypnotic behavior for the manipulation of emotions is considerable (Zimbardo, Maslach and Marshall, 1972). Of course, maladaptive emotions constitute the aversive core of most neurotic symptoms (e.g., performance anxiety, hostility, guilt, depression, etc.), and hypnotic manipulation could be a useful adjunct to behavioral interventions like systematic desensitization, assertive training, and graded-task assignment (Seligman, 1973).

(3) Wickramasekera (1970 a, b) suggests that the hypnotic relationship appears to lead to an *increase in social reinforcer effectiveness*. A patient who has participated in a successful and personally relevant experience, (e.g., analgesia, profound relaxation, an hallucination, or a catalepsy) with an operator nearly always emerges with a new sense of awe and respect for the operator. In other words, an emotionally charged relationship is set up which can be used to potentiate any appropriate behavior therapy technique.

(4) Many neurotic symptoms such as phobias and anxiety states involve a psychological (perceptual-cognitive) and consequently a physio-

logical orientation that sensitizes the patient to stress. This hyperalert psychological orientation together with a learned tendency to "catastrophize" cognitively (Ellis, 1963) predisposes the patient to excessive sympathetic nervous system arousal and increases the probability of chronically high levels of stress maintained across a variety of situations. In the symptomatic control of psychosomatic disorders, it may be important to train the patient to *"let go"* of his typical vigilant, hyperalert orientation. The focus of the retraining should be on modifying the central *appraisal* function (Arnold, 1960) in emotional behavior. This central appraisal function appears to be most directly altered with the type of Stoic philosophy and logical analysis proposed by Albert Ellis (1963). This attack and alteration of the appraisal function may be most effective if careful attention is paid to the previously stated conditions that potentiate verbal instruction. It has been shown (Lader and Mathews, 1968) that "anxious patients" demonstrate a higher level of arousal than normals. The level of arousal was measured by the frequency of spontaneous skin conductance fluctuations and the rate of habituation to an auditory stimulus in subjects diagnosed clinically as "anxious" and "normal." In fact, patients labeled "anxiety state" showed more fluctuations in skin conductance and habituated more slowly than patients with specific phobias. Unless such a hypervigilant orientation and associated high level of arousal can be altered downwards, even minimal stress can set in motion a "positive feedback mechanism" which can induce a panic reaction and increase the probability of relapse even after effective therapy.

The research of Schachter (1964) and Valins (1970) has demonstrated the importance of cognitive and perceptual variables in emotional arousal. Hypnosis appears to produce greater tolerance for logical inconsistencies and novelty at the perceptual cognitive level (Orne, 1959). Hence, hypnosis may have the potential for shaping sustained attitudes of quiet confidence, low physiological arousal, and "passive volition," which are important in the permanent modification of phobic anxiety states and the technology of effective biofeedback training. Clinical experience with biofeedback procedures for the control of muscle contraction (Budzynski et al., 1970; Wickramasekera, 1972b, 1973b) or migraine headache (Wickramasekera, 1973c) demonstrate that it is important for the patient to develop a subjective attitude of "passive volition." Passive volition is more an attitudinal than a physical orientation towards a goal. It appears that the alterations in consciousness associated with hypnotic induction and relaxation may catalyze the onset of the type of passive volition that facilitates the control of autonomic functions like temperature regulation (Roberts, Kewman, and McDonald, 1973; Maslach, Marshall, and Zimbardo, 1972).

The article by Spiegel (1972) implies that an individual's hypnotic susceptibility can be rapidly estimated (within 5 to 10 seconds). This measurement procedure is relatively objective, can be standardized, and appears on preliminary observation (in our laboratory) to correlate positively with the longer measurement scale (50 minutes) produced by the Stanford laboratory (Weitzenhoffer and Hilgard, 1959). Brief tests like the Spiegel Scale encourage the clinical use of hypnosis. Research like my own on the modification of hypnotizability (Wickramasekera, 1970c, 1973a) and that of other investigators suggests that eventually clinically usable procedures for increasing the hypnotizability of individuals may be available. The articles on smoking (Spiegel, 1970) and blepharospasm (Wickramasekera, 1974b) illustrate how hypnotic and behavior therapeutic techniques can be woven into a total treatment package for individual patients. Clinical experience indicates that hypnosis can have powerful motivational (Hilgard, 1964; Orne, 1970) relevance to a therapy program. The incentive properties of hypnosis can be expressed through the creation and manipulation of expectancies plus the mood altering possibilities of hypnotic procedures.

In summary, it appears that hypnotic procedures arrange for the presence of several powerful overlapping psychological conditions that increase the probability of altering a variety of complex human behaviors. These conditions are initial voluntary participation, structuring of expectations, the manipulation of transference, attention, social reinforcement, informational feedback, sensory restriction, relaxation, and finally "permission" to ignore objective reality.

References

Agras, S., Leitenberg, H., & Barlow, D. Social reinforcement and the modification of agoraphobia. *Archives of General Psychiatry,* 1968, *19,* 423-427.

Agras, S., Leitenberg, H., Barlow, D., & Thompson, L. Instructions and reinforcement in the modification of neurotic behavior. *American Journal of Psychiatry,* 1969, *125,* 1435-1439.

Arnold, M. *Emotion and Personality.* 2 vol. New York: Columbia University Press, 1960.

Barber, T. *Hypnosis: A scientific approach.* New York: Von Nostrand Reinhold, 1969.

Barber, T., & Hahn, K. Hypnotic induction and relaxation: An experimental study. *Archives of General Psychiatry,* 1963, *8,* 295-300.

Beary, J., Benson, H., & Klemchuk, H. A simple psychophysiologic technique which elicits the hypometabolic changes of the relaxation response. *Psychosomatic Medicine,* 36, No. 2, 1974.

Benson, H., Beary, J., & Carol M. The relaxation response. *Psychiatry,* 1974, *37,* 37-46.

Benson, H., Rosner, B., Marzetta, B., & Klemchuk, H. Decreased blood-pressure in pharmacologically treated hypertensive patients who regularly elicited the relaxation response. *The Lancet,* February, 1974.

Bergin, A., & Strupp, H. *Changing frontiers in the science of psychotherapy.* Chicago: Aldine, 1972.

Bernstein, D., & Neitzel, M. Procedural variation in behavioral avoidance tests. *Journal of Consulting and Clinical Psychology,* 1973, *41,* 165-174.

Bertini, M, Lewis, H. B., and Witkin, H. A., Some preliminary observations with an experimental procedure for the study of hypnagogic and related phenomena. In C. T. Tart (Ed.) *Altered States of Consciousness,* 1969 New York: John Wiley and Sons.

Borkovec, T. The role of expectancy and physiological feedback in fear research: A review with specific reference to subject characteristics. *Behavior Therapy,* 1973, *4,* 491-505.

Brehm, J., & Cohen, A. *Exploration in cognitive dissonance.* New York: Wiley, 1962.

Budzynski, T.H. Some applications of biofeedback produced twilight states. In D. Shapiro et al. (Eds.), *Biofeedback and self control 1972.* Chicago: Aldine, 1973.

Budzynski, T., Stoyva, J., & Adler, C. Feedback induced muscle relaxation, application to tension headache. *Journal of Behavior Therapy and Experimental Psychiatry,* 1970, *1,* 205-211.

Bush, H.D. The effects of chronic morphine administration on intracranial self-stimulation in the rat. Unpublished master's thesis, Bradley University, 1974.

Davison, G. Counter-control in behavior modification. In L.A. Hamerlynch, L.C. Handy, & E. Mash (Eds), *Behavior change methodology concepts and practice.* Champaign, Ill.: Research Press, 1973.

Eisenberger, R. Is there deprivation-satiation function for social approval? *Psychological Bulletin,* 1970, *74* (4), 225-275.

Ellis, A. *Reason and emotion in psychotherapy.* New York: Lyle Stuart, 1963.

Festinger, L. *A theory of cognitive dissonance.* Stanford: Stanford University Press, 1957.

Foulkes, D. *The psychology of sleep.* New York: Scribners, 1966.

Frank, J. *Persuasion and healing: A comparative study of psychotherapy.* Baltimore: Johns-Hopkins Press, 1961.

Freud, S. *Collected papers.* Vol. 1, New York: Basic Books, 1959.

Galin, D., & Ornstein, R. Lateral specialization of cognitive mode: EEG study. *Psychophysiology,* 1972, *9,* 412-418.

Gardner, G. The psychotherapeutic relationship. *Psychological Bulletin,* 1964, *61,* 426-437.

Garrett, B.L., & Silver, M.P. The use of EMG and alpha biofeedback to relieve test anxiety in college students. Unpublished paper, n.d.

Goldstein, A. *Therapist patient expectancies in psychotherapy.* Elmsford, N.Y.: Pergamon, 1962.

Goldstein, A. *Psychotherapeutic attraction.* Elmsford, N.Y.: Pergamon, 1971.

Goldstein, A. *Structured learning therapy.* New York: Academic Press, 1973.

Goldstein, A., Heller, K., & Sechrest, L. *Psychotherapy and the psychology of behavior change.* New York: Wiley, 1966.

Heath, R.G., & Moan, C.E. Septal stimulation for the initiation of heterosexual behavior in a homosexual male. *Behavior Therapy and Experimental Psychiatry,* 1972, 3, 23-30.

Hilgard, E. The motivational relevance of hypnosis. In D. Levine (Ed.), *Nebraska Symposium on motivation.* Lincoln: University of Nebraska Press, 1964.

Hilgard, E. *Hypnotic susceptibility.* New York: Harcourt, Brace & World, 1965.

Hilgard, E. Pain as a puzzle for psychology and physiology. *American Psychologist,* 1969, *24* (2), 103-113.

Hoehn-Saric, R., Frank, J., Imber, S., Nash, E., Stone, A., & Battle, C. Systematic preparation of patients for psychotherapy: I. Effects on therapy, behavior and outcome. *Journal of Psychiatric Research,* 1964, *2,* 267-281.

Hunsicker, J., Nelson, T., & Reid, L. Two kinds of intracranial stimulation as counter-conditioners of persisting avoidance in rats. *Physiological Psychology,* 1973, *1,* 227-230.

Kazdin, A. The effects of suggestion and pretesting on avoidance reduction in fearful subjects. *Journal of Behavior Therapy and Experimental Psychiatry,* 1973, 4, 213-221.

Kelly, G. *The psychology of personal constructs.* New York: W.W. Norton, 1955.

Kidder, L. On becoming hypnotized: How skeptics become convinced: A case of attitude change? *American Journal of Clinical Hypnosis,* 1973, *16,* (1).

Kimble, G. *Conditioning and learning.* London: Methuen, 1961.

Lader, M., & Mathews, A. A physiological model of phobic anxiety and desensitization. *Behavior Research and Therapy,* 1968.

Lang, P. The application of psychophysiological methods to the study of psychotherapy and behavior modification. In A.E. Bergin and S.L. Garfield (Eds.), *Handbook of psychotherapy and behavior change.* New York: Wiley, 1971.

Lazarus, A., & Ambrovitz, A. The use of "emotive imagery" in the treatment of children's phobias. *Journal of Mental Science,* 1962, *108,* 191-195.

Leitenberg, H., Agras, W., Thompson, L., & Wright, D. Feedback in behavior modification: An experimental analysis of two phobic cases. *Journal of Applied Behavior Analysis,* 1968, *1,* 131-137.

Lewisohn, P., & Shaw, D. Feedback about interpersonal behavior as an agent of behavior change: A case study in the treatment of depression. *Psychotherapy and Psychosomatics*, 1969, *17*, 82-88.

Lindgren, H.C. *Educational psychology in the classroom.* 4th ed. New York: Wiley, 1972.

Lipsitz, D., & Gilner, F. Drive level and incentive in systematic desensitization. Unpublished paper, n.d.

Maslach, C., Marshall, G., & Zimbardo, P. Hypnotic control of peripheral skin temperature: A case report. *Psychophysiology*, 1972, *9*, 600-605.

Mathews, A. Psychophysiological approaches to the investigation of desensitization and related procedures. *Psychological Bulletin*, 1971, *76*, 73-91.

McFall, R. The effects of self-monitoring on normal smoking behavior. *Journal of Consulting and Clinical Psychology*, 1970, *35*, 135-142.

Milgrim, S. Behavioral study of obedience. *Journal of Abnormal and Social Psychology*, 1963, 67, 371-378.

Milner, B. Interhemispheric differences in the localization of psychological processes in man. *British Medical Bulletin*, 1971, 27 (3), 272-277.

Mischel, W. On the empirical dilemmas of psychodynamic approaches: Issues and alternatives. *Journal of Abnormal Psychology*, 1973, *82*, 335-344.

Mowrer, O. *The new group therapy.* Princeton, N.J.: Van Nostrand, 1964.

Murray, E., & Jacobson, L. The nature of learning in traditional and behavioral psychotherapy. In A.E. Bergin & S.L. Garfield (Eds.), Handbook of psychotherapy and behavior change. New York: Wiley, 1971.

Nakamura, C., & Broen, W. Further study of the effects of low drive states on competing responses. *Journal of Experimental Psychology*, 1965, *70*, 434-436.

Orne, M.T., The nature of hypnosis: Artifact and essence, *Journal of Abnormal and Social Psychology*, 1959, 58, 277-299.

Orne, M. Hypnosis, motivation and the ecological validity of the psychological experiment. In W.J. Arnold & M.M. Page (Eds.), *Nebraska Symposium on Motivation.* Lincoln: University of Nebraska Press, 1970.

Orne, M., Sheehan, I., & Evans, F. Occurrence of post hypnotic behavior outside the experimental setting. *Journal of Personality and Social Psychology*, 1968, *9*, 189-196.

Ornstein, R. *The psychology of consciousness.* New York: Viking, 1973.

Paul, G. Physiological effects of relaxation training and hypnotic suggestion. *Journal of Abnormal Psychology*, 1969, *74*, 425-437.

Perls, F. *Gestalt therapy verbatim.* Lafayette, Ca.: Real People Press, 1969.

Powers, W. *Behavior: The control of perception.* Chicago: Aldine, 1973.

Rachman, S. The role of muscular relaxation in desensitization therapy. *Behavior Research and Therapy*, 1968, *6*, 159-166.

Reid, L., Miller, H., Stone, D., Monico, K., Rassel, L., Taylor, C., & Sautter, F. Methods of deconditioning persisting avoidance. *JSAS Catalog of Selected Documents in Psychology*, 1973, *3*, 120.

Roberts, A., Kewman, D., & McDonald, H. Voluntary control of skin temperature: Unilateral changes using hypnosis and feedback. *Journal of Abnormal Psychology*, 1973, *82* (1), 163-168.

Rosenthal, R. *Experimenter effects in behavioral research.* New York: Appleton-Century Crofts, 1966.

Sarbin, T., & Andersen, M. Role-theoretical analysis of hypnotic behavior. In J.E. Gordon, *Handbook of Clinical and Experimental Hypnosis.* New York: Macmillan, 1967.

Sarbin, T., & Slagle, R. Hypnosis and psychophysiological outcomes. In E. Fromm & R. Shor, *Hypnosis research developments and perspectives.* Chicago: Aldine-Atherton, 1972.

Sachs, L. Construing hypnosis as modifiable behavior. In A. Jacobs (Ed.), *Psychology of private events.* New York: Academic Press, 1971.

Schachter, S. The interaction of cognitive and physiological determinants of emotional state. *Advances in experimental social psychology,* 1964, *1,* 49-80.

Seligman, M. Fall into helplessness. *Psychology Today,* 1973, *7,* 43-48.

Shapiro, A. Placebo effects in medicines, psychotherapy, and psychoanalysis. In A. Bergin & S. Garfield, *Handbook of psychotherapy and behavior change.* New York: Wiley, 1971.

Spence, K. *Behavior theory and conditioning.* New Haven: Yale University Press, 1956.

Sperry, R. The great cerebral commissure. *Scientific American,* 1964, *210* (1), 42-52.

Spiegel, H. A single treatment method to stop smoking using ancillary self hypnosis. *International Journal of Clinical and Experimental Hypnosis,* 1970, *18,* 235-250.

Spiegel, H. An eye-roll test of hypnotizability. *American Journal of Clinical Hypnosis,* 1972, *15,* 25-28.

Strupp, H., & Bloxom, A. Preparing lower class patients for group psychotherapy. *Journal of Consulting and Clinical Psychology,* 1973, *41,* 373-384.

Suedfeld, P. Changes in intellectual performance and in susceptibility to influence. In J.P. Zubek, *Sensory deprivation fifteen years of research.* New York: Appleton-Century Crofts, 1969.

Szasz, T. *The myth of mental illness.* New York: Harper & Row, 1961.

Terrace, H. Stimulus control. In W.K. Honig (Ed.), *Operant Behavior: Areas of Research and Application.* New York: Meredith Publishing Co., 1966.

Thistlewaite, D. Effects of social recognition upon the educational motivation of talented youth. *Journal of Educational Psychology,* 1959, *50,* 111-116.

Thompson, C. Introduction. In B. Wolstein, *Transference.* New York: Grune & Stratton, 1954.

Tori, C., & Worell, L. Reduction of human avoidant behavior: A comparison of counterconditioning, expectancy and cognitive information approaches. *Journal of Consulting and Clinical Psychology,* 1973, *41* (2), 269-278.

Travis, T., et al. Subjective aspects of the alpha enhancement situation. Unpublished paper, 1973.

Truax, C., Wargo, D., Carkhuff, R., Kodman, F., & Moles, E. Changes in self-concepts during group psychotherapy as a function of alternate sessions and vicarious therapy pretraining in institutionalized juvenile delinquents. *Journal of Consulting Psychology,* 1966, *30,* 309-314.

Truax, C., & Mitchell, K. Research on certain therapist interpersonal skills in relation to process and outcome. In A. Bergin & S. Garfield. (Eds.), *Handbook of psychotherapy and behavior change.* New York: Wiley, 1971.

Valenstein, E. *Brain control.* New York: Wiley, 1973.

Valins, S. The perception and labeling of bodily changes as determinants of emotional behavior. In P. Black (Ed.), *Physiological correlates of emotion.* New York: Academic Press, 1970.

Wallace, R. Physiological effects of trancendental meditation. *Science,* 1970, *167,* 1751-1754.

Weitzenhoffer, A. Eye blink rate and hypnosis: Preliminary findings. *Perceptual Motor Skills,* 1969, *38,* 671-676.

Weitzenhoffer, A., & Hilgard, E. *The Stanford Hypnotic Susceptibility Scales, Forms A & B.* Palo Alto, Ca.: Consulting Psychologists Press, 1959.

Wickramasekera, I. Reinforcement and/or transference in hypnosis and psychotherapy, a hypothesis. *American Journal of Clinical Hypnosis,* 1970, *12* (3), 137-140(a).

Wickramasekera, I. The effects of hypnosis and a control procedure on verbal conditioning. Unpublished manuscript, 1970. (b)

Wickramasekera, I. Effects of sensory restriction on susceptibility to hypnosis: A hypothesis and more preliminary data. *Journal of Abnormal Psychology,* 1970, *76* (1), 69-75. (c)

Wickramasekera, I. Goals and some methods in psychotherapy: Hypnosis and isolation. *American Journal of Clinical Hypnosis,* 1970, *13* (2), 95-100.(d)

Wickramasekera, I. Effects of "hypnosis" and task motivational instructions in attempting to influence the "voluntary" self-deprivation of money. *Journal of Personality and Social Psychology,* 1971, *19* (3), 311-314.

Wickramasekera, I. Instructions and EMG feedback in systematic desensitization: A case report. *Behavior Therapy,* 1972, *3* (3), 460-465. (a)

Wickramasekera, I. EMG feedback training and tension headache: Preliminary observations. *American Journal of Clinical Hypnosis,* 1972, *15,* 83-85. (b)

Wickramasekera, I. The effects of EMG feedback on hypnotic susceptibility. *Journal of Abnormal Psychology,* 1973, *82,* 74-77. (a)

Wickramasekera, I. Application of verbal instructions and EMG feedback training to the management of tension headache: Preliminary observations. *Headache,* 1973, 13 (2), 74-76. (b)

Wickramasekera, I. Temperature feedback for the control of migraine. *Behavior Therapy and Experimental Psychiatry,* 1973, *4,* 343-345. (c)

Wickramasekera, I. Broad spectrum behavior therapy for blepharospasm, *International Journal of Clinical and Experimental Hypnosis,* 1974, *3,* 209.

Wilkins, W. Desensitization: Social and cognitive factors underlying the effectiveness of Wolpe's procedure. *Psychological Bulletin,* 1971, *76,* 311-317.

Wolpe, J. *The practice of behavior therapy.* New York: Pergamon, 1969.

Wolpe, J., & Lazarus, A. *Behavior therapy techniques.* Oxford: Pergamon Press, 1966.

Wolpin, M., & Raines, J. Visual imagery expected roles and extinction. *Behavior Research and Therapy,* 1966, *54,* 55-58.

Zimbardo, P., Maslach, C., & Marshall, G. Hypnosis and the psychology of cognitive and behavioral control. In E. Fromm & R. Shor (Eds.), *Hypnosis: Research developments and perspectives.* Chicago: Aldine, 1972.

Zimbardo, P., Marshall, G., White, G., & Maslach, C. Objective assessment of hypnotically induced time distortion. *Science,* 1973, *181,* 4096.

Zubek, J. *Behavioral and physiological effects of prolonged sensory and perceptual deprivation: A review.* John P. Zubek, 1973.

An Eye-Roll Test
for Hypnotizability

Herbert Spiegel
Department of Psychiatry
College of Physicians and Surgeons
Columbia University
New York

In the course of informal clinical observation over the years, one phenomenon seemed to emerge with striking regularity. Those subjects who turned out to be deeply hypnotizable had impressive capacity to roll their eyes upward. Extra-ocular eye movements seemed more mobile and expressive. In contrast, those patients who turned out to be non-hypnotizable, did not in general, show this mobile extra-ocular movement.

After informal testing over a two-year period showed an apparent correlation, a more systematic study ensued.

This is a report of 2000 consecutive cases from October 1968 to June 1970 in which the same trance induction procedure was used by the examiner. Usually, one or more other physicians were present during the test procedure. In all cases, the induction was done in the clinical context as preparation for a psychotherapeutic procedure. All patients had clearly specific goals for which the hypnosis was being used. In no instance was the hypnotic induction done as an experiment simply to study the phenomenon of hypnosis itself, thereby differentiating these data from customary experimental data about hypnosis.

The trance state was graded on a 0-5 scale by means of a 10-minute Hypnotic Induction Profile procedure which is reported in detail elsewhere (Spiegel, 1970).

The Profile measures and correlates the pattern of neurophysiological response to signals for eye movements, arm levitaion, post-hypnotic subjective sensations, post-hypnotic motor compliance, ability to report with candor, cut-off compliance, and the degree of amnesia to the cut-off signal.

Definition of Hypnosis

Hypnosis is not sleep. Whatever sleep is, hypnosis is not (Anand et al., 1961). In an operational sense, hypnosis is a response to a signal from another or to an inner signal, which activates a capacity for a shift of awareness in the subject and permits a more intensive concentration upon a designated goal direction. This shift of attention is constantly sensitive to and responsive to cues from the hypnotist or the subject himself if properly trained.

More succinctly, hypnosis is a dynamic state of attentive, responsive concentration, even to the point of dissociation.

Test Procedure

The patient is asked to:

1. "Hold your head looking straight forward;
2. While holding your head in that position, look upward toward your eyebrows—now toward the top of your head (Up-Gaze);
3. While continuing to look upward, at the same time close your eyelids slowly (Roll) (Figure 1);
4. Now, open your eyes and let your eyes come back into focus."

The Up-Gaze and Roll are scored on a 0—4 scale.

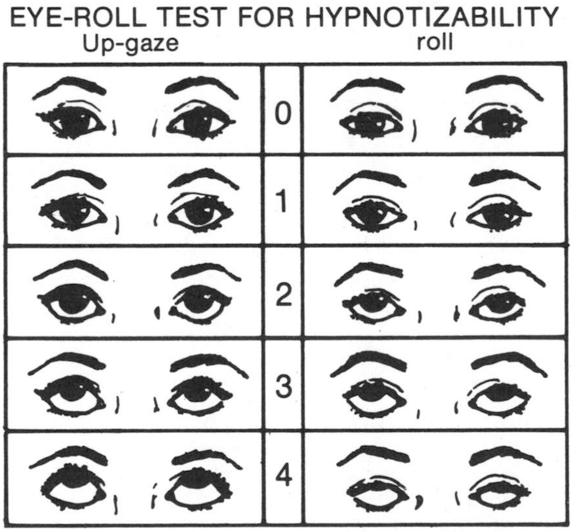

FIGURE 1. Eye-roll test for hypnotizability.

The amount of sclera visible between the lower eyelid and the lower edge of the cornea is the most practical measurement. A secondary measurement is upward movement of the cornea under the upper eyelid. Sometimes, during the Up—Gaze or Roll, an internal squint occurs. The degree varies on a 1—3 scale (Figure 2). The Squint score adds to the significance of the Up-Gaze and Roll score. (For example, an Up-Gaze 2 with a Roll 1 and Squint 2 is operationally equivalent to a Roll 3, or, Up-Grade 2, Roll 3.) This is a clinical "soft focus" observation which does not require discrete linear quantifications with optical measurement instruments. The entire procedure can be done in about five seconds.

EYE-ROLL TEST (SQUINT)

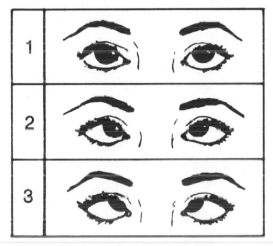

FIGURE 2. Eye-roll test (squint).

Results (Table 1)

1. Trance capacity was measured in terms of the Hypnotic Induction Profile which can be elicited in 5 to 10 minutes.

2. In about 75% of the 2000 consecutive cases, a five second examination of the Eye Roll Sign, graded from 0—4, accurately predicted hypnotic trance capacity (Figure 3).

3. In one out of four cases, the positive Eye Roll Sign was misleading (Figure 3).

4. The Hypnotic Induction Profile filtered out these false positive eye signs.

TABLE 1

HYPNOTIC INDUCTION PROFILE—2000 CASES

	Grade*	No. of Cases	% of Cases
Correlate with Eye Roll	1	183	9.2
	2	490	24.5
	3	447	22.4
	4—5	246	12.3
	0	114	5.5
No Correlation with Eye Roll	Decrement & Erratic	510	25.2
	Misc. (Unclassifiable)	12	0.6
Total		2002	99.7**

* Grades 1, 2, 3, 4-5, and 0 correlate with Eye Roll. Decrement & Erratic do not.
** Rounding error.

5. Ninety-nine percent of the hypnotizable group showed a positive Eye Roll Sign, *i.e.,* scored above zero. Less than 1 percent of the hypnotizable group had a grade 0 Roll.

6. Using the above measurements, in a series of 2000 consecutive psychotherapy cases:

a. About seven out of ten patients were hypnotizable to some degree.

b. About one out of eight was extremely hypnotizable.

Theoretical Speculations

1. The remarkable correlation between the Eye Roll and hypnotizability suggests that trance capacity is either genetically determined or learned so early in life at something like an imprint level that the circuitry is essentially physiological or structural rather than psychological (Spiegel, 1965).

2. Now that we know something about the nature of sleep, it is clear that whatever sleep is, hypnosis is not. Hypnosis is characterized by a contraction of peripheral awareness and an increase in focal attention. The essence of hypnosis is related to the ability to concentrate in an attentive, responsive manner, even to the point of dissociation. When the sleep concept of hypnosis was abandoned, this test discovery followed.

3. It is generally observed that when a person wants to concen-

HYPNOTIZABILITY DISTRIBUTION
2000 CONSECUTIVE THERAPY CASES

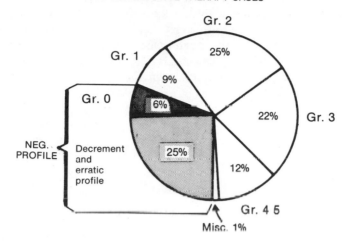

FIGURE 3. Hypnotizability distribution.

trate intensely without interference, one postural stance is to look upward. Sometimes this is followed by eye closure and is consistent with the need to reduce peripheral awareness to facilitate focal attention. The Eye Roll test is an extension of this.

4. Alpha rhythms are associated with attentive, meditative states of concentration (Wallace, 1970).

5. Vertical up-gaze is associated with alpha rhythm. Vertical movement also has bilateral representation; thus, more integration, in contrast to horizontal eye movement which has unilateral representation. Mentation defects involve bilateral cerebrums (Mulholland & Evans, 1966).

6. This Eye Roll test seems to tap a capacity for experiencing a mode which seems related to Primary Process in the psychoanalytic sense. Yet it is an organized aspect of what can be an overall chaotic clinical mosaic.

7. Understanding hypnotic phenomena requires an understanding of the physiological factors in memory, concentration, and amnesia. Until we know these, data like this eye-roll correlation contribute to our peripheral knowledge.

Conclusions and Implications

1. Quick appraisals for hypnotizability are now feasible. In 5 to 10 seconds, a highly probable estimation can be made. The degree of Eye

Roll roughly correlates with hypnotizability. In 5—10 minutes the Hypnotic Induction Profile measurement can provide the clinician an opportunity to grade this capacity with sharper focus and more certainty.

2. In the past, a serious deterrent for using hypnosis in therapy was the claim that it took too much time to determine with whom it could be used. The Eye Roll sign and the Hypnotic Induction Profile not only answer that complaint, but they open the way to use hypnosis more frequently to accelerate primary treatment strategies.

References

Anand, B. K., China, G. S., & Sing, B. Some aspects of electroencephalographic studies in Yogis. *Electroencephalography and Clinic Neurophysiology*, 1961, *13*, 452-456.

Mulholland, T., & Evans, C. Oculomotor function and the alpha-activation cycle. *Nature*, 1966, *211*, 1278-1279.

Spiegel, H. Imprinting, hypnotizability and learning as factors in the psychotherapeutic process. *American Journal of Clinical Hypnosis*, 1965, *7*, 221-225.

Spiegel, H. & Bridger, A. A. *Manual for hypnotic induction profile.* New York, N.Y.: Soni Medica, Inc, 1970.

Wallace, R. K. Physiological effects of transcendental meditation. *Science*, 1970, *167*, 1751-1754.

Effects of Sensory Restriction on Susceptibility to Hypnosis: A Hypothesis and More Preliminary Data

Ian Wickramasekera
University of Illinois
College of Medicine
Peoria

The psychoanalytic theory of Gill and Brenman (1959) predicts that a prior sensory restriction procedure will enhance susceptibility to hypnosis. A series of experiments with children and adults (Adams, 1964; Adams, Robertson, & Cooper, 1963; Bexton, Heron, & Scott, 1954; Cooper, Adams & Gibby, 1962; Gaines & Vetter, 1968; Gerwirtz & Baer, 1958a, 1958b; Gibby, Adams, & Carrera, 1960; Heron, 1961; Pavio, 1963; Staples & Walters, 1961; Stevenson & Odom, 1962; Suedfeld, 1964; Walters & Karal, 1960; Walters, Marshall, & Shooter, 1960; Walters & Ray, 1960) stemming from what may broadly be termed a social learning orientation has found that prior social restriction and sensory deprivation procedures used as "setting events" (Kantor, 1959) seem to enhance the acquisition of a wide range of responses (e.g., simple psychomotor tasks, verbal conditioning, suggestibility in the autokinetic situation, susceptibility to social influence, and susceptibility to propaganda, and psychotherapy). Restricting social stimuli may differ from restricting sensory stimuli on a number of dimensions, but it is tentatively hypothesized that sensory restriction is a quantitatively stronger treatment than the restriction of social stimuli.

There have been at least two interpretations of these results: *(a)* An interpretation consistent with the Gewirtz and Baer (1958b) hypothesis suggests that the restriction of social stimuli is the crucial procedure and that the reinforcer value of social stimuli may be altered by deprivation and satiation procedures. *(b)* Walters et al. (1960) have hypothesized that isolation and sensory deprivation procedures activate anxiety, and it is this which causes the facilitation effect.

A pilot study (Wickramasekera, 1969a) appeared to suggest that sensory restriction increased hypnotic susceptibility in a sample of female college students. Since the first draft of this paper was written, it has been brought to my attention that a very similar study (Pena, 1963) also found that "perceptual isolation" increased hypnotic susceptibility as measured by the Stanford Hypnotic Susceptibility Scale. The Pena study used 45 male prisoners, divided into one control and two experimental groups. The experimental Groups 2 and 3 were exposed to 1½ and 3 hours of sensory restriction (visual, auditory, and kinesthetic modalities), respectively, and immediately retested for hypnotic susceptibility. The control group was simply retested 24 hours later. The results of this study indicated that all three groups showed statistically significant gains in hypnotizability, but that the enhancement scores of the three groups were ordered in the direction which is consistent with the hypothesis. Group III obtained the greatest enhancement and the control group the lowest [Pena, 1963, p. 69].

The enhancement scores of Group 3 (3 hours of sensory restriction) were significantly greater than those of Group 2 (1½ hours of sensory restriction) and Group 1 (control group). But Group 2 and Group 1 did not differ significantly in terms of gain. Pena concluded that "stress and body image distortions as products of perceptual isolation were associated with the enhancement of hypnotizability [p. 70]." The procedure used with the control group appears to be unsatisfactory as even the author pointed out. The present writer recognized a similar weakness in his own pilot study (Wickramasekera, 1969a), and in a separate paper (Wickramasekera, 1969b) he proposed some theoretical reasons for using a different control procedure in research on sensory restriction.

Based on Hull's (1933) view that hypnosis shares parameters with learning, three hypotheses were formulated: *(a)* A prior sensory restriction procedure would enhance susceptibility to hypnosis. *(b)* A prior treatment which combined sensory restriction and "anxiety" (a set of pretreatment verbal instructions) arousal will enhance susceptibility to hypnosis to an even more significant degree. *(c)* There will be no enhancement of hypnotic susceptibility in a control group that experienced neither prior sensory restriction nor "anxiety" arousal.

Method

Hypnotic susceptibility was measured with the Stanford Hypnotic Susceptibility Scale (SHSS). Forms A and B of the Stanford scale are essentially parallel forms. An operational definition of hypnotic susceptibility which permits behavioral measurement is given as "the number of times the subject acts like a hypnotized person when hypnosis is induced by a standard procedure [Weitzenhoffer & Hilgard, 1959, p. 5]." The scale is composed of 12 "work samples," items which are presented to *S* within a standardized hypnosis induction. The reliability (Hilgard, 1965, p. 69) and validity (Hilgard, 1965, pp. 216-217) of the scale were reported to be adequate for research purposes.

TABLE 1

COMPARISON OF GROUPS WITH REGARD TO MEAN AGE, IQ, AND EDUCATION

Group	Mean		
	Age	IQ	Education
1 (Control)	19.06	111.6	9.2
2	19.40	112.00	9.60
3	19.26	111.13	8.86
Combined	19.24	111.57	9.22

Subjects

A total of 45 male Caucasian prisoners of a state reformatory in a midwestern state were *S*s in the study. Prisoners who were convicted for homicide or with any previous known psychiatric history, sex offenses, or who were physically handicapped or mentally subnormal (IQ below 90) were eliminated from the pool of potential *S*s. A decision was made to drop any *S*s chosen for the study who, before the pretest or between pretesting and posttesting, spent any time in solitary. The *S*s were screened for age, IQ, and educational achievement from prison records. After the screening, a pool of 65 *S*s was assembled and asked to volunteer for a psychological experiment, the nature of which was not specified. Volunteers were promised two packets of cigarettes as a reward for their participation. They were asked to volunteer 2—3 hours of their time for an interesting and important psychological experiment. The volunteers were then told that the study involved the induction of hypnosis, and those who did not want to participate were invited to leave. Only 2 *S*s withdrew from the study at this point. Forty-five *S*s from the pool of 51 *S*s were randomly assigned to one of the three groups of 15 *S*s each. No information about the sensory restriction procedure was conveyed to *S*s until they were seen individually.

As can be seen in Table 1, there is very little difference among the groups with regard to mean age, education, and Beta IQ. It seems safe to assume that the three groups were random samples from the same population insofar as these three variables are concerned.

Apparatus

Sensory restriction conditions were established by using padded earphones, white noise, goggles and cotton gloves. The need for silence and immobility was stressed.

The experimental treatment rooms were two large offices furnished with only two chairs and a table. There were no pictures or other ornamentation in the room. Two overhead parallel fluorescent lamps were switched on at all times.

The Ss wore goggles whose lenses were removed and replaced with heavy black cardboard discs to keep out light. They also wore loose-fitting heavy cotton gloves which reached their wrists.

Procedure

All Ss in the three groups received Form A of the SHSS during their first interview. Twenty-four hours later, all Ss were retested on Form B. Hence, it is to be noted that all Ss were tested and retested with equivalent time intervals. The standardized induction of hypnosis consumes about 45—50 minutes on each testing. The experimental design of this study used 45 Ss randomly assigned to three groups of 15 Ss each.

Group 1, the control group, experienced no sensory restriction prior to retesting on Form B. When they entered the sensory restriction chamber prior to retesting on Form B, they were read the following instructions:

Today you will do nothing for one hour before you are tested again for hypnotic susceptibility. You may look at the magazines on this table and listen to the radio on these earphones for one hour before we are ready to work with you in the next room.

The E then sat down in front of the S, proceeded to read a magazine, and generally discouraged conversation or verbal responses from S by responding to any questions with a repetition of the foregoing instructions. The Ss in this control group spent 1 hour sitting on the same chair used in sensory restriction, listening to music from a local radio station, and looking at magazines. At the termination of 1 hour, the control Ss were wide awake and were all read the following instructions: "Please come with me now to the next room so that I may retest you for hypnotic susceptibility."

After each *S* in Group 2 was seated on the chair, the following instructions were read verbatim to him:

Today you will do nothing for one hour before you are tested again for hypnotic susceptibility. You will sit in the chair and wear these gloves, headphones, and goggles. It is very important that you do not speak, touch your body, or move during this one-hour period. I will remove the apparatus when your hour is up. Try not to fall asleep; I will be in this room with you at all times.

All questions from *S*s were responded to by repeating the relevant passages of the above instructions. The apparatus was then put on *S*, and *E* sat down in front of the *S* about 5 ft. from him. At the end of 1 hour, the headphones, gloves, and goggles were removed in that sequence. The following instructions were then read to *S*: "Please follow me now to the office next door so that we may begin the retesting of your hypnotic susceptibility."

The time spent moving from the termination of sensory restriction to the initiation of Form B of the SHSS ranged 1—2 minutes for *S*s in all three groups. All *S*s in Group 2 conformed to the request for silence and immobility except for sporadic movements.

When each *S* in Group 3 entered the sensory restriction room, he was read the following instructions:

Today you will do nothing for one hour before you are tested again for hypnotic susceptibility. You will sit in this chair and wear these headphones, gloves, and goggles for one hour. It is very important that you do not speak, touch your body, or move during this one-hour period. You may at times feel that you are going "stir crazy" and you may even hear or see and feel unusual *things* during this period. But do not be afraid of them, I will be here in this room at all times watching you and ready to help you if you should need help. I will be watching you at all times and I assure you that no harm will come to you. It is very important that you remain in this apparatus for one hour.

The demand for silence was conformed to by only seven *S*s. Eight *S*s broke silence from one to four times for brief periods, requesting that the apparatus be removed. All these requests were responded to by a momentary removal of one earphone and the statement, "Please hang on a little longer," or "It is very important that you hang on a little longer."

The demand for immobility was violated by all *S*s in Group 3, and considerable sporadic small and large muscle movements were noted. But *E* was able to keep the apparatus on all *S*s until the full 60 minutes were up.

The *E* did all the testing, both in the sensory restriction and hypnosis induction situations. To avoid biases due to change in test administration skill resulting from increasing practice on the part of *E*, one *S* from each group was tested at each sitting (e.g., one *S* from each group, then a second, etc., i.e., 1,2,3,1,2,3,etc.).

Hypotheses

1. There will be no significant difference between Form A and Form B scores for *S*s in the control group (Group 1 *S*s).
2. The Forms B and B-A (difference) scores will be significantly larger in experimental groups (Groups 2 and 3) than in the control group (Group 1).
3. The B-A scores in Group 3 will be significantly larger than those in Group 2.

Results

This study was designed to determine if sensory restriction and "anxiety" arousal are associated with the enhancement of hypnotic susceptibility. One-tailed tests of significance were used since the experimental hypotheses specified the direction of the score changes.

The data from the SHSS were analyzed with nonparametric (Siegel, 1956) tests for the following reasons: first, because the data from the SHSS are at best ordinal in nature; second because not enough is yet known about the distribution of this type of data (Hilgard, 1965); and, finally, because the use of such statistics involves less restrictive assumptions than parametric statistics.

In order to determine if any of the groups manifested changes in hypnotizability in either direction between pretesting and posttesting, the Wilcoxon matched-pairs signed-ranks test was applied. The control group demonstrated no statistically significant changes, but both experimental groups demonstrated an enhancement of hypnotic susceptibility significant beyond the .005 level.

To determine if there were any statistically significant differences between the three sets of scores (Forms A, B, and B-A) compared together, the Kruskal-Wallis one-way analysis of variance test was applied to Form A scores, Form B scores, and Form B-A scores.

The Form A or pretest scores were compared to determine if the three groups were equated in terms of initial susceptibility, and they were found not to differ to a statistically significant degree (Ho accepted at .05 level). A similar analysis of the posttreatment (B scores) and B-A scores demonstrated a difference statistically significant beyond the .001 level.

The ranked enhancement (B-A) scores of Groups 1 and 2, 1 and 3, and 3 and 2 were compared by means of the Mann-Whitney *U* test. The enhancement scores of Groups 1 and 2 and 1 and 3 demonstrated differences statistically significant beyond the .002 level. The enhancement scores of Group 3 were not significantly higher than those of Group 2 ($p<.10$). For ordinal data of this type and considering the grossness of the measuring device (SHSS), such a difference may be a meaningful one.

The results of the present study and the previous pilot study (Wickramasekera, 1969a) by the present author generally support the earlier findings of Pena (1963). But they do not confirm the Pena study in at least two important respects. In neither of our studies did we find a statistically significant increase in hypnotizability in the control group even though the length of time between pretesting and posttesting was similar to that used in the Pena study (1963). The second major respect in which the present findings conflict with the Pena study is that the Pena study suggests that 1½ hours of sensory restriction may not be adequate to demonstrate a statistically significant gain in hypnotizability. Both studies done by the present writer suggest that a period of sensory restriction, even as brief as ½ hour, may be sufficient to escalate hypnotizability. This situation suggests that the duration of sensory restriction per se may be only one of the crucial variables involved in this procedure. The rather weak attempt to manipulate *S* expectancies in the context of the present study appears to confirm, at least in terms of a trend, the role of expectancies when hypnotizability is the depended variable. The review by Zuckerman (1969) suggested that *S* expectancies may play a major role in the more general effects of sensory restriction procedures. Another factor which may complicate the interpretation of the results of these three similar studies is chronological age (Hilgard, 1965). There was in excess of a 10-year difference between the mean age of *S*s in the Pena study and in both studies done by the present author.

Hence, in summary, it may be stated that the first two formal experimental hypotheses were clearly supported by the results of the present study. But the status of the third hypothesis is dubious.

Discussion

In view of the nature and small size of this sample, caution is required in drawing conclusions and generalizing from these data. A previous pilot study (Wickramasekera, 1969a) with a sample of 16 female undergraduates produced similar "enhancement effects" in the experimental group.

In this study, the variable which has been termed "need for social approval" could not be controlled statistically. An attempt was made to control for it experimentally, but there is no indication of the degree to which the experimental control through randomization was achieved.

An effort was made to make the control procedure as similar as possible to the experimental procedures without actually involving sensory restriction. But the experimental hypotheses may still have been implicitly conveyed (Orne, 1959) to Ss by even the minor differences in the control and experimental procedures.

The independent variable in this study, sensory restriction, is a very gross one, and there is a clear need for more precise experimental parametric studies of it. Also, the possibility of E bias in the administration of even a standardized scale like the SHSS must be considered.

The voluntary submission of the experimental Ss to an unpleasant procedure like sensory restriction may have increased the general interpersonal influence of E. A future control for this may include subjecting a control group to an equally unpleasant procedure which does not include sensory restriction per se.

This study appears to suggest that sensory restriction may increase hypnotic susceptibility. Until recently (Pascal & Salzburg, 1959; Sachs & Anderson, 1967), hypnotizability has been regarded as generally unmodifiable (Hilgard, 1965).

If hypnotic susceptibility is increased by a procedure that also enhances verbal conditioning and simple learning, it suggests that hypnosis may share parameters with learning and motivation. This, of course, was the direction of Clark Hull's (1933) pioneering research in experimental hypnosis.

A series of reports (Frank, 1965; Goldstein, 1962; Jackson, 1960; Orne, 1962, 1964; Platonov, 1959) have indicated the power of "demand characteristics" (Orne, 1959), or expectancies stemming from explicit or implicit suggestions, to affect the results of both psychological experiments and psychotherapy. Imber, Frank, Nash, and Gliedman (1956) have reported a positive relationship between suggestibility and stay in psychotherapy. Heller (1963) implied that "good" psychotherapy patients and "good" Ss in laboratory social psychological research on persuasion are notably similar. Frank (1965) has reported that psychotherapeutic gains effected by an inert placebo have been maintained up to 5 years. Frank, Nash, Stone, and Imber (1963) reported a significant overall improvement in 109 psychiatric outpatients receiving a placebo. Paul (1966) reported that a placebo treatment was as powerful a tool as psychologists using an "insight" focused treatment procedure. Rosenthal and Fodes (1963) reported that expectancies affect even laboratory research with animals.

The placebo effect is a uniquely psychological effect, and, hence, it makes sense to use it rather than eliminate it in psychological treatment procedures (Patterson, 1966). Krasner and Ullman (1965) noted that "It seems reasonable to maximize placebo effects in the treatment situation to increase the likelihood of client change [p. 230]." Freud's recognition of the importance of what today is called the "placebo effect" is clearly indicated by the following statements:

> In the first place, let me remind you that psychotherapy is in no way a modern method of healing . . . in order to effect a cure a condition of "expectant faith" was induced in sick persons. . . . We have learned to use the word "suggestion" for this phenomenon, and Mobius has taught us that the unreliability which we deplore in so many of our therapeutic measures may be traced back actually to the disturbing influence of this very powerful factor. . . . Is it not then a justifiable endeavor on the part of a physician to seek to control this factor, to use it with a purpose, and to direct and strengthen it? This and nothing else is what scientific psychotherapy proposes [1959, pp. 250-251].

Hypnosis is one of the oldest purely psychological techniques for manipulating human expectancies. But the fact that under normal circumstances only a limited number of people are hypnotizable contributed to its neglect. The development of routine rapid techniques (sensory restriction) of increasing the proportion of hypnotizable patients may render hypnosis more widely usable as a pretreatment procedure. Essentially, it is suggested that patient expectancies be appropriately "primed" through hypnosis prior to actual treatment to increase the patient's readiness for the kinds of learning that await him in psychotherapy, or that hypnosis be used to increase the therapist's reinforcer value to the client.

Susceptibility to social influence and to propaganda have been shown to be enhanced by isolation procedures, and the anxiety arousal interpretation of this effect seems to have the widest support. If prior isolation procedures can also be shown to facilitate the effects of psychotherapy and counseling, then there would be movement made in the direction of demonstrating that such apparently discontinuous procedures as psychotherapy, hypnosis, thought reform (Frank, 1965), or "brainwashing," counseling, and verbal conditioning share at least one gross motivational parameter. Clinical lore (Wolberg, 1954) and theory (Freud, 1959; Rogers, 1951) already suggest that a minimum level of patient anxiety is necessary for a positive psychotherapeutic outcome.

Mowrer (1960) has previously suggested that all learning is "sign learning" and that effective manipulation of the contingencies of fear and hope facilitate learning. The use of isolation and hypnosis as "setting events" (Kantor, 1959) aimed at such contingencies may do something to increase the effectiveness of current psychological treatment procedures. Specifically, hypnosis may be used systematically to heighten the therapist's reinforcer value (hope), and sensory restriction may be used when necessary to induce the level of anxiety arousal or social deprivation which will most accelerate the rate of therapeutic learning.

References

Adams, H. B. Therapeutic potentialities of sensory deprivation procedures. *International Mental Health Research Newsletter,* 1964, *6,* 7-9.

Adams, H. B., Robertson, M. H., & Cooper, G. D. Facilitating therapeutic personality changes in psychiatric patients by sensory deprivation methods. Paper presented at the meeting of the 18th International Congress of Psychology, Washington, D. C., August 1963.

Bexton, W. H., Heron, W., & Scott, T. H. Effects of decreased variation in sensory environment. *Canadian Journal Psychology,* 1954, *8,* 70-76.

Cooper, G. D., Adams, H. B., & Gibby, R. G. Ego strength changes following perceptual deprivation. *Archives of General Psychiatry,* 1962, *7,* 75-79.

Frank, J. D. *Persuasion and healing.* New York: Schocken Books, 1965.

Frank, J. D., Nash, E. H., Stone, A. R., & Imber, S. D. Immediate and long-term symptomatic course of psychiatric outpatients. *American Journal Psychiatry,* 1963, *120,* 429-439.

Freud, S. *Collected papers,* Vol. 1. New York: Basic Books, 1959.

Gaines, L. S., & Vetter, H. J. Sensory deprivation and psychotherapy. *Psychotherapy: Theory, Research and Practice,* 1968, *5,* 7-12.

Gewirtz, J. L. & Baer, D. M. The effect of brief social deprivation on behaviors for a social reinforcer. *Journal of Abnormal and Social Psychology,* 1958, *56,* 49-56. (a)

Gewirtz, J. L., & Baer, D. M. Deprivation and satiation of social reinforcers as drive conditions. *Journal of Abnormal and Social Psychology,* 1958, *57,* 165-172. (b)

Gibby, R. G., Adams, H. B., & Carrera, R. N. Therapeutic changes in psychiatric patients following partial sensory deprivation. *Archives of General Psychiatry,* 1960, *3,* 57-64.

Gill, M. N., & Brenman, M. *Hypnosis and related states: Psychoanalytic studies in regression.* New York: International Universities Press, 1959.

Goldstein, A. P. *Therapist-patient expectancies in psychotherapy.* New York: Pergamon, 1962.

Heller, K. Experimental analogues of psychotherapy: The clinic relevance of laboratory findings of social influence. *Journal of Nervous and Mental Disease,* 1963, *137,* 420-426.

Heron, W. Cognitive and physiological effects of perceptual isolation. In P. Solomon (Ed.), *Sensory deprivation.* Cambridge, Mass.: Harvard University Press, 1961.

Hilgard, E. R. *Hypnotic-susceptibility.* New York: Harcourt, Brace & World, 1965.

Hull, C. L. *Hypnosis and suggestibility: An experimental approach.* New York: Appleton-Century, 1933.

Imber, S. D., Frank, J. D., Nash, E. H., & Gliedman, L. H. Suggestibility, social class and the acceptance of psychotherapy. *Journal of Clinical Psychology,* 1956, *12,* 341-344.

Jackson, C. W. An exploratory study of the role of suggestion in research on sensory deprivation. Unpublished doctoral dissertation, University of Michigan, 1960.

Kantor, J. R. *Interbehavioral psychology.* (2nd ed.) Bloomington, Ind.: Principia Press, 1959.

Krasner, L., & Ullman, L. P. (Eds.), *Research in behavior modification.* New York: Holt, Rinehart & Winston, 1965.

Mowrer, O. H. *Learning theory and behavior.* New York: Wiley, 1960.

Orne, M. T. The nature of hypnosis: Artifact and essence. *Journal of Abnormal and Social Psychology,* 1959, *58,* 277-299.

Orne, M. T. On the social psychology of the psychological experiment. *American Psychologist,* 1962, *17,* 776-783.

Orne, M. T., & Scheibe, K. E. The contribution of nondeprivation factors in the production of sensory deprivation effects. *Journal of Abnormal and Social Psychology,* 1964, *68,* 8-12.

Pascal, G. R., & Salzberg, H. C. A systematic approach to inducing hypnotic behavior. *International Journal of Clinical and Experimental Hypnosis,* 1959, *7,* 161-167.

Patterson, C. H. *Theories of counseling and psychotherapy.* New York: Harper & Row, 1966.

Paul, G. L. *Insight vs. desensitization.* Stanford, Calif.: Stanford University Press, 1966.

Pavio, A. Audience influence, social isolation, and speech. *Journal of Abnormal and Social Psychology,* 1963, *67,* 247-253.

Pena, F. Perceptual isolation and hypnotic susceptibility. Unpublished doctoral dissertation, Washington State University, 1963.

Platonov, H. I. *The word as a physiological and therapeutic factor.* (2nd ed.) Moscow: Foreign Languages Publishing House, 1959.

Rogers, C. R. *Client-centered therapy.* Boston: Houghton Mifflin, 1951.

Rosenthal, R., & Fodes, K. L. The effect of experimenter bias on the performance of the albino rat. *Behavioral Science,* 1963, *8,* 183-189.

Sachs, L. B., & Anderson, W. L. Modification of hypnotic susceptibility. *International Journal of Clinical and Experimental Hypnosis,* 1967, *4,* 172-180.

Siegel, S. *Nonparametric statistics.* New York: McGraw-Hill, 1956.

Staples, F. R., & Walters, R. A. Anxiety, birth order and susceptibility to social influence. *Journal of Abnormal and Social Psychology,* 1961, *62,* 716-719.

Stevenson, H. W., & Odom, R. D. The effectiveness of social reinforcement following two conditions of deprivation. *Journal of Abnormal and Social Psychology,* 1962, *65,* 429-430.

Suedfeld, P. Attitude manipulation in restricted environments. *Journals of Abnormal and Social Psychology,* 1964, *68,* 242-247.

Walters, R. H., & Karal, P. Social deprivation and verbal behavior. *Journal of Personality,* 1960, *28,* 89-107.

Walters, R. H., Marshall, W. E., & Shooter, J. R. Anxiety, isolation, and susceptibility to social influence. *Journal of Personality,* 1960, *28,* 518-529.

Walters, R. H., & Quinn, M. T. The effects of social and sensory deprivation on autokinetic judgments. *Journal of Personality,* 1960, *28,* 210-219.

Walters, R. H., & Ray, E. Anxiety, social isolation, and reinforcer effectiveness. *Journal of Personality,* 1960, *28,* 358-367.

Weitzenhoffer, A. M., & Hilgard, E. R. *Stanford Hypnotic Susceptibility Scale, Forms A and B.* Palo Alto, Calif.: Consulting Psychologists Press, 1959.

Wickramasekera, I. The effects of sensory restriction on susceptibility to hypnosis, a hypothesis and some preliminary data. *International Journal of Clinical Experimental Hypnosis,* 1969, *17,* 217-224(a).

Wickramasekera, I. Reinforcement and/or transference in hypnosis and psychotherapy: A hypothesis. *American Journal of Clinical Hypnosis,* 1969, *12,* 137-140. (b)

Wolberg, L. R. *The technique of psychotherapy.* New York: Grune & Stratton, 1954.

Zuckerman, M. Variables affecting deprivation results. In J. Zubek (Ed.), *Sensory deprivation, fifteen years of research.* New York: Appleton-Century-Crofts, 1969.

The Modification of Hypnotic Behavior or Extending the Verbal Control of Complex Human Behavior

Ian Wickramasekera

University of Illinois
College of Medicine
Peoria

Until recently, hypnotizability has been regarded as relatively unmodifiable behavior (Hilgard, 1965; Shor, Orne and O'Connell, 1966; London, 1969; Gill and Brenman, 1959). Several psychotherapist-hypnotists have implied that hypnotizability can be significantly altered (Bernheim, 1884; Erickson, 1952; Moll, 1958). It appears likely that the early interpersonal techniques (Gill and Brenman, 1959; As, Hilgard, and Weitzenhoffer, 1963) used to modify hypnotizability were relatively ineffective because the specific experiential behavioral targets of change were poorly defined and the interventions unsystematic. Recently the following procedures have been found to be promising approaches to disinhibiting or shaping-up expanded hypnotic repertoires: 1) verbally and behaviorally (modeling) presented instructions and training directed at private events, (e.g., attention, imagery, misconception, critical thinking, sensory focus, and comfort under conditions of fading reality orientation); 2) training in interpersonal risk-taking, closeness, self-disclosure, and arranging the conditions for "trust"; 3) special procedures intended to alter perception (sensory deprivation and psychedelic drugs); 4) biofeedback training procedures (EEG and EMG).

Shor, Orne, and O'Connell (1966) have stated that it is important to distinguish between variations in hypnotic performance and the modification of hypnotizability per se. But it is important to note that all statements about changes in hypnotizability are necessarily inferences from performance because hypnotizability per se, like learning, is an unobservable construct. From a practical standpoint, it is important to know

1) if the four general types of prehypnotic procedures identified above will reliably expand hypnotic behavior (response to test suggestions) above baseline levels;

2) if the expanded hypnotic repertoire will generalize to a standard induction procedure minus the special prehypnotic procedures;

3) if changes induced in hypnotic performance in the laboratory will generalize to the clinical situation;

4) if prehypnotic procedures that are reliably effective in the laboratory will also be reliably effective in the clinic.

It is also important to know if these four general types of hypnosis increasing interventions have the most impact on initially (baseline measurement) low or moderately hypnotizable subjects. It would also be useful to know which technique to use with which type of subject and which experimental procedures are most suitable for shaping-up or disinhibiting which hypnotic phenomena. Unfortunately, secure answers to all the above questions are not yet in.

The procedures to be outlined below appear to increase significantly the probability of boosting hypnotic performances above baseline levels by facilitating the subject's skill in manipulating internal events or by educating him subjectively. Through subjective education or the development of effective and reliable skills in controlling private events (thoughts and their physiological consequences), the range of personal self-management and control may be expanded beyond the limits that are environmentally imposed. It is probable that if subjective education is made part of the regular elementary and secondary school curricula there will be a less sharp drop-off in longitudinal curves of hypnotizability and related phenomena from childhood to adulthood. It is also possible that the average adult who comes to the psychotherapist will bring with him more subjective skills and a higher baseline of subjective education, which, of course, may improve the prognosis for therapy. Hypnotic training, biofeedback, transcendental meditation, and related procedures may contribute to a technology of subjective education.

The following techniques appear to increase the probability of disinhibiting hypnotic experience:

(1) *Verbally and behaviorally (modeling) presented systematic instructions and training directed at private events.* It has been shown that modifying a subject's expectations regarding hypnosis either in the direction of inculcating positive attitudes or correcting misconceptions can

increase hypnotizability. Positive attitudes may be induced by defining the situations as easy to respond to, a pleasant and interesting experience, and a consent situation (Barber and Calverley, 1964, 1966; Diamond, 1972). Positive expectations may also be experimentally induced by manipulating a subject's estimates of his own ability to respond (Wilson, 1967; Gandolfo, 1971; Gregory and Diamond, 1973). For example, Wilson (1967) used unobtrusive types of "prompts" (e.g., hidden lights, etc.) to increase the probability that the subject would experience hypnotic suggestions. Gregory and Diamond (1973) used false personality test results to alter in a positive direction a subject's expectation of hypnotic experience.

Positive attitudes toward hypnosis may also be elicited by exposing hypnotic subjects to a very susceptible hypnotic model who verbalizes his or her subjective experiences, sensations, and responses to the discrete hypnotic suggestions. Inviting the subjects whose hypnotizability is to be increased to question the highly susceptible hypnotic model raises the probability of increasing hypnotizability. A model who has high status in a context that is relevant to the hypnotic subject appears to contribute to the enhancement of hypnotizability (De Voge and Sachs, 1973). In general, exposing hypnotic subjects to a highly susceptible hypnotic model, who openly verbalizes his or her subjective reactions to hypnosis and who responds freely to questions will increase the probability of hypnotic responses in participating observers (Zimbardo, Rapaport and Baron, 1969; Marshall and Diamond, 1969; Diamond, 1972; De Voge and Sachs, 1973; De Stefano, 1971).

The alteration of misconceptions regarding hypnosis and provision of counterinformation will also raise the probability of hypnotic response (Cronin, Spanos and Barber, 1971; Diamond, 1972; Gregory and Diamond, 1973; Diamond and Harada, 1973). Exposure of misconceptions and provision of counterinformation may be provided by written instructions on paper, by the observation and questioning of a highly susceptible hypnotic model, or by looking at a responsive hypnotic model on videotape. Extinguishing anxieties which stem from misconceptions like loss of consciousness, loss of personal self-control, inability to wake from hypnosis, and so forth is also a powerful cognitive procedure to increase hypnotizability.

The systematic provision of information and training (self-paced successive approximations) on what to do internally (privately and experientially) provided by a responsive hypnotic model or through verbal instructions will also increase hypnotizability (Pascal and Salzberg, 1959; Sachs and Anderson, 1967; Zimbardo, Rapaport and Baron, 1969; Diamond, 1972; Gregory and Diamond, 1973; Diamond and Harada, 1973; Sachs, 1970). The following are effective procedures: 1) provision of a clear verbal concept of the desired sensory experience; 2) the use of "prompts" to shape up vivid sensory experiences (e.g., to acquaint subject with immediate sensations of heaviness, place a heavy weight on hands); 3) self-paced successive approximations using just noticeable-difference (JND) steps; 4) structuring the procedure to place the subject in a double-bind situation where he has to validate his subjective report with increased objective performance. In essence, this is a cognitive dissonance procedure; 5) inviting the subject to imagine vividly, to suspend reality orientation and critical judgment and to permit himself to become totally absorbed (e.g., like at an exciting movie); 6) verbal reinforcement of hypnotic responsivity; 7) eliciting the subject's active responsible participation by the use of task relevant motivational instructions presented either verbally or in the form of a programmed text (Havens, 1973).

(2) *Training intra- and interpersonal risk-taking.* I hypothesize that systematically increasing a subject's personal risk-taking behavior will increase hypnotizability. This increase in risk-taking behavior may be induced by increasing his confidence in the outcome and/or by lifting his intrapersonal inhibitions (defensiveness) to risk-taking. Confidence in outcome may be shaped with first a continuous reinforcement schedule and eventually a variable reinforcement schedule. The resulting positive expectancy and the conditions for "trust" are prompts and props which may be faded after risk-taking behaviors are internalized and have become high-probability events under appropriate conditions. Specifically it is predicted that any manipulations that increase confidence and trust in the self or confidence and trust in a specific person in the social environment will increase hypnotizability.

In terms of increasing hypnotizability by arranging conditions for "trust" (Wickramasekera, 1973) and confidence in an individual in the social environment, it has been shown that a hypnotist who speaks in a forceful voice (Barber and Calverley, 1964b), behaves warmly (Greenberg and Land, 1971), and who is perceived by the subject (through instructional and situational manipulations) to be an experienced expert (Balaschak, Blocker, Rossiter and Perin, 1972; Wuraftic, 1971; Small and Kramer, 1969; Coe, Bailey, Hall, Howard, Janda, Kobayashi and Parker, 1970) elicits greater hypnotizability. It is hypothesized that systematic provision of the "core conditions" at high levels plus increasing patient "self-exploration" (Truax and Carkhuff, 1965) will also increase hypnotizability in that interpersonal context by reducing defensiveness and resistance.

Hypnotizability may also be increased by increasing confidence in the self (mature self-confidence). Tart (1970) found that a nine-month training program that stressed interpersonal risk-taking (encounter groups and Gestalt therapy) and subjective experiential experimentation (directed imagery and sensory awareness) at Esalen Institute increased hypnotizability as measured by the Stanford Scales. If high interpersonal and intrapersonal trust are an important aspect of both positive mental health and hypnotizability, then the generally poorer·hypnotizability of psychiatric patients is partially explained (Gill and Brenman, 1959; Barber, Karacan and Calverley, 1964; Webb and Nesmith, 1964). The clinical-empirical observation (Hilgard, 1965) that adventurous behavior is correlated with hypnotizability may be explained by postulating a risk-taking construct that may facilitate both behaviors (mental health behaviors and hypnotizability). It is hypothesized that a systematic program of subjectively-oriented personal and social risk-taking which incorporates the elements of successive approximation, reinforcement, and corrective feedback will increase the probability of hypnotic behavior.

(3) *Special procedures to alter perception.* It is probable that impairing reality testing with psychedelic drugs and/or sensory deprivation will increase hypnotizability by inhibiting left cerebral hemisphere functions like sequential, analytic, and critical-judgmental verbal operations (Sperry, 1964; Milner, 1971; Galin and Ornstein, 1972; Gassaniea, 1967). In terms of the effects of psychedelic drugs, it has been shown that both hypnotic phenomena and hypnotizability may be enhanced by LSD-25 (Fogel and Hoffer, 1962; Levine, Ludwig and Lyle, 1963; Levine and Ludwig, 1965; Sjoberg and Hollister, 1965; Netz, Morten and Sundwall, 1968; Negz and Engstrom, 1968; Middefell, 1967; Ulett, Akpinar and Itil, 1972) and mescaline (Sjoberg and Hollister, 1965). Two recent studies report a high degree of association between self-reported use of marijuana, LSD, mescaline and psilocybin, and hypnotizability scores on the Harvard Group Scale (Show and Orne, 1962; Van Nuys, 1972; Franzini and McDonald, 1973). It is possible that prior use of marijuana and/or psychedelic drugs creates a sense of familiarity and comfort with right hemispheric mental functions and inhibits chronic vigilance and analytic thinking. The disinhibition of these mental functions creates an intrapersonal condition that increases the probability of entry into the hypnotic experience.

Sensory deprivation and restriction procedures appear to be a promising technique of increasing hypnotizability (Pena, 1963; Wickramasekera, 1969, 1970; Sanders and Rehyer, 1969), at least temporarily. Pena (1963) found that three hours of sensory restriction increased hypnotizability in a prison population. Wickramasekera (1969) found that thirty minutes of sensory restriction were sufficient to increase hypnotizability in a college female population, and later Wickramasekera (1970) found that one hour of sensory restriction increased hypnotizability in a group of male prisoners who were generally younger than Pena's (1963) subjects. Sanders and

Rehyer (1969) reported that four to six hours of sensory restriction significantly increased the hypnotizability of previously resistant subjects. In the above studies, sensory restriction or perceptual deprivation (Zubek, 1973) was imposed on the visual, auditory, and tactual-kinesthetic sensory systems to varying extents and with varied instrumentation (sensory deprivation chamber, wearing goggles constructed to decompose visual patterns, or listening to "white" noise through headphones). Under the above conditions, many subjects spontaneously reported hallucinatory experiences. The above sensory restriction studies used control groups, but there were no tests for transfer of the increased hypnotizability outside the laboratory or to the later points in time.

(4) *Biofeedback training procedures (EEG and EMG)*. Some studies appear to show a relationship between the duration of EEG alpha and hypnotic susceptibility (Galbraith, London, Leibovitz, Cooper and Hart, 1970; London, Hart and Lebovitz, 1968). The biofeedback training procedure (Barber et al., 1971) was used by Engstrom, London and Hart (1970) to demonstrate that six sessions of contingent alpha feedback training was productive of greater increases in hypnotic susceptibility than six sessions of noncontingent alpha feedback training. It appeared from verbal reports that the "alpha-on" state and hypnosis were subjectively similar. In a single blind study, Wickramasekera (1971) showed that six sessions of contingent EMG-feedback training increased hypnotizability more significantly than an equal number of sessions of noncontingent EMG feedback training. In a double blind study, Wickramesekera (1973) replicated the above results with another sample of college students of identical age and sex. Ten sessions of shorter (30 minutes) EMG-feedback training were used in the replication study. Currently we are collecting data on pre- and postmeasures of hypnotizability in patients who are learning temperature control with feedback for the management of migraine. These data appear to confirm the hypothesis that any procedure that increases comfort and skill in the self-control of internal responses increases the probability of hypnotic behavior.

In summary, then, it appears that certain procedures and environmental arrangements increase the probability of hypnotic experience. These arrangements appear to alter perception externally or to increase comfort and skill in subjective functioning. The technology of experimental hypnosis is only one of the streams converging to improve the general technology of subjective education. The availability of reliable and effective procedures to elicit or shape subjective responses (private events) may contribute saliently to a precise and powerful future technology for the control of complex human behavior.

References

As, A., Hilgard, E. R., & Weitzenhoffer, A. M. An attempt at experimental modification of hypnotizability through repeated individualized hypnotic experience. *Scandinavian Journal of Psychology*, 1963, 4:81-89.

Balaschak, B.; Blocker, K.; Rossiter, T.; & Perin, C. T. The influence of race and expressed experience of the hypnotist on hypnotic susceptibility. *International Journal of Clinical and Experimental Hypnosis*, 1972, 20, 38-45.

Barber, T. X., & Calverley, D. S. Comparative effects on "hypnotic-like" suggestibility of recorded and spoken suggestions. *Journal of Consulting Psychology*, 1964, 28, 384. (a)

Barber, T. X., & Calverley, D. S. Effect of E's tone of voice on "hypnotic-like" suggestibility. *Psychological Reports*, 1964, 15, 139-144. (b)

Barber, T. X.; Karacan, I.; & Calverley, D. S. Hypnotizability and suggestibility in chronic schizophrenics. *Archives General Psychiatry*, 1964, 11, 439.

Barber, T. X.; Ascher, L. M.; & Mavroides, M. Effects of practice on hypnotic suggestibility: A re-evaluation of Hull's postulates. *American Journal of Clinical Hypnosis*, 1971, 14, 48-53.

Bernheim, H. M. *De la suggestion dans l'etat hypnotique et dans l'etat de veille*. Paris: Librairie Scientifique et Philosophique, 1884.

Coe, W. C.; Bailey, J. R.; Hall, J. C.; Howard, M. L.; Janda R. L.; Kobayashi, K.; & Parker, M. D. Hypnosis as role enactment: The role-location variable. *Proceedings*, APA, 1970, 5, 839-840.

Cronin, D. M.; Spanos, N. P.; & Barber, T. X. Augmenting hypnotic suggestibility by providing favorable information about hypnosis. *American Journal of Clinical Hypnosis*, 1971, 13, 259-264.

De Stefano, M. G. The modeling of hypnotic behavior. Paper presented at the Annual Meeting of the Society for Clinical and Experimental Hypnosis, University of Chicago, October, 1971.

De Voge, J. T., & Sachs, L. B. The modification of hypnotic susceptibility through imitative behavior. *International Journal of Clinical and Experimental Psychology*, 1973, 21, 70-77.

Diamond, M. J. The use of observationally presented information to modify hypnotic susceptibility. *Journal of Abnormal Psychology*, 1972, 79, 174-180.

Diamond, M. J., & Harada, D. The use of direct instructions to modify hypnotic susceptibility. Unpublished manuscript, University of Hawaii, 1973.

Engstrom, D. R., London, P., & Hart, J. T. EEG alpha feedback training and hypnotic susceptibility. *Proceedings, APA*, 1970, 5, 837-838.

Erickson, M. H. Deep hypnosis and its induction. In L. M. Cron (Ed.), *Experimental Hypnosis*. New York: Macmillan, 1952, pp. 70-112.

Franzini, L. R., & McDonald, R. D. Marijuana usage and hypnotic susceptibility. *Journal of Consulting and Clinical Psychology*, 1973, 40, 176-180.

Fogel, S., & Hoffer, A. The use of hypnosis to interrupt and to reproduce an LSD-25 experience. *Journal of Clinical and Experimental Psychopathology*, 1962, *23*, 11-16.

Galbraith, G., London, P., Leibovitz, M., Cooper, L., & Hart, J. An electro-encephalographic study of hypnotic susceptibility. *Journal of Comparative and Physiological Psychology*, 1970.

Gandolfo, R. L. Role of expectancy, amnesia, and hypnotic induction in the performance of posthypnotic behavior. *Journal of Abnormal Psychology*, 1971, *77*, 324-328.

Galin, D., & Ornstein, R. E. Lateral specialization of cognitive mode: An EEG study. *Psychophysiology*, 1972, *9*, 412-418.

Gazzaniga, M. S. The split brain in man. *Scientific American*, 1967, *217*, 24-29.

Gill, M. M., & Brenman, M. *Hypnosis and Related States*. New York: International Universities Press, 1959.

Greenberg, R. P., & Land, J. M. Influence of some hypnotist and subject variables on hypnotic susceptibility. *Journal of Consulting and Clinical Psychology*, 1971, *37*, 111-115.

Gregory, J., & Diamond, M. J. Increasing hypnotic susceptibility by means of positive expectancies and written instructions. *Journal of Abnormal Psychology*, 1973, n.p.

Havens, R. Using modeling and information to modify hypnotizability. Unpublished doctoral dissertation, West Virginia University, 1973.

Hilgard, E. R. *Hypnotic Susceptibility*. New York: Harcourt, Brace & World, 1965.

Levine, J., & Ludwig, A. M. Alterations in consciousness produced by combinations of LSD, hypnosis, and psychotherapy. *Psychopharmocologia*, 1965, *7*, 123-137.

Levine, J., Ludwig, A. M., & Lyle, W. H. The controlled psychedelic state. *American Journal of Clinical Hypnosis*, 1963, *6*, 163-164.

London, P. *Behavior Control*, New York: Harper & Row, 1969.

London, P.; Hart, J.; & Lebovitz, M. EEG alpha rhythms and hypnotic susceptibility. *Nature*, 1968, *219*, 71-72.

Marshall, G. D., & Diamond, M. J. Increasing hypnotic susceptibility through modeling. Unpublished manuscript, Stanford University, 1969.

Middlefell, R. the effects of LSD on body sway suggestibility in a group of hospital patients. *British Journal of Psychiatry*, 1967, *113*, 227-280.

Milner, B. Interhemispheric differences in the localization of psychological processes in man. *British Medical Bulletin*, 1971, *27*, (3), 272-277.

Moll, A. *The study of hypnosis*. New York: Julian Press, 1958.

Netz, B.; Morten, S.; & Sundwall, A. Lysergic acid diethylamide (LSD-25) and intellectual functions, hypnotic susceptibility, and sympatho adrenmedullary activity. A pilot study. MPI B-rapport nr 19, 1968, Stocholm: Militurpsykologiska Institutet.

Orne, M. T. The nature of hypnosis: Artifact and essence. *Journal of Abnormal and Social Psychology*, 1959, *58*, 277-299.

Pascal, G. R., & Salzberg, H. C. A systematic approach to inducing hypnotic behavior. *International Journal of Clinical and Experimental Hypnosis*, 1959, *7*, 161-167.

Pena, F. Perceptual isolation and hypnotic susceptibility. Unpublished doctoral dissertation, Washington State University, 1963.

Sachs, L. B. Comparison of hypnotic analgesia and hypnotic relaxation during stimulation by a continuous pain source. *Journal of Abnormal Psychology*, 1970, *76*, 206-210.

Sachs, L. B. Construing hypnosis as modifiable behavior. In A. Jacobs & L. Sachs (Eds.), *Psychology of private events*. New York: Academic Press, 1971.

Sanders, R. S., & Reyher, J. Sensory deprivation and the enhancement of hypnotic susceptibility. *Journal of Abnormal Psychology,* 1969, *74,* 375-381.

Shor, R. E., & Orne, E. C. *The Harvard Group Scale of Hypnotic Susceptibility, Form A.* Palo Alto, California: Consulting Psychologists Press, 1962.

Shor, R. E,, Orne, M. T., & O'Connell, D. N. Psychological correlates of plateau hypnotizability in a special volunteer sample. *Journal of Personality and Social Psychology,* 1966, *3,* 80-95.

Sjoberg, B. M., & Hollister, L. E. The effects of psychotomimetic drugs on primary suggestibility *Psychopharmacologia,* 1965, *8,* 251-262.

Small, M. M., & Kramer, E. Hypnotic susceptibility as a function of the prestige of the hypnotist. *International Journal of Clinical and Experimental Hypnosis,* 1969, *17,* 251-256.

Sperry, R. W. The great cerebral commissure. *Scientific American,* 1964, *210,* 42-52.

Tart, C. T. Increases in hypnotizability resulting from a prolonged program for enhancing personal growth. *Journal of Abnormal Psychology,* 1970, *75,* 260-266.

Truax, C. B., & Carkhuff, R. R. Experimental manipulation of therapeutic conditions. *Journal of Consulting Psychology,* 1967, *29,* 119-124.

Ulett, G. A.; Akpinar, S.; & Itil, T. M. Hypnosis: Physiological, pharmacological reality. *American Journal of Psychiatry,* 1972, *128,* 33-39.

Van Nuys, D. Meditation, attention, and hypnotic susceptibility: A correlational study. *International Journal of Experimental Hypnosis,* 1972.

Webb, R. A., & Nesmith, C. C. A normative study of suggestability in a mental patient population. *International Journal of Clinical and Experimental Hypnosis,* 1964, *12,* 181-183.

Wickramasekera, I. The effects of sensory restriction of susceptibility to hypnosis: A hypothesis, some preliminary data, and theoretical speculation. *International Journal of Clinical and Experimental Hypnosis,* 1969, *17,* 217-224.

Wickramasekera, I. Effects of sensory restriction on susceptibility to hypnosis: A hypothesis and more preliminary data. *Journal of Abnormal Psychology,* 1970, *76,* 69-75.

Wickramasekera, I. Effects of "hypnosis" and task motivational instructions in attempting to influence the "voluntary" self-deprivation of money. *Journal of Personality and Social Psychology,* 1971, *19,* 311-314.

Wickramasekera, I. The effects of EMG feedback on hypnotic susceptibility: More preliminary data. *Journal of Abnormal Psychology,* (In Press).

Wilson, D. L. The role of confirmation of expectancies in hypnotic induction. Unpublished doctoral dissertation, University of North Carolina, 1967.

Wuraftic, R. D. Effects of experimenter status on hypnosis and suggestibility. Unpublished doctoral dissertation, University of Tennessee, 1971.

Zimbardo, P. G.; Rapaport, C.; & Baron, J. Pain control by hypnotic induction of motivational states. In P. G. Zimbardo (Ed.), *The cognitive control of motivation.* Glenview, Ill.: Scott, Foresman, & Company, 1969.

Zubek, J. P. Behavioral and physiological effects of prolonged sensory and perceptual deprivation: A review. In J. Rasmussen (Ed.), *Man in Isolation and Confinement.* Chicago: Aldine, 1973.

Hypnotic Control of Peripheral Skin Temperature: A Case Report

Christina Maslach,
Department of Psychology
University of California
Berkeley
Gary Marshall, and
Philip G. Zimbardo
Department of Psychology
Stanford University

Maintenance of a relatively constant level of body temperature is a vital physiological function. It is so efficient and automatic that we become aware of the process only when pathological internal conditions cause us to react with fever or chills, and when extremes of environmental conditions markedly alter the skin temperature of our limbs. To what extent can such a basic regulatory function be brought under volitional control?

Luria (1969) performed an experiment dealing with this question, in which he studied the mental feats of a man with eidetic imagery. Apparently, his subject could induce such vivid visual images that they exerted a profound influence on his behavior. When he was instructed to modify the skin temperature in his hands, he was able to make one hand hotter than it had been by two degrees, while the other became colder by one and a half degrees. These bilateral changes were attributed by the subject to the "reality" of his visual images, which consisted of putting one hand on a hot stove while holding a piece of ice in the other hand. Is such a phenomenon replicable with "normal" individuals not born with the remarkably developed eidetic ability of this man? We were led to believe so on the basis of converging research findings in the areas of visceral learning, cognitive control of motivation, and hypnosis.

Neal Miller and his associates at Rockefeller University (1969a, 1969b) have recently demonstrated that the control over skeletal muscle responses through operant conditioning procedures can be extended to responses of the glands and viscera. Their work has generated the powerful conclusion that any discriminable response which is emitted by any part of the body can be learned if its occurrence is followed by reinforcement. These results are extended in the work of Zimbardo and his colleagues (1969) which experimentally demonstrates that biological drives, as well as social motives, may be brought under the control of cognitive variables such as choice and justification, even in the absence of external reinforcers.

It appeared to us that hypnosis: a) is a state in which the effects of cognitive processes on bodily functioning are amplified; b) enables the subject to perceive the locus of causality for mind and body control as more internally centered and volitional; c) is often accompanied by a heightened sense of visual imagery; and d) can lead to intensive concentration and elimination of distractions. For these reasons, it should be possible for well-trained hypnotic subjects to gain control over regulation of their own skin temperature without either external reinforcement or even external feedback. While there have been some attempts to control temperature through hypnosis or other methods (Barber, 1970; Green, Green, & Walters, 1970), they have often lacked adequate controls and tend to focus only on unilateral changes.

Our present study was exploratory in nature and attempted to demonstrate that hypnotic subjects would be able to achieve simultaneous alteration of skin temperature in opposite directions in their two hands, which waking control subjects would not. The bilateral difference of one hand becoming hotter than normal, while the other gets colder, was chosen in order to rule out any simple notion of general activation or prior learning and to control for any naturally occurring changes in skin temperature. We also attempted to rule out other alternative explanations of changes in skin temperature by keeping environmental conditions constant and by minimizing overt skeletal responses on the part of the subjects.

Method

Subjects

All of the subjects (with the exception of the junior author—PGZ) were undergraduate paid volunteers from the introductory psychology course at Stanford University. Three of the Ss received hypnotic training prior to the experiment, while the remaining six Ss did not. The training averaged about ten hours per person and was usually conducted in small groups. It was permissive in orientation, stressing the *S*'s ability to achieve self-hypnosis, and involved several criterion tests.

Procedure

The *S*s were individually tested in the Laboratory of Dermatology Research at the Stanford Medical Center. The ambient temperature in this room was automatically regulated to maintain a constant level. Ten thermocouples of copper constantin were taped to identical sites on the ventral surface of the two hands and forearms of the *S*. Both room and skin temperatures were continuously monitored by a Honeywell recording system. The *S*s lay on a bed with their arms resting comfortably at their sides and with open palms extended upward in exactly the same position. This posture was maintained throughout the session, and there was no overt body movement.

For the hypnotic *S*s, the experiment began with approximately 10 minutes of hypnotic induction. The remainder of the session was identical for both hypnotic and waking control *S*s. They were first asked to focus attention on their hands, and were then told to make an arbitrarily selected hand hotter, and the other colder, than normal. Accompanying this last, brief instruction were suggestions of several images which could be useful in producing this effect, as well as encouragement to generate personal imagery and commands which might be necessary to achieve the desired result. The *S* lay in silence for the duration of the testing sessions (which averaged about 10 minutes). The final instruction was to normalize the temperature in both hands by returning it to the initial baseline level. Each of the *S*s participated in 2 such sessions. In addition, 1 of the *S*s completed 2 sessions utilizing auto-hypnosis, a procedure in which the *S* provides the instructions to himself.

Results

All of the hypnotic *S*s demonstrated the ability to produce bilateral changes in skin temperature. Large differences (as much as 4^0 C) between identical skin sites on opposite hands appeared within 2 min of the verbal suggestion, were maintained for the entire testing period, and then were rapidly eliminated upon the suggestion to normalize skin temperature. Temperature decreases in the "cold" hand were generally much larger than the increases in the "hot" hand, the largest decrease being 7^0 C, while the largest increase was 2^0 C. In contrast, none of the waking control *S*s was

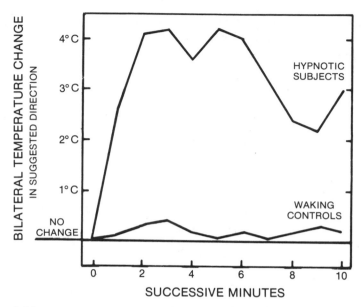

FIGURE 1. Mean algebraic sum of bilateral skin temperature differences ("successful" directional changes in each hand were weighted positively, while changes which were opposite to the suggested direction were weighted negatively).

able to achieve such significant bilateral changes in the temperature of their hands. Any temperature change that they did exhibit was usually in the same direction for both hands (rather than in opposite directions), thus yielding close to a zero score for bilateral change (see Figure 1). The difference between these control scores and the consistently large bilateral changes of the hypnotic Ss is highly significant ($t = 14.27$, $df = 7$, $p < .001$). All of the hand thermocouples reflected these successful bilateral changes, while the forearm thermocouples showed no temperature changes at all, thus indicating the specificity of this hypnotic control process. Also, the performance of the hypnotic Ss showed an improvement from the first to the second session; this was not true of the control Ss.

When the individual patterns of reaction in the hypnotized Ss are examined, the degree of control that they were able to exert becomes even more apparent. The S's data shown in Figure 2 reveal how, following the suggestion to make her left hand colder and right hand hotter (opposite to their relative baseline position), she rapidly "drove" them in the appropriate directions. After maintaining the separation for more than 10 minutes, she re-established the initial baseline difference as soon as she was given the instruction to normalize her skin temperature. Since there was no overlap in the temperature distributions of the two hands, the obtained differences from minute 4 to minute 16 were extremely significant (within-subject t = 20.18, df = 12, p <.001).

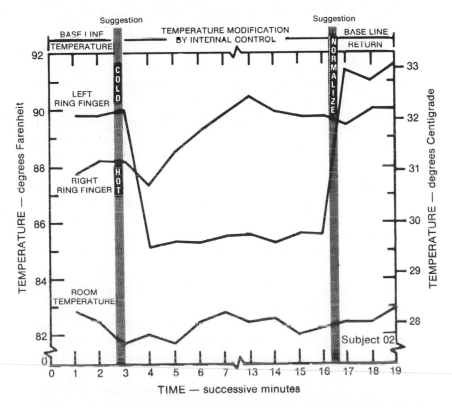

FIGURE 2. Simultaneous modification of skin temperature in opposite directions in the right and left hands (omitted minutes 8-12 are no different from the rest of the modification period).

Both the hypnotic and waking control Ss reported trying hard to meet the experimental demand. Several of the control Ss even believed that they had successfully completed the task, although as noted earlier, their largest bilateral difference was very slight. All Ss also reported that they had generated assorted imagery to help them produce changes in their skin temperature. Some of the imagery involved realistic experiences, such as having one hand in a bucket of ice water and the other under a heat lamp, while other imagery had a more symbolic or fantasy quality. In addition, Ss also used image-less "commands" given independently to each hand (i.e., "you become hot, you become cold").

In the initial pre-test, verbal feedback was given to the Ss when they had succeeded in producing the bilateral difference in temperature. Such feedback had an unexpected negative effect, resulting in the "loss" of the attained difference, and was subsequently eliminated in the experimental sessions. It may be that the intensive concentration required to achieve the unusual performance demanded in this study was disturbed by having to attend to and process the informational input from the experimenter. In a sense, the feedback, although supportive, operated as a distractor to attenuate the obtained differences in skin temperature. The ability of hypnotic Ss to perform successfully this task without feedback is particularly evident in the data of the S using auto-hypnosis, who was able to produce bilateral differences in skin temperature without the aid of any external demands, feedback, or extrinsic sources of reinforcement.

Discussion

Although we are not in a position to characterize the underlying physiological mechanisms responsible for the bilateral control of skin temperature which we have shown, we believe that the role of hypnosis in the process is quite understandable. The research by Miller on visceral learning has stressed the important function served by curare in paralyzing the skeletal musculature of the animals. At first, this methodological control was thought to be necessary only to rule out possible influences of skeletal musculature on glandular and visceral responding. However, it now appears that curarizing the animals "may help to maintain a constant stimulus situation and/or to shift the animal's attention from distracting skeletal activities to the relevant visceral ones [Miller, 1969b, p. 19]."

We would argue that the effects of hypnosis are analogous to those of curare, since hypnosis provides a set of training conditions which permit a greater than normal degree of generalized relaxation, removal of distracting stimuli, and enhanced concentration upon a given, relevant dimension. Hypnotic training may also aid in the control of experiential, behavioral, and physiological processes by increasing the subject's confidence in his ability to exert such control, and by altering consciousness to the point that words and images can be more readily translated into a code language to which he is physiologically responsive.

To us, the significance of research in this area is less in understanding how hypnosis per se operates, but rather how human beings "naturally" learn to induce ulcers, tachycardia, excessive and uncontrolled sweating, and other forms of psychosomatic illness. Miller's work suggests that the intervention and modification of such reactions follow priniciples of operant conditioning. Our work·adds the possibility that the sources of reinforcement in both producing and changing psychosomatic symptoma- tology may be cognitive in nature. In a recent clinical application of these ideas (Sargent, J. D., Green, E. E., & Walters, E. D. unpublished research report entitled, "Preliminary Report on the Use of Autogenic Feedback Techniques in the Treatment of Migraine and Tension Headaches," 1971) patients are trying to reduce their migraine headaches by learning how to control voluntarily their blood flow and skin temperature via biofeedback techniques. Therapeutic control may thus be best achieved by combining the precision of reinforcement contingencies with the power of a more pervasive cognitive approach to dealing with such mind-body interactions.

References

Barber, T. X. *LSD, marihuana, yoga and hypnosis.* Chicago: Aldine Publishing Co., 1970.

Green, E. E., Green, A. M., & Walters, E. D. Self-regulation of internal states. In J. Rose (Ed.), *Progress of cybernetics: Proceedings of the International Congress of Cybernetics, London, 1969.* London: Gordon and Breach, 1970.

Luria, A. R. *The mind of a mnemonist.* New York: Discus Books, 1969.

Miller, N. E. Learning of visceral and glandular responses. *Science,* 1969, *163,* 434-445. (a)

Miller, N. E. Autonomic learning: Clinical and physiological implications. Invited lecture at the XIX International Congress of Psychology, London, 1969. (b)

Zimbardo, P. G. *The cognitive control of motivation.* Glenview, Ill.: Scott, Foresman and Co., 1969.

Note: This study was financially supported by an Office of Naval Research grant N000 14-67-A-0112-0041 to Philip G. Zimbardo, supplemented by funds from an NIMH grant 03859-09 to Ernest R. Hilgard.

Objective Assessment of Hypnotically-Induced Time Distortion

Philip G. Zimbardo, Gary Marshall, and Greg White
Psychology Department
Stanford University
Stanford
Christina Maslach
Psychology Department
University of California
Berkeley

Time perception is one of the most important, although least studied, consequences of the socialization process. Infants and children, whose behavior is primarily under the control of biological and situational exigencies, must be taught to develop a temporal perspective in which the immediacy of the experienced reality of the present is constrained by the hypothetical constructs of past and future. Society thereby transforms idiosyncratic, impulsive, and potentially disruptive behavior into approved, predictable, controllable reactions through the time-bound mechanisms of responsibility, obligation, guilt, incentive, and delayed gratification (1). The social acceptability of such reactions often depends on their rate of emission as much as upon other qualitative aspects. Thus, we develop, in addition to a sense of temporal perspective, a time sense of personal tempo, which involves both the estimation of the rate at which events are (or should be) occurring and affective reactions to different rates of stimulus input (2).

The learned correspondence between our subjective time sense and objective clock time can be disrupted by the physiological and psychological changes that accompany some types of mental illness, emotional arousal, body temperature variations, and drug-induced reactions (3).

However, it is possible to modify either temporal perspective or tempo within a controlled experimental paradigm by means of hypnosis. Our previous research demonstrates the marked changes in cognition, affect, and action that result when hypnotized subjects internalize the instruction to experience a sense of "expanded present" (4). However, the data used to document such changes in this and related studies (5) have been too subjective and gross. In the present study we attempted to alter personal tempo and measure the behavioral consequences with precise, objective techniques.

The experience of tempo was systematically varied (speeded up or slowed down) by time-distorting instructions administered to hypnotic subjects and controls. If effective, such a manipulation should generate asynchronicity between clock time and the subjective passage of time. This asynchronous responding was assessed by means of the objective precision of a specially designed operant conditioning and recording apparatus. As predicted, the operant behavior of these hypnotized subjects was significantly altered relative to their own normal baseline and also to that of subjects in two control conditions.

The volunteer subjects were 36 Stanford University undergraduates of both sexes, who were selected from among the high scorers on a modified version of the Harvard group scale of hypnotic susceptibility (6) administered in their introductory psychology class. They were each randomly assigned to one of three treatments: hypnosis, hypnotic role-playing, and waking nonhypnotized controls. Before the experiment, the hypnosis group underwent a 10-hour training program designed to teach them to relax deeply; to concentrate; to experience distortions in perception, memory, and causal attribution; and to induce autohypnosis. The other subjects received no prior training. During the experiment, the testing procedure was identical for all subjects; an experimenter who was unaware of the experimental treatment delivered the standardized instructions to the subject, who sat isolated in an acoustic chamber. A second experimenter induced a state of hypnotic relaxation in the hypnosis group and instructed the hypnotic role-playing subjects to try their best to simulate the reactions of hypnotic subjects, to behave as if they were really hypnotized throughout the study. The waking controls were told only to relax for a period of time equivalent to that given to subjects in the other two treatments.

Subjects were taught to press a telegraph key at different rates in order to illuminate various target lights in an array of ten colored lights. In the first of five 2-minute trials, a comfortable operant rate of responding was established, and it became obvious to the subject that the sequential onset and offset of the lights was controlled by response rate. The functional relationship between response rate and change in the light stimulus was determined by relay circuits in the apparatus and can be characterized as a "conjugate" schedule of reinforcement *(7)*. This schedule creates a dynamic interplay between behavior and a selected environmental event—the stimulus event changing continually as response rate varies. Pressing the key at a faster or slower rate than that required to illuminate the target stimulus light turned on one of the other lights in the array. It was only by empirically determining the rate appropriate to reach a particular target and then by maintaining that rate consistently that a subject could satisfy the task demand, "to keep light X illuminated as long as possible."

Of the remaining four trials, the first and third were baseline and the second and fourth were experimental. On one baseline trial, each subject was instructed to keep the red light illuminated, which required three presses per second. On the other baseline trial a faster rate of six responses per second was required to maintain the illumination of a blue light. Interspersed between these baseline trials and the experimental trials were the instructions to modify personal tempo. After being told about the differences between clock and subjective time, all subjects were instructed to alter their perception of tempo, by experiencing time as slowing down ("so that a second will seem like a minute, and a minute will seem like an hour"), and also by experiencing time as speeding up. Between these two tempo modification instructions, subjects were told to normalize their experience of time. The order in which these two tempo instructions (slower and faster) were given to each subject was counterbalanced across conditions (and did not have a significant effect upon the task behavior). A cumulative recorder provided an ongoing display of the subject's response rate and indicated whether responding was on- or off-target. In addition, an event recorder and electronic timers indicated to the experimenter the sequence and duration of the stimulus light levels being activated by variations in rate of responding.

The reinforcer for maintaining a particular target light level is probably the sense of competence a subject feels in being able to satisfy the experimenter's demand to do so. Knowledge of being off-target should serve as a negative reinforcer and guide efforts to modify responding to achieve the positive consequences of on-target performance. Such performance depends primarily upon two variables: a stable, veridical sense of personal tempo and the environmental feedback necessary for monitoring the effects of different response rates. Our tempo instructions, in conjunction with hypnosis, were designed to alter the first of these, and variation in feedback was introduced to alter the second. Within our repeated-measurements factorial design, the array of lights remained functional during the experimental periods for half the subjects (objective feedback), and they were extinguished during the experimental periods for the other subjects in each of the three conditions (no feedback). Those in the no feedback condition had to rely entirely on their memory of the previously appropriate baseline rates that they were asked to reproduce in the experimental periods, while objective feedback subjects had direct access to the external information provided by the illuminated array.

Since the electronic relay circuits in the apparatus function on fixed, real-time parameters, a subject operating on a subjective time dimension not in synchrony with clock time would have difficulty satisfying the task demand of achieving and maintaining a particular state of the apparatus. The absence of feedback frees task behavior from reality demands, thereby generating considerable asynchronous responding. But off-target responding can result from either intentionally altering response rate (without changing time sense) or altering personal tempo and thus indirectly affecting response rate. Feedback serves as a reality monitor to create a conflict only in subjects motivated to change their response rate voluntarily while also being motivated to maintain the target light level. For those who have internalized an altered sense of tempo, there is not a conflict between two competing motivations but rather an inability to perform the task successfully because of thieir altered cognitive state. They should continue to respond asynchronously even in the presence of feedback; the intentional responders should resolve their conflict in the direction of the most salient reinforcer—being on-target.

Only the hypnotic subjects were reliably able to translate the verbal suggestion of asynchronicity between clock time and personal time into behavioral "reality." This is shown in comparisons of mean rates of response, percentage of total time on- and off-target, mean deviation in individual response rates from baseline to experimental response levels, and in even the more subtle measures of variability—in displacement of the response distribution.

The sequence of responding for a typical hypnotic subject is shown in the cumulative response curves in Figure 1. From an initially low operant level, the subject responds appropriately to the rate demands imposed by

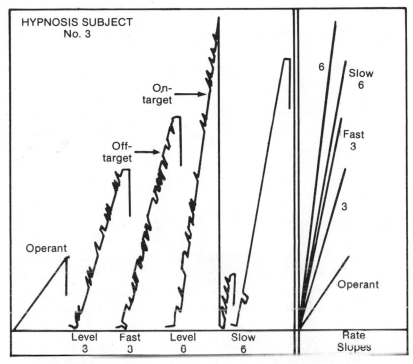

FIGURE 1. Cumulative records of representative hypnotized subject during each of five 2-minute test periods. The slope of the curve indicates rate of responding. Superimposed on this curve are upward and downward deflections; downward deflections signify when response rate is synchronized with target stimulus rate (*on-target* arrow), and upward deflections indicate asynchrony (*off-target* arrow).

target levels 3 and 6, being on target most of the time. Instructions to speed up time result in a steeper slope, while instructions to slow tempo lower the response rate. In this case, the slopes of the response curves for the two altered time periods almost converge. The substantial percentage of time the subject is responding at off-target rate levels reveals the extent of asynchronicity between his altered experience of tempo and the constant rate requirements programmed into the apparatus.

Our research design permits both within- and between-subject comparisons. During baseline trials, there were no reliable differences on any measure between groups. An analysis of variance performed on the mean deviation in operant rate from baseline to experimental responding (Table 1) demonstrates a highly significant treatment effect ($P<.001$), and also a feedback effect ($P<.001$) *(8)*. Deviation from target level (combined across

TABLE 1.

TEMPO MODIFICATION. DATA ARE MEAN DEVIATIONS
IN THE RATE FROM BASELINE PERFORMANCE

Treatment	N	No feedback	Objective feedback	Combined
Hypnotized	12	.534	.233	.38*
Role-players	12	.299	.004	.15**
Waking controls	12	.023	.043	.03
		$P < .025$	$P < .005$	$P < .001$

* $P < .01$ for comparison with role players; $P < .001$ for comparison with waking controls.
** Comparison with waking controls not significant.

feedback conditions) significantly differentiated between the hypnotized subjects and those in the other two conditions. The marked deviations from target levels in the no feedback condition were attenuated by providing external feedback. However, as predicted, this feedback served primarily to differentiate between the hypnotized and role-playing subjects. It totally eliminated the asynchrony in responding among the role-players, but the reduced asynchrony of the hypnotized subjects was still substantially different from the other two controls ($P < .005$). Any volitional effect of responding to the tempo instructions as if they were direct suggestions to vary response rate thus appears limited to the no feedback condition. When confronted with information about the consequences of one's behavior, the controls responded with appropriate synchrony, the hypnotized subjects did not. Neither direction of tempo modification (slower or faster) nor target light response level (low or high) was significant.

Perhaps the most convincing data of the extent to which hypnotic subjects altered their sense of personal tempo come from analyses of the pattern of off-target response variability. This measure of variability is the frequency of recorded shifts from one stimulus level to another. The underlying variability in response rate could lead to shifts either around the target level or to shifts around off-target levels. For example, if the target level were 6, shifts to levels 5 or 7 or from them back to 6 would represent around-target shifts. Off-target shifts would be between 7 and higher levels (faster tempo) and between 5 and lower levels (slower tempo). There are no overall differences in total variation between treatments. However, there are significant differences between the hypnotized subjects and controls in the specific pattern of variability ($P<.001$, by Scheffe multiple *t*-test comparisons). The response distribution for the hypnotized subjects was displaced to off-target stimulus levels (in the experimentally appropriate direction), while that of the controls stabilized around the target levels. Thus, in the no feedback condition in which response variability was greatest, subtracting each subject's frequency of off-target shifts from baseline trials to experimental trials resulted in a group mean of +31.0 for the hypnosis condition, but only +1.5 for role-players and -5.0 for nonhypnotized waking controls.

To underscore the critical role of hypnosis in creating a cognitive state receptive to this time distortion manipulation, a subgroup of the role-playing subjects was subsequently given our program of hypnotic training and retested with the hypnotic induction. Four of the five subjects showed sizable changes in the suggested direction. While there were no differences in their standard baseline performance between earlier role-playing trials and these hypnosis trials, there were significant experimental trial differences due to the greater effectiveness of the time-distorting instructions when they were hypnotized (mean deviation in rate: +.51 for level 6, $P<.05$; and +.38 for level 3, $P<.10$).

Interviews and questionnaire responses of the hypnotic subjects indicated that they indeed tried to satisfy the experimenter's demand to keep the target light illuminated, but found they were unable to do so effectively. Their modified sense of personal tempo became a stable reference against which they judged environmental changes. As a result, they believed that the experimenters were covertly altering the apparatus to make their task more difficult (a situational error). By contrast, in an earlier study *(9)* in which clock time had been covertly altered by the researchers, subjects attributed discrepancies between clock and personal time to their own lack of ability in time estimation (a dispositional error).

We believe that a wide range of behaviors and physiological reactions which are under temporal control, such as drug addiction, depression, emotional arousal, and hypertension, may be modified by altering one's sense of personal tempo.

References and Notes

1. W. Mischel, *Progr. Exp. Pers. Res. 3*, 85 (1966).

2. R. E. Ornstein, *On the Experience of Time* (Penguin, Baltimore, 1970); W. Durr, in *The Voices of Time*, J. T. Fraser, Ed., (Braziller, New York, 1966), pp. 180-200.

3. R. Fischer, in "Interdisciplinary perspectives of time," R. Fischer, Ed. [*Ann. N. Y. Acad. Sci. Sci. 138*, 440-488 (1967)]; J. Cohen, *Psychological Time in Health and Disease* (Thomas, Springfield, Ill., 1967); S. Newell, in *The Future of Time*, H. Yaker, H. Osmond, F. Cheek, Eds. (Doubleday, New York, 1971), pp. 351-388.

4. P. G. Zimbardo, G. Marshall, C. Maslach, *J. Appl. Soc. Psychol. 1*, 305 (1972); B. S. Aaronson, in *The Future of Time*, H. Yaker, H. Osmond, F. Cheek, Eds. (Doubleday, New York, 1971), pp. 405-436.

5. L. F. Cooper and M. H. Erickson, *Bull. Georgetown Univ. Med. Cent. 4*, 50 (1950); T. X. Barber and D. S. Calverly, *Arch. Gen. Psychiat. 10*, 209 (1964); W. E. Edmonston, Jr., and J. R. Erbeck, *Amer. J. Clin. Hypn. 10*, 79 (1967).

6. R. E. Shor and E. C. Orne, *The Harvard Group Scale of Hypnotic Susceptibility, Form A* (Consulting Psychologists, Palo Alto, Calif., 1962).

7. O. R. Lindsley, *Science 126*, 1290 (1957); P. G. Zimbardo, E. B. Ebbesen, S. C. Fraser, *J. Pers. Soc. Psychol.*, in press.

8. Analysis of this data was performed by Perry Gluckman of the Center for Advanced Study in the Behavioral Sciences (CASBS) by using Anovar BMDO 6V and 2V computer programs. The statistical advice of Lincoln Moses is also gratefully acknowledged.

9. K. H. Craik and T. R. Sarbin, *Percept. Mot. Skills 16*, 597 (1963).

Note: This study was supported by Office of Naval Research grant N00014-67-A-0112-0041.

The Effects of Hypnosis and a Control Procedure on Verbal Conditioning: A Hypothesis, Some Preliminary Data, and Theoretical Speculation*

Ian Wickramasekera
University of Illinois
College of Medicine
Peoria

Abstract

The hypothesis tested in this study was that a prior hypnotic relationship with an experimenter (E) would facilitate the immediately subsequent verbal conditioning out of "hypnosis," of the same subject to a greater degree than an equivalent control procedure not defined to the subject as "hypnosis". The hypothesis appears to be partially confirmed. The implications of such a procedure for psychotherapy or behavior therapy are discussed.

Holz and Azrin (1966) noted that the results of verbal conditioning experiments have not been "substantial or consistent." From a methodological point of view, they questioned the adequacy of the social reinforcers used and suggested the potential importance of the nature of the interaction between experimenter and subject. They also recognized the importance of instructions and their roles as discriminative stimuli in conditioning situations. Their logical analysis of the problems of response class, thematic control, and response units while intellectually interesting has not discouraged empirical studies.

---

*Paper presented at the meeting of the American Psychological Association, Miami, September, 1970.

Krasner (1965) defines verbal conditioning as "the systematic application of social reinforcements to influence the probability of another person emitting a specifiable verbal behavior." The effects of a "hypnotic relationship" on susceptibility to verbal conditioning seem worth investigating for several reasons:

1. In the context of a set of procedures labelled "hypnosis" with highly suggestible subjects, suggestions given may lead to unusual effects, for example, physiological changes, etc., (Barber, 1969) which may increase the attention value and prestige of the "hypnotist."

2. Recently Cairns (1969) has hypothesized that at least with human subjects, instructions and attention may be major variables in enhancing the strength of social reinforcers or prestige factors. Barber's (1969) empirical formulation of "hypnosis" regards attention and instructions as major antecedent variables.

3. Two previous studies (Wickramasekera, 1969a, 1970) appeared to indicate that sensory restriction procedures increase "hypnotic" susceptibility, as measured by the Stanford Scales, and hypothesized that the "hypnotic relationship" may lead to an increase in the social reinforcer value or prestige of an experimenter.

4. Freud and nearly all other traditional psychotherapists recognize the "relationship," or more specifically the "transference" aspect of it, as the major vehicle for reshaping "personality." The "transference" which Freud (1938) later came to recognize as a form of hypnotic relationship, established the analyst as an influential person in the patient's life. A "hypnotic relationship" is a miniature telescoped model of a "transference" (Gill and Brenman 1959), according to one psychoanalytic theory of hypnosis. In a theoretical paper (Wickramasekera 1969b) it was hypothesized that the major effect of the "positive transference relationship" was to increase the analyst's prestige or social reinforcer value, which in turn increased the analyst's ability to manipulate the behavior of the analysand. If this is true then "hypnotic relationship" should increase postinduction susceptibility to verbal conditioning.

Quay (1959) demonstrated that "highly personal and emotionally charged memories can be manipulated by another person in an interview with very minimal verbal participation selectively placed after certain classes of these memories" (p. 257). The present study was conceptualized as a replication and extension of the Quay (1959) study. In his study, "thirty-four college students were asked to recall events from their early childhood. After a baseline was established in an initial operant period, sixteen of the Ss were reinforced by E saying uh-huh for memories concerned with members of *S*'s family. Eighteen of the *S*'s were reinforced for memories not concerned with the family. In both groups the reinforcing stimulus served to increase the proportion of memories in the reinforced category when the reinforcement period was compared to the operant period" (p. 257). The recall of early childhood memories plays a major role in psychoanalytic therapy. Quay (1959) suggested that the prestige of the experimenter could be a factor in the effectiveness of the verbal conditioning. The present study attempted to focus on this prestige variable, conceptualizing it in terms of the strength of social reinforcement. The purpose of this study was to compare the effectiveness of two procedures ("hypnosis" vs. task motivational instructions) which appear to generate prestige. The specific hypothesis tested in this study was that a prior "hypnotic induction" by an experimenter (E) would facilitate the immediately subsequent verbal conditioning out of "hypnosis," of the same subject to a greater degree than an equivalent control procedure (Task Motivational Instructions) not defined to the subject as "hypnosis."

Subjects

The subjects in the study were 36 female junior college students, 18-20 years of age, who volunteered to participate in a study of "hypnosis, concentration, and memory." Subjects were screened for hypnotic susceptibility on the Harvard Scale, which was administered by a male research assistant. Subjects were confined to those with scores between 9-12 on the Harvard Scale (superior hypnotic subjects). Subjects reporting current psychiatric contacts or with a record (in University Record Office) of psychiatric problems were eliminated from the pool of subjects.

Design and Procedure

This entire study, except for the preliminary screening, was conducted in E's office at the Mental Health Clinic.

An equal number of subjects were assigned randomly to a hypnosis group, (N = 18), and a task-motivational group, (N = 18). Within each of the above major groups, subjects were assigned equally and randomly to two subgroups ("family memories," N = 9, "nonfamily memories," N = 9). During the following conditioning procedure, subjects were instructed to verbalize events from their early childhood as they came to mind. A baseline was established for each subject in a free operant period; then a minimal level of verbal reinforcement (experimenter saying uh-huh) was introduced to reinforce selected memory topics. The hypnosis or task motivational instructions were presented immediately before or after the baseline procedure in counterbalanced order.

The hypnotic procedure consisted of administering the standardized hypnotic induction procedure described by Barber (1969) and followed immediately by the Barber Suggestibility Scale (1969). The control procedure consisted of administering the task-motivational instructions described by Barber (1969), followed immediately by the Barber Suggestibility Scale. The only departure from the specific procedures described by Barber was to tell the subjects in the control group before administering the task motivational instructions that they would not be hypnotized. This is crucial because the definition of the situation as "hypnosis" is one of the effective independent variables in the hypnotic induction (Barber 1969). Only the objective part of the Barber Suggestibility Scale was scored. Subjects were out of hypnosis during the verbal conditioning and no posthypnotic suggestions relevant to verbal conditioning or anything else were given when the subjects were in hypnosis. As in the Quay study, the reinforcing stimulus was a flat, non committal "uh-huh" spoken in a low conversational tone. All subjects were seated on a recliner facing away from E during all the procedures. The responses of all subjects were tape-recorded.

The hypnosis group (N = 18) was composed of nine subjects one subgroup for which memories concerned with their families were reinforced and nine subjects in a second subgroup for which memories concerned with people and events outside the family were reinforced. The task motivational group (N = 18) was identically composed and treated with respect to the above reinforcement procedures.

The procedure described by Quay (1959) was used to establish the reliability of the family and nonfamily classes of memories. The reliability of the categories was found to be high and they were found to provide adequate initial operant levels.

The experimental period was divided into two half-hour sessions generally one week apart. The first ten minutes of the first half hour were used to establish the operant level (relative frequency) of the memory category to be reinforced. This procedure served to make each subject his own control. At the end of the first half hour, the subject was interrupted and asked to return one week later for another half hour. The Ss in the task motivational subgroups (family vs. non family) and the hypnosis subgroups (family vs. nonfamily were all treated in the manner described above.

Apart from the insertion of the hypnosis and task-motivational procedures prior to the reinforcement procedure, the present study is identical in
method to the Quay study.

Results

Reliability of memory categories:

Quay reported that the classification of memories of E when tested by a
second judge showed a percentage of agreement that ranged between 90%
and 100%, with a mean of 96%. Using a similar procedure for the present data
the range of agreement was between 100% and 92% with a mean of 94%.

Comparison of Operant
and Reinforcement Periods:

In order to test the hypothesis that reinforcement would increase the
frequency of memories in the reinforced category, family or nonfamily, the
relative proportion in the free operant period was compared to the relative
proportion in the reinforcement period. The reinforcement period was
defined as that part of the total experimental hour which followed the
delivery of the second reinforcement.

The task-motivational group was composed of two subgroups. In the
family subgroup, seven of the nine subjects gave a higher proportion of
family memories after reinforcement. The probability of this event as
indicated by a one-tailed sign test is .09 (Siegel 1956). A one-tailed test was
used because the direction of the change was predicted. For the nonfamily
group, eight of the nine subjects gave a higher proportion of nonfamily
memories after reinforcement. This event has a probability of .02 with a one-
tailed sign test.

In both of the hypnosis subgroups, *all* the subjects (nine out of nine)
gave a higher proportion of memories in the reinforced category. The
probability of these events as indicated by one-tailed sign tests were both
.002.

It should be noted that while both types of subgroups are experimental
groups, the mutually exclusive, all-inclusive nature of the memory
categories makes them at the same time control groups for each other. As
Quay noted "if one should argue that the relative frequency of family
memories would naturally rise as a result of S becoming more at ease with E
as the interview proceeded, then one must also explain the drop in relative
frequency of family memories when nonfamily memories are reinforced
(1959, p. 256)."

Comparison of Hypnosis
and Control Treatments

The magnitude of the change (from baseline to reinforcement) ranged from — .31 to .30 in the task-motivational group and from .04 to .44 in the hypnosis group. Nonsignificant Mann-Whitney U tests (Siegel 1956) indicate that the amount of change was not related to the categories family and nonfamily in the task-motivational and hypnosis groups respectively.

For family memories, there was no significant difference during the operant period between the task-motivation and hypnosis groups. For family memories after reinforcement, there was a difference between the task-motivation and hypnosis groups significant at the .02 level (Mann-Whitney U test). For nonfamily memories there was no significant difference during the operant period between the task-motivation and hypnosis groups. For nonfamily memories after reinforcement, the difference between the hypnosis and task-motivation groups was significantly only at the .10 level (Mann-Whitney U test).

The following observations are on subjects reinforced for producing family memories in the task-motivation group. The subject that conditioned the most poorly produced nine family memories during the operant period and twenty family memories during the reinforcement period. On the other hand, the subject that conditioned the best produced seven family memories during the operant period and thirty-eight family memories during the reinforcement period. The following results were obtained from subjects reinforced for producing nonfamily memories in the task-motivation group. The subject that conditioned the most poorly produced six nonfamily memories during the operant period and twenty-eight nonfamily memories during the reinforcement period. On the other hand, the subject that conditioned the best produced six nonfamily memories during the operant period and forty-one nonfamily memories during the reinforcement period.

The following results stem from subjects in the hypnosis group who were reinforced for producing family memories. The subject who conditioned most poorly produced seven family memories during the operant period and twenty-nine family memories during the reinforcement period. The subject who conditioned best produced six family memories during the operant period and sixty-five family memories during the reinforcement period. The following results were obtained from subjects in the hypnosis group who were reinforced for producing nonfamily memories. The subjects who conditioned the most poorly produced twelve nonfamily memories during the operant period and thirty-six nonfamily memories during the reinforcement period. The subject who conditioned the best produced ten nonfamily memories during the operant period and fifty-eight nonfamily memories during the reinforcement period.

Quay reports that of thirty subjects who returned a post experimental questionnaire, only one person indicated an "awareness" of the contingency between his response and the reinforcing stimulus.

The issue of subject awareness or ability to verbalize the response reinforcement contingency was not evaluated because of the unavoidable delay (to avoid revealing the purpose of this study to those Ss who had as yet not participated) in checking for awareness, and because in the context of a study like this, awareness would have to be inferred from subject responses to progressively more suggestive interview questions (Bandura, 1969) with at best an unreliable procedure (Weinstein and Lawson, 1963).

There were no significant differences (Mann-Whitney U test) on the Barber Suggestibility Scale between the family and nonfamily subgroups both in the task-motivational and in the hypnosis treatments. There were also no significant differences (Mann-Whitney U test) on the Barber Suggestibility Scale between the task-motivation groups (composed of combined subgroups of family and nonfamily) and the hypnosis groups (also composed of combined subgroups of family and nonfamily).

Discussion and
Theoretical Speculation

The results of this study should be interpreted cautiously because of the possibility of experimenter bias and these results should be regarded as only suggestive. But the topic of this study seems a very crucial one for behavior therapy.

Previous studies (Clark and Long, 1964) have not been able to demonstrate a consistent relationship between conditionability and suggestibility. In the present study, highly suggestible subjects were found to be also verbally conditionable. Highly suggestible subjects may be conceptualized as subjects very responsive to instructional sets or susceptible to control by verbal stimuli.

It is hypothesized that a subject who scores high on a hypnotic or suggestibility scale is a subject whose behavior in general is highly susceptible to control by verbal stimuli. The subject's experience of the unusual effects of the hypnotist's words on his behavior increases the hypnotist's attention value, prestige, or social-reinforcer effectiveness. It was hypothesized that after such a sequence of events, the hypnotist's ability to condition the subject's verbal or nonverbal behavior will be generally increased. It appears that for some human subjects, cognitive variables (instructional sets) may be complexly related to reinforcement variables. This implies that a highly suggestible subject may condition or learn poorly if his superior susceptibility to control by instructional sets is not used.

A number of studies with children and adults have sought to increase the strength of social reinforcers. The results of these studies have been interpreted in terms of the deprivation of social stimuli (Gewirtz and Baer, 1958), the manipulation of anxiety (Walters and Ray, 1960). There have been informal attempts to increase a therapist's reinforcer value by his association with primary reinforcers (Patterson, 1965a, 1965b).

The present study suggests that a set of interactions between E and S labelled "hypnosis" may increase the effectiveness with which E can later condition some aspects of the verbal behavior of certain subjects. The

TABLE 1
GENERAL EXPERIMENTAL DESIGN

Harvard Group Scale N = 36	Task Motivation Group N = 18	"Family Memories" Group N = 9
		"Non-Family Memories" Group N = 9
	Hypnotic Induction Group N = 18	"Family Memories" Group N = 9
		"Non-Family Memories" Group N = 9

process through which the experimenter's behaviors become more effective may simply be that the *S* pays more attention to the E's behavior. As Cairns (1969) suggests, "The seemingly contradictory operations of (a) interacting with the child in a threatening fashion, (b) interacting in a friendly fashion, and (c) not interacting at all have been shown to be successful in making the experimenter's comments more effective. Possibly these disparate procedures work by virtue of a common mechanism: whether or not they serve to heighten the probability that the child attends to the experimenter's behavior. Once this orientation is accomplished, regardless of the operations required to bring it about, the effectiveness of the comments will be enhanced (p. 13)."

The above formulation is not inconsistent with the clinical observation that before the psychotherapist, witch-doctor, brain-washer, or counselor can effectively influence the behavior of a subject he needs to become a "significant person" in the subject's life. *S* then becomes and stays more accurately tuned in to the behaviors of E. It does not seem impossible to define and measure operationally such a concept, even in a traditional therapy session, with measures like eye fixation, postural orientation, and so forth.

It has been hypothesized (Wickramasekera, 1969 b) that the effective element in the establishment and analysis of "transference" in psychoanalytic therapy was the arrangement of procedures to increase the analyst's social-reinforcer value and the use of this increased influence to shape the behavior of the patient. Psychoanalytic theory considers a hypnotic induction as the temporary establishment of a "transference relationship" (Gill and Brenman 1959; Weitzenhoffer, 1957). In a sense then the present study represents a miniature analogue of the psychoanalytic situation and demonstrates the reliability with which the content of verbal behavior can be influenced in a relatively brief period of time.

It is also interesting to note that Barber's task-motivational instructions were associated with significant conditioning effects almost equal to those associated with labeling a procedure, "hypnosis." The prediction from Barber's formulation would appear to be that defining the pre-reinforcement interaction to the subject as hypnosis or task-motivational instructions would not lead to any differences in postinteraction susceptibility to verbal conditioning.

In view of the unreliability (Holz and Azrin, 1966) of verbal conditioning phenomena particularly when minimal reinforces (uh-huh) are used, it would be interesting to determine if task-motivational instructions and the

BSS would be significantly more effective than a no-treatment (no instructions or interactions prior to verbal conditioning) control. If it is, we may have in hypnosis and task-motivational instructions, relatively objective procedures that appear to increase the reliability with which verbal conditioning can be demonstrated.

References

Bandura, A. *Principles of behavior modification.* New York: Holt, 1969.

Barber, T. X. *Hypnosis: A scientific approach.* New York: Van Nostrand, 1969.

Barber, T. X., & Silver, M. J. Fact, fiction, and the experimenter bias effect. *Psychological Bulletin Monograph,* Vol. 70, No. 6, Part 6, Part 2, Dec., 1968.

Barber, T. X.; Calverley, D. S.; Forgione, A.; McPeake, J. D.; Chaves, J. F.; & Bowen, B. Five attempts to replicate the experimenter bias effect. *Journal of Consulting and Clinical Psychology,* 1969, *33,* 1-6.

Cairns, R. B. Towards an alternative to the concepts of dependency and attachment. Paper read at the Society for Research in Child Development, Santa Monica, California, March 28, 1969.

Clark, J. P., & Long, T. E. On the lack of relationships between hypnotizability and the response to verbal conditioning. *Psychol. Rep. 1964, 72, 14, 103-105.*

Freud, S. *A general introduction to psychoanalysis.* New York: Garden City Publishing Co., 1938.

Gewirtz, J. L., & Bauer, D. M. Deprivation and satiation of social reinforcers as drive conditions. *J. Abnorm. Soc. Psychol.,* 1958, *57,* 165-172.

Gill, M. G., & Brenman, M. Hypnosis and related states. New York: Int. Univ. Press, 1959.

Holz, W. C., & Azrin, N. H. Conditioning human verbal behavior. In W. K. Honig (Ed.), *Operant behavior.* New York: Appleton-Century-Crofts, 1966.

Krasner, L. Verbal conditioning and psychotherapy. In L. Krasner & L. P. Ullman (Eds.), *Research in Behavior Modification.* New York: Holt, 1965.

Patterson, G. R. A learning theory approach to the treatment of the school phobic child. In L. P. Ullman and L. Krasner (Eds.), *Case Studies in behavior modification.* New York: Holt, 1965. (a)

Patterson, G. R. An application of conditioning techniques to the behavior of a hyperactive child. In L. P. Ullman and L. Krasner (Eds.), *Case studies in behavior modification.* New York: Holt, 1965. (b).

Quay, H. The effects of verbal reinforcement on the recall of early memories. *J. Abnorm. Soc. Psychol.,* 1959, *59,* 254-257.

Rosenthal, R. *Experimenter effects in behavioral research.* New York: Appleton-Century-Crofts, 1966.

Sarbin, T. R., & Andersen, M. L. Role-theoretical analysis of hypnotic behavior. In J. E. Gordon (Ed.), *Handbook of clinical and experimental hypnosis.* New York: Macmillan, 1967.

Sears, R. R. A theoretical framework for personality and social behavior. *American Psychologist,* 1951, *6,* 476-483.

Siegel, S. *Non-parametric statistics.* New York: McGraw, 1956.

Ullman, L. P., & Krasner, L. *A psychological approach to abnormal behavior.* Englewood Cliffs, N. J.: Prentice-Hall, 1959.

Walters, R. H., & Ray, E. Anxiety, social isolation, and reinforcement effectiveness. *J. Pers.,* 1960, *28,* 358-367.

Weinstein, W. K., & Lawson, R. The effect of experimentally induced "awareness" upon performance in free operant verbal conditioning and on subsequent tests of "awareness." *Journal of Psychology,* 1963, *56,* 203-211.

Weitzenhoffer, A. M. *General Techniques of Hypnotism.* New York: Grune and Stratton, Inc., 1957.

Wickramasekera, I. The effects of sensory restriction on susceptibility to hypnosis: A hypothesis, some preliminary data, and theoretical speculation. *Int. J. Clin. Exp. Hypnosis,* 1969, *17,* 217-224. (a)

Wickramasekera, I. Reinforcement and/or transference in psychotherapy and hypnosis. *American Journal of Clinical Hypnosis,* 1969, *12,* 137-139 (b)

Wickramasekera, I. The effects of sensory restriction on susceptibility to hypnosis. A hypothesis and more preliminary data. *J. Abnorm. Psychol.,* 1970, *76,* 69-75.

Effects of "Hypnosis" and Task Motivational Instructions in Attempting to Influence the "Voluntary" Self-Deprivation of Money

Ian Wickramasekera
University of Illinois
College of Medicine
Peoria

A posthypnotic suggestion refers to a suggestion given to a hypnotized person to behave in a specified manner after the termination of the trance [Barber, 1962, p. 321]." Erickson and Erickson (1941) have described posthypnotic behavior as being involuntary, quasi-automatic, and compulsive. Barber (1969) has challenged the above view and stated: "A hypnotic induction (and presumed "hypnotic trance state") is not necessary to elicit compliance with a suggestion to perform specified acts, post-experimentally [p. 205]."

Two hypotheses can be derived from the above empirical generalization. The first hypothesis stated by Barber (1969) was: "It can be hypothesized that hypnotic and non-hypnotic subjects will not comply with suggestions to carry out post-experimental acts if they are led to believe that the experimenter will not know whether or not they complied [p. 205]." A study by Orne, Sheehan, and Evans (1968) claims to have demonstrated that the posthypnotic behavior of excellent hypnotic subjects is independent of the knowledge or presence of the experimenter. In the Orne et al. study, the posthypnotic test was administered by the experimenter's secretary. Hence, the subjects had reason to believe that she would report their responses to the experimenter. It appears therefore that Barber's (1969) hypothesis was not adequately tested by the Orne et al. study.

A second hypothesis is that there will be no statistically significant difference between hypnotized and nonhypnotized excellent hypnotic subjects on a postexperimental act if they are similarly selected and treated. The present study tested this second hypothesis.

Method

Subjects

The subjects in this study were undergraduate college students, white females, between the ages of 18 and 20, who agreed to participate in a "hypnosis-imagination emotional arousal study" for the payment of $5. Subjects were told specifically that they would not be paid for the group screening on the Harvard scale (used as a preliminary test to select subjects with superior hypnotic ability) and that the author intended to measure with the galvanic skin response the degree of emotional arousal when certain events were imagined. From the large pool of subjects who offered themselves for group screening, the first 20 subjects who scored between 10 and 12 on the Harvard scale were selected for the study. The 20 subjects were randomly assigned equally to control and experimental groups. All 20 subjects were told: "You will be paid $5 for your participation in this emotional arousal study, immediately after your individual session with me." All procedures were administered by the author.

The subjects assigned to the hypnosis group were "induced" individu-

TABLE 1

NUMBER OF HOURS THAT ELAPSED SINCE DELIVERY OF THE SUGGESTION AND REQUEST FOR THE PAYMENT CHECK IN THE HYPNOSIS AND TASK MOTIVATIONAL GROUPS

Subject	Hypnosis group	Task motivational group
1	312	22
2	172	200
3	196	29
4	213	30
5	288	46
6	129	38
7	330	112
8	312	143
9	240	21
10	360	6

ally with the Barber (1969) hypnotic induction procedure and then given the following suggestions from the Stanford Hypnotic Susceptibility Scale (Form C and Profile Scale) and the Barber Suggestibility Scale: *(a)* thirst hallucination (1 minute), *(b)* taste hallucination (2½ minutes), *(c)* hand analgesia (1½ minutes), *(d)* heat hallucination (2 minutes), and *(e)* a posthypnotic suggestion.

Subjects in the control group were individually administered the Barber task motivation instructions (see Barber, 1969, p. 46) and told: "Please close your eyes, and imagine what I ask you to, without being hypnotized. It is important that you do not become hypnotized." Control subjects were asked to imagine the following scenes: *(a)* drinking their favorite beverage (1 minute), *(b)* eating their favorite food (2½ minutes), *(c)* putting on their favorite clothes (1½ minutes), *(d)* taking a warm shower (2 minutes), and *(e)* posthypnotic suggestion.

The following posthypnotic suggestion was read to both the control and experimental subjects:

> Please pay close attention to what I am going to say to you now. In a few minutes I will ask you to open your eyes. You will then have the opportunity to collect $5 for your participation in this study. After you open your eyes you will start to feel something very interesting. You will notice no desire to accept payment for your participation in this pleasant and unusual study. In fact, you will even feel a certain pride in giving freely of your time for the advancement of science. You will not want to cheapen what you have done today by placing a price on it. You will find it much easier and more personally satisfying to ignore entirely the fact that you previously agreed to take money for the privilege of participating in this study. You will feel a certain pride in your inner freedom to refuse money for your participation in this test of your imagination.

All subjects were connected to a galvanic skin response machine (LaFayette Model 760C) before the induction procedure. The following instructions were read to both the control and experimental subjects after they had opened their eyes:

> Thank you for your participation in this study. Your $5 is in an envelope with your name on it on the table in the next room. You may pick it up on your way out or you can have it mailed to you by calling this number (they were handed the experimenter's telephone number at his home) any time of the night or day. If you have not called me within 15 days, I will assume that you do not want the money, and I will dispose of it.

Results

The data analyzed in this study consisted of the *number of hours* elapsed between the delivery of the posthypnotic suggestion and the receipt of the telephone call from the subject requesting that her check be mailed (see Table 1). This type of data can be regarded as interval scale data, but to avoid the restrictive assumptions associated with parametric statistical procedures and because of the very small size of the present sample, the data were analyzed with the Wilcoxon matched-pairs signed-ranks test. The test indicated a statistically significant difference between the data for the hypnotic group and the "task motivational" group. Since the direction of the difference was predicted beforehand, the null hypothesis was rejected at the .005 level for a one-tailed test. No checks were picked up on the way out, immediately after the experimental or control procedures. One subject did not request payment at the end of the experimental period and refused payment even afterward.

Discussion

Currently, there appears to be no objective independent means of inferring the existence of an altered hypnotic state of consciousness. A small number of imaginative experiments (Bower & Pribram; Deckert, 1964; Parrish, Lundy, & Leibowitz, 1969) suggest a direction from which this kind of independent specification may come. It appears, however, that recent reviews do not mention these studies in the above specific context.

From the point of view of controlling and predicting the behavior of the subjects in this study, the determination of whether or not they were hypnotized does not seem important, but what appears to be demonstrated is that there is a difference in the degree of subject compliance with verbal instructions when such instructions are given within the context of a procedure labeled hypnosis, as compared with the same instructions given within the context of a procedure not labeled hypnosis.

It may be argued that this study simply illustrates compliant behavior. This is specifically what the author was attempting to demonstrate and measure. Future studies can test the strength of similarly developed compliant behaviors by manipulating upward the quantity of money or the quantity of time associated with the verbal suggestions (i.e., $100 and a 30-day deadline, etc.). The voluntary-involuntary dimension formulation, although an intellectually interesting one, does not seem to have much relevance to the practical problems of the stimulus control of behavior.

It may also be argued that the procedure used with control subjects reduced their motivation to comply with the posthypnotic suggestion. For example, screening the controls with a hypnotic procedure, but failing to test them with it, may have been a "letdown" for them. On the other hand, it may be argued that it made the experiment more interesting to them because they were exposed to a variety of procedures (hypnotic instructions plus task motivational instructions). If the experience of the control subject was more interesting, it was better fitted to the common rationale (e.g., since this was an interesting experience, you should not accept payment for participating in it) which the subjects were offered for complying with the posthypnotic suggestion. Hence, it may be argued that rather than being let down, they had a motivational advantage over the hypnotic subjects.

It has been empirically demonstrated (Barber, 1969) that task motivational instructions can elicit a degree of compliance equal to hypnotic instructions. In the present study, such task motivational instructions were used to elicit posthypnotic compliance. Hence, the control subjects were treated with a procedure that has appeared to be equally powerful. The speculation that changing motivational procedures (hypnotic screening to task motivational instructions) reduces the probability of compliance remains to be empirically demonstrated.

It may also be argued that since the control subjects were not hypnotized, they were not led to believe that the experimenter expected them to comply with the posthypnotic suggestion. For example, telling the control subjects not to become hypnotized may have implied that they were not expected to comply with the posthypnotic suggestion. Also, the control subjects were given tests that were similar to but different from those that were given to the hypnotic subjects. It may be argued that these tests were less pleasant than those that were given to the hypnotic subjects. If they were experienced as less pleasant, this may have implied to the control subjects that the rationale for complying with the posthypnotic suggestion was not intended to apply to them. From the above rationale, it may be inferred that the experimenter was covertly telling the control subjects in at least two ways that he did not expect them to comply with his posthypnotic suggestion.

First, it is a matter of empirical fact that all of the control subjects complied to some degree with the posthypnotic suggestion. Second, it is also a fact that three of the control subjects complied almost as well as those exposed to hypnotic instructions. Hence, the data suggest that all control subjects knew that they were expected to comply with the posthypnotic suggestion.

Third, an attempt was made to disguise the purpose of this experiment by presenting it as a test of "hypnosis, imagination, and emotional arousal." But there is no indication of how effective a disguise it was. When informally questioned after the 15-day deadline, only one subject (in the experimental group) stated that she believed that the experiment was primarily intended to test the strength of a posthypnotic suggestion. The posthypnotic suggestion was carefully worded to avoid any implication that compliance with it was contingent on the experience of hypnosis. Compliance was related implicitly to the satisfaction derived from participation in a pleasant and interesting experience, and not necessarily a hypnotic one. But there appear to be no independent objective means of determining how the subjects interpreted these instructions. Apart from all the above possible inferences and speculations, the empirical observation was that the verbal suggestion given within the context of a procedure labeled hypnosis appears to have been more effective than within the context of the control procedure.

This study suggests that it may be empirically more productive to think of hypnosis as a socially learned type of cognitive set about hypnotic behavior, and that this cognitive set can be the starting point for some subjects for profound psychophysiological and motivational alterations. Hence, even if the belief in hypnosis as an "altered state" turns out to be a delusion (e.g., like certain religious and scientific beliefs), it may be a useful delusion, in that it may be used to provide some people with a rationale for extending themselves in ways in which they would not usually. Beliefs that can have profound physical and motivational consequences are clearly powerful tools for behavioral engineers and clinicians.

It would appear that the major role of money in the posthypnotic suggestion gives the suggestion a peculiarly relevant and "life-like" quality insofar às the behavior of the college undergraduate is concerned. Requesting subjects to "voluntarily" deprive themselves of a generalized reinforcer (Skinner, 1953), in this case, money, makes provision for the demonstration of the effectiveness of verbal stimulus control over a wide range of alternative behaviors and motivational contingencies. The apparent demonstration of the continued effectiveness of verbal instructions after the subject had returned to his natural habitat and the artifacts and props of the experimental situation were "faded" seems to suggest that verbal instructions given within the context of an operation labeled hypnosis become peculiarly effective.

A very important result of this study is that, with one exception, the desire to be paid eventually became stronger than the desire to comply with the posthypnotic suggestion. This result illustrates the limits of a single cognitive structuring procedure conducted within the context of a broader procedure labeled hypnosis. It also suggests ways (e.g., individualized rationales and reinforcement schedules) in which more durable cognitive sets may be programmed and measured objectively after the individual has returned to his natural habitat. It would be interesting to know how long such "self-deprivation" of "self-control" can be maintained with individualized reinforcement schedules or boosters.

After the termination of the experimental period, a check was mailed to the subject who had not received payment for participation. The check was returned by the experimental subject and had to be mailed to her several times before she finally accepted it.

References

Barber, T. X. Toward a theory of hypnosis: Post-hypnotic behavior. *Archives of General Psychiatry,* 1962, *7,* 321-342.

Barber, T. X. *Hypnosis: A scientific approach.* New York: Von Nostrand Reinhold, 1969.

Bower, G., & Pribram, K. Unpublished manuscript. Cited by E. Hilgard, *Hypnotic susceptibility.* New York: Harcourt, Brace & World, 1965.

Deckert, G. H. Pursuit eye movements on the absence of a moving visual stimulus. *Science,* 1964, *143,* 1192-1193.

Erickson, M. H., & Erickson, E. M. Concerning the nature and character of posthypnotic behavior. *Journal of General Psychology,* 1941, *24,* 95-133.

Orne, M. T., Sheehan, P. W., & Evans, F. J. Occurrence of posthypnotic behavior outside the experimental setting. *Journal of Personality and Social Psychology,* 1968, *9,* 189-196.

Parrish, M., Lundy, R. M., & Leibowitz, H. W. Effect of hypnotic regression on the magnitude of the Ponzo and Poggendorff illusions. *Journal of Abnormal Psychology,* 1969, *74,* 693-698.

Skinner, B. F. *Science and human behavior.* New York: Macmillan, 1953.

A Single-Treatment Method to Stop Smoking Using Ancillary Self-Hypnosis

Herbert Spiegel
Columbia University
New York City

How do you help the smoker who wants to stop? This problem has become an urgent one because of what is now known about the physical damage done to the body by nicotine and tars. As evidence has accumulated, patients in ever larger numbers have wanted to stop smoking. In fact, the American Cancer Society (1968) estimates twenty-one million Americans had stopped smoking as of October, 1968. But what of the many who want to stop but seem unable to do so? Their repeated failures tend to frustrate physicians concerned about this problem. Eventually, many physicians stop telling their patients about the dangers of smoking. The usual suggestion to "cut down" may assuage a physician's conscience, but, in truth, it merely conveys an ill-disguised helplessness. Patients perceive this suggestion as the mildest of rebukes and one that merely telegraphs the message: "I am resigned to the reality that you are unable to stop smoking."

Because of this generally defeatist attitude, a new approach is needed to help patients stop one of the most prevalent and corrosive habits of our day. To achieve this objective, the present author has developed an affirmative treatment that includes hypnosis as a useful ancillary technique. However, before physicians can use this method effectively, they need to understand whom they can help. There are three general types of "hard-core smokers."

(a) There are smokers who decide to stop smoking and do so successfully. They have confronted themselves with the facts of smoking, and, because they respect their bodies, they decide to protect themselves from further poisoning. For this fortunate group the problem is solved without treatment.

(b) Some smokers acknowledge the danger, yet continue to smoke *because* cigarettes are poisonous. They are like drinkers who continue to drink despite their knowledge of the deleterious effect of alcohol. This group generally resists treatment.

(c) The group that demands the most serious attention consists of those hard-core smokers who want to stop smoking, but who cannot do so despite repeated attempts. This group needs something besides repeated admonitions or standard scare tactics. Physicians can provide practical and immediate aid, because when these hard-core smokers cry out for help, they mean it.

This continuing study deals with patients in group *c,* a random sample of private patients voluntarily seeking treatment. It demonstrates that a treatment approach which provides immediate impact will help to motivate the hard-core smoker who wants to give up his habit. Since 1963, the author has been modifying and refining a treatment technique which relies on hypnosis as a significant, although not indispensable, part of therapy. So far, 615 smokers have been treated, primarily by reinforcement of their already existing resources for self-preservation. The following preliminary report describes this approach and its effects at least 6 months after the single-treatment session. One-, two-, and three-year follow-ups are also planned and will be reported.

Method

In 1963, during the early development of this approach, no limit was set on the number of treatment sessions, but it soon became apparent that the absence of such a limit encouraged the patient to delay confrontation of the smoking problem. The ritual of coming to see the doctor became a substitute for authentic effort. Consequently, patients were informed in advance that there would be a three-session limit to treatment. Those who were able to stop smoking did so, but usually only after the second or third session.

The treatment procedure was then further refined and reduced to one session. If the treatment worked, it worked right away; if there was a delayed response, it occurred without further contact with the therapist.

The Patients

Since the initiation of single-session therapy for termination of smoking, 615 consecutive patients have been treated. Evaluations were made 6 months or more after therapy. All patients were adult. About half were male and half were female, ranging from 20 to 67 years old. Some of these patients had been smoking at least one pack of cigarettes per day for 30 to 40 years. At the age of 57, one male patient reported that he had been smoking since the age of ten, and was averaging three packs a day. Most of the smokers had tried other methods such as medications or smoking clinics. Almost without exception, each patient in the study had been exposed to a fear and/or aversion technique before coming to this treatment. All were private patients who voluntarily asked for help to stop smoking.

Treatment Considerations

The primary strategy in this treatment is the three-point affirmation by the patient of a commitment to respect and protect his body. Hypnosis, at best, is an ancillary, facilitating technique. It aids in creating an expectant, receptive state of attention and aroused concentration that permits a new perspective on the old smoking habit. The treatment described in this paper uses hypnosis, but any other procedure that arouses the undivided attention and concentration of a patient may serve as well.

What we are grappling with is control of a habit or an urge. One way to attempt to control is to say "don't." The person accustomed to freedom resents the idea of permanent prohibition; however, free people can be induced to change when they are *for* something. It is, therefore, more logical, and more consistent with human nature, to focus on protecting the body from poison instead of concentrating on not smoking. The emphasis is placed on positive reinforcement. To concentrate on not smoking is to increase preoccupation with it.

When the patient accepts the commitment to respect his body, he distracts his attention from the urge to smoke. He now experiences two urges simultaneously— the urge to smoke and the urge to protect his body. By locking them together and emphasizing respect for his body, he concurrently ignores the urge to smoke. Any urge when repeatedly not satisfied and ignored will eventually wither away.

Technique

First, a brief clinical history of the patient is obtained. This history must include the number of years the patient has been smoking and the maximum, minimum, and average number of cigarettes used per day. Has the patient ever been able to stop smoking for any length of time? What physical symptoms are apparent now? What precipitated the decision to look for help at this particular time? Who else in the household smokes besides the patient?

Then the patient is tested for hypnotizability—for his ability to concentrate in an attentive manner, receptive to signals from the doctor. But the general approach need not be changed if a patient cannot be hypnotized. Hypnotizability gives the treatment greater impact or extra leverage; however, sufficient motivation can compensate for a patient's inability to be hypnotized.

After being hypnotized, the patient is asked to close his eyes and concentrate on these three basic points:

1. For your body, smoking is a poison. You are composed of a number of components, the most important of which is your body. Smoking is not so much a poison for you as it is for your body.

2. You cannot live without your body. Your body is a precious physical plant through which you experience life.

3. To the extent thay you want to live, you owe your body respect and protection. This is your way of acknowledging the fragile, precious nature of your body and, at the same time, your way of seeing yourself as your body's keeper. You are in truth your body's keeper. When you make this commitment to respect your body, you have within you the power to have smoked your last cigarette.

Once the patient learns the physiological and subjective sensations that identify the hypnotized state, he is immediately shown how to induce this state of receptive attention by himself and how to bring himself out of self-hypnosis.

The three basic points, the crux of treatment, are then repeated and elaborated. The therapist demonstrates the sequence of trance induction so that the patient can watch it. The patient then induces self-hypnosis several times under the therapist's supervision and repeats the three basic points of treatment each time. Following this procedure, the patient practices the exercise several times by himself. The therapist then shows the patient a camouflage technique so that reinforcement excercises can be done for 15 to 20 seconds any number of times daily without attracting attention, even if strangers are present. Finally, an abbreviated secondary reinforcement gesture, like stroking the side of the face, is demonstrated. This demonstration concludes the 45-minute session.

The following is an illustrative transcript of a hypnosis induction procedure and the training instructions to stop smoking.
    Doctor: All right, would you please sit in this chair. [Doctor sits to the

patient's left side, facing him.] Get as comfortable as you can. Put each arm on the arm of the chair.

Now, look at me. As you hold your head in that position, I am going to count to three. One, look up toward your eyebrows. Try to look up still more and as you continue to look up, two, close your eyelids slowly. Keep your eyes rolled upward, and take a deep breath. Hold. Now, three, exhale, let your eyes relax. Keep your eyes closed and let your body float. Imagine yourself floating, floating down right through the chair. There will be something pleasant and welcome about this feeling of floating.

As you concentrate on the floating, I am going to concentrate on your left hand. Shortly I am going to stroke your middle finger. After I do, you will develop movement sensations in that finger. Then the movements will spread, causing your left hand to feel light and buoyant and you will let it float upward.

Ready [Doctor strokes middle finger and forearm], first one finger, then another, and as the restless movements develop, your left hand will float upward, your elbow bend,. and your forearm lift into an upright position. Now permit your hand to feel like a buoyant balloon and let it float upward. Try to feel this contradictory sensation of your body floating down and your hand floating up, all the way up, higher and higher.

I am going to position your arm in this manner [elbow bent resting on chair and forearm raised] and your hand will remain in this upright position even after I give the signal for your eyes to open. In fact, after your eyes open, even when I put your hand down, it will float right back up to where it is now.

You will find something amusing about this sensation. Later, when I touch your left elbow, your usual sensation and control will return.

In the future, each time you get the signal for the trance experience, at the count of one, your eyes will roll upward, by the count of three, your eyes will close, and you will float into a relaxed trance state. Each time you will find the experience easier and easier.

Now I am going to count backwards. Three, get ready. Two, again roll up your eyes with your eyelids closed and do it now, and one, let them open slowly. Stay in this position and describe what physical sensations your are aware of now in your left arm and hand.

Patient: It feels very light. It feels like I am not holding it up there.

Doctor: All right. Are you aware of any tingling sensations?

Pt: You, a slight tingling sensation. It's as though my hand wasn't there.

Dr: Does your left hand feel as if it is not as much a part of your body as your right hand?

Pt: Yes.

Dr: [Doctor grasps patient's left hand and puts it down. After 5-second pause, if hand does not levitate, he continues:] Now turn your head and look at your left hand. Watch what is going to happen. [The left hand rises to an upright position.] How would you describe that?

Pt: [Laughing] Very funny.

Dr: While it remains in this upright position, by way of comparison, raise your right arm. Now put your right arm down. Are you aware of a difference in the sensation of your right arm going up as compared to your left arm?

Pt: Very funny.

Dr: How would you describe the difference?

Pt: Well, my right arm went up easily. Like I said, "Go up," and it went up. The other sort of raised very gradually by itself.

Dr: Would you say that there is a difference in your sense of control in one hand?

Pt: Yes.

Dr: Where do you have more control?

Pt: In my right hand.

Dr: [Doctor touches patient's left elbow and puts patient's forearm down to arm rest.] Now, make a fist. Open. Are you aware of a change in sensation now in your left arm?

Pt: Yes, it is regular. Like it has come back to my control.

Dr.: The usual sensations have returned. You see the hypnosis that was there is gone. Do you have any idea what caused it to go away?

Pt: You brought it down, made me make a fist and it was gone.

Dr: Now you see what it is like to be hypnotized. It is not sleep, but rather a way of shifting attention. Like shifting gears. It is another method of concentration. And a helpful feature about hypnosis is that you shift attention and get into this state of receptivity, you become more sensitive to your own thoughts than you usually are. For that reason each time you repeat this exercise, it has more impact. You become more receptive to your own thoughts. You are able to step aside, take a fresh point of view about this habit, mobilize your resources, and do something about it in a new way. This is how it is done.

I am going to count to three. Follow this sequence again. One, look up toward your eyebrows, all the way up; two, close your eyelids, take a deep breath; three, exhale, let your eyes relax and let your body float.

And as you feel yourself floating, you permit one hand or the other to feel like a buoyant balloon and allow it to float upward. As it does, your elbow bends and your forearm floats into an upright position. Sometimes you may get a feeling of a magnetic pull on the back of your hand as it goes up. When your hand reaches this upright position, it becomes for you a signal to enter a state of meditation.

In this state of meditation, you concentrate on the feeling of floating and, at the same time, concentrate on these three critical points:

The first point is: *For your body, smoking is a poison.* You are composed of a number of components, the most important of which is your body. Smoking is not so much a poison for you as it is for your body specifically.

The second point is: *You cannot live without your body.* Your body is a precious physical plant through which you experience life.

The third point is: *To the extent that you want to live, you owe your body respect and protection.* This is your way of acknowledging the fragile, precious nature of your body, and, at the same time, your way of seeing yourself as your body's keeper. You are in truth your body's keeper. When you make this commitment to respect your body, you have within you the power to have smoked your last cigarette.

Notice how this strategy puts the emphasis on what you are *for,* rather than what you are *against.* It is true that smoking is a poison and you are against it, but the emphasis is upon the commitment to respect your body. As a consequence of your commitment, it becomes natural for you to protect your body against the poison of further smoking.

Observe that when you make this commitment to respect your body, you incorporate with it a view toward eating and drinking which reflects your respect for your body. As a result, each eating and drinking experience in itself becomes an exercise in disciplined concern for your body. You can, if you wish, use this same exercise to maintain your ideal weight while protecting your body against the poison of further smoking.

Now I propose that in the beginning you do these exercises as often as ten different times a day, preferably every 1 to 2 hours. At first the exercise takes about a minute, but as you become more expert, you can do it in much less time.

The exercise is as follows:

You sit or lie down and, to yourself, you count to three. At one, you do one thing; at two, you do two things; and at three, you do three things. At one, look up toward your eyebrows; at two, close your eyelids and take a deep breath; and at three, exhale, let your eyes relax and let your body float.

As you feel yourself floating, you permit one hand or the other to feel like a buoyant balloon and let it float upward as your hand is now. When it reaches this upright position, it becomes the signal for you to enter a state of meditation.

In this state of meditation you concentrate on these three critical points:

One: For your body, not for you, for your body smoking is a poison.

Two: You need your body to live.

Three: You owe your body this respect and protection.

Reflect on the implications of these three points and then bring yourself out of this state of concentration called self-hypnosis by counting backwards in this manner.

Now, three, get ready, Two, with your eyelids closed, roll up your eyes (and do it now). And, one, let your eyelids open slowly. Then when your eyes are back in focus, slowly make a fist with the hand that is up and as you open your fist slowly, your usual sensation and control return. Let your hand float downward. That is the end of the exercise, but you retain a general feeling of floating.

[Patient now out of formal trance state.]

By doing the exercise ten different times each day, you can float into this state of buoyant repose. Give yourself this island of time. Twenty seconds, ten times a day, in which you use this state of extra receptivity to re-imprint these three critical points. *For your body, smoking is a poison. You need your body to live. You owe your body this respect and protection.* Reflect upon it, then float back up to your usual state of awareness, and get on with what you ordinarily do.

Now, if I had my way, I would ask you to spend the next week in a tobacco shop in order to emphasize the point that the issue is not the presence of tobacco, but rather your private commitment to your body, even in the presence of tobacco. For that reason, it is not necessary to throw cigarettes away. It is just as well to have them around. It is not necessary to ask people not to smoke in your presence. It is just as well that they do because the showdown is between you and your body even in the presence of smokers. This is a private understanding between you and your body.

One of the most frequent mistakes that people make when they try to stop smoking is to put the emphasis on *not* smoking. For example, "I must not smoke. I should not smoke. I won't smoke." This kind of thinking is dead wrong. It makes about as much sense as concentrating on not having an itching sensation on your nose. What happens if you concentrate on not having an itch? Right! You have it! The same thing happens with smoking. If you concentrate on not smoking, you end up more preoccupied than ever with smoking. Free people resent being told what *not* to do on a permanent basis, even if you tell it to yourself, but a free person is able to change on the basis of something he is *for.* So if you look at this as a promise to protect your body, this can result in not smoking, but you experience it as "yes" rather than "don't."

It means looking at yourself in a double sense: you on one hand, your body on the other. You are your body's keeper. Your body is your physical plant. And there is something both innocent and helpless about your body. When you put poison into your body, it can do nothing but accept it and make the best of it. When you realize that you are the one putting the poison there, you have some questions to ask yourself. Are you for your body or are you not? Are you for living or are you not? If the answer is no, then keep smoking.

But, if the answer is yes, you have a built-in obligation to give your body the respect and protection it deserves. You see how different that is from saying, "I will not smoke"?

In essence, this is an art form, the art of controlling an urge. If you mean to control an urge, don't fight it. The more you fight it, the more prominent it will become. Instead, learn to ignore it. Here is a way to do it.

When an urge to smoke occurs, admit it, but, at the same time, acknowledge that you have this commitment to respect your body. Thus, you have two urges at the same time: the urge to smoke and the urge to respect your body. *Lock them together.* By emphasizing respect for your body, you simultaneously ignore the urge to smoke. If you lock together two contradictory urges and focus on one, you must, at the same time, ignore the other.

We know this much about urges. *If you repeatedly deny satisfaction to an urge, biological or psychological, by ignoring it, the urge eventually withers away.* This is true even with something as strong as hunger. When Gandhi went on his hunger strikes, he did not concentrate on not eating. He concentrated on arousing public opinion for his cause. Not eating was an incidental aspect of his strategy. As a result, days later, even though weak from starvation, he observed that his appetite was gone. His urge to eat disappeared. Similarly, by concentrating on this new sense of protection for your body, the urge to smoke is ignored and eventually it disappears.

[The doctor himself performs the sequence of trance induction to allow the patient to watch it. Then, the patient repeats it again while the doctor supervises with directions.]

Suppose 1 to 2 hours have elapsed and you want to do a reinforcement exercise, and you do not have privacy. You do not want to attract attention with your hand up in the air. Here is a camouflaged way to do it. Make two changes. Close your eyelids first and then roll your eyes up. This way the upward eyeroll is private. Second, instead of raising your forearm straight up, bring your hand to your forehead in a position of concentration.

Repeat to yourself: *For my body, smoking is a poison. I need my body to live. I owe my body this respect and protection.* Once you have mastered it, the exercise takes about 20 seconds. An observer would assume that you are concentrating on something, and that is preceisely what you are doing. Self-hypnosis is disciplined concentration.

So far we have discussed the exercise as a basic body defense system. Doing the exercise every 1 or 2 hours is like programming a computer. By imprinting this program on your brain, you have a private computer that sets your primary policy.

Finally, there is a secondary defense. Suppose you find your hand reaching for a cigarette, or you find yourself thinking about smoking. Instead of fighting it, do this quickly. Bring your hand up and stroke the side of your face. This gesture reactivates the last time you did the exercise. It reactivates the third point, which is *I owe my body this respect and protection.* The reason for doing the exercise every 1 to 2 hours is that you always have a recent exercise to which you can refer.

If you fight it, you are missing the message. But if you keep reinforcing this affirmation to respect and protect your body, you have something going for you. Good luck!

Follow-up

As patients left, they were given a stamped, self-addressed postcard which they were asked to fill in and mail in about a week. The postcard read:

HAVE STOPPED_____

NOT SURE YET_____

STILL SMOKED_____

COMMENTS:

NAME _____

Six months after treatment, a questionnaire (Table 1) was sent to all treated patients, with a covering memo stating, "This Research Project is concerned with evaluating the effectiveness of your efforts at controlling the cigarette smoking habit. Your cooperation and response can be of value to others in resolving this important health problem."

TABLE 1
SIX MONTH FOLLOW-UP QUESTIONNAIRE
STOP-SMOKING FOLLOW-UP
(Please check appropriate answers)

NAME:_____ DATE:_____

1. Have you stopped smoking since last seen by Doctor? Yes____ No____
   If No: Cigarette____ Cigar ___ Pipe ___
   How much are you smoking now?
   When did you start to smoke again?
2. What were your physical and emotional reactions after the treatment session?
   a) Immediately afterwards?
   b) Now?
3. Have you used the self-hypnosis exercises? Yes____ No____
   a) How often?
   b) For how long after treatment did you use it?
4. If still smoking, in your opinion, what is the reason?
5. Has your urge to smoke been affected? Yes____ No____
   If so, how?
6. If you have stopped smoking, do you feel that you will be able to continue this way?
   Certain____ Doubtful____
7. If you are still smoking, do you have any desire to stop now?
8. Over-all comments (use other side if necessary):

TABLE 2

RESULTS OF SINGLE-SESSION HYPNOSIS THERAPY TO TERMINATE
SMOKING—SIX-MONTH FOLLOW-UP SURVEY OF 615 PATIENTS

Response	N	%
Stopped smoking (6 months or longer)	121	20
Resumes smoking		
in less than a week	32	
in about: one week	39	
one month	19	
2 months	16	
3 months	8	
4 months	3	
5 months	3	
6 months	1	
Total resumed smoking	121	20
Continued smoking (no impact[a])	29	4
Total treatment failures	150	24
No response to follow-up questionnaire (assumed treatment failure)	344	56

Note.—Only 271 (44%) of 615 patients returned their 6-month follow-up questionnaires by the cut-off date, May 9, 1969.

[a] Impact of therapy was measured by (a) the length of time the patient stopped smoking and (b) the decrease in the number of cigarettes smoked. There was some impact on 80% of the negative responders and on 90% of all those who returned questionnaires.

Results

Survey questionnaires were sent to the 615 patients who were ready for a 6-month follow-up. By the cut-off date, May 9, 1969, 271 patients (44%) had responded. (All data are documented in writing. Protocols and patients' written responses are available for serious research groups.

Not smoking at all 6 months after treatment was the single criterion for effective treatment. Nothing else was considered a positive result. *Reduction of the number of cigarettes smoked, although it demonstrated a measurable impact of treatment, was still considered a negative result.*

Assuming that all those who did not respond (344 patients) had resumed smoking, the results are as follows (see Table 2):

1. Six months or more after a single treatment, at least one out of five, or 20%, of 615 patients were still not smoking (see Figure 1). One of these patients had not smoked since 1964—the longest period of abstinence in this series.

2. Therapy had some effect on at least another 20% of the 615 patients. This was shown by a decrease in the number of cigarettes smoked

SIX-MONTH FOLLOW-UP
TOTAL CASES TREATED — 615

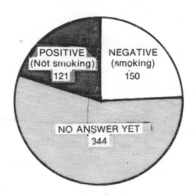

FIGURE 1.

IMPACT IN NEGATIVE CATEGORY

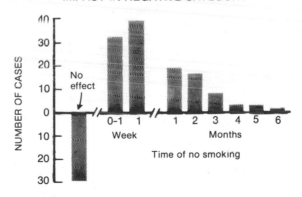

FIGURE 2.

or by the length of time, from 1 day up to 6 months, for which the patient had stopped smoking.

      3. There was a reported impact of treatment on 90% of those who returned the questionnaire, 243 of 271 patients (see Figure 2).

      Although it was assumed that all non responders were treatment failures (see Table 2), information filtering back through other patients indicated that this was not so. There appeared to be several varieties of reasons for not answering the questionnaire: (a) Some people refused to answer questionnaires on principle. Although they were not smoking, they did not bother to respond. (b) Some who had given up cigarettes did not want to give credit to the treatment or satisfaction to the therapist. (c) A number of patients did cheat a bit at first, but later stopped smoking entirely. Although they had stopped smoking completely, they did not answer the questionnaire because they did not want to lie. (d) Several patients felt that since they had paid for the treatment they did not have to give out any information. (e) And some who were not smoking after six months still were not sure that they could continue to abstain, and therefore did not want to respond.

Discussion

      The difficulties of getting people to stop smoking are well-known, but this does not mean that physicians must give up the attempt. Claims for results of previous treatment approaches have ranged from the totally ineffective to a 90% success rate. However, follow-up studies have failed to substantiate the successes claimed (Bernstein, 1969). A new approach to both treatment and follow-up is needed.

      The advantages of the single-session psychotherapy reported on in this paper reside in its simplicity and strategy. The approach to the patient is affirmative and protective; no scare or pressure tactics are used. Furthermore, there is no coercion whatever. The technique requires only one 45-minute period of the physician's time—a small expenditure for a worthwhile result, the immediate salvaging of one confirmed smoker in five. Follow-up is uncomplicated, does not require the patient to pay a return visit, and can be done by mail.

      There was no evidence of harmful effects observed in those who stopped smoking (Spiegel, 1967). Those who are really harmed are the individuals who continue to smoke. The lack of coercion acts as a screening device to rule out all those who are not sufficiently motivated.

Secondary Responses

The secondary effects are best understood if we separate the main issue—whether or not the patient smokes—from the secondary issue, how he reacts to his smoking or not smoking.

Secondary responses were not consistent. Some used overeating as an excuse to resume smoking; others lost weight when they stopped smoking. There were a variety of somatic complaints. Some had symptoms such as sweating, dizziness, palpitations, insomnia, irritability, anxiety, and depression when they stopped smoking; *others had the same symptoms if they resumed smoking*. Some blamed the doctor for their failure, others praised him for their success, but most reacted with a sense of personal involvement. Some patients felt relieved and resigned when they returned to smoking; others who stopped developed a sense of well-being, even euphoria. On occasion, this expansive feeling produced a "ripple effect" that led to new mastery experiences (Spiegel & Linn, 1969). One woman felt so exuberant when she learned that she could control her smoking that she spontaneously overcame a 20-year-old fear of riding escalators and elevators.

Future Directions

A number of problems remain unresolved and deserve further attention.

1. Can more people be salvaged if repeat sessions occur? To what extent, on the other hand, do we encourage avoidance of confrontation by having more than one session? The impact on those who resume smoking before the end of 6 months is impressive enough to pursue this treatment approach further. Further study may give us clues as to when to reinforce those who still have the operational potential to stop smoking entirely.

2. Can one delineate the significant forces and strategies of this approach clearly enough to study its effects with control groups? Such a study is now being planned.

3. Can this response, or a better response, be evoked without hypnosis, or on a group basis? Can it be obtained by use of records, tapes, movies, or television? The logistics of personnel time alone make it imperative that such possibilities be investigated.

4. The implications of these findings excite more interest in the question of psychodynamic insight as a condition for desirable change. The direct impact awareness of the conseqences of a habit may be enough to evoke permanent change for many.

5. A related issue is the importance of the example set by admired public figures, leaders, parents, teachers, etc., who improve the general atmosphere of respecting and protecting the body against smoking. For example, if Johnny Carson simply stopped smoking while on camera, he would contribute precious support to the health of his audience. The propaganda effect of the public media and legislation is a serious reinforcement dynamism for the group that needs constant support. Those who failed to give up the smoking habit, but had a partial response to treatment, would especially benefit.

Further reports of this continuing study, including 1-, 2-, and 3-year follow-ups of these and other patients, will be reported in the future.

Summary and Conclusions

This initial report discusses the first 615 patients attempting to terminate the smoking habit who have been treated in one 45-minute session of psychotherapy reinforced by hypnosis. Follow-up questionnaires were sent to patients who had had this impact therapy 6 months or more before the questionnaire date.

Of the 271 patients who returned the questionnaire by the cut-off date, 121 hard-core smokers (who had repeatedly tried and failed to stop smoking before) were able to stop for at least 6 months. Another 120 persons reduced their smoking to varying degrees, while 29 patients showed no response whatever to treatment. The 344 persons who failed to return their questionnaires must be presumed treatment failures, even though there is evidence to suggest that some of these were actually treatment successes.

These results suggest that every habitual smoker who is motivated to stop ought to be exposed to the impact of this procedure or its equivalent. In this way, at least the one out of five who is capable of responding right away can be salvaged.

References

American Cancer Society. *1969 Cancer facts and figures.* New York: Author, 1968.

Bernstein, D. A. Modification of smoking behavior: An evaluative review. *Psychol. Bull.,* 1969, *71,* 418-440.

Spiegel, H. Is symptom removal dangerous? *Amer. J. Psychiat.,* 1967, *123,* 1279-1283.

Spiegel, H., & Linn, L. The "ripple effect" following adjunct hypnosis in analytic psychotherapy. *Amer. J. Psychiat.,* 1969, *126,* 53-58.

Broad-Spectrum Behavior Therapy for Blepharospasm

Ian Wickramasekera
University of Illinois
College of Medicine
Peoria

This case study describes the apparently successful treatment of a case of blepharospasm. The blepharospasm apparently did not respond to analytic psychotherapy which had previously been attempted in this case. The dynamics and etiology of the symptoms seemed clear to the previous therapist, present therapist, and to the patient. Combining hypnosis and behavior therapy in the manner calculated to strengthen the ego appears to have been the critical therapeutic intervention, in this case.

The patient is a small, but chunky, 45-year-old, white, divorced female who was referred for hypnotherapy because she had failed to respond to a variety of medications and intensive, insight-oriented psychotherapeutic procedures over a two-and-one-half-year period. The major presenting symptom which had stubbornly resisted treatment was a blepharospasm or severe eye blink tic. The symptom started about two and a half years ago and it apparently had grown progressively worse. By the time the patient consulted me, she could not drive, could not walk outside her home unassisted, and was led into my office by a female friend. Apparently, the rate and duration of the blink was so high that the patient's eyes were closed most of the time. She was, for all practical purposes, blind outside her home. Patient wore dark glasses because she stated the sunlight bothered her eyes. After she was helped into a chair in front of me and her female friend had withdrawn, reluctantly at my request, I asked the patient to remove her dark glasses, which she did under protest. She then elaborated the following history in her first two sessions with me.

As a child, her family (mother, one younger brother, and herself) had been abandoned by her father. The patient described her father up to the point of his departure as a loving and industrious man. She stated that she did not expect him to take off and she never found out why he abandoned his family. Because the patient was the oldest child, she had to quit high school, which she dearly loved, and support the family by working at the job which she held till the time of her present symptoms.

At the age of twenty-five, she married a man who was active like herself in the youth program of a Fundamentalist Christian Church. She stated that though she was allowed to keep her job all through her marriage, her husband dominated their social and recreational life. All her hours away from work and her vacation were spent doing the things he valued with the friends he liked. Their social and sexual relationships were always on his terms. She apparently responded to this situation by becoming increasingly absorbed in her work, in the youth camp, and in scout activities connected with their church. She had recognized during her previous therapy that conflict was very aversive to her and that she avoided it.

In retrospect, she recognized that over the years of marriage, she and her husband had drifted farther apart but that neither of them took the initiative to try to stop the process. She also felt that he blamed her for not becoming pregnant, though they were never certain as to which one was the sterile member.

After about five years of infertility, they decided to raise foster children, but her husband would permit only older girls, between the ages of ten to sixteen years. Together they raised several female foster-children. After about twelve years of raising foster-children, the patient stated that she refused to have any more of them in her house, mainly because she felt that she and her husband had never had any time together by themselves. She recalled that before the foster-children, there were the church activities which kept them apart. At this time, there was an attractive young female adolescent who needed a foster home, but the patient was opposed to taking her in. The patient claimed her husband insisted and told her that unless she accepted the girl, he would move out and raise the girl himself, at which point, the patient backed off and reluctantly accepted the girl into her house.

The patient claimed that she resented the young female right from the beginnning and never established a close relationship with her as she had done with the previous foster-children. Patient claimed that she recognized that this only drove the foster-child and her husband closer together. She recalls that over the years, the situation deteriorated to such a point that when she would enter a room, frequently her husband and the girl would stop talking, which, of course, made the patient uneasy, uncomfortable, and suspicious. Patient claimed that she felt uneasy with this situation but did not know what to do to change it. Patient stated that her husband bitterly complained of her indifference to him and the girl. Patient said that she suspected that her 46-year-old husband and the 16-year-old foster-child were closer than they should be, but she never suspected that they were sexually intimate. Hence, it appears that her passive resistance only isolated her even more in her own home and drove her husband and foster-child together. She was apparently too insecure to risk open conflict and possibly abandonment by her husband, as her mother had been abandoned by her father.

The patient wanted to think that her husband's interest in the girl was only fatherly. One evening he told her that the girl was pregnant by him and that the two of them intended to move out of the house the next morning and that he intended divorcing her and marrying the girl. The patient claimed that she took the news in stunned silence, but did not try to prevent their leaving the next morning. After they left, she attempted to kill herself in the garage by starting the motor of the car with the garage door closed. Apparently, she fell forward on the steering wheel and activated the horn, alerting the neighbors. She woke up in the emergency room of a general hospital. Later she was moved to the psychiatric ward, severely depressed, and received a course of electroshock therapy. Patient claimed that after her release from the hospital, she attempted to go back to work but was unable to function on the job because she could not keep her eyes open. Patient stated that the blepharospasm became progressively worse until one day when she was driving to the grocery store, she became involved in a near fatal accident. She sought psychiatric treatment again (chemotherapy and intensive psychotherapy) without positive outcome. Apparently she accepted the symptom and developed a close relationship with a young, obese, female neighbor (Linda) on whom she had come to depend more and more to drive and to lead her around outside her house.

In time, she came to have a sexual relationship with Linda, but claimed that she played a passive role in this sexual liaison. At the time she consulted me, she was deeply into the sexual relationship with the young woman and was also leaning on her for nearly all her excursions outside her house. Patient had no social relationship apart from the one she had with this girl; her church and social activities had also ceased. She claimed that all her neighbors and church members uniformly blamed her ex-husband for the divorce and were full of pity for her. She remembers feeling vaguely uncomfortable with this outpouring of sympathy for her. It did help her, however, during the divorce to strip her husband of everything that they had built together materially when they were married. It seemed to me that she felt some sense of guilt for the way her marriage had drifted and for the harsh judgment her community had inflicted on her ex-husband, his infant, and young wife.

The patient then began to tell me how long she had worked at her previous job before her illness and how important the job and her friends used to be to her. She stated that she was concerned that in the last two years so much had changed on the job that she did not know if she could cope with the changes. She stated that on two previous occasions, she had tried to go back to work on a full-time basis, but that her eyes had become worse and that she had had to quit. I told her during the second session that I agreed with her that the work there in the mail room was probably now too difficult for her to comprehend or to cope with and that, if she insisted on going back to work, I would require that her employer take her back on a part-time basis, if at all. I added that I would call the medical authorities at the plant and insist that she was too sick to be considered for any full-time employment and that if she did not cooperate with me in these measures, I would have to terminate her treatment.

One aspect of her nonverbal behavior in the consulting room attracted my attention. I noticed even during her first session with me that the frequency of blinking seemed to increase when I addressed the patient and seemed to decrease when she was addressing me. I opened the third session of treatment by asking her what her immediate short-term and long-term goals were. After a few moments of silence, she stated that she wanted to be able to go places outside the home unassisted. I next asked her if she could be more concrete and specific about what she wanted to be able to accomplish in the next two weeks. In response she stated that she wanted to (1) be able to do her own marketing; (2) drive her own car; (3) be able to walk around her neighborhood unassisted.

After a few moments of silence, I asked her what she would like to accomplish in the long-run and, after some delay and extended verbal self-exploration, she stated that she would like to be able to (1) pick up and complete her high school education at the point she had dropped it twenty-five years ago and hopefully secure a high school diploma; (2) return to work; (3) become again involved in youth and social activities in her church.

I told her that the idea of securing a high school diploma seemed like a good and sensible one, but since she was on permanent disability insurance and apparently living well on it, I could see no sensible reason she had for even contemplating returning to work. The patient appeared surprised at the second part of my response since she apparently expected me to pressure her to go back to work like her previous therapists and employer. Apparently, there had been quite a bit of pressure to get her off her disability status.

The patient then began to tell me again how long she had worked at her previous job before her illness and how important it and her friends at work used to be to her and how much she desired to return to work. It appeared that her anxiety regarding her ability to function on the job, if she returned to work, was at least one factor retarding her motivation to recover from the blepharospasm and that this avoidance was also being reinforced by her disability status and checks. I therefore explored with her tentatively the possibility of systematically desensitizing her apprehension about returning to work and the work situation. When it became clear to the patient that she would have to learn progressive muscular relaxation, which apparently she regarded as a passive and supine inter-personal posture, I noted that she seemed resistant and insisted that she was the type of person who could not sit still in a chair and needed to be active and busy. In view of the clear message that she did not want to sit passively in a chair during systematic desensitization and because I had noticed earlier that activity on my part and passivity on her part seemed to increase the blepharospasm, it seemed that the only effective intervention in the short run would be one in which she played an active role and in which she felt that she was challenged. Of course, there is also material in her background to indicate that men were not to be trusted (her father and her husband) or be allowed much influence over her life.

I tried to make it clear to her that I would not allow her to return to work in the short run, even if she should recover, because I felt it would deflate the pressure to perform visually, which subjectively seemed very real to her. I decided to use a hypnotic intervention, which was what she was expecting originally anyway. Hypnosis was induced with the hand levitation method and deepened with a procedure with which she counted backwards quietly in her mind from 20 to 0. When she appeared to be in about a medium level of trance, I said to her, **"I want you now to recall the specific short-term goals you wanted to accomplish in the next two weeks. Please recall them now and concentrate on them. I want you to think carefully about each of them and to picture each one in your mind, to notice, and to recognize how important it is**

to you to accomplish these steps you have described to me. I will now be quiet for a while and you can get into concentrating and picturing even more clearly these goals in your head." After about three minutes of silence, I asked her to tell me while still in the trance what kinds of things she needed to do in general to accomplish the above three goals in he next two weeks. She stated that she needed to (1) act more "independently," (2) lean less on Linda; (3) get off the medications which she had been phasing off for two years; (4) forget her past and stop feeling sorry for herself. I told her to pick the easiest one of these four methods and to commit herself right now to implementing it. I told her that if she acted upon my suggestion that she implement at least one of the above four methods, she would require no help in walking into my office next Saturday. In fact, each week she might want to commit herself to concentrating on working harder on changing the other three weaknesses in her life.

The patient walked into her fourth session unassisted, but still wearing her dark glasses. After she was seated across from me, she removed her glasses, spontaneously sat back in the reclining chair (which she had never done in previous sessions), and smiled broadly at me. She opened the session by saying that her eyes were very much improved since she had decided to get off the medication which she had been taking in reduced doses in the past two and one-half years. She stated that the medication had kept her mind in a fog and that not only could she see better but her mind was much clearer and sharper and that she felt excited about putting her brain to work to secure a high school diploma. She reminded me that in adolescence she had always been a straight A student and her mind felt so bright now that she felt almost invincible. I gave her the name of the counselor at the local Adult Education Extension Center and suggested he might be a person to help her to start exploring the possibilities of returning to school. I did not probe her explanation of her symptomatic improvement, but I closed the session by suggesting to her that when she was able to drive herself alone to my office, she would be approaching the point where she did not need to consult me anymore. The purpose of this statement was to reinforce a specific treatment goal and to indicate to her indirectly that I stood ready even now to return to her the influence over her which she had given me. The patient made no mention of hypnosis during this session and hypnosis was not mentioned hereafter by either of us. We both knew that her medication had been both altered and stopped several times before without symptomatic change, but neither of us mentioned this little inconsistency, because it seemed we both recognized her need for this rationalization and had tacitly agreed to an innocent pact of mutual ignorance.

In the following fifteen sessions, the patient made rapid changes in her lifestyle. She enrolled in a crash two-month program to prepare herself for the G.E.D. and graduated with the highest scores made by anyone in her class. Her relationship with Linda deteriorated slowly as I helped her to focus on its unhealthy aspects and as her own sense of self-reliance and confidence surfaced. She walked into my office one day and told me that she had decided to clean out her closets and that she had found and burnt a lot of old letters from her ex-husband, letters that he had written her during and before their marriage. It was approaching Christmas, and she said that she felt lonely, but that she had to get rid of these old memories. She was surprised that she did not weep more than she did while looking at the letters. At Christmas she accepted an expensive gift from Linda and felt very guilty about accepting it. After a few sessions of assertive training, she returned the gift to Linda. I noticed that even though Linda continued to drive the patient to our sessions, she no longer came into my waiting room, but would wait for the patient outside in the car. The patient and Linda shared a part-time job selling Avon cosmetics. The patient's role was to sit in the car getting the merchandise together while Linda drove from house to house and walked from door to door delivering the merchandise. Since the patient's eyes had improved, I asked her if she would be willing to try driving the car on the short trips from house to house to give her the feel of being behind the wheel again. Even though the patient was clearly uneasy about trying to drive again because of her previous near fatal accident, she agreed to try this *in vivo* desensitization procedure. Apparently it worked out well and by the twelfth therapy session, she was doing all the driving on the Avon route. When under pressure at school, the blinking would worsen, but only temporarily, and she would complain that her mind felt foggy. Soon after she graduated at the top of her class, she asked me to explore the possibility of getting her back to work on a part-time basis. I arranged to phase her back in small steps into the work situation and within a month she was working again full-time at her previous job. She now drove herself regularly to our sessions and, by mutual agreement, we decided to see each other only on a monthly basis. Patient continued to make progress both vocationally and socially. She was promoted on her job and had returned to social activities at church. The most striking change that occurred was in her attitude toward her ex-husband; her previous bitterness seemed to yield to a sense of real compassion for him and for his family. She joined an older adult social-dating group. At this time, she terminated treatment. Follow-ups done six months, and one year after termination, indicated the complete absence of the blepharospasm and no evidence of symptom substitution. In fact, the patient's life had expanded into several new social, vocational, and personal dimensions. While the initial therapeutic goal was symptomatic improvement, the focus of treatment shifted rapidly away from her symptom and towards enhancing and expanding the patient's intellectual and social skills and stimulating risk-taking behaviors and generally more self-affirmative behaviors which enlarged and redefined her capacity for joy.

The psychoanalyst who had treated her previously had interpreted her blepharospasm as symbolic of her reluctance to confront reality. The interpretation was probably quite accurate, but it seemed highly improbable that the patient would improve symptomatically till she was able to find an alternative resource (e.g. her "mind") around which to rally and concretize (e.g., a high school diploma) her discontent and restlessness with the cramped and stifling context of her life. Apparently in some personally meaningful way, her intellect provided her with a point of reference within herself which was fundamentally dependable and which enabled her to pick up a thread from her life which she had dropped twenty-five years ago and to go on to use it to broaden the base of her self-reliance and personal worth. It appeared that hypnosis catalyzed her previous therapeutic learning and focused her attention on her need to evolve alternative strategies of adaptation to her loneliness. The behavioristic focus of treatment may have encouraged her to translate her previous therapeutic insights into the concrete and specific substance and shape of actions which behaviorally defined her commitment to intervene in her own life and which concurrently propelled her life forward. Research in psychotherapy (Truax and Carkhuff, 1964) has indicated the power of the concrete and specific dimension in therapeutic influence. The fact that the present therapist was a man—a reasonably dependable and trustworthy one—may have enabled the patient vicariously to complete "unfinished business" (Perls, 1969) with her husband and father.

References

Perls, Frederick. *Gestalt Therapy*. New York: Julian Press, 1969.

Truax, C. B., and Carkhuff, R. R. Concreteness: A neglected variable in research in psychotherapy. *Journal of Clinical Psychology*, 1964, *20*, 264-267.

Reinforcement and/or Transference in Hypnosis and Psychotherapy: A Hypothesis

Ian Wickramasekera
University of Illinois
College of Medicine
Peoria

The psychoanalytic model of hypnosis of Gill and Brenman (1959) would predict an enhancement of hypnotic susceptibility by sensory restriction procedures. From their model it may be deduced that sensory restriction would intensify the kind of "regression" occurring under hypnosis. Curiously enough, a social-learning motivational model would seem to lead to an identical prediction, but for different reasons. A series of experiments with children and adults based on social-learning model (Gewirtz and Baer, 1958a, b; Stevenson and Odom, 1962; Staples and Walters, 1961; Walters and Karal, 1960; Walters and Ray, 1960; Walters, Marshall and Shooter, 1960; Pavio, 1963; Suedfeld, 1964; Bexton, Heron, and Scott, 1954; Heron, 1961; Gibby, Adams, and Carrera, 1960; and Copper, Adams, and Gibby, 1962) have shown that social isolation and sensory restriction procedures enhance the acquisition of simple psychomotor tasks, verbal conditioning, suggestibility in the autokinetic situation, susceptibility to social influence, and susceptibility to propaganda and psychotherapy. Susceptibility to hypnosis has also recently been shown to be enhanced by sensory restriction procedures (Wickramasekera, 1969 a, b).

There have been two types of interpretations of these findings: (a) Gewirtz and Baer (1958b) hypothesize the operation of a "social drive" which like organic drives is subject to deprivation and satiation effects. In other words, social reinforcers ("good," "fine," etc.) like food are subject to deprivation and satiation procedures. The actual Gewirtz and Baer procedure appears to bear some similarity to the sensory deprivation procedures, but there are major differences in terms of the duration of the procedure, the lack of unusual apparatus, and, finally, the age of the subjects involved. It may be tentatively hypothesized that sensory restriction is a quantitatively stronger treatment than the restriction of social stimuli in the Gewirtz and Baer procedure. (b) Walters, et al. (1960) have hypothesized that isolation and sensory deprivation procedures activate anxiety, and it is this which causes the facilitation effects. The systematic research of Spence, et al., (1954) suggests that anxiety arousal may facilitate learning up to a point.

"Freud and nearly every other orthodox psychoanalyst have taken the position that hypnosis is nothing more or less than a transference manifestation [Weitzenhoffer, 1957, p. 61]." This suggests that procedures that would intensify the positive transference would enhance hypnotic susceptibility. Weitzenhoffer goes on to quote Freud as saying "what he (Bernheim) called suggestibility is nothing else than the tendency to transference . . . we have to admit that we have only abandoned hypnosis in our methods to discover suggestion again in the shape of transference [Weitzenhoffer, 1957, p. 61]."

The concept of transference includes the concept of reinforcement and histories of reinforcement in relation to specific "significant others." It may be hypothesized that one of the purposes of transference establishment is to enable the psychoanalyst to draw on the greater reinforcement values possessed by the parental figures. In other words, it is hypothesized that the psychoanalyst deliberately fosters the transference to accomplish what, in terms of operant conditioning, would be termed increasing his reinforcement value so that he will be more effective in shaping the patient's behaviors. The actual procedures set up to enable the patient to associate the therapist with significant others involve environmental operations that induce ambiguity (Bordin, 1955) in the relationship. The greater the degree of ambiguity in the relationship the fewer the opportunities for the patient to discriminate between the therapist and his own parents, and consequently the greater the probability of generalization. Hence, it seems that clinical procedures that maximize ambiguity become the machinery through which the therapist is enabled to draw on the powerful reinforcer values possessed by the patient's parents. The attempts to manipulate the transference through procedures like "abstinence" (Fenichel, 1945) amount, in the language of operant conditioning, to "setting conditions" (Kantor, 1959) to increase or decrease the reinforcer value of a class of stimuli.

The concept of transference in Freudian theory is broader than that of reinforcement in operant conditioning. The increase of the analyst's reinforcement value through transference establishment may be only one of the effective consequences of transference establishment, or it may be the only effective consequence which makes possible the modification of the patient's cognitive, affective, and motor responses. The other associated operations and procedures may be "superstitious" in the sense in which Skinner (1953) has used the concept. It is hypothesized that the increase in the therapist's reinforcement value renders the patient more susceptible to the interpersonal influence of the therapist, be it exerted in the form of psychoanalysis, psychotherapy, hypnosis, conditioning, or "thought reform [Frank, 1961]." Frank (1961) has noted similarities between the psychoanalytic and "thought reform" situations. The transference relationship is believed to lead to the revivification of memories and experiences that serve the purpose of insight and working through of neurotic defenses. Quay (1959) has experimentally demonstrated that it is possible, through selective reinforcement, to influence the nature of early memories "recalled." Dinoff, *et al.* (1960) demonstrated that reinforcement could be used to direct the verbalizations of subjects into any one of three areas congruent with the therapist's "theoretical biases." Rosenthal (1955) found that "improved" patients changed their "moral" values in the direction of the therapist. Sheehan (1953) and Graham (1960) report that "successful patients' Rorschach responses became increasingly like those of their therapist. Stekel (1951) observes that the patient's dreams always confirm the theoretical formulations of their therapist. Gill and Brenman (1948), discussing research on psychoanalytic psychotherapy, say that it is "inevitably influenced by the therapist's views . . . the subtleties of showing interest in certain kinds of material, often not consciously detected either by therapist or patient, are manifold." The personal analysis, which is supposed to control this tendency, may be regarded as a procedure for sensitizing and reinforcing the trainee in certain ways of conceptualizing experience and programming the trainee to reinforce systematically these formulations in himself and others.

Early client-centered theory, even more than psychoanalytic theory, denied any attempt to influence or control the patient's behaviors. Yet, recent analyses (Truax, 1966) of Rogers' own therapy tapes suggest that much verbal conditioning and selective reinforcement occurs in client-centered therapy. It is predicted that similar analyses of psychoanalytic training and therapy tapes will empirically demonstrate that much covert and overt influencing occurs in the psychoanalytic transference situation. The essential implication of the above suggestions is that once the therapist has increased his reinforcement value through association with "significant others" in the patient's past, he is able, through the types of expectations (Goldstein, 1962) and "demand characteristics [Orne, 1959]" he structures in the treatment situation, to influence the verbalizations, memories, feelings, and "insights" produced by the patient.

The tendency to transference may evoke the "placebo effect" (Shapiro, 1960) even in brief human relationships, providing one party to the relationship with considerable influence over the behavior of the other. The operation of a "placebo effect" may indicate that the influencer's reinforcement value has increased in the relationship. Attention, since it is a precondition for any specific reinforcement, acquires reinforcing properties and is, hence, called a conditioned generalized reinforcer (Skinner, 1953). Krasner (1962) seems to suggest that attention is the essence of the "placebo effect." In addition, behaviors like therapist enthusiasm and confident manner (which may have been paired with a wide range of effective deliveries of specific reinforcers) may also be generalized conditioned reinforcers. Sensory deprivation procedures place conditioned generalized reinforcers, such as attention particularly, on deprivation schedules and hence tend to escalate their reinforcement value.

It is possible that one of the merits of attempting to formulate salient clinical phenomena (e.g., transference) in terms of the concepts of the experimental psychology of learning is that controlled observation and manipulation of the phenomena may be stimulated. Its relationship to other experimentally well-established principles (e.g., the schedules of reinforcement) may eventually lead to the separation of what is effective from what is merely superstitious (Skinner, 1953) in clinical practice.

In summary, it appears that both a social-learning motivational model and a psychoanalytic formulation of transference in terms of reinforcement lead to identical predictions regarding certain hypnotic susceptibility phenomena. From the above formulation, it would be predicted that verbal or nonverbal operant conditioning, hypnotic susceptibility, and the establishment of a positive transference would all be facilitated in the adult human being by involving experimental subjects in a prior social and sensory restriction treatment.

References

Baxton, W.H., Heron, W., and Scott, T.H. Effects of decreased variation in sensory environment. *Canadian Journal of Psychology,* 1954, 8, 70-76.

Bordin, E.S. *Psychological counseling.* New York: Appleton-Century-Crofts, 1955.

Cooper, G.D., Adams, H.B., and Gibby, R.G. Ego strength changes following perceptual deprivation. *Archives of General Psychiatry,* 1962, 7, 75-79.

Dinoff, M., Rickard, H.C., Salzberg, H., and Sipprelle, C.N. An experimental analogue of three psychotherapeutic approaches. *Journal of Clinical Psychology,* 1960, 16, 70-73.

Fenichel, Otto. *The psychoanalytic theory of neurosis.* London: Routledge and Kegan Paul, 1963.

Frank, J.D. *Persuasion and healing: A comparative study of psychotherapy.* Baltimore: Johns Hopkins Press, 1961.

Gewirtz, J.L., and Baer, D.M. The effect of brief social deprivation on behaviors for a social reinforcer. *Journal of Abnormal and Social Psychology,* 1958, 56, 49-56. (a)

Gewirtz, J.L., and Baer, D.M. Deprivation and satiation of social reinforcers as drive conditions. *Journal of Abnormal and Social Psychology,* 1958, 57, 165-172. (b)

Gibby, R.G., Adams, H.B., and Carrera, R.N. Therapeutic changes in psychiatric patients following partial sensory deprivation. *Archives of General Psychiatry,* 1960, 3, 57-64.

Gill, M.G., and Brenman, Margaret. Research in psychotherapy. *American Journal of Orthopsychiatry,* 1948, 18, 100-110.

Gill, M.G., and Brenman, Margaret. *Hypnosis and related states: Psychoanalytic studies in regression.* New York: International Universities Press, 1959.

Goldstein, A.P. *Therapist-patient expectancies in psychotherapy.* New York: Pergamon, 1962.

Graham, S.R. The influence of therapist character structure upon Rorschach changes in the course of psychotherapy. *American Psychologist,* 1960, 15, 415. (Abstract)

Heron, W. Cognitive and physiological effects of perceptual isolation. In P. Solomon (Ed.), *Sensory deprivation.* Cambridge: Harvard Univ. Press, 1961.

Kantor, J.R. *Interbehavioral psychology,* 2nd ed. Bloomington, Ind.: Principia Press, 1959.

Krasner, L. The therapist as a social reinforcement machine. In H.H. Strupp and L. Luborsky (Eds.), *Research in psychotherapy.* Washington, D.C.. American Psychological Association, 1962, 2, 61-94.

Orne, M.T. The demand characteristics of an experimental design and their implications. Paper presented at American Psychological Association, Cincinnati, Sept., 1959.

Pavio, A. Audience influence, social isolation and speech. *Journal of Abnormal and Social Psychology,* 1963, 67, 247-253.

Quay, H.C. The effect of verbal reinforcement on the recall of early memories. *Journal of Abnormal and Social Psychology,* 1958, 59, 254-257.

Rosenthal, D. Changes in some moral values following psychotherapy. *Journal of Consulting Psychology,* 1955, 19, 431-436.

Shapiro, A.K. A contribution to a history of the placebo effect. *Behavioral Science,* 1960, 5, 109-135.

Sheehan, J.G. Rorschach changes during psychotherapy in relation to personality of the therapist. *American Psychologist,* 1953, 8, 434. (Abstract)

Skinner, B.F. *Science and human behavior.* New York: Macmillan, 1953.

Spence, K.W., Farber, I.D., and Taylor, E. The relation of electric shock and anxiety to level of performance in eyelid conditioning. *Journal of Experimental Psychology,* 1954, 48, 404-408.

Staples, F.R., and Walters, R.A. Anxiety, birth, order and susceptibility to social influence. *Journal of Abnormal and Social Psychology,* 1961, 62, 716-719.

Stekel, W. *How to understand your dreams.* New York: Eton, 1951.

Stevenson, H.W., and Odom, R.D. The effectiveness of social reinforcement following two conditions of deprivation. *Journal of Abnormal and Social Psychology,* 1962, 65, 429-430.

Suedfeld, P. Attitude manipulation in restricted environments. *Journal of Abnormal and Social Psychology,* 1964, 68, 242-247.

Truax, C.B. Reinforcement and non-reinforcement in Rogerian psychotherapy. *Journal of Abnormal Psychology,* 1966, 71, 1-9.

Walters, R.H., and Karal, P. Social deprivation and verbal behavior. *Journal of Personality,* 1960, 28, 89-107.

Walters, R.H., Marshall, W.E., and Shooter, J.R. Anxiety, isolation and susceptibility to social influence. *Journal of Personality,* 1960, 28, 518-529.

Walters, R.H., and Ray, E. Anxiety, social isolation and reinforcer effectiveness. *Journal of Personality,* 1960, 28, 358-367.

Weitzenhoffer, A.M. *General techniques of hypnotism.* New York: Grune and Stratton, Inc., 1957.

Wickramasekera, I. The effects of sensory restriction on susceptibility to hypnosis. International Journal of Clinical and Experimental Hypnosis. (In press)

Wickramasekera, I. The effects of sensory restriction on susceptibility to hypnosis. A hypothesis and more preliminary data. (Unpublished manuscript)

Goals and Some Methods in Psychotherapy: Hypnosis and Isolation

Ian Wickramasekera
University of Illinois
College of Medicine
Peoria

Recently, there has been a growing recognition that all psychological treatment procedures (psychotherapy, counseling, behavior therapy, psychoanalysis, modern and primitive religious healing [Frank, 1965]), and thought reform or brainwashing (Frank, 1965), which are aimed at either "personality" reconstruction or behavior change, involve the direct or indirect manipulation of values (Rosenthal, 1955; Mowrer, 1964; Patterson, 1958; Dreikurs, 1950; Szasz, 1961; London, 1964; Frank, 1965; Ellis, 1962).

It seems that the label a psychological procedure acquires is largely a function of the cultural value context in which it is practiced, and the degree to which the culturally sanctioned agent of change (psychotherapist, interrogator, witch doctor, or behavior therapist) sincerely believes he is promoting the subject's welfare. A conventional procedure like psychoanalysis would be regarded as "brainwashing" in the Soviet Union while a procedure like thought reform (Frank, 1965), which the Chinese Communists regard as rehabilitative, is considered "brainwashing" in the United States.

It would seem that one major dimension of similarity in "brainwashing" on one hand, and psychotherapy and counseling on the other, is the degree to which the agent of change (psychotherapist, counselor, brainwasher, witch doctor) sincerely believes he is promoting the welfare of the subject. The dimension can be operationally defined to some degree in terms of a scale like the Therapist Self-Congruence Scale (Truax, 1962; Truax & Carkhuff, 1963). This matter of therapist sincerity or genuineness is the old issue of the Inquisition vs. Protestantism in which the Catholics regarded their procedures as laudable since they were intended to promote the welfare of the subject's soul (we would today probably talk about a self), but the Protestants regarded the procedures as cruel and diabolical.

In general, behavior therapists, witch doctors, and interrogators seem to produce quicker and more dramatic results, probably because they actively manipulate a wider range of significant environmental contingencies. One important way in which behavior therapists may be distinguished from witch doctors, etc., is the degree to which they employ effective as opposed to "superstitious" (Skinner, 1953) procedures to induce behavior change.

It has been suggested that the voluntary-involuntary dimension (Krasner, 1962) be used to distinguish psychotherapy from brainwashing. Apart from the fact that a great many involuntary patients (institutionalized psychotics, children, and mental defectives) are receiving "psychotherapy," the increasing use of positive reinforcement in behavior modification makes the question of volition academic. As Skinner (1948) has said, "We can achieve a sort of control under which the controlled . . . nevertheless *feel free.* . . . By careful cultural design, we control not the final behavior but the *inclination* to behave—the motives, the desires, the wishes. . . . The curious thing is that in that case the question of freedom never arises [p. 262]." The exclusive contingent use of conditioned generalized positive reinforcers in the form of the "core conditions" (Truax & Carkhuff, 1965) within traditional psychotherapy can render the process of manipulation so covert that "awareness" (Roe, 1959) of being changed will give the subject no protection. The traditional therapist will generally confine himself to relatively unsystematic non-contingent manipulations of social reinforcers inside his office. However, the behavior therapist will, when necessary, invade the patient's natural habitat (Bijou, 1966), his home, office, etc., to ensure the systematic contingent manipulation of environmental factors to induce behavior change. The insight therapies (London, 1964) tend to be covertly manipulative and to induce change at a rate so slow that it is generally imperceptible. The behavior therapies are overtly manipulative and apparently are still reporting dramatic behavior changes. For these reasons, the behavior therapist is more visibly involved in "meddling with values" or even "brainwashing."

If effectiveness of behavior change is the major criterion for evaluating the use of a procedure, then sensory restriction (Gaines & Vetter, 1968; Goldstein, *et al.,* 1966), improved techniques of "punishment" (Azrin &

Holz, 1966), etc., may come into wider use. The increasing use of overtly manipulative procedures by psychotherapists brings into the open the conflict between the professed concern of therapists for individual freedom of choice and the control of individual behavior by such procedures, a conflict which has not been clearly recognized and faced by many therapists.

A series of reports (Orne, 1962, 1964; Jackson, 1960; Goldstein, 1962; Frank, 1965; Platonov, 1959) have indicated the power of "demand characteristics" (Orne, 1959a), or expectancies stemming from explicit or implicit suggestions, to affect the results of both psychological experiments and psychotherapy. Imber, *et al.,* (1956) have reported a positive relationship between suggestibility and stay in psychotherapy. Heller (1963) implies that "good" psychotherapy patients and "good" subjects in laboratory social psychological research on persuasion are notably similar. Frank (1965) has reported that psychotherapeutic gains effected by an inert placebo have been maintained up to five years. Frank, Nash, Stone, and Imber (1963) reported a significant overall improvement in 109 psychiatric outpatients receiving a placebo. Paul (1964) reports that a placebo treatment was as powerful a therapeutic tool as experienced psychologists using an "insight" oriented treatment procedure. Rosenthal and Fode (1963) report that expectancies affect even laboratory research with animals.

The placebo effect is a uniquely and purely psychological effect, and, hence, it makes sense to use it rather than eliminate it is psychological treatment procedures (Patterson, 1966). Krasner and Ullman (1965) note that "It seems reasonable to maximize placebo effects in the treatment situation to increase the likelihood of client change [p. 230]." Freud's recognition of the importance of what today is called the "placebo effect" is clearly indicated by the following statements. "In order to effect a cure a condition of 'expectant faith' was induced in sick persons. . . . We have learned to use the word 'suggestion' for this phenomenon, and Mobius has taught us that the unreliability which we deplore in so many of our therapeutic measures may be traced back actually to the disturbing influence of this very powerful factor . . . it is disadvantageous, however, to leave entirely in the hands of the patient what the mental factor in your treatment of him shall be. In this way it is uncontrollable; it can neither be measured nor intensified. Is it not then a justifiable endeavor on the part of a physician to seek to control this factor, to use it with a purpose, and to direct and strengthen it? This and nothing else is what scientific psychotherapy proposes [1959, pp. 250-251]." Hypnosis provides a convenient means of manipulating the faith, hope, and trust which are the essence of the placebo effect. Hypnosis is one of the oldest purely psychological techniques for manipulating human expectancies. But the fact that under normal circumstances only a limited number of people are deeply hypnotizable contributed to its neglect. But if routine, rapid techniques (sensory restriction) of increasing the proportion of hypnotizable patients can be developed (Wickramasekera, 1969, 1970), hypnosis may become more widely usable as a pretreatment procedure.

The present writer has, in two controlled laboratory studies (Wickramasekera, 1969, 1970,), demonstrated with a total population of 61 nonpsychiatric subjects that a brief period (one-half to one hour) of sensory restriction will significantly increase hypnotic susceptibility as measured by Forms A and B of the Stanford Hypnotic Susceptibility Scale. Sensory restriction was induced with the use of padded earphones which delivered white noise; the subjects also wore goggles and cotton gloves. The lenses were removed from the goggles and replaced with heavy black cardboard discs to keep out light. The subjects wore loose-fitting heavy cotton gloves which reached to their wrists. They were strictly forbidden to touch or scratch their bodies and were seated in stuffed easy chairs.

A pre-treatment hypnotic induction and demonstration of appropriate but unusual sensory or motor phenomena within hypnosis may be a powerful priming operation prior to actual psychotherapy. In the language of operant conditioning it may be described as increasing the experimenter's reinforcer value or, in conventional psychiatric terms, may be called increasing the therapist's interpersonal influence or power in the patient's eyes.

The patient's subjective experience of the therapist's power may be used to shape the patient's expectation of recovery and hope for the future. Hence, within the context of a trusting relationship with a person who is already recognized as a socially sanctioned healer, hypnosis can become a powerful instrument in the crucial early sessions of treatment, for even temporarily freeing the patient from his burden of past defeats and expectation of future failures. It is important to note that the appearance of the therapist's omnipotence and patient powerlessness is an illusion, and that the therapist "does not actually acquire the power that the patient ascribes to him [Orne, 1962, p. 81]."

Essentially, we are suggesting that patient expectancies be appropriately "primed" prior to actual treatment to increase the patient's readiness for the kinds of learning that await him in psychotherapy, or in other words, that hypnosis be used to increase the therapist's reinforcer value to the client.

Susceptibility to social influence and to propaganda have been shown to be enhanced by isolation procedures (Gewirtz & Baer, 1958; Stevenson & Odom, 1962; Staples & Walters, 1961; Walters & Karal, 1960; Walters & Ray, 1960; Walters, Marshall, & Shooter, 1960; Pavio, 1963; Suedfeld, 1964; Bexton, Heron, & Scott, 1954; Heron, 1961; Gibby, Adams, & Carrera, 1960; and Cooper, Adams, & Gibby, 1962), and the anxiety arousal interpretation of this effect seems to have the widest support. If prior isolation procedures can also be shown to facilitate the effects of psychotherapy and counseling, then a start would have been made in the direction of demonstrating that such apparently discontinuous procedures as psychotherapy, hypnosis, thought reform (Frank, 1965) or "brainwashing," counseling, and verbal conditioning share at least one gross motivational parameter. Clinical lore (Wolberg, 1967) and theory (Freud, 1959; Roger, 1951) already suggest that a minimum level of patient *anxiety* is necessary for a positive psychotherapeutic outcome. The patient's susceptibility to influence may be increased by the patient's involvement in a pretherapy isolation procedure (Goldstein *et al.,* 1966).

Presently, both jailors and, in practice, educational behaviorists appear to be using isolation procedures as punishment, in the sense in which the term is defined by Azrin and Holz (1966). Ferster (1958) has shown that the onset of "a pre-time-out-or-reinforcement stimulus" operates like punishment (Azrin & Holz, 1966) to inhibit responses associated with the pre-time-out stimulus. When these procedures are used in penal institutions, they are called confinement in the "hole," and when used in university-related laboratory schools, they are called placement in the "time-out" room. Isolation, if used differently, may also have some value as a "setting event" (Kantor, 1959) in addition to its function as a punishment procedure.

Mowrer (1960) has previously suggested that all learning is "sign learning" and that effective manipulation of the contingencies of "fear" and "hope" facilitate learning. The use of priming procedures like isolation and hypnosis are aimed at such contingencies, and their use may do something to increase the effectiveness of current psychological treatment procedures. Specifically, hypnosis may be used to heighten the patient's faith and hope in the therapist, and sensory restriction may be used when necessary to induce the level of anxiety arousal or social deprivation, which will most accelerate the rate of therapeutic learning.

Traditional therapists, probably primarily because of their ineffectiveness and self-delusion, have only slowly recognized the extent to which they shape their successful client's values and, through their changed values, their specific behavioral goals. It is becoming increasingly clear that every effective therapeutic act shapes the client's values through what we choose to change and what we do not choose to change in clients, through our rationale (however esoteric and implausible) for the success of our behavioral procedures, and finally through the images of man (Patterson, 1966) and cultural stereotypes unintended but implicit in the tools of our trade (couches, shock generator, hypnosis, tests, M and M's, conversation, etc.).

It may be that certain therapeutic methods (overtly manipulative and aversive) are incompatible with certain therapeutic goals (the shaping of an independent person), but this is an empirical question to be resolved by evidence rather than speculation; for example, comparative studies of relevant aspects of the consequences of "successful" treatment in behavior modification and more "insight" oriented therapies.

In a recent conversation (Evans, 1968) Skinner noted that he and Rogers are essentially in agreement on goals. "I'd like people to be approximately as Rogers wants them to be. . . . We agree on our goals; we each want people to be free of the control exercised by others—free of the education they have had, so that they profit by it but are not bound by it [p. 7]." It is the central point of this paper that such a goal may be only relatively attainable, if not impossible to achieve, in any truly meaningful sense because of the inherent nature of the human predicament.

In summary, it is suggested that isolation and hypnosis may take their place among other tools for increasing the client's readiness for the kinds of value manipulations (Dreikurs, 1950; Mowrer, 1960, 1964; Ellis, 1962; Szasz, 1961; London, 1964) which, when culturally approved, are called psychotherapy, counseling or social rehabilitation, but when culturally disapproved, are described as "brainwashing."

References

Azrin, N.H., & Holz, W.C. Punishment. In W.K. Honig (Ed.), *Operant Behavior, Areas of Research and Application.* New York: Appleton-Century-Crofts, 1966.

Bexton, W.H., Heron, W., & Scott, T.H. Effects of decreased variation in sensory environment. *Canadian Journal of Psychology,* 1954, 8, 70-76.

Bijou, S.W. Implications of behavioral science for counseling and guidance. In J.D. Krumboltz (Ed.), *Revolution in Counseling.* Boston: Houghton Mifflin, 1966.

Cooper, G.D., Adams, H.B., & Gibby, R.G. Ego strength changes following perceptual deprivation. *Archives of General Psychiatry,* 1962, 7, 75-79.

Dreikurs, R. *Fundamentals of Adlerian psychology.* New York: Greenberg, 1950.

Ellis, A. *Reason and emotion in psychotherapy.* New York: Lyle Stuart, Inc., 1962.

Evans, R.T. Dialogue with B.F. Skinner. *Psychiatric and Social Science Review.* 1968, 2, 12.

Ferster, C.B. Control of behavior in chimpanzees and pigeons by timeout from positive reinforcement. *Psychological Monographs,* 1958, 72 (Whole No. 461).

Frank, J.D., Nash, E.H., Stone, A.R., & Imber, S.D. Immediate and long-term symptomatic course of psychiatric outpatients. *American Journal of Psychiatry,* 1963, 120, 429-439.

Frank, J.D. *Persuasion and healing.* New York: Schocken Books, 1965.

Freud, S. *Collected papers, Volume I.* New York: Basic Books, 1959.

Gaines, L.S., & Vetter, H.J. Sensory deprivation and psychotherapy. *Psychotherapy: Theory, Research and Practice.* 1968, 5, 1.

Gewirtz, J.L., & Baer, D.M. The effect of brief social deprivation on behaviors for a social reinforcer. *Journal of Abnormal and Social Psychology,* 1958, 56, 49-56.

Gewirtz, J.L., Baer, D.M., Roth, E., & Chaya, F. *Child Development,* 1958, 29, 149-152.

Gibby, R.G., Adams, H.B., & Carrera, R.N. Therapeutic changes in psychiatric patients following partial sensory deprivation. *Archives of General Psychiatry,* 1960, 3, 37-64.

Goldstein, A.P. *Therapist-patient expectancies in psychotherapy.* New York: Pergamon, 1962.

Goldstein, A.P., Heller, K., & Sechrest, L.B. *Psychotherapy and the psychology of behavior change,* New York: Wiley, 1966.

Heller, K. Experimental analogues of psychotherapy: The clinical relevance of laboratory findings of social influence. *Journal of Nervous and Mental Disease,* 1963, 137, 420-426.

Heron, W. Cognitive and physiological effects of perceptual isolation. In P. Solomon (Ed.), *Sensory Deprivation.* Cambridge: Harvard University Press, 1961.

Imber, S.E., *et al.* Suggestibility, social class and the acceptance of psychotherapy. *Journal of Clinical Psychology,* 1956, 12, 341-344.

Jackson, C.W. An exploratory study of the role of suggestion in research on sensory deprivation. Unpublished doctoral dissertation, University of Michigan, 1960.

Kantor, J.R. *Interbehavioral psychology.* (2nd Ed.), Bloomington, Ind.: Principia Press, 1959.

Krasner, L. Behavior control and social responsibility, *American Psychologist,* 1962, 17, 199-204.

Krasner, L., & Ullman, L.P. (Ed.). *Research in behavior modification.* New York: Holt, Rinehart and Winston, 1965.

London, P. *The modes and morals of psychotherapy.* New York: Holt, Rinehart, and Winston, 1964.

Mowrer, O.H. *Learning theory and behavior.* New York: Wiley, 1960.

Mowrer, O.H. *The new group therapy.* Princeton, N.H.: Van Nostrand, 1964.

Orne, M.T. The demand characteristics of an experimental design and their implications. Paper presented at American Psychological Association, Cincinnati, September, 1959. (a)

Orne, M.T. The nature of hypnosis: Artifact and essence. *Journal of Abnormal and Social Psychology,* 1959, 58, 277-299. (b)

Orne, M.T. On the social psychology of the psychological experiment. *American Psychologist,* 1962, 17, 776-783.

Orne, M.T., & Scheibe, K.E. The contribution of nondeprivation factors in the production of sensory deprivation effects. *Journal of Abnormal and Social Psychology,* 1964, 68, 8-12.

Patterson, C.H. *Theories of counseling and psychotherapy.* New York: Harper and Row, 1966.

Patterson, C.H. The place of values in counseling and psychotherapy. *Journal of Counseling Psychology,* 1958, 5, 216-223.

Paul, G.L. Effects of insight, desensitization and attention-placebo treatment of anxiety: An approach to outcome research in psychotherapy. Unpublished doctoral dissertation, University of Illinois, 1964.

Pavio, A. Audience influence, social isolation and speech. *Journal of Abnormal and Social Psychology,* 1963, 67, 247-253.

Platonov, H.I. *The word as a physiological and therapeutic factor.* (2nd ed.). Moscow: Foreign Languages Publishing House, 1959.

Roe, A. Man's forgotten weapon. *American Psychologist,* 1959, 14, 261-266.

Rogers, C.R. *Client-centered therapy.* Boston: Houghton Mifflin Company, 1951.

Rosenthal, D. Changes in some moral values following psychotherapy. *Journal of Consulting Psychology,* 1955, 19, 431-436.

Rosenthal, R., & Fodes, K.L. The effect of experimenter bias on the performance of the albino rat. *Behavioral Science,* 1963, 8, 183-189.

Skinner, G.W. *Walden two.* New York: Macmillan, 1948.

Skinner, G.F. *Science and human behavior.* New York: Macmillan, 1953.

Staples, F.R., & Walters, R.A. Anxiety, birth order and susceptibility to social influence. *Journal of Abnormal and Social Psychology.* 1961, 62, 716-719.

Stevenson, H.W., & Odom, R.D. The effectiveness of social reinforcement following two conditions of deprivation. *Journal of Abnormal and Social Psychology,* 1962, 65, 429-430.

Suedfeld, P. Attitude manipulation in restricted environments. *Journal of Abnormal and Social Psychology,* 1964, 68, 242-247.

Szasz, T.S. *The myth of mental illness.* New York: Hoeber, 1961.

Truax, C.B. A tentative scale for the measurement of therapist genuineness or self-congruence. *Discussion Papers, Wisconsin Psychiatric Institute,* University of Wisconsin, 1962.

Truax, C.B., and Carkhuff, R.R. The process of psychotherapeutic personality change. *Academic Assembly on Clinical Psychology.* McGill University, Montreal, Canada, 1963.

Truax, C.B., and Carkhuff, R.R. Experimental manipulation of therapeutic conditions. *Journal of Consulting Psychology,* 1965, 29, 119-124.

Walters, R.H., and Karal, P. Social deprivation and verbal behavior. *Journal of Personality,* 1960, 28, 89-107.

Walters, R.H., Marshall, W.E., and Shooter, J.R. Anxiety, isolation and susceptibility to social influence. *Journal of Personality,* 1960, 28, 518-529.

Walters, R.H., and Ray, E. Anxiety, social isolation and reinforcer effectiveness. *Journal of Personality,* 1960, 28, 358-367.

Wickramasekera, I. The effects of sensory restriction on susceptibility to hypnosis. *International Journal of Clinical and Experimental Hypnosis,* 1969, 17, 217-224.

Wickramasekera, I. The effects of sensory restriction on susceptibility to hypnosis: A hypothesis and more preliminary data. *Journal of Abnormal Psychology,* 1970, 76, (1), 69-75.

Wolberg, L.R. *The technique of psychotherapy* (2nd Ed.). New York: Grune and Stratton, 1967.

Conclusion— Biofeedback, Behavior Therapy and Hypnosis: Convergences and the Placebo Response

Biofeedback, Behavior Therapy and Hypnosis: Convergences and the Placebo Response

Ian Wickramasekera
University of Illinois
College of Medicine
Peoria

Laboratory Roots

Biofeedback, behavior therapy, and hypnosis share several common features. All three technologies have been inspired, developed out of, or maintained roots in the experimental laboratory. Biofeedback is supposed to have grown out of the application of operant conditioning principles to physiological responses occurring within the skin. Today, it appears that the type of process that occurs in human clinical biofeedback training is incompletely understood and probably more complex than current conceptual-empirical formulations of operant conditioning. But in general, it is true that biofeedback technology has grown out of the laboratories of electrical engineers and psychophysiologists.

The hypotheses, techniques, and rationales of behavior therapists have been inspired by laboratory investigators like Watson, Skinner, Hull, and Mowrer. The effective intervention procedures of behavior therapy are rationalized in terms of laboratory studies of conditioning and learning to which they bear some superficial similarity. But even more importantly, behavior therapists define their dependent variables (outcomes) and independent variables (treatment techniques) in ways that permit controlled observation and manipulation. Hence, the topic of behavior change is defined by behavior therapists in a manner which makes it amenable to investigation with laboratory methods.

The laboratory study of hypnotic behavior dates back to the pioneering systematic investigations of Clark Hull (1933). The experimental tradition in hypnosis has been almost self-conscious, as evidenced by the fact that experimentally- and clinically-oriented hypnotists generally belong to different national hypnotic societies. In spite of this clinical-versus-laboratory distinction in hypnosis, in recent years, clinicians and experimentalists have come to greater mutual appreciation of each other's procedures and behaviors (not explanations or theories). Laboratory hypnosis has made major contributions to the thinking and practice of sophisticated clinicians by producing scales for identifying and measuring individual differences in susceptibility to hypnosis (Hilgard and Weitzenhoffer, 1959; Barber, 1969; Spiegel, 1972). The laboratory studies have also sought to identify the verbal and situational-environmental conditions under which hypnotic behaviors are likely to be emitted or elicited (Barber, 1969). Laboratory studies have identified some of the parameters of hypnotic behavior (Hilgard, 1965) and developed techniques for increasing hypnotic susceptibility (Wickramasekera, 1973c). It is an optimistic sign that biofeedback, behavior therapy, and hypnosis maintain a close relationship with the laboratory, because the scientific method is the only effective current antidote for superstitious clinical behavior, surplus theory, dogmatism, and blockages to corrective empirical feedback, fresh observation, hypothesis formation, and hypothesis testing. At some future time, of course, the scientific method, as currently conceived, may become an impediment to progress in these fields, but today it facilitates the advance of these three technologies.

Specification of Independent Variables

Biofeedback, behavior therapy, and hypnosis appear to share a second feature. All three approaches appear to attend to the need to specify the independent variables (procedures, instructions, hardware) and the sequence in which the components of the independent variables (treatment) are implemented. This concern for specification of treatment components and sequences may stem from laboratory roots or collaterals of these three technologies. To the clinician, careful specification of treatment techniques has great practical utility because it facilitiates implementation and replication of treatment. The clinician's primary activity consists of controlling and predicting the behavior of individual patients. Reliable and precise treatment outcomes require careful specifications of repeatable interventions under known conditions, with reliably recognizable diagnostic groups (specification of for whom the procedures are indicated and contraindicated). A recent article on the treatment of exhibitionism (Wickramasekera,

1972a) illustrates an approximation to the above ideal. The article describes a procedure to inhibit rapidly (within two-sessions) and permanently indecent exposure with internalized aversion. The paper describes the type of patient in whom such internalized aversion may be installed without the use of electric shock (or other noxious stimuli) and also specifies what situational-environmental arrangements should be made to install internalized aversion.

Specification of Dependent Variables

Biofeedback, behavior therapy, and hypnosis share a third common feature. All three technologies tend to focus on relatively circumscribed, specific symptoms which are either directly or indirectly observable (verbal report or with instruments, e.g., EMG responses). The decision to deal with limited behaviors, one at a time, and to define them in ways that are either directly or indirectly (with electronic instruments) detectable and trackable ensures that corrective feedback can occur in hypothesis testing and that effective interventions can be separated from ineffective ones. As illustrated in this book, in clinical application of biofeedback, headache pain is specified in terms of verbal ratings of pain intensity, the duration (in hours) of pain and the correlated EMG or temperature activity. (Wickramasekera, 1972b; 1973d; 1974b). In behavior therapy, as illustrated in the second part of this book, the symptom may be defined in terms of the number of homosexual episodes (Colson, 1972), the number of masturbations with homosexual fantasies (Evans, 1968), or the number of exhibitionistic episodes (Wickramasekera, 1972a). In clinical hypnosis, the focus is also generally on specific symptoms (but may include more general constructs like ego-strengthening) like blepharospasm (Wickramasekera, 1974a), or number of cigarettes smoked (Spiegel, 1970).

Procedural Approach to Cognition

Biofeedback, behavior therapy, and hypnosis share a fourth common feature. All three procedures seek either directly or indirectly to manipulate cognition, but their approach to cognition is behavioral, procedural, or involves hardware. In a sense, they seek to study "soft" phenomena with objective, repeatable and hard tools (electrical instruments). This approach may do violence to the complexity of the soft phenomena (consciousness, moods, thoughts), but at least it may result in repeatable and reliable consequences under known conditions of observation and manipulation. Hence, the number of unknowns will hopefully be reduced. The study of soft phenomena with soft methods (Rorschach, T.A.T., etc.) is often productive of mush. Cognitive activity and consciousness appear to be hooked up to both motor and visceral response systems. The latter system appears to exert critical control of neurotic and psychosomatic symptoms. The development of effective and reliable procedures to manipulate cognition may lead to a major breakthrough in the explanation, control, and prediction of complex human behavior. It may be said that biofeedback, behavior therapy, and hypnosis are contributing to the effort to put a handle on cognition.

Explicit Psychophysiological Approach

Biofeedback, behavior therapy, and hypnosis share a fifth common feature. All three technologies attend carefully to the physiological-autonomic consequences of verbal and motor events. Biofeedback is most directly concerned with this dimension because of its preoccupation with the physiological consequences of psychological events. Biofeedback suggests that psychological changes appear to cause physiological changes and vice versa. Hence, the direction of control may be bilateral. Behavior therapists (Wolpe, 1958; Paul, 1969; Mathews, 1971; Wickramasekera, 1973b) have recognized the importance of physiological states of low arousal in modifying maladaptive behaviors (phobias, anxiety states, etc.). Behavior therapists have stated that the cognitive, visceral, and motor response systems may not change at equal rates, nor do they respond equally to the same intervention (Lang, 1969). Hence, we may have to design interventions which are maximally effective for each response system.

Hypnotic-induction procedures stress the role of cognitively-initiated physiological relaxation and sensory restriction (close eyes, sleep, or sit quietly) in deepening hypnotic states. Hypnosis is also the oldest technique for psychologically modifying visceral-physiological responses in clinical situations (the management of pain, bleeding, hypertension, blisters, etc). The psychophysiological stress in behavior therapy, biofeedback, and hypnosis has contributed to the "return" of the body to psychological methods of modifying maladaptive behavior. There is both a conceptual and technical emphasis on psychophysiology in behavior therapy, biofeedback and hypnosis.

Information About Consequences

Biofeedback, behavior therapy, and hypnosis share a sixth common feature. The role of informational feedback and reinforcement (incentives) is stressed in all three technologies. In a more technical sense, the role of the confirmation or disconfirmation of expectancies is critical in successful biofeedback training, in behavior therapy (Murray and Jacobson, 1971), and in hypnosis (Orne, 1959b). The importance of informational feedback is coming into increasing recognition in behavior therapy (Murray and Jacobson, 1971; Borkovec, 1973) and is, of course, basic to biofeedback (Wickramasekera 1973e). The importance of reinforcement, in an incentive sense, is recognized in behavior therapy by careful attention to the contingencies of reinforcement (Skinner, 1953). In experimental and clinical hypnosis, explicit and implicit structuring of expectancies occur, and social reinforcement for appropriate hypnotic behavior is contingently dispensed, but probably less systematically than in behavior therapy. In the clinical biofeedback situation, escape from an internally aversive event (headache pain) may be used to motivate training, or the production of a positive psychological state of consciousness (e.g., euphoria) may motivate training behavior.

Expanding the Boundaries of Self-Control

Biofeedback, behavior therapy, and hypnosis share a seventh common feature. All three procedures appear to have enlarged the boundaries of self-control. Biofeedback and hypnosis appear to be generating a technology for the self-control of the internal environment (thoughts, emotions, moods, motivational states, and visceral responses). For example, biofeedback has enabled patients to control their EMG activity (Wickramasekera, 1972b; Garrett and Silver, 1974), heart rate (Blanchard et al., 1974) and EEG responses (Garrett and Silver, 1974). Hypnosis has enabled patients to control their body temperature (Maslach et al., 1972; Roberts et al., 1973), and pain responses (Hilgard, 1969). Behavior therapy is currently developing a set of procedures for the self-control of responses to aversive events. As two recent case studies illustrate, systematic desensitization can provide a method of controlling a patient's response to internal or external aversive stimuli in the form of an examination situation (Wickramasekera, 1972c) or an unpleasant obsessive thought (Wickramasekera, 1970).

Behavior therapy also appears to be developing promising techniques in altering response to appetitive stimuli (e.g., sex, food, etc.). Self-monitoring (Johnson and White, 1971) and self-management (Mahoney and Thoresen, 1972) may enable a subject to alter his responses to a wide range of situations and stimuli which typically exert strong control over behavior (e.g., cigarettes and food). Self-control procedures, like covert sensitization, self-instruction (Meichenbaum, 1973) and the alteration of eating habits (Stunkard, 1972), appear to enable a person to control his or her reactions in the presence of food, sexual, and other stimuli. In clinical practice, the above procedures are not always effective. All three interventions lean heavily on verbal instructions and talking to oneself in self-regulatory ways. It is possible that a more complete knowledge of the conditions under which verbal instructions are potentiated may increase the effectiveness and reliability of the above procedures. Section III which deals with hypnosis is concerned with the specification of conditions that potentiate verbal instruction.

Wider Applicability

Biofeedback, behavior therapy, and hypnosis have an eighth feature in common. All three techniques appear to be applicable to a wider range of patients than psychodynamically-oriented insight therapy does. Insight-oriented psychotherapy appears to be limited in its effectiveness to adult, white, successful, educated, intelligent, Protestant, middle-class, or wealthy patients (Schofield, 1964; Goldstein, 1973). Biofeedback has been used successfully with animals (Barber et al., 1972) and, hence, there is no reason to assume that it is beyond the learning capacities of mental defectives, children, the poor, the illiterate, and underprivileged minorities. Behavior therapy has been successfully used with the retarded, delinquent, and with children (Ullman and Krasner, 1966). It also appears to be a promising approach to the poor, the illiterate, and underprivileged (Goldstein, 1973). Hypnosis has traditionally been the treatment of choice of patients whose life circumstances (poverty, long working hours, etc.) and values lead them to seek short-term circumscribed solutions to their emotional and behavioral problems. Because of the rapid and apparently "miraculous" emotional and behavioral changes that sometimes occur with highly hypnotizable and motivated patients, hypnosis is frequently the psychological treatment of choice of lower socioeconomic groups.

Potentiating the Placebo Response

Biofeedback, behavior therapy, and hypnosis also share a ninth feature. All these techniques have contributed in strengthening the placebo response, (Wickramasekera 1973b), which is probably the most basic and ultimately important variable in all psychological methods of treatment. According to Shapiro (1971), a placebo is "any therapy, or that component of any therapy, that is deliberately used for its nonspecific, psychologic, or psychophysiologic effect, or that is used for its presumed specific effect on a patient, symptom, or illness, but which, unknown to patient and therapist, is without specific activity for the condition treated." The essential features of the definition are (1) a psychological effect; (2) that is nonspecific to a particular disease; and (3) that is mediated through an inert substance or procedure. The following variables have been found to reliably influence placebo effects (Shapiro, 1971): (1)acute anxiety and/or depression in the patient; (2) patient expectations about what is effective therapy; (3) therapist variables such as empathy, prestige, warmth, etc. Shapiro also reported a lack of relationship between suggestibility as measured by laboratory tests and the clinical placebo response. He noted that a laboratory test of suggestibility may not be a valid test of such a relationship.

A placebo response may be redefined as a change in a visceral or behavioral response due to a psychological effect that is mediated through a high-credibility instructional set or a set of high-credibility verbal inferences by the patient about therapeutic elements (in a person; procedures and context) in the clinical situation. In final analysis, the verbal instructions given to the patient and the cognitive inferences (the verbal instructions he gives himself) he himself makes about the total clinical situation become the determinant of whether the placebo reaction will be positive, negative, or neutral, and whether reaction will be strong or weak. The above issue functionally overlaps with asking what are the conditions under which verbal instructions are potentiated or what are the conditions under which hypnotizability is increased?

It appears that the placebo response in the clinical situation depends for its strength and reliability on at least two factors. First, the confidence the patient has in psychological science in general. In the long run, this depends on the specific effectiveness and the scientific image of the field. It is to the scientific image of psychology that behavior therapy and biofeedback contribute. This factor sets a socially learned lower limit to the confidence a patient brings to any psychological practitioner. The second factor in the placebo response, in this context, has to do with how effectively the psychological factor is managed in order to maximize its power and consistency with the specific treatment components (e.g., reinforcement, informational feedback, etc.). The literature on the modification of hypnotic susceptibility (Wickramasekera, 1973c) appears to suggest that there are some preferred ways of delivering verbal instructions and arranging situational cues to stimulate the patient to make the kinds of verbal inferences which will maximize placebo effects. Behavior therapy and biofeedback may have also increased the probability of stronger placebo effects by strengthening the scientific base (specific effects, careful attention to the optimal conditions for acquisition and extinction of learning, e.g., reinforcement, feedback, etc.) and credibility of psychological therapy. Also, the "hardware" (impressive electronic instruments) and rituals (graphing, quantifying, etc.) of behavior therapy and biofeedback look like those of "hard" science. Hypnosis research has contributed to maximizing placebo effects by identifying some of the conditions for maximizing the impact of verbal events (Wickramasekera, 1973c).

It may be asserted that biofeedback, behavior therapy, and hypnosis have all contributed to a common technology concerned with increasing the generality and stabilizing the power of the placebo response. The verbal or instructional control of complex human behavior has been advanced by all three technologies. Each of them has added knowledge about the techniques and conditions under which the verbal-cognitive control of behavior may be reliably and generally increased. For example, biofeedback technology has provided hardware and training procedures to control physiological functions instructionally-cognitively. Behavior therapy studies (Wilkins, 1971; Borkovec, 1973; Murray and Jacobson, 1971) have shown how operant and respondent reinforcement procedures and modelling can add to the strength of powerful explicit or implicit expectational structuring. In hypnotic research, the power of implicit subject expectations was recognized early and labeled "demand characteristics" (Orne, 1959a). Effective arrangement of demand characteristics was shown to elicit even some of the bizarre phenomena of sensory deprivation (Orne and Scheibe, 1964) and the control for demand characteristics has become a basic control in current clinical-social psychological research. Expectation can play a powerful role when cogently structured and related to real patient needs (Goldstein, 1962) in psychological therapy. Hypnotic research has in even more specific and direct ways sought to determine the conditions under which the verbal control of complex human behaviors (hypnotic behavior) may be increased. The discovery of conditions and procedures to increase hypnotizability (Wickramasekera, 1973c) potentially increases the generality, reliability, and power of the placebo response as defined above.

There has never been anything intrinsically "bad" about the placebo response; it has simply been unreliable and transitory in its effects and unidentifiable in advance. Hence, it has confounded physical and chemical studies with humans. If more reliable, powerful, sturdy, and quantifiable placebos may be developed, they may be incorporated rather than eliminated from clinical interventions. Hence, we may be on the road to doing something about the problem that Freud (1959) recognized in the following terms, "In order to effect a cure, a condition of 'expectant faith' was induced in sick persons . . . We have learned to use the word 'suggestion' for this phenomenon, and Mobius has taught us that the unreliability which we deplore in so many of our therapeutic measures may be traced back actually to the disturbing influence of this very powerful factor . . . it is disadvantageous, however, to leave entirely in the hands of the patient what the mental factor in your treatment of him shall be. In this way it is uncontrollable; it can neither be measured nor intensified. Is it not then a justifiable endeavor on the part of a physician to seek to control this factor, to use it with a purpose, and to direct and strengthen it? This and nothing else is what scientific psychotherapy proposes."

If biofeedback technology, behavior therapy, hypnosis, and other self-control procedures like transcendental meditation are incorporated into public education in the elementary and secondary school level, then larger segments of the population may emerge with greater instructional control of their internal environments. Current public education stresses only "objective education," or control of external environmental events. "Subjective education" or the effective, reliable verbal control of the internal environment (moods, perceptions, thoughts, visceral responses) is at least as important for total effective human functioning. Maladaptive cognitions, perceptions, values, emotions, and visceral responses, appear to constitute the core of functional psychopathology. The effective alteration of these "private events" is central to any effective psychological treatment package. Subjective education may strengthen the cortical control of behavior and the Thought rather than being precariously perched on the shifting shoulders of visceral and motor responses may come to have a firmer grip on both response systems.

Finally, there is a sense in which all three procedures—biofeedback, behavior therapy, and hypnosis—are supplementary and complementary. An example from our current clinical treatment program will illustrate this point. After the careful diagnostic screening and baseline observation of a tension headache patient is completed (Wickramasekera, 1972b), a nonresearch patient is processed in the following manner. He is given carefully selected articles about biofeedback from the popular press (e.g., *Time, New Yorker, Playboy*) to read. This reading, in general, creates a positive and credible expectational set. Articles are selected from a folder to fit the patient's comprehension and sophistication level. Next, the patient is given a pep talk not labeled "hypnosis," but with careful attention to the verbal instructions and situational arrangements which hypnotic research has found to increase the effectiveness of verbal interventions and instructions.

The primary purpose of this treatment component is to secure the patient's commitment to training and to give him responsibility to make the treatment work.

Just before the patient commences training, he observes a videotape of a successful patient going through the steps of biofeedback training. The purpose of this step is to alleviate any residual anxiety the patient may feel about an unfamiliar procedure and to give the patient a clear knowledge of what is expected of him and what he must do to participate actively and responsibly in his treatment. During the biofeedback training procedure, information feedback is provided, and social reinforcements are contingently dispensed to maintain training efforts on a successive approximation (shaped) training schedule in which frustration and failure are minimized. The latter operations are suggested by the literature of behavior therapy. Hence, the total treatment package includes elements of hypnosis, biofeedback, and behavior therapy. Systematic structuring of expectations enhances and channels motivation, and secures commitment to clearly specified therapeutic goals. To increase the probability of goal attainment, careful attention is given to the optimal conditions for learning and generalization. The above procedures describe how instructional (Hypnosis), informational feedback (Biofeedback), and reinforcement (Behavior Therapy) components can be used to *detach* stress from behavior.

The Aversive Behavior Rehearsal (Wickramasekera, 1972) procedure describes ways in which instructional components (Hypnosis), informational feedback components (Biofeedback-videotape and psychophysiological feedback report), and reinforcement components (Behavior Therapy) can be integrated to *attach* stress to behavior.

In conclusion, it appears that the creative and systematic manipulation of antecedents (instructions, explicit or implicit expectations) and consequences (informational feedback and positive or negative incentives) can be used to *confer* on human behavior a semblance of order, predictability, and control.

References

Barber, T.X. *Hypnosis: A scientific approach.* New York, Van Nostrand Reinhold, 1969

Barber, T.X., et al. (Eds). *Biofeedback and self-control, 1971.* Chicago: Aldine, 1972.

Blanchard, E.B., Scott, R.W., Young, L.D., & Edmundson, E. The unit of measurement in behavioral approach to clinical cardiac control. Unpublished paper, 1974

Borkovec, T.D. The role of expectancy and physiological feedback in fear research. *Behavior Therapy,* 1973, *4,* 491-505.

Colson, C.E. Olfactory aversion therapy for homosexual behavior. *Journal of Behavior Therapy and Experimental Psychiatry.* 1972, *3,* 185-187.

Evans, D.R. Masturbatory fantasy and sexual deviation. *Behavior Therapy,* 1968, *6,* 17-19.

Freud, S. *Collected papers* (Vol. 1). New York: Basic Books, 1959.

Garrett, B.C., & Silver, M.P. The use of EMG and alpha biofeedback to relieve test anxiety in college students. Unpublished paper, 1974.

Goldstein, A.P. *Therapist-patient expectancies in psychotherapy.* Elmsford, N.Y.: Pergamon, 1962.

Goldstein, A.P. *Structured learning therapy.* New York: Academic Press, 1973.

Hilgard, E.R. *Hypnotic susceptibility.* New York: Harcourt, Brace and World, 1965.

Hilgard, E.R. Pain as a puzzle for psychology and physiology. *American Psychologist,* 1969, *24* (2), 103-113.

Hilgard, E.R., & Weitzenhoffer, A. Stanford Hypnotic Susceptibility Scale Forms, B. Palo Alto, Ca.: Consulting Psychologists Press, 1959

Hull, C.L. *Hypnosis and suggestibility: An experimental approach.* New York: Appleton-Century, 1933.

Johnson, S.M., & White, G. Self observation as an agent of behavioral change. *Behavior Therapy,* 1971, *2* (4), 488-497

Lang, P.J. The mechanics of desensitization and the laboratory study of human fear. In C. M. Franks (Ed.), *Behavior therapy appraisal and status.* New York: McGraw-Hill, 1969.

Mahoney, M.J., & Thoresen, C.E. Behavioral self-control: Power to the person. Unpublished manuscript, 1972.

Mathews, A.W. Psychophysiological approaches to the investigation of desensitization and related procedures. *Psychological Bulletin, 1971, 76,* 73-91.

Maslach, C., Marshall, G., & Zimbardo, P. Hynotic control of peripheral skin temperature: A case report. *Psychophysiology,* 1972, *9,* 600-605.

Meichenbaum, D.H. Cognitive factors in behavioral modification: Modifying what clients say to themselves. In C.M. Franks & G.T. Wilson (Eds.), *Annual Review of Behavior Therapy,* 1973. New York: Brunner-Mazel, 1973.

Murray, E.J., & Jacobson, L.I. The nature of learning in traditional and behavioral psychotherapy. In E.E. Bergin & S.L. Garfield (Eds.), *Handbook of psychotherapy and behavior change.* New York: John Wiley, 1971.

Orne, M.T. The demand characteristics of an experimental design and their implications. Paper presented at a meeting of the American Psychological Association, Cincinnati, September 1959. (a)

Orne, M.T. The nature of hypnosis: Artifact and essence. *Journal of Abnormal Psychology,* 1959, *58,* 277-299. (b)

Orne, M.T., & Scheibe, E.H. The contribution of non-deprivation factors in the production of sensory deprivation effects. *Journal of Abnormal Psychology,* 1964, *68,* 3-12.

Paul, G.L. Physiological effects of relaxation training and hypnotic suggestion. *Journal of Abnormal Psychology,* 1969, *74,* 425-437.

Roberts, A.H., Kewman, D.G., & MacDonald, H. Voluntary control of skin temperature: Unilateral changes using hypnosis and feedback. *Journal of Abnormal Psychology,* 1973, *82* (1), 163-168.

Schofield, W. *Psychotherapy: The purchase of a friendship.* Englewood Cliffs, N.J.: Prentice-Hall, 1964.

Shapiro, A.K. Placebo effects in medicine, psychotherapy and psychoanalysis. In A.E. Bergin & S.L. Garfield (Eds.), *Handbook of psychotherapy and behavior change.* New York: John Wiley, 1971.

Skinner, B.F. *Science and human behavior.* New York: Macmillan, 1953.

Spiegel, H. A single treatment method to stop smoking using ancillary self-hypnosis. *International Journal of Clinical and Experimental Hypnosis,* 1970, *18,* 235-250.

Spiegel, H. An eye-roll test of hypnotizability. *American Journal of Clinical Hypnosis,* 1972, *15,* 25-28.

Stunkard, A. New therapies for the eating disorder. *Archives of General Psychiatry,* 1972, *26,* 391-399.

Ullman, L.P., & Krasner, L. *Case studies in behavior modification.* New York: Holt, Rinehart and Winston, 1965.

Wickramasekera, I. Desensitization, re-sensitization and desensitization again. *Behavior Therapy and Experimental Psychiatry,* 1970, *1,* 257-262.

Wickramasekera, I. A technique for controlling a certain type of sexual exhibitionism. *Psychotherapy: Theory, Research and Practice,* 1972, *9* (3), 207-210. (a)

Wickramasekera, I. EMG feedback training and tension headache: Preliminary observations. *American Journal of Clinical Hypnosis,* 1972, *15,* 83-85. (b)

Wickramasekera, I. Instructions and EMG feedback in systematic desensitization: A case report. *Behavior Therapy,* 1972, *3,* 460-465. (c)

Wickramasekera, I. On the apparent instrusion of a recurring nightmare into an EMG feedback training procedure. Unpublished paper, 1973. (a)

Wickramasekera, I. Verbal instructions, hypnosis, and behavior change. Unpublished paper, 1973. (b)

Wickramasekera, I. The modification of hypnotic behavior. Unpublished paper, 1973. (c)

Wickramasekera, I. Application of verbal instructions and EMG feedback training to the management of tension headache: Preliminary observations. *Headache,* 1973, *15* (2), 74-76. (d)

Wickramasekera, I. The effects of EMG feedback on hypnotic susceptibility. *Journal of Abnormal Psychology*, 1973, *82*, 74-77.(e)

Wickramasekera, I. Broad spectrum behavior therapy for blepharospasm. *International Journal of Clinical and Experimental Hypnosis*, 1974, *22*, 201-209. (a)

Wickramasekera, I. Temperature feedback for the control of migraine. *Behavior Therapy and Experimental Psychiatry*, 1974, *4*, 343-345. (b)

Wilkins, W. Desensitization: Social· and cognitive factors underlying the effectiveness of Wolpe's procedure. *Psychological Bulletin*, 1971, *76*, 311-317.

Wolpe, J. *Psychotherapy by reciprocal inhibition.* Stanford, Ca.: Stanford University Press, 1958.